THE EUROPEAN UNION'S EXTERNAL ACTION IN TIMES OF CRISIS

The Lisbon Treaty modified the legal framework of EU external action, and these innovations must be applied in a period of deep economic and financial crisis interacting with other more specific crises affecting the EU's external activities. This volume investigates the recent institutional and substantive developments in EU external relations law and practice in this context of multiple crises for the EU. The economic and financial crisis has a major impact on EU external action, but other crises too affect this sensitive area of the EU's activity and the book takes them into account. For instance, there is a crisis in the relationship between EU law and international law after the ECJ judgment in the *Kadi* case. In addition to exploring these questions, the volume also examines questions of legitimacy in fields such as foreign investment protection and arbitration. Representing the output of a powerful research team composed of leading scholars in the field this comprehensive collection will appeal to both an expert and non-expert readership.

Volume 63 in the Series Modern Studies in European Law

Modern Studies in European Law
Recent titles in this series:

The European Court of Justice and External Relations: Constitutional Challenges
Edited by Marise Cremona and Anne Thies

A Critique of Codification
Leone Niglia

Protecting Vulnerable Groups: The European Human Rights Framework
Edited by Francesca Ippolito and Sara Iglesias Sanchez

EU International Relations Law Second Edition
Panos Koutrakos

Fundamental Rights in the EU: A Matter for Two Courts
Edited by Sonia Morano-Foadi and Lucy Vickers

What Form of Government for the European Union and the Eurozone?
Federico Fabbrini, Ernst Hirsch Ballin and Han Somsen

The UK and European Human Rights: A Strained Relationship?
Edited by Katja S Ziegler, Elizabeth Wicks and Loveday Hodson

The European Union in International Organisations and Global Governance: Recent Developments
Edited by Christine Kaddous

Nudge and the Law: What Can EU Law Learn From Behavioural Sciences?
Edited by Alberto Alemanno and Anne-Lise Sibony

Fundamental Rights in EU Internal Market Legislation
Vasiliki Kosta

Uniformity of Customs Administration in the European Union
Kathrin Limbach

The Impact of Union Citizenship on the EU's Market Freedoms
Alina Tryfonidou

Equal Citizenship and Its Limits in EU Law
Päivi Johanna Neuvonen

European Law on Unfair Commercial Practices and Contract Law
Mateja Durovic

For the complete list of titles in this series, see 'Modern Studies in European Law' link at www.hartpub.co.uk/books/series.asp

The European Union's External Action in Times of Crisis

Edited by
Piet Eeckhout and Manuel López-Escudero

•HART•
PUBLISHING
OXFORD AND PORTLAND, OREGON
2016

Hart Publishing
An imprint of Bloomsbury Publishing Plc

Hart Publishing Ltd
Kemp House
Chawley Park
Cumnor Hill
Oxford OX2 9PH
UK

Bloomsbury Publishing Plc
50 Bedford Square
London
WC1B 3DP
UK

www.hartpub.co.uk
www.bloomsbury.com

Published in North America (US and Canada) by
Hart Publishing
c/o International Specialized Book Services
920 NE 58th Avenue, Suite 300
Portland, OR 97213-3786
USA

www.isbs.com

First published 2016

British Library Cataloguing-in-Publication Data
A catalogue record for this book is available from the British Library.

ISBN: HB: 978-1-50990-055-8
ePDF: 978-1-50990-056-5
ePub: 978-1-50990-057-2

Library of Congress Cataloging-in-Publication Data

Names: Eeckhout, Piet, editor. | López-Escudero, Manuel, editor.

Title: The European Union's external action in times of crisis / Edited by Piet Eeckhout and Manuel López-Escudero.

Description: Portland, Oregon : Hart Publishing, 2016. | Series: Modern studies in European law ; 63 | Includes bibliographical references and index.

Identifiers: LCCN 2016028880 (print) | LCCN 2016029334 (ebook) | ISBN 9781509900558 (hardback : alk. paper) | ISBN 9781509900572 (Epub)

Subjects: LCSH: International and municipal law—European Union countries. | European Union countries—Foreign relations—Law and legislation. | European Union. | International cooperation—European Union countries.

Classification: LCC KJE5057 .E925 2016 (print) | LCC KJE5057 (ebook) | DDC 341.242/2—dc23

LC record available at https://lccn.loc.gov/2016028880

Series: Series Modern Studies in European Law, volume 63

Typeset by Compuscript Ltd, Shannon
Printed and bound in Great Britain by
CPI Group (UK) Ltd, Croydon CR0 4YY

Contents

List of Abbreviations

ACC	Arms Control Coalition
ACP	African, Caribbean, and Pacific Group of States
ACTA	Anti-Counterfeiting Trade Agreement
AEO	Authorised Economic Operator
AETR	Accord Européen sur les Transports Routiers
AFET	Committee on Foreign Affairs (European Parliament)
AFSJ	Area of Freedom, Security and Justice
AGRI	Agriculture and Fisheries Council
AMISOM	African Union's Mission in Somalia
ASA	Association and Stabilisation Agreement
ASEAN	Association of Southeast Asian Nations
ATA	US-EU Air Transport Agreement
ATAA	Air Transport Association of America
ATT	Arms Trade Treaty
AU	African Union
BCBS	Basel Committee on Banking Supervision
BIS	Bank for International Settlements
BITs	Bilateral investment treaties
BOs	Broadcasting organisations
BRICs	Brazil, the Russian Federation, India, China
BTSD	Board on Trade and Sustainable Development
BTWC	Biological and Toxin Weapons Convention
CAAT	Campaign Against Arms Trade
CARICOM	Caribbean Community
CARIFORUM	(The Forum of the Caribbean Group of African, Caribbean and Pacific (ACP) States)
CCP	Common Commercial Policy

CEAS	Common European Asylum System
CEPS	Centre for European Policy Studies
CETA	Comprehensive Economic and Trade Agreement EU-Canada
CFI	Former Court of First Instance (now General Court)
CFSP	Common Foreign and Security Policy
CITES	Convention on International Trade in Endangered Species of Wild Fauna and Flora
CJEU	Court of Justice of the European Union
CMFB	Committee on Monetary Financial and Balance of Payments Statistics
COHOM	Working Party on Human Rights (Council of the European Union)
CONUN	United Nations Working Party (Council of the European Union)
COPs	Conference of Parties (Multilateral environmental agreements)
CSCE	Conference on Security and Co-operation in Europe
CSDP	Common Security and Defence Policy
DCFTA	Deep and Comprehensive Free Trade Agreements
DG	Directorate General
DHS	United States Department of Homeland Security
DSB	Dispute Settlement Body
EBRD	European Bank for Reconstruction and Development
EC	European Community
ECB	European Central Bank
ECFR	European Council on Foreign Relations
ECHR	European Convention on Human Rights
ECJ	European Court of Justice (European Union)
ECtHR	European Court of Human Rights
ECOSOC	United Nations Economic and Social Council
ECOWAS	Economic Community of West African States
ECSC	European Coal and Steel Community
EDPS	European Data Protection Supervisor
EEA	European Economic Area
EEC	European Economic Community

EEAS	European External Action Service
EFC	Economic and Financial Committee
EFSF	European Financial Stability Facility
EFSM	European Financial Stabilisation Mechanism
EFTA	European Free Trade Association
EGF	European Gendarmerie Force
ELFAA	European Low Fares Airline Association
EMA	Euro-Mediterranean Association
EMDCs	Emerging markets and developing countries
EMU	Economic and Monetary Union
ENP	European Neighbourhood Policy
EP	European Parliament
EPA	European Partnership Agreements
ERM	Exchange Rate Mechanism
ERTA	European Road Transport Agreement
ESA	Eastern and Southern African (ESA) European Partnership Agreement
ESM	European Stability Mechanism
ESS	European Security Strategy
ETS	Greenhouse gas emissions trading schemes
EU	European Union
EUKFTA	European Union-Korea Free Trade Agreement
EUNAVFOR	European Union Naval Force
EUPOL	European Union Police Mission in Afghanistan
EUPM	European Union Police Mission
EURIMF	EU Representatives to the IMF
EURODAD	European Network on Debt and Development
EUSEC	European Union Mission to provide advice and assistance for security sector reform in the Democratic Republic of the Congo
EUSFTA	European Union-Singapore Free Trade Agreement
EUSRs	European Union Special Representatives
EWG	Eurogroup Working Group

FAC	Foreign Affairs Council
FAFA	European Union-United Nations Financial and Administrative Framework Agreement
FAO	Food and Agriculture Organization (of the UN)
FDI	Foreign Direct Investment
FRA	Fundamental Rights Agency (European Union)
FREMP	Working Party on Fundamental Rights, Citizens' Rights and Free Movement of Persons (Council of the European Union)
FRONTEX	European Agency for the Management of Operational Cooperation at the External Borders
FSAP	Financial Sector Assessment Program
FSB	Financial Stability Board
FSJ	Area of Freedom, Security and Justice
FTA	Free Trade Agreement
GATS	General Agreement on Trade in Services
GATT	General Agreement on Tariffs and Trade
GCC	Gulf Cooperation Council
GDP	Gross Domestic Product
GIs	Geographical indications
GPA	WTO Agreement on Government Procurement
G-77	The Group of 77
GRIP	Groupe d'Information et Recherche sur la Paix et la Sécurité
GRULAC	Group of Latin American and Caribbean States
GSP +	Enhanced preferences
HCHR	High Commissioner for Human Rights
HR	High Representative of the European Union for Foreign Affairs and Security Policy
HRC	Human Rights Council
IAEA	International Atomic Energy Agency
IANSA	International Action Network on Small Arms
IATA	International Air Transport Association
IBA	International Bar Association

ICANN	Internet Corporation for Assigned Names and Numbers
ICAO	International Civil Aviation Organisation
ICC	International Chamber of Commerce
ICSID	International Centre for Settlement of Investment Disputes
IEC	International Electrotechnical Commission
IETF	Internet Engineering Task Force
IFAD	International Fund for Agricultural Development
IHL	International Humanitarian Law
ILC	International Law Commission
ILO	International Labour Organization
IMCO	Committee on the Internal Market and Consumer Protection (European Parliament)
IMF	International Monetary Fund
IMO	International Maritime Organization
INTA	Committee on International Trade (European Parliament)
IOs	International Organizations
IOSCO	International Organization of Securities Commissions
IPRs	Intellectual Property Rights
ISDS	Investor-state dispute settlement (tribunals)
ISO	International Organization for Standardization
ISOC	Internet Society
ISP	Internet service providers
JHA	Justice and Home Affairs
JURI	Committee on Legal Affairs (European Parliament)
LBS	Protocol for the Protection of the Mediterranean Sea Against Pollution from Land-based Sources and Activities
LIBE	Committee on Civil Liberties, Justice and Home Affairs (European Parliament)
LTTE	Liberation Tigers of Tamil Eelam
MARPOL	International Convention for the Prevention of Pollution from Ships
MDGs	Millennium Development Goals
MEAs	Multilateral environmental agreements

MEPs	Members of the European Parliament
MFA	Macro-Financial Assistance
MFF	Multiannual Financial Framework
MFN	Most Favoured Nation
MISCA	International Support Mission to the Central African Republic
MONUC	United Nations Mission in the Democratic Republic of the Congo
MOPs	Meeting of Parties (Multilateral environmental agreements)
MOU	Memorandum of Understanding
MS	Member States
NAFTA	North American Free Trade Agreement
NATO	North Atlantic Treaty Organization
NGOs	Non-Governmental Organizations
NTBs	Non-tariff barriers
OAS	Organization of American States
OCHA	United Nations Office for the Coordination of Humanitarian Affairs
ODSG	OCHA Donor Support Group
OECD	Organisation for Economic Cooperation and Development
OIC	Organisation Islamic Cooperation
OPCW	Organisation for the Prohibition of Chemical Weapons
OSCE	Organisation for Security and Co-operation in Europe
PCA	Partnership and Cooperation Agreement
PDRK	People's Democratic Republic of Korea (North Korea)
PNR	Passenger Name Record
PPP	Purchasing Power Parity
PSC	Political and Security Committee
QMV	Qualified Majority Voting
REIO	Regional Economic Integration Organisation
RELEX	Working Party of Foreign Relations Counsellors (Council of the European Union)
RTA	Regional Trade Agreements
SAA	Stabilisation and Association Agreements

SALW	Small Arms and Light Weapons
SC	United Nations Security Council
SCIMF	Sub-committee on IMF matters and related issues
SCM	Agreement on Subsidies and Countervailing Measures
SDGs	Sustainable Development Goals
SDR	Special Drawing Right
SGP	Stability and Growth Pact
SIPRI	Stockholm International Peace Research Institute
SMEs	Small and Medium Enterprises
SPSs	Sanitary and Phytosanitary Measures
SWIFT	Society for Worldwide Interbank Financial Telecommunication
TBTs	Technical Barriers to Trade
TEC	Treaty establishing the European Community
TEEC	Treaty establishing the European Economic Community
TEU	Treaty of the European Union
TFEU	Treaty on the Functioning of the European Union
TRIPS	Trade-Related Aspects of Intellectual Property Rights
TTIP	Transatlantic Trade and Investment Partnership EU-US
UDHR	Universal Declaration of Human Rights
UN	United Nations
UNAMA	United Nations Assistance Mission in Afghanistan
UNCITRAL	United Nations Commission on International Trade Law
UNCLOS	United Nations Convention on the Law of the Sea
UNCTAD	United Nations Conference on Trade and Development
UNDP	United Nations Development Programme
UNECE	United Nations Economic Commission for Europe
UNEP	United Nations Environment Programme
UNESCO	United Nations Educational, Scientific and Cultural Organization
UNFCCC	United Nations Framework Convention on Climate Change
UNFPA	United Nations Population Fund
UNHCR	United Nations High Commissioner for Refugees

UNGA	United Nations General Assembly
UNICEF	United Nations Children's Fund
UNMIBH	United Nations Mission in Bosnia-Herzegovina
UNPOS	United Nations Political Office for Somalia
UNROCA	United Nations Register of Conventional Arms
UNRWA	United Nations Relief and Works Agency for Palestine Refugees in the Near East
UNSC	United Nations Security Council
UPR	Universal Periodic Review
WCO	World Customs Organization
WCT	WIPO Copyright Treaty
WFP	World Food Programme
WFSA	World Forum on the Future of Sport Shooting Activities
WHO	World Health Organization
WIPO	World Intellectual Property Organisation
WPPT	WIPO Performances and Phonograms Treaty
WTO	World Trade Organization

List of Contributors

Steven Blockmans, Senior Research Fellow, Centre for European Policy Studies (Brussels), Professor of EU External Relations Law and Governance, University of Amsterdam, and member of the governing board of the Centre for the Law of EU External Relations (CLEER), The Hague.

Enzo Cannizzaro, Professor of International and European Law, University of Rome 'La Sapienza'.

Dominique Carreau, Professor Emeritus of Public International Law, Université Paris-I Panthéon-Sorbonne.

Fernando Castillo de la Torre, Legal Adviser, Legal Service, European Commission.

Anna-Luise Chané, Research Fellow and PhD Candidate, Leuven Centre for Global Governance Studies—Institute for International Law, Katholieke Universiteit Leuven.

Javier Diez-Hochleitner, Professor of Public International Law, Autónoma University of Madrid.

Piet Eeckhout, Professor of EU Law, University College London.

Ricardo Gosalbo-Bono, Director in the Legal Service of the Council of the EU and Professor of Law at the Vrije Universiteit Brussel (VUB).

Christine Kaddous, Professor of EU Law, University of Geneva, Jean Monnet Chair ad personam, Director of the Centre d'études juridiques européennes, Jean Monnet Centre of Excellence of the University of Geneva.

Manuel López-Escudero, Professor of EU Law and Public International Law, University of Granada, Legal Secretary of the Court of Justice of the European Union, Luxembourg, and Co-editor of the *Revista de Derecho Comunitario Europeo.*

José Rafael Marín Aís, PhD Lecturer in Public International Law and European Union Law, University of Granada.

Inmaculada Marrero Rocha, Tenured Professor of International Relations, University of Granada.

José Martín y Pérez de Nanclares, Professor of Public International Law, University of Salamanca. Currently Head of the International Law Division at the Spanish Ministry of Foreign Affairs and Cooperation.

Frederik Naert, Member of the Legal Service of the Council of the EU and an affiliated senior researcher at the Katholieke Universiteit Leuven.

Ricardo Passos, Director of the External Relations Team at the Legal Service of the European Parliament.

Carmela Pérez Bernáldez, Senior Lecturer in Public International Law, University of Granada.

Javier Roldán Barbero, Professor of Public International Law, University of Granada.

Antonio Segura Serrano, Tenured Professor of Public International Law, University of Granada.

Ramses A Wessel, Professor of International and European Institutional Law, Centre for European Studies, University of Twente, The Netherlands and member of the governing board of the Centre for the Law of EU External Relations (CLEER), The Hague.

Jan Wouters, Professor of EU Law and International Law and Jean Monnet Chair ad personam, Director, Leuven Centre for Global Governance Studies—Institute for International Law, KU Leuven and Visiting Professor, College of Europe (Bruges), Sciences Po (Paris) and Luiss (Rome).

Table of Cases

International Courts and Tribunals and Other International Adjudicatory Bodies

International Court of Justice

Advisory opinions:

Judgments:

Separate opinions

European Commission of Human Rights

Decisions

European Court of Human Rights

Judgments:

Human Rights Committee:

General Comments:

International Centre for Settlement of Investment Disputes (ICSID)

Decisions:

International Criminal Court for the Former Yugoslavia

Judgments:

Uncitral arbitral tribunals

Decisions

WTO Dispute Settlement Mechanisms

WTO Panels

European Union Courts

Court of Justice of the European Union

General Court (former Court of First Instance)

Judgments

Court of Justice

Opinions

Judgments

Orders

Case Law of Domestic Courts

Germany

German Constitutional Court

United States

United States Supreme Court

Part I

Introduction

Introduction

PIET EECKHOUT AND MANUEL LOPEZ-ESCUDERO[1]

Content

AS WE WRITE the introduction to this volume on the many legal dimensions of the European Union's 'external action', the crises engulfing the EU are not abating. The term 'external action', as a common denominator for the set of EU policies which are focused on the outside world, was introduced by the Lisbon Treaty. When that Treaty entered into force—in late 2009—the 2008 financial crisis was wreaking havoc. It subsequently morphed into the sovereign debt and Eurozone crises, whose effects were by no means confined to monetary matters. The EU's haphazard response, the intergovernmental instruments which were created (such as the ESM), the untransparent and contested role of the troika, the austerity orthodoxy, and the lack of solidarity all contributed to a legitimacy crisis which shakes the EU in its very foundations. Add to this the threat of 'Brexit', and the ongoing refugee crisis which undermines Schengen, one of the EU's core achievements and policies. Nor is the outside world offering much comfort. Indeed the refugee crisis is in large measure a result of the EU's unstable Eastern and Southern borders, and Europe does not need a resurgent Russia, seeking to protect (and reconstitute?) its spheres of interest with policies which are diametrically opposed to the EU's ethos.

In the EU, crisis does not equal inaction. All of the above crises have triggered a panoply of responses, political, legal, and institutional. The questions which are raised are rather about the adequacy of those responses, their substance and effectiveness, and indeed their legitimacy. This comment extends to the EU's external

[1] Piet Eeckhout, Professor of EU Law, University College London.
Manuel López-Escudero, Professor of EU Law and Public International Law, University of Granada, Legal Secretary of the ECJ.

action; although at least in the English language 'external action' is rather inelegant, and not a term of art, it does capture the frenetic activity which the EU often displays, also in the external sphere and at international level. Many contributions to this volume evidence the scope and depth of EU external action, and its capacity to grow and extend to new areas.

It is, however, less clear whether the growth of EU external action is of the right kind, in order to meet the crises. The EU's unstable neighbourhood calls for a more robust Common Foreign and Security Policy (CFSP), but Gosalbo Bono and Naert—insiders as Council lawyers—deplore the EU's failure to strengthen the CFSP, and 'the practical reduction of the external action of the EU to a policy of sanctions'. The CFSP continues to be a 'fledgling' policy (to use a euphemism), and the intended institutional strengthening by the Lisbon Treaty has not as yet been delivered. The refugee crisis, on the other hand, calls for a much more coherent migration and asylum policy, but Martín y Pérez de Nanclares shows that external action in the sphere of the Area of Freedom Security and Justice (AFSJ) remains *à la carte*, based on unstable foundations, and lacking in clear policy directions. The Lisbon Treaty may have removed the three-pillar structure of the EU, yet it is clear that the formerly intergovernmental pillars, CFSP and AFSJ, continue to be more intergovernmental indeed, and less effective.

It is also clear that the growth of EU external action continues to be mainly of a normative kind, and is not matched by a clear EU voice and position in international politics. Indeed, the non-expert reader of these lines will no doubt be puzzled by the claim of rapidly growing external action, since most of it remains below the radar of daily media reporting, with its reduction of international politics to events, soundbites, and conflicts between nations and entities as games between unitary players. Whether this below-the-radar nature of EU external action—which continues to conform to the Normative Power Europe concept[2]—equals ineffectiveness, is not so clear though.

The normative nature of EU external action results in a constant stream of legal developments and issues, which occupy an increasing share of EU law analysis. This volume aims to contribute to such analysis. The contributors are not confined to academia, but include leading lawyers in the EU institutions and at a national level. This introduction cannot do justice to the richness of the material, analysis, and commentary which follow it. There are nevertheless a number of themes which we should like to highlight. They are three in number, and concern the continued significance of questions of EU external competence; the problematic relationship between EU law and international law, particularly as a result of the case-law of the EU Court of Justice (CJEU); and the unsettled nature of institutional questions, including questions of external representation and particiation in international dispute settlement.

[2] I Manner, 'Normative Power Europe: A Contradiction in Terms?' (2002) 40 *Journal of Common Market Studies* 235.

A. Questions of Competence

Questions of EU external competence have always occupied a central place in EU external relations law. Notwithstanding the valiant attempt by the Treaty of Lisbon to codify the relevant principles, and to provide for more coherence, those questions remain as alive as ever. This can be seen in the contributions by lawyers of the institutions: Gosalbo Bono and Naert of the Council, Passos of the European Parliament, and Castillo de la Torre of the Commission. Those contributions demonstrate the extent to which this area of law continues to be conflicted, with diametrically opposed views by the Council and the Commission. Gosalbo Bono and Naert argue that the Treaty of Lisbon sought to introduce some competence-restrictive provisions (and suggest that the CJEU ignores them in its latest case law). Castillo de la Torre, on the other hand, takes a broad view of the EU's external competences. It seems that this is an institutionally engrained battleground. Ever since the first cases on competence, *AETR* and *Opinion 1/75*,[3] the Commission and the Council lawyers have harboured these fundamentally different conceptions. For the Council it is important to respect the desire of at least a number of Member States to circumscribe EU competences, and to maintain a space for those States to be international actors in their own right. For the Commission those Member States are really only concerned about issues of national prestige, and do little more than to hinder EU activity. That does not mean that this trench war does not evolve. The Parliament is becoming a much more significant player, particularly through its ability to consent to, or indeed reject, international agreements which the EU seeks to conclude. The Parliament also advocates wide EU competences. And it has to be said that the CJEU is increasingly willing to go along with the Commission's and the Parliament's conceptions, particularly in its case law on implied powers. But the practice does not necessarily follow: mixed agreements are as popular as ever, in the Council, and the resistant case law does not manage to rein in the practice of mixity.

In this respect we venture a comment on Castillo de la Torre's argument that mixity signifies de facto unanimity, as all Member States need to conclude the agreement, whereas under shared EU competences Council decision-making is, as a rule, subject to qualified-majority voting. Where mixity is legally unnecessary, QMV is substituted with unanimity. That is true, but there is a significant difference between the conclusion of an international agreement and the adoption of EU legislation which counterbalances this phenomenon to some degree. EU legislation is proposed by the Commission, and can then be amended by the Parliament and the Council. International agreements, by contrast, are negotiated by the Commission—admittedly under the direction of the Council—but are nevertheless primarily a Commission product. Parliament and Council cannot

[3] Case 22/70 *Commission v Council (AETR)*, EU:C:1971:32 and Opinion 1/75 re Export Credits, EU:C:1975:145.

really amend the final product. In that sense de facto unanimity (or perhaps better consensus) among the Member States does not completely disturb the balance between the supranational and the intergovernmental.

Several contributions engage with susbtantive questions and areas of external competence. Carreau's paper on the EU's participation in the international monetary and financial system unearths the many questions of EU competence which are unanswered with respect to such participation. Kaddous carefully describes the road which EU trade policy has travelled over the decades. It is an impressive trajectory, with the extension to trade in services, intellectual property and foreign direct investment. Dyed-in-the-wool external relations lawyers may recall that at the Maastricht intergovernmental competence the Commission proposed to convert the common commercial policy to a 'common external economic policy', but was laughed out of the room. Yet the current scope of the common commercial policy is getting a lot closer to such a full external economic policy. Segura Serrano's impressive dissection of recent preferential trade agreements which the EU concludes, and which takes the EU-Singapore FTA as a case study, exemplifies the practice of putting together such a policy, built around a wide conception of commercial policy.

But it is not all about competence creep.[4] The paper by Cannizzaro offers a most insightful dissection of the interface between the CFSP and the EU's substantive external policies—including the so-called bridge of Article 215 TFEU in the sphere of sanctions ('restrictive measures'). His analysis shows the unresolved nature of the attempt to find some kind of legally enforceable balance between the open-ended and intergovernmental CFSP and the substantively defined supranational EU policies. There is no indication here that the balance is shifting towards the supranational.

B. Autonomy from International Law?

In Opinion 2/13 regarding EU accession to the ECHR the CJEU emphasised the autonomy of EU law, and constructed it as an autonomy from both national and international law. The Opinion is referred to in several contributions, and was not wholly unexpected. The CJEU case law on international law of the last decade or so is often criticised for not being *völkerrechtsfreundlich*. Some contributors to this volume also rehearse this theme. It is remarkable that even Council lawyers—Gosalbo Bono and Naert—consider that the case law 'disproportionately magnifies the autonomy and purity of the EU legal order over other legal orders', and express disappointment (Chapter one). Diez-Hochleitern is less explicit in his analysis of the compatibility of investor-state dispute settlement (ISDS) with EU

[4] To borrow from S Weatherill, 'Competence Creep and Competence Control' (2004) 23 *Yearbook of European Law* 1.

law, yet the autonomy concept which he advocates is one which allows the EU to become a player in ISDS (Chapter fourteen). Of course, the latter is contested also for other reasons, but the author offers a spirited, reasoned, and reasonable defence. Leaving the political contestation to one side, we do note here that the kind of autonomy from international law which the CJEU articulated in Opinion 2/13 appears to make it difficult for the EU to participate in 'mixed' systems of dispute settlement (involving both the EU and the Member States).[5] This is because of the Court's aversion against an international tribunal interpreting EU law, and allocating responsibility to either the EU or a Member State.

Cannizzaro returns to the famous *Kadi* litigation (Chapter seventeen), and although he is positive about the fact that the EU assumed jurisdiction in that case, and reviewed Mr Kadi's listing, he considers that the international-law route ought to have been chosen: the Court should have reviewed the international validity of the relevant Security Council resolution.

Eeckhout (Chapter four) and Neframi (Chapter five), on the other hand, are more sanguine about the CJEU case law, and emphasise the fundamental openness towards international law. Neframi offers a refined analysis of the difference in treatment between international agreements and customary international law. Even if the latter is incapable of having direct effect, it pervades EU law.

These are all fascinating debates, but what is in our view most notable throughout this volume is the enormous contrast between the CJEU's emphasis on autonomy, marking a distance from international law, and the EU's growing participation in international law-making. Wessel and Blockmans present a very informed assessment of the interaction between the EU and international organisations (IOs), and the extent to which decisions of IOs influence and affect EU law (Chapter six). The authors are critical of the autonomy concept, and their near empirical approach shows that excessive autonomy would hinder EU participation in the work of IOs. Roldán Barbero discusses the many connections between EU law and international agreements concluded by the Member States: even where the EU is not itself a party, there is an intricate web of such connections (Chapter seven). Marín Aís identifies the EU's contribution to the formation of customary international law in the field of human rights (Chapter eight). His analysis exemplifies how strongly EU human rights law is integrated with international and (non-EU) European human rights law. Pérez Bernárdez's chapter shows that, notwithstanding the EU's status limitations in the UN, as a mere observer, there is unified action in the sphere of human rights (Chapter ten). She rightly emphasises universality and is hopeful about the contribution which the EU is capable of making to global respect for universal rights. The contribution by Wouters and Chané (Chapter nine) also evidences the extent to which the EU is active in the multilateral UN framework. And Marreo Rocha's comprehensive account (Chapter eighteen) of how the EU is contributing to arms trade control reveals that even in areas

[5] Opinion 2/13 re Accession to the ECHR, EU:C:2014:2454.

which used to be the jealous guard of national sovereignty, the EU has become a global actor.

The conclusion is thus that at policy-making level the EU embraces international law, and aims to be faithful to the goal set in Article 3(5) TEU of contributing to the strict observance and development of international law. This introduction is not the place to develop a further critique on the CJEU's autonomy case law, but it seems clear from both the TEU and the EU's policies that an excessive emphasis on autonomy does not fit the EU's living constitution.

C. Institutional Issues Remain Alive

The Lisbon Treaty was advertised as a grand settlement of EU institutional issues. In the sphere of external action it was welcomed as a strong attempt to reinforce the institutional set-up, through the enhanced role of the High Representative (HR) and the creation of the External Action Service (EEAS). The HR's 'double-hatting', and the staffing of the EEAS would contribute to greater coherence of EU external action, and to less institutional strife. However, there is no agreement among the contributors to this volume that those goals have been met, and that the current institutional arrangements are satisfactory.

We have already noted the extent to which the Council and Commission lawyers continue to disagree on competence issues, in much the same way as throughout the EU's history. The chapter by Passos (Chapter two) shows the extent to which the Parliament has also become a significant player, and though its greater role in EU external action can only be applauded, it also leads to more inter-institutional disputes. And how about the HR and the EEAS? Gosalbo Bono and Naert are critical of the Lisbon innovations (Chapter one). They speak of an overburdened HR, a struggling EEAS, and a more confused system of EU external representation due to the Lisbon Treaty's assigning of the such representation to multiple actors.

But the picture is mixed. Wouters and Chané (Chapter nine) are more positive about the reformed institutional structure, and like Pérez Bernárdez (Chapter ten) they see more unified action in the UN. López-Escudero, on the other hand, rightly laments the painstakingly slow progress in establishing a stronger EU representation in the IMF (Chapter twelve). It is indeed an anachronism that the world's second currency does not have its own IMF seat. Like in many other organizations, the EU needs to live with second-best solutions of representation through the Member States. The Kissinger urban myth of who to call in Europe continues to reflect a genuine problem, perhaps more than ever. The issue is not that there is *no* number to call; it is that there are so many of them: those of the Commission and European Council Presidents; of the Member States' presidencies; of the HR; of the Eurogroup President; and of the Member States' political leaders.

The approach towards international dispute settlement can also be counted among the institutional issues. It is really only in the WTO that things have worked well, with a unified EU. Free-trade agreements concluded by the EU each have their own dispute settlement system, but they are rarely used, if ever. Nor are there any other multilateral systems in which the EU participates and is an active player. In our view, the litmus test for how the EU's participation in dispute settlement develops, revolves around its new FDI policy, and the embrace—or not—of ISDS. The chapter by Diez-Hochleitern is an excellent guide to the issues which this embrace raises (Chapter fourteen). Obviously, the ongoing TTIP negotiations are crucial in this respect.

D. Some Final Remarks

Many more themes are touched upon and discussed throughout the contributions that follow, and this introduction cannot do them all justice. The three themes which we have highlighted do show the constancy of 'the law' in EU external action. It is becoming a mature field of EU law, even if it continues to be dynamic and littered with new or unresolved questions. Such maturity is helpful in times of crisis. The actions and responses of the institutions are embedded in a constitutional and legal framework which guarantees some level of effectiveness and legitimacy. It is however also clear that, as noted above, this strong framework is not matched by a visible political persona for the EU as an international actor. There is only so much the law on its own can do, and the extent to which the EU continues to develop as an international actor will be to a large degree dependent on political decisions and developments, including in times of multiple crises.

Part II

The EU Institutional System for External Action at Work

1

The Reluctant (Lisbon) Treaty and Its Implementation in the Practice of the Council

RICARDO GOSALBO-BONO AND FREDERIK NAERT[1]

Content:

I. INTRODUCTION

IN THIS CONTRIBUTION, we will discuss a number of selected legal and institutional issues concerning EU external relations, with particular attention to the practice of the Council of the EU. The issues covered are by no means the only ones that pose challenges. They have been selected because of their broad impact, fundamental nature, and the particular questions that they raise in practice.

[1] Ricardo Gosalbo-Bono is Former Director in the Legal Service of the Council of the EU and Professor of Law at the Vrije Universiteit Brussel, (VUB).

The Treaty of Lisbon introduced a significant number of changes to the Treaties. They have been analysed extensively in doctrine[2] and need not be repeated here. However, it is pertinent to briefly highlight those changes which in the practice of EU external relations have been particularly problematic.[3]

II. AN EFFECTIVE TREATY?

In the wake of the failure of the planned Constitutional Treaty, one of the key objectives which led to the conclusion of the Treaty of Lisbon, was to respond to a widely recognised need to achieve greater coherence and consistency in the field of external relations.[4] For that purpose, the Lisbon Treaty introduced changes of a structural nature that 'serve to consolidate, streamline and clarify the provisions on the EU's external relations', but which, however, 'do not change the overall objectives of the EU's external policies'.[5] In order to rationalise EU external action, which was before Lisbon based on a three pillar structure, the Lisbon Treaty merged pillars one (Community) and three (Police and Judicial Cooperation in Criminal Matters) but maintained special arrangements for the Common Foreign and Security Policy (CFSP); transferred the former provisions on the CFSP objectives into a new chapter entitled 'General Provisions on the Union's External Action' covering the whole of EU external action; and added a new Article 21 TEU setting out the principles underpinning the external action of the EU which, in addition to preserving pre-Lisbon provisions now also include explicit references to the consolidation and support for the principles of international law, to multilateral cooperation and to the prevention of conflicts. Finally, it incorporated into the TFEU a Part V which brings together the main external policy areas belonging to the former community competences and other external policy matters except for the CFSP.

Dr Frederik Naert is a member of the Legal Service of the Council of the EU and an affiliated senior researcher at the Katholieke Universiteit Leuven. The views expressed are solely those of the authors and do not bind the Council or its Legal Service.

[2] For an insider's view, see J-C Piris, *The Lisbon Treaty. A Legal and Political Analysis* (Cambridge, Cambridge University Press, 2010).

[3] See also PJ Cardwell, *EU External Relations Law and Policy in the Post-Lisbon Era* (Berlin/The Hague, Springer/TMC Asser Press, 2012) and J Wouters, D Coppens and B De Meester, 'External Relations after the Lisbon Treaty' in S Griller and J Ziller (eds), *The Lisbon Treaty—EU Constitutionalism without a Constitutional Treaty?* (Vienna, Springer, 2008) 143.

[4] See Piris (n 2 above) 238 and 241–43. The main recital of the Treaty of Lisbon reads as follows: 'DESIRING to complete the process started by the Treaty of Amsterdam and by the Treaty of Nice with a view to enhancing the efficiency and democratic legitimacy of the Union and to improving the coherence of its action'. The latter aspect is not limited to the Union's external action but applies especially in this field.

[5] See UK House of Lords, Select Committee on European Union, Session 2007–08, Tenth Report, *The Treaty of Lisbon: an Impact Assessment*, March 2008: www.publications.parliament.uk/pa/ld200708/ldselect/ldeucom/62/62.pdf, chapter 7, points 7.1–7.16, especially point 7.16.

More specifically, the Lisbon Treaty provides for:[6]

- horizontal overall objectives for all EU external relations in Articles 3(5) and 21 TEU and Article 205 TFEU;
- the attribution of multiple roles to the High Representative of the Union for Foreign Affairs and Security Policy ('High Representative' or 'HR') *intuitu personae*, namely Presidency of the Foreign Affairs Council (FAC), Vice-Presidency of the Commission, and HR proper (relating to CFSP matters), assisted by a European External Action Service (EEAS) (Articles 18 and 27 TEU);
- increased participation of the European Parliament (EP) in decision-making, notably in relation to international agreements (the conclusion of a substantial number of which now requires the consent of the EP pursuant to Article 218(6) TFEU) and as regards the common commercial policy, the scope of which has been substantially enlarged (Article 207 TFEU);[7]
- a unified procedure for negotiating and concluding international agreements, including in the field of the CFSP, albeit with different modalities (Article 218 TFEU and Article 207 TFEU on the common commercial policy);
- a permanent chair for the FAC, namely the High Representative, and for the European Council, namely its President;
- the introduction of innovations in/amendments to the provisions on the CFSP, which remains essentially a distinct policy 'subject to specific rules and procedures' with a very limited role for the Court of Justice of the European Union (Court of Justice, CJEU, the Court or EU Court),[8] the European Parliament and the European Commission (Article 24(1) TEU);
- the introduction of innovations in/amendments to the provisions on the Common Security and Defence Policy (CSDP), including the role of the High Representative, the increase in cases of decision-making by qualified majority voting, even if it remains the exception (Article 31 TEU), a mutual assistance clause in case of armed aggression against a Member State (Article 42(7) TEU), the primary law anchoring of the European Defence Agency (Article 45 TEU), the 'Permanent Structured Cooperation' (Article 46 TEU) and the authorisation to create a start-up fund for expenditure for (preparatory activities for) CSDP tasks which are not charged to the Union budget (Article 41(3) TEU);

[6] For a thorough analysis, see ibid, chapter 7.

[7] See generally M Bungenberg, 'Going Global? The EU Common Commercial Policy After Lisbon' (2010) 1 *European Yearbook of International Economic Law* 123; A Dimopoulos, 'The Effects of the Lisbon Treaty on the Principles and Objectives of the Common Commercial Policy' (2010) 15 *European Foreign Affairs Review* 153; M Krajewski, 'The Reform of the Common Commercial Policy' in A Biondi and P Eeckhout (eds), *European Union Law after the Treaty of Lisbon* (Oxford, Oxford University Press, 2012) 292; and G Villalta Puig and B Al-Haddab, 'The Common Commercial Policy after Lisbon: an Analysis of the Reforms' (2011) 36 *European Law Review* 289.

[8] The CJEU is not competent on CFSP issues, with the exception of its jurisdiction to monitor compliance with Art 40 TEU and to review the legality of certain CFSP decisions imposing restrictive measures against individuals or entities (see Art 275 TFEU). The topic of restrictive measures is addressed below.

— a revised provision on the relationship between the CFSP and other Union policies (Article 40 TEU) which now not only protects the non-CFSP Union policies from encroachment by CFSP measures, but also vice versa, ie it requires mutual non-interference between the CFSP and other Union policies;
— a 'solidarity clause' laid down in Article 222 TFEU, imposing assistance by the Union and the Member States if a Member State is the object of a terrorist attack or the victim of a natural or man-made disaster—although this clause in fact appears primarily to have an internal dimension.

These Treaty amendments remain modest in comparison with those of the failed Constitutional Treaty in the field of external relations, which inter alia envisaged the role of High Representative for the Common Foreign and Security Policy as amalgamated with the role of the Commissioner for External Relations and which would have created a new Union Minister for Foreign Affairs who would also be a Vice President of the Commission responsible for coordinating foreign policy across the Union, and representing the EU abroad in areas where there is a Union position.

On a number of issues the text of the Treaty of Lisbon was a compromise text reflecting quite diverse positions of Member States, and these differences of opinion have resurfaced in relation to the interpretation and implementation of certain provisions, for instance in relation to the setting up of the European External Action Service (EEAS) and have affected the willingness to make use of some of the possibilities offered by the Treaty of Lisbon (eg the establishment of the permanent structured cooperation pursuant to Article 46 TEU or the creation of the start-up fund pursuant to Article 41(3) TEU).

Moreover, the Treaty of Lisbon contains clear provisions/declarations to better define, and thereby circumscribe, the powers of the Union (Article 4(1) TEU; Article 2(2) TFEU as regards the shared competences of the EU; Article 4(3) and (4) TFEU as regards parallel competences; and Declaration Nos 13 and 14 on the CFSP). This was an important point for a number of Member States, not least in order to ensure that they remained the 'Masters of the Treaties', notably in response to certain case law of the EU Court such as Opinion 1/94 on the question whether the Union had exclusive competence to conclude the WTO Agreement and its Annexes,[9] and the *ECOWAS* judgment whereby the Court annulled

[9] Opinion 1/94 of 15 November 1994 *on the competence of the Community to conclude agreements concerning services and the protection of intellectual property* [1994] ECR I-5267. Some scholars have argued that the CJEU has on occasion wrestled some control over the Treaties from Member States. See eg G Conway, 'Conflicts of Competence Norms in EU Law and the Legal Reasoning of the ECJ' (2010) 11 *German Law Journal* 966, 995–1005 (available online at: www.germanlawjournal.com/pdfs/Vol11-No9/PDF_Vol_11_No_09_966-1005_Conway.pdf). On p 999, Conway writes that: 'In Opinion 1/91, the ECJ did appear to act as a supra-constitutional body, since it ruled out the apparent adoption by the constituent power of the EC, ie the Member States, of a body with overlapping competence with the Community. The ECJ thus seemed to implicitly posit the existence of some lex superior higher even than the Treaty. This suggests that although the Community originated in an act of the Member States, the Member States are no longer fully "masters of the Treaties"'. Compare K Alter, 'Who are "Masters of the Treaties"? European Governments and the European Court of Justice' (1998) 52 *International Organization* 121; V Constantinesco, 'The ECJ as Law-maker: Praeter aut Contra Legem?' in D O'Keeffe

a CFSP Council decision that supported the moratorium on small arms and light weapons because the Court considered that whenever a measure could be founded within both the CFSP and within the Community pillar, it should always be adopted within the latter ('the first pillar always wins').[10] This circumscription of Union powers is particularly visible in relation to the competences of the Union and has influenced the position and practice of the Council.

By contrast, the Commission has adopted a strategy to interpret and apply the new provisions of the Treaties widely, thereby reducing, if not completely suppressing, existing competences of the Member States in the field of external relations.[11] Moreover, the Commission has reserved an important role for legal action in its strategy, bringing a series of cases against the Council (some examples are discussed below), in an effort to seek the endorsement of the Commission's wide interpretation by the CJEU.[12]

Likewise, the European Parliament has sought to maximise its powers and role (eg in relation to the EEAS and international agreements) and has also brought several actions against the Council before the CJEU (see the examples below). The EP had some notable political success in this respect in relation to the Commission, as reflected in their bilateral inter-institutional agreement,[13] which has, however, been criticised by the Council.[14]

and A Bavasso (eds), *Judicial Review in European Law: Essays in Honour of Lord Slynn* (The Hague, Kluwer Law International, 2001) 73; and G Conway, *The Limits of Legal Reasoning and the European Court of Justice* (Cambridge, Cambridge University Press, 2012).

[10] Case C-91/05 *Commission v Council (ECOWAS)* [2008] ECR I-3651. See C Hillion and R Wessel, 'Competence Distribution in EU External Relations after ECOWAS: Clarification or Continued Fuzziness?' (2009) 46 *Common Market Law Review* 551.

[11] Another, horizontal front (also involving the EP) has been the choice/difference between delegated acts and implementing acts under Arts 290 and 291 TFEU, as well as the scope of implementing acts. See eg the CJEU's judgment of 18 March 2014 in Case C-427/12 *Commission v Parliament and Council (Biocides)* (EU:C:2014:170); its judgment of 15 October 2014 in Case C-65/13 *Parliament v Commission* (EU:C:2014:2289); and its judgment of 16 July 2015 in Case C-88/14 *Commission v Parliament and Council* (EU:C:2015:499). In fact, this issue was one of the main difficulties in the negotiations over the most recent external financial instruments.

[12] For a recent example, see the decision of the Commission to ask the CJEU for an opinion on the trade agreement with Singapore which has been initialed. See 'Singapore: The Commission to Request a Court of Justice Opinion on the trade deal', Commission press release of 30 October 2014.

[13] Framework Agreement on relations between the European Parliament and the Commission [2010] OJ L304/47. For instance, this Framework Agreement refers to equal treatment by the Commission of the EP and the Council (eg in recital E and point 9), despite the fact that both of the latter institutions have different prerogatives. See the opinion of the Council Legal Service included in Council doc 15018/10 of 18 October 2010, p 11, para 7.

[14] The Council has stated that: 'The Council notes that several provisions of the Framework Agreement have the effect of modifying the institutional balance set out in the Treaties in force, according the European Parliament prerogatives that are not provided for in the Treaties and limiting the autonomy of the Commission and its President. The Council is particularly concerned by the provisions on international agreements, infringement proceedings against Member States and transmission of classified information to the European Parliament. The Framework Agreement cannot be applied to the Council. The Council will submit to the Court of Justice any act or action of the European Parliament or of the Commission performed in application of the provisions of the Framework Agreement that would have an effect contrary to the interests of the Council and the prerogatives conferred upon it by the

Divergent institutional positions on many fronts have resulted in serious inter-institutional conflicts, the resolution of which has required the investment of much time and effort which could have been devoted to the substance of EU external action and its external delivery. It has also significantly affected the degree of cooperation. Some of the examples given below illustrate this.

III. THE PROBLEMATIC AND DISPUTED FIELD OF COMPETENCES AND THE ISSUE OF MIXITY

For the first time in the constitutional history of the EU, the Treaty of Lisbon sets out explicitly constitutional principles that—except for the principle of conferral[15]—have always been implicit in the Treaties: the Union may only exercise such competences (ie the powers in specified areas of responsibility) as the Member States have conferred on it—the principle of conferral (Articles 4 and 5 TEU)—and all other competences remain with the Member States, which may decide to reduce the competences of the Union (Article 48(2) TEU).[16] This is also the subject of Declaration No 18 in relation to the delimitation of competences[17] and is reflected in Protocol No 25 on the exercise of shared competence.

The Lisbon Treaty 'seeks to describe and codifies the division of competences between the Union and the Member States' 'for decision-making in a particular policy field' (Articles 4 and 5 TEU and new Title I TFEU).[18] In particular, in the field of foreign relations, while expanding the scope of some EU competences (eg foreign direct investments, intellectual property, humanitarian aid, the solidarity clause), the Treaty of Lisbon safeguards the external competences of the

Treaties' (see Council doc 15172/10, p 17). See also Council doc 15018/10 of 18 October 2010 and V Pop, 'Member States Threaten MEPs and Commission with Legal Case', *EU Observer*, 21 October 2010: euobserver.com/institutional/31098.

[15] Ever since the creation of the European Communities it has been made clear that the Union only has those competences which have been conferred on it by the Treaties: see already explicitly Art 4(1) *in fine* TEEC and see generally G De Baere, *Constitutional Principles of EU External Relations* (Oxford, Oxford University Press, 2008) 9–32. The Court of Justice has also acknowledged the pivotal nature of the principle of conferral, a principle that has informed the life of the EU since its evolution in different configurations (see eg Opinion 2/94 of 28 March 1996 *on Accession by the Community to the European Convention for the Protection of Human Rights and Fundamental Freedoms*, para 23), as have the constitutional or supreme courts of the Member States, with nuances, in their decisions relating to who is the final arbiter on the delimitation of competences between the EU and its Member States (for a recent discussion in relation to the case law of the German Constitutional Court, see eg D Murswiek, 'ECB, ECJ, Democracy, and the Federal Constitutional Court: Notes on the Federal Constitutional Court's Referral Order from 14 January 2014' (2014) 15 *German Law Journal* 147 (available online at: www.germanlawjournal.com/pdfs/Vol15-No2/PDF_Vol_15_No_03_Murswiek.pdf), especially 156–66).

[16] See UK House of Lords, Select Committee on European Union, Tenth Report, above n 5, points 2.21–2.23 and 2.42.

[17] The first paragraph of this Declaration reads as follows: 'in accordance with the system of division of competences between the Union and the Member States as provided for in the [TEU] and the [TFEU], competences not conferred upon the Union in the Treaties remain with the Member States'.

[18] See UK House of Lords, Select Committee on European Union, above n 5, point 2.21.

Member States. Thus, Article 5 TEU provides that 'The limits of Union competences are governed by the principle of conferral', according to which 'the Union shall act only within the limits of the competences conferred upon it by the Member States in the Treaties to attain the objectives set out therein'. 'For the first time and in the clearest terms' Article 4 TEU provides that 'competences not conferred upon the Union in the Treaties remain with the Member States' and that the Union 'shall respect' the Member States' 'essential State functions, including ensuring the territorial integrity of the State, maintaining law and order and safeguarding national security. In particular, national security remains the sole responsibility of each Member State'.[19] Article 5 TEU clarifies, in more detail than in previous treaties, that

> in areas which do not fall within its exclusive competence, the Union shall act only if and insofar as the objectives of the proposed action cannot be sufficiently achieved by the Member States, either at central level or at regional and local level

(the principle of subsidiarity, referring, for the first time, also to the sub-State level) and that the 'Union action shall not exceed what is necessary to achieve the objectives of the Treaties' (the principle of proportionality).[20] The practical application of the subsidiarity and proportionality principles is laid down in Protocol No 2, which gives national parliaments 'power to police the principle of subsidiarity' and is annexed to the Treaties.[21]

The TFEU 'determines the areas of, delimitation of, and arrangements for exercising [the Union's] competences' (Article 1). Article 2 TFEU lays down further details on the Union's competences so that when the Treaties confer on the Union exclusive competence in a specific area, only the Union may legislate and adopt legally binding acts, 'the Member States being able to do so themselves only if so empowered by the Union or for the implementation of acts of the Union' (para 1). When the Treaties confer on the Union a competence shared with the Member States in a specific area, the Union and the Member States may legislate and adopt legally binding acts in that area and the 'Member States shall exercise their competence to the extent that the Union has not exercised its competence' (para 2). The 'Member States shall exercise their competence again to the extent that the Union has decided to cease exercising its competence' (para 2).

As regards the field of external relations, Article 216(1) TFEU explicitly echoes the principle of conferral, in the light of compliance with the principles of subsidiarity and proportionality, in the following terms:

> The Union may conclude an agreement with one or more third countries or international organisations where the Treaties so provide or where the conclusion of an agreement is necessary in order to achieve, within the framework of the Union's policies, one of the objectives referred to in the Treaties, or is provided for in a legally binding Union act or is likely to affect common rules or alter their scope.

[19] ibid, point 2.22.
[20] ibid, point 2.23.
[21] ibid, point 2.23.

Moreover, Article 352(2) and (3) TFEU, which confers upon the Union the power to adopt measures to achieve Union objectives where the Treaties do not provide for specific powers, now contains specific and explicit limits with regard to its scope (cf its predecessor provision ex-Article 308 TEC).[22] In addition, the rules which some Member States have put in place to implement this provision at their level[23] have introduced significant thresholds and requirements that undoubtedly make recourse to Article 352 TFEU much more exceptional than it had been in the past. By making these powers explicit, and by circumscribing them, there will probably be less room for innovative expansions of EU powers.

Again, for the first time in the constitutional history of the EU, the Treaty of Lisbon sets out categories of competences and refers to competences in the descriptions of each category by more or less broadly defined areas.[24] The categories largely reflect the provisions of the former TEC setting out the competences, and the case law of the EU Court as it has examined those provisions over the years.[25] Most areas of EU activity are defined as shared competences, as Article 4 TFEU expressly provides that the list of areas contained therein is illustrative, not exhaustive.[26]

Indeed, leaving aside competence for the CFSP (see below), the TFEU recognises three types of Union competence: exclusive competence, shared competence, and supporting competence. Where the Union has exclusive competence (see Article 2(1) TFEU), 'only the Union' can legislate and adopt legally binding acts (the principle of subsidiarity does not apply), 'the Member States being able to do so themselves only if so empowered by the Union or for the implementation of Union acts' (Article 2(1) TFEU); the areas of exclusive competence are well established in Article 3 TFEU which lays down the list of areas of exclusive competence and defines the grounds on which the EU may acquire exclusive competence as a result of the development of EU law, reflecting the case law of the EU Court.[27] Shared competence exists where the Union and its Member States are both able to act. In practice, the 'principal areas' of shared competence are laid down in

[22] At least its limits have been more explicitly and clearly reflected in the text: see notably paras 2 and 3 of Art 352.

[23] For the UK, see notably the European Union Act 2011 (c 12) (see: services.parliament.uk/bills/2010-11/europeanunion.html). For Germany, see the 'Lisbon accompanying laws' of 22 September 2009, BGBl I, respectively pp 3022, 3026 and 3031 (including *Gesetz über die Wahrnehmung der Integrationsverantwortung des Bundestages und des Bundesrates in Angelegenheiten der Europäischen Union*, subsequently amended by Art 1 of the *Gesetz zur Umsetzung der Grundgesetzänderungen für die Ratifizierung des Vertrags von Lissabon* of 1 December 2009, BGBl I, p 3822). This legislation was adopted in response to the 'Lisbon judgment' of the German Constitutional Court of 30 June 2009 (2 BvE 2/08).

[24] See UK House of Lords, Select Committee on European Union, above n 5, point 2.28.

[25] ibid, point 2.43.

[26] ibid, point 2.43.

[27] Pursuant to para 2 of Art 3 TFEU the Union: 'also has exclusive competence for the conclusion of an international agreement when its conclusion is provided for in a legislative act of the Union or is necessary to enable the Union to exercise its internal competence, or in so far as its conclusion may affect common rules or alter their scope'.

Article 4 TFEU; in those cases, 'the Member States shall exercise their competence to the extent that the Union has not exercised its competence' and they 'shall again exercise their competence to the extent that the Union has decided to cease exercising its competence' (Article 2(2) TFEU). In addition, Protocol No 25 on the exercise of shared competence annexed to the Lisbon Treaty provides that 'when the Union has taken action in a certain area [of shared competence], the scope of this exercise of competence only covers those elements governed by the Union act in question and therefore does not cover the whole area'. Member States are therefore free to act in the same area, as long as they do not enact legislation that is not in line with EU law or principles. Finally, the Union has competence to carry out actions to support, coordinate or supplement the actions of Member States in certain areas. This EU supporting competence may include adopting incentive measures and making recommendations but it does not supersede the competence of Member States to act and must not entail the harmonisation of national laws (Article 2(5) TFEU).

However, the Treaty of Lisbon lists setting out the division of policy areas into these types of competence, despite their transparent and codifying achievements, are short and do not cover every aspect of Union activity. For the detailed determination of each competence, reference is made in Article 2(6) TFEU to 'the provisions of the Treaties relating to each area'. Thus, eg the existing provisions on the common commercial policy are amended to also refer to foreign direct investment (Article 207 TFEU).

The ability to repatriate competences, which has been referred to as 'the mirror image of conferral',[28] is included in the Treaties for the first time under the Lisbon Treaty reforms. Thus Declaration No 18 relating to the delimitation of competences 'underlines' that competences not conferred upon the Union in the Treaties 'remain with the Member States' and goes into more detail about shared competence, explaining that

> When the Treaties confer on the Union a competence shared with the Member States in a specific area, the Member States shall exercise their competence to the extent that the Union has not exercised, or has decided to cease exercising, its competence. The latter situation arises when the relevant EU institutions decide to repeal a legislative act, in particular better to ensure constant respect for the principles of subsidiarity and proportionality. The Council may, at the initiative of one or several of its members (representatives of Member States) and in accordance with Article 241 of the [TFEU], request the Commission to submit proposals for repealing a legislative act. The Conference welcomes the Commission's declaration that it will devote particular attention to these requests. Equally, the representatives of the governments of the Member States, meeting in an Intergovernmental Conference, in accordance with the ordinary revision procedure provided for in Article 48(2) to (5) of the [TEU], may decide to amend the Treaties upon which the Union is founded, including either to increase or to reduce the competences conferred on the Union in the said Treaties.

[28] See UK House of Lords, Select Committee on European Union (n 5 above), point 2.30.

This Declaration states explicitly what has been the obvious nature of the EU competences since the creation of the EU (even though it is and has been regarded as blasphemy in some circles),[29] namely that the EU does not determine its own remit—the Member States do (they are the 'Masters of the Treaties')—and that, since the European Union does not have the sovereign 'competence of competences', every competence that the European Union has is conferred on it by Member States and that such competence can be taken away by the same Member States.[30]

The above provisions on the delimitation and division of competences have become a contentious issue in particular because, despite the objective of 'an ever closer Union among the peoples of Europe' (Article 1, second paragraph, TEU) this does not appear to imply an increased use of conferred Union competences (see the above quoted Declaration No 18).[31]

In particular, the exact determination of the extent to which the Union's competences have been extended by the Lisbon Treaty has proven to be difficult in practice. The Treaty includes new articles formally specifying new competences, but some of these largely confirm areas of competence in which the Union has already legislated on a different legal basis. Competence is also extended less visibly by amendments to pre-existing articles, but again, the significance of such changes has been perceived differently by the EU institutions and by the Member States (some of which consider that the explicit division of competences in the Lisbon Treaty is meant to prevent 'competence creep').

However, as past practice has shown, in the Court of Justice's task to ensure 'that in the interpretation and application of the Treaties the law is observed' (Article 19(1)) TEU), the case law of the Court makes clear that the definition of shared competences implies that when the European Union legislates over one of them, the Member States lose their power to legislate in that area (the doctrine of the 'occupied territory') thus converting the shared competence into a mere residual competence. Indeed, the Court of Justice has recently been called upon more often to address the Treaties' provisions regarding competences and these Articles have been increasingly interpreted by the Court of Justice in a way that has attracted strong criticism. For instance, the CJEU has indicated that it does not necessarily see some of the above-mentioned provisions as restricting the scope of its pre-Lisbon case law. In particular, in its recent Opinion 1/13 *on the Convention on the civil aspects of international child abduction*, the Court has held that the question when the conclusion of an international agreement may affect common rules or alter the scope of common rules for the purpose of determining the exclusive competence of the Union must be examined in the light of the case law of the EU

[29] ibid, point 2.31.

[30] ibid, point 2.31.

[31] See its second and third paragraphs cited above. The possibility to reduce the competences conferred on the EU goes further than no longer exercising a competence. Moreover, there is now also the explicit possibility for a Member State to withdraw from the Union (Art 50 TEU). It is expected that the UK will trigger this provision following the outcome of its 23 June 2016 referendum.

Court, according to which there is a risk that common EU rules may be adversely affected by international commitments undertaken by the Member States, or that the scope of those rules may be altered where those commitments fall within the scope of those rules. The Court added that a 'finding that there is such a risk does not presuppose that the areas covered by the international commitments and those covered by the EU rules coincide fully' and that 'the scope of EU rules may be affected or altered by international commitments where such commitments are concerned with an area which is already covered to a large extent by such rules', emphasising that 'that circumstance remains relevant, in the context of Article 3(2) TFEU, for the purpose of ascertaining whether the condition pertaining to the risk of EU common rules being affected, or of their scope being altered, is met'.[32]

By contrast, the practice of the Council has shown an attachment to the literal meaning of the provisions of the Treaty of Lisbon, reflecting the views of most (and on occasion all) Member States that any competence not yet exercised by the Union, even for specific aspects in a field largely regulated by the Union, remains with the Member States and that it is an entirely discretionary and political choice whether in any given case the Union chooses to exercise a shared competence, or not to do so.

The issue of 'mixed agreements', ie agreements which contain provisions relating to matters within the competence of the European Union and also provisions relating to matters within the competence of the Member States, or indeed agreements in the fields where both the EU and its Member States have a competence,[33] requires special consideration. The Council and its Member States frequently have recourse to the conclusion of mixed agreements even in cases where an agreement could be concluded by the Union alone if it were decided that it should exercise certain competences (eg CFSP).

In those situations, dual decisions by the EU and the Member States are needed. More specifically, in several cases both a Council decision in relation to Union competences and a Member States decision ('decision of the representatives of the governments of Member States, meeting within the Council') for matters within Member States' competence, including shared non-exercised competences, have been adopted authorising the opening of negotiations, designating the negotiator/negotiating team and issuing negotiating directives.[34] In some cases this has also

[32] Opinion 1/13 of 14 October 2014 *on the Convention on the civil aspects of international child abduction*, EU:C:2014:2303, paras 69–90, especially paras 71–73.

[33] See also R Gosalbo Bono, 'The Organization of the External Relations of the European Union in the Treaty of Lisbon' in P Koutrakos (ed), *The European Union's External Relations a Year After Lisbon*, CLEER Working Paper 2011/3: www.asser.nl/upload/documents/772011_51358CLEER%20WP%20 2011-3%20-%20KOUTRAKOS.pdf, pp 29–33, as well as A Dashwood, 'Mixity in the Era of the Treaty of Lisbon' in C Hillion and P Koutrakos (eds), *Mixed Agreements Revisited. The EU and its Member States in the World* (Oxford, Hart Publishing, 2010) 351, 351 ('There is … nothing in the Treaty of Lisbon that can be seen as deliberately designed either to facilitate or to impede recourse to mixity') and A Rosas, 'The Future of Mixity', in ibid, 367, 367 ('Mixity is here to stay').

[34] See eg Council Decision authorising the opening of negotiations with the Republic of Kazakhstan for an enhanced Partnership and Cooperation Agreement between the European Union and

been done for signature and provisional application.[35] Leaving aside the question whether such decisions can be combined in a 'hybrid' decision of the Council and the Member States,[36] the point of interest here is that by doing so, Member States seem to wish to very explicitly indicate that a competence is not being exercised,[37] even though they are willing to allow the Commission to negotiate on matters falling within such competences in some cases.[38]

its Member States, of the one part, and the Republic of Kazakhstan, of the other part (Council doc 8282/11 of 13 April 2011) and Decision of the representatives of the governments of Member States, meeting within the Council, authorising the European Commission to negotiate, on behalf of the Member States, the provisions of an enhanced Partnership and Cooperation Agreement between the European Union and its Member States, of the one part, and the Republic of Kazakhstan, of the other part, that fall within the competences of the Member States (Council doc 8283/11 of 13 April 2011). Such dual decisions were also adopted, inter alia, in relation to the negotiations for horizontal agreements with Georgia, Armenia, Azerbaijan and Australia (for the latter, see Council doc 14658/11 of 4 October 2011).

[35] See the Decision 2011/708/EU of the Council and of the Representatives of the Governments of the Member States of the European Union, meeting within the Council of 16 June 2011 on the signing, on behalf of the Union, and provisional application of the Air Transport Agreement between the United States of America, of the first part, the European Union and its Member States, of the second part, Iceland, of the third part, and the Kingdom of Norway, of the fourth part; and on the signing, on behalf of the Union, and provisional application of the related Ancillary Agreement [2011] OJ L283/1. Usually, Member States sign mixed agreements without any formal joint decision to this effect.

[36] The Decision cited in the preceding note was challenged before the CJEU by the Commission in Case C-28/12 *Commission v Council*, seeking the annulment of that Decision. In essence, the Commission took the view that such a single hybrid decision wrongly involves the Member States in the adoption of a Union act and that this results in changing the voting rule from qualified majority to unanimity. By contrast, the Council and Member States considered that the two distinct components of this Decision are adopted by different voting rules and that a hybrid decision reflects the requirement of the unity in external representation, notably where Union and Member State competences are inextricably linked. In its judgment of 28 April 2015, the Court held that: 'the contested decision was adopted by means of a single procedure applied to the two acts … However, the act concerning the provisional application of the agreements at issue by the Member States entails consensus of the representatives of those States, and therefore their unanimous agreement, whereas Article 218(8) TFEU provides that the Council must act, on behalf of the European Union, by a qualified majority. The two different acts, brought together in the contested decision, cannot therefore be validly adopted under a single procedure' (para 52).

[37] Prior to the entry into force of the Treaty of Lisbon, for mixed horizontal agreements (such as association agreements, partnership and cooperation agreements or framework agreements) there was usually only a single decision (often not even in the form of a formal decision) adopted by the Council designating the Commission and the Presidency (the latter for the former Titles V and VI TEU), but these agreements were invariably mixed and it was understood that there was an implicit parallel decision by Member States. See eg the decision on Council Negotiating Directives for a new Agreement to provide a comprehensive framework for EU/Russia relations and related note to the Council set out in Council doc 8829/08 of 28 April 2008 (partially declassified in Council doc 8829/08 EXT 2 of 22 December 2009).

[38] See the example of the Member States' decision concerning Kazakhstan (above n 34), Art 1(1). Note that this provision nevertheless also entails a (limited) role for the (rotating) Presidency of the Council (Art 1(2): 'A representative of the Presidency of the Council will accompany the Commission in the negotiations for matters falling within the competences of the Member States') and states that it is 'without prejudice to future decisions of the Member States relating to the designation of their representative on matters falling within their competences' (Art 1(3)). In certain other cases, especially for sectoral agreements, Member States have designated the Presidency to negotiate for matters within their competence. For a controversial case (an agreement on Mercury in the environment field), see eg T Corthaut and D Van Eeckhoutte, 'Legal Aspects of EU Participation in Global Environmental

The Commission has in several cases proposed negotiating directives for 'EU-only' agreements, ie non-mixed agreements to which only the Union and not the Member States would be a party. However, this has been almost systematically rejected by the Council. In particular, Member States within the Council have repeatedly chosen not to exercise shared competences which had not already been exercised, have considered that some elements of envisaged agreements fall within exclusive Member State competence, and/or have chosen not to exercise the Union's CFSP competence (see below), in order to maintain their presence and participation alongside that of the Union. This pattern can be identified both with regard to 'horizontal' agreements (eg association agreements, partnership and cooperation agreements) and agreements dealing with particular policies (eg environment or transport). In some cases, the Commission has challenged the relevant Council (and Member States') decision(s) before the Court of Justice. One exception is the stabilisation and association agreement with Kosovo,[39] but this is due to the fact that for some Member States which have not recognised Kosovo as an independent State, a mixed agreement would imply a recognition of the independence of Kosovo by all the contracting parties and thus mixity was not acceptable in this case.

As its recent rulings demonstrate, the Court of Justice appears unaffected by the restrictive provisions of the Treaty of Lisbon and continues to reinforce and expand its traditional views on the scope of EU competences. Thus in its recent ruling of 4 September 2014 on the international convention for the protection of neighbouring rights of broadcasting organisations,[40] the Court held, in relation to Article 3(2) TFEU, that 'the scope of common EU rules may be affected or altered by [international] commitments also where those commitments fall within an area which is already largely covered by such rules' (para 70), and considered that a more restrictive interpretation under Protocol No 25 on the exercise of shared competences (see above) did not affect this finding, since that Protocol

> seeks to define the scope of the exercise by the European Union of a shared competence … which was conferred on it by the Treaties, and not to limit the scope of the exclusive

Governance under the UN Umbrella' in J Wouters et al (eds), *The European Union and Multilateral Governance* (Basingstoke, Palgrave Macmillan, 2012) 145; G De Baere, 'Mercury Rising: The European Union and the International Negotiations for a Globally Binding Instrument on Mercury' (2012) 37 *European Law Review* 640; G De Baere, 'International Negotiations Post-Lisbon: A Case Study of the Union's External Environmental Policy' in P Koutrakos (ed) (n 32 above) 97; and J Wouters and T Ramopoulos, *Revisiting the Lisbon Treaty's Constitutional Design of EU External Relations*, Leuven Centre for Global Governance Studies Working Paper No 119, September 2013: www.fp7-frame.eu/wp-content/materiale/w-papers/WP119-Wouters-Ramopoulos.pdf, p 20. See also M Gatti and P Manzini, 'External representation of the European Union in the conclusion of international agreements' (2012) 49 *Common Market Law Review* 1703, 1711–23.

[39] See Council Decision (EU) 2015/1988 of 22 October 2015 on the signing, on behalf of the Union, of the Stabilisation and Association Agreement between the European Union and the European Atomic Energy Community, of the one part, and Kosovo*, of the other part (*This designation is without prejudice to positions on status, and is in line with UNSCR 1244/1999 and the ICJ Opinion on the Kosovo declaration of independence), OJ L 290, 6.11.2015, p 4.

[40] Case C-114/12 *Commission v Council*, judgment of 4 September 2014 (EU:C:2014:2151).

> external competence of the European Union in the cases referred to in Article 3(2) TFEU (paragraph 73).[41]

It concluded that

> the content of the negotiations for a Convention ... falls within an area covered to a large extent by common EU rules and ... those negotiations may affect common EU rules or alter their scope. Therefore, those negotiations fall within the exclusive competence of the European Union (paragraph 102).

Despite the rulings of the Court of Justice interpreting extensively the scope of competences of the EU in the field of external relations, it appears doubtful that the Council and its Member States will change their position about mixity, a practice that, reinforced with provisional application, is founded on the fundamental principle of conferral and which in their view has proven to be very useful. There can be little doubt about the legal validity of the practice, since it has been validated by the Court of Justice,[42] which has established that mixed agreements are an integral part of the EU legal order[43] and has emphasised the need for common action, or sincere cooperation, by the Union and the Member States 'in close association' with each other in the negotiation and implementation of such agreements. This duty of sincere or close cooperation follows from what the Court has called the 'requirement of unity in the international representation of the Union',[44] which is one of the fundamental principles of the external relations of the Union. Consequently, mixed agreements remain one of the most distinctive features of the external relations law and practice of the European Union.

The operation of the treaty provisions on the CFSP within the practice of mixity requires specific consideration.

IV. THE CFSP: A DISTINCT PILLAR WITH UNACHIEVED POTENTIAL

With the Treaty of Lisbon, the CFSP has remained 'subject to specific rules and procedures' (Article 24 TEU), which differentiates it from other external policy areas, in particular as regards decision-making procedures and the distribution of powers between the institutions.

[41] That finding is far from obvious in relation to the specific type of exclusive competence under Art 3(2) TFEU, namely one based on the prior exercise of Union competence resulting in common rules, including in areas of shared competence. The latter are subject to Protocol No 25 and it is not clear why the rule set out therein should apply to internal aspects of such policies but not their external ones.

[42] Case 12/86 *Demirel v Stadt Schwäbisch Gmünd* [1987] ECR 3719. In this case the Court used the term 'mixed agreement' to describe the Association Agreement between the Community and the Member States on the one hand and Turkey on the other.

[43] Case C-431/05 *Merck Genericos—Produtos Farmacêuticos Lda v Merck & Co Inc* [2007] ECR I-7001, paras 33–48.

[44] See eg Ruling 1/78 (*Re Draft Convention on the Physical Protection of Nuclear Materials*) [1978] ECR 2151, paras 34–36.

Under the Treaty of Lisbon, the CFSP continues to be based on European Council and Council 'decisions' (no longer named 'joint actions' and 'common positions') acting unanimously as a general rule even if abstentions are possible. Furthermore, when abstaining in a vote Member States are entitled to make a formal declaration in which case they are not obliged to apply that decision but have to accept that the decision commits the Union and that they have to refrain from any action likely to conflict with or impede the Union action based on that decision (Article 31(1), second subparagraph, TEU); this is usually referred to as 'constructive abstention' and sometimes (also) as 'qualified abstention',[45] a description which captures its less constructive nature in comparison with normal abstention).

The Treaty of Lisbon also maintains the exceptional cases in which the rule of qualified majority voting (QMV) is provided for, while adding new possibilities for the adoption by QMV, namely: for decisions defining an EU action or proposal submitted by the HR when the European Council has specifically requested it; for the establishment of 'the start-up fund' for the financing of preparatory activities and planned CSDP tasks whenever they cannot be charged to the Union budget (Article 41(3) TEU); for the decision defining the statute of the European Defence Agency (Article 45(2) TEU); and for the decision establishing the 'permanent structured cooperation' (Article 46(2) TEU; see below). However, QMV does not apply to decisions having military or defence implications other than these three cases, and decisions taken by QMV are subject to an 'emergency brake' procedure which allows a Member State to delay their adoption for 'vital and stated reasons of national policy', in which case the Council may request their adoption by the European Council acting unanimously (Article 31(2) *in fine* TEU).

The Treaty of Lisbon has also made clear that CFSP decisions, although binding and committing the Member States (Articles 28(2) and 29 TEU), are not legislative acts since they are not adopted in accordance with the legislative procedure. The scope and nature of CFSP powers/competences remain the same as before Lisbon and continue to be subject to the general principle of conferral (Article 5 TEU) and to the exclusion of the notion of exclusive competence (the doctrine of 'occupied territory' does not apply to CFSP). The Lisbon Treaty puts special emphasis on the preservation of national sovereignty in the CFSP (Declaration Nos 13 and 14).

The Court of Justice lacks jurisdiction over CFSP provisions save for its role in ensuring 'mutual respect' between CFSP and other EU policies (Article 40 TEU) and for the power of review by the Court of the legality of certain restrictive measures against natural or legal persons (Article 275 TFEU). The Commission has lost all power with regard to CFSP save for the implementation of the EU budget, while the right of initiative in the CFSP is shared between the HR (which may be

[45] See eg M Cremona, 'Enhanced Cooperation and the European Foreign and Security and Defence Policy' in JM Beneyto (ed), *Unity and Flexibility in the Future of the European Union: the Challenge of Enhanced Cooperation* (Madrid, CEU Ediciones, 2009) (available at: www.ceuediciones.es/documents/ebookceuediciones1.pdf) 75, 87.

supported by the Commission) and the Member States (Article 30(1) TEU). There is 'oversight' by the European Parliament limited to it being regularly consulted by the HR 'on the main aspects and the basic choices of the common foreign and security and the common security and defence policy'; to being informed by the HR of 'how those policies evolve' (Article 36 TEU); and being 'immediately and fully informed' at all stages of the procedures relating to the negotiation, signature, conclusion and implementation of CFSP international agreements (Article 218(10) TFEU).

The issue of the exercise by the EU of powers relating to the CFSP in horizontal agreements warrants some remarks. The general practice of the Council in most international agreements has been that foreign policy and external security issues have not been included as competences exercised under the CFSP Treaty provisions but rather as part of Member States' competence.[46] This has been so despite the fact that, with the entry into force of the Treaty of Lisbon, the exercise of CFSP powers in EU agreements has been facilitated by the merger of the Communities and the Union and the indication in the Treaties that an agreement could cover both CFSP matters and matters falling within other Union competences.[47]

While the Council has not generally availed itself of this opportunity as regards the signature and conclusion of agreements,[48] for the purposes of negotiations of international agreements, the Council has on several occasions designated the High Representative as the negotiator for matters falling within the CFSP in the Council decision authorising the opening of negotiations for matters within *Union* competence.[49] Moreover, the Council has shown that it considers that it is possible to conclude an agreement combining the legal basis of the CFSP with that of another Union policy such as development.[50] However, at the stages of signature and conclusion, the Council has opted for not accepting that the CFSP competence should be exercised by the Union, leaving it to be exercised by the Member States as part of national competences in mixed agreements. Exceptions to this practice are the recent decisions on the signature and provisional

[46] Prior to the entry into force of the Treaty of Lisbon, none of the agreements were concluded also by the Union (as opposed to the Community/Communities).

[47] See para (3) of Art 218 TFEU.

[48] See eg the Council Decision 2012/272/EU of 14 May 2012 on the signing, on behalf of the Union, of the Framework Agreement on Partnership and Cooperation between the European Union and its Member States, of the one part, and the Republic of the Philippines, of the other part [2012] OJ L134/3 (this decision was annulled in Case C-377/12 *Commission v Council*, judgment of 11 June 2014 (EU:C:2014:1903) on grounds not affecting this point). Decision 2012/272/EU did not include a CFSP legal basis although the agreement (for the text, see Council doc 15616/10 of 21 January 2011) contains provisions on foreign policy and security cooperation.

[49] See the example of the Council decision concerning Kazakhstan (above n 34), Art 2(2).

[50] See Council Decision 2012/308/CFSP of 26 April 2012 on the accession of the European Union to the Treaty of Amity and Cooperation in Southeast Asia [2012] OJ L154/1. This decision was based on Arts 37 and 31(1) TEU as well as Arts 209 and 212 in conjunction with Art 218(6)(a) and Art 218(8), second subparagraph, TFEU.

application of the association agreements with Ukraine, Georgia and Moldova.[51] These were justified by a strong political desire to swiftly provisionally apply the political parts of these agreements, especially the one with Ukraine. This swift provisional application was not considered practicable if the foreign policy provisions would have been exercised as part of Member State competence, since the constitutional traditions of several Member States do not allow for provisional application and since it often takes several years before all Member States have concluded their ratification procedures for such agreements. But it has not been envisaged that the CFSP legal basis will be included in the EU decision to conclude this agreement with Ukraine, which will remain a mixed agreement,[52] in contrast with the association agreement with Kosovo which—in order to avoid the difficulties derived from the recognition of Kosovo as a sovereign State raised by several Member States—will be concluded as an EU-only agreement and founded inter alia on the CFSP Treaty provisions.[53]

The frequent preference of the Member States for mixity as regards CFSP issues is difficult to explain on legal grounds, taking account of the specific nature of the CFSP and the Treaty provisions pertaining thereto, which offer all possible prerogatives for the control by the Member States through unanimous decision-making in the Council,[54] the absence of a doctrine of 'occupied territory' in the field of the

[51] For Ukraine, see Council Decision 2014/295/EU of 17 March 2014 on the signing, on behalf of the European Union, and provisional application of the Association Agreement between the European Union and the European Atomic Energy Community and their Member States, of the one part, and Ukraine, of the other part, as regards the Preamble, Article 1, and Titles I, II and VII thereof [2014] OJ L161/1 (citing Arts 31(1) and 37 TEU as substantive legal bases, in addition to Art 217 TFEU; furthermore Art 4 of Decision 2014/295/EU identifies the provisions to be provisionally applied 'only to the extent that they cover matters falling within the Union's competence, including matters falling within the Union's competence to define and implement a common foreign and security policy'). For the text of the Agreement between the European Union and its Member States, of the one part, and Ukraine, of the other part, see *ibid*, p 3. See furthermore Council Decision 2014/494/EU of 16 June 2014 on the signing, on behalf of the European Union, and provisional application of the Association Agreement between the European Union and the European Atomic Energy Community and their Member States, of the one part, and Georgia, of the other part [2014] OJ L261/1 and Council Decision 2014/492/EU of 16 June 2014 on the signing, on behalf of the European Union, and provisional application of the Association Agreement between the European Union and the European Atomic Energy Community and their Member States, of the one part, and the Republic of Moldova, of the other part [2014] OJ L260/1.

[52] See the draft Council Decision on the conclusion, on behalf of the European Union, of the Association Agreement between the European Union and the European Atomic Energy Community and their Member States, of the one part, and Ukraine, of the other part, with the exception of the provisions relating to the treatment of third-country nationals legally employed as workers in the territory of the other party (Council doc 13613/3/13 of 20 June 2014), which contains no reference to Art 37 TEU.

[53] See n 39 above and accompanying text.

[54] See eg the UK's review of the balance of competences in this respect: UK Government, *Review of the Balance of Competences between the United Kingdom and the European Union. Foreign Policy*, 22 July 2013: www.gov.uk/government/consultations/foreign-policy-report-review-of-the-balance-of-competences (eg the executive summary says on p 5 that 'The majority of the evidence affirmed that, in CFSP … the balance of competence lies squarely with the Member States. All significant decisions are made by unanimity, so each Member State has a power of veto' and point 6.4 of the conclusions on p 88 states that 'The majority of our evidence judged that Member States were firmly in charge of the [CFSP] … and could act unilaterally when they judged fit'). See also Wouters and Ramopoulos (n 36

CFSP and its specific feature that when the CFSP is exercised it does not in any way prevent Member States from continuing to exercise their foreign policies (see Declaration Nos 13 and 14 concerning the CFSP).[55] Actually, as regards the latter trait, CFSP competence can be assimilated to the so-called 'parallel' competences[56] which exist for non-CFSP matters in the areas of research, technological development and space as well as development cooperation and humanitarian aid, for which 'the exercise of that competence shall not result in Member States being prevented from exercising theirs' (paras (3) and (4) of Article 4 TFEU). Moreover, in practice, the implementation of the foreign policy parts of such agreements essentially concerns matters on which there is a Union CFSP position or action. Thus, it may be concluded that the reluctance of the Member States to agree to the exercise by the EU of its CFSP competence in international agreements appears mainly due to general political considerations, ie a preference by the Member States to emphasise their own presence in the framework of mostly horizontal international agreements, thus ensuring that such horizontal agreements remain mixed. It remains to be seen whether the challenges of obtaining timely ratification by all Member States, as illustrated by the recent referendum in the Netherlands in which a majority of those who voted opposed ratification of the association agreement with Ukraine, will lead to changes in this respect.

The security and defence provisions of the Treaty of Lisbon also merit special consideration. With the Treaty of Lisbon the former European Security and Defence Policy (ESDP) has been renamed the Common Security and Defence Policy (CSDP) without changing the policy materially, while in parallel recognising the role of NATO in the defence policy of certain Member States. However, there is one significant material change: the new Article 42(7) provides for a 'mutual aid and assistance' duty between Member States whenever one of them 'is the victim of an armed aggression on its territory'. This obligation falls on each Member State individually and not on the EU and its institutions; thus the provision does not transform the EU into a military alliance for collective defence rivalling NATO. This differs from the defence implications of the 'solidarity clause' contained in Article 222 TFEU, according to which, when a Member State is the object of a

above) 9–10. The limited exceptions to unanimity voting in CFSP matters mentioned above have never been applied in practice.

[55] The former inter alia states that 'the provisions in the [TEU] covering the [CFSP], including the creation of the office of High Representative … and the establishment of an External Action Service, do not affect the responsibilities of the Member States, as they currently exist, for the formulation and conduct of their foreign policy nor of their national representation in third countries and international organisations' and the latter that 'In addition to the specific rules and procedures referred to in paragraph 1 of Article 24 of the [TEU], … the provisions covering the [CFSP] including in relation to the High Representative … and the External Action Service will not affect the existing legal basis, responsibilities, and powers of each Member State in relation to the formulation and conduct of its foreign policy, its national diplomatic service, relations with third countries and participation in international organisations, including a Member State's membership of the Security Council of the United Nations'.

[56] See also R Wessel, 'The EU As a Party to International Agreements: Shared Competences, Mixed Responsibilities' in A Dashwood and M Maresceau (eds), *Law and Practice of EU External Relations: Salient Features of a Changing Landscape* (Cambridge, Cambridge University Press, 2011) 152, 157.

terrorist attack or the victim of a natural or man-made disaster both the Member States and the Union must assist the Member State concerned, at its request and in its territory, including by mobilising all the instruments at the disposal of the EU and the military resources made available by the Member States. The mutual assistance clause was invoked for the first time following the terrorist attacks in Paris on 13 November 2015. France presented a request for assistance from the other Member States under this provision during the Foreign Affairs Council on 17 November 2015. All Ministers expressed their support to France and their readiness to provide assistance.[57]

There is a new provision (Article 46 TEU) allowing for a form of institutionalised cooperation, called 'Permanent Structured Cooperation', whereby the Council, acting by QMV, authorises a number of Member States (there is no minimum threshold) to develop their military capabilities—focusing on military equipment programmes—and to provide combat units for EU missions. According to Protocol No 10 relating to permanent structured cooperation, the latter would allow the EU to assume fully its responsibilities within the international community, including in response to requests from the UN, by improving the capabilities of the Member States to deploy forces to the theatre of operations in third countries. However, this cooperation has not yet been implemented, which is striking considering that decisions are to be taken by QMV—a flexibility expressly provided for in order to prevent an individual Member State from blocking the establishment of such a structured cooperation, from blocking another Member States from subsequently joining the structured cooperation, or from blocking the suspension of a non-performing Member State.

The Permanent Structured Cooperation should not be confused with the so-called 'enhanced cooperation', a form of institutionalised cooperation introduced initially for non-CFSP policies by the Treaty of Amsterdam, then extended by the Treaty of Nice to CFSP policies other than matters having military and defence implications, and finally again extended to all matters including those having military or defence implications by the Treaty of Lisbon (Article 20 TEU and Articles 326 to 334 TFEU). Enhanced cooperation is a procedure whereby a minimum of nine Member States are allowed to establish advanced integration or cooperation in an area (so far it has taken place in non-CFSP areas such as divorce law, patents, and the financial transaction tax) within EU structures but without the other Member States being involved. As regards the CFSP, enhanced cooperation is decided by the Council acting unanimously. So far, enhanced cooperation in the field of CFSP has not been in demand owing perhaps to the need to maintain credibility and unity in EU external action while military and defence matters are already intrinsically differentiated.

[57] See the Outcome of this Council Meeting in doc 14120/15, p 6 ('*French President François Hollande had invoked article 42(7) of the Treaty on European Union, requesting bilateral aid and assistance from the other EU member states. Ministers expressed their unanimous and full support for France and their readiness to provide all the necessary aid and assistance. …*').

Another example of flexibility not yet implemented is provided in Article 44 TEU, according to which the Council may entrust the implementation of a CSDP task to a 'group of Member States' which are willing and have the necessary capability for such a task. It is clear that CSDP operations under this provision remain Union CSDP operations under the responsibility and control of the Council.[58] To some extent, a shared understanding of the modalities for implementing this provision has been developed, based on discussions in several preparatory bodies of the Council.[59] A key question is the balance between the elements to be adopted by the Council (including objectives, scope and general conditions for implementation) and those entrusted to the group of Member States which will implement the task and agree amongst themselves on its management. While a shared understanding may emerge from these discussions, it is ultimately in the implementation in a specific case that the exact modalities will be determined.

The provision in the Lisbon Treaty to establish by qualified majority a financial 'start-up fund' has also not yet been applied. This financial facility is meant to be used when there is an urgent need for financing initiatives in the framework of the CFSP and in particular for preparatory activities when those tasks cannot be charged to the Union budget (Article 41(3) TEU). Similarly, the Council has not adopted a decision establishing procedures for rapid access to appropriations in the Union budget for urgent financing of CFSP activities, in particular for preparatory activities for CSDP tasks pursuant to Article 41(3) TEU.

The Lisbon Treaty has also codified several existing practices: it has introduced a specific legal basis for the European Defence Agency (Articles 42(3) and 45 TEU) and has codified the scope of the crisis management operations that were available to the EU before Lisbon (often referred to as the Petersberg tasks) while explicitly including a wider range of tasks (in a non-exhaustive manner) covering 'joint disarmament operations', 'military advice and assistance tasks', conflict prevention tasks, and 'post-conflict stabilisation', and also contributing 'to the fight against terrorism, including by supporting third countries in combatting terrorism in their territories' (Article 43). This new language also reflects the evolution of the practice in UN Peace Operations, which the EU is frequently called upon to support. However, it is well known that over the last years the EU has been modest in availing itself of these possibilities (there are a few recent examples such as Ukraine and the Central African Republic).

The EU has not yet laid down the provisions implementing the specific legal basis for protecting data processed by Member States when acting in the context

[58] Art 44(1) TEU provides for entrusting this mandate to a group of Member States 'Within the framework of the decisions adopted in accordance with Article 43', and pursuant to Art 44(2) the *Council* shall adopt the necessary decisions if the completion of the task entails 'major consequences' or requires 'amendment of the objective, scope and conditions determined for the task'.

[59] For a discussion, see eg T Tardy, *In Groups We Trust—Implementing Article 44 of the Lisbon Treaty*, EU ISS Brief No 27, October 2014: www.iss.europa.eu/uploads/media/Brief_27_Article_44.pdf. For a legal analysis, see Legal Service contribution 'on the conditions and modalities of recourse to Article 44 TEU—entrusting the implementation of a CSDP task to a group of Member States', Council doc 5225/15 of 13 January 2015.

of the CFSP (Article 39 TEU).[60] In the absence of such a decision, Member States apply their national rules, which must comply with the relevant provisions of the European Convention on Human Rights (ECHR) and of the Charter of Fundamental Rights.

Finally, from an institutional point of view, the Treaty of Lisbon did put the potential for improving the effectiveness and coherence of EU external action in the hands of a 'triple-hatted' HR, as mentioned in Section II. This issue requires special consideration.

V. AN OVERBURDENED AND CHALLENGED HIGH REPRESENTATIVE?

The functions of the HR include the responsibilities of the presidency of the FAC (Article 18(3) TEU), being 'responsible within the Commission for responsibilities incumbent on it in external relations and for coordinating other aspects of the Union's external action' (Article 18(4) TEU) and the role of initiator and implementer in the field of CFSP (Articles 18(2) and 27 TEU), including conducting political dialogue with third parties on the Union's behalf. The triple-hatted function is conferred on the HR *intuitu personae* (strictly with that officer-holder); there is no provision in the Treaties allowing for the creation of deputies to the HR. In practice the HR has experienced difficulties in fulfilling all of her expanded powers. Furthermore, the HR has been challenged in her relations with the Council (eg in the case of EU Special Representatives (EUSRs))[61] and the Commission (eg by decisions taken by Commission President Barroso at the start of the Commission's post-Lisbon mandate and by legal proceedings in which the Commission essentially disavowed actions of the HR).[62]

Difficulties have arisen in the implementation of one of the objectives of the Treaty of Lisbon: the strengthening of the EU's external action by reinforcing the coherence between different EU external competences. Several treaty amendments aim to further these tasks and this objective. In particular pursuant to Article 21(3) TEU the HR assists the Council and the Commission in their responsibilities in ensuring consistency between the different areas of the EU's external action. The HR fulfils this function by, eg, participating as HR proper in the Trade configuration of the FAC, which is chaired by the rotating Presidency.[63] The introduction of

[60] Discussions have taken place on the scope of this provision in specific cases but these have not resulted in any agreement so far.

[61] Acrimonious discussions have repeatedly taken place on the issue of EUSRs, with the Council generally being in favour of maintaining a significant number of EUSRs (with a degree of cohesion seldom seen in other matters) while HR Ashton was much less keen on doing so. See also below nn 82–85 and accompanying text.

[62] See below, respectively nn 69–72 and accompanying text and n 68.

[63] See the statement in the footnote at the end of Art 2(5) of the Council's Rules of Procedure (annexed to Council Decision 2009/937/EU of 1 December 2009 adopting the Council's Rules of Procedure [2009] OJ L325/35; last amended by Council Decision 2014/692/EU, Euratom of 29 September

horizontal overall objectives for all EU external relations in Article 3(5) TEU and especially in Article 21 TEU was also meant to help, even if within this framework each specific policy retains its own objectives and is subject to its own procedures. It is only the CFSP which no longer has distinct objectives: Article 23 TEU merely provides that the Union's action in the area of the CFSP 'shall be guided by the principles, shall pursue the objectives of, and be conducted in accordance with, the general provisions' common to all EU external relations; and Article 24(1), first sentence, TEU provides that the 'Union's competence in matters of [CFSP] shall cover all areas of foreign policy and all questions relating to the Union's security'. This does not make the delimitation between the CFSP and other Union policies easier,[64] for the drafters of the Treaty of Lisbon surely were aware of the fact that having distinct competences, procedures and actors could entail challenges for ensuring coherent EU external action.[65] An illustration of the practical difficulties encountered is provided by the EU's 'comprehensive approach' (to external conflict and crises):[66] owing to the need to achieve common objectives while respecting the distribution of competences between the different areas, it has not been easy to ensure smooth transitions from CSDP missions to non-CFSP assistance programmes under the EU's external financial instruments and/or to ensure that both these measures are used in a complementary way. This challenge has inter alia manifested itself in the framework of efforts to 'train and equip' security forces of third countries—an issue currently being discussed under the label 'capacity building for security and development'.[67]

2014 [2014] OJ L289/18): 'When the [FAC] is convened to discuss common commercial policy issues, its President will ask to be replaced by the six-monthly Presidency as provided for in Article 2(5), second subparagraph'.

[64] See eg P Van Elsuwege, 'EU External Action after the Collapse of the Pillar Structure. In Search of a New Balance between Delimitation and Consistency' (2010) 47 *Common Market Law Review* 987 and P Van Elsuwege, 'The Interface between the Area of Freedom, Security and Justice and the Common Foreign and Security Policy of the European Union: Legal Constraints to Political Objectives' in R Holzacker and P Luif (eds), *Freedom, Security and Justice in the European Union: Internal and External Dimensions of Increased Cooperation after the Lisbon Treaty* (New York, Springer, 2013) 119. See also below nn 137, 152 and 260–61 on Cases C-658/11, C-130/10 and C-263/14.

[65] See also Wouters and Ramopoulos (n 38 above) 9–14.

[66] After lengthy preparations this '*comprehensive approach*' was set out in the Joint Communication by the High Representative and the European Commission on 'The EU's Comprehensive Approach to External Conflict and Crises', JOIN(2013) 30 final of 11 December 2013, and endorsed in the Council Conclusions of 12 May 2014 on the EU's comprehensive approach. According to the latter, 'the comprehensive approach is both a general working method and a set of concrete measures and processes to improve how the EU, based on a common strategic vision and drawing on its wide array of existing tools and instruments, collectively can develop, embed and deliver more coherent and more effective policies, working practices, actions and results' (para 2).

[67] See eg para 7 of the Conclusions of the 19–20 December 2013 European Council (EUCO 217/13); para 16 of the Council Conclusions on CSDP of 18 May 2015 (doc 8971/15); The Joint Communication to the European Parliament and the Council, Capacity building in support of security and development—Enabling partners to prevent and manage crises (JOIN (2015)17 and doc 8504/15) and 'Capacity building in support of security and development—Implementation Plan—Non-paper by the EEAS and Commission services' (doc 13869/15).

The final provision of Article 18(4) TEU is also telling:

> The [HR] shall be one of the Vice-Presidents of the Commission. He shall ensure the consistency of the Union's external action. He shall be responsible within the Commission for responsibilities incumbent on it in external relations and for coordinating other aspects of the Union's external action. In exercising these responsibilities within the Commission, and only for these responsibilities, the [HR] shall be bound by Commission procedures to the extent that this is consistent with paragraphs 2 [ie the conduct of CFSP by the HR] and 3 [ie the Presidency of the FAC].

This provision demonstrates very clearly that although the three functions are united in a single person, they are not governed by the same rules. In particular, in her 'CFSP functions' and as FAC Chair, the HR is not subject to Commission rules (which, inter alia, ensure in Article 17(3) TEU that the Commissioners cannot receive instructions from the governments of the Member States). Obviously, given the aim to ensure consistency, the HR needs to act coherently in her different capacities. However, this does not give the Commission (as a collegiate body) a veto right over measures taken in the HR's non-Commission functions. In practice, some legal difficulties have arisen from the acts of the HR in the exercise of her different functions.[68]

It has been argued that a series of decisions and measures adopted by Commission President Barroso at the start of his post-Lisbon mandate limited the potential of the HR to fully exercise her responsibilities as Vice-President of the Commission pursuant to Article 18(3) TEU.[69]

Indeed, in the HR report *EEAS Review*, published in July 2013 pursuant to Article 13(3) of Council Decision 2010/427/EU of 26 July 2010 establishing the organisation and functioning of the European External Action Service,[70] various recommendations were made with a view to better ensuring the full exercise of the function of Vice-President coordinator of external action within the Commission.[71] In its conclusions in this review, the Council inter alia underlined

[68] By way of example, in Case C-658/11 *Parliament v Council*, judgment of 24 June 2014 (EU:C:2014:2025), the Commission intervened before the CJEU in support of an action for annulment which the EP had brought against the Council, acting on (and consistent with) a proposal by the HR (in relation to an agreement between the EU and Mauritius on the conditions of transfer to Mauritius of suspected pirates captured by the EU's counter-piracy operation Atalanta). Thus the Commission expressed its disagreement with the HR. Arguably, the HR could have sought to intervene in the case in support of the Council.

[69] For an account of these early decision and measures, see L Erkelens and S Blockmans, 'Setting up the European External Action Service: an Act of Institutional Balance' (2012) 8 *European Constitutional Law Review* 246, 249–54 (also available at: www.asser.nl/upload/documents/1272012_125753cleer2012-1web.pdf), under section 2 entitled 'Bureaucratic manoeuvres of the President of the Commission'.

[70] [2010] OJ L201/30.

[71] *EEAS Review* (2013). See eeas.europa.eu/library/publications/2013/3/2013_eeas_review_en.pdf. The report comprises an analysis of how the EEAS has been functioning as well as a series of short- and medium-term recommendations. See pp 7–9 and 13 on Relations with the Commission, as well as short-term recommendations 9 and 12–14 (at p 16) and medium-term recommendations 3–4 (p 18). Compare with the recommendations in the European Court of Auditors' report on the EEAS, below

'the importance to ensure fully the coordination role of the [HR] as Vice President of the Commission in the field of external relations within the Commission in line with Article 18(4) of the TEU'.[72] It is to be expected that the new organisation of the Commission under its President Juncker—with clusters under the leadership of Vice-Presidents, including the HR[73]—should permit the second HR to effectively make better use of her role within the Commission.

With regard to the functions of the HR proper ('CFSP functions'), Article 27 TEU provides that:

> (1) The [HR] ... shall contribute through his proposals to the development of the [CFSP] and shall ensure implementation of the decisions adopted by the European Council and the Council.
>
> (2) The [HR] shall represent the Union for matters relating to the [CFSP]. He shall conduct political dialogue with third parties on the Union's behalf and shall express the Union's position in international organisations and at international conferences.[74]

It would exceed the scope of this contribution to address this role at any level of detail. However, a few points and practical experiences are worth mentioning.

First, the Treaty of Lisbon has introduced a right of initiative by the HR in CFSP matters (while the Commission has lost that right),[75] in principle alongside the right of initiative of Member States (Articles 30(1) and 42(4) TEU), but in some cases in the form of an exclusive right of initiative, eg on international agreements

n 98, pp 24–25. For a legal analysis, see EEAS Review—indications relating to the legal and institutional issues raised by the recommendations, Council doc 14458/13 of 4 October 2013 and S Blockmans and C Hillion (eds), *EEAS 2.0: A Legal Commentary on Council Decision 2010/427/EU Establishing the Organisation and Functioning of the European External Action Service* (Brussels, CEPS, February 2013), available at: www.ceps.eu/system/files/EEAS%202.0.pdf. For a further analysis of the EEAS Review, including contributions made in its preparation phase, see eg S Duke, 'Reflections on the EEAS Review' (2014) 19 *European Foreign Affairs Review* 23; S Blockmans and C Hillion (eds), *EEAS 2.0: Recommendations for the amendment of Council Decision 2010/427/EU on the European External Action Service*, November 2013, CEPS special report No 78: www.ceps.eu/book/eeas-20-recommendations-amendment-council-decision-2010427eu-european-external-action-service; B Van Vooren, J Wouters, G De Baere and K Raube, *The EEAS post-Lisbon: Achievements, Challenges and Opportunities*, Report for the Foreign Affairs Committee of the European Parliament, February 2013: www.europarl.europa.eu/RegData/etudes/etudes/join/2013/457111/EXPO-AFET_ET(2013)457111_EN.pdf and See also S Lehne, *More Action, Better Service. How to Strengthen the European External Action Service*, Carnegie Endowment Policy Outlook, 16 December 2011: carnegieendowment.org/files/CEIP_Outlook_EAS-Lehne_C.pdf.

[72] These conclusions were adopted by the General Affairs Council (it was a deliberate choice that it was not the FAC) of 17 December 2013, see: www.consilium.europa.eu/uedocs/cms_data/docs/pressdata/EN/genaff/140141.pdf (quote from para 6). The review was extensively discussed in a series of COREPER meetings.

[73] See ec.europa.eu/about/juncker-commission/structure/index_en.htm and especially the final page of the 'structure' at: ec.europa.eu/archives/juncker-commission/docs/structure_en.pdf.

[74] See also Art 26(3) TEU: 'The [CFSP] shall be put into effect by the [HR] and by the Member States, using national and Union resources' and Art 24(1) TEU: 'The [CFSP] shall be put into effect by the [HR] ... and by Member States, in accordance with the Treaties'.

[75] It may however support proposals of the HR: see Art 30(1) TEU.

in the field of the CFSP,[76] on the appointment of EUSRs[77] and on the establishment of the start-up fund in the field of the CSDP.[78] Also, decisions on restrictive measures under Article 215 TFEU implementing CFSP decisions in this field can only be adopted on a joint proposal from the HR and the Commission. Similarly, the arrangements for the implementation by the Union of the solidarity clause in the cases of terrorist attacks and of natural or non-made disasters 'shall be defined by a decision adopted by the Council acting on a joint proposal by the Commission and the [HR]' (Article 222(3) TFEU).[79]

Secondly, the HR represents the Union on CFSP matters, a role that prior to the Treaty of Lisbon was exercised by the (rotating) Presidency of the Council. In this respect, Article 34(2) TEU specifically provides that

> When the Union has defined a position on a subject which is on the United Nations Security Council agenda, those Member States which sit on the Security Council shall request that the [HR] be invited to present the Union's position.

While the HR has addressed the Security Council on some occasions,[80] the practice of requesting her participation in Security Council meetings has not been systematic.[81] In any case, the HR does not enjoy a representational exclusive prerogative since the President of the European Council 'shall, at his level and in that capacity, ensure the external representation of the Union on issues concerning its [CFSP], without prejudice to the powers of the [HR]' (Article 15(6) TEU)[82] (see below).

Furthermore, Article 33 TEU maintains the possibility for the Council, on a proposal by the HR, to appoint EUSRs, who 'shall carry out [their] mandate under the authority of the [HR]'. In the course of the negotiations that led to the establishment of the EEAS (see below), consideration was given to integrating the EUSRs, or their functions, into the EEAS.[83] However, this option was not retained inter alia for legal reasons. Indeed, given the existence of a separate Treaty provision and the powers of the Council to define the mandate and modalities of the EUSRs, it is doubtful whether the EUSRs could be fully integrated into the EEAS,

[76] See Art 218, paras (3), (5) and (6) TFEU (while this is not explicitly stated in Art 218, it is clear that the negotiator on CFSP matters can only be the HR).

[77] Art 33 TEU.

[78] Art 41(3) TEU. Some other decisions in the field of the CSDP require consultation of the HR.

[79] See also Council Decision 2014/415/EU of 24 June 2014 on the arrangements for the implementation by the Union of the solidarity clause [2014] OJ L192/53.

[80] eg on 13 February 2013 and 14 February 2014, both on EU-UN cooperation, see; www.consilium.europa.eu/uedocs/cms_Data/docs/pressdata/EN/foraff/135451.pdf and: eeas.europa.eu/top_stories/2014/170214_ca_un_en.htm.

[81] This would certainly be the case if 'a Union position' were not deemed to refer only to positions laid down in a Council decision (see Art 29 TEU—'common positions' as they were known prior to the Lisbon Treaty), as opposed to those expressed in other forms such as Council conclusions (which are used far more frequently). Yet even if one interprets positions more restrictively, this is not applied in practice (eg the HR would need to speak in most sanctions discussions, which she does not do).

[82] Note that the HR shall take part in the work of the European Council (Art 15(2) TEU).

[83] See eg the Presidency Report to the European Council on the European External Action Service, Council doc 14930/09 of 23 October 2009, para 14.

which operates under the exclusive authority of the HR.[84] On the occasion of the EEAS review,[85] the Council underlined its 'continuing commitment to the role of [EUSRs] as a valuable instrument of EU foreign policy' and stressed 'the need to enhance overall efficiency and accountability, as well as to ensure coordination and coherence with all other EU actors, emphasising the importance of close cooperation with the EEAS'.[86]

The HR chairs the FAC[87] and her representatives chair most of the preparatory bodies of the Council dealing with external relations. These include, inter alia, the Political and Security Committee (PSC), the Committee for Civilian Aspects of Crisis Management, the Political Military Group, the Working Parties dealing with disarmament and non-proliferation and the geographical Working Parties. These representatives of the HR become EEAS staff upon their appointment as chairs (if they are not so already).[88] By contrast, some preparatory bodies in the field of external relations are still chaired by the rotating Presidency (eg those dealing with trade, development, humanitarian aid, public international law, external aspects of terrorism and the foreign relations counsellors working party (RELEX)[89]) or by elected chairs.[90] It should be noted that, in addition to those external relations working parties not chaired by representatives of the HR, COREPER (Committee of Permanent Representatives) is chaired by the rotating Presidency. These divisions have given rise to practical difficulties which are resolved by the coordination of work in PSC and COREPER between the 'EEAS' and 'rotating' chairs/Presidencies, an important coordination that takes place in the context of the preparatory work of the FAC. The HR's report on the EEAS review proposed to extend the arrangement of 'EEAS chairs' to all external relations working parties,[91] a proposal that might be reconsidered by the review to take place by the end of 2015, when 'the Council may discuss, as appropriate, the chairmanship of preparatory bodies of the Council on the basis of an assessment of the current arrangements'.[92]

[84] In particular, EUSRs are appointed and operate under Art 33 TEU, whereas the EEAS is established pursuant to Art 27 TEU. Furthermore, EUSRs are appointed by Council, whereas EEAS staff are appointed by the EEAS (more specifically by its appointing authority). See also Blockmans and Hillion (eds) (n 71 above ('recommendations')), p 10.

[85] *EEAS Review* (above n 71), pp 4–5 as well as short-term recommendation 4 (p 16).

[86] Council conclusions (n 72 above), para 4. Furthermore, the Council has resisted attempts to transfer the budget line for EUSRs from the CFSP budget line to the EEAS administrative budget line.

[87] See also Art 16(9) TEU.

[88] See Arts 2 and 4 of European Council Decision of 1 December 2009 on the exercise of the Presidency of the Council [2009] OJ L315/50 and Art 4 of and Annex II to Council Decision 2009/908/EU of 1 December 2009 laying down measures for the implementation of the European Council Decision on the exercise of the Presidency of the Council, and on the chairmanship of preparatory bodies of the Council [2009] OJ L322/28. For the most recent version of the List of Council preparatory bodies, see Council doc 5183/16 of 18 January 2016.

[89] RELEX deals with legal acts and financial issues.

[90] The chairs of the EU Military Committee and its Working Group are elected by the EUMC and appointed by Council COREPER respectively.

[91] Above n 71, p 6 as well as short-term recommendation 1 (p 16).

[92] Council conclusions (n 72 above), para 11. No changes have been made so far.

The Lisbon Treaty attributes the three functions of the HR *intuitu personae*, ie to him/her alone, and provides that they have to be exercised separately without mixing the institutions and representational functions concerned (Articles 18, 27 and 40 TEU). Since the HR cannot always personally exercise each of these functions, the question has arisen whether it is possible for the HR to have deputies or, if this is impossible, to have arrangements for the replacement of the High Representative.[93] The HR report on the EEAS review refers to

> The current arrangements ... to deputise for the [HR] when she is unable to attend a particular meeting or event are ad-hoc and involve the Minister of the rotating Presidency, Members of the Commission with geographic responsibilities, senior EEAS officials and EUSRs[94]

and in practice, as Commission Vice-President, the HR has been replaced by other Commissioners, whereas in her capacity as FAC chair and her CFSP functions (which prior to Lisbon were exercised both by the rotating Presidency and by the HR), the HR has been replaced (at least at ministerial level) by a Foreign Minister of a Member State, usually the one holding the rotating Presidency of the Council.[95] The EEAS review recommends to 'Clarify [the] system of political deput(ies) for the [HR] (either within EEAS structures or through clearer responsibility for HRVP over other Commissioners)' and recommends to 'Conclude formal arrangements for existing practice where Foreign Ministers, members of the Commission and senior EEAS officials can deputise for the HRVP (including having formal representation rights in EP, Council and Commission meetings)'.[96] The Council did not express a view on this in its conclusions on the EEAS review but the arrangements for the new Commission do reflect to some extent the above recommendation.[97] So what role is there for the EEAS?

VI. THE STRUGGLING EUROPEAN EXTERNAL ACTION SERVICE (EEAS)

A two-fold rationale led the Lisbon Treaty drafters to provide for the establishment of the EEAS: to assist the HR in her/his expanded role, and to represent the Union abroad.

[93] See also Wouters and Ramopoulos (n 38 above) 14–15.

[94] Above n 71 above, p 13.

[95] In conformity with Arts 5(2) and 20(2) of the Council's Rules of Procedure (n 63 above).

[96] Above n 71, medium-term recommendation 3 (p 18). On p 13, the review adds that: 'An alternative model would be to create a new formal deputy HR/VP position(s). This would have a strong political and symbolic impact and reflect practice in most national Foreign Ministries ... It would however be more complex in institutional terms because of the absence of a clear legal basis in the Treaty, and in relation to the debate on the composition of the Commission'. It is indeed doubtful whether a deputy High Representative position or positions could be created without Treaty change, as the Treaties entrust the prerogatives only to the HR herself. See also Blockmans and Hillion (eds) (n 71 above; 'recommendations'), p 4.

[97] See above n 73 and accompanying text: for a number of Commissioners, the organigram / structure indicates with an * that 'The HRVP may ask this Commissioner (and other Commissioners) to deputise for her *in areas related to Commission competence*'. (emphasis added)

In principle while exercising her functions as chair of the FAC, the HR is assisted by the General Secretariat of the Council, and as Vice-President of the Commission the HR is assisted by the Commission services, but in her CFSP functions the HR is assisted by the EEAS. This service

> shall work in cooperation with the diplomatic services of the Member States and shall comprise officials from relevant departments of the General Secretariat of the Council and of the Commission as well as staff seconded from national diplomatic services of the Member States. The organisation and functioning of the European External Action Service shall be established by a decision of the Council. The Council shall act on a proposal from the [HR] after consulting the [EP] and after obtaining the consent of the Commission (Article 27(3) TEU).

More explicitly, Article 2 of the Council Decision of 26 July 2010 establishing the organisation and functioning of the European External Action Service,[98] provides that:

> 1. The EEAS shall support the High Representative in fulfilling his/her mandates as outlined, notably, in Articles 18 and 27 TEU:
>   — in fulfilling his/her mandate to conduct the [CFSP] of the [EU], including the [CSDP], to contribute by his/her proposals to the development of that policy, which he/she shall carry out as mandated by the Council and to ensure the consistency of the Union's external action,
>   — in his/her capacity as President of the [FAC], without prejudice to the normal tasks of the General Secretariat of the Council,
>   — in his/her capacity as Vice-President of the Commission for fulfilling within the Commission the responsibilities incumbent on it in external relations, and in coordinating other aspects of the Union's external action, without prejudice to the normal tasks of the services of the Commission.
> 2. The EEAS shall assist the President of the European Council, the President of the Commission, and the Commission in the exercise of their respective functions in the area of external relations.[99]

It is understood that the assistance provided by the EEAS cannot be at the expense of the general assistance provided to the HR by the Secretariat General of the Council and the services of the Commission respectively for the HR's functions as FAC chair and as Vice-President of the Commission. Otherwise Article 2 would be incompatible with the Treaty since Article 240(2) TFEU provides that the Council is 'assisted by a General Secretariat, under the responsibility of a Secretary General appointed by the Council'. The same applies to the Vice President coordinating

[98] See generally B Van Vooren, 'A Legal-Institutional Perspective on the European Union External Action Service' (2011) 48 *Common Market Law Review* 475 and Erkelens and Blockmans (n 69 above). For a rather critical analysis, see also European Court of Auditors, Special Report No 11/2014, *The Establishment of the European External Action Service*, June 2014: www.eca.europa.eu/Lists/ECADocuments/SR14_11/SR14_11_EN.pdf.

[99] For a detailed and comprehensive legal analysis, see Blockmans and Hillion (eds) (n 71 above).

role within the Commission, for which assistance is provided by the Commission services (eg DG Trade). Nevertheless, it is clear that in practice the role of the EEAS has not been limited to the CFSP (eg the EEAS has had a major role in the elaboration and implementation of action covering issues relating to both non-CFSP (development and humanitarian aid) and CFSP policies under the so-called 'comprehensive approach'), with the sole exception of trade.

The practice with regard to the role of Union delegations is worth mentioning. Pursuant to Article 1(4) of the EEAS Decision, 'The EEAS shall be made up of a central administration and of the Union Delegations to third countries and to international organisations'; it was therefore decided that Union delegations in third countries and at international organisations, which represent the Union 'shall be placed under the authority of the [HR]' pursuant to Article 221 TFEU and would be part of the EEAS. The role of EU delegations, as well as the procedure for deciding on their opening and closure and rules on their functioning are laid down in detail in Article 5 of this Decision, paragraph 6 of which provides that

> The [HR] shall enter into the necessary arrangements with the host country, the international organisation, or the third country concerned. In particular, the [HR] shall take the necessary measures to ensure that host States grant the Union delegations, their staff and their property, privileges and immunities equivalent to those referred to in the Vienna Convention on Diplomatic Relations of 18 April 1961.

The implementation of this provision has given rise to the question of the status of such arrangements and their relationship to Article 218 TFEU,[100] for, if such arrangements are legally binding, they would constitute international agreements which should be concluded by the *Union* in accordance with Article 218 TFEU.[101]

In particular, the role of EU delegations in relation to consular protection has been the subject of considerable debate. Article 5(10) of Council Decision 2010/427/EU provides in this respect that

> The Union delegations shall, acting in accordance with the third paragraph of Article 35 TEU, and upon request by Member States, support the Member States in their diplomatic relations and in their role of providing consular protection to citizens of the Union in third countries on a resource-neutral basis.

In this regard, the Council conclusions on the EEAS review indicate that

> While recognising that consular protection remains a national competence, the Council agrees to further explore, on the basis set out in the Treaties and relevant legal framework,

[100] Compare ibid, p 35 and n 107 below (on agreements concluded by Europol). See also Gatti and Manzini (n 38 above) 1731.

[101] However, the Commission habitually concluded arrangements itself as regards its delegations abroad prior to the Treaty of Lisbon. See A-P Allo, 'Les accords administratifs entre l'Union européenne et les organisations internationales' in D Dormoy (ed), *L'Union europeenne et les organisations internationales* (Brussels, Bruylant, 1997) 56; I MacLeod, ID Henry and S Huett, *The External Relations of the European Communities* (Oxford, Clarendon Press, 1996) 166–67; and D Verwey, *The European Community, the European Union and the Law of Treaties* (The Hague, TMC Asser Press, 2004) 97–99 and 217.

> including Council Decision 2010/427/EU, possibilities for developing, in line with Article 5(10) of the latter, the role of EU Delegations in facilitating and supporting coordination between Member States in their role of providing consular protection to citizens of the Union in third countries, also taking into account lessons learnt from previous crises and the experience of local consular cooperation initiatives.

The question of the external representation of the European Union has proven to be particularly difficult in practice, and requires special consideration.

VII. A CONFUSING EXTERNAL REPRESENTATION

One of the reasons for the conferral of a triple-hatted function on the High Representative was to end the external representation of the EU by the former '*troika*',[102] as the latter did not prove effective in transmitting a single EU voice to the outside world. In practice the new arrangements for the external representation provided by the Treaty of Lisbon have given rise to serious difficulties since, instead of simplifying and unifying the external representation, the Treaty of Lisbon has made it more complex by assigning the role of external representation of the Union to multiple actors.

First, the task of external representation of the Union in the field of the CFSP is attributed to the HR (Article 27(2) TEU) as well as to the President of the European Council (Article 15(5) TEU). In addition, Article 33 TEU provides that the Council may appoint EUSRs, who shall carry out their mandate under the authority of the HR (see also above). In this respect, it is worth noting that some EUSRs have been 'double-hatted', ie they were/are also the Head of an EU Delegation in order to provide synergies and limit the multiplication of EU representatives.[103]

Secondly, pursuant to Article 17(1) TEU, 'With the exception of the [CFSP], and other cases provided for in the Treaties, [the Commission] shall ensure the Union's external representation'. This general rule also applies in the area of Freedom, Security and Justice (FSJ), which—unlike the CFSP—is no longer subject to any specific rules or procedures in this respect.

Other cases of external representation provided for in the Treaties include the role of EU Delegations. Pursuant to Article 221(1) TFEU 'Union delegations in third countries and at international organisations shall represent the Union' (Article 221(2) TEU adds that they 'shall be placed under the authority of the

[102] Namely the Secretary-General of the Council/High Representative for the Common Foreign and Security Policy, the (Foreign Minister of the rotating) Presidency of the Council and the external relations Commissioner.

[103] For a pre-Lisbon example, see the EU representation to the African Union (see: www.eeas.europa.eu/policies/eu-special-representatives/koen-vervaeke/index_en.htm). For a recent example, see the EUSR and Head of the EU Delegation to Bosnia and Herzegovina (see: europa.ba/Default.aspx?id=6&lang=EN).

[HR]'; see also above).[104] It is clear that this power is not limited to the CFSP and allows delegations to represent the Union in any area of EU competence. It is also clear that this is a concurrent power, which does not prevent the other actors from representing the Union in a country or international organisation where the EU has a delegation.[105]

Thirdly, for the sake of completeness, it should be noted that, pursuant to Article 138(2) TFEU, 'The Council, on a proposal from the Commission, may adopt appropriate measures to ensure unified representation within the international financial institutions and conferences. The Council shall act after consulting the European Central Bank' (only members of the Council representing Member States whose currency is the euro are to take part in the vote). This has not yet been implemented.

Fourthly, a number of EU agencies also have distinct rules on *their* external representation.[106] For instance, Europol and Eurojust maintain cooperation with third States and international organisations, including an element of representation; thus pursuant to Article 38(6) of the 2009 Council Decision on Europol, 'The Director shall be Europol's legal representative' and some external relations capacity has been conferred on Europol, including for the negotiation and the conclusion of international agreements.[107]

Fifthly, while the above distinct rules apply to the representation of the Union within its competences, they do not apply to the representation of the Member States, which is not addressed in the Treaties, and which, as indicated above, in the view of the Member States and the Council, includes shared competences not yet exercised by the Union. In these cases, Declaration No 13 indicates that the CFSP provisions do not affect 'the responsibilities of the Member States ... for the formulation and conduct of their foreign policy nor of their national representation in third countries and international organisations' and Declaration

[104] Upon the entry into force of the Treaty of Lisbon, the former Commission delegations became EU delegations. See also the Draft notification to third parties before the entry into force of the Treaty of Lisbon, Council doc 16654/1/09 of 27 November 2009, final sentence on p 2 and first sentence on p 4. See also the periodic overview of the 'EU Diplomatic Representation in third countries'. For the first half of 2015 this is set out in Council doc 17034/14 of 17 December 2014 (no subsequent updates appear to have been made). This document includes a list of countries in which the EU is represented by a Member State because of the absence of an EU delegation.

[105] See R Gosalbo Bono (n 33 above) 35.

[106] See more generally A Ott, E Vos and F Coman-Kund, *EU Agencies and Their International Mandate: A New Category of Global Actors?*, CLEER Working Paper 2013/7: www.asser.nl/upload/documents/20140106T113002-cleer_13-7_web.pdf.

[107] Council Decision 2009/371/JHA of 6 April 2009 establishing the European Police Office (Europol) [2009] OJ L121/37. See especially Art 23 and Art 26(1), points (a) and (b) thereof. However, there is disagreement between the institutions as to Europol's power to conclude international agreements. See: www.statewatch.org/news/2013/nov/europol-third-states-ep.htm and Case C-363/14 *Parliament v Council,*), in which the Parliament sought the annulment of Council Implementing Decision 2014/269/EU of 6 May 2014 amending Decision 2009/935/JHA as regards the list of third States and organisations with which Europol shall conclude agreements ([2014] OJ L138/104). In its judgment of 10 September 2015 (EU:C:2015:579), the Court dismissed the action, including on the basis of the Protocol on transitional provisions.

No 14 contains similar wording. Thus the Member States can choose who represents them; in practice they can represent themselves or authorise the rotating Presidency, the Commission or the HR to do so.[108]

Sixthly, it is also worth mentioning the specific case of EU representation in bilateral joint bodies established on the basis of agreements between the EU (previously the European Communities), together with its Member States, on the one hand, and a third State (or group of third States) on the other hand. Such bodies have been established in particular under Partnership and Cooperation Agreements and Association Agreements, and typically include, among others, a Council (usually meeting at ministerial level) and a Committee. The ministerial level Councils supervise the application and implementation of the agreement in the light of its objectives and examine any major issue arising in the framework of the agreement as well as any other bilateral or international issue of common interest. They are usually entitled to take binding decisions, especially in the case of association Councils; they usually consist, on the 'EU side', of 'the members of the Council and members of the Commission' (there are variations), reflecting the mixed nature of the agreement. On the EU side the joint Councils are chaired by the Presidency of the Council of the EU. The lower level joint committees assisting the joint Council in the performance of its duties usually consist of 'representatives of (the) members of the Council and representatives of members of the Commission', in principle at senior civil servant level;[109] on the EU side, the joint committees are chaired by representatives of the Commission.

In the case of mixed agreements, this established practice is likely to continue.[110] After Lisbon the HR chairs the association or other joint Council meetings in her capacity as president of the FAC when the EU side has to chair them.[111] Since the

[108] This is reflected in the 2011 General Arrangements on EU Statements in Multilateral Organisations, Council doc 15901/11 of 24 October 2011, under point 3 ('Member States agree on a case by case basis whether and how to co-ordinate and be represented externally. The Member States may request EU actors or a Member State, notably the Member State holding the rotating Presidency of the Council, to do so on their behalf'). See also Gosalbo Bono (n 33 above) 30–32. Compare Wouters and Ramopoulos (n 38 above) 12–13.

[109] See Gosalbo Bono (n 33 above) 32–33.

[110] See eg Arts 120(1) and 122(1) of the Stabilisation and Association Agreement between the European Communities and their Member States of the one part, and the Republic of Serbia, of the other part [2013] OJ L278/16 ('The Stabilisation and Association Council shall consist of the members of the Council of the [EU] and members of the European Commission, on the one hand, and of members of the Government of Serbia on the other' and 'a Stabilisation and Association Committee, composed of representatives of the Council of the [EU][*] and of representatives of the European Commission, on the one hand, and of representatives of the Government of Serbia on the other'; * note that the wording here differs slightly from the usual wording 'representatives of *the members of* the Council').

[111] eg Council and Commission Decision 2013/489/EU, Euratom of 22 July 2013 establishing the position to be taken on behalf of the European Union and the European Atomic Energy Community within the EU-Serbia Stabilisation and Association Council concerning a Decision of the EU-Serbia Stabilisation and Association Council adopting its rules of procedure [2013] OJ L278/1: in Art 1 of the annexed rules of procedure, it is stated that '[t]he Stabilisation and Association Council shall be chaired alternately for periods of 12 months by the President of the Foreign Affairs Council of the European Union, on behalf of the European Union and its Member States and the European Atomic Energy Community'. See also Art 3(2) of Council and Commission Decision 2013/490/EU, Euratom of 22 July

joint Councils are presided over by the chair of the FAC, the rotating Presidency of the Council has to replace the absent HR.

The Treaty of Lisbon is deliberately ambiguous in the way it addresses the mechanics of the relations between the institutions and the HR: in her task of ensuring the external representation of the Union on issues concerning the CFSP (Article 27(2) TEU), the HR has to 'cohabit' with the President of the European Council (who ensures an identical external representation 'at his level and in that capacity' in accordance with Article 15(6) *in fine* TEU) and the President of the Commission (who also has coordinating powers within the Commission and represents the Union externally on non-CFSP issues at his level). Consequently, the Treaty of Lisbon has in practice added difficulties. On the one hand, it has created a new 'triangle' which experiences not only overlapping but also overcrowding since there are at present no fewer than three senior figures exercising relevant functions in the field of external representation: the President of the European Council, the President of the European Commission and the High Representative. There is in addition the Head of the State or Government of the rotating Presidency of the Council, which represents the Member States whenever there is mixity and this representation has been agreed. If necessary, this Head of State or Government also replaces the President of the European Council.[112] Furthermore, the President of the European Parliament has participated in some external representation activities (eg at the summit launching the Eastern Partnership).

It is clear from the rules as described above that the Treaty of Lisbon has failed to simplify or unify the Union's external representation, since the Union itself as well as the Union with its Member States, may be represented by more than one person/institution. Under these circumstances, cooperation between all those involved is therefore essential. This was obvious to the drafters of the Treaty of Lisbon and they inserted several provisions aimed at ensuring coordination.[113]

2013 on the conclusion of the Stabilisation and Association Agreement between the European Communities and their Member States, of the one part, and the Republic of Serbia, of the other part [2013] OJ L278/14 ('The President of the Council shall, in accordance with Article 120 of the Agreement, preside over the Stabilisation and Association Council. A representative of the Commission shall preside over the Stabilisation and Association Committee, in accordance with the Rules of Procedure thereof').

[112] See Art 2(4) of the Rules of Procedure of the European Council, adopted by and annexed to European Council Decision 2009/882/EU of 1 December 2009 [2009] OJ L315/51.

[113] See especially the following five provisions of the Treaty of Lisbon: 'Pursuant to the principle of sincere cooperation, the Union and the Member States shall, in full mutual respect, assist each other in carrying out tasks which flow from the Treaties. The Member States shall take any appropriate measure, general or particular, to ensure fulfilment of the obligations arising out of the Treaties or resulting from the acts of the institutions of the Union. The Member States shall facilitate the achievement of the Union's tasks and refrain from any measure which could jeopardise the attainment of the Union's objectives'. (Art 4(3) TFEU); 'The Member States shall support the Union's external and security policy actively and unreservedly in a spirit of loyalty and mutual solidarity and shall comply with the Union's action in this area. The Member States shall … refrain from any action which is contrary to the interests of the Union or likely to impair its effectiveness as a cohesive force in international relations'. (Art 24(3) TEU); 'The [HR] shall … ensure the consistency of the Union's external action. He shall be responsible within the Commission for responsibilities incumbent on it in external relations and for coordinating other aspects of the Union's external action'. (Art 18(4) TEU); 'The diplomatic and consular missions

In particular, all those concerned, ie both EU institutions or actors and Member States, are under a duty to sincerely cooperate,[114] a duty which stems directly from the principle of loyal cooperation (Article 4(3) TEU)[115] and results from the requirement of unity in the external representation of the Union and the Member States.[116] The Court of Justice has applied cooperation duties in the management of mixed agreements which, in the view of the Court, impose a close association between the Union and its Member States in the process of negotiation and conclusion of international agreements and in the fulfilment of the obligations stemming from them.[117] These duties are 'best efforts' procedural obligations of information, reporting and consultation as well as arrangements for sharing the exercise of competences, aiming at ensuring the unity of external representation both in its internal implications[118] and in its external dimension.[119] In the framework of EU external relations, the cooperation duty of the Member States requires 'close cooperation between the [Member States] and the [Union] institutions'[120] with the aim of obtaining a concerted action at the international level, since unilateral action by a Member State 'is likely to compromise the principle of unity in international representation of the Union and its Member States and weaken their negotiating power'.[121]

The implementation of cooperation duties between EU institutions under EU law corresponds to the implementation of the principle of good faith under international law as regards EU external representation: on the basis of the respective competences and prerogatives, through coordination and cooperation, pragmatic and reasonable solutions must be sought, even though this has proven to be quite a challenge.

of the Member States and the Union delegations in third countries and international conferences, and their representations to international organisations, shall cooperate in ensuring that decisions defining Union positions and actions adopted pursuant to this Chapter are complied with and implemented. They shall step up cooperation by exchanging information and carrying out joint assessments'. (Art 35 TEU); 'Union delegations shall … act in close cooperation with Member States' diplomatic and consular missions.' (Art 221(2) TEU).

[114] See eg F Casolari, 'The Principle of Loyal Co-operation: A 'Master Key' for EU External Representation?' and P Van Elsuwege and H Merket, 'The Role of the Court of Justice in Ensuring the Unity of the EU's External Representation' in S Blockmans and R Wessel (eds), *Principles and Practices of EU External Representation*, CLEER Working Paper 2012/5: www.asser.nl/upload/documents/20120911T102448-cleer2012-5book_web.pdf, respectively pp 11–35 and 37–57.

[115] See Case C-459/03 *Commission v Ireland (Mox Plant)* [2006] ECR I-4635.

[116] Opinion 2/91 of 19 March 1993, *Convention No 170 of the International Labour Organization concerning safety in the use of chemicals at work* [1993] ECR I-1061, para 36. See also Opinion 1/94 (n 8 above), para 108 and Opinion 2/00 of 6 December 2001, *Cartagena Protocol* [2001] ECR I-9713, para 18.

[117] Ruling 1/78 of 14 November 1978, *Re Draft Convention on the Physical Protection of Nuclear Materials* [1978] ECR 2151.

[118] Joined Cases C-300/98 and C-392/98 *Parfums Christian Dior SA v TUK Consultancy BV* and *Assco Gerüste GmbH v Wilhelm Layher GmbH & Co KG* [2000] ECR I-11307.

[119] Case C-25/94 *Commission v Council (FAO Case)*. [1996] ECR I-1469

[120] The so-called Inland Waterways cases: Case C-266/03 *Commission v Luxemburg* [2005] ECR I-4805, para 60, and Case C-433/03 *Commission v Germany*, [2005] ECR I-6985, para 66.

[121] Case C-246/07 *Commission v Sweden (PFOS)* [2010] ECR I-3317, para 104.

In particular, beyond the question of 'who represents', there is the sensitive issue of 'what constitutes representation', in particular in relation to the 'determination of the Union's position' and the issue of 'what constitutes coordination'. The Treaties make an important distinction between who represents the Union, and who decides on the substance of the position of the Union which is to be expressed by the Union's representative(s). This distinction is very clear throughout Article 218 TFEU in relation to the negotiation, signature and conclusion of international agreements. All key decisions (authorising the opening of negotiations, adopting negotiating directives (optional), approving signature (and, where relevant, provisional application) and conclusion) are taken by the Council.

Similarly, Article 218(9) TFEU provides that

> The Council, on a proposal from the Commission or the [HR] ... shall adopt a decision suspending application of an agreement and establishing the positions to be adopted on the Union's behalf in a body set up by an agreement, when that body is called upon to adopt acts having legal effects, with the exception of acts supplementing or amending the institutional framework of the agreement.

This is mirrored in Article 29 TEU as regards the CFSP: 'The Council shall adopt decisions which shall define the approach of the Union to a particular matter of a geographical or thematic nature' (formerly 'common positions'). These provisions reflect the institutional balance laid down in Articles 16 and 17 TEU (leaving aside the involvement of the Parliament here): while the Commission proposes, represents and implements (on non-CFSP issues),[122] the Council has a treaty-making and policy-making role.[123]

However, in practice, the drawing of this distinction and its consequences have been the subject of considerable discussion and controversy between the institutions. This has been the case in relation to the scope of positions having legal effects under Article 218(9) TFEU: does this provision only cover cases in which the Union is a party to an agreement establishing a body entitled to take decisions? The Court has recently held in Case C-399/12 concerning the International Organisation of Vine and Wine that the provisions of Article 218(9) cover cases where the Union takes a position without being a party,[124] and the Court has provided guidance with regard to the meaning and scope of the terms 'having legal effects' in Article 218(9) TFEU, which must be interpreted widely beyond the more restricted scope of 'binding' legal effects.[125] It is probably fair to say that the main

[122] See Art 17(1) TEU: the Commission shall: 'take appropriate initiatives ... It shall ... execute the budget and manage programmes. It shall exercise coordinating, executive and management functions, as laid down in the Treaties. With the exception of the [CFSP], and other cases provided for in the Treaties, it shall ensure the Union's external representation. It shall initiate the Union's annual and multiannual programming'.

[123] Pursuant to Art 16(1) TEU, the Council shall 'carry out policy-making and coordinating functions as laid down in the Treaties'.

[124] Case C-399/12 *Germany v Council*, judgment of 7 October 2014 (EU:C:2014:2258), paras 48–55.

[125] ibid, paras 56–66.

difficulties have arisen on positions that do not concern the adoption of acts having legal effects (see further below).

Another source of difficulty has been the question whether statements are made on behalf of the Union and/or on behalf of the Member States,[126] which is a question of competence (see above) that led to the adoption of 'General Arrangements' on EU statements in multilateral organisations.[127]

There are also differences between the Council, the Commission and the HR/EEAS on the issue of when the Commission and/or HR can express EU positions on the basis of previously agreed EU policies, and when they need to seek Council approval of a position (eg in the practice of statements and declarations made by the HR in the field of the CFSP).[128] The CJEU has only provided limited guidance in this respect so far.[129]

[126] For an example of how the competence issue was addressed in one case concerning legally binding arrangements, see Council Decision 2007/668/EC of 25 June 2007 on the exercise of rights and obligations akin to membership ad interim by the European Community in the World Customs Organisation [2007] OJ L274/11. Recital 8 thereof states that 'For matters falling under [EC] competence a [EC] position must be established. For matters falling partly within [EC] competence, Member States should strive to adopt a common position to ensure the unity of external representation of the [EC] and its Member States'.).

[127] 'EU Statements in Multilateral Organisations—General Arrangements', Council doc 15901/11 of 24 October 2011 and COR 1. These arrangements, reviewed in early 2012, inter alia set out when statements should be delivered on behalf of the Union and/or its Member States. Separate arrangements continue to exist for some international organisations, including some which can adopt decisions having legal effects. For an example, see the arrangements on the Food and Agriculture Organisation (FAO), which are currently being discussed in view of their updating. See The role of the European Union in the Food and Agriculture Organisation (FAO) after the Treaty of Lisbon: Updated Declaration of Competences and new arrangements between the Council and the Commission for the exercise of membership rights of the EU and its Member States, COM(2013) 333 final of 25 May 2013 and the correlation table in Council doc 15019/13 of 8 November 2013 (after more than 3 years, there is still no internal agreement within the Union on these revised arrangements and the more recent documents are not public).

[128] See eg the Annual report from the High Representative of the European Union for Foreign Affairs and Security Policy to the European Parliament covering the year 2012 (Council doc 14924/13 of 16 October 2013), the introductory part to Annex III ('HR Declarations on behalf of the EU: reflect the official position of the EU and are issued under the HR's authority with prior consultation of the Member States. Where no such official position exists, these Declarations are agreed by Member States within the Council' and 'HR Statements: used most frequently to respond to events requiring quick EU reaction and issued under the HR's authority without formal consultation of the Member States').

[129] Case C-73/14 about a Commission statement to the International Tribunal for the Law of the Sea. In its application, the Council requested the Court to annul the Commission's decision of 29 November 2013 to submit the 'Written statement on behalf of the European Union' to the International Tribunal for the Law of the Sea in Case 21 without the Council's approval and against the Council's will. The Council considered that the Commission infringed the principle of distribution of powers and the principle of institutional balance since the position to be expressed on behalf of the Union before this Tribunal should have been established by the Council in accordance with Art 218(9) TFEU and since the Commission infringed Art 16(1) TEU by usurping the policy-making functions which belong to the Council. It also considered that the Commission infringed the principle of sincere cooperation. In its judgment of 6 October 2015 (EU:C:2015:663) the Court dismissed the action. It inter alia held that submissions before a court were not positions adopted in a body set up by an agreement and that in this particular case, the purpose of the statement was not to formulate policy.

Particular difficulties have arisen with regard to the scope and meaning of Article 220 TFEU which provides that the EU shall 'establish all appropriate forms of cooperation' with the UN and its specialised agencies, the Council of Europe, the Organisation for Security and Cooperation in Europe and the Organisation for Economic Cooperation and Development and 'shall maintain such relations as are appropriate with other international organisations'. The implementation of this provision is for 'The High Representative ... and the Commission' and the practical difficulties which have arisen concern the issue of how much autonomy the Commission and the High Representative have in developing these relations with international organisations, and in particular whether the provision of Article 220 TFEU constitutes a distinct legal basis that can be used independently of, or together with, Article 218 TFEU.[130] Within this context, one specific case subject to discussion concerns possible additional participatory rights for the European Union within the formal and informal bodies of the United Nations High Commissioner for Refugees.[131]

Finally, there is the issue of coordination between the different actors.[132] The Treaty is largely silent on how coordination must be organised. In principle coordination usually implies an organisation of the different actors and elements of the activity in order to allow them to work together and obtain the most effective result and thus covers the distribution of presentational and supporting tasks, and the appropriateness and timing of (oral) interventions. This coordination usually takes place 'locally' (eg in New York or Geneva)[133] and is important and necessary.[134] However, it cannot replace the determination or adaptation of the contents

[130] See eg the UK statement reproduced in Council doc 13375/13, p 31: 'The UK strongly welcomes the Draft Agreement between the European Union and the European Organisation for the Safety of Air Navigation providing a general framework for enhanced cooperation ... However, the UK objects to the inclusion of the citation of Articles 218 and 220 TFEU in the recitals to the Draft Agreement ... The UK does not consider that the citation of Article 220 in the Draft Agreement is correct in this context. Article 220 concerns administrative cooperation between the EU and international organisations, but is not the appropriate legal base under the TFEU for the negotiation of legally binding agreements with international organisations on behalf of the EU'.

[131] See Council documents 12765/14; 13046/14 and 13046/14 REV 1 (September 2014), as well as the Press release of the Council meeting on 25–26 September 2014 (Council doc 13437/1/14, p 18). See notably the UK statement in Annex II to doc 13046/14 REV 1 ('The [UK] reiterates its understanding that the Coreper ... adopted this text in order to allow the Commission and EEAS to conduct initial discussions with the UNHCR on possible options to achieve such additional rights, but that this did not constitute a formal mandate to negotiate any changes'). This subsequently led to Council Decision (EU) 2015/1817 of 6 October 2015 on the position to be adopted on behalf of the European Union in the 66th session of the Executive Committee of the Programme of the United Nations High Commissioner for Refugees, [2015] OJ L 264/13, adopted under Article 218(9) TFEU. However, for reasons external to the EU, the UNHCR bodies have not yet granted the requested participation rights so far (it is hoped that this will be possible by the end of 2016).

[132] See Gosalbo Bono (n 33 above) 35–36.

[133] See also the periodic overview of the 'EU Diplomatic Representation in third countries', above n 104. In para 3 of the document for the first half of 2015, it is stated that 'The responsibility of representation *and coordination* on behalf of the EU has been performed by a number of Union delegations as of 1 January 2010 or later'. (emphasis added)

[134] See also 'EU Statements in Multilateral Organisations—General Arrangements' (n 125 above).

of EU positions by the relevant EU institutions, eg the Council as the policy-making body. Of course whenever the coordination implies limited refinements or minor adaptations, they can be agreed by Member States' local representatives under the coordination of the Presidency, in a configuration closely resembling that of the Council (and its working parties). Note that in the CFSP, Article 34(1) TFEU provides that 'Member States shall coordinate their action in international organisations and at international conferences. They shall uphold the Union's positions in such forums. The [HR] … shall organise this coordination'.

Another area which has given rise to a series of legal challenges and court cases, is that of international agreements and other international instruments.

VIII. DISPUTES CONCERNING THE PRACTICE OF INTERNATIONAL AGREEMENTS AND OTHER INTERNATIONAL INSTRUMENTS

In addition to issues of mixity and competence (see above), one particular challenge has been the choice and combination of legal bases.[135] This is of course an issue which has been with us since long before the Treaty of Lisbon. However, some of the amendments introduced by the Treaty of Lisbon have given rise to additional difficulties.

One important challenge is the opt-outs of the UK, Ireland and Denmark from measures adopted within the Area of Freedom, Security and Justice (FSJ) (Articles 67 to 89 TFEU) when horizontal international agreements include provisions in this area. In those situations Protocols Nos 21 and 22 to the Lisbon Treaty contain constitutional rights and duties for the three Member States not to take part in the adoption of FSJ measures, to remain outside EU law, or in the case of UK and Ireland a choice to 'opt in'. Are the traditional criteria on the choice of legal bases (such as 'the centre of gravity' or the 'accessory/secondary' methods) affected when agreements contain FSJ measures? In particular, when multiple policy areas are involved, can the FSJ areas which affect the above-mentioned constitutional Protocols ever be 'secondary' to the prevailing legal basis or bases resulting from the centre of gravity? If the answer were positive, it would mean that the Member States concerned by the Protocols would in fact be deprived of their prerogatives ensured by primary law not to participate in measures adopted under this policy when they are combined with other measures and are deemed to be only secondary to other policies pursued by those other measures.

The Court of Justice has made it clear that it will not give any special consideration to these primary law rights of these three Member States and will simply

[135] See eg G De Baere, 'From "Don't Mention the Titanium Dioxide Judgment" to "I Mentioned it Once, But I Think I Got Away with It All Right": Reflections on the Choice of Legal Basis in EU External Relations after the Legal Basis for Restrictive Measures Judgment' (2013) 15 *Cambridge Yearbook of European Legal Studies* 537 and M Klamert, 'Conflicts of Legal Basis: No Legality and No Basis but a Bright Future under the Lisbon Treaty?' (2010) 35 *European Law Review* 497.

apply its traditional case law (centre of gravity, ancillary or secondary dimensions, '*accessoire*', etc) on the choice of legal bases.[136] The same applies to the choice of legal bases whenever CFSP measures apply together with non-CFSP measures.[137] It should be noted that the practice of the Member States concerned by the Protocols has so far been not to accept the reasoning of the Court[138] and to continue invoking their constitutional rights under the Protocols even in cases in which the FSJ dimension is only secondary.[139]

The Court has also indicated more generally that the centre of gravity test which it had already applied to sectoral agreements (eg in the choice of an environment and/or trade legal basis)[140] also applies to horizontal international agreements. This follows in particular from its judgment of 11 June 2014 in the *Philippines case* (Case C-377/12, *Commission v Council*). In this judgment the Court rejected the addition of specific sectoral legal bases to the 'development'—which it apparently considers to be of a more general nature—and 'trade' legal bases in the Framework Agreement on Partnership and Cooperation (PCA) with the Philippines, which is a horizontal agreement.

In this recent case law, the Court thereby sets aside its previous case law, in which the Court upheld that the conclusion of horizontal international agreements required the insertion of as many legal bases as competences were exercised.[141] However, the Court does not seem to apply its new approach consistently.

[136] See notably Case C-656/11 *United Kingdom v Council*, judgment of 27 February 2014 (EU:C:2014:97), para 49 ('Nor is the legality of the choice of the legal basis for a European Union measure affected by the consequence that the choice may have as regards whether Protocol No 21, and Protocol No 22 on the position of Denmark ... apply') and Case C-81/13 *United Kingdom v Council*, judgment of 18 December 2014 (EU:C:2014:2449), para 37 ('Protocol No 21 is not capable of having any effect whatsoever on the question of the correct legal basis') as well as Case C-377/12 *Commission v Council*, judgment of 11 June 2014 (*Philippines case*) (EU:C:2014:1903), paras 34–60, especially paras 57–60. For a further case on the delimitation between the FSJ and other Union policies, see Case C-431/11 *United Kingdom v Council*, judgment of 26 September 2013, paras 45–68.

[137] Case C-658/11 *Parliament v Council*, judgment of 24 June 2014 (EU:C:2014:2025), para 45.

[138] For a brief critical analysis by a commentator on the Advocate General's opinion on this point in the *Philippines case* (which was in the same vein as the judgment but addressed the issue explicitly), see S Peers, 'Is Readmission Linked to development?', 23 January 2014: eulawanalysis.blogspot.be/2014/01/is-readmission-linked-to-development.html. Note, however, that in para 77 of his Opinion of 23 January 2014 in this case, Advocate General Mengozzi considered that the prerogatives of those Member States would be preserved when the Union would conclude the re-admission agreement referred to in Article 26 of the PCA, as the re-admission agreement would be concluded on the basis of Art 79 TFEU (EU:C:2014:29).

[139] For an example, albeit prior to the *Philippines* judgment, see eg the Statement by the UK upon the adoption of Council Decision 2014/164/EU of 11 February 2014 on the conclusion, on behalf of the European Union, of the Protocol against the Illicit Manufacturing of and Trafficking in Firearms, Their Parts and Components and Ammunition, supplementing the United Nations Convention against Transnational Organized Crime [2014] OJ L89/7, reproduced in Council doc 10191/1/14 REV 1, p 11.

[140] See eg Opinion 2/00 of 6 December 2001 (*Cartagena Protocol*) [2001] ECR I-9713, paras 23 and 42. For an example of a dual legal basis, see eg Case C-94/03 *Commission v Council* [2006] ECR I-1 (*Rotterdam Convention*).

[141] See Opinion 1/94 (n 9 above). The Court held that the competence was mixed and that the Union competence was based not only on the common commercial policy under Art 113 TEC (as in force at the time). Indeed, no less than 11 substantive legal bases (Arts 43, 54, 57, 66, 75, 84(2), 99,

In particular, in its judgment of 18 December 2014 in Case C-81/13, *United Kingdom v Council*, relating to the decision on the position on the coordination of social security systems to be taken by the EU within the Association Council with Turkey, the Court held that the correct legal bases would have been the combination of Article 217 TFEU (the general legal basis for association agreements) and Article 48 TFEU (the specific legal basis for social security measures necessary to provide freedom of movement for workers).[142] As a result, choosing the correct legal basis or bases for international agreements and decisions on EU positions remains a significant challenge.[143]

Another aspect of this issue concerns the decision-making process: in the situation where a JFS legal basis is required in combination with another (non-JFS) legal basis, can these legal bases be combined in a single Council decision on signature or conclusion of an agreement, or do the decisions need to be split into two decisions? The question has arisen because the Council is composed differently under the respective legal bases since Denmark and—depending on the case—the UK and Ireland, do not take part in the adoption of FSJ measures. The practice of the Council is not uniform in this respect:[144] in a number of cases such decisions have been 'split',[145] whereas in other cases they have not.[146] This practice derives

100, 100a, 113, and 235 TEC as in force at the time) were included in Council Decision 94/800/EC of 22 December 1994 concerning the conclusion on behalf of the European Community, as regards matters within its competence, of the agreements reached in the Uruguay Round multilateral negotiations (1986–1994) [1994] OJ L336/1 following their implicit approval by the Court in this Opinion.

[142] C-81/13, *United Kingdom v Council* (EU:C:2014:2449). See especially paras 62 ('the Council is entitled, on the basis of Article 217 TFEU, to adopt a measure in the framework of an association agreement on condition that that measure relates to a specific area of EU competence and is also founded ... on the legal basis corresponding, in the light in particular of its aim and content, to that area') and 63.

[143] Furthermore, in recent case law the Court seems to give more weight to the objective of a measure than to its content: see eg Case C-43/12 *Commission v Parliament and Council*, judgment of 6 May 2014 (EU:C:2014:298).

[144] For an example of the UK position, see the Statement by the UK mentioned above in n 137: 'the UK considers that the Council Decision should have been split into two, to cover both the non-Title V, and the Title V, aspects of the Firearms Protocol'. Compare the Commission's statement reproduced in Council doc 13375/13, p 6: 'insofar as the splitting of the Decision intends to reflect the different voting requirements pursuant to the application of Protocol 21, the Commission notes that a Decision authorising negotiation of an international agreement is not a "measure" in the sense of that Protocol. Accordingly, it is not appropriate to split the Decision authorising negotiations'.

[145] eg in relation to the conclusion of the 2002 Protocol to the Athens Convention relating to the Carriage of Passengers and their Luggage by Sea (see Council Decisions 2012/22/EU and 2012/23/EU of 12 December 2011 concerning the accession of the European Union to the Protocol of 2002 to the Athens Convention relating to the Carriage of Passengers and their Luggage by Sea, 1974, respectively with the exception of Articles 10 and 11 thereof and as regards Articles 10 and 11 thereof [2012] OJ L8, respectively p 1 and p 13) and of the Association Agreement with Ukraine (see above nn 51–52). By contrast, in the case of the Framework Agreement on Partnership and Cooperation with the Philippines, an FSJ legal basis was contained in the Council decision together with other legal bases (but the Court rejected the addition of the FSJ and other sectoral legal bases, holding that only the development and trade legal bases were correct; see n 136 above for the judgment in that case).

[146] See eg Council Decision 2012/418/EU of 21 December 2011 on the signing, on behalf of the European Union, and provisional application of certain provisions of the Partnership and Cooperation Agreement between the European Union and its Member States, of the one part, and the Republic of Iraq, of the other part [2012] OJ L204/18.

from the principle of the autonomy of the Council to organise its internal work taking into account the particular circumstances of each case.

The designation of the negotiator or head of the negotiating team has also proven challenging.[147] In addition to the question of mixity and the possible role of the Member State exercising the rotating Presidency of the Council (see above), the respective roles of the Commission and HR/EEAS are laid down in Article 218(3) TFEU which provides that

> The Commission, or the [HR] … where the agreement envisaged relates exclusively or principally to the [CFSP], shall submit recommendations to the Council, which shall adopt a decision authorising the opening of negotiations and, depending on the subject of the agreement envisaged, nominating the Union negotiator or the head of the Union's negotiating team.

In cases where the Council has designated both the Commission and the HR, the Council has appointed one of them as head of the Union's negotiating team[148] and has left to the HR (and through her the EEAS) and the Commission the freedom to arrange their cooperation and coordination throughout the process of negotiation. In practice, in some cases, the Commission appears to have given the lead to the EEAS even where the Commission has been designated as head of the negotiating team, at least in terms of the actual negotiations.[149] Part of the explanation for this practice resides in the fact that the Commission no longer has geographical desks (these were all transferred to the EEAS upon the establishment of the latter) and the Commission has designated the most relevant thematic Directorate General as its lead service for each geographical area.

Divergent positions between the institutions have manifested themselves in other areas, including as regards the extent to which the Council may issue instructions to the Commission when authorising it to open negotiations and/or when adopting negotiating directives;[150] as regards the need for or utility of

[147] Compare the analysis of Gatti and Manzini (n 38 above) 1703, especially 1707–10 and 1720–23.

[148] See eg the Council decision on the negotiations with Kazakhstan, above n 34, Art 2(1).

[149] Compare the case study by H Kostanyan in 'Examining the Discretion of the EEAS: What Power to Act in the EU-Moldova Association Agreement?' (2014) 19 *European Foreign Affairs Review* 373.

[150] In Case C-425/13 *Commission v Council*, the Commission sought the annulment of the Council Decision authorising the opening of negotiations on linking the EU emissions trading scheme with an emissions trading system in Australia (Council doc 8568/13 (not public) and ADD 1 DCL 1 (annexed negotiating directives, including 'procedure for negotiations'; now declassified)), claiming that the obligations imposed in that decision on the Commission as negotiator and the role assigned to the special committee violate Arts 218 and 295 TFEU and Art 13(2) TEU. See also the Commission's statement upon the adoption of this decision (Council doc 8805/13 ADD 1). The statement by the Council in response is not public (Council doc 8805/13 ADD 2). In its judgment of 16 July 2015 (EU:C:2015:483), the Court upheld the Council decision except for the part which provided that '[w]here appropriate, detailed negotiating positions of the Union shall be established within the special committee referred to in Article 1(2) or within the Council'. The Court inter alia held that 'Article 218(4) TFEU must be interpreted as empowering the Council to set out, in the negotiating directives, procedural arrangements governing the process for the provision of information, for communication and for consultation between the special committee and the Commission' (para 78). Compare Gatti and Manzini (n 38 above) 1710–11.

decisions authorising the opening of negotiations to identify the substantive legal bases concerned;[151] and as regards the extent of the obligation to keep the EP fully and immediately informed of all steps in the procedure under Article 218(10) TFEU.[152]

Furthermore, the Council practice concerning international agreements has been extended to non-binding arrangements and other international instruments. While the Lisbon Treaty maintains the premise that EU external action is an extension of internal policies, with a focus on legislative measures and binding international agreements, international relations are not only conducted though international agreements but involve a multitude of instruments. Many of these are not specifically provided for in the Treaties, which raises the question of what rules and procedures govern the adoption of such instruments. Two examples illustrate this issue. The first illustration is the status of non-binding international arrangements, such as memoranda of understanding; in particular, the foundational instruments of both the Eastern Partnership and the Union for the Mediterranean are considered not to be legally binding and have not been adopted under Article 218 TFEU;[153] obviously, what matters here (both under EU law and under international law) is not the name,[154] but whether or not such an arrangement contains obligations of a legal nature.[155] If it does, it is a legal

[151] The Council's more recent practice is to increasingly identify the substantive legal bases but the Commission considers that this is not necessary. On the latter, see eg the Commission's statement reproduced in Council doc 10191/1/14 REV 1, p 18 ('The Commission does not consider it necessary that a Council Decision authorising the opening of negotiations indicates a substantive legal basis').

[152] See Cases C-658/11 *Parliament v Council*, judgment of 24 June 2014 (EU:C:2014:2025) and C-263/14, *Parliament v Council*, judgment of 14 June 2016 (EU:C:2016:435). In the former case, the Court ruled inter alia that the Council had not immediately informed the EP about the decision on signature and conclusion of the agreement concerned and it annulled the decision on that ground, while maintaining its effects. In the latter case, the EP is asked the Court to endorse a very broad reading of its right to be informed on negotiations. In both cases the Commission intervened in support of the Parliament and issues were also raised in relation to the scope of the CFSP and its delimitation with the FSJ as well as the consent of the EP under Art 218(6) TFEU. In her opinion of 28 October 2015 (EU:C:2015:729), Advocate General Kokott took the view that the Council had correctly relied on a CFSP legal basis but had not sufficiently informed the EP. The Court took the same view.

[153] For the Eastern Partnership, see the Joint Declaration of the Prague Eastern Partnership Summit of 7 May 2009, available at: www.eeas.europa.eu/eastern/docs/index_en.htm. See also B Van Vooren, 'A Case-Study for "Soft Law" in EU External Relations: The European Neighbourhood Policy' (2009) 34 *European Law Review* 696. For the Union for the Mediterranean, see the Joint Declaration of the Paris Summit for the Mediterranean of 13 July 2008, available at: ufmsecretariat.org/history/.

[154] In the field of energy, such arrangements have often been called a memorandum of understanding. In the field of migration, they have eg been called mobility partnerships, one of the instruments used within the framework of the EU's Global Approach to Migration and Mobility (see: ec.europa.eu/dgs/home-affairs/what-we-do/policies/international-affairs/global-approach-to-migration/index_en.htm). In other cases, they have taken the form of joint declarations.

[155] See eg Opinion 1/75 of 11 November 1975, *Draft Understanding on a Local Cost Standard drawn up under the auspices of the OECD* [1975] ECR 1359–60 ('In its reference to an "agreement", the second subparagraph of Article 228(1) of the Treaty uses the expression in a general sense to indicate any undertaking entered into by entities subject to international law which has binding force, whatever its formal designation'). See also the ICJ, *Maritime Delimitation and Territorial Questions between Qatar and Bahrain (Qatar v Bahrain)*, judgment of 1 July 1994, paras 23–30.

agreement subject to Article 218 TFEU. If it does not, Article 218 TFEU does not apply as such[156] and it is less clear what rules apply in such cases. The practice has been that Article 218 TFEU has not been applied to such arrangements. Instead, they have been concluded/signed by the Commission and usually, depending on their substance, with a varying degree of involvement of the Council. In some cases the Council, or one of its preparatory bodies, has merely been informed at some point in the process, whereas in other cases the Council has approved the conclusion of such arrangements. The Council's position is that whenever such arrangements include political commitments by the Union, it requires approval by Council, given the Council's policy-making role under Article 16(1) TEU.[157] The Commission appears to share this position to some extent, except that it does not consider that such approval is necessary where the commitments reflect existing EU policy. But the Commission's practice has not always been consistent in terms of involvement of the Council.

The second illustration is provided by EU unilateral declarations. Although used less frequently, at least as regards declarations that seek to create legal rights, one such declaration concerning the granting of access to EU waters to Venezuela has been the subject of a case before the CJEU.[158] One of the questions raised was whether such an instrument must be adopted under Article 218 TFEU in a somewhat modified form, or under the procedure applicable to internal acts (usually a legislative procedure).[159] The Court did not settle this issue as it concluded that

[156] See Case C-233/02 *France v Commission* [2004] ECR I-2759, para 45.

[157] See also M Gatti and P Manzini (n 37 above) 1732–33. See especially the pending Case C-660/13 *Council v Commission*. In that case, the Council sought the annulment of the Commission's decision C(2013) 6355 final of 3 October 2013 on the signature of the Addendum to the Memorandum of Understanding on a Swiss financial contribution. The Council considered that this decision without prior authorisation by the Council infringed the principle of distribution of powers contained in Article 13(2) TEU and, consequently, the principle of institutional balance and that the Commission's course of action leading to the adoption of the decision and the signature of the Addendum infringed the principle of sincere cooperation contained in Article 13(2) TEU. In her opinion of 26 November 2015 (EU:C:2015:787), Advocate General Sharpston took the view that 'the decision on whether or not to approve and sign a non-binding international agreement with a third State belongs to the Council' (para 117). Similar questions arise in relation to positions taken in the framework of international organisations where the conditions of Art 218(9) TFEU are not met. See also above on case C-73/14 *Council v Commission* (above n 129). It is worth noting that in Case C-233/02 *France v Commission* (n 156 above), para 40, the Court stated that its judgment in that case 'cannot be construed as upholding the Commission's argument that the fact that a measure such as the Guidelines is not binding is sufficient to confer on that institution the competence to adopt it'.

[158] See Joined Cases C-103/12 *Parliament v Council* and C-165/12, *Commission v Council* (EU:C:2014:2400). The act at issue in that case is Council Decision 2012/19/EU of 16 December 2011 on the approval, on behalf of the European Union, of the Declaration on the granting of fishing opportunities in EU waters to fishing vessels flying the flag of the Bolivarian Republic of Venezuela in the exclusive economic zone off the coast of French Guiana [2011] OJ L6/8. This Decision refers to Art 43(3), in conjunction with point (b) of Art 218(6) TFEU.

[159] In her opinion of 15 May 2014 (EU:C:2014:334), Advocate General Sharpston took the view that such acts are subject to Art 218 TFEU by analogy, while excluding the possibility that they would fall under para (9) of this Article (paras 96–123).

the declaration and its acceptance by Venezuela 'must be regarded, taken together, as an agreement concluded between those two parties' and that the declaration at issue was 'a constituent element of an international agreement' that fell 'within the scope of Article 218 TFEU'.[160]

The participation of the EU in international institutions has also proven interesting in the post-Lisbon practice[161] and requires special consideration.

IX. AN UNSATISFACTORY EU PARTICIPATION IN INTERNATIONAL ORGANISATIONS

While the Union is a full member of some international organisations, eg the WTO and the FAO, in many other cases it has obtained lesser participation rights, such as observer status. This situation has given rise to a number of issues.

In view of the wide scope of Union competence, there would seem to be, potentially, a vast number of international organisations which deal at least in part with matters falling within Union competences, such as the International Maritime Organization[162] and the International Civil Aviation Organization.[163] Does the Union need to seek membership in all these cases?[164] Or should it only be concerned with organisations dealing with exclusive Union competences—including competences that have become exclusive because they have been internally exercised in accordance with the *ERTA* doctrine?[165] In which circumstances is it sufficient that the EU acts through its Member States?

In the case of exclusive competence the Member States are under an obligation to take all appropriate measures to ensure fulfilment of the obligations arising from the Treaties, to facilitate the achievement of the Union's tasks, and to abstain

[160] Judgment of 26 November 2014, especially paras 67–73 and 82–85. The Court added that Art 218 TFEU: 'governs the negotiation and the conclusion of agreements between the European Union and third countries or international organisations, the expression "agreement", in accordance with the case-law, being understood in a general sense to indicate any undertaking entered into by entities subject to international law which has binding force, whatever its formal designation'.

[161] See eg R Wessel, 'The Legal Framework for the Participation of the European Union in International Institutions' (2011) 33 *European Integration* 621 and (on the pre-Lisbon situation) F Hoffmeister, 'Outsider of Frontrunner? Recent Developments under International and European Law on the Status of the European Union in International Organizations and Treaty Bodies' (2007) 44 *Common Market Law Review* 41.

[162] On the EU and the IMO, see L Nengye and F Maes, 'Legal Constraints to the European Union's Accession to the International Maritime Organization' (2012) 43 *Journal of Maritime Law and Commerce* 279: www.vliz.be/imisdocs/publications/247600.pdf.

[163] In relation to ICAO, see also B Van Vooren and R Wessel, 'Diplomatic Ambitions of the European Union versus the Reality of International Law' (2013) 20 *Journal of European Public Policy* 1354–56.

[164] See generally M Emerson et al, *Upgrading the EU's Role as Global Actor: Institutions, Law and the Restructuring of European Diplomacy* (Brussels, CEPS, 2011): www.ceps.eu/book/upgrading-eus-role-global-actor-institutions-law-and-restructuring-european-diplomacy.

[165] Case 22/70 *Commission v Council (European Agreement on Road Transport)* [1971] ECR 263.

from any measure which could jeopardise the attainment of the objectives of the Treaties. Any

> unilateral action by the Member States in this regard, even if it were collective and concerted action, would have the effect of calling into question certain of the essential functions of the Community and in addition of affecting detrimentally its independent action in external relations.[166]

This includes an obligation of means ('*obligation de moyens*') to allow the EU to be able to be represented by its institutions and actors. However, in many cases, the constitutions of such organisations provide for membership of States exclusively. In the latter situations, whenever the Union has exclusive competence, the Member States may be empowered by the Union to act on behalf of the EU (Article 2(1) TFEU).

Where the constitutions of international organisations have allowed for EU membership, or it was proposed to amend them to that effect, it is probably fair to say that in some cases, at least some Member States have not been particularly supportive,[167] either when the Council has received proposals from the Commission recommending that the EU should seek membership, or when the EU has agreed to seek membership but its final acceptance has depended upon the persuasion of the non-EU members of the organisation concerned. Both aspects are a classic application of the duty of sincere cooperation.

Yet, the greatest challenge remains when the other non-EU States which are members of the international organisation concerned object to the accession of the EU and are in a position to prevent the Union from joining that organisation,[168] or seek to obtain a price for Union membership which may be very costly.[169]

There are two examples in the framework of the UN which illustrate the difficulties which the EU has sometimes faced in attempting to obtain an appropriate status in certain international organisations or bodies. The first one is the difficulties experienced in order to obtain an enhanced observer status for the EU at the

[166] Ruling 1/78 of 14 November 1978 *pursuant to Art 103 of the Euratom Treaty* [1978] ECR 2151, para 33.

[167] Emerson et al (n 164 above) 44–45, although it is not clear whether the authors refer to EU Member States or those of the organisations concerned. See also Nengye and Maes (n 162 above) 280 and 288 and Van Vooren and Wessel (n 163 above) 1354 (who speak about 'the apparent willingness of some member states to back-track what could be gained from the Lisbon Treaty' and a 'deep schism between the EU and its member states' and consider that 'realizing the potential from the Lisbon Treaty is not without obstacles imposed by the member states').

[168] Compare Van Vooren and Wessel (n 163 above) 1350–67.

[169] Incidentally, it would appear that very serious external obstacles arise more in such cases than in the cases of multilateral international agreements on substantive areas of international law that do not set up an international organisation or of which such setting up is not the main focus. The Union is a party to a number of such agreements, such as the UN Convention on the Law of the Sea (although this treaty does set up some international bodies), a number of international agreements in the field of the environment, and recently also some human rights treaties (the UN Disabilities Convention; the accession to the ECHR was at an advanced stage but has suffered a serious set-back in the form of the CJEU's negative Opinion 2/13 of 18 December 2014; see below). In most cases this is on the basis of a clause in the agreement allowing for membership of Regional Economic (Integration) Organisations.

UN General Assembly.[170] The second, less recent, one is the discussions over EC/EU representation in the UN Peacebuilding Commission.[171]

In particular, the issue of the EU status at the UN remains controversial. The EU is not a member of the UN. However, it has obtained the status of 'enhanced' observer 'in the sessions and work of the General Assembly and its committees and working groups, in international meetings and conferences convened under the auspices of the Assembly and in United Nations conferences' (Resolution 65/276, adopted by the UN General Assembly (UNGA) on 3 May 2011). This Resolution was adopted, not without difficulties, the EU having undertaken long and laborious negotiations with a number of States, in particular those belonging to the Caribbean Community (CARICOM), which were mindful of the preservation of their status quo in the UNGA, a status quo which, in their view, did not allow for distinctions between observers or, as they perceived it, the incorporation of non-State entities as full members 'by the back door' since 'the parameters for the conferral of any special privileges to a non-State observer remained the supremacy of the Charter', and required 'the strict observance of the rules of procedure as well as the established practices of the General Assembly'.[172] These difficulties were overcome only after the EU and its Member States agreed to 'water-down' a more ambitious initial draft resolution and to incorporate in the adopted resolution explicit language 'reaffirming' that 'the General Assembly is an intergovernmental body whose membership is limited to States that are Members of the United Nations', and 'recognising' that other 'regional organizations' might get equal treatment in the UNGA whenever such a case would be considered.[173] The Resolution justifies the new status of the EU in the UNGA bearing in mind that, as a result of the entry into force of the Lisbon Treaty, the EU had replaced/succeeded the European Community; that it was 'a party to many instruments concluded under the auspices of the UN'; that it was already 'an observer or participant in the work of several UN specialized agencies and bodies'; and that it had a new external institutional representation (ie the President of the European Council, the High Representative, the European Commission, and Union delegations) (preambular paragraphs of Resolution 65/276).

The interesting conditions under which the new enhanced observer status of the EU has to be exercised ('modalities') are set out in the Annex to the Resolution. According to these modalities the representatives of the EU enjoy several rights,

[170] This status was finally granted in UN General Assembly Resolution 65/276 of 3 May 2011, UN Doc A/65/l.64/Rev.1. For an insider's view, see P Serrano de Haro, *Participation of the EU in the work of the UN: General Assembly Resolution 65/276*, CLEER Working Paper 2012/4: www.asser.nl/upload/documents/20120620T112233-cleer2012-4web.pdf.

[171] For a partial account revealing some of the external difficulties (leaving aside the prior internal discussions), see Council doc 11134/07 of 22 June 2007 on 'EU/EC Representation in the Peacebuilding Commission—Nameplate'.

[172] Official Records of the Sixty-fifth session of the UN General Assembly, Doc A/65/PV.88 p 5.

[173] UNGA Resolution 65/276 of 3 May 2011, operative paras 1 and 3.

'in order to present positions of the [EU] and its member States as agreed by them'; in particular, they are:

(a) Allowed to be inscribed on the list of speakers among representatives of major groups, in order to make interventions;
(b) Invited to participate in the general debate of the General Assembly, in accordance with the order of precedence as established in the practice for participating observers and the level of participation;
(c) Permitted to have its communications relating to the sessions and work of the General Assembly and to the sessions and work of all international meetings and conferences convened under the auspices of the Assembly and of [UN] conferences, circulated directly, and without intermediary, as documents of the Assembly, meeting or conference;

and what is more important

(d) Also permitted to present proposals and amendments orally as agreed by the States members of the [EU]; such proposals and amendments shall be put to a vote only at the request of a Member State; [and]
(e) Allowed to exercise the right of reply regarding positions of the [EU] as decided by the presiding officer; such right of reply shall be restricted to one intervention per item.

Otherwise the status of the EU in the UNGA is limited in that, in practice and in law, the representatives of the EU in the UNGA sit 'among the observers', which means that in principle they can only intervene after the UN Member States unless the EU speaks through the EU Member State which holds the rotating presidency of the Council, in which case the EU voice is heard as part of the intervention of that State. In addition, as is the case of all observers, the representatives of the EU do not have the 'the right to vote, to co-sponsor draft resolutions or decisions, or to put forward candidates'.[174] Also, at the start of each session of the UNGA, the President of the UNGA gives a precursory explanation or recalls the resolution on the status of the EU before the EU takes the floor.

These modalities have been the subject of further clarification by the UN Secretary-General in his Note of 1 June 2011 to the UNGA, which has specified that, in practice: (a) the inscription of the EU on the list of speakers among representatives of major groups, will be 'in the order in which the [EU] signifies its desire to speak'; (b) in the order of precedence for participation in the general debate of the UNGA, the EU will follow after the interventions of the Member States of the UN, the Holy See and Palestine; (c) while the representatives of the EU will be permitted to present proposals and amendments orally, action and voting on the EU's oral proposal or amendment will be taken 'only at the request of a Member State in accordance with the relevant rules and the Rules of Procedure of the UNGA', and in any case the representatives of the EU 'will not have the right to

[174] See Annex to the Resolution entitled 'Participation of the European Union in the work of the United Nations'.

submit proposals or amendments for circulation as an official document'; (d) the representatives of the EU are seated among the observers, who come 'after Member States, non-Member States and Palestine'; and (e) in addition to not disposing of the right to vote, 'including in elections', and the right to co-sponsor a draft resolution, decision or amendment, 'the representatives of the [EU] may neither submit the [EU]'s own candidacy for any election or appointment nor submit the names of candidates for any election or appointment' and

> will not have the right to raise points of order, to challenge or appeal the rulings of the presiding officer or to make procedural motions including the adjournment of debate, the closure of debate and the suspension or adjournment of the meeting.[175]

These restrictions have led to criticisms by some commentators who have argued that the UNGA Resolution and its practical modalities which qualify the actual participation rights of the Union in the everyday work of the UNGA and, thereby, its capacity to influence decisions of the UNGA, have failed to meet the Lisbon Treaty objective of stronger external representation of the EU.[176] This criticism does not take account of the fact that a successful negotiation does not depend on internal factors only but in particular on external ones: the EU's intention to upgrade its status faced an unprecedented level of resistance, mainly from the Caribbean and African countries.

In contrast with the UNGA, there is an absence of any status for the EU in the UN Security Council (UNSC). However, Article 34 TEU explicitly provides that

> when the Union has defined a position on a subject which is on the United Nations Security Council agenda, those Member States which [are] on the Security Council shall request that the High Representative be invited to present the European Union positions.

This provision, which codifies an existing practice initiated when Javier Solana was HR, does not of course change the right of the UK and France to sit as permanent members of the UNSC and does not affect their individual votes and rights of veto within the UNSC (nor the rights of other EU Member States which may be non-permanent members of the UNSC). Although the invitation to the HR to speak in the UNSC is dependent upon the unanimous acceptance of all the members of the Security Council, Article 34 TEU is worded so as to ensure that a request to the UNSC is made for it to issue an invitation to the HR to present the Union's position, and that the EU positions are made known to the UNSC even in the absence of the HR: on the one hand, Article 34 TEU provides that

> When the Union has defined a position on a subject which is on the [UN] Security Council agenda, those Member States which sit on the Security Council shall request that the High Representative be invited to present the Union's position;

175 Note by the Secretary-General, UNGA Doc A/65/856 of 1 June 2011, para 12.

176 See J Wouters, J Odermatt and T Ramopoulos, *The Status of the European Union at the United Nations after the General Assembly Resolution of 3 May 2011* (Leuven, Katholieke Universiteit Leuven, Centre for Global Governance Studies, July 2011).

on the other hand, it indicates that

> Member States which are also members of the [UN] Security Council will concert and keep the other Member States and the [High Representative] fully informed. Member States which are members of the Security Council will, in the execution of their functions, defend the positions and the interests of the Union, without prejudice to their responsibilities under the provisions of the [UN] Charter.

The final assessment on the EU membership of international organisations may, as indicated above, be more of a political nature: what concessions should the EU accept in return for third States' acceptance of EU membership? If the price is too high, membership may ultimately not be beneficial to the EU and its Member States.[177] As the example of the UN indicates, in cases where EU membership cannot be obtained, it may be necessary to settle for lesser participation rights[178] and/or to rely on Member States acting in the interests of the Union where they are so authorised. For an example of the latter, one may refer to cases in which the Union has authorised the Member States to ratify agreements in the interests of the Union.[179]

Finally, problems may also arise when Union competence expands and leads to a situation in which Member States should no longer be parties to an international agreement or members of an international organisation alongside the Union.[180]

[177] Regional settings may include specific challenges in this respect. In particular, if the EU has a number of votes equivalent to that of its Member States, it has or would have a majority of votes in virtually any European international organisation. This raised some challenges in the framework of the pending EU accession to the ECHR and it was agreed that the Rules of the Committee of Ministers for the supervision of the execution of judgments and of the terms of friendly settlements should be amended to avoid a situation where the Union and its Member States could systematically veto any measures relating to cases concerning them. See Council of Europe Doc 47+1(2013)008rev2 of 10 June 2013: www.coe.int/t/dghl/standardsetting/hrpolicy/Accession/Meeting_reports/47_1(2013)008rev2_EN.pdf, 30–32 (explanatory report). However, the fate of this accession after Opinion 2/13 of the CJEU remains to be seen (see below).

[178] For an example of such participation rights (*in casu* as an interim solution), see Council Decision 2007/668/EC of 25 June 2007 on the exercise of rights and obligations akin to membership ad interim by the European Community in the World Customs Organisation [2007] OJ L274/11.

[179] eg Council Decision 2007/431/EC of 7 June 2007 authorising Member States to ratify, in the interests of the European Community, the Maritime Labour Convention, 2006, of the International Labour Organization [2007] OJ L161/40; and Council Decision 2014/165/EU of 3 March 2014 authorising Member States to ratify, in the interests of the European Union, the Arms Trade Treaty [2014] OJ L89/44.

[180] This is probably an exceptional situation but it is worth mentioning the case of the European Convention on the legal protection of services based on, or consisting of, conditional access, Strasbourg, 24 January 2001, CETS 178: conventions.coe.int/Treaty/en/Treaties/html/178.htm. Pursuant to Article 9(2) of this Convention, at multilateral consultation meetings 'Concerning questions within its competence, the European Community shall exercise its right to vote and cast a number of votes equal to the number of its member States that are Parties to the Convention'. Furthermore, pursuant to Article 10(3) thereof, 'Any amendment … can be adopted by a majority of two-thirds of the States which have ratified the Convention'. Some Member States are parties to this Convention but it now falls entirely within the exclusive competence of the Union (see Case C-137/12 *Commission v Council*, judgment of 22 October 2013). However, if Member States withdrew from the Convention, this would only leave the Union as a party, in addition to non-EU Council of Europe State parties, and this poses a problem in terms of the application of these two provisions. If applied literally, it would leave the

X. THE QUESTION OF THE LEGALITY OF RESTRICTIVE MEASURES

The EU considers that restrictive measures (often referred to as 'sanctions') providing for the interruption or reduction, in part or completely, of political, economic and/or financial relations with third countries are an essential tool in order to achieve the EU's objectives under the CFSP. In general terms, the EU imposes restrictive measures to bring about a change in policy or activity by the target country, part of a country, the government, entities or individuals. They are a preventive, non-punitive instrument which allows the EU to respond swiftly to political challenges and developments. The political objectives and criteria of the restrictive measures are defined in EU legal acts. They are used as part of an integrated and comprehensive policy approach, in the framework of the EU's overall foreign policy strategies, involving political dialogue, complementary efforts and other instruments.[181]

The EU has very frequently imposed a wide range of restrictive measures: diplomatic sanctions (expulsion of diplomats, severing of diplomatic ties, suspension of official visits); suspension of cooperation with a third country; boycotts of sport or cultural events; trade sanctions (general or specific trade sanctions, arms embargoes); financial sanctions (freezing of funds or economic resources, prohibition on financial transactions, restrictions on export credits or investment); and restrictions on admission (visa and travel bans). These sanctions have very often included restrictive measures against natural or legal persons and groups or non-State entities.[182]

Union without any vote in multilateral consultation meetings. This issue is under discussion. See also the Commission statement in Council doc 8421/14 ADD 1 of 4 April 2014 and the declaration by the Union annexed to Council doc 7597/1/14 of 27 November 2014, as well as the statements set out in Council doc 16170/14 ADD 1 of 28 November 2014 (the latter is not public).

[181] See: www.eeas.europa.eu/cfsp/sanctions/index_en.htm (including an overview of EU restrictive measures and a regularly updated table at: www.eeas.europa.eu/cfsp/sanctions/docs/measures_en.pdf). At the time of writing, some 2300 persons and entities were designated under these measures under some 30 different sanctions regimes. See generally F Giumelli, *How EU Sanctions Work: A New Narrative*, EU ISS Chaillot Paper No 129, May 2013: www.iss.europa.eu/uploads/media/Chaillot_129.pdf; C Beaucillon, *Comment choisir ses mesures restrictives? Guide pratique des sanctions de l'UE*, EU Institute for Security Studies *Occasional Paper* No 100, December 2012: www.iss.europa.eu/uploads/media/op100.pdf and K Gebert, *Shooting in the Dark? EU Sanctions Policies*, European Council on Foreign Relations Policy Brief January 2013: www.ecfr.eu/page/-/ECFR71_SANCTIONS_BRIEF_AW.pdf. For a legal analysis, see I Cameron (ed), *EU Sanctions: Law and Policy Issues concerning Restrictive Measures* (Cambridge, Intersentia, 2013); C Eckes, *EU Counter-Terrorist Policies and Fundamental Rights: the Case of Individual Sanctions* (Oxford, Oxford University Press, 2009); and C Eckes, 'EU Restrictive Measures against Natural and Legal Persons: from Counterterrorist to Third Country sanctions' (2014) 51 *Common Market Law Review* 869.

[182] Restrictive measures in force cover the following countries: Afghanistan, Belarus, Bosnia and Herzegovina, Burma, Central African Republic, China, Democratic Republic of Congo, Egypt, Eritrea, Republic of Guinea (Conakry), Guinea Bissau, Haiti, Iran, Iraq, Ivory Coast, Democratic People's Republic of Korea, Lebanon, Liberia, Libya, Moldova, Myanmar (Burma), Russian Federation, Serbia and Montenegro, Somalia, South Sudan, Sudan, Syria, Tunisia, Ukraine, USA and Zimbabwe. Restrictive measures also target natural and legal persons in those countries and terrorist groups (ie Al Qaeda, Hamas etc). This list does not include the types of sanctions decided in the framework of

The EU practice on restrictive measures dates back to well before the Treaty of Lisbon and comprises all the CFSP decisions or Common Positions and other legal acts based on the Treaties, including those CFSP acts which merely provide for measures for which no specific Regulation was adopted, such as restrictions on admission of persons (visa or travel bans). The Treaty of Lisbon codifies existing practice, provides an explicit legal basis for restrictive measures against natural or legal persons and groups or non-State entities in Article 215(2) TFEU[183] and extends the CJEU's jurisdiction to cover also the review of the legality of CFSP acts enacting such measures against natural or legal persons, under the conditions of Article 263, fourth paragraph, TFEU (see Article 275, second paragraph TFEU). These persons and entities are the subject of targeted ('*smart*') financial sanctions which comprise an obligation to freeze all funds and economic resources of the targeted persons and entities and a prohibition on making funds or economic resources available directly or indirectly to or for the benefit of these persons and entities.

Certain EU measures are imposed by resolutions adopted by the UN Security Council under Chapter VII of the UN Charter. The EU may, however, decide to apply autonomous measures in addition to the UN's measures or adopt completely autonomous restrictive measures on its own. EU autonomous sanctions or EU additions to UN sanctions are reviewed at regular intervals in order to ensure that measures are adjusted as needed, in line with developments affecting the stated objectives and the effectiveness of the measures. Where individuals or entities are subject to targeted restrictive measures the EU lays down clear criteria, tailored to the specific case, for the purposes of determining who should be listed (and de-listed).

The introduction and implementation of restrictive measures is subject to strict legal conditions: they must respect human rights and fundamental freedoms, in particular the rights of the defence and the right to an effective remedy. In addition the measures imposed must always be proportionate to their objective. Finally, the measures and their implementation must be carried out in accordance with international law (including the international obligations of the EU and its Member States derived from the WTO Agreements).

It may be recalled that in its (second) *Kadi* judgment of 18 July 2013, the Court of Justice has codified the EU fundamental rights requirements with regard to the listings of persons subject to restrictive measures. In essence, the Court of Justice has held that the

> Courts of the [EU] must, in accordance with the powers conferred on them by the Treaties, ensure the review, in principle the full review, of the lawfulness of all Union

European Political Cooperation (prior to November 1993), restrictions not enacted by a CFSP Decision, or the suspension or termination of bilateral agreements and suspension or termination of cooperation with third countries.

[183] Compare the *Kadi I* judgments (below n 209) as regards the pre-Lisbon situation.

> acts in the light of the fundamental rights forming an integral part of the [EU] legal order, including review of such measures as are designed to give effect to resolutions adopted by the Security Council under Chapter VII of the Charter of the United Nations (paragraph 97).[184]

Those fundamental rights include, inter alia, respect for the rights of the defence (Article 41(2) of the Charter of Fundamental Rights of the European Union),[185] and the right to effective judicial protection (Article 47 of the Charter).[186] The rights of the defence include the right to be heard and the right to have access to the file (ie the documents which the Council and/or the Commission hold on a given person or entity in relation to its designation), 'subject to legitimate interests in maintaining confidentiality' (*Kadi*, para 99). The right to effective judicial protection requires that 'the person concerned must be able to ascertain the reasons upon which the decision taken in relation to him is based, either by reading the decision itself or by requesting and obtaining disclosure of those reasons' (ibid, para 100). Although Article 52(1) of the Charter allows limitations on the exercise of the rights enshrined in the Charter, these limitations are subject 'to the conditions that the limitation concerned respects the essence of the fundamental right in question and subject to the principle of proportionality, that it is necessary and genuinely meets objectives of general interest recognised by the [EU]' (ibid, para 101).[187] In any case these limitations must be examined 'in relation to the specific circumstances of each particular case' (ibid, para 102),[188] which includes consideration of 'the nature of the act at issue, the context of its adoption and the legal rules governing the matter in question' (ibid).[189]

In concreto, as regards the implementation of the rights of the defence, Article 296 TFEU imposes an 'obligation to state the reasons' which implies 'in all circumstances' that there is a 'statement of reasons' identifying the individual, and providing the 'specific and concrete reasons why the competent authorities consider that the individual concerned must be subject to restrictive measures' (ibid, para 116).[190] In addition, compliance with the rights of the defence requires that the competent Union authority 'must ensure that that individual is placed in a position in which he may effectively make known his views on the grounds advanced

[184] Joined Cases C-584/10 P, C-593/10 P and C-595/10 P *European Commission and Others v Kadi*, judgment of 18 July 2013 (EU:C:2013:518). See also, to that effect, Joined Cases C-399/06 P *Faraj Hassan v Council and Commission* and C-403/06 P *Chafiq Ayadi v Council* [2009] ECR I-11393, para 71; and C-548/09 P *Bank Melli Iran v Council* [2011] ECR I-11381, para 105.

[185] See, to that effect, Case C-27/09 P *France v People's Mojahedin Organization of Iran* [2011] ECR I-13427, para 66.

[186] See Case C-300/11 *ZZ v Secretary of State for the Home Department*, judgment of 4 June 2013 (not yet reported), para 53 and case law cited therein.

[187] See also ibid (*ZZ*), para 51.

[188] See, to that effect, Case C-110/10 P *Solvay v Commission* [2011] ECR I-10439, para 63.

[189] See, to that effect, as regards compliance with the duty to state reasons, the judgments of 15 November 2012 in Joined Cases C-539/10 P and C-550/10 P *Al-Aqsa v Council* and *Netherlands v Al-Aqsa*, paras 139 and 140 (EU:C:2012:711); and in Case C-417/11 P *Council v Bamba*, para 53 (EU:C:2012:718).

[190] See, to that effect, *Al-Aqsa*, paras 140 and 142, and *Bamba*, paras 49–53 (both n 189 above).

against him' (ibid, para 112),[191] and examines, 'carefully and impartially, whether the alleged reasons are well founded, in the light of those comments and any exculpatory evidence provided with those comments' (ibid, para 114).[192] As regards the implementation of the right to effective judicial protection, the listed person is entitled to a review by the Courts of the EU in the event that the person concerned challenges the lawfulness of the decision to list or maintain the listing, and this review 'must extend to whether rules as to procedure and rules as to competence, including whether or not the legal basis is adequate, are observed' (ibid, para 117).[193] The Courts of the EU must, further, 'determine' whether the competent EU authority has complied with all the procedural safeguards included in the rights of the defence, and the obligation to state reasons laid down in Article 296 TFEU, in particular, 'whether the reasons relied on are sufficiently detailed and specific' (ibid, para 118). The effectiveness of the judicial review also requires that—as part of the review of the lawfulness of the grounds which are the basis of the decision to list or to maintain the listing of a given person—the Courts of the EU 'ensure that that decision, which affects that person individually' (ibid, para 119),[194] is taken on a 'sufficiently solid factual basis' (ibid)[195] and that requires 'a verification of the factual allegations in the summary of reasons underpinning that decision' (ibid)[196] because the

> judicial review cannot be restricted to an assessment of the cogency in the abstract of the reasons relied on, but must concern whether those reasons, or, at the very least, one of those reasons, deemed sufficient in itself to support that decision, is substantiated (ibid).

To that end, it is for the Courts of the EU, in order to carry out that examination, 'to request the competent [EU] authority, when necessary, to produce information or evidence, confidential or not, relevant to such an examination' (ibid, para 120). In particular, it is necessary that 'the information or evidence produced should support the reasons relied on against the person concerned' (ibid, para 122). If the competent EU authority finds itself unable to comply with the request by the Courts of the EU, 'it is then the duty of those Courts to base their decision solely on the material which has been disclosed to them' and if that material 'is insufficient' to allow a finding that a reason is well founded, the Courts of the EU 'shall

[191] See, to that effect, Case C-32/95 P *Commission v Lisrestal and Others* [1996] ECR I-5373, para 21; Case C-462/98 P *Mediocurso v Commission* [2000] ECR I-7183, para 36; and Case C-277/11 *MM v Minister for Justice, Equality and Law Reform, Ireland and Attorney General*, judgment of 22 November 2012 (EU:C:2012:744) para 87 and the case law cited therein.

[192] See, by analogy, Case C-269/90 *Technische Universität München v Hauptzollamt München-Mitte* [1991] ECR I-5469, para 14; Case C-525/04 P *Spain v Lenzing* [2007] ECR I-9947, para 58, and *MM v Minister for Justice, Equality and Law Reform, Ireland and Attorney General* (n 191 above), para 88.

[193] See, to that effect, by analogy, Case C-376/10 P *Tay Za v Council*, judgment of 13 March 2012 (EU:C:2012:138), paras 46–72.

[194] See, to that effect, Joined Cases C-478/11 P to C-482/11 P *Gbagbo and Others v Council*, judgment of 23 April 2013 (EU:C:2013:258), para 56.

[195] See, to that effect, *Al-Aqsa* (n 189 above), para 68.

[196] See to that effect, Case C-550/09 *Criminal proceedings against E and F* [2010] ECR I-6213, para 57.

disregard that reason as a possible basis for the contested decision to list or maintain a listing' (ibid, para 123). However, if the competent EU authority provides relevant information or evidence, the Courts of the EU must then

> determine whether the facts alleged are made out in the light of that information or evidence and assess the probative value of that information or evidence in the circumstances of the particular case and in the light of any observations submitted in relation to them by, among others, the person concerned (ibid, para 124).

Whenever overriding considerations to do with the security of the EU or of its Member States or with the conduct of their international relations may preclude the disclosure of some information or some evidence to the person concerned,

> it is none the less the task of the Courts of the [EU], before whom the secrecy or confidentiality of that information or evidence is no valid objection, to apply, in the course of the judicial review to be carried out, techniques which accommodate, on the one hand, legitimate security considerations about the nature and sources of information taken into account in the adoption of the act concerned and, on the other, the need sufficiently to guarantee to an individual respect for his procedural rights, such as the right to be heard and the requirement for an adversarial process (ibid, para 125).

To that end, it is for the Courts of the EU, when carrying out an examination of all the matters of fact or law produced by the competent EU authority, 'to determine whether the reasons relied on by that authority as grounds to preclude that disclosure are well founded' (ibid, para 126). If the Courts of the EU conclude that those reasons do not preclude disclosure, or at the very least partial disclosure, of the information or evidence concerned, the EU Court 'shall give the competent [EU] authority the opportunity to make such disclosure to the person concerned' and if that authority does not permit the disclosure of that information or evidence, in whole or in part, 'the Courts of the [EU] shall then undertake an examination of the lawfulness of the contested measure solely on the basis of the material which has been disclosed' (ibid, para 127). If it turns out that the reasons relied on by the competent EU authority do indeed preclude the disclosure to the person concerned of information or evidence produced before the Courts of the EU, it is for the EU Courts

> to strike an appropriate balance between the requirements attached to the right to effective judicial protection, in particular respect for the principle of an adversarial process, and those flowing from the security of the European Union or its Member States or the conduct of their international relations (ibid, para 128).

In order to strike such a balance, it is 'legitimate to consider possibilities such as the disclosure of a summary outlining the information's content or that of the evidence in question', and irrespective of whether such possibilities are pursued,

> it is for the Courts of the European Union to assess whether and to what the extent the failure to disclose confidential information or evidence to the person concerned and his consequential inability to submit his observations on them are such as to affect the probative value of the confidential evidence (ibid, para 129).

The Rules of Procedure of the General Court as recently amended now include a provision specifically addressing the possible recourse to classified information.[197]

With such a series of specific and detailed fundamental rights requirements for the listings, and the ample powers that the EU Courts reserve to themselves with regard to the review of their legality, it comes as no surprise that measures against individuals and entities have given rise to an increasing number of cases[198] brought before the EU Courts. The case law has clarified a number of issues by now[199] and the Council has adapted its practice accordingly.[200]

Nevertheless, a number of challenges remain. The most difficult issue is probably that of the proof required to substantiate the reasons given for designating an individual or entity. Taking account of the limited means of gathering information on situations in countries in which the governments oppose the restrictive measures, and the fact that some of the information which is relevant is classified,[201] this is likely to remain a difficulty.[202] This question is distinct from that of the adequacy of the reasons, which is also frequently contested but on which grounds there have been fewer annulments by the EU jurisdictions (the reasons for designation have in many cases become considerably more specific and concrete). Another persistent challenge concerns UN-based restrictive measures, where respect for human rights must be reconciled with obligations to comply with UN Security Council decisions (see below). It may also be noted that the Council was recently ordered to pay damages in a restrictive measures case for the first time.[203] Furthermore, in two recent judgments relating to restrictive measures against terrorist groups under Common Position 2001/931/CFSP and Regulation (EC)

[197] See Article 105 of these Rules of Procedure, [2015] OJ L 105/1. However, this provision will only apply once the Court has adopted security rules (see Article 227(3)), which the Court has not yet done. A corresponding amendment to the Rules of Procedure of the Court of Justice is under discussion.

[198] At the time of writing, some 120 restrictive measures cases against the Council were pending.

[199] See generally the doctrine cited in n 181 above. See also: europeansanctions.com/.

[200] This is inter alia reflected in the (updated) Guidelines on implementation and evaluation of restrictive measures (sanctions) in the framework of the EU Common Foreign and Security Policy, Council doc 11205/12 and CORs 1 and 2. See also more recently 'Restrictive measures (Sanctions)—Update of the EU Best Practices for the effective implementation of restrictive measure', Council doc 7383/1/15 of 24 March 2015.

[201] Article 105 of the General Court's Rules of Procedure as amended in 2015 ([2015] OJ L105, 23.4.2015, p 1), entitled 'Treatment of information or material pertaining to the security of the Union or that of one or more of its Member States or to the conduct of their international relations', now addresses the handling of classified information in proceedings before the Court.

[202] For a good discussion, see A Cuyvers, '"Give Me One Good Reason": The Unified Standard of Review for Sanctions after Kadi II' (2014) 51 *Common Market Law Review* 1759.

[203] Case T-384/11 *Safa Nicu Sepahan v Council*, judgment of 25 November 2014 (EU:C:2014:986). However, it should be noted that the General Court has recently ruled that an action for damages in relation to a CFSP act on restrictive measures does not fall within the Court's jurisdiction as the second paragraph of Article 275 TFEU only covers *actions for annulment* brought by individuals, under the conditions set out in the fourth paragraph of Article 263 TFEU, against restrictive measures adopted by the Council: see the judgment of 18 February 2016 in Case T-328/14, *Mahmoud Jannatian v Council* (EU:T:2016:86), paras 30–31.

No 2580/2001,[204] the General Court annulled the designations of Hamas and of the Tamil Tigers (LTTE).[205] Under this Common Position (and Regulation), certain measures are taken against listed persons, groups and entities involved in terrorist acts as defined therein. The list is

> drawn up on the basis of precise information or material in the relevant file which indicates that a decision has been taken by a competent authority in respect of the persons, groups and entities concerned, irrespective of whether it concerns the instigation of investigations or prosecution for a terrorist act, an attempt to perpetrate, participate in or facilitate such an act based on serious and credible evidence or clues, or condemnation for such deeds (Article 1(4)).

In both judgments the General Court annulled the listings purely for reasons related to the procedure used for their adoption. In *Hamas*, the Court considered that the Council had not demonstrated that the decisions of the competent national authorities invoked as a basis for the designation of Hamas fell within the scope of the Common Position (as it did not identify the facts underlying those decisions) and that the Council could not rely on elements that were not contained in such decisions, including open source material, even for decisions to maintain the listing of Hamas (as opposed to its initial designation). In the *LTTE* case, the Court found the same defects and furthermore considered that the Council had not demonstrated in the statement of reasons that it had verified that a decision of a competent authority of a third State, upon which the Council had relied, fell within the scope of the Common Position and that the third State in question ensured protection of the rights of defence and a right to effective judicial protection equivalent to that guaranteed at EU level (paragraphs 138–147), while accepting that the Council can rely on third State decisions when they meet the conditions (paragraphs 126–136).

The judicial practice of restrictive measures has also contributed to shape fundamental aspects of the relationship between international law and EU law.

XI. THE CONTENTIOUS RULINGS OF THE CJEU IN THE FIELD OF EXTERNAL RELATIONS

There is one aspect in the case law of the EU Court that merits special consideration[206] and that concerns the Court's recent case law on the relationship

[204] Common Position 2001/931/CFSP of 27 December 2001 on the application of specific measures to combat terrorism ([2001] OJ L344/93) and Regulation (EC) No 2580/2001 of 27 December 2001 on specific restrictive measures directed against certain persons and entities with a view to combating terrorism ([2001] OJ L344/70), as amended.

[205] Case T-400/10 *Hamas v Council*, judgment of 17 December 2014 (EU:C:2014:1095) and Joined Cases T-208/11 and T-508/11 *Liberation Tigers of Tamil Eelam (LTTE) v Council*, judgment of 16 October 2014 (EU:C:2014:885). The Council has lodged an appeal against both of these judgments (Cases C-599/14 P and C-79/15 P).

[206] See more generally M Cremona and A Thies (eds), *The European Court of Justice and External Relations: Constitutional Challenges* (Oxford, Hart Publishing, 2014).

between international law and EU law, in particular with regard to the interpretation and application of rules of international law by the Court, including both the provisions in international agreements and customary international law.[207] In this respect, the case law of the EU Court has arguably evolved over time: while some of the early case law emphasised the specific nature of Community law by distinguishing it from general international law, later case law appeared to show a greater openness towards international law, eg by interpreting EU law in accordance with international law ('*Völkerrechtsfreundliche Auslegung*').[208] However, during the last few years the Court seems to have reversed this trend and a number of decisions indicate a renewed focus on the autonomy of EU law.

This is for instance reflected in the judgments of the CJEU in the two *Kadi* appeals,[209] which have been exhaustively discussed in numerous publications some of which are very critical with regard to the Court's consideration of the status under EU law of the UNSC resolutions adopted under Chapter VII of the UN Charter.[210] It may be recalled that in its judgment of 3 September 2008 in this case (*Kadi I*),[211] the Court held, in essence, that the obligations imposed 'by an international agreement' such as the UN Charter cannot have the effect of prejudicing the constitutional principles of the TEC, which include the principle that all EU acts must respect fundamental rights—that respect constituting a condition of their lawfulness which it is for the Court to review within the framework of the complete system of legal remedies established by that Treaty. The Court held further

[207] See generally E Cannizzaro, P Palchetti and R Wessel (eds), *International Law as Law of the European Union* (Leiden, Martinus Nijhoff, 2011).

[208] See Cases C-70/94 *Fritz Werner Industrie-Ausrüstungen GmbH v Germany* [1995] ECR I-3189, para 23; C-83/94, *Leifer* [1995] ECR I-3231, para 24; and C-53/96 *Hermès International v FHT Marketing Choice BV* [1998] ECR I-3603, para 28. See R Gosalbo Bono, 'Some Reflections on the CFSP Legal Order' (2006) 43 *Common Market Law Review* 366 and F Naert, *International Law Aspects of the EU's Security and Defence Policy, with a Particular Focus on the Law of Armed Conflict and Human Rights* (Antwerp, Intersentia, 2010) 375–76, with further references (the thesis on which this book is based, is available online at: lirias.kuleuven.be/bitstream/1979/1986/1/Doctoraatsthesis_Frederik_Naert_08-09-2008_final.pdf).

[209] See Joined Cases C-402/05 P and C-415/05 P *Yassin Abdullah Kadi and Al Barakaat International Foundation v Council and Commission* [2008] ECR I-6351 (*Kadi I*) (appeal against Case T-315/01 *Kadi v Council and Commission* [2005] ECR II-3649) and Joined Cases C-595/10 P, C-593/10 P and C-584/10 P *Commission and Others v Yassin Abdullah Kadi*, 18 July 2013 (*Kadi II*) (appeal against Case T-85/09 *Yassin Abdullah Kadi v Commission* [2010] ECR II-5177).

[210] C Tomuschat, 'The *Kadi* Case: What Relationship is there between the Universal Legal Order under the Auspices of the United Nations and the EU Legal Order?' (2009) 28 *Yearbook of European Law* 654, especially 658. P Margulies, 'Aftermath of an Unwise Decision: The U.N. Terrorist Sanctions Regime after Kadi II' (2014) 6 *Amsterdam Law Forum* 51, argues that the Court failed to display an appropriate level of deference to the decisions of the UNSC sanctions committee. Some authors refer to the 'intransigence' of the Court with regard to the protection of human rights: see H Rouidi, 'L'arrêt de la CJCE du 3 septembre 2008—vers un modus operandi de l'exécution communautaire des résolutions onusiennes?' (2009) *Revue de science criminelle et de droit pénal comparé* 75, 75. Other, less critical, authors consider that the EU Court indicated a possible opening to allow for precedence of UN Security Council measures, if sufficient human rights guarantees are created: see eg J Kokott and C Sobotta, 'The Kadi Case—Constitutional Core Values and International Law—Finding the Balance?' (2012) 23 *European Journal of International Law* 1015.

[211] Above n 209.

that, notwithstanding the fact that undertakings given in the UN context must be observed when implementing Security Council resolutions, it does not follow from the principles governing the international legal order under the UN that an act adopted by the EU to implement such a resolution thereby enjoys immunity from jurisdiction, and the Court added that there is no basis for such immunity in the EC Treaty. In those circumstances the Court has held that 'the Courts of the [EU] must ensure the review, in principle the full review, of the lawfulness of all [EU] acts in the light of fundamental rights, including where such acts are designed to implement Security Council resolutions'.[212]

What makes the rulings in *Kadi* exceptional is that the international obligations derived from the binding resolutions of the UN Security Council acting under Chapter VII of the UN Charter—which according to the General Court bound the Union by virtue of its '*competence liée*' (mandatory duty)[213]—were relegated by the Court of Justice to the premises of its well-known case law concerning ordinary international agreements, thus distancing itself from the traditional and constant general legal wisdom that the UN Charter is no ordinary international agreement and that its universal acceptance and its supremacy clause (Article 103 UN Charter) make it the highest authority of international law, even the 'constitution of the International Community' for an important number of internationalists.[214] The Court's dualist approach in *Kadi* has been described as 'unfaithful to its traditional fidelity to public international law',[215] and 'inserting itself in the tradition of nationalism'.[216] Even if the *Kadi* case law was interpreted as open to allowing for precedence of UNSC measures if an 'equivalent protection' of human rights were created by the UNSC[217] (which has not been the case so far), such an interpretation, in the line of the *Bosphorus* case law by the European Court of Human Rights,[218] does not change the main message of the Court which still remains that

212 *Kadi II*, 18 July 2013 (n 209 above), para 23.

213 Case T-184/95 *Dorsch Consult Ingenieurgesellschaft mbH v Council and Commission* [1998] ECR II-667, para 74.

214 R Chemain and A Pellet (eds), *La Charte des Nations Unies, constitution mondiale? Actes du colloque du CEDIN—Paris X du 24 juin 2005* (Paris, Pedone, 2006).

215 G De Búrca, 'The European Court of Justice and the International Legal Order After Kadi' (2010) *Harvard International Law Journal* 44 *et seq*, as cited by Kokott and Sobotta (n 210 above) 1015.

216 B Fassbender, 'Triepel in Luxemburg. Die dualistische Sicht des Verhältnisses zwischen Europa- und Völkerrecht in der "Kadi-Rechtsprechung" des EuGH als Problem des Selbstverständnisses der Europäischen Union' (2010) 63 *Die Öffentliche Verwaltung* 333, 340, as cited by Kokott and Sobotta (n 210 above) 1015.

217 A Rosas, 'Counter-Terrorism and the Rule of Law: Issues of Judicial Control' in AM Salinas de Frías, KLH Samuel and ND White (eds), *Counter-Terrorism: International Law and Practice* (Oxford, Oxford University Press, 2012) 83, 107.

218 In that case the European Court of Human Rights held that the transfer of public authority to an international organisation is in compliance with the ECHR 'as long as the relevant organisation is considered to protect fundamental rights … in a manner which can be considered at least equivalent to that for which the Convention provides'. See ECtHR, *Bosphorus Hava Yolları Turizm ve Ticaret Anonim Şirketi v Ireland*, Application No 45036/98, (2006) 42 EHRR 1, para 155. See K Kuhnert, 'Bosphorus—Double standards in European human rights protection?' (2006) 2 *Utrecht Law Review* 177.

the autonomy of the EU legal order is more important than its integration into an overarching international legal order.[219]

The *Kadi* judgments confirm that 'a dramatic uprising is taking place in the jurisprudential conception of the relationship between [EU] law and international law', which traditionally has been governed by the monist principle that international law is part of EU law, a principle 'already deeply shaken by the WTO saga'.[220] Indeed it will be recalled that the Court of Justice held that, given their nature and purpose, the WTO agreements are not in principle among the rules in the light of which the Court is to review the legality of measures adopted by the EU institutions.[221] Having noted that the system resulting from the WTO agreements accorded considerable importance to negotiation between the parties,[222] the Court found that to require courts to refrain from applying rules of domestic law which are inconsistent with the WTO agreements would have the consequence of depriving the legislative or executive organs of the contracting parties of the possibility (afforded in particular by the Understanding on Rules and Procedures Governing the Settlement of Disputes, which forms Annex 2 to the Agreement establishing the WTO, 'the Dispute Settlement Understanding') of entering into a negotiated arrangement even on a temporary basis.[223] Furthermore, the Court held that to accept that the Courts of the EU have the direct responsibility for ensuring that EU law complies with the WTO rules 'would deprive the [EU]'s legislative or executive bodies of the discretion which the equivalent bodies of the [EU]'s commercial partners enjoy',[224] considering in particular that some of the most important commercial partners of the EU 'have concluded from the subject-matter and purpose of the WTO agreements that they are not among the rules applicable by their courts when reviewing the legality of their rules of domestic law' and that 'such lack of reciprocity, if admitted, would risk introducing an anomaly in the application of the WTO rules'.[225] The Court considers that it can

[219] The Kadi II judgment 'does not provide a proper interface between international law and EU law, due to the asymmetric relations between the EU and the UN legal orders': M Wimmer, 'Inward- and Outward-Looking Rationales behind Kadi II' (2014) 21 *Maastricht Journal of European & Comparative Law* 676, 678.

[220] X, *International Law in the EC Legal Order: the Contribution of the Intertanko Case*: www.scienzegiuridiche.uniroma1.it/sites/default/files/docenti/cannizzaro/intertanko-case.pdf (in relation to the *Intertanko* case (n 233) discussed below).

[221] See Case C-149/96 *Portugal v Council* [1999] ECR I-8395, para 47; Case C-307/99, *OGT Fruchthandelsgesellschaft mbH v Hauptzollamt Hamburg-St Annen*, Order of 2 May 2001, para 24; Cases C-27/00 and C-122/00 *R v Secretary of State for the Environment, Transport and the Regions, ex parte Omega Air Ltd and Others* [2002] ECR I-2569, para 93; Case C-76/00 P *Petrotub and Republica v Council* [2003] ECR I-79, para 53; Case C-93/02 P *Biret International v Council* [2003] ECR I-10497, para 52; and Case C-377/02 *Léon Van Parys NV v Belgisch Interventie- en Restitutiebureau (BIRB)* [2005] ECR I-1465, para 39.

[222] See *Portugal v Council* (n 221 above), para 36.

[223] See *Portugal v Council* (n 221), para 40, and *Van Parys* (n 221 above), para 48.

[224] See the recent confirmation of the now well established principles in the preliminary ruling of 18 December 2014 in Case C-306/13 *LVP NV v Belgische Staat*, para 46.

[225] See *Portugal v Council* (n 221 above), paras 43–46; *Van Parys* (n 221 above), para 53; and Joined Cases C-120/06 P and C-121/06 P *Fabbrica italiana accumulatori motocarri Montecchio SpA (FIAMM) and Others v Council and Commission* [2008] ECR I-6513, para 119.

review the legality of the EU measure at issue in the light of the WTO rules only 'where the [EU] intends to implement a particular obligation assumed in the context of the WTO or where the [EU] measure refers expressly to specific provisions of the WTO agreements'.[226] More recently, the CJEU has confirmed in the last of the series of 'Bananas' cases that

> the provisions of the WTO Agreements, are not such as to create rights which individuals might rely on directly before a national court in order to oppose the application of the customs tariff rate of EUR 176 per tonne, laid down in Article 1(1) of Council Regulation (EC) No 1964/2005 of 29 November 2005 on the tariff rates for bananas.[227]

When the WTO case law was analysed it was understood by the commentators (those who approved as well as those who disapproved of the restrictive view taken by the Court) that the approach of the Court was 'exceptional' and responded to the idiosyncratic nature of the legal regime laid down by the WTO treaties.[228] Indeed, ever since the *International Fruit* cases,[229] the CJEU had ruled out the automatic effect of WTO rules in the Union legal order,[230] but it was common wisdom that it was not expected that the Court would expand the scope of its WTO case law to other agreements. This exception appeared to be confirmed by the Court in the *Simutenkov* case in which it held that 'it is clear from the Court's case law that when an agreement establishes cooperation between the parties, some of the provisions of that agreement may … directly govern the legal position of individuals'.[231]

However, in the 2008 *Intertanko* judgment the Court extended to the Convention on the Law of the Sea the special treatment accorded to the WTO agreements. In this case, the Court was to decide, in a preliminary ruling, whether Directive 2005/35/EC on ship-source pollution and on the introduction of penalties for infringements was—with regard to the liability regime for accidental discharges that it established—in breach of two international conventions: the

[226] See recently Case C-306/13 (n 224 above), para 47. See also with regard to the General Agreement on Tariffs and Trade of 1947, the judgments in Case 70/87 *Fediol v Commission* [1989] ECR 1781, paras 19–22; and Case C-69/89 *Nakajima v Council* [1991] ECR I-2069, para 31, and, with regard to the WTO agreements, the judgments in *Portugal v Council* (n 221 above), para 49; *Biret International v Council* (n 221 above), para 53; and *Van Parys* (n 221 above), para 40.

[227] Case C-306/13 (n 224 above), para 60.

[228] See eg M Bronckers, 'The Effect of the WTO in European Court Litigation' (2005) 40 *Texas Law Journal* 443, 443 and S Peers, 'Fundamental Right or Political Whim? WTO Law and the European Court of Justice' in G de Burca and J Scott (eds), *The EU and WTO: Legal and Constitutional Issues* (Oxford, Hart Publishing, 2001) 111, 111.

[229] Joined Cases 21 to 24/72 *International Fruit Company NV and others v Produktschap voor Groenten en Fruit* [1972] ECR 1219.

[230] The Court has accepted WTO rules only in exceptional cases as a yardstick for the legality of EU law, namely when EU law was meant to implement a particular obligation entered into within the framework of the WTO (Case C-69/89 *Nakajima v Council* [1991] ECR I-2069, paras 27–31), or when it explicitly refers to specific provisions of WTO law (Case 70/87 *Fediol v Commission* [1989] ECR 1781, paras 19–22).

[231] Case C-265/03 *Simutenkov v Ministerio de Educación y Cultura and Real Federación Española de Fútbol* [2005] ECR I-2579.

United Nations Convention on the Law of the Sea (UNCLOS), to which the EU and its Member States are parties, and the International Convention for the Prevention of Pollution from ships (MARPOL),[232] to which only the Member States are parties because that Convention does not provide for membership of regional/international organisations. The Court held that review of the validity of a Union measure in the light of those conventions and, in general, the rules of international law, was subject to the double condition on the one hand of the EU being bound by those rules and on the other hand, of the nature and broad logic of the act of international law in question which should not preclude such review of validity by the Court and whose provisions appear to be unconditional and sufficiently precise in their contents. With regard to the Marpol Convention, the Court indicated that since the EU was not a contracting party the mere fact that the Directive in question incorporated certain rules of the Convention was not sufficient to afford the Court the possibility of reviewing the legality of the Directive in the light of that Convention. With regard to UNCLOS, the Court, while recognising that the provisions of the Convention did form an integral part of the EU legal order, also concluded that it was not able to assess the Directive's validity in the light of the Convention because the latter did not establish rules intended to apply directly and immediately to individuals nor did it confer upon them individual rights or freedoms capable of being relied upon against States, irrespective of the position of the flag State.[233]

It is interesting to note the difference in the argumentation of the Court between the WTO cases and the *Intertanko* case. On the one hand, the lack of effect of WTO rules is traditionally traced back to their reciprocal character (in *Portugal v Council* the Court had held that

> the WTO … is founded … on the principle of negotiations with a view to entering into reciprocal and mutually advantageous arrangements and is thus distinguished, from the viewpoint of the Community, from the arrangements concluded between the Community and non-Member countries which introduce a certain asymmetry of obligations or create special relations of integration with the Community)[234]

and the lack of domestic remedies for violating agreements is seen as justified in order to avoid interference with the remedies provided for in the international legal order. On the other hand, in the *Intertanko* case the Court appears to insist rather on the inter-State character of the obligations flowing from the UNCLOS and on substantive considerations, in particular that agreements which do not aim to produce rights and duties for individuals in the international legal order do not entail rights and duties for individuals in the Union legal order. The question has been raised whether it is 'reasonable to make the existence of internal effects

[232] International Convention for the Prevention of Pollution from Ships, signed in London on 2 November 1973, as supplemented by the Protocol of 17 February 1978.

[233] Case C-308/06 *The Queen on the application of International Association of Independent Tanker owners (Intertanko) v Secretary of State for Transport* [2008] ECR I-4057.

[234] Case C-149/96 *Portugal v Council* [1999] ECR I-8395, para 42.

of international agreements conditional upon whether the agreement is intended to create rights and duties for individuals in the international legal order'.[235] In the present state of development of international law, this circumstance is very rare and would amount to a broad denial of the relevance of international agreements in the Union legal order. The distinction established in its *Portugal v Council* case law has been regarded by some as 'dangerously close to a political preference for regional integration over a multilateral framework based on non-discrimination'.[236] Furthermore, the approach of the Court appears to distance itself from the traditionally agreed monistic conception adopted in paragraph (2) of Article 216 TFEU (formerly Article 300(7) of the EC Treaty), according to which 'agreements concluded by the Union are binding upon the institutions and the Member States'. This cannot merely mean that international law must have the same content in both the international and EU legal orders but rather that it is possible for international law to introduce its normative content directly in the domestic legal order. Both the monistic and dualistic approach (both doctrines are increasingly becoming irrelevant in a world of plural legal orders)[237] traditionally employed to determine the effect of international law within the national legal system share a common methodology, namely that application of international obligations within domestic jurisdictions, either directly or through implementing legislation, is part of the process of implementation of the international obligations.[238]

The controversial shift by the Court of Justice from monism to dualism continues. Indeed, in its recent judgment of 13 January 2015 on the Aarhus Convention, the Court has confirmed that it will only examine the validity of a legal act of the Union in the light of an international agreement in the exceptional cases set out in the *Nakajima* and *Fediol* judgments[239] where the nature and the broad logic of the agreement do not preclude this and where, in addition, the provisions of that agreement appear, as regards their content, to be unconditional and sufficiently precise.[240] This philosophy also inspired earlier case law on compensation for air transport passengers.[241] In *IATA*,[242] the Court held that certain categories

[235] See X (n 220 above). See also R Wessel, 'Reconsidering the Relationship between International and EU Law: Towards a Content-Based Approach?' in Cannizzaro, Palchetti and Wessel (eds) (n 207 above) 7, 12.

[236] P Eeckhout, *External Relations of the European Union: Legal and Constitutional Foundations* (Oxford, Oxford University Press, 2004) 312.

[237] Von Bogdandy has described monism and dualism as 'zombies of another time' that 'should be laid to rest or deconstructed': see A Von Bogdandy, 'Pluralism, Direct Effect, and Ultimate Say: on the Relationship between International and Domestic Constitutional Law' (2008) 6 *International Journal of Constitutional Law* 397, 400.

[238] See X (n 220 above).

[239] See above n 230.

[240] Judgment in Joined Cases C-404/12 P *Commission v Stichting Natuur en Milieu and Pesticide Action Network Europe*, and C-405/12 P, *Council v Stichting Natuur en Milieu and Pesticide Action Network* (EU:C:2015:5).

[241] See eg R Lawson and T Marland, 'The Montreal Convention 1999 and the Decisions of the ECJ in the Cases of IATA and Sturgeon—in Harmony or Discord?' (2011) 36 *Air and Space Law* 99.

[242] Case C-344/04 *The Queen on the application of International Air Transport Association and European Low Fares Airline Association v Department for Transport* [2006] ECR I-403, especially paras 34–48.

of compensation towards air passengers provided for under Regulation (EC) No 261/2004[243] were not contrary to the Montreal Convention, which limits such categories of compensation.[244] A case which has given rise to particular criticism outside the Union is the *Air Transport Association of America* judgment on the issue of the compatibility of the EU's greenhouse gas emission allowance trading, with various rules and principles of international law.[245]

[243] Regulation (EC) No 261/2004 of the European Parliament and of the Council of 11 February 2004 establishing common rules on compensation and assistance to passengers in the event of denied boarding and of cancellation or long delay of flights, and repealing Regulation (EEC) No 295/91 [2004] OJ L46/1.

[244] Convention for the Unification of Certain Rules for International Carriage by Air ('the Montreal Convention'). In *IATA* the Court accepted that it could review the legality of the Regulation in the light of this Convention 'since, first, neither the nature nor the broad logic of the Convention precludes this and, second, [the] three articles [at stake] appear, as regards their content, to be unconditional and sufficiently precise' (para 39), but it interpreted the Convention in a rather unusual manner, creating a distinction not made in the Convention between two types of compensation: on the one hand, action taken by the public authorities to redress, in a standardised and immediate manner, the damage that is constituted by the inconvenience that delay in the carriage of passengers by air causes; and on the other hand, individual damage, inherent in the reason for travelling, redress for which can only be the subject of compensation granted subsequently on an individual basis (eg in the framework of actions for damages before the courts) (paras 43–48). The case law of the EU Court in this field is also controversial from another angle. In particular, in Joined Cases C-402/07 and C-432/07 *Sturgeon and others v Condor Flugdienst GmbH* and *Böck and Lepuschitz v Air France SA*, 19 November 2009, especially paras 27–69, the Court equated certain flight delays to flight cancellations for the purposes of compensation under Regulation (EC) No 261/2004 in a manner which was arguably contrary to the (text of the) Regulation. The Court relied on the principle of equal treatment to reach this conclusion. By contrast, Advocate General Sharpston, in her opinion of 2 July 2009 had argued that 'cancellation' and 'delay' were distinguishable but that the distinction was unlawful because it breached the principle of equality (paras 31–66). For a defence and explanation of this judgment, see Judge Lenaerts, now President of the Court, in a lecture on theories and methods of adjudication and interpretation delivered at Academy of European Law's Summer Course on the Law of the European Union in July 2013 and available at: www.youtube.com/watch?v=DOdnDKoPmN8 (between minutes 39:30 and 47 into the presentation, especially around minutes 43–47, where he admits the very limited support for the Court's findings to be found in the text of the Regulation (only thin support in recitals) but invokes the *travaux préparatoires* and interpretation in accordance with the principle of equality as preferable to annulment for violation of that principle). The reliance on *travaux préparatoires* raises questions where these are used to support positions proposed by the Commission but rejected by the co-legislators.

[245] Case C-366/10 *Air Transport Association of America and Others v Secretary of State for Energy and Climate Change* [2011] ECR I-13755. The Court upheld the legality of the contested Directive. For criticism, see eg BF Havel and JQ Mulligan, 'Flying too high? Extraterritoriality and the EU Emissions Trading Scheme: the Air Transport Association of America judgment', 2 February 2012: eutopialaw.com/2012/02/02/958/. Compare the annotation by B Mayer in (2012) 49 *Common Market Law Review* 1113. They key issues for the purposes of the present chapter are the Court's findings on which international law rules or principles could be invoked to contest the legality of the EU legal act at issue (following the earlier case law of the EU Court, it held inter alia that the provisions of the Chicago Convention were not among these rules as the Union itself is not a party to it) and whether the allowance trading scheme which was unilaterally enacted by the Union (as multilateral efforts had not been successful) could cover those parts of flights which take place outside the airspace of the EU Member States, including flights by aircraft registered in third States, without violating these international law rules and principles (notably the principle that each State has complete and exclusive sovereignty over its airspace, the principle that no State may validly purport to subject any part of the high seas to its sovereignty, and the principle which guarantees freedom to fly over the high seas). The Court upheld the legality of the allowance trading scheme and found that it did not violate these rules and principles.

A further example of difficulties with the interpretation and application of international law concerns the conditions for subsidiary protection under Directive 2004/83/EC on minimum standards for the qualification and status of third country nationals or stateless persons as refugees or as persons who otherwise need international protection and the content of the protection granted.[246] In *Aboubacar Diakité* the Court interpreted the notion of 'internal armed conflict' in an overly broad manner,[247] adopting an interpretation which was not supported by the text of the Directive, nor by the intent of the legislator, and which is inconsistent with any existing definition of the notion of internal armed conflict under international humanitarian law.[248]

An important recent example of the somewhat dismissive attitude towards (regional) international law in the name of the autonomy of EU law is Opinion 2/13 of 18 December 2014. In this opinion, the CJEU considered that the draft agreement on the EU accession to the ECHR setting out the specific arrangements for that accession was not compatible with EU law. This may not have come entirely as a surprise as there have always been doubts about such an accession in some quarters[249] and the Court is known to have a particular sensitivity as regards its own prerogatives.[250] Nevertheless, the Lisbon Treaty introduced amendments to the Treaties specifically to overcome a previous opinion of the Court holding that the EC did not have the competence to accede to the ECHR[251] and Article 6(2) TEU now contains a clear obligation to accede to the ECHR. Furthermore, great efforts had been made to accommodate the wishes which the

[246] Council Directive 2004/83/EC of 29 April 2004 on minimum standards for the qualification and status of third country nationals or stateless persons as refugees or as persons who otherwise need international protection and the content of the protection granted [2004] OJ L304/12, and corrigendum [2005] OJ L204/24.

[247] Case C-285/12 *Aboubacar Diakité v Commissaire général aux réfugiés et aux apatrides*, judgment of 30 January 2014 (EU:C:2014:39), paras 17–35.

[248] In paras 20–21, the Court deduces from the use of the notion 'internal armed conflict', as opposed to the international humanitarian law (IHL) concept of 'armed conflict not of an international character' that the EU legislature wished to grant subsidiary protection not only to persons affected by 'armed conflict not of an international character', as defined in IHL, but also to persons affected by internal armed conflict, without it being necessary for all the criteria referred to in Common Article 3 of the four Geneva Conventions to be satisfied. However, the Court does not offer any evidence that the legislator in fact intended this notion to mean anything different than 'armed conflict not of an international character'. It is very much doubtful that this was the intent. Moreover, while notions used in the Directive may be autonomous and would not violate or affect IHL, it can hardly have been the intent that a new notion of armed conflict should be developed without any guidance as to what this notion means. In fact, the Court simply referred to the 'usual meaning in everyday language' of 'internal armed conflict' and found that this is 'a situation in which a State's armed forces confront one or more armed groups or in which two or more armed groups confront each other' (paras 27–28).

[249] By way of example, at the oral public hearing in these proceedings, one of the judges even openly asked why the EU should accede to the ECHR.

[250] See eg Opinion 1/91 of 14 December 1991 (*Draft agreement relating to the creation of the European Economic Area*), paras 30–65 and Opinion 1/09 of 8 March 2011 (*Agreement creating a Unified Patent Litigation System*), paras 66–89.

[251] Opinion 2/94 of 28 March 1996 on *Accession by the Community to the European Convention for the Protection of Human Rights and Fundamental Freedoms*.

Court had expressed beforehand, and the main other institutions (Council, EP and Commission) as well as all Member State (the authors of the Treaties, who presumably envisaged that the accession could take place without the need for any additional Treaty changes and the great majority of which intervened in the proceedings) unanimously considered that the draft agreement was compatible with the Treaties. Moreover, given the importance which the Court attaches to human rights in its case law, notably in *Kadi* (see above), one might have expected that this was the one area of international law where a defensive posture was least necessary. Yet none of these considerations were able to persuade the Court that the arrangements which had been negotiated were compatible with the Treaties. By contrast, in her 'view' of 13 June 2014 (but only released on the day of the opinion), Advocate General Kokott took the view that the draft accession agreement was compatible with the Treaties, provided that certain issues were adequately addressed in the further process.[252] It is telling that most of the early commentaries are very critical of the Court's Opinion 2/13.[253]

The opinion is very sweeping in terms of the number of objections raised by the Court[254] and the fundamental nature of some of them. In addition, while it remains to be seen how the institutions concerned and the Member States will react, given this sweeping scope, it seems unlikely that renegotiating the agreement would succeed. The number and nature of the concessions that would have to be obtained are unlikely to be acceptable for the other Council of Europe members and the question arises whether some of them would be compatible with the fundamental principles underlying the ECHR. If this assessment should prove to be correct, ultimately a further Treaty amendment would be necessary. In that case either the accession could be abandoned or the conditions of accession as well as any necessary Treaty changes could be laid down in primary law. Furthermore, the opinion raises some questions about the status of human rights in EU law, as the Court suggests that other principles or rules of EU law may prevail over strict compliance with human rights, including those set out in the ECHR, eg in the area of FSJ.[255] This is questionable and would appear to be at odds with the status which the Court accorded to human rights in *Kadi*. Finally, the opinion clearly demonstrates an extreme attachment to the autonomy of EU law and the Court's

[252] EU:C:2014:2475.

[253] See eg S Peers, 'The CJEU and the EU's Accession to the ECHR: a Clear and Present Danger to Human Rights Protection', 18 December 2014: eulawanalysis.blogspot.no/2014/12/the-cjeu-and-eus-accession-to-echr.html; J Morijn, 'After Opinion 2/13: How to Move on in Strasbourg and Brussels?', 5 January 2015: eutopialaw.com/2015/01/05/after-opinion-213-how-to-move-on-in-strasbourg-and-brussels/; JP Jacqué, 'L'avis 2/13 CJUE. Non à l'adhésion à la Convention européenne des droits de l'homme?, 23 December 2014: www.droit-union-europeenne.be/412337458; and A Buyse, 'CJEU Rules: Draft Agreement on EU Accession to ECHR Incompatible with EU Law', 20 December 2014: echrblog.blogspot.be/2014/12/cjeu-rules-draft-agreement-on-eu.html.

[254] These inter alia include a number of issues that could perfectly well—and, ironically, more autonomously—have been addressed in internal EU acts and arrangements, such as the issue of Art 344 TFEU.

[255] See paras 170–172 and 191–194. See also paras 187–190.

role, with little regard for international law and certain other Treaty provisions (including those on the CFSP).[256]

This series of disappointing cases on the status of international law within the EU legal order appears to be justified on a defensive, narrow and partisan conception of the EU legal order, conceived as superior to and more legitimate than any other, including the UN Charter or the ECHR, in which the Court of Justice has reserved for itself the final say. Beyond its constitutional assessment, the comparative lawyer cannot avoid referring to the more mature openness that most national legal orders permit with regard to the effects of international law within their legal systems. It suffices to refer to the doctrines of 'internal effect' or '*invocabilité*' that international agreements have within some domestic legal orders of EU Member States even without actually having direct effect.[257] For instance, in Germany there is the concept of '*interne Geltung*' or 'internal validity', which describes the principle of internal automatic validity that international agreements have within the domestic legal order from the moment of their incorporation, a validity that does

[256] See paras 249–257. Since the Treaties require accession to the ECHR and did not exclude any area of competence from this accession while continuing to exclude the jurisdiction of the CJEU over most CFSP measures, it is difficult to understand how it can be contrary to the Treaties that the European Court of Human Rights would be competent in cases concerning CFSP measures in which the CJEU is not competent precisely by virtue of the Treaties. Moreover, the Court apparently prefers that Union actions in the area of the CFSP are not subject to any international judicial review at all as regards their compatibility with human rights rather than having such judicial review without its own involvement. In any event, it cannot be excluded that the European Court of Human Rights will consider that it is competent to review CFSP acts through cases brought against one or more Member States. The CJEU has clarified and may further clarify the scope of its jurisdiction in the area of the CFSP in a number of recent and pending cases, in particular Cases C-658/11 *Parliament v Council*, judgment of 24 June 2014 (EU:C:2014:2025—at para 73 the Court held that 'it cannot be argued that the scope of the limitation, by way of derogation, on the Court's jurisdiction envisaged in the final sentence of the second subparagraph of Article 24(1) TEU and in Article 275 TFEU goes so far as to preclude the Court from having jurisdiction to interpret and apply a provision such as Article 218 TFEU which does not fall within the CFSP, even though it lays down the procedure on the basis of which an act falling within the CFSP has been adopted'); C-439/13 P *Elitaliana v Eulex Kosovo* (procurement in a civilian CSDP mission—in its judgment of 12 November 2015 (EU:C:2015:753), the Court held that it was competent to verify compliance with horizontal EU financial regulations also in the CFSP context); C-455/14 P *H v Council and Commission* (treatment of a Member State official seconded to a civilian CSDP mission—in his opinion of 7 April 2016 (EU:C:2016:212), Advocate General Wahl took the view that the Court did not have jurisdiction) and C-72/15 *OJSC Rosneft Oil Co v HM Treasury and Others* (reference for a preliminary ruling from a UK court on the validity and interpretation of several Council acts relating to restrictive measures, including CFSP decisions—in his opinion of 31 May 2016 (EU:C:2016:381), Advocate General Wathelet took the view that the EU Courts have jurisdiction 'to review the compliance with Article 40 TEU of all CFSP acts (either in an action for annulment or in preliminary ruling proceedings) … as well as to review the legality of CFSP decisions adopted by the Council in accordance with Chapter 2 of Title V of the EU Treaty which provide for restrictive measures against natural or legal persons (again, either in an action for annulment or in preliminary ruling proceedings) …'). See also the 'view' of Advocate General Kokott of 13 June 2014 in the Opinion 2/13 proceedings (EU:C:2014:2475) and the General Court's judgment of 18 February 2016 in Case T-328/14, *Mahmoud Jannatian v Council* (EU:T:2016:86), paras 30-31 (above n 203).

[257] P Manin, 'L'influence du droit international sur la jurisprudence communautaire' in J-C Gautron and L Grard (eds), *Droit international et droit communautaire. Perspectives actuelles. Société Française pour le Droit International. Colloque de Bordeaux* (Paris, Pedone, 2000) 153, 163 *et seq*.

not depend on the self-executing nature of an agreement or its direct effect.[258] Also, some authors have pointed out the usefulness of the principle of interpreting domestic law in a manner consistent with international law, which is possible even in situations where an international instrument has no internal effect, for instance in the interest of avoiding incurring responsibility under international law.[259] In particular, the wording of Article 216(2) TFEU permits a wider interpretation than the doctrine of reciprocity developed by the Court of Justice in *Portugal v Council*,[260] and, within this framework, consideration could be given to the elaboration of a more sophisticated doctrine of direct effect limited to certain types of international agreements.[261]

Finally, the judgment of the General Court of 10 December 2015 in Case T-512/12, *Front Polisario v Council* must be mentioned.[262] This judgment is extraordinary for several reasons. First, the case raises important legal questions in the field of the relationship between European Union law and international law most of which are either ignored or resolved by the General Court in an unsatisfactory way. Secondly, the General Court, invoking questionable reasons, admits the capacity of the Polisario Front to institute proceedings as a legal person directly and individually concerned, under article 263 TFEU, by the Decision of 8 March 2012 on the conclusion of an agreement in the form of an Exchange of Letters between the European Union and the Kingdom of Morocco. Thirdly, for the first time ever an individual applicant has been able to bring an action for annulment and has obtained the annulment of a decision of conclusion of an international agreement between the European Union and a third State.[263] Fourthly, for the first time the European Union judge has laid down a duty, for the Council, to examine carefully and impartially, prior to the conclusion of an international agreement, all the relevant elements to ensure that the potential implementation of such agreement does not lead to, or indirectly encourages, the violation of the fundamental rights of the people of a disputed territory, or benefits therefrom, and in particular the rights derived from the principle of permanent sovereignty over natural resources as a corollary of the principle of self-determination. Fifth, the General Court omits in its judgment to consider the legal consequences, under international law, of the annulment of a domestic decision that expresses the consent of the European Union to be bound by an international treaty. Sixth, the judgment

[258] W Schroeder and H Selmayr, 'Die EG, das GATT und die Vollzugslehre' (1998) 53 *Juristenzeitung* 344, 345 *et seq*.

[259] R Uerpmann, 'Völker- und Europarecht im innerstaatlichen Recht' in C Grewe and C Gusy (eds), *Französisches Staatsdenken* (Baden-Baden, Nomos, 2002) 196, 200.

[260] *Portugal v Council* (n 234 above). See J Klabbers, 'International Law in Community Law: the Law and Politics of Direct Effect' (2002) 21 *Yearbook of European Law* 263, 270 *et seq*.

[261] Criteria for making a distinction have been suggested, eg by A Von Bogdandy, 'Legal Equality, Legal Certainty and Subsidiarity in Transnational Economic Law' in A Von Bogdandy et al (eds), *European Integration and International Coordination:* Studies in Transnational Economic Law in Honour of Claus-Dieter Ehlermann (The Hague, Kluwer Law International, 2002) 13, 35.

[262] EU:T:2015:953. The appeal brought by the Council against this judgment is pending.

[263] The Court also incorrectly qualifies that decision as a legislative act.

of the General Court does not set any limitation ratione temporis on the effects of the judgment and, therefore, fails to ensure the necessary legal certainty, in particular for the economic operators, as regards the applicability of the international commitments entered into by the European Union within the Union's legal order.

Beyond the relationship between the EU and the international legal orders, there exists a second issue in the case law that remains controversial: the delimitation between the CFSP and other Union (formerly Community) competences. In particular, in its 2008 *ECOWAS* judgment, the Court annulled a Council decision dealing with the fight against small arms and light weapons, on the basis that it pursued not only security but also development policies and therefore could, pursuant to ex Article 47 TEU, not be adopted solely under the CFSP.[264] This judgment was widely seen by the Council and the Member States as having distorted the real security objective pursued by the decision and its weight compared to any beneficial effect on development. There is no doubt that it was partially in response to this judgment that the Treaty of Lisbon amended ex Article 47 TEU, now Article 40 TEU, from a unilateral protection of the Community against encroachment by CFSP measures to a mutual non-interference between CFSP measures and measures adopted under other Union policies.

The Court does appear to have noticed this and seems to have started to acknowledge and respect the scope of the CFSP. For instance, in its judgment on Regulations (EC) No 881/2002 and (EU) No 1286/2009 about restrictive measures directed against certain persons and entities associated with Usama bin Laden, the Al-Qaeda network and the Taliban, the Court accepted that these measures fell within the CFSP and were correctly adopted under Article 215 TFEU rather than Article 75 TFEU.[265] Also, in the *Mauritius pirate transfer agreement* case, it ruled that the agreement at issue in that case, providing for the transfer to Mauritius of suspected pirates arrested by an EU military operation, fell within the CFSP.[266]

Since, as indicated above, there is no consistency in the case law of the EU Court with regard to the method for determining the choice of legal bases for the conclusion of international agreements, determining the legal bases for EU international agreements remains a somewhat uncertain endeavour.

These developments are unfortunate, since the case law of the EU Court in the field of EU external relations is important not only in view of the traditional

264 Case C-91/05 *Commission v Council* (*ECOWAS*) [2008] ECR I-3651. ('Economic Community of West African States').

265 Case C-130/10 *Parliament v Council*, judgment of 19 July 2012 (EU:C:2012:472).

266 Case C-658/11 *Parliament v Council*, judgment of 24 June 2014 (EU:C:2014:2025). The judgment is not entirely clear on the legal bases point, as the EP had focused its arguments on its consent under Art 218(6) TFEU and had argued that this could be dissociated from the substantive legal bases. On the latter, the EP argued that the agreement also related to JFS and development policy but admitted that these were only secondary objectives. On the basis of the latter, the Court ruled that the use of an exclusively CFSP substantive legal basis was correct (paras 43–62). In a similar case, C-263/14 *Parliament v Council*, the EP argued that the FSJ objective is not secondary and that two JFS legal bases are also required. In her opinion of 28 October 2015 (EU:C:2015:729), Advocate General Kokott took the view that the Council had correctly relied on a CFSP legal basis. In its judgment of 14 June 2016 (EU:C:2016:435), the Court took the same view.

development of EU law by the Court of Justice, but particularly so in a field in which relations between the institutions and the Member States are, unfortunately, often marked by significant and long-running divergent positions. In this regard, the Court of Justice is seen as the final arbiter, a role that in its interpretation and application of EU law, must effectively be carried out respecting the institutional balance, the limits on the competences of the Union laid down in the Treaties and 'the strict observance and the development of international law' (Article 3(5) TEU), which is now a fundamental objective of the Union's external relations expressly incorporated by the Treaty of Lisbon.

XII. FINAL REMARKS

The aim of the Lisbon Treaty to strengthen the EU's external policies and action has been hampered by several obstacles, which in part result from this same Treaty. The Treaty of Lisbon has suffered from its 'reluctant' conclusion in the wake of the failure of the planned Constitutional Treaty, as illustrated by the extremely difficult process of negotiation and national ratification. The implementation of the Treaty of Lisbon has also been 'reluctant', as shown not only by the practical confirmation of the relative value of its sectoral, modest amendments in comparison with the failed Constitutional Treaty, but also by the repentance, almost regret, of some of those Member States which contributed to its birth as they have sought only a limited use of its potential. As two commentators put it, there is an 'apparent willingness of some member states to back-track what could be gained from the Lisbon Treaty in terms of unified EU diplomatic representation' and

> Turf wars may exist intra-institutionally, but they seem minor in comparison to the deep schism between the EU and its member states. In this respect, the example of the ICAO has shown that realizing the potential from the Lisbon Treaty is not without obstacles imposed by the member states, possibly even wanting to roll back further well-entrenched principles of EU external relations law.[267]

In particular, the implementation of the Treaty of Lisbon has been and remains problematic because, as illustrated in this chapter, both the EU institutions and (at least some of) the Member States have refused to apply the Treaty as it was intended to be applied. This has led to inter-institutional conflicts (essentially between the Council, the European Parliament and the Commission) and a marked lack of political will towards the Treaty's execution on the part of the Member States. The manifestation of the absence of political will is evidenced by a preference of the 'big' Member States to impose their own influence within the EU rather than to work for strengthening the presence of the EU on the international scene, as well as by contradictions in the positions of some of the medium-sized and 'smaller'

[267] B Van Vooren and R Wessel (n 163 above) 1354 and 1363.

Member States which, while consistently supporting a stronger EU role, refuse to make the necessary means available to the EU.

When the political will for EU action was found, even if frequently half-hearted, the Council has tended to be very literal in its interpretation of the external relations provisions of the Treaty: it has systematically favoured unanimity in its decision-making irrespective of the qualified majority voting rule laid down in the Treaties, has made mixity prevalent, and has demonstrated a lack of enthusiasm to apply some of the innovative amendments introduced by the Lisbon Treaty. Specific problems have arisen when Union competence expands and leads to a situation in which Member States are no longer accepted to be parties to an international agreement or to remain members of an international organisation alongside the Union.[268] In particular in the field of the CFSP there is little progress in the development of armament, military and defence cooperation between the Member States. Furthermore the Council has not enacted specific CFSP rules on data protection, the Permanent Structured Cooperation, or the Start-up Fund, and, more significantly, the Union's action has not been successful when there has not been an identification of the 'common interests' of all the EU actors involved. The European Council has notoriously failed to identify these 'strategic interests and objectives of the Union' (Article 22 TEU).[269] As has been pointed out by analysts,[270] the achievements of the CFSP have been lacklustre as shown by the scarcity of EU crisis management operations since 2009; the residual, even ancillary role of the EU in the Middle East; the limited number of updated, general and country strategies; and the practical reduction of the external action of the EU to a policy of sanctions.

Meanwhile, the European Parliament has continued to adhere to its well-known method of seizing any opportunity to increase its powers beyond the scope of the provisions of the Treaties, in particular throughout the process of elaboration, negotiation and conclusion of international agreements, including in the field of CFSP (eg the *Pirate Transfer Agreements* cases).[271]

The Commission has adopted a maximalist strategy in its adherence to its version of a teleological interpretation of the provisions of the Treaties, as if the failed Constitutional Treaty had been in force, and in its reluctance to accord sufficient value to the explicit Lisbon Treaty provisions aiming at safeguarding the remaining competences of the Member States and the distribution of powers between the Council and the Commission in the field of external relations. For example, the Commission has favoured the conclusion of EU-only agreements, as well as

[268] See eg above n 180 about the European Convention on the legal protection of services based on, or consisting of, conditional access.

[269] Instead, documents of a (more or less) strategic nature have been adopted at the level of the Council, eg the strategic framework for the Horn of Africa.

[270] P de Boissieu, T de Brujin, A Vitorino and S Wall, *L'action extérieure de l'Union européenne: cause perdue ou dernière chance?*, Synopia/nouvelle gouvernance, September 2014: www.synopia.fr/laction-exterieure-de-lunion-europeenne-cause-perdue-ou-derniere-chance/.

[271] Above n 266.

an interpretation of EU external representation in the international scene which includes not only the usual official role of speaking on behalf of the EU, but also the power to determine the policies of the EU, in practice depriving the Council of its role as the policy-making institution pursuant to the Treaties. The Commission's maximalist interpretation and application of the Lisbon Treaty's external relations provisions and its frequent uncompromising approach has proven to be counterproductive as it has only contributed to a hardening of the antagonistic positions of the Member States, and consequently also of the Council, in several fields.

The HR has been overburdened and her scope of action limited by both the Council and the Commission. The HR, who is assisted by an EEAS with a very limited budget, has no decision-making power (since the latter belongs to the Council) and the multiple functions attributed *intuitu personae* to the HR in the Treaties (ie chairing the FAC, coordinating all EU external action as Vice-President within the Commission, representing the EU for matters relating to the CFSP, making proposals to develop the CFSP, implementing CFSP decisions, conducting political dialogue with third parties, assisting the Council and the Commission in ensuring consistency between the different areas of EU external action, and taking part in the work of the European Council) are impossible to perform at the same time by the same person.

The Court of Justice, in its role of ensuring that in the interpretation and application of the Treaties the law is observed, has systematically upheld the so-called 'Community method' in questions relating to the choice of legal bases, irrespective of the policy field involved. This has been at the expense for example of the Treaty provisions providing that the CFSP is governed by 'specific rules and procedures' (as demonstrated in *ECOWAS* case)[272] and of the primary law nature of the protocols in the field of the area of FSJ (as shown in the *Convention for the protection of neighbouring rights of broadcasting organisations* or the *Philippines* cases).[273] In addition, the Court of Justice, in its continued application of the criterion based on the centre of gravity for the choice of legal bases, has consistently favoured the prevalence of the general/horizontal legal basis even where a specific and exceptional legal basis existed. Finally, the Court of Justice appears to be on the defensive in its reassessment of the relations between the EU, national and international legal orders when it disproportionally magnifies the autonomy and purity of the EU legal order over the other legal orders, as if the former was superior to the latter or as if the EU legal order needed to be protected from (phantom) enemies or as if the EU legal order lacked the maturity to benefit from outside influences, with the resulting risks of impermeability and opaqueness. The case law of the EU Court has been a source of concern for the Member

[272] Above nn 10 and 264.

[273] Above respectively nn 40–41 and accompanying text on the one hand, and nn 136, 138, 140 and accompanying text and n 145 on the other hand.

States and the subject of some criticism in legal circles (eg the *Kadi* and *Intertanko* cases[274] and Opinion 2/13).[275]

International developments are such that the European Union cannot afford to spend so much of its energy on infighting rather than on the proper conduct of its external relations. There is little trust between the Commission, the EEAS, the Council Secretariat and the national administrations; the Member States systematically fight for the preservation of the intergovernmental method in order to escape the control of the 'Brussels bureaucracy', while those who uphold the supranational method have shown a radicalism and inflexibility which has led to a break in the link between the internal and the external action of the EU as well as to a disconnect between national diplomacies and the Commission and EEAS, even though the EEAS was meant to become precisely the coordinator of the EU and national actors, instead of becoming the 29th Foreign Office.

A way out from these dysfunctional trends which does not require Treaty amendments, is to abide by and apply the principles of sincere cooperation, loyalty, and the unity of external representation, which are useful tools to overcome the challenges posed by the present divergent inter-institutional positions and protracted fights. The external action of the EU can only be successful if it is the result of a harmonious synthesis of a combined implementation of all the means offered in the Treaties by EU institutions and organs, and the Member States.[276]

[274] Above respectively n 209 and *passim* in sections X and XI on the one hand, and nn 233–236 and accompanying text on the other hand.

[275] See above nn 249–256 and accompanying text.

[276] This comes at a time when the EU faces one of the worst ever crises, both economic and political, of its existence and has to meet the challenge posed by its promises of a 'European perspective' towards its neighbours of the East and of the Western Balkans.

2

The External Powers of the European Parliament

RICARDO PASSOS[1]

Content:

[1] Director of the External Relations Team at the Legal Service of the European Parliament. The opinions expressed in the chapter are purely personal and cannot be considered as of the responsibility of the European Parliament or its Legal Service.

I. INTRODUCTION

IT IS WELL known that the European Parliament's role in the European Union's external action has changed dramatically with the entry into force of the Treaty of Lisbon. One could say that this role may be scrutinised as 'before and after' the Treaty of Lisbon.

Before 1 December 2009, it was only in some exceptional cases that Parliament had to give its consent before an agreement could be concluded by the Council. These cases (four) were explicitly mentioned in Article 300(3) TEC: association agreements (Article 310 TEC); agreements establishing a specific institutional framework by organising cooperation procedures; agreements having notable budgetary implications; and agreements entailing amendment of an act adopted under the co-decision procedure. These were the exceptions to the general rule. The position of the Parliament was rather weak in this context: mere consultation as a general rule; and no say on trade agreements, on agreements relating to the Common Foreign and Security Policy (CFSP) or relating to Justice and Home Affairs (JHA). On the CFSP, Parliament was merely entitled to be 'regularly informed' in accordance with Article 21 TEU (before the Treaty of Lisbon).

All this changed with the Treaty of Lisbon, following the important work achieved in this area by the European Convention in 2002–03. Instead of 'consultation', Parliament's consent is now the rule. This had an enormous impact, particularly concerning trade, fisheries and JHA (especially data protection) agreements.

Parliament immediately exercised its new powers. Yet, contrary to what some would have thought, it has used them with a high sense of responsibility, fully aware of the consequences of its decisions withholding consent. In a total of 241[2] agreements concluded since the entry into force of the Treaty of Lisbon, Parliament refused consent in only three cases, for legitimate and understandable reasons.

The first case related to the 'Swift agreement' with the United States. During the whole process of negotiation, Parliament complained that it was not sufficiently informed, and expressed concern on the substance of some of the provisions relating to data protection. The Parliament was not informed because, before the Treaty of Lisbon, agreements related to JHA (Third Pillar) were negotiated by the Presidency of the Council, generally assisted by the Commission, and Parliament was not even consulted. It happened, however, that on 30 November 2009, the Council did not succeed in concluding the agreement under the Treaty of Nice and that on the next day, 1 December 2009, the Treaty of Lisbon entered into force.

Parliament also refused consent in two other cases concerning the ACTA Agreement and the EU-Morocco Agreement (Second Protocol), for different reasons.

Almost seven years have elapsed following the entry into force of the Treaty of Lisbon. It is now a good opportunity to try to make an evaluation of how Parliament has exercised its new external powers. In particular, it seems opportune to assess whether or not it became an actor in the shaping of the EU external action.

[2] On 1 July 2016.

In that context, in the light of the experience of the last seven years, it is worth revisiting the issues that can be raised concerning the interpretation of Article 218 TFEU, which lays down the procedure for the negotiation, conclusion and suspension of international agreements concluded by the Union.

II. EVALUATION OF PARLIAMENT'S ROLE AFTER THE TREATY OF LISBON: HAS IT BEEN DECISIVE IN THE SHAPING OF THE EU EXTERNAL ACTION?

The question is simple: does the fact that Parliament in general has the power to give consent before an agreement can be concluded by the Council mean that Parliament actually manages to have an influence on the very content of this international agreement?

It is true that Article 218 TFEU does not explicitly say that Parliament shall be involved in the procedure for the opening of the negotiations, nor for the choice of the negotiator, nor for the setting of the negotiating directives. Yet, it does contain a provision of great significance on the whole process, and that is Article 218(10) TFEU.

According to this provision 'the European Parliament shall be immediately and fully informed at all stages of the procedure'. The Parliament contends that the *ratio legis* of this provision is not to allow the Parliament to passively take note of the actions of the other institutions during the negotiations, but to afford it the opportunity of bringing some influence to bear on the Commission and the Council as regards the content of the agreement, in order to facilitate the consent to the final text. The essence of the consent procedure is thus that the Parliament plays already an active role during the phase of the procedure where the text is being shaped. This role of the Parliament during the negotiations preceding its consent may, to a certain extent, be compared to its position in legislative procedures where the Parliament is called upon to give consent, in particular concerning the adoption of the Regulation on the Multiannual Financial Framework (MFF). Indeed, Article 312(5) TFEU requires the cooperation of the institutions throughout the procedure. Should this provision be interpreted as establishing a specific procedure only, or could it rather be considered as an illustration of the requirement of active cooperation by institutions in proceedings where the treaty foresees Parliament's consent? This latter interpretation can be defended and it can be argued that Article 312(5) TFEU reflects the need for close cooperation, which applies by analogy to international agreements. Otherwise, why does Article 218(10) TFEU require that 'immediate' and 'full' information be given to the Parliament during the negotiations, if it were for the Parliament to remain passive during the whole negotiating process?

We will now consider the three international agreements where the European Parliament withheld consent during the last six years and the concrete advantages which resulted from the Parliament's position.

In Section II.B, we will examine the influence that the Parliament actually has had during the negotiation of international agreements.

A. The Cases in which Parliament Withheld its Consent: Consequences

i. The SWIFT Agreement with the United States (February 2010)[3]

(a) The Decision Not to Give Consent Relating to the First SWIFT Agreement of 2009

The facts were largely made public at the time. Following the terrorist attacks of 11 September 2001, the US Government initiated the Terrorist Finance Tracking Program (TFTP) aimed at fighting against the financing of terrorism all over the world. The US Treasury Department issued subpoenas to the SWIFT Centre in the US to obtain financial messaging data. The US SWIFT Centre had servers that contained the same information as the EU SWIFT Centre, and as a result, the Treasury Department could have access to the financial transfers made by many Europeans.[4]

This situation gave rise to concern in the EU when it became known, because the US authorities were having access to the data. The Article 29 Working Group (established by Directive 95/46/EC)[5] considered that the transfer of personal data to the US by SWIFT constituted a violation of Directive 95/46. The European Parliament showed its preoccupation with this situation in a resolution of 6 July 2006 and called for explanations by the Commission, the Council and the European Central Bank about the existence of this secret agreement between SWIFT and the US government. It stressed that the information stored by SWIFT to which the US authorities have had access concerned hundreds of thousands of EU citizens, as European banks use SWIFT messaging for the worldwide transfer of funds between banks. These transfers of personal data to third States should be subject to national and EU legislation, which provides that any transfer must be authorised by a judicial authority and that any derogation from this principle must be proportional and founded on a law or an international agreement. In its resolution, Parliament referred to the need to respect Article 8 of the European Convention on Human Rights (ECHR) and Article 13 of Directive 95/46/EC for transfer of personal data to third countries.[6]

[3] There are three articles particularly interesting on the rejection by the Parliament of the 2009 SWIFT Agreement written by: J Santos Vara, 'The Role of the European Parliament in the Conclusion of the Transatlantic Agreements on the Transfer of Personal Data after Lisbon' *CLEER* Working Papers No 2013/2; M Cremona, 'Justice and Home Affairs in a Globalised World: Ambitions and Reality in the tale of the EU-US SWIFT Agreement' Institute for European Integration Research, Austrian Academy of Sciences, *Working paper No 04/2011* (available at: www.ideas;repc.org/p/erp/eifxxx/p0022.html); and J Monar, 'The rejection of the EU-SWIFT Interim Agreement by the European Parliament: A Historic Vote and its Implications' (2010) 15 *European Foreign Affairs Review* 143–51.

[4] SWIFT is a cooperative that offers the transfer of financial managing data to bank entities. More than 9,000 banking organisations in 280 countries use SWIFT every day to exchange financial messages. SWIFT is based in Belgium, but is organised in regions: America, Asia Pacific, Europe, Middle East and Africa.

[5] Directive 95/46/EC of the European Parliament and of the Council on the protection of individuals with regard to the processing of personal data and on the free movement of such data, [1995] OJ L281/23.

[6] European Parliament Resolution of 6 July 2006 on the interception of bank transfer data from the SWIFT system by the US secret services, [2006] OJ C303E/651.

In another resolution of 14 February 2007, Parliament called for the conclusion of an international agreement with the US to end legal uncertainty regarding data sharing and transfer between the EU and the US.[7]

On 27 July 2009, the Council authorised the Presidency, assisted by the Commission, to open negotiations for an agreement between the EU and the US on the processing and transfer of Financial Messaging Data, on the basis of former Articles 24 and 38 TEU (ex-Third Pillar), which did not foresee the participation of the European Parliament. The agreement would allow the US to request providers, including SWIFT, to make available to the US Treasury financial payment messaging data stored in the EU.

Parliament made strong protests on the lack of sufficient information during the negotiations. In a resolution adopted on 1 September 2009—before the entry into force of the Treaty of Lisbon—Parliament claimed that the agreement should contain a certain number of provisions ensuring in particular that:

— the data are transferred and processed only for the purposes of fighting terrorism, as envisaged in Article 1 of Council Framework Decision 2002/475/JHA of 13 June 2002 on combatting terrorism,[8] and that they relate to individuals or terrorist organisations recognised as such also by the EU;
— the transfer requests are based on specific, targeted cases, limited in time and subject to judicial authorisation;
— EU citizens are granted the same defence rights as exist in the EU and that the legality and proportionality of the data transfers are open to judicial review in the US;
— the reciprocity mechanism is strictly adhered to, obliging the US authorities to transfer financial messaging data to the competent EU authorities upon request;
— the agreement is expressly set up for an intermediate period by means of a 'sunset clause', not exceeding 12 months;
— the interim agreement clearly provides for the US authorities to be notified after the entry into force of the Treaty of Lisbon and that a possible new agreement will be negotiated under the new EU legal framework, fully involving the European Parliament and national parliaments.[9]

The Council did not take Parliament's requests fully into account. Plausibly, its idea was to sign and conclude the interim agreement before the Treaty of Lisbon entered into force. The agreement was signed by the Council on 30 November

[7] European Parliament Resolution of 14 February 2007 on SWIFT, the PNR agreement and the transatlantic dialogue on these issues, P6_TA (2007)0039, [2007] OJ C287E/349. In this resolution, Parliament also called on the Commission to analyse the potential for economic and business espionage stemming from the current design of payment systems in the broadest sense.

[8] [2002] OJ L164/3.

[9] Resolution of 17 September 2009 on the envisaged international agreement to make available to the United States Treasury Department financial payment messaging data to prevent and combat terrorism and terrorist financing, in particular para 7, P7_TA(2009)0016.

2009, with provisional application as from 1 February 2010, pending its entry into force and for a maximum duration of nine months, until 1 October 2010. Yet there was no unanimity within the Council to proceed to the conclusion of the agreement,[10] and the next day the Treaty of Lisbon entered into force.

Thus, on 17 December 2009, the Commission had to submit a proposal to the Council for the conclusion of the agreement, but on the basis of the new provisions of the Treaty of Lisbon. The legal bases mentioned in the proposal were the following: Articles 82(1)(d), 87(2)(a) and 218(6)(a) TFEU.[11]

Vested with its new powers, the responsible parliamentary committee, the EP Committee on Civil Liberties, Justice and Home Affairs (LIBE) considered that not only was there a lack of information during the whole negotiating process but also that Parliament's requests were not duly taken into account. In addition, Parliament did not appreciate the fact that the Council decided to apply the agreement provisionally until 1 October 2010 and presented it thus as a 'fait accompli', which could not be renegotiated.

On these grounds, in spite of enormous pressure without precedent put on its President and Members by the American government and by the Spanish Presidency (not to mention pressure from some of the Member States on individual MEPs), Parliament decided on 11 February 2010 not to give consent to the interim agreement.[12] With this vote,[13] the provisional application of the interim agreement came to an end, in conformity with the Vienna Convention on the Law of the Treaties.[14] The US was informed by the Council. For the first time, in application of the Treaty of Lisbon (Article 218(6)(v) TFEU) Parliament did not give its consent to an international agreement to be concluded by the EU.

(b) The Consequences of the Non-consent: Renegotiation of a New Agreement, the 2010 SWIFT Agreement

The Commission submitted on 24 March 2010 to the Council a new proposal of negotiating directives. On 5 May 2010, Parliament adopted a resolution on this proposal[15] and showed satisfaction with the level of information provided by the Commission.

[10] Some Member States had serious misgivings about the agreement, namely Austria, Germany, Greece and Hungary. See for further developments, J Monar, 'The rejection of the EU-SWIFT Interim Agreement by the European Parliament: A Historic Vote and its Implications', n 3 above, p 146.

[11] COM(2009) 0703 final.

[12] A7-0013/2010.

[13] 378 in favour of the recommendation from LIBE to reject consent, 196 against and 31 abstentions.

[14] Art 25 of the Convention reads as follows: '1. A treaty or a part of a treaty is applied provisionally pending its entry into force if: (a) the treaty itself so provides; or (b) the negotiating States have in some other manner so agreed. 2. Unless the treaty otherwise provides or the negotiating States have otherwise agreed, the provisional application of a treaty or a part of a treaty with respect to a State shall be terminated if that State notifies the other States between which the treaty is being applied provisionally of its intention not to become a party to the treaty'.

[15] P7_TA(2010)0143.

Eventually, Parliament gave its consent to the new agreement on 8 July 2010,[16] which was concluded by the Council on 13 July 2010.[17]

It should be noted that not all the concerns expressed by the Parliament were met. In particular, the system is still based on the bulk transfer of data and not on targeted searches, and the storing for five years of non-extracted data is allowed. More importantly, it does not contain sufficient judicial review because the agreement 'shall not create or confer any right or benefit on any person or entity' (Article 20(1)). In this respect, the European Data Protection Supervisor pointed out that, given that current US privacy laws only create rights for US citizens and permanent residents, the position of EU citizens remains unclear. He referred to Article 20(1) of the Agreement and underlined that, according to the US Privacy Act, a request for access to one's records is only possible for 'a citizen of the US or an alien lawfully admitted for permanent residence'.[18]

If one compares the first and the second agreements, it can be considered that the result, as a whole, is nonetheless positive for the Parliament, taking into account the following improvements:

- it includes a clearer definition of terrorism based on the Union's 2002 Framework Decision;
- it stipulates that Europol shall verify whether the requests comply with the agreement (Article 4(4));
- it regulates onward transfer (Article 7);
- it contains detailed regulation of the rights to verification, erasure or blocking (Articles 15 and 16);
- an independent person is appointed by the European Commission to monitor the use of the data, in order to prevent misuse of data (eg industrial espionage)(Article 12).

Another positive consequence of the refusal to give consent was the fact that the Council declared to the Parliament that it was available to negotiate an inter-institutional agreement about the transmission of classified information to the Parliament. This inter-institutional agreement was concluded on 12 March 2014 and entered into force on 1 April 2014.[19]

[16] P7_TA-PROV(2010)0279.

[17] Council Decision 2010/412/EU, [2010] OJ L195/3.

[18] Opinion of the EDPS on the Swift Agreement, [2010] OJ C355/10. It seems that, in the meantime, the pressure put by the EU on the US to extend privacy protection rights to EU citizens (this protection to date only applies to US citizens) is beginning to find a solution, because the US administration promised to pass legislation granting EU citizens many of the privacy protection rights enjoyed by US citizens. The proposed law would apply to data on EU citizens being transferred to the US for law enforcement purposes. See Ewen MacAskill, 'US to extend privacy protection rights to EU citizens' *The Guardian*, (London, 25 June 2014) www.theguardian.com/world/2014/jun/25/us-privacy-protection-rights-europe.

[19] Interinstitutional Agreement of 12 March 2014 between the European Parliament and the Council concerning the forwarding to and handling by the European Parliament of classified information held by the Council on matters other than those in the area of the common foreign and security policy, [2014] OJ C95/1.

ii. The Second Protocol to the Fisheries Agreement with Morocco (December 2011)

(a) The Decision Not to Give Consent

On 22 May 2006, the Union concluded a Fisheries and Partnership Agreement with Morocco, which entered into force on 28 February 2007. This agreement entailed a first Protocol establishing the fishing capacities and the financial compensation for a non-renewable period of four years (28 February 2007–28 February 2011).[20]

A second Protocol was signed on 13 July 2011 concerning a one-year extension of the first Protocol. It established the financial contribution from the EU at €36.1 million per year. The decision on the signature foresaw its provisional application until 27 February 2012. On 29 September 2011, the Parliament considered a request by the Fisheries Committee with a view to obtaining an opinion by the Court of Justice on the compatibility of the envisaged Second Protocol with the Treaties, in particular concerning the question whether fishing in the Western Sahara waters was in conformity with international law principles. The Parliament rejected this recommendation and decided not to request a preliminary opinion of the Court of Justice, in conformity with Article 218(11) TFEU.

Subsequently, on 14 December 2011, the Parliament rejected the Second Protocol[21] and its provisional application was immediately terminated. The rejection was motivated mainly by economic, environmental and political reasons. From an economic perspective, on the basis of an outside evaluation report of the first four years (2007–11) ordered by the Commission, it was considered that the cost of the agreement was very high in relation to the fisheries opportunities. The EU fleets estimated turnover was €30.2 million, a figure well below the level of the EU financial contribution (€36.1 million).

Concerning the environmental concerns, it was stressed that the Protocol did not guarantee the sustainability of the stocks exploited.

From a political perspective, Parliament reckoned that there were legal issues with regard to Western Sahara. The issue at hand concerns whether or not the Agreement directly benefits the Saharawi people.[22] The Parliament's Legal Service was consulted in 2009 and recalled that under international law, Western Sahara has the status of a Non-Self-Governing Territory within the meaning of Article 73 of the UN Charter. Morocco is the de facto administrator of the territory. The Legal Service added that compliance with international law requires that economic activities related to the natural resources of a Non-Self-Governing Territory are

[20] Regulation 764/2006, [2006] OJ L141/1.

[21] 326 votes in favour, 296 against and 58 abstentions, P7_TA (2011)0569.

[22] See Recommendation from Carl Haglund, Rapporteur of the Committee on Fisheries, A7-0394/2011.

carried out for the benefit of the people of such territory, and in accordance with their wishes. In the event that it could not be demonstrated that the agreement was implemented in conformity with the principles of international law concerning the rights of the Saharawi people over their natural resources, the EU should refrain from allowing vessels to fish in the waters of Western Sahara by requesting fishing licences only for fishing zones that are situated in the waters off Morocco.[23] One of the difficulties in this context was that, according to Article 6 of the Protocol, the Moroccan authorities have full discretion in their use of the financial contribution, with no specific obligation to use part of the contribution in the Western Sahara territory to benefit the local population.

The Rapporteur of the Fisheries Committee, Mr Haglund, considered that the Protocol did not contain the relevant documentation clarifying this sensitive question. He proposed therefore to his committee that the Parliament should decline to give consent. He was not followed by the Fisheries Committee, which proposed to give consent, but was eventually followed by the Parliament.

Following this vote, Parliament adopted, on the same day (14 December 2011), a resolution on the future Protocol setting out the fishing opportunities and financial compensation provided for in the Fisheries Agreement with Morocco.[24] In this resolution, Parliament presented in a way its 'conditions' for giving consent to a future protocol. Concerning the economic requirements, Parliament called on the Commission 'to ensure that any future Protocol is economically, ecologically and socially sustainable'. Concerning the political and legal issues relating to the local populations in Western Sahara, the resolution, without mentioning this territory, insisted that the Protocol 'fully respects international law and benefits all the local population groups affected'. In this context, it insisted on having effective oversight mechanisms to ensure that funds earmarked for development, and in particular for infrastructure improvements in the fisheries sector, are used properly.[25]

(b) The Consequences of the Non-consent: The Renegotiation of a New Protocol

The Commission negotiated a new protocol claiming that it took into account the main three concerns expressed by the Parliament. It improved significantly

[23] See Opinion of the Committee on Development annexed to the recommendation from Carl Haglund, Rapporteur of the Committee on Fisheries, A7-0394/2011, p 11.

[24] Resolution of 14 December 2011, P7_TA (2011)0573.

[25] The rapporteur was very critical of the Commission because the Protocol was officially referred to the Parliament only in June 2011: this was three months after it had been initiated, enabling the de facto continuation of fishing activities since the termination of the First Protocol in February 2011, without Parliament having the opportunity to express itself. Thus, the Parliament in its resolution also 'called on the Commission to move the negotiations on a new Protocol forward in order to rule out any situation in which the Protocol has to be applied provisionally because Parliament has not yet given its consent'.

the cost-benefit ratio, increasing the fishing opportunities and at the same time reducing the amount of the EU annual financial contribution, from €36.1 to €30 million (€16 million is linked with the access and €14 million for the development and implementation of the Moroccan fisheries policy). It also indicated that the fishing activities are dependent on sound and scientific advice. Finally, concerning the delicate issue of Western Sahara, the new text requires Morocco to provide regular, detailed reports on the use of the financial contribution for the fisheries sector, including the economic and social benefits on a geographical basis, and providing for a mechanism for the possible suspension of the Protocol, including in the event of violations of human rights and democratic principles.

The new Protocol was initialled on 24 July 2013, followed by the Council Decision of 15 November 2013 on its signature. Taking on board the recommendation of the Parliament, no provisional application of the Protocol was foreseen before its final conclusion after the Parliament's consent.

On 10 December 2013, Parliament gave consent to the new text of the Second Protocol.[26] This time, three parliamentary committees (Fisheries, Development and Budgets) made the same proposal, even though within some political groups (in particular the Greens, GUE and ALDE) there was still a strong reluctance to accept the Protocol. The Rapporteur, Ms Carmen Fraga, considered that, even though there are some aspects that the fisheries sector hopes to modify in the Joint Committee established in the Agreement, the new protocol contains huge improvements and highlights the efforts made to respond to Parliament's concerns, in particular from an economic and financial point of view, and in terms of social and environmental sustainability.

In order to respond to the criticism made regarding a lack of sufficient control of the implementation of the agreement, including on the financial benefits to the local Saharawi population, the resolution entails the following paragraph:

> Recalls the European Parliament's right to be kept punctually and fully informed about the application of the Protocol and its results, and therefore insists once again that representatives of the European Parliament should have the opportunity to attend meetings of the Joint Committee provided for in Article 10 of the Fisheries Agreement as observers. Further calls for Parliament to be provided with documentation on the guidelines, objectives and indicators concerning the chapter relating to support for the fisheries sector in Morocco, and all information necessary for the proper monitoring of the aspects included in Article 6 of the Protocol,[27] including the final report that Morocco is to submit on the implementation of the sectorial support programme.[28]

[26] 310 in favour, 204 against and 4 abstentions, Resolution P7_TA (2013)0522 of 10 December 2013, and minutes of the sitting of that day, Annex 1, results of votes, item 4.

[27] According to this provision, Morocco is required to provide regular and detailed reports on the use of the financial contribution for the fisheries sector development, including in respect of the economic and social benefits for the local population on a geographic basis.

[28] Resolution P7_TA(2013)0522 of 10 December 2013, para 2.

The Council concluded the Protocol on 16 December 2013 for a period of four years (15 July 2014–15 July 2018).[29]

As for the consequences of the rejection by the Parliament of the first version of the Protocol, one can notice that the cost-benefit ratio has certainly improved: the fishing opportunities have been increased by 33 per cent and, at the same time, the annual financial contribution has dropped from €36.1 million to €30 million per year (a reduction of 17 per cent). The question remains whether the protocol will be implemented in a way which could be considered as compatible with the principles of international law given the specific status of the Western Saharan in international law. This issue is not clearly dealt with either in the Partnership and Fisheries Agreement or in this Second Protocol, which do not explicitly mention the waters of Western Sahara (some MEPs were rather in favour of completely excluding fishing in the Western Sahara waters). However, the Parliament has accepted that, even if this territory is not mentioned explicitly in Article 6 of the Protocol, Morocco has to provide information to the Joint Committee on the impact of the financial contributions allocated for specific projects, taking into account also their geographical contribution. Moreover, it was also advanced as an argument for accepting the agreement that, in case the implementation of the Protocol raises difficulties, the latter can be suspended 'if the dispute between the two parties is deemed to be serious and if the consultations held within the Joint Committee … have not resulted in an amicable settlement' (Article 8(2) of the Protocol). In this regard, the Parliament insisted, as mentioned before, on being fully informed about the application of the Protocol and its results, and that its own representatives could attend the meetings of the Joint Committee. This is new and was put forward as a condition of accepting the Protocol. It is still early to make a first evaluation in particular concerning the impact of the Protocol on the local people of Western Sahara, but it is to be expected that the Fisheries Committee will seriously scrutinise the implementation of the Protocol. Obviously, Parliament was aware of all the implications of its vote and the approval of the Protocol has to be considered as the result of a political choice.[30]

[29] Council Decision on the conclusion, on behalf of the European Union, of the Protocol between the European Union and the Kingdom of Morocco setting out the fishing opportunities and financial contribution provided for in the Fisheries Partnership Agreement in force between the two parties, [2013] OJ L349/1.

[30] On 14 March 2014, the Front Polisario lodged an action before the General Court of the European Union against the Council, seeking the annulment of Council Decision of 16 December 2013 (Case T-180/14 *Front Polisario v Council*). The Front Polisario contests the legality of the act. It alleged inter alia that the decision breached the UNCLOS, in so far as it allows the entry into force of a protocol by which the EU and Morocco set fishing quotas for waters not under their sovereignty and authorise the EU vessels to exploit fisheries resources under the sole sovereignty of the Sahrawi people. It claimed also an infringement of Art 73 of the Charter of UN, because it was not consulted. The Commission intervened in support of the Council. This case was pending at the time of writing.

In the meantime, the General Court of the European Union decided another case (Case T-512/12) also brought by the Front Polisario against the Council seeking the annulment of Council Decision 2012/497/EU on the conclusion of the Agreement between the EU and Morocco on the liberalisation *iii. The Anti-Counterfeiting Trade Agreement (ACTA)*

The Agreement was born out of the frustration of the major industrialised economies with lack of progress on monitoring and norm-setting on the enforcement of intellectual property rights (IPR) in multilateral fora. In the WTO Council for TRIPS, Brazil, India and China have constantly blocked the inclusion of enforcement as a permanent agenda item. At the World Intellectual Property Organization (WIPO), enforcement issues were relegated to a purely advisory committee. ACTA was justified by the need to find a multilateral enforcement of IPR, as well as the need to fight increasing volumes of counterfeit and pirated products. It contains provisions in several areas, such as: civil enforcement, border measures, criminal enforcement, enforcement of IPR in the digital environment, measures to improve the enforcement practices and international cooperation.

Initial intentions to negotiate such an agreement started in 2005 by Japan and later in 2006 by the United States. Formal negotiations were launched in October 2007 and concluded in October 2010 in Tokyo. The negotiating parties included: Australia, Canada, Japan, the Republic of Korea, Morocco, New Zealand, Singapore, Switzerland, Mexico, the United States and the European Union. Countries like China, Brazil and India did not participate.

On 24 June 2011, the Commission submitted to the Council a proposal for a Council Decision authorising the signing and a proposal for a Council Decision concluding the Agreement.[31] The Commission proposed the agreement as a mixed agreement. It declared that the Agreement contains a number of provisions on criminal enforcement (Article 83(2) TFEU) and that the Commission has opted not to propose that the EU exercise its potential competence, but rather the Member States. This option was possibly justified by the sensitivity of the issue for the Member States. It was also in practice logical so as to underline that the part of the agreement relating to criminal enforcement had actually been negotiated by the Member States under their national responsibility.

of agricultural and fishery products. By Judgment of 10 December 2015, the General Court annulled the Council Decision, because the Council failed to fulfil its obligation to examine all the elements of the case before adopting its decision. The General Court considered that:' Given the fact, inter alia, that the sovereignty of the Kingdom of Morocco over Western Sahara is not recognised by the European Union or its Member States, or more generally by the UN, and the absence of any international mandate capable of justifying Moroccan presence on that territory, the Council, in the examination of all the relevant facts of the present case, with a view to exercising its wide discretion as to whether or not to conclude an agreement with the Kingdom of Morocco which may also apply to Western Sahara, should have satisfied itself that there was no evidence of an exploitation of the natural resources of the territory of Western Sahara under Moroccan control likely to be to the detriment of its inhabitants and to infringe their fundamental rights. The Council cannot merely conclude that it is for the Kingdom of Morocco to ensure that no exploitation of that nature takes place'. (EU:T: paragraph 241). The Council lodged an appeal against this judgment before the ECJ, which is pending. The Commission intervened in support of the Council in both proceedings.

[31] COM(2011)37 final and COM(2011)380 final.

On 16 December 2011, the Council adopted the decision for the Union to sign ACTA and on 14 February 2012 it requested the consent of the Parliament in order to conclude the Agreement. Yet, a number of Member States did not sign (Cyprus, Estonia, Germany, the Netherlands and Slovakia), which was already an indication that they were not feeling very comfortable with the Agreement.[32]

Indeed, an unprecedented wave of protests and demonstrations by internet users, particularly in Eastern Europe and Germany, expressed strong criticism against the Agreement. Very active NGOs expressed concern on a certain number of issues, including the potential negative effect of ACTA on fundamental rights, the risk that ACTA would have an effect on internet access for consumers that infringe the Agreement, or the possibility of imposing liability on internet service providers that carry content that infringes the Agreement, or the possible negative effect of ACTA on access to medicines in the EU and in third countries. Several MEPs echoed this criticism and the Parliament also protested several times about not being fully informed about the negotiations, as required by Article 218(10) TFEU.[33]

Also, the responsible committee in the Parliament, the Committee on International Trade (INTA), ordered a study in June 2011 elaborated by several academics containing an assessment on ACTA, which was rather negative in some regards.[34] An opinion was also produced on 8 October 2011 by Professors Korff (London Metropolitan University) and Ian Brown (Oxford Internet Institute, University of Oxford) at the request of a political group (the Greens) about the compatibility of ACTA with the ECHR and the EU Charter of Fundamental Rights. This opinion concluded that ACTA 'seriously threatens fundamental rights in the EU'. Attached to this was another opinion by 30 different academics from different Member States, advising the Parliament to withhold consent.[35]

On 24 April 2012, the European Data Protection Supervisor (EDPS) issued an opinion on ACTA on his own initiative. He pointed out that:

> The Agreement is unclear about the scope of enforcement measures ... The notion of 'commercial scale' in Article 23 of the Agreement is not defined with sufficient precision ... The Agreement does not contain sufficient limitations and safeguards in respect of the implementation of measures that entail the monitoring of electronic communications networks on a large scale. In particular, it does not lay out

[32] F Hoffmeister, 'The deep and comprehensive free trade agreements of the European Union—concept and challenges' in M Cremona and T Takács (eds), *Trade liberalisation and standardisation—new directions in the 'low politics of EU foreign policy*, CLEER Working Papers 2013/6, p 21.

[33] Resolution of 10 March 2010 on the transparency and state of play of the ACTA negotiations (P7_TA(2010)0058); Declaration of the Parliament of 9 September 2010 on the lack of transparent process for the ACTA and potentially objectionable content (P7_TA(2010)0317); Resolution of 24 November 2010 on ACTA (P7_TA(2010)0432).

[34] Directorate-General for External Policies of the Union, Policy Department, see: www.europarl.europa.eu/RegData/etudes/etudes/join/2011/433859/EXPO-INTA_ET(2011)433859_EN.pdf.

[35] www.iri.uni-hannover.de/acta-1668.html.

safeguards such as the respect of the rights to privacy and data protection, effective judicial protection, due process, and the respect of the principle of the presumption of innocence.[36]

In an attempt to allay the concerns expressed in the public debate, the Commission requested on 10 May 2012 an opinion of the Court of Justice, pursuant to Article 218(11) TFEU on the question whether the envisaged ACTA Agreement was compatible with the Treaties and in particular with the Charter of Fundamental Rights. This move was justified, because in purely legal terms the arguments advanced against the agreement did not seem very solid.

Yet the Parliament preferred not to wait for the Court's opinion, and on 4 July 2012 decided to withhold its consent. The Rapporteur of the responsible committee (INTA), Mr David Martin, recommended not giving consent,[37] and his recommendation was followed by the Parliament.[38] There was a massive vote from the Socialists, Greens and Communists against the Agreement. Parliament seemed not so much concerned with the economic advantages of the agreement but rather with the alleged risks of violation of civil rights. The Rapporteur used the following formula:

> A vague text is dangerous. We cannot guarantee that civil liberties will be robustly protected by the ACTA provisions. When it comes down to protecting intellectual property rights or protecting civil liberties, civil liberties should always be central to the concern of this House.[39]

Actually, it turned out that the debate was not so much in favour of or against giving consent, but rather on withholding consent or waiting for the opinion of the Court of Justice on the compatibility of ACTA with the Treaties.[40]

Several reasons can be mentioned to justify Parliament's vote not to give consent:

— the most substantial reason was the dissatisfaction with the content of the agreement and the lack of precision of certain provisions concerning, in particular: the scope of the enforcement measures (no specific definition of 'commercial scale'), the types of mechanisms that could be put in place to implement the agreement and the need to specify more clearly the safeguards against the misuse of personal data and to protect the right of defence, the notion of 'competent authority' (Article 27(4)) and the need to stipulate that the disclosure of personal data of alleged infringers should only take place under the control of judicial authorities. It was also considered disproportionate that the enforcement cooperation mechanisms entail the

[36] secure.edps.europa.eu/EDPSWEB/webdav/shared/Documents/Consultation/Opinions/2012/12-04-24_ACTA_EN.pdf, p 16. The EDPS had issued a previous opinion in February 2010, also on his own initiative, on a previous draft of the Agreement ([2010] OJ C147/1).

[37] Actually, not only INTA—the lead committee—recommended to the Parliament not to give consent, but also the other four parliamentary committees involved (LIBE, JURI, IMCO and DEVE).

[38] 255 in favour of giving consent, 420 against and 9 abstentions P7_TA(2012)0287.

[39] P7_TA(2012)0287.

[40] During the debate, Vital Moreira, Chairman of INTA, contrary to his committee, pleaded in favour of giving consent to ACTA.

processing by internet service providers (ISP) of personal data for the purpose of monitoring individuals' behaviour. This was mentioned by the Rapporteur who said during the debate that 'it is not the role of the ISPs to police internet, and we should not be privatising law enforcement in this way';
— the fact that the purpose of ACTA was to promote to third countries rules on criminal enforcement which have not yet been agreed internally within the EU law. Even if the agreement was presented as a mixed agreement in order to quieten concerns regarding criminal enforcement, this does not alter a perception that the EU was involved in designing rules intended to apply to others, which were not yet established by the EU itself[41] (even though this is legally possible, as the EU may modify EU secondary law by concluding an international agreement);
— the impressive mobilisation of the civil society, in particular some NGOs and scholars, against ACTA (a petition of over 2.8 million online petitioners against ACTA was sent to the Parliament);
— the two opinions of the European Data Supervisor, which contained strong reservations about ACTA;
— last, but not least, the criticism concerning the fact that the agreement was negotiated behind closed doors, and that the Parliament, and the public in general, were not sufficiently informed about its possible implications.

This last aspect contributed decisively to the perception that the Agreement contained parts which were negative for internet users. This was naturally also exploited by those who were against it, with a simple argument: if there is no issue of compatibility with EU law (including the Charter on Fundamental Rights) why is the Commission hiding the negotiations? Parliament also complained that it had only received the Agreement at a very late stage where there was not much possibility to request any changes to the text. It is true though that the Commissioner, Mr De Gucht, endeavoured to inform INTA about the evolution of negotiations, but this was not considered enough by the MEPs.

This is a more general issue, which was also patent with the SWIFT Agreement. If the Parliament is not properly informed, the chances that such an agreement will be rejected are real. Surely the Commission and the Council will have to reckon much more with the Parliament's interests and this not only at the conclusion stage but also at the negotiating stage. In the case of ACTA, Parliament indeed received a draft text of 2 October 2010, but in reality it had no chance to influence the contents of the Agreement. At the end, it echoed the widespread wave of criticism by public opinion in many Member States. The issue naturally became political; facing such hostile public opinion[42] (Parliament as echoing the

[41] M Cremona, 'The EU's international regulatory policy, democratic accountability and the ACTA: a cautionary tale' in M Cremona and T Takács (eds), *Trade liberalisation and standardisation—new directions in the 'low politics of EU foreign policy'*, *CLEER Working Papers* 2013/6, p 74.

[42] It should be noted however that on 24 November 2010, Parliament considered that ACTA was 'a step in the right direction', but asked the Commission to accede to a certain number of commitments (P7_TA(2010)0432).

vox populi), and being also concerned with the implications of ACTA (even if some were not justified with solid legal arguments), the majority against consent was visible. In this regard, the request by the Commission to receive an opinion by the Court came too late (the Commission withdrew it in December 2012).

The consequences of the non-conclusion of ACTA are not easy to evaluate. It is not like the two preceding cases where the Commission launched negotiations to achieve a new agreement corresponding to the wishes of the Parliament. This seems rather unrealistic concerning another ACTA agreement. It is for the moment unacceptable to the Parliament that in future bilateral agreements with third States, the Commission may reintroduce 'ACTA clauses'. This was criticised in the trade agreement with Canada. According to Hoffmeister, following the non-consent by the Parliament, the Commission has reviewed the entire IPR chapter in its on-going negotiations. He suggests that in relation to criminal enforcement, it will be for the Presidency of the Council and for the Member States to decide on the future approach to be taken.[43] Maybe the Parliament could be called on to play a role in this regard. One possible way out is to elaborate the EU's own rules on the protection of intellectual property in the Union, including the chapter on criminal enforcement, and only then launch negotiations for a new multilateral agreement. This would have the merit of adopting rules under the ordinary legislative procedure, and in a transparent way.[44]

B. The Influence of the Parliament in the Negotiation of International Agreements

i. More Democracy in the EU External Action

The refusal of consent should remain exceptional, because it affects the stability of the position of the Union on the international scene. As indicated before, the cases of non-consent are indeed exceptional (three cases in 241 agreements on which Parliament did not give consent).

What is important is that the institutions work closely in a spirit of good cooperation, in the same line as they cooperate in the ordinary legislative procedures. Even though the procedures are different, in practical terms 'consent' and

[43] F Hoffmeister, 'The deep and comprehensive free trade agreements of the European Union—concept and challenges' see fn 32 above, p 22.

[44] The Commission is putting forward a toolbox to ensure greater respect for IPR in the EU. An international level strategy is also part of the package, which will be implemented in 2016. In a Communication from 1 July 2014, the Commission indicates that it will seek to obtain an agreement between the different stakeholders (online advertising agencies and payment services carriers) to remove counterfeiting from internet trade. The aim is to deny those contravening IPR their sources of revenue. The Commission is hoping to assess the lie of the land to extend reimbursement systems relating to certain credit cards when accidentally purchasing counterfeit goods. A Green Paper will set out concrete measures to be carried out to this end and to help provide funding to SMEs so that they can protect themselves against IPR infringements (on the basis of best practice in Member States). The

'ordinary legislative procedure' may be compared to the extent they both require a 'joint decision'.

Concerning the perception of the role of the Parliament in the EU external action, it can be reckoned that a lot of progress has been made. When the Treaty of Lisbon entered into force, some expressed fears that the consent procedure, especially for trade agreements, would be a catastrophe. That is really not the case. The parliamentary committees have in the last seven years developed their work rather seriously and are in general working well with the Commission and the Council.

Differences of views on the substance of the envisaged agreements are natural, that is part of the democratic scrutiny by the Parliament. The problem that remains is still the incomplete flow of information. It is true that sometimes radical positions are expressed on both sides—some want a complete secrecy of negotiations, and some MEPs want complete transparency. There is surely a need to find an appropriate balance, and in particular to find proceedings aiming at securing the confidentiality of information, when this is necessary.

In any case, it should be stressed that the involvement of Parliament implies more openness and more information for public opinion about on-going negotiations. This is the lesson to be taken from the negotiations on the SWIFT Agreement, and especially on the ACTA Agreement. This impact is even more visible with the on-going negotiations concerning the Transatlantic Trade and Investment Partnership (TTIP) between the EU and the United States.[45] The fact that the Parliament had to give consent brought the impact of the agreements to the knowledge of the citizens. The whole purpose of the changes in the Treaty reinforcing the role of the Parliament is indeed to enable more democracy and open debate about the EU external policies.

As for the procedure involving Parliament, at the stage of the opening of the negotiations, the parliamentary committees should have been informed already by the Commission (or by the European External Action Service (EEAS), if the agreement is to be negotiated by it because it relates principally to the CFSP). It may happen that the Parliament considers that the negotiations are premature or inopportune. In that case, the Parliament may adopt a resolution explicitly asking the Council not to authorise the opening of negotiations.[46]

At the stage of the negotiations, when the committees receive the draft negotiating directives from the Commission (or through the EEAS)—which is

proposed strategy also includes an external dimension through which the Commission is proposing the continuation of multilateral efforts to improve the international framework for IPR and to ensure that the chapters on IPR in bilateral trade agreements guarantee appropriate protection for rights holders. It also seeks to collaborate with non-EU trade partners by way of dialogue and working groups on intellectual property issues.

[45] See on the transparency of the negotiations, M Cremona, 'Guest Editorial: Negotiating the Transatlantic Trade and Investment Partnership (TTIP)' (2015) 52 *Common Market Law Review* 351–62.

[46] European Parliament Resolution of 13 June 2012 on EU trade negotiations with Japan, P7_TA(2012)026. In that case, the Parliament wanted to examine first the negotiating directives proposed by the Commission.

sent to the Council—they may utilise the period of time (around three months) needed by the Council to take a Decision, to adopt a resolution on the very content of the draft negotiating directives. In this resolution, the Parliament generally indicates the matters it wishes to have included in the agreement. Sometimes the Parliament indicates, more or less explicitly, the 'conditions' of giving consent (eg Resolutions on the free trade agreement with Japan,[47] on the agreement with China,[48] or on the Transatlantic Trade and Investment Partnership negotiations (TTIP), where the Parliament requested the exclusion of the audio-visual sector from the negotiating mandate).[49] The fact that a resolution is adopted by the Parliament has the consequence that much will be debated in public (this may raise the issue whether it is always appropriate to disclose in this way the full content of the negotiating directives). Moreover, the committees regularly organise hearings or workshops concerning on-going international agreements. For example, concerning the TTIP agreement, not only the responsible committee (INTA), but also all the other concerned committees have organised hearings on the subject-matter of the agreement related to their own competences. These hearings related in particular to the Investor-State Dispute Settlement (ISDS) (in the meantime replaced by another system of dispute settlement, the Investment Court System (ICS), see below), to the regulatory cooperation envisaged in the agreement, as well as to its implications in specific areas, such as agriculture, industry, health services, data protection, etc.

ii. The Involvement of Parliament in the Shaping of Some International Agreements

Parliament generally succeeds in influencing the content of international agreements in the following areas of concern:

(a) First of all, by insisting on the inclusion of human rights clauses, considered as an essential element of the agreement. These clauses are generally inserted in association agreements but also in some trade agreements. Taking the example of the Trade Agreement with Colombia and Peru, the following observations can be made:
  — The Agreement contains a specific provision on human rights, which reads:

    > Respect for democratic principles and fundamental rights as laid down in the Universal Declaration of Human Rights and for the principles of the rule of law, underpins the internal and international policies of the parties. Respect for these principles constitutes an essential element of the agreement. Failure

[47] 2010/2152(INI).

[48] Resolution of 9 October 1013 on the EU-China negotiations for a bilateral investment agreement, 20132674(RSP).

[49] 2013/2558(RSP).

to respect these principles constitutes a 'material breach' of the agreement, which would give rise to the termination or the suspension of the agreement, partially or totally (Article 1);[50]

— The Parliament insists on a monitoring system involving the civil society;
— The Parliament will hold public hearings both within its premises and in the capital of the country concerned; following the hearings, the Parliament wishes to obtain a written report to be submitted to the responsible committee on the application of the agreement.[51]

Failure to respect human rights and democratic principles would constitute a 'material breach' of the agreement which, under public international law, could give rise to the adoption of appropriate measures, including the possibility to terminate or to suspend partially or totally the agreement (eg Article 8 of the trade agreement with Colombia and Peru). As the European Parliament has pointed out on various occasions in relation to human rights clauses, it is essential that proper monitoring of the respect of human rights by all signatory parties is ensured and that the practical enforceability of the human rights clause is guaranteed. Parliament insists that the agreements establish a bilateral organ with the power to suspend the agreement if there is a violation of the human rights clause.[52,53]

(b) Inclusion in the agreement of chapters on environment, sustainable development and labour standards.

Parliament condemns adamantly child labour in countries where this may exist and declares clearly that it can only give consent if International Labour Organization (ILO) observers are granted access in order to eradicate this practice.[54] The Parliament also insists on incorporating in bilateral free trade agreements a chapter dealing with sustainable development, including labour rights. Moreover, it takes the view that the social clauses in trade agreements should be complemented by the incorporation of the concept of corporate social responsibility, which concerns the behaviour of corporations.[55]

In the trade agreement with Colombia and Peru, the parties commit to promote the effective implementation of core ILO Conventions, including freedom of association and the effective recognition of the right of collective

[50] P7_TA-PROV(2012)0148.

[51] Resolution of 13 June 2012 on EU trade agreement with Colombia and Peru, P7_TA(0249).

[52] Lorand Bartels, *The European Parliament's role in relation to human rights in trade and investment agreements* (Directorate-General for External Policies, February 2014) p 23.

[53] The Association Agreements EU-Morocco and EU-Lebanon foresee that the Association Council established a subcommittee on Human Rights, Democracy and Governance, which monitors the implementation of the human rights clauses, [2003] OJ L79/14 and [2012] OJ L290/18.

[54] European Parliament resolution of 15 December 2011 on the EC-Uzbekistan partnership and cooperation agreement and bilateral trade in textiles, P7_TA(2011)0586, para 2.

[55] European Parliament Resolution of 25 November 2010 on corporate social responsibility in international trade agreements, P7_TA(2010)0446, para 8.

bargaining. There are also wordings to incorporate the obligations set out in multilateral environmental agreements. Parties undertake not to lower their levels of environmental protection to attract investment or fail to enforce labour and environmental standards in a manner that affects trade between the parties. While this chapter is legally binding, it is, however, not subject to the dispute settlement mechanism.

(c) Defence of specific economic sectorial interests of the Union

1. *The FTA with Korea*

Concerning the Free Trade Agreement with Korea, the Parliament and the Council adopted a regulation implementing the bilateral safeguard clause included in the agreement.[56] Safeguard measures may only be considered if the product in question is imported into the Union in such increased quantities as to cause (or threaten to cause) serious injury to Union producers of like competitive products. Annexed to this regulation, the Parliament and the Commission adopted a joint statement enabling the Parliament to ask the Commission to initiate safeguard investigations (concerning the car and textile industries, in particular). The Commission will carefully examine whether the conditions under the regulation are fulfilled. If that is not the case, the Commission will present a report to the responsible committee of the European Parliament (INTA) justifying its position.

The Parliament had a significant influence because the implementation of the safeguard clause of this agreement was adopted by ordinary legislative procedure. Parliament has shown a particular interest for the protection of the car industry.[57]

2. *The TTIP*

One of the basic aims of the negotiations will be on investment liberalisation and protection provisions. As mentioned in the negotiating directives adopted by the Council on 17 June 2013 'the inclusion of investment protection and investor-to-state dispute settlement (ISDS) will depend on whether a satisfactory solution meeting the EU interests concerning the issues covered by paragraph 23, is achieved'.[58] In this paragraph, reference is made to the fact

[56] Regulation (EU) No 511/2011 of the European Parliament and of the Council of 11 May 2011 implementing the bilateral safeguard clause of the Free Trade Agreement between the European Union and its Member States and the Republic of Korea, [2011] OJ L145/19.

[57] A similar strategy was adopted concerning the Free Trade Agreement with Colombia and Peru. A regulation was adopted by the Parliament and the Council implementing a bilateral safeguard clause and stabilisation mechanism for bananas in conformity with the ordinary legislative procedure. A Joint Declaration annexed to this regulation reads as follows: 'If the European Parliament adopts a recommendation to initiate a safeguard investigation, the Commission will examine the request. If the Commission considers that the conditions in regulation … are not fulfilled, it will present a report to INTA including an explanation of all the factors relevant to the initiation of such an investigation'.

[58] Document ST 11103/13 of 9 October 2014, p 8.

> that such mechanism should be without prejudice to the right of the EU and the Member States to adopt and enforce measures necessary to pursue legitimate public policy objectives such as social, environment, security, stability of the financial system, public health and safety, in a non-discriminatory manner.
>
> This matter is of deep concern to the Parliament. It has been argued that sometimes the rulings taken by arbitrators are problematic, in particular when the State is condemned to pay damages due to the effects of legislation on the investors' rights. Such rulings may thus have a chilling effect to the extent that may potentially limit the State's power to regulate.

States may prefer not to regulate an issue simply from fear of litigation. Also, it has been said that the risk may exist that foreign controlled firms will locate operations in certain countries in order to access specific rights under an investment agreement. Also, some say that arbitrators may have already provided counsel to the parties, and thus are not presenting the required impartiality.

At the instigation of the INTA Committee, the Commission has presented a concept paper to it in May 2015 foreseeing the creation of one permanent court with the arbitrators being qualified to hold judicial office in their home jurisdiction or a similar qualification.

After much work involving the opinions of 13 different committees, the INTA Committee submitted a report to the Plenary, which was adopted on 8 July 2015, by a comfortable majority (436 in favour, 241 against and 32 abstentions).[59] The purpose of this resolution is to transmit to the Commission, as negotiator, a certain number of recommendations, which the Parliament wishes to be included in the final text of the agreement. These recommendations relate to the scope of the agreement, the market access, regulatory cooperation, rules, transparency, civil society information, public and political outreach. On the ISDS issue, the following paragraph was adopted by the Parliament:

> (xv) to ensure that foreign investors are treated in a non-discriminatory fashion, while benefiting from no greater rights than domestic investors, and *to replace the ISDS-system with a new system* for resolving disputes between investors and states which is subject to democratic principles and scrutiny, where potential cases are treated in a transparent manner by publicly appointed, independent professional judges in public hearings and which includes an appellate mechanism, where consistency of judicial decisions is ensured, the jurisdiction of courts of the EU and of the Member States is respected, and *where private interests cannot undermine public policy objectives* (emphasis added).

On 12 November 2015, the Commission submitted a written proposal on the resolution of investment disputes replacing the ISDS mechanism by a new mechanism, the Investment Court System (ICS). According to this proposal, a tribunal of first instance is established, composed of fifteen Judges (five shall be nationals

[59] P8_TA-PROV(2015)0252.

of a Member State of the EU, five shall be nationals of the US and five shall be nationals of third countries). The judges shall be available at all times and on short notice, and shall stay abreast of dispute settlement activities under the Agreement. A permanent Appeal Tribunal (composed of six Members, two of each component) is also established to hear appeals from the awards issued by the first instance tribunal. On the applicable law, it is laid down that the Tribunal shall apply the provisions of the agreement and other rules of international law applicable between the parties, but that the domestic law of the parties shall not be part of the applicable law. Moreover, a provision was inserted on transparency applying to the disputes. This new mechanism has now been inserted in two international agreements signed by the Council (the trade agreement with Vietnam and the Comprehensive, Economic and Trade Agreement with Canada (CETA)),[60] but is yet to be transmitted to the Parliament for consent. It is not discounted that the compatibility of this mechanism with the Treaties will eventually be brought before the ECJ for an opinion in accordance with Article 218(11) TFEU.

III. SOME RECENT LEGAL ISSUES RELATED TO ARTICLE 218 TFEU

Article 218 is a new provision of the TFEU, which succeeds Article 300 EC Treaty. With the abolition of the 'pillars', a single provision establishes the procedure for the negotiation and conclusion of all EU international agreements (Articles 24 and 38 of the TEU relating to the AFSJ and CFSP were suppressed). This simplification does not imply the same procedure for all the international agreements. The CFSP agreements have a specific regime.

Soon after the entry into force of the Treaty of Lisbon, it became apparent that the implementation of this provision encompasses important choices about the competences of the Union vis-à-vis the Member States (EU-only agreements or mixed agreements), the respective role of the institutions, the position of the Commission as negotiator, the role of the Parliament when it is called upon to give consent or not, and also how Parliament's right to be informed about the negotiation and conclusion of international agreements (and their suspension) shall be implemented. These questions reflect generally disputes about the shaping of the Union external policy, and the need to secure the proper institutional balance. For that reason, it is not surprising that the Court of Justice had been called on to provide guidance in some aspects. As the Court of Justice emphasised, 'the question of the extent of the powers of the European Union institutions in the field of external action is not only of considerable practical importance, but has constitutional significance'.[61] In recent years, it is noticeable that in the context of external relations some Member States now

[60] http://trade.ec.europa.eu/doclib/docs/2015/september/tradoc_153807.pdf

[61] See Opinion 1/08 of 30 November 2009, [2009] ECR I-11129, para 110.

question the very new provisions created by them in the Treaty of Lisbon relating in particular to the competence to conclude international agreements (exclusive or shared) and the procedure provided for in Article 218 TFEU.[62]

The following issues seem of particular interest:

- the role of the Commission as negotiator;
- mixed agreements and the question whether the Council can take hybrid decisions jointly with the Member States;
- the need to involve the Parliament in the provisional application of the agreements;
- the choice of the legal basis covering at the same time TFEU and CFSP policies;
- the scope of the obligation to inform the Parliament (Article 218(10) TFEU).

A. The Role of the Commission as Negotiator: Case C-425/13, *Commission v Council*

The Commission plays a crucial role in the conduct of the external action of the Union. Leaving aside the area of CFSP, in all the other areas, the Commission has the power of initiative. According to Article 218 TFEU, it is the Council that authorises the opening of negotiations, adopts negotiating directives, authorises the signature, decides on the provisional application and concludes the agreement. However, the Council cannot act without a proposal from the Commission. Beyond the right of initiative, it is the Commission that negotiates the agreement and initials the text, once the negotiations are concluded (once again excluding the case of the CFSP agreements).[63]

The question is to assess what margin of negotiation the Commission has.

The Commission must indeed consult with a 'special committee' during the negotiations (Article 218(4) TFEU). Concerning trade agreements, the treaty is more precise. Article 207(3) third subparagraph, TFEU reads as follows:

> The Commission shall conduct these negotiations in consultation with a special committee appointed by the Council to assist the Commission in this task and within the framework of such directives as the Council may issue to it. The Commission shall report regularly to the special committee and to the European Parliament on the progress of negotiations.

In practical terms, the Commission not only has to consult with the 'special committee', but also to report regularly to it on the evolution of the negotiations.

[62] See Peter Jan Kuijper, From the Board: Litigation on External Relations Powers after Lisbon: The Member States Reject Their Own Treaty, *Legal Issues of Economic Integration* 43, no. 1 (2016): 1-14.

[63] The initialling of the text is the act whereby the negotiators authenticate the text resulting from the negotiations. This phase of the procedure forms part of the negotiation. This should not be confused with the signature of the agreement.

In addition, according to Article 218(10) TFEU, the Commission is obliged to inform immediately and fully the European Parliament about the opening of the negotiations and their evolution. This is an essential procedural requirement, as the Court underlined in its Judgment of 24 June 2014 in Case C-658/11 *European Parliament v Council of the European Union* (which will be analysed further in this chapter). Also, the Framework Agreement of 2010 on relations between the European Parliament and the Commission stipulates that the Commission has to keep Parliament regularly and promptly informed about the conduct of negotiations until the agreement is initialled, and explains whether and how Parliament's comments were incorporated in the texts under negotiation and, if not, why.[64]

The Commission is thus under an obligation to cooperate closely both with the Council (through the special committee) and with the Parliament (generally through the responsible committee). In its responsibility as negotiator, the Commission acts with an *obligation de résultat*, that is to say with a view to enabling the Parliament to eventually give consent and the Council to conclude the agreement. The Commission can thus not go manifestly beyond the negotiating directives or the requests put forward by the Parliament; otherwise it takes a serious risk that the negotiations will not be successful through Parliament's consent and the conclusion of the agreement by the Council. This being said, it is inherent to the role of negotiator to have a certain margin of discretion. Otherwise, one could not speak of a proper 'negotiation'. Concessions may need to be made and complete or partial refusals and counter-proposals are part of the exercise, provided that both the negotiating directives allowed by the Council and the positions of the Parliament are taken into account. This margin should be accepted, and the Commission should be fully in its role when it negotiates, seeking the best result for the Union interests. The Commission, when it negotiates an agreement, represents the European Union and does not act in the name and on behalf of the Council or the European Parliament. In this context, the Commission may also be in a position to try to find a common denominator of the, often varying, interests of the Members States.[65]

Another matter is when the Council, while adopting the negotiating directives, establishes in the same decision binding mechanisms with the possible result of limiting considerably or even depriving the Commission of its margin of negotiation. In that case, the question is whether the Council, in this way, is not violating the rights of the Commission as negotiator, and at the same time placing the latter in a very delicate situation vis-à-vis the Parliament as being practically obliged to refuse any wish the Parliament may have formulated during the negotiations. Such a scenario needs to be scrutinised, in particular under the principle of conferral of powers on each institution (Article 13(2) TEU), the principle

[64] Framework Agreement on relations between the European Parliament and the Commission, Annex 3 on the negotiation and conclusion of international agreements, point 3, [2010] OJ L304/47.

[65] P Eeckhout, *External Relations of the European Union, second edition* (Oxford, Oxford University Press, 2011) 197.

of institutional balance, and in general as to how Article 218(2) and (4) TFEU should be interpreted.

These questions are not purely theoretical. Concerning the mutual recognition between the EU scheme and other greenhouse gas emissions trading schemes (ETS), the EU opened negotiations with Australia. On 13 May 2013, the Council adopted a decision appointing a special committee and establishing the negotiating directives. Section A of the Annex containing the negotiating directives establishes the procedure for negotiations. In particular, it is laid down that 'detailed negotiating positions of the Union shall be established within the special committee or within the Council'. Moreover, 'each negotiating session shall be preceded by a meeting within the special committee in order to identify the key issues and establish negotiating positions or guidance, as appropriate'. The Commission reacted in vain against this text, before it was adopted by the Council.

On 24 July 2013, the Commission brought annulment proceedings before the Court against the Council.[66] The Commission argued in substance that the Council power to issue negotiating directives does not include the establishment of the negotiating procedure. The negotiating directives concern the policy options and objectives to be achieved during the negotiations, but not the internal procedures. Moreover, Article 218(2) and (4) TFEU do not foresee that the Council may establish detailed negotiating positions during the negotiations, as laid down in the contested decision. According to the Commission, once the Council has authorised the Commission to negotiate, the Council has no direct decision-making role during the negotiations. Only the 'special committee' is involved, but as a consultative organ. Therefore, the Commission claimed that insofar as the decision empowered the special committee to adopt detailed negotiating positions, which are intended to be binding on the Commission, the Council violated Article 218(2) and (4) TFEU.

The European Parliament decided to intervene in this case in support of the Commission.[67] It was Parliament's understanding that the Council decision did not respect Article 218(2) and (4) TFEU because it placed the Commission under a legal obligation simply to implement positions taken by the special committee or by the Council during the negotiations. The Parliament acknowledged that this special committee or the Council may take political positions during the negotiations vis-à-vis the Commission, but these positions cannot be issued as legally binding. Indeed, if that were the case, then the position of the Parliament and its margin of influence on the negotiations would be completely jeopardised. That would be contrary to the principle of institutional balance and against the Treaties, because the right of the Parliament to be informed implies that the Parliament should be in a 'position to exercise democratic scrutiny of the European external

[66] Case C-425/13, *Commission v Council*, [2013] OJ C274/17.

[67] Poland, the Czech Republic, Sweden, Netherlands, Germany, United Kingdom, France and Denmark intervened in support of the Council.

action'.[68] In this regard, the Framework Agreement between the Commission and the Parliament of 2010 foresees that the Commission 'shall take due account of Parliament's comments throughout the negotiations'.

This was an important case about the prerogatives of the Commission as negotiator within the meaning of Article 218(4) TFEU. It was also about how to secure the principle of conferral of powers on the institutions and the principle of institutional balance.

On 17 March 2015, Advocate General Melchior Wathelet delivered his opinion[69] and concluded that Annex A of the Council Decision should be annulled (or, alternatively, the whole Council Decision). He pointed out that negotiating directives are meant to relate to the strategic choices and substantive objectives to be defended during the negotiations (paragraph 89). On the question whether negotiating directives may contain procedural provisions, like those contained in the contested decision, he considered that the Council cannot on the basis of Article 218(2) to (4) TFEU, unilaterally impose on the Commission a detailed procedure for the conduct of negotiations. In so doing the Council transformed itself into a true negotiator and encroached upon the Commission's powers (paragraph 87). He emphasised that Section A of the Annex to the contested decision confers on the special committee decision-making powers in the conduct of the negotiations, whereas Article 218 TFEU provides that this committee has a merely consultative role.

On the principle of institutional balance, the Advocate General examined the argument put forward by the Council and by most of the Member States intervening, according to which the raison d'être of negotiating directives (and of the special committee) was to 'avoid a politically unacceptable fait accompli, since such an outcome could jeopardise the very approval of the agreement itself' (paragraph 117). It is true that the Parliament raised a similar argument on the purpose of being fully informed about the negotiations and give an input during the latter, so that the consent of the Parliament is not put at risk. In response to this argument, Advocate General Whatelet emphasised that the power of the Council to adopt negotiating directives 'cannot be interpreted as eliminating the Commission's task of leading the negotiations and its right of initiative once the negotiations are concluded' (paragraph 119). The Council has no power to compel the Commission to make a proposal which will obtain the necessary majority within the Council (paragraph 120).

This is surely correct, but it cannot be, in my view, underestimated that full information and to a certain extent a certain involvement of the Council (and of the Parliament) during the negotiations may eventually influence the positive conclusion (or approval by the Parliament) of the agreement, without questioning the institutional autonomy of the Commission recognised in Article 218 TFEU. Indeed, the involvement of Parliament and Council during the negotiations stems

[68] Judgment of 24 June 2014, Case C-658/11, *Parliament v Council*, para 79 (EU:C:2014:2025).

[69] Opinion of AG Wathelet, delivered 17 March 2015, *Commission v Council*, EU:C:2015:174.

from the principle of sincere cooperation and can be seen as part of the procedure of negotiation. Besides, it is not disputed that the Commission has the responsibility to negotiate an agreement 'which best serves the interests of the European Union' before submitting it to the Council for concluding the agreement (with the necessary approval of the Parliament).

In this context, the Advocate General added that 'the Commission must be free to decide that it is not in the general interest of the European Union wholly to follow the opinion of the special committee, which could be dictated purely by national interests' (paragraph 182).

In its judgment of 16 July 2015,[70] the Court of Justice annulled the most controversial parts of the negotiating directives, namely the part stating that 'where appropriate, detailed negotiating positions of the Union shall be established within the special committee … or within the Council' (Annex to the Council Decision, second sentence of paragraph 1 of Section A) and the words 'and establish negotiating positions' (in paragraph 3 of Section A).

The Court held that Article 218 (4) TFEU must be interpreted as empowering the Council to set out, in the negotiating directives, procedural arrangements governing the process for the provision of information, for communication and for consultation between the special committee and the Commission, as such rules meet the objective of ensuring proper cooperation at the internal level (those parts of the Council Decision were thus upheld). However, the Court considered that the parts of the Decision empowering the special committee or the Council to adopt positions with binding effects on the Commission, as negotiator, violated Article 218(4) TFEU. First, the special committee cannot adopt detailed negotiating positions, because its role should remain consultative, as required by Article 218(4) TFEU. Secondly, this provision does not confer on the Council the power to impose 'detailed negotiating positions' on the negotiator. In doing so the Council also infringed the principle of institutional balance, as the Parliament had claimed.

In this judgment the Court clarified the demarcation of powers conferred on the Commission (which applies by analogy to the EEAS), the supervisory committee appointed by the Council and the Council. The Commission is obliged to provide to the special committee all the information necessary for it to monitor the progress on the negotiations; the Commission can also be requested to provide that information to the Council, so that the latter can have a clear knowledge of the course of the negotiations and be in a position to conclude or not the agreement at a later stage. Yet, what stems clearly from the judgment is that neither the special committee nor the Council can adopt positions which are binding on the Commission, as negotiator. The latter's autonomous role during the negotiations as promoting the general interest of the Union, in accordance with Article 17(1) TEU, is thus explicitly acknowledged by the Court. As for the Parliament, the Court did not need to consider its position in the negotiating process. It can

[70] EU:C:2015:483.

however be emphasised that, according to Article 218(10) TFEU, Parliament shall be immediately and fully informed by the Commission (or the EEAS) of the negotiations and their evolution. It is surely entitled to make known its views to the Commission about the agreement at stake, but these positions are of a political nature, and by no means legally binding, even if they can influence the subsequent decision of the Parliament to give consent or not to a specific agreement.

B. Mixed Agreements: The Decisions Taken Jointly by the Council with the Member States

The objective of more efficiency and more simplification in the EU external action, as foreseen by the Treaty of Lisbon, did not result in a reduction of mixed agreements, even though all the actors are aware that these agreements can only enter into force after having been ratified by the EU and by all the Member States, with the delays that these national ratifications imply (and the complexity of the national procedures applicable, when a referendum is required). However, even in the case of mixed agreements, one might have thought that with the number of Member States increasing, it would have been possible to entrust the Commission as representing the Union as a whole, so that the latter would speak with more visibility and efficiency with one voice on the international scene.

After the entry into force of the Lisbon Treaty, the Union competence in the field of the common commercial policy fully covers trade in services, the commercial aspects of intellectual property rights and foreign direct investment. So there is much less need for mixity, at least in legal terms.[71] In practice, there appears to be a tendency to limit the participation of the EU to what is strictly necessary, that is, the exercise of its exclusive competence or at least to leave it open to what extent the non-exclusive EU competences have actually been exercised.[72] Even if it would be desirable, with time, to reduce the number of mixed agreements in a Union of 28 Member States,[73] it is not certain that this will happen in the near future.

In reality, since 2009, the number of mixed agreements seems to have increased, and even those agreements which could be concluded as EU-only agreements are negotiated from the very beginning as mixed, sometimes through the inclusion of a chapter with limited relevance in the light of the global content of the agreement, where the Member States can justify a national competence or where this competence is shared.[74] It seems also that this strategy is in some cases launched

[71] C Timmermans, 'The Court of Justice and Mixed Agreements' in *The Court of Justice and the Construction of Europe: Analysis and Perspectives on Sixty Years of Case Law* (Berlin, Springer Verlag, 2013) 659, 672.

[72] Ibid, 661.

[73] Ibid, 672.

[74] One of the difficulties with mixed agreements is the delimitation between the EU competence and the Member States' competence. This becomes even more complex when the Member States

by national parliaments in some Member States wishing to have their say concerning agreements of considerable political importance (eg TTIP). The Council seems to follow this trend and sometimes modifies the Commission proposal with a view to creating a mixed agreement.[75]

This being said, when mixed agreements are negotiated, close cooperation must exist between the Commission, representing the EU and focusing on the EU part of the agreement, and the Member States (generally represented by the rotating Presidency, even if representatives of Member States may also be present). That obligation to cooperate flows from the requirement of unity in the international representation of the Community.[76] In order to optimise their cooperation, Member States meet within the Council, with the advantage of the latter's expertise.

In this context, in two instances such cooperation has been developed so closely that Member States and the Council decided to adopt jointly a decision opening negotiations concerning a mixed agreement, and in another instance they also took a joint decision relating to the signature of a mixed agreement. These 'hybrid' decisions are not foreseen in the Treaties. For that reason, and in order to prevent a generalisation of such a practice, the Commission brought these two decisions before the Court of Justice.

i. Case C-114/12, Concerning a Hybrid Act on the Opening of Negotiations of a Mixed Agreement

In this case, the Council and the Representatives of the Member States (meeting in the Council as representatives of their governments) took a decision on 19 December 2011 authorising the Commission to negotiate a Convention of the Council of Europe on the protection of the rights of broadcasting organisations.[77] The Commission seeks the annulment of this Decision mainly on three grounds: first, the agreement should not be mixed, because the Union has exclusive external competence in this area (on the grounds that the subject-matter of the Convention falls within the scope of existing directives), secondly, the decision violates Article 218(2) TFEU and Article 13(2) TEU since only the Council could adopt the decision, and thirdly, it violates Article 218(8) TFEU and Article 16(3) TEU

participate in a mixed agreement because their competence is shared with that of the EU and the EU competence is not of an exclusive nature, and they prefer to continue exercising their competence instead of allowing the EU to use its competence: Timmermans, 'The Court of Justice and Mixed Agreements' in *The Court of Justice and the Construction of Europe: Analysis and perspectives on Sixty Years of Case Law*, n 71 above, p 670.

[75] Trade agreement with Colombia and Peru, where initially the Commission considered that it was a pure EU agreement (COM(2011) 570 of 22.09.2001), whereas the Council eventually considered that the agreement was mixed (Decision of the Council of 31 May 2012, [2012] OJ L354/1). The Parliament had no say in the whole question, before being invited to give consent.

[76] Opinion 2/91, *Re ILO Convention No 170 on Safety in the Use of Chemicals at Work*, [1993] ECR I-1061.

[77] [2012] OJ C138/5.

because the decision should have been adopted by qualified majority and not by unanimity, which is the practical effect of merging an EU decision and an intergovernmental decision into a hybrid act.

In this regard, the Commission claims that the Council deprived the procedure in Article 218(8) TFEU of its substance, undermined the effectiveness of the decision-making process, and may possibly have affected the content of the Decision by adopting it subject to a stricter majority. The Parliament shared completely the arguments concerning the very content and equilibrium foreseen in Article 218 TFEU, and decided to intervene before the Court of Justice in support of the Commission.[78] From Parliament's perspective, by adding an intergovernmental part to the decision, the Council is enabling the Member States to determine the content of that decision by being involved in its adoption, and thus also conditioning the Commission's role as negotiator of the agreement, and weakening indirectly the margin of influence of the Parliament.

On 3 April 2014, Advocate General Sharpston issued her opinion on this case.[79] Concerning the competence to negotiate the Convention of the Council of Europe, she considered that it was not demonstrated that the EU competence is exclusive because it was not clear that the conclusion of the entire Convention 'may affect common rules or alter their scope' within the meaning of Article 3(2) TFEU. However on the other pleas, concerning in particular Article 218(2) and (8) TFEU, she fully supports the Commission (and Parliament's) arguments concerning Article 218 TFEU. She recalls that it follows from the division of external competences that the EU and the Member States must cooperate in the negotiation, conclusion and implementation of the international agreement. The fact that an international agreement is mixed does not alter the fact that only EU law can govern the EU's participation in that agreement. She stresses that Article 218(2) TFEU makes it clear that only the Council is competent to authorise the EU to negotiate, to adopt negotiating directives and to authorise the signature and the conclusion of an international agreement between the EU and third countries or international organisations. The rules governing the EU decision-making are not at the disposal of the Member States or of the institutions themselves and, in accordance with the principle of conferral in Article 13(2) TEU, the Council cannot involve the Member States in a decision-making procedure, where the Treaties provide otherwise.

Concerning the alleged violation of Article 218(8) TFEU on an obligation to vote by qualified majority within the Council, Advocate-General Sharpston also upholds the Commission (and Parliament's) arguments. She pointed out that this type of hybrid act is not comparable to an act which, due to its content, has a dual legal basis, one of which requires unanimity and the other qualified majority. The Treaties provide for a single voting rule to be applied to the Council's decision to authorise the opening of negotiations. Since the decision

[78] The Czech, German, Netherlands, Polish and United Kingdom governments intervened in support of the Council.

[79] EU:C:2014:224.

does indeed contain both an intergovernmental act and an EU act and was nevertheless adopted by a single vote, it cannot have been adopted by qualified majority, as required by Article 218(8) TFEU, but it must have been approved by unanimity.

In this regard, she takes fully into account the impact of unanimity voting in the very content of a decision. She writes:

> Of course, it is true that unanimity includes majority. However, that does not mean that unanimity makes no difference to the content of a decision. A decision on which all can agree or to which no one is opposed is not necessarily the same as a decision on which a qualified majority can agree. For example, the content of a decision which can command a qualified majority might need to be watered down in order to be approved unanimously or without any opposition (paragraph 189).

By its judgment of 4 September 2014,[80] the Court of Justice annulled the disputed Decision adopted jointly by the Council and the Member States. It considered that only the Council could have adopted the decision because the Union has exclusive external competence. The negotiations within the Council of Europe on the protection of neighbouring rights of broadcasting organisations being based on the EU *acquis* in this area, the Court considered that the Council violated Article 3(2) TFEU. For that reason, the Court did not consider necessary to examine the other pleas relating to Article 218 TFEU'.

ii. Case C-28/12 Concerning a Hybrid Act on the Signature and Provisional Application of Two Mixed Agreements

This case is different from the abovementioned Case C-425/13 in two regards: first, it does not raise the issue whether the agreement relates to the exclusive competence of the EU, and secondly, it does not relate to the opening of negotiations but to the decision on the signature and provisional application of a mixed agreement. Otherwise, the arguments advanced by the Commission on this case are comparable to those developed in the previous case.

On 16 June 2011, departing from the Commission proposal the Council and the Representatives of the Governments of the Member States of the European Union meeting within the Council adopted a decision on the signing, on behalf of the Union, and provisional application of the Air Transport Agreement between the United States of America, the EU and its Member States, Iceland and Norway, as well as the signing and provisional application of the Ancillary Agreement thereto. This ancillary Agreement on the application of the Air Transport Agreement aims at maintaining the bilateral nature of the procedure for adopting measures implementing the initial Air Transport Agreement and provides that the Commission represents the States in these procedures. It should be noted that on 2 May 2011

[80] EU:C:2014:2151.

the Commission submitted a proposal to be adopted by the Council alone. It is not disputed that the nature of these two agreements is mixed.

The Commission introduced an action before the Court of Justice seeking the annulment of this decision.[81] The Commission argues, first, that by adopting the contested decision the Council has violated Article 13(2) TEU in conjunction with Article 218(2) and (5) TFEU, in so far as it transpires from Article 218(2) and (5) TFEU that the Council is the institution designated to authorise the signing and provisional application of agreements. Therefore, the decision should have been solely taken by the Council and not jointly with the Member States, meeting within the Council. The Commission also argues that by adopting the contested decision, the Council violated Article 218(8) TFEU, pursuant to which '[t]he Council shall act by qualified majority'. The decision of the Member States, meeting within the Council, is not a decision of the Council, but an act taken by the Member States' representatives collectively as members of their governments and not in their capacity as members of the Council. Due to its nature, such an act requires unanimity. As a result, taking both decisions as one and making it subject to unanimity divests the qualified majority rule set out in the first subparagraph of Article 218(8) TFEU of its very nature.

The Parliament also decided to intervene in this case in support of the Commission, basically because, according to Article 218(2) TFEU, only the Council is competent to authorise the signature of the agreement, even when the agreement is mixed, and the Council must act within the limits of its competence under the principle of conferral (Article 13(2) TEU). In addition, as in the previous case, by adopting a decision containing both an intergovernmental act and an EU act, the Council could only decide unanimously, whereas it should have adopted its decision by qualified majority vote. The Parliament argued that this practice constituted an encroachment by the Member States on a procedure where only the three EU institutions were entitled to act, and was undermining the institutional balance required by the treaties.

In his opinion of 29 January 2015, Advocate General Mengozzi makes an important contribution on the interpretation of Article 218 TFEU, in particular concerning mixed agreements and their provisional application.[82] He pointed out that the contested decision, as a hybrid act, was an act which is not provided for by the treaties. He added that Article 218 TFEU makes no provision for the Member States, as such, to have a role in the procedure for the adoption of acts which the EU has to take in the various stages of the procedure laid down in Article 218 TFEU.

On the merging in the same decision of an EU act and an act of the competence of the Member States, he pointed out that the legal basis mentioned in the decision did not really determine the voting rule necessary for the adoption of the hybrid act. As a consequence of the merging, the qualified majority voting was divested of its

[81] Case C-28/12 *Commission v Council*, [2012] OJ C73/23.
[82] EU:C:2015:43.

substance because the Council in fact decided by common accord. He formulated his conclusion on this issue, as follows:

> I believe that to accept such a merger could … constitute a dangerous precedent of contamination of the autonomous decision-making process of the EU institutions that is liable, therefore, to cause damage to the autonomy of the EU as a specific legal system (para 80).

In its judgment of 28 April 2015 the Court (Grand Chamber) followed the Advocate General and annulled the decision adopted jointly by the Council and the Member States on the signing and provisional application of the agreement on Air Transport with the USA, as well as the decision on the Ancillary Agreement, on the ground that it violated Article 218(2), (5) and (8) TFEU, and Article 13(2) TEU.[83]

The Court noted that the disputed decision in fact merges two different acts without it being possible to discern which act reflects the will of the Council and which the will of the Member States. As a consequence, the Member States participated in the adoption of the act relating to the signature of the agreements on behalf of the EU and their provisional application by it, although such an act could only be adopted by the Council. The latter was also involved in the act concerning the provisional application of the agreements by the Member States, and had no competence to that effect, such act falling within the scope of internal law of each State, and then international law.

Besides, the Court also considered that Article 218(8) TFEU was violated because the act was adopted under a single procedure, whereby the Council should act by qualified majority, but due to the merger it acted by unanimity.

Finally, in response to the argument that the contested decision reflects the duty of cooperation in the field of mixed agreements, the Court considered that 'that principle cannot justify the Council setting itself free from compliance with the procedural rules and voting arrangements laid down in Article 218 TFEU' (para 55).

C. The Need to Involve the Parliament in the Provisional Application of the Agreements

Several questions may be raised in this context, namely: how to evaluate the EU part when a decision is taken by the Council on provisional application of a mixed agreement? How to link this question with the consent of the Parliament? Should the provisional application only start after consent has been decided by Parliament? Does the Parliament have a role on the determination of the provisions of the agreement to which provisional application applies? What procedures should be put in place with a view to enabling the Parliament to have a say before the Council decides on the provisional application?

83 EU:C:2015:282.

The purpose of provisional application is to give immediate effect to all or some of the substantive provisions of a treaty without waiting for the completion and effects of the formal requirement for entry into force contained therein. The Vienna Convention on the Law of the Treaties of 1969 foresees the possibility that an agreement (or part of it) be applied provisionally, if that is provided for in the agreement or is the will of the parties (Article 25(1)). This is justified in cases where the ratification process is expected to take some time (eg to complete the constitutional procedures for the ratification, multilateral agreements) or for other reasons (urgency or as a matter of precaution to build trust in highly sensitive agreements).[84] In the case of the Association Agreement with Ukraine, the provisional application was foreseen in view of advancing an early reform impact.[85]

In the European Union, the provisional application was often used, even before it was established in the Treaties.[86] This practice was criticised by the Parliament, with the argument that a fait accompli was placed before it and yet it was obliged to take the provisional application into account as a budgetary authority.[87] The Treaty of Amsterdam inserted a specific provision stipulating that the Council decision on the signing of an agreement may be accompanied by a decision on provisional application, but in that case 'the European Parliament shall be immediately and fully informed of any decision under this paragraph concerning the provisional application and suspension of agreements' (Article 300(2), third subparagraph). Yet only very exceptionally was the Parliament given the opportunity to respond on the provisional application in cases where consent was required.[88]

The non-involvement of Parliament was explained by the fact that the provisional application was generally used for the trade part of mixed agreements, on which Parliament had had no say before the Treaty of Lisbon.[89] Yet in some EU-only agreements (eg fisheries agreements), the provisional application had immediate budgetary consequences, which the Parliament had to accept, even

[84] United Nations, General Assembly, International Law Commission, 65th session, first report on the provisional application of treaties, prepared by Juan Manuel Gómez Robledo, Special Rapporteur, 3 June 2013, (doc A/cn.4/664).

[85] Proposal for a Council Decision of 15 May 2013, COM(2013) 289 final, p 2; this proposal was submitted before the crisis.

[86] 200 times between 1976 and 1990, see G Garzón Clariana, 'L'application provisoire des accords internationaux de la Communauté' in *30 ans d'études juridiques européennes au Collège d'Europe, Liber Professorum 1973/74-2003/04, Cahiers du Collège d'Europe* (Berlin, Peter Lang, 2005) 482. Between 2004 and 2009, the provisional application was used 80 times. Since 2009 on average one third of the agreements concluded by the EU are applied provisionally.

[87] G Garzón Clariana, ibid, p 482.

[88] See the Energy Charter Treaty in 1994, where the Commission decided to consult the Parliament on the provisional application because the Parliament would subsequently have to give its consent (see report of MT Estevan Bolea, [1994] OJ L380/1). This agreement is rather exceptional, because the decision on the conclusion was adopted by the Council and the Commission, since it related to the three Treaties (EC, ECSC and Euratom), [1998] OJ L69/1.

[89] C Flaesch-Mougin and I Bosse-Platière, 'L'application provisoire des accords internationaux' in *The European Union in the world: essays in honour of Marc Maresceau* (Leiden, Martinus Nijhoff Publishers, 2014).

without being able to express its possible reservations, and in some cases the Parliament had the power not to give consent (eg Fisheries Agreement with Morocco).

Apart from that, it is true that in the Treaty of Amsterdam the role of the European Parliament was not very important concerning the negotiation and conclusion of international agreements.[90] Its role only changed substantially with the Treaty of Lisbon, as mentioned before. As a consequence, the Parliament now has to give consent basically to all trade agreements and mixed agreements concerning a TFEU policy. Yet the Treaty of Lisbon did not extend the new powers of the Parliament to the provisional application of agreements, at least not explicitly in a specific provision.

According to Article 218(5) TFEU 'the Council, on a proposal by the negotiator, shall adopt a decision authorising the signing of the agreement and, if necessary, its provisional application before entry into force'. The crucial provision in this regard is Article 218(10) TFEU, which holds that 'the Parliament shall be immediately and fully informed at all stages of the procedure', that is to say, also concerning the provisional application.

The *effet utile* of this requirement of information is that the fait accompli shall not be put before Parliament, but that it shall be placed in a situation where it will have the opportunity to express its views about the provisional application, before the latter is decided by the Council. This is particularly important because if an agreement is already provisionally applied, the non-consent of the Parliament immediately terminates its application.[91] This happened with the SWIFT Agreement and with the Second Protocol annexed to the Fisheries Agreement with Morocco, as explained above. In both cases, the Council decided on the provisional application, without seeking the views of the Parliament in advance, and eventually the negative vote had the effect of terminating these agreements.

In these two instances, the Parliament criticised the fact that its consent was to a certain extent made more difficult because the agreements were already provisionally applied (in particular if several months have elapsed before the Parliament's consent is requested by the Council). Indeed, in some cases, the agreement in question is provisionally applied for several years. How can the Parliament then take the responsibility of rejecting the agreement years later and thus terminate its effects?[92] Even if the Parliament is surely free to reject such an agreement, the

[90] Except association agreements or agreements modifying an act adopted under the co-decision procedure or establishing an institutional framework or with notable financial implications.

[91] According to Art 25(2) of the Vienna Convention on the Law of the Treaties: 'Unless the treaty otherwise provides or the negotiating States and negotiating organizations … have otherwise agreed, the provisional application of a treaty or a part of a treaty with respect to a State or an international organization shall be terminated if that State or that organization notifies the States and organizations with regard to which the treaty is being provisionally applied of its intention not to become a party to the treaty'.

[92] For example, the Council adopted a decision on signature and provisional application of the Framework Agreement with the Republic of Korea on 10 May 2010 (Council Decision 2012/40/EU, [2013] OJ L20/1), but this Agreement was only transmitted to Parliament in order to obtain its consent on 12 February 2014. Parliament gave its consent on 16 April 2014 and the Council concluded the agreement on 12 May 2014.

impact of its vote risks frustrating considerably the legitimate expectations created by the Council, and this raises an obvious political issue.

It should be underlined that this has a very negative impact on the stability of international relations and on the legitimate expectations of the third countries and private companies and citizens benefiting from the envisaged agreement.[93] This kind of disruption should be avoided by any means and the principle of mutual sincere cooperation among institutions (Article 13(2) TEU) should apply fully.

Another criticism is about the scope of the provisional application concerning mixed agreements. This application concerns only the part of the agreement falling within the EU competence, and the decision establishing the provisions of the agreement which can (or cannot) be applied provisionally raises political and legal issues because the boundary between EU and Member States jurisdiction is often a complex task, and can end up by creating legal uncertainty for the parties of the agreement and persons or economic operators. Some examples demonstrate these difficulties.[94] The first refers to the use of a general and rather imprecise clause, reading as follows: '*the agreement shall be applied provisionally only in so far as it concerns matters falling within the Union competence*', without specifying which are those matters.[95] In other instances, the agreement itself empowers the Union to indicate the parts of the agreement which will be applied provisionally, and the decision on the signature and provisional application indicates these parts and provisions.[96] The decision concerning the Association Agreement with Chile indicates the articles which will be applied provisionally. By contrast, the decision on the Trade Agreement with Colombia and Peru and the Free Trade Agreement with Korea indicate the provisions which shall not be applied provisionally.[97] This may result in some difficulties of interpretation, or more importantly, in some inconsistencies: for example, in some cases the 'human rights clauses'—dear to the Parliament—are applied provisionally (eg Partnership and cooperation Agreement with Iraq, Trade Agreement with Peru and Colombia), whereas in other agreements they are not (Association Agreement with Central America).[98] This obviously has a political impact on the EU relationship with these

[93] Especially taking into account the fact that, under international law, the Union has to respect its obligations resulting from an agreement provisionally applied (O Dörr and K Schmalenbach, *Vienna Convention on the Law of the Treaties, A commentary* (Berlin, Springer Verlag, 2012) 420; also G Garzón Clariana, n 86 above, p 482).

[94] This problem does not exist in EU-only agreements, because for them the provisional application relates to the whole agreement (eg the protocol annexed to the Morocco Fisheries Agreement or the provisional application of an EU agreement with several third States concerning the points system applicable to heavy goods vehicles travelling through Austria during a certain period of time, [2004] OJ L169/13).

[95] Art 117 of the Partnership and Cooperation Agreement with Iraq, Council Decision of 21 December 2011, [2012] OJ L204/18; ibid with the agreement of Economic Partnership Agreement with CARIFORUM, Article 4 of the Council Decision, [2008] OJ L289/1.

[96] Art 486(4) of the Association Agreement between the European Union and its Member States, of the one part, and Ukraine, of the other part, [2014] OJ L161/3–2137.

[97] [2012] OJ L354/1 and [2011] OJ L127/1, respectively.

[98] Council Decision of 25 June 2012, [2012] OJ L346/1.

countries because in case of violation of these clauses, the suspension of the agreement can be decided, and yet the Parliament is just not aware of the reasons for this divergence of approach.[99]

A proper involvement of the Parliament is therefore indispensable. Now that its consent is generalised, the provisional application should be considered as closely linked with the very scope of the consent. The Court acknowledged the enhanced role of the Parliament in the Mauritius Judgment (which will be developed below in this chapter), when it held that the Parliament is entitled to exercise its right of scrutiny and to make known its views in the phase preceding the conclusion of an agreement. This is exactly the case with provisional application. In its relations with the Commission, according to the existing Framework Agreement between the two institutions, the latter 'shall inform Parliament as early as possible when it intends to propose its provisional application to the Council and the reasons therefor, unless reasons of urgency preclude it from doing so' (Annex 3, point 7). What matters is that the Parliament is not only informed, but that it is given the opportunity to issue its views in a timely manner on the provisional application of an agreement, before the Council takes its decision. This is particularly meaningful when a choice is made on the parts of the agreement which are to be applied provisionally in mixed agreements (see the complex problems on the provisional application of the Ukraine Association Agreement).

In order to achieve this goal, cooperation is needed between the three institutions on the implementation of Article 218(5) TFEU. Two possibilities may be advanced for involvement of the Parliament:

(a) One possibility would be that the Commission presents two separate proposals to the Council: one on the signature of the agreement and another proposal for a Council decision on the provisional application, after having taken into account the position of the Parliament on this proposal. It is true that Article 218(5) TFEU may be interpreted as if the signature and provisional application were part of the same decision, but it can be argued that proceeding in two phases does not go against this provision. This procedure would have the advantage of involving the Parliament, at an early stage, in the decision applying an agreement provisionally. Indeed, if the Parliament adopts a resolution—on the basis of the proposal on the signature transmitted to it by the Commission, in accordance with Article 218(10) TFEU—stating that it may decline its consent, the Commission should in that case rather prefer not to propose the provisional application to the Council. It is understood that the Council can only decide on the provisional application if the Commission makes such a proposal, even though the Council may modify it.

(b) Another possibility is that the Commission submits at the same time to the Council two proposals: one concerning the signature and provisional

[99] C Flaesch-Mougin and I Bosse-Platière, 'L'application provisoire des accords internationaux', n 89 above.

application and a second one concerning the conclusion of the agreement. The first proposal does not indicate the exact date when the agreement would start being applied provisionally, with a view to enabling the Parliament to express its position on the question whether or not the agreement would be applied provisionally. The first proposal could mention that the notification indicating the date of the beginning of the provisional application will be transmitted to the third country subsequently. It could be agreed that this notification will be transmitted at a certain date or after the Parliament has given its consent. This procedure has the advantage of not starting the provisional application if the Parliament withholds consent. It has the inconvenience that the Parliament is not in a position to express its views on the very question of the provisional application and its scope, but only on the consent to the agreement.

This latter procedure has been applied already. For example concerning the Association Agreement with Ukraine, the Commission made the following suggestion in its proposal of 15 May 2013 on the signing and provisional application of the Agreement:

> with a view to taking into account the enhanced role of the European Parliament, the Commission considers that the Council should send the notification referred to in Article 486(4) of the Agreement[100] only after a certain lapse of time so as to allow the European Parliament to express its views.[101]

However, on 17 March and 23 June 2014, the Council adopted its decisions on the signing and provisional application modifying the scope of the latter and it did not make any reference to the Commission's suggestion.[102] In this particular case, where the Council changed substantially the provisions of the agreement to be applied provisionally, Parliament was merely informed. It eventually supported the provisional application, basically on political grounds.[103]

In the Free Trade Agreement with Korea,[104] in the Multipartite Trade Agreement with Colombia and Peru[105] and in the Association Agreement with

[100] Article 486(4) of the Association Agreement with Ukraine reads as follows: 'The provisional application shall be effective from the first day of the second month following the date of receipt by the Depositary of the following:—the Union's notification on the completion of the procedures necessary for this purpose, indicating the parts of the Agreement that shall be provisionally applied; and—Ukraine's deposit of the instrument of ratification in accordance with its procedures and applicable legislation'.

[101] Proposal for a Council Decision of 15.05.2013, COM(2013) 289 final, p 6.

[102] Council Decision of 15 March 2014, 2013/0155(NLE).

[103] European Parliament resolution of 17 July 2014 on Ukraine, para 1, P8_TA-PROV(2014)0009.

[104] Council Decision of 16 September 2010, doc 2011/265/UE ([2011] OJ L127/1). In its proposal for the signature and provisional application, the Commission used the same language as in the Association Agreement with Ukraine (COM(2010) 136 final). The Council adopted its decision on 16 September 2010 and the Parliament gave its consent on 17 February 2011 (P7_TA(2011)0063). The notification to Korea was only transmitted on 1 July 2011 ([2011] OJ L168/1), after Parliament's consent.

[105] The two Commission proposals (COM(2011) 570 final and COM(2011) 569 final) were submitted on 22 September 2011, the Council decided on 31 May 2012 ([2012] OJ L354/1), the

Central America,[106] the Council notified the third countries in question starting the provisional application only after the consent had been given by the Parliament.[107] However, in the Partnership and Cooperation Agreement with Iraq, the Council made the notification for the provisional application of the agreement with effect from 1 August 2012, before the Parliament gave its consent. In this case, moreover, the provisional application implies the establishment of an institutional framework (Cooperation Council and a Cooperation Committee).[108]

Both procedures indicated in (a) and (b) are legally possible but the first—which has not yet been used—offers better involvement of the Parliament in the decision-making process relating to the provisional application.

In this context, it is worth mentioning that concerning trade agreements, the Commissioner responsible, Cecilia Malmström, made a clear commitment to the Parliament during the hearing as Commissioner-designate in Summer of 2014. She gave the following written answer on this matter:

> I am ready, when proposing decisions to sign politically important trade agreements which fall under my responsibility, to ask Council to delay provisional application until the European Parliament has given its consent. However, we need certain flexibility in applying such a practice as there will always be occasions where the urgency of a particular file, or its technical character, mean that it is unwarranted to delay its application pending EP's consent.[109]

She reassured again the INTA MEPs on her commitment in a recent "structural dialogue" of 21 April 2016 (which is taken place on a periodical and regular basis).

D. The Choice of the Legal Basis Covering at the Same Time TFEU Policies and CFSP

The Court of Justice applies its well-established case law on the choice of the legal basis to agreements concerning at the same time TFEU and CFSP policies. According to this case law:

> [T]he choice of the legal basis for an EU measure must rest on objective factors amenable to judicial review, which include the aim and content of that measure. If examination of a measure reveals that it pursues two aims or that it has two components, and if one of

Parliament gave its consent on 11 December 2012 (P7_TA-PROV(2012)0481). According to Art 3(2) of the Council's Decision, 'In order to determine the date of the provisional application of the agreement, the Council shall fix the date by which the notification referred to in Article 330(3) thereof is to be sent to Colombia and Peru'. This notification was transmitted after the consent of the Parliament.

[106] Council Decision of 21 December 2011, doc 2012/418/UE ([2012] OJ L204/18).

[107] In these two agreements Parliament and Council had to adopt under the ordinary legislative procedure regulations aiming at implementing the safeguard clauses contained in the agreements.

[108] See C Flaesch-Mougin and I Bosse-Platière, 'L'application provisoire des accords internationaux', in *The European Union in the world: essays in honour of Marc Maresceau*, n 89 above, p 16.

[109] http://www.europarl.europa.eu/meetdocs/2014_2019/documents/inta/dv/malmstrom_/malmstrom_en.pdf

> those aims or components is identifiable as the main one, whereas the other is merely incidental, the measure must be founded on a single legal basis, namely that required by the main or predominant aim or component.[110]

It is thus necessary to identify if there is a main aim or component. If this relates to the CFSP, then the single legal basis relating to CFSP shall be used.

The attempt by Parliament to use a stricter test for the interpretation of the word 'exclusively' was not successful. Article 218(5) TFEU states that except where agreements relate exclusively to CFSP, Parliament has to give consent or be consulted. The word 'exclusively' seems, at least when taken literally, stricter than the word 'principal' or 'main'. Yet, the Court has considered that the word 'exclusively' within the meaning of Article 218(6) TFEU does not, itself, permit one interpretation of that provision.[111] It recalls that 'symmetry' has to be observed

> between the procedure for adopting EU measures internally and the procedure for adopting international agreements in order to guarantee that the Parliament and the Council enjoy the same powers in relation to a given field, in compliance with the institutional balance provided for by the Treaties.[112]

In the *Mauritius case*, the Court thus decided that the Council Decision could be based on Article 37 TEU alone. This case law implies that an agreement relating principally to CFSP, but with a part relating to TFEU, can be founded on Article 37 TEU alone, that is to say, without any involvement of the European Parliament in its conclusion.[113]

By the same token, agreements that relate mainly to TFEU policies, but also incidentally to CFSP policies, should be based on TFEU legal basis only.[114]

For this reason, it is questionable that the Council has decided to use the CFSP legal basis (Articles 31(1) and 37 TEU) in its decisions on the signing and provisional application of the Association Agreements with Ukraine, Moldova and Georgia, which should be based on Article 217 TFEU alone. The Court's ruling in the *Philippines case* reinforces this assertion.[115] In this case, the Court held that the concept of development cooperation within the meaning of Article 209 TFEU encompasses a wide range of specific areas and that there was no need to add other legal bases relating to the re-admission of nationals, transport and environment.

[110] European Court of Justice, Judgment of 24 June 2014, *Parliament v Council* in Case C-658/11, *Parliament v Council*, EU:C:2014:2025, para 41.

[111] Ibid, para 49.

[112] Ibid, para 56.

[113] Since 1 December 2009, the Council has adopted 30 agreements based on Art 37 TEU. They concern: the status of mission agreements with third States that host CSDP missions (five agreements), framework agreements on the participation of third States in the CSDP (eleven agreements), exchange of classified information (four agreements) and transfer of suspected pirates (two agreements).

[114] There are quite a few examples: Stabilisation and Association Agreement with Montenegro, Stabilisation and Association Agreement with Serbia, Partnership and Cooperation Agreement with Iraq and Association Agreement with Central America. They all contain provisions relating to CFSP, which are considered incidental.

[115] Judgment of 11 June 2014 in Case C-377/12, *Commission v Council* (EU:C:2014:1903).

If this is the case for Article 209 TFEU, it is even more so in relation to Article 217 TFEU, concerning association agreements, because this provision 'necessarily empowers the Union to guarantee commitments towards non-member countries in all the fields covered by the Treaties'.[116]

E. The Scope of the Obligation to Inform the Parliament (Article 218(10) TFEU)

According to Article 218(10) TFEU 'The Parliament shall be immediately and fully informed at all stages of the procedures'.

Since the entry into force of the Treaty of Lisbon, Parliament has insisted that the right to be immediately and fully informed surely implies that the Parliament should not remain passive, waiting to be informed by the Commission or the Council, but rather that it implies also the right to express its views on the matters, after being informed.

In other words, Parliament is entitled to be informed about the opening of negotiations, the draft and the negotiating directives, the texts under discussion during the negotiations, the draft and the decision on the signature, the draft and the decision on the provisional application, the draft and the decision on the conclusion and the draft and the decision on the suspension of an international agreement. For each of 'these stages of the procedure', the Parliament is entitled to express its views, which may have consequences on the very position eventually adopted by the Commission or the Council.

This is what the Court acknowledged in the *Mauritius case*, which related to CFSP. The Court said first of all that:

> If the Parliament is not immediately and fully informed at all stages of the procedure in accordance with Article 218(10) TFEU, including that preceding the conclusion of the agreement, it is not in a position to exercise the right of scrutiny which the Treaties have conferred on it in relation to the CFSP or, where appropriate, to make known its views as regards, in particular, the correct legal basis for the act concerned. The infringement of that information requirement impinges, in those circumstances, on the Parliament's performance of its duties in relation to the CFSP, and therefore constitutes an infringement of an essential procedural requirement.[117]

On this latter aspect, the Court underlined that the infringement of an essential procedural requirement leads to nullity of the measure thereby vitiated. It recalled, in this context, that the involvement of the Parliament is an expression of the democratic principle on which the EU is founded, that the people should participate in the exercise of power through the intermediary of a representative assembly (paragraph 81).

[116] Case 12/86 *Demirel v Stadt Schwäbisch Gmünd* [1987] ECR 3719, para 9; see also the conclusions of Advocate General Kokott in Case C-431/11, *United Kingdom v Council*, para 57.

[117] Ibid, para 86.

This judgment acknowledges the enhancement of the role of the Parliament in the shaping of the EU external action, which is established in the Treaty of Lisbon without prejudice to the powers and autonomy of the Commission as negotiator, as was recognised by the Court of justice in the above-mentioned case C-425/13. If this is true for CFSP matters, it is a fortiori true for the agreements relating to TFEU policies, on which in general Parliament has the right of consent. The consequence is thus that EU external action will be more democratic, more transparent and more open to public scrutiny.

Advocate General Kokott developed further the scope of Article 218(10) TFEU in her conclusions concerning a similar agreement between the EU and Tanzania (Case C-263/14).[118] She underlined that the transparency created by informing the Parliament immediately and fully at all stages of the procedure is in itself an element of democratic control which has an inherent value. This transparency also ensures that the elected representatives of the citizens of the EU have an opportunity, in full knowledge of the facts, to have a public debate on foreign policy matters (the agreement with Tanzania is based on CFSP legal basis) and to scrutinise the entire procedure for the conclusion of an international agreement critically. She emphasised that "*in this way they can also endeavour, entirely legitimately, to influence the content of the planned agreement, even if from a formal perspective the agreement can be concluded without their consent or consultation*".[119]

In its judgment of 14 June 2016, the Court has not only confirmed Advocate General's approach, but even developed further the role of the Parliament in the EU's external action.

The Court reiterated that the purpose of the requirement to inform the Parliament fully and immediately is to allow the Parliament not only to check the appropriate legal basis for measures adopted (in the present case, as part of the CFSP), but 'to exercise its own powers with full knowledge of the EU's external action as a whole' (paragraph 71). In this context, the Court added that in this way Parliament can play its role in contributing to ensure the coherence and consistency between the different areas of the EU's external action, in accordance with Article 21(3) TEU.

With respect to the scope of the information obligation covered by Article 218(10) TFEU, the Court made clear that this 'includes, inter alia, the authorisation to open negotiations, the definition of the negotiating directives, the nomination of the Union negotiator and, in some cases, the designation of a special committee, the completion of negotiations, the authorisation to sign the agreement, where necessary, the decision on the provisional application of the agreement before its entry into force and the conclusion of the agreement'.

The Court underlined further that the requirement to inform the Parliament extends also to the 'intermediate results reached by the negotiations' (paragraph 77).

[118] C-263/14, *European Parliament v Council*, EU:C:2015:729.
[119] Ibid, para 79.

It goes without saying that this involvement or input of Parliament during the negotiations in the shaping of the planned agreement is surely more important where Parliament has right of consent, as we mentioned already.

It is now for the institutions to agree on the modalities to implement Article 218(10) TFEU, as interpreted by the Court.

Also, as far as the EEAS is concerned, the VPHR, Ms Mogherini, is currently negotiating with the Chairman of the AFET Committee, Mr Brok, about the modalities to implement fully the Court's judgment.

In the context of the election of the Commission, Parliament usually revises the framework agreement on relations between the two institutions. The last Framework Agreement was adopted in 2010.[120] This time, it is not foreseen to modify it. Instead, the three institutions have adopted an Interinstitutional agreement (IIA) on Better Law-making, in accordance with Article 295 TFEU, replacing a previous agreement of 16 December 2003.[121] This agreement was signed by the three institutions on 13 April 2016.

It refers primarily to the improvement of the legislative making process, in particular relating to the following elements: programming, impact assessment, public consultation, ex-post evaluation, legislative instruments, delegated and implementing acts, transparency of the legislative process and implementation and application of EU legislation and simplification.[122]

Concerning international agreements, the IIA states that:

> The three institutions acknowledge the importance of ensuring that each Instittuion can exercise its rights and fulfil its obligations enshrined in the Treaties as interpreted by the Court of Justice of the European Union regarding the negotiation and conclusion of international agreements.
>
> The three institutions commit to meet within six months after the entry into force of this Agreement in order to negotiate improved practical arrangements for ccoperation and information-sharing within the framework of the Treaties, as interpreted by the Court of Justice of the European Union.[123]

This would offer an opportunity to establish or re-examine provisions concerning the implementation of Article 218 TFEU. Some issues need particular attention, such as:

- the modalities for informing the Parliament immediately and fully about the opening of negotiations, giving it a chance to express its views before the latter is decided;
- the provisional application of the agreement, where the role of the Parliament has not been so far fully taken into account;

[120] [2010] OJ L304/47.
[121] OJ C 321, 31.12.2003, p.1.
[122] http://data.consilium.europa.eu/doc/document/ST-15506-2015-INIT/en/pdf
[123] Ibidem, para 40.

— the transmission of information relating to the negotiation of the agreements. This information needs to be comprehensive, and the fact that it is allegedly 'confidential' should not have a negative impact on the exercise of the right of the Parliament to be informed; Parliament should always be in a position to, in full knowledge of the facts, influence the very content of the planned agreement;
— the implementation of the agreement, in particular concerning the clauses on which the Parliament has put more weight;
— on the basis of the information provided on the implementation of the agreements, the involvement of the Parliament on their possible suspension.

It goes without saying that this applies to the Commission (or the High Representative) and to the Council. An inter-institutional agreement also exists between the Parliament and the Council concerning classified information held by the Council on matters other than those in the area of CFSP.[124] This agreement may also need to be revisited. Finally, an agreement should be negotiated with the Council concerning the transmission of information relating to CFSP matters. The Judgments of the Court in the *Mauritius* case and in the Tanzania case shed new light and makes this negotiation timelier.

[124] See n 19 above.

3

The Court of Justice and External Competences After Lisbon: Some Reflections on the Latest Case Law

FERNANDO CASTILLO DE LA TORRE[1]

To Gregorio. The best of us

Content:

[1] Legal Adviser, Legal Service, European Commission. The author has represented the Commission in some of the cases analyzed in this chapter. The present chapter however reflects exclusively the personal opinions of the author and not those of the European Commission or its Legal Service.

I. INTRODUCTION

ONE OF THE objectives of the Treaty of Lisbon was to streamline the external relations area in order to be able to 'speak with one voice'. The post of High Representative was created for CFSP. Competences and rules on external representation were also clarified. The external policy is much more visible in the revised Treaties. Consistency was meant to be ensured by bringing together the various aspects of the external action of the EU, with a number of common provisions. The issue had become important in the area of external relations, where Member States were keen on preserving (or at least pretending to preserve) a space for national decision-making.

The objective was not fully achieved. Certainly some legal concepts were made more explicit, and the legal consequences of certain categories of competences were made clear. Yet, speaking with one voice is in practice the case mainly in areas where the EU is considered to have exclusive competences. Outside them a cacophony remains where Member States, for reasons of national prestige, rarely give up their alleged right to speak and vote. In the definition of competences some ambiguities remained and, partly as a consequence of the Euro-scepticism that was becoming prevalent among certain governments, the practice in the implementation of the new Treaties has not lived up to the expectations.

Inter-institutional disputes have become more frequent than ever, and issues which could have remained largely uncontested a decade ago are now controversial, giving the impression that some Member States took the opportunity of the Treaty of Lisbon to take a step back in the European integration, and not the opposite. Some of these disputes have, quite logically, reached the Court of Justice, which has delivered over the last few years a number of important judgments. This chapter will provide some reflections on these recent judgments, trying to make sense of them in the current context and considering its implications for the practice of mixity in the conclusion of international agreements. These reflections will not be exhaustive, as some significant issues relating to external competences will not be covered.

The general provisions on competences of the Treaty of Lisbon apply also to external relations. One should distinguish between exclusive, shared, parallel and supporting competences, and the type of competence will determine whether it is the Union alone, or the Union with Member States that will negotiate and conclude the international agreement in question. It is important to briefly recall the provisions at issue, as the Treaty of Lisbon has slightly amended them. Article 2(1) TFEU provides that

> [w]hen the Treaties confer on the Union exclusive competence in a specific area, only the Union may legislate and adopt legally binding acts, the Member States being able to do so themselves only if so empowered by the Union or for the implementation of Union acts.

Article 2(2) TFEU provides that

> [w]hen the Treaties confer on the Union a competence shared with the Member States in a specific area, the Union and the Member States may legislate and adopt legally binding

> acts in that area. The Member States shall exercise their competence to the extent that the Union has not exercised its competence. The Member States shall again exercise their competence to the extent that the Union has decided to cease exercising its competence.

Protocol No 25, on the exercise of shared competence, contains a sole article:

> With reference to Article 2(2) [TFEU] on shared competence, when the Union has taken action in a certain area, the scope of this exercise of competence only covers those elements governed by the Union act in question and therefore does not cover the whole area.

Article 3(1) TFEU defines several areas as being within the exclusive competence of the Union. Amongst them the 'common commercial policy' is mentioned. Article 3(2) TFEU, which defines the areas of the Union's exclusive competence on top of those mentioned in the first paragraph, provides that:

> The Union shall also have exclusive competence for the conclusion of an international agreement when its conclusion is provided for in a legislative act of the Union or is necessary to enable the Union to exercise its internal competence, or in so far as its conclusion may affect common rules or alter their scope.

Pursuant to Article 216(1) TFEU:

> The Union may conclude an agreement with one or more third countries or international organisations where the Treaties so provide or where the conclusion of an agreement is necessary in order to achieve, within the framework of the Union's policies, one of the objectives referred to in the Treaties, or is provided for in a legally binding Union act or is likely to affect common rules or alter their scope.

II. THE *RENAISSANCE* OF COMMON COMMERCIAL POLICY

Before examining the recent case law on the nature and scope of implied competences under Article 3(2) TFEU, it is worth examining briefly the most recent case law on commercial policy, which is covered by Article 3(1) TFEU. It is by relying on explicitly exclusive policies that mixity is avoided in certain cases. Two recent judgments have rejected a narrow view of common commercial policy.

A. *Daiichi*

In *Daiichi*, the referring court asked essentially whether Article 27 of the TRIPs Agreement fell within a field for which the Member States have primary competence and, if so, whether the national courts may accord that provision direct effect subject to the conditions laid down by national law.[2] The Court noted that Article 207(1) TFEU, which entered into force on 1 December 2009, differs noticeably

[2] Case C-414/11, *Daiichi Sankyo Co Ltd and Another v DEMO Anonymos Viomichaniki kai Emporiki Etairia Farmakon*, EU:C:2013:520.

from the provisions it essentially replaced, in particular those in Article 133(1), (5), first subparagraph, (6), second subparagraph, and (7) EC. It differs even more from the provision that was in force when the TRIPs Agreement was concluded, namely Article 113 of the EC Treaty (subsequently, after amendment, Article 133 EC).[3] It considered that, in view of that significant development of primary law, the question of the distribution of the competences of the EU and the Member States had to be examined on the basis of the Treaty now in force.[4]

Interpreting the expression 'the commercial aspects of intellectual property', it recalled that the mere fact that an act of the EU, such as an agreement concluded by it, is liable to have implications for international trade is not enough for it to be concluded that the act must be classified as falling within the common commercial policy. An EU act falls within the common commercial policy if it relates specifically to international trade in that it is essentially intended to promote, facilitate or govern trade and has direct and immediate effects on trade. Of the rules adopted by the EU in the field of intellectual property, only those with a specific link to international trade are capable of falling within the concept of 'commercial aspects of intellectual property' in Article 207(1) TFEU and hence the field of the common commercial policy.[5]

For the Court such was the case with the rules in the TRIPs Agreement. Although those rules do not relate to the details, as regards customs or otherwise, of operations of international trade as such, they have a specific link with international trade. The TRIPs Agreement is an integral part of the WTO system and is one of the principal multilateral agreements on which that system is based. The specific character of the link with international trade is illustrated in particular by the fact that the Understanding on Rules and Procedures governing the settlement of disputes—which forms Annex 2 to the WTO Agreement and applies to the TRIPs Agreement—authorises under Article 22(3) the cross-suspension of concessions between that agreement and the other principal multilateral agreements of which the WTO Agreement consists. Moreover, the Court of Justice considered that the authors of the TFEU could not have been unaware that the terms thus used in Article 207(1) TFEU correspond almost exactly to the very title of the TRIPs Agreement.

The Court of Justice admitted that it remained altogether open to the EU, after the entry into force of the TFEU, to legislate on the subject of intellectual property rights by virtue of competence relating to the field of the internal market. However, acts adopted on that basis and intended to have validity specifically for the EU will have to comply with the rules concerning the availability, scope and use of intellectual property rights in the TRIPs Agreement, as those rules are still, as previously, intended to standardise certain rules on the subject at world level and thereby to facilitate international trade. Consequently, to regard the rules on

[3] Ibid paras 46–47.

[4] Ibid para 48.

[5] Ibid paras 51–52.

patentable subject-matter in Article 27 of the TRIPs Agreement as falling within the field of the common commercial policy rather than the field of the internal market correctly reflects the fact that the context of those rules is the liberalisation of international trade, not the harmonisation of the laws of the Member States of the EU.[6]

B. The *Conditional Access Services* Judgment

The second big step was the judgment in the *Conditional Access Services* case.[7] This was also the first direct dispute on the scope of Article 3(2) TFEU, but the Commission's primary position, finally upheld by the Court, was that the agreement fell in the commercial policy area, and was therefore already covered by Article 3(1) TFEU. The Court of Justice followed that approach and the interpretation of Article 3(2) TFEU was not finally examined.

The case concerned the legality of Council Decision 2011/853/EU of 29 November 2011 on the signing, on behalf of the Union, of the European Convention on the legal protection of services based on, or consisting of, conditional access.[8] Well before then, the European Parliament and the Council had adopted Directive 98/84/EC on the legal protection of services based on, or consisting of, conditional access.[9] The Commission, supported by the Parliament, submitted in essence that, in the light of the aim and content of the Convention, the contested decision came primarily under the common commercial policy and only incidentally under the internal market policy. By contrast, the Council and the Member States intervening in support of it contended that the Convention—in view of both its aim and its content—and, by extension, the contested decision were essentially linked to the internal market policy and only incidentally linked to the common commercial policy.

The Court of Justice agreed with the Commission. The Convention established a regulatory framework which is almost identical to that provided for in Directive 98/84. The Explanatory Report on the Convention stated that the aim of the Convention was to ensure a similar minimum level of protection for the services concerned across Europe and thus to provide a valuable complement to Directive 98/84. According to the Explanatory Report and the explanatory memorandum accompanying the proposal for a decision, it was necessary, by means of the Convention, to extend beyond the European Union the legal protection introduced by Directive 98/84, because many European non-member countries may be bases for the manufacture, marketing and distribution, by a parallel 'industry', of devices

[6] Ibid paras 58–60.

[7] Case C-137/12, *Commission v Council*, judgment of 22 October 2013, EU:C:2013:675.

[8] Council Decision 2011/853/EU of 29 November 2011 on the signing, on behalf of the Union, of the European Convention on the legal protection of services based on, or consisting of, conditional access ([2011] OJ L336/1).

[9] [1998] OJ L320/54

which make it possible to gain unauthorised access to conditional access services, since legal protection in those countries against such acts of piracy is either ineffective or non-existent. In that context, the signing of the Convention on behalf of the EU was undertaken with a view to encouraging broader ratification of the Convention by Member States of the Council of Europe. While Directive 98/84 is intended to ensure adequate legal protection at EU level for the services concerned in order to promote trade in those services within the internal market, the contested decision was intended to introduce similar protection in European non-member countries, in order to promote the supply of such services to those States by EU service providers. That objective, which can be seen from the recitals to the contested decision, read in conjunction with the Convention, was considered to be the primary objective of that decision, and therefore has a specific connection with international trade in those services, by dint of which it can legitimately be linked to the common commercial policy.

The Court of Justice rejected several counter-arguments. First, the aim of approximating the legislation of the contracting parties, referred to in the second sentence of Article 1 of the Convention, is irrelevant. It follows from Article 11(4) of the Convention that, in their mutual relations, the Member States of the EU are to apply EU rules and are not therefore to apply the rules established by the Convention except where there is no EU rule governing the particular subject area concerned. Article 11(4) of the Convention confirms that, since the approximation of the legislation of Member States in the field concerned has already been largely achieved by Directive 98/84, the primary objective of the Convention is not to improve the functioning of the internal market, but to extend legal protection of the relevant services beyond the territory of the EU. The reference made in the Convention to approximation of the legislation of the contracting parties is a reference to *a means of achieving* the objectives of the Convention, rather than to one of its actual aims.

Secondly, it considered that the aim of prohibiting the export of illicit devices to the EU Union from European non-member countries in order to ensure the proper functioning of the internal market is not capable of calling into question the existence of a specific link between the contested decision and the common commercial policy. By contrast, a ban on the export of illicit devices to the EU concerns the defence of the EU's global interests and falls, by its very nature, within the ambit of the common commercial policy.[10]

Thirdly, as regards the argument that, unlike Directive 98/84, the Convention includes certain provisions—Articles 6 and 8—which relate to seizure and confiscation measures and to international cooperation between the contracting parties, the Court noted that those provisions are intended generally to ensure effective legal protection for conditional access services throughout the territories of those parties. Accordingly, they help to achieve the primary objective of

[10] Case C-137/12, *Commission v Council*, judgment of 13 July 2013, EU:C:2013:675, paras 68–69.

the contested decision, read in conjunction with the Convention. If Articles 6 and 8 of the Convention are also supposed to improve the conditions for the functioning of the internal market by clarifying the definition of the sanctions provided for under Article 5 of Directive 98/84, that objective is purely incidental to the primary objective of the contested decision.[11] The supposedly criminal-law nature of the seizure and confiscation measures provided for under the Convention was also considered to be immaterial, since quite apart from the fact that the Convention provisions do not require the sanctions and measures referred to therein to be exclusively of a criminal-law nature, that argument does not explain why Article 114 TFEU would be the correct legal basis in the circumstances.

Finally, the Court also rejected the argument made at the hearing to the effect that Protocol No 21 on the position of the United Kingdom and Ireland in respect of the area of freedom, security and justice and Protocol No 22 on the position of Denmark, which are annexed to the TEU and the TFEU, had an influence on the choice of legal basis. The Court recalled that it is the legal basis for a measure which determines the protocols to be applied, and not vice versa.

C. Conclusions and Prospects

This case law, especially the *Daiichi* judgment, is sometimes dismissed by some Member States as concerning only the WTO area. This is obviously incorrect. First, the judgment in *Regione autonoma Friuli-Venezia Giulia and Agenzia regionale per lo sviluppo rurale (ERSA)*,[12] is relevant in this context. It was examined whether Article 133, the predecessor of Article 207 TFEU, could be the legal basis of an EC–Hungary Agreement on wines. The question was specifically asked 'in view of the fact that that agreement contains rules governing the protection of geographical names which have intellectual and commercial property significance'.[13] The Court found that the principal objective of such agreements was to promote trade between the Contracting Parties by facilitating on a reciprocal basis, on the one hand, the marketing of wines originating in the third countries concerned by guaranteeing those wines the same protection as that provided for in respect of quality wines of Community origin and, on the other, the marketing in those third countries of wines originating in the Community. The guarantee of reciprocal protection for certain geographical indications was an 'instrument directly affecting trade in wines'. This shows that the protection of intellectual property may be covered by the common commercial policy even if the agreement is not concluded within the framework of WTO.

[11] Ibid paras 70–71.

[12] Judgment in Case C-347/03, *Regione autonoma Friuli-Venezia Giulia and Agenzia regionale per lo sviluppo rurale (ERSA) v Ministero delle Politiche Agricole e Forestali*, judgment of 12 May 2005, EU:C:2005:285, paras 71–83.

[13] Ibid para 71.

For example, the signature of the Marrakesh Treaty, administered by WIPO, is based on both Article 207 and 114 TFEU.[14] WIPO and TRIPs are not two worlds apart. Some international treaties administered by WIPO (or provisions thereof) are to be complied with as a result of provisions included in the TRIPS Agreement, and they are, therefore, applicable as part of the Union common commercial policy.[15] The Court of Justice has ruled that the primary objective of the TRIPs Agreement is 'to strengthen and harmonise the protection of intellectual property on a worldwide scale'.[16]

Secondly, the *Conditional Access Services* case confirms that trade in services is covered by Article 207 TFEU even if the international agreement is not concluded in the framework of WTO. The primary objective of the Convention being the supply of services to and from non-EU countries, the reference to the approximation of the contracting parties' legislation appeared to be a mere reference to a means of achieving that objective, rather than an objective as such. In the same vein, Article 207 TFEU also covers the setting of international standards in the field of intellectual property where it appears to be a mere means of achieving the objective of the liberalisation of international trade, rather than an objective as such.

One could argue that the acid test for examining whether Article 207 applies, instead of Article 114 TFEU, can often consist in examining how important it is that third parties ratify the international treaty. Article 114 TFEU concerns harmonisation within the EU. In the context of an international agreement which pursues the objective of harmonising the laws and regulations of Member States it is of very limited relevance whether third countries ratify the agreement or not. The 'harmonising effect' is achieved by the ratification by the EU as such. Whether there are five or 50 contracting parties to an international treaty is not really relevant when the objective of its conclusion is 'internal'. If, by contrast, for the conclusion by the EU to achieve its purpose it is also important that the Treaty is ratified by as many parties as possible, this is a strong indication that the trade element is dominant.[17] This is very clearly formulated by the Court of Justice in the *Conditional Access Services* judgment, where it considered that the aim of the

[14] Council Decision 2014/221/EU of 14 April 2014 on the signing, on behalf of the European Union, of the Marrakesh Treaty to Facilitate Access to Published Works for Persons who are Blind, Visually Impaired, or otherwise Print Disabled ([2014] OJ L115/1).

[15] For example, Article 9(1) of the TRIPs Agreement provides: 'Members shall comply with Articles 1 through 21 of the Berne Convention (1971) and the Appendix thereto. However, Members shall not have rights or obligations under this Agreement in respect of the rights conferred under Article 6b is of that Convention or of the rights derived therefrom.' On treaties which are rendered applicable by virtue of the TRIPs Agreement, see, for example, Case C-180/11, *Bericap Záródástechnikai*, EU:C:2012:717, paras 70-75; Case C-406/10, *SAS Institute*, EU:C:2012:259, para 34.

[16] See Case C-245/02, *Anheuser-Busch*, EU:C:2004:717, para 65, and Case C-414/11 *Daiichi Sankyo and Sanofi-Aventis Deutschland*, EU:C:2013:520, para 58.

[17] In some recent cases in WIPO, such as the Marrakesh Treaty to Facilitate Access to Published Works for Persons who are Blind, Visually Impaired, or otherwise Print Disabled (COM(2014) 638 final) or the review of the Lisbon Agreement on Appellations of Origin and Geographical Indications (negotiations authorised by Council on 8 May 2015), the objective of the agreements is to facilitate export and import of format copies from and to third countries and to promote exports respectively.

conclusion of the Convention on the legal protection of conditional access services by the EU was to encourage conclusion of that Convention by third parties.

III. ARTICLES 3(2) AND 216(1) TFEU

External relations are the only area where implied competences have become a central element of the constitutional framework. Historically when competence was not explicit, in the sense that the Treaties did not provide for the possibility to conclude international agreements in pursuance of a certain objective, it could only be implicit. Only a limited number of provisions under the original Treaties provided for the possibility of concluding international agreements. However, the Court of Justice very soon in its case law developed the principle of implied competences, which meant that the EU could conclude international agreements even where this was not explicitly provided for in the Treaties. The Court of Justice developed the concept as a manifestation of the principle of effectiveness.[18] However, later case law created some degree of confusion, and exclusive competence started being regarded as somewhat exceptional in nature.[19]

Article 216 TFEU now more explicitly provides that international agreements may be concluded outside areas where such possibility is specifically provided for. Although referring to the 'necessity' of such agreements to pursue the objectives of the Treaties, the wording is different from that in Article 3(2) TFEU when defining exclusive competences. The normative options when trying to regulate in a specific area are not limited to the adoption of 'internal' legislation, but rather the EU can also regulate through the adoption of international agreements, and this in all areas of the EU policies. Self-evidently, Article 3(2) TFEU will apply in areas which are not covered by Article 3(1), ie areas of shared competence, as any shared competence may become exclusive after its exercise.

A. The Case Law Before the Treaty of Lisbon

i. Exclusive Competence

In paragraph 17 of the *AETR* judgment,[20] the Court established the principle that, where common rules have been adopted, the Member States no longer have the

See, for geographical indications, judgment in Case C-347/03, *Regione autonoma Friuli-Venezia Giulia and Agenzia regionale per lo sviluppo rurale (ERSA)*, n 12 above, paras 71–83.

[18] G De Baere, *Constitutional Principles of EU External Relations* (Oxford, Oxford University Press, 2008) 17.

[19] M Cremona, 'EU External Relations: Unity and Conferral of Powers' in L Azoulai, *The Question of Competence in the European Union* (Oxford, Oxford University Press, 2014) 65, 68.

[20] Case 22/70, *Commission v Council—European Agreement on Road Transport (AETR)*, EU:C:1971:32, para 16.

right, acting individually or even collectively, to undertake obligations with non-member countries which affect those rules. In paragraph 11 of Opinion 2/91, the Court stated that that principle also applies where rules have been adopted in areas falling outside common policies and, in particular, in areas where there are harmonising measures. Giving its opinion on Part III of Convention No 170 of the International Labour Organization concerning safety in the use of chemicals at work, which is an area already 'largely covered by Community rules', the Court took account of the fact that those rules had been progressively adopted with a view to achieving an ever greater degree of harmonisation designed to remove barriers to trade resulting from differences in legislation from one Member State to another. It concluded that that part of that Convention was such as to affect those Union rules and that consequently Member States could not undertake such commitments outside the framework of the Union.[21]

In the *Open Skies* judgments,[22] the Court recalled three situations in which it recognised exclusive Union competence:

> where the international commitments fall within the scope of the common rules (*AETR* judgment, paragraph 30), or in any event within an area which is already largely covered by such rules (Opinion 2/91, paragraph 25). In the latter case, the Court has held that Member States may not enter into international commitments outside the framework of the Community institutions, even if there is no contradiction between those commitments and the common rules (Opinion 2/91, paragraphs 25 and 26).[23]
>
> whenever the Community has included in its internal legislative acts provisions relating to the treatment of nationals of non-member countries or expressly conferred on its institutions powers to negotiate with non-member countries, it acquires an exclusive external competence in the spheres covered by those acts (Opinion 1/94, paragraph 95; Opinion 2/92, paragraph 33).[24]
>
> even in the absence of any express provision authorising its institutions to negotiate with non-member countries, where the Community has achieved complete harmonisation in a given area, because the common rules thus adopted could be affected within the meaning of the *AETR* judgment if the Member States retained freedom to negotiate with non-member countries (Opinion 1/94, paragraph 96; Opinion 2/92, paragraph 33).[25]

The Court of Justice recalled in its Opinion 1/03 that those three situations are, however, only examples, formulated in the light of the particular contexts with which the Court was concerned.[26] So, in a nutshell, there is exclusive competence

[21] Opinion 2/91, EU:C:1993:106, paras 25 and 26.

[22] Case C-467/98 *Commission v Denmark*, EU:C:2002:625, and Case C-476/98 *Commission v Germany* EU:C:2002:631.

[23] Case C-476/98 *Commission v Germany*, judgment of 5 November 2002, EU:C:2002:631, para 108.

[24] Ibid para 109.

[25] Ibid para 110.

[26] Opinion 1/03 of 7 February 2006—*Competence of the Community to conclude the new Lugano Convention on jurisdiction and the recognition and enforcement of judgments in civil and commercial matters*, EU:C:2006:81, para 121.

when 'the international commitments fall within the scope of the common rules',[27] or in any event within 'an area which is already largely covered by such rules'.[28] Member States may not enter into international commitments outside the framework of the Union institutions, even if there is no contradiction between those commitments and the common rules.[29] It is not necessary for the areas covered by the international agreement and the EU legislation 'to coincide fully'.[30] Ruling in more general terms, the Court has found there to be exclusive Union competence in particular 'where the conclusion of an agreement by the Member States is incompatible with the unity of the common market and the uniform application of Community law'[31] or where,

> given the nature of the existing Community provisions, such as legislative measures containing clauses relating to complete harmonisation of a particular issue, any agreement in that area would necessarily affect the Community rules within the meaning of the *AETR* judgment.[32]

In short, as the Court of Justice concluded in Opinion 1/03, it is essential to ensure a uniform and consistent application of the Union rules and the proper functioning of the system which they establish in order to preserve the full effectiveness of Union law.[33]

As the Court of Justice summarised in Opinion 1/03:

> a comprehensive and detailed analysis must be carried out to determine whether the Community has the competence to conclude an international agreement and whether that competence is exclusive. In doing so, account must be taken not only of the area covered by the Community rules and by the provisions of the agreement envisaged, insofar as the latter are known, but also of the nature and content of those rules and those provisions, to ensure that the agreement is not capable of undermining the uniform and consistent application of the Community rules and the proper functioning of the system which they establish.[34]

ii. Non-exclusive Competence

Although much of the case law from *AETR* to Opinion 1/03 was devoted to ascertaining whether competence was exclusive, the Court of Justice also recognised

[27] Case 22/70, *Commission v Council (AETR)*, EU:C:1971:32, para 30.

[28] Opinion 2/91 of 19 March 1993, *delivered pursuant to the second subparagraph of Article 228 (1) of the EEC Treaty—Convention No 170 of the International Labour Organization concerning safety in the use of chemicals at work.* EU:C:1993:106, para 25; C-476/98, *Commission v Germany*, para 108.

[29] Opinion 2/91, EU:C:1993:106, paras 25 and 26.

[30] Opinion 1/03, EU:C:2006:81, para 126.

[31] Case 22/70, *Commission v Council (AETR)*, EU:C:1971:32, para 31; Opinion 1/03, EU:C:2006:81, para 123.

[32] See, Opinion 1/03, EU:C:2006:81, para 122.

[33] Opinion 1/03, EU:C:2006:81, para 128.

[34] Ibid para 133.

the existence of competence to conclude international agreements which may not be exclusive, but shared or parallel. The 'exclusive' nature of the competence was not mentioned in Opinion 1/76[35] (it was only in Opinion 1/94 that the Court of Justice interpreted Opinion 1/76 as acknowledging exclusive competence), and in Opinion 2/91 the Court of Justice made a distinction between the existence of competence and its 'exclusive or non-exclusive' nature,[36] and referred to areas of 'shared' competence where the 'negotiation and implementation of the agreement require joint action by the Community and the Member States'.[37]

In reality, as noted elsewhere, in *AETR* the Court took two decisions: that the Union could conclude agreements in areas which such agreements were not mentioned and that the EU had acquired exclusive competence.[38] Although *AETR* was quite clear, later references to exclusive competences were the source of some confusion and, for some, they serve no conceivable purpose.[39] The problem comes from the fact that Opinion 1/94 added confusion as the Court of Justice appeared to have equated implied competence with exclusive competence. The Commission's position in that case is often mentioned as the origin of the Court's final approach, but a careful reading of the question put to the Court (and the pleadings in the case) shows that the Commission was asking first whether the Union had 'competence' to conclude the agreement. It is only the third question that was devoted to the issue whether Member States' ability to conclude the WTO was affected. The Court of Justice, having to quickly decide the case, 'reinterpreted' the Commission's position as requesting a finding on whether competence was exclusive or not.

Practical examples of non-exclusive competences can be seen in pre-Lisbon case law. The Court of Justice rebutted arguments to the effect that a development cooperation agreement had to be mixed in *Portugal v Council*.[40] This is a clear case of affirmation of competence that could be exercised 'alone', even if it was not exclusive. In the *MOX* case the Court of Justice recalled that

> the question as to whether a provision of a mixed agreement comes within the competence of the Community is one which related to the attribution and, thus, the very existence of that competence, and not to its exclusive or shared nature.

It added that EU external competence in regard to protection of the marine environment

> is not, in principle, contingent on the adoption of measures of secondary law covering the area in question and liable to be affected if Member States were to take part in the

[35] Opinion 1/76 of 26 April 1977, *given purusant to Article 228 (1) of the EEC Treaty—'Draft Agreement establishing a European laying-up fund for inland waterway vessels'*, EU:C:1977:63.

[36] Opinion 2/91, EU:C:1993:106. See also Opinion 1/03, EU:C:2006:81, para 115.

[37] Opinion 2/91, EU:C:1993:106, paras 12.

[38] P Eeckhout, 'Exclusive External Competences: Constructing the EU as an International Actor' in A Rosas and others (eds), *The Court of Justice and the Construction of Europe—Analyses and Perspectives on Sixty Years of Case-law* (Berlin, Springer, 2013) 613, 627.

[39] Ibid 628; P Eeckhout, *EU External Relations Law*, 2nd edn (Oxford, OUP, 2011) chapter 3.

[40] Case C-268/94, *Portugal v Council*, EU:C:1996:461.

> procedure for concluding the agreement in question, within the terms of the principle formulated by the Court in paragraph 17 of the AETR judgment. The Community can enter into agreements in the area of environmental protection even if the specific matters covered by those agreements are not yet, or are only very partially, the subject of rules at Community level, which by reason of that fact, are not likely to be affected.[41]

The Court considered it necessary to establish whether and to what extent the Community, by becoming a party to the Convention, 'elected to exercise its external competence in matters of environmental protection'.[42] The Court referred to the Declaration of Community competence, which formed part of the Community's instrument of formal confirmation and that specifies the extent and the nature of the areas of competence transferred by the Member States to the Community in the matters dealt with by the Convention in respect of which the Community accepts the rights and obligations provided for by that convention.

For the Court, the declaration

> confirm[ed] that a transfer of areas of shared competence, in particular in regard to the prevention of marine pollution, took place within the framework of the Convention, and without any of the Community rules concerned being affected, within the terms of the principle set out in the *AETR* judgment.[43]

However, 'that passage of the Declaration of Community competence makes the transfer of areas of shared competence subject to the existence of Community rules, even though it is not necessary that those rules be affected'.[44] It followed that, within the specific context of the Convention, a finding that there has been a transfer to the Community of areas of shared competence was contingent on the existence of Community rules within the areas covered by the Convention provisions in issue, irrespective of what might otherwise be the scope and nature of those rules. The Court, after examining EU law as it stood at the time, concluded that

> [t]he Convention provisions on the prevention of marine pollution relied on by Ireland, which clearly cover a significant part of the dispute relating to the MOX plant, come within the scope of Community competence which the Community has elected to exercise by becoming a party to the Convention.[45]

The judgment appears, however, to be incorrect insofar as it uses the term 'transfer' of competence to describe what is simply the exercise of competence. By exercising shared competence the competence is not 'transferred', as it is already a competence of the EU. This language shows that the legal characterisation of shared competences was not fully articulated before the Treaty of Lisbon.

[41] Case C-459/03, *Commission v Ireland*, judgment of 30 May 2006, EU:C:2006:345, paras 94–95.
[42] Ibid para 96.
[43] Ibid para 105.
[44] Ibid para 106.
[45] Ibid para 120.

Similar findings could be found in the *Étang de Berre* judgment. The Court of Justice clearly stated that the Barcelona Convention[46] and the LBS Protocol[47] were concluded by the Community and its Member States under shared competence.[48] The Court also stated that the provisions of the Barcelona Convention and the LBS Protocol 'without doubt cover a field which falls in large measure within Community competence'.[49] Furthermore the Court stated that the 'environmental protection, which is the subject matter of the Convention and the Protocol, is in very large measure regulated by Community legislation, including with regard to the protection of waters against pollution'.[50] The fact that discharges of fresh water and alluvia into the marine environment, which were at issue in that case, had not yet been the subject of Community legislation was not capable of calling that finding into question.[51]

B. The Case Law After the Treaty of Lisbon

i. Pringle

In *Pringle* the Court of Justice was confronted for the first time with the interpretation of Article 3(2) TFEU, but very incidentally. The referring court asked whether the European Stability Mechanism (ESM) Treaty was an international agreement the operation of which may affect the common rules on economic and monetary policy. Interestingly, some of the parties sending observations (including the Commission) considered that Article 3(2) TFEU did not apply. The Court of Justice did not agree. For the Court it followed from that provision 'that Member States are prohibited from concluding an agreement *between themselves* which might affect common rules or alter their scope' (emphasis added).[52] However, the arguments put forward in this context had not demonstrated that an agreement such as the ESM Treaty would have such effects.

The Court held that since the European Financial Stability Facility was established by the Member States whose currency is the euro, outside the framework of the Union, the assumption by the ESM of the tasks conferred on the EFSF is not

[46] Convention for the protection of the Mediterranean Sea against pollution, signed at Barcelona on 16 February 1976 and approved on behalf of the European Economic Community by Council Decision 77/585/EEC of 25 July 1977 ([1977] OJ L240/1).

[47] Protocol for the protection of the Mediterranean Sea against pollution from land-based sources, signed at Athens on 17 May 1980 and approved on behalf of the European Economic Community by Council Decision 83/101/EEC of 28 February 1983 ([1983] OJ L67/1).

[48] Judgment in Case C-239/03, *Commission v France* (*Étang de Berre*), judgment of 7 October 2004, EU:C:2004:598, para 24.

[49] Ibid para 27.

[50] Ibid para 28.

[51] Ibid para 30.

[52] Case C-370/12, *Pringle v Government of Ireland, Ireland and Attorney-General*, judgment of 27 November 2012, EU:C:2012:756, para 101.

such as to affect common rules of the Union or alter their scope. The establishment of the ESM does not affect the power of the Union to grant, on the basis of Article 122(2) TFEU, ad hoc financial assistance to a Member State when it is found that that Member State is in difficulties or is seriously threatened with severe difficulties caused by natural disasters or exceptional occurrences beyond its control. Moreover, since neither Article 122(2) TFEU nor any other provision of the EU and FEU Treaties confers a specific power on the Union to establish a permanent stability mechanism such as the ESM, the Member States are entitled, in the light of Articles 4(1) TEU and 5(2) TEU, to act in this area. The conclusion and ratification of the ESM Treaty by the Member States whose currency is the euro therefore does not jeopardise in any way the objective pursued by Article 122(2) TEU or by Council Regulation establishing a European financial stabilisation mechanism,[53] adopted on the basis of that provision, and does not prevent the Union from exercising its own competences in the defence of the common interest. Consequently, Article 3(2) TFEU does not preclude either the conclusion of an agreement such as the ESM Treaty by the Member States whose currency is the euro or their ratification of it.

ii. The Conditional Access Services *Judgment*

The issue of the application of Article 3(2) TFEU was not finally decided in the *conditional access services* judgment. Yet, the Commission relied on Article 3(2) TFEU in the alternative. The Opinion of Advocate-general Kokott is worth mentioning since she discussed this alternative argument and concluded that exclusive competence could result from Article 3(2) (if the legal basis was to be 114 TFEU and not 207 TFEU). She noted that

> the risk of common rules being affected cannot be ruled out solely because the substance of the rules of an international agreement is largely similar to that of the provisions existing within the Union. Even where they are substantively similar, the discretion enjoyed by the Union legislature is reduced where commitments are entered into vis-à-vis third countries under international law.[54]

She focused on the confiscation measures under Article 6 of the Convention, and in respect of international cooperation under Article 8 of the Convention in so far as it concerns confiscation measures within the meaning of Article 6. In the view of the Council, these two points in particular made it necessary to regard the Convention as a mixed agreement. The Advocate-general did not follow completely the Commission on this point, as she saw no risk of Article 5(1) of the directive being affected by Articles 6 and 8 of the Convention. Article 5(1) of Directive 98/84 contains only a very general and rudimentary obligation for the Member States to

[53] Council Regulation (EU) No 407/2010 of 11 May 2010 establishing a European financial stabilisation mechanism ([2010] OJ L118/1).

[54] Opinion in Case C-137/12, *Commission v Council*, EU:C:2013:441, para 101.

provide for sanctions which must 'be effective, dissuasive and proportionate to the potential impact of the infringing activity'. The Member States enjoy a broad discretion in laying down appropriate sanctions in their national legal orders. These may include the seizure and confiscation of items, but this is *not mandatory* under the directive. For her,

> ultimately, the Member States only take a joint measure to fulfil their duty under Article 5(1) of Directive 98/84 to provide for effective, dissuasive and proportionate sanctions where they—on their own or with the participation of third countries—conclude an international agreement which prescribes mandatory confiscation measures, as is the case with Article 6 of the Convention. The Member States then simply exercise the discretion which they enjoy as EU law stands at present and, moreover, contribute to the attainment of the objectives of Directive 98/84.[55]

Nevertheless, she reached a similar outcome. She considered that even if Articles 6 and 8 of the Convention did not per se entail a risk of Article 5(1) of Directive 98/84 being affected, the Convention as a whole might still fall within the Union's exclusive competence. The Union must be considered to have exclusive competence to conclude an agreement, according to settled case law, wherever it concerns an area which is already covered to a large extent by Community rules. She rejected the argument that this case law was no longer relevant following the entry into force of the Treaty of Lisbon. For her there was 'absolutely nothing to suggest that the authors of the Treaty of Lisbon wished to make such a restriction'. She added that

> the Council failed to provide any specific evidence in support of its view, for example from the preparatory work for the European Convention on the Treaty establishing a Constitution for Europe or from the preparatory work for the Treaty of Lisbon.[56]

She considered that no different conclusion could be drawn from Protocol No 25. For her,

> according to its wording, Protocol No 25 relates only to the exercise of the Union's *shared competence* within the meaning of Article 2(2) TFEU and not to the scope of its *exclusive competence* within the meaning of Article 2(1) TFEU. There is *a fortiori* no evidence to suggest that with that Protocol the authors of the Treaty of Lisbon specifically intended to restrict, whether directly or indirectly, the scope of the Union's exclusive competence to conclude agreements under the third variant of Article 3(2) TFEU. An argument against such a restriction is not least the fact that there is no reference to Article 3(2) TFEU in Protocol No 25.[57]

She considered that a risk of common rules being affected or their scope altered can arise where an international agreement contains provisions whose substance is 'closely connected' with Community rules which already to a large extent govern the subject in question in EU law. Such Community rules can be adversely affected

[55] Ibid para 108.
[56] Ibid para 111.
[57] Ibid para 115.

by an international agreement even if the Community rules and the international agreement do not regulate precisely the same 'elements' (within the meaning of the Protocol No 25).[58] She considered that the Union legislature has already harmonised the area to a large extent within the Union by adopting Directive 98/84. It certainly did not merely adopt minimum standards, but made many aspects of that area subject to full harmonisation. She added that

> the fact that in Article 5(1) of Directive 98/84 the Union legislature allowed the Member States broad discretion in the choice of sanctions does not militate against the assumption that the area of the legal protection of services based on, or consisting of, conditional access, *when seen as a whole*, is already governed to a large extent by EU law.[59]

Therefore, she concluded that the conditions laid down in the third variant of Article 3(2) TFEU, as clarified in case law, were satisfied.

iii. The Broadcasters *Judgment*

Since the Court of Justice did not take a position in the *conditional access* case, judgment in *Broadcasters* discussed for the first time the issue of the impact of Protocol No 25.[60] The Court could not escape the question whether its own case law prior to the Lisbon Treaty still applied where harmonisation was not exhaustive.[61] It was again argued by the Council and some Member States that Protocol No 25 should be understood as limiting the applicability of some aspects of pre-Lisbon case law, in particular Opinion 2/91. After recalling the context of the case, it is important to examine the findings in the judgment in view of the arguments exchanged by the parties, and the Opinion of the Advocate-General, as it is only by comparing them that the impact of the judgment can be better understood.

The EU had been at the forefront of international developments in the area of copyright and related rights developments in international law, influencing standards agreed in the Council of Europe and WIPO.[62] Conversely, any improvement

[58] Ibid para 116.

[59] Ibid para 121.

[60] Case C-114/12, *Commission v Council* (*Broadcasters*), judgment of 4 September 2014, EU:C:2014:2151.

[61] The Court annulled the contested decision on the basis of the first plea, and accordingly did not address the second and third pleas which challenged the hybrid form of the contested decision.

[62] The Rome Convention for the Protection of Performers, Producers of Phonograms and Broadcasting Organisations of 26 October 1961 (Rome Convention) introduced rights for broadcasting organisations for the fixation of their broadcasts, and also for record producers and also for performers where performances are carried by broadcasting organisations. Whilst the EU is not a Contracting Party to the Rome Convention, under Article 5 of Protocol 28 to the EEA Agreement, the Contracting Parties undertook to obtain their adherence before 1 January 1995 to the Rome Convention. Following the Berne Convention and the Rome Convention, a number of other instruments have since been adopted in the context of the Council of Europe or at worldwide level. The most significant of these have been the TRIPS Agreement, the WCT, and the WIPO Performances and Phonograms Treaty (WPPT) 1996. Of these only the TRIPS Agreement provides specifically for the rights of broadcasting organisations. The TRIPS Agreement does not provide for any greater protection than the Rome Convention and indeed specifically refers back to the Rome Convention (Article 14(3)). Both the Rome Convention and the TRIPS Agreement are limited to traditional broadcasting by wireless means.

in the standard of protection for all categories of rights-holders at international level is normally translated into EU law. As regards the case at issue, the EU had led for years the efforts to protect the rights of a particular category of rights-holders, namely broadcasting organisations (BOs), for which the EU has a system of rights that goes well beyond international law.[63]

The judgment needs be understood also in the context of recent case law of the Court in this area.[64] The Court's recent case law has severely curtailed that freedom in three key respects. The Court has ensured that notions that are not defined and which make no reference to national law become autonomous concepts of EU law, which are often interpreted relying on the case law applicable to other rights, in order to ensure 'unity and coherence'.[65] The Court has tended to view significant aspects of the protection accorded to right-holders by the *acquis* as maximum harmonisation, and any discretion or options left to Member States in the *acquis* have been narrowly interpreted and can only be applied consistently with EU law.[66] Taken together this means that EU law leaves limited scope for Member States' own action in the area of intellectual property rights. In addition, it also means that Member States have lost the freedom which they enjoyed under international law to regulate certain matters where to do so would be inconsistent with EU law. The Convention to be negotiated in the Council of Europe was to be based on the EU *acquis* for BOs, with some possible improvements on a few

[63] Notwithstanding the fact that neither the WCT nor the WPPT updated the rights of broadcasting organisations, the EU took the opportunity to grant more extensive rights to broadcasting organisations. The rights of broadcasting organisations have been harmonised to a very great extent by Directives 2006/115/EC on rental right and lending right and on certain rights related to copyright in the field of intellectual property ([2006] OJ L376, 27.12.2006, p 28), 2006/116/EC on the term of protection of copyright and certain related rights ([2006] OJ L372, 27.12.2006, p 12), 93/83/EEC on the coordination of certain rules concerning copyright and rights related to copyright applicable to satellite broadcasting and cable retransmission and 2001/29/EC on the harmonisation of certain aspects of copyright and related rights in the information society. Unlike authors' rights protection, the protection of related rights is not made conditional upon the existence of a standard of originality but rather on the personal or commercial investment of the related rights-holders. Broadcasters are granted certain neighbouring rights to protect the 'product', namely the broadcasting 'output', against certain acts whereby a third party is considered to derive undue fair commercial profit from the broadcasters' investment.

[64] Member States have traditionally considered that the EU *acquis* on intellectual property leaves them quite a significant discretion or leeway on how to regulate certain matters, or define certain concepts and in particular to maintain in their law the notions that were traditionally inspired by international law in the area of intellectual property such as the Berne Convention which gave contracting parties freedom to regulate certain matters including amongst themselves.

[65] The Court of Justice has held that in view of the requirements deriving from the unity and coherence of the legal order of the European Union, the terms used by one directive relating to intellectual property must be interpreted in the light of the rules and principles established by other directives relating to intellectual property (Case C-5/08 *Infopaq International A/S v Danske Dagblades Forening*, judgment of 16 July 2009, EU:C:2009:465, paras 35 and 36; judgment in Joined Cases C-431/09 and C-432/09 *Airfield NV and Another v Belgische Vereniging van Auteurs, Componisten en Uitgevers CVBA (Sabam)* and *Airfield NV v Agicoa Belgium BVBA*, judgment of 13 October 2011, EU:C:2011:648, para 44).

[66] Case C-466/12, *Svensson and Others v Retriever Sverige AB*, judgment of 13 February 2014, EU:C:2014:76, paras 33–41.

points. This made the case an ideal one by which to test the principles underlying the *AETR* jurisprudence.

As regards the relevant test, the judgment follows the Commission's position as regards the Treaty of Lisbon: Protocol No 25 is irrelevant in this context, and there is no reason to deviate from prior case law.[67] The position of the Advocate-general was more ambiguous. She made a lengthy examination of the test under Article 3(2) TFEU.[68] In principle she did not consider that the Lisbon Treaty had overruled or changed in any way the existing pre-Lisbon test. However, on closer examination she considered that being 'largely covered' was not enough to automatically conclude that there was exclusive competence,[69] and at paragraphs 108–109 of the Opinion she developed a test which is reminiscent of the Council position. She proposed to reject the plea if 'in at least one respect Member States retain competence'. This more restrictive test is the one she relies upon later in her Opinion. Her analysis focuses on whether rules are 'minimum rules'. She finds a couple of instances, and considers therefore that competence is not exclusive. More importantly, she makes it clear that the freedom which is left by a minimum rule implies the freedom to act either by legislation or by concluding an international agreement:

> [t]hus, EU law does not yet regulate 'at least' the right of retransmission by wire or cable, whereas the Convention might do so and the Member States are currently authorised to provide for it in their own jurisdiction. Whether they do so on their own initiative or as a result of an international commitment makes no difference in that regard.[70]

She also considered that there is no difference between enlarging a right or giving greater protection to the right as defined in EU law.

It is important to examine how EU law was found by the Court to be affected or altered in this case. There was no disagreement about the fact that for many points EU law was affected, as the Court points out at paragraph 88. The Council and Member States submitted that there was no exclusive competence for the whole Convention because there were a few points where, in their view, EU law would not be affected, either because there was no 'common rule' or because the rule was of minimum harmonisation. The judgment concludes that for each single point common rules could be affected or their scope altered. It is interesting to examine each point, and the differences from the Advocate-General's analysis.

On the very notion of 'broadcasting organisation' and where it might, for the purposes of the future convention in question, be defined in a broad sense so as to extend to web or 'simulcasting' broadcasters, the Advocate-General remained ambiguous. She appeared to accept that there is exclusive competence if an 'absolute category' is agreed that is 'wider' than the broadcasting organisations that are

[67] Case C-114/12, *Commission v Council*, judgment of 4 September, EU:C:2014:2151, paras 66–73.
[68] Opinion in Case C-114/12, EU:C:2014:224, paras 81–114.
[69] Ibid para 107.
[70] Ibid para 150.

right-holders under the EU Directives, but if the definition does not change and is not exhaustive, this 'may not be the case'.[71] However, it should be noted that although the term 'broadcasting organisation' appears in several places in the EU *acquis* it is not defined. It should be treated as an autonomous notion of EU law. Accordingly, the judgment is more clear-cut: any negotiation on a definition of the 'broadcasting organisation' affects EU law as it would define the notion and scope of that particular right-holder or, in the words of the Court 'would have a horizontal effect on the scope of the body of common EU rules relating to the protection of neighbouring rights of such organisations'.[72]

For re-transmission by wire or cable which is not expressly covered by a specific rule of EU law, the Advocate-General considered that whether this would be a different right or an enlargement of existing rights does not matter: Member States are left with the possibility to provide for enlarged protection, so there is no exclusive competence. The judgment, following the Commission, considered that (a) enlarging the scope of a right by including 'wire and cable' is 'capable of altering the scope of the common EU rules on the right of retransmission',[73] and (b) in any event transmission over the wire was partly covered by other rights with which the re-transmission right interacts.[74]

On the protection of pre-broadcast signal, the Advocate-General considered that if the approach of the Convention was to cover such signal by existing rights (by enlarging the definitions or similar ways), there would be exclusive competence,[75] but if a distinct right was created the reason why there would be exclusive competence was not apparent to her.[76] The Commission had argued that the choice between options was for the EU to take, even if certain options could be said to affect EU law more than others. The judgment recalls that one of the approaches, namely the extension of the term 'broadcasts' to pre-broadcast signals in such a way as to include those signals in the scope of protection of the various rights conferred on broadcasting organisations, would 'undeniably be capable of altering, in a horizontal manner, the scope of the common EU rules in the area concerned'.[77] The other approaches are considered simply 'hypothetical' and the Court does not deal with them.[78]

For certain other aspects which appeared to be controversial, the Court considered, as the Advocate-General did, that there was no evidence that they were covered by the negotiations.[79] For the rest (rights of fixation, reproduction,

[71] Ibid para 156.

[72] Case C-114/12, *Commission v Council*, EU:C:2014:2151, para 87.

[73] Ibid para 92.

[74] Ibid para 93.

[75] Opinion in Case C-114/12, delivered 3 April 2014, EU:C:2014:224, para 154.

[76] Opinion in Case C-114/12, EU:C:2014:224, para 155.

[77] Case C-114/12, *Commission v Council*, EU:C:2014:2151, para 98.

[78] Ibid para 99.

[79] For the possible extension of the right of communication to the public to include places accessible to the public without payment of an entrance fee, both the Advocate-General (para 150) and the Court (paras 94–96) consider that there was no evidence that such an extension was the subject of the

distribution and making available to the public, limitations and exception, term of protection, protection of technological measures and rights-management information) both the Advocate-General's Opinion,[80] and the judgment[81] considered that it was not disputed that EU law could be affected.

The Court also refers to the *Étang de Berre* judgment at paragraphs 83–84 (which defined the area as that of 'water pollution') and the interaction with copyright at paragraph 93. This shows that despite the fact that it delineates the 'area' which is relevant for the analysis (of whether the 'area' is 'largely covered') as that of the rights for BOs (paragraphs 78–83, even if the area may be 'distributed' between several directives), the Court will not take a narrow view of the area of EU law which may be relevant for the analysis, contrary to what some Member States and the Council were contending.

The overall examination shows that the judgment covers the different aspects of protection of the rights of the BOs (the right-holder, the subject-matter and the form of exploitation):

- It considers that the definition of the right-holder may be affected if there is a discussion at international level about the definition of the right-holder, regardless of whether the international definition is wider or more restrictive. Any definition will influence the EU definition.
- It considers that if the subject-matter of protection is extended (pre-broadcast signal), EU law is affected.
- It considers that if the right granted is extended to cover other forms of exploitation (possible extension of retransmission right to wire and cable), EU law is affected.

iv. The Opinion on the 1980 Hague Convention

Opinion 1/13 offered the Court of Justice the opportunity to address a somewhat unusual situation. The Hague Convention of 25 October 1980 on the civil aspects of international child abduction (the 1980 Convention or the Convention) sets out to combat the wrongful removal or retention of children. To this end the Convention establishes a system of cooperation between authorities designated by the Contracting States, and in order to ensure that rights of custody and access are effectively respected, it provides for an expedited procedure to secure the prompt return of children to the Contracting State of their habitual residence.

negotiation. On the other hand, the Court does state that the existing rule in the EU *acquis* has a precise 'material scope' and that this material scope should not be confused with a minimum requirement (para 91). On enforcement, both Advocate-General (para 158) and the Court's judgment (para 100) agree that there was no basis for considering that criminal sanctions would be negotiated.

[80] Opinion in Case C-114/12, EU:C:2014:224, paras 151–152, 157 and 159–160.

[81] Case C-114/12, *Commission v Council*, EU:C:2014:2151, para 88.

The objective is to restore the status quo by immediately returning a child who has been wrongfully removed or retained.[82]

All the Member States are parties to the 1980 Convention. The EU is not a party thereto.[83] Article 38(4) of the 1980 Convention stipulates that the Convention applies between the acceding country and such Contracting States as will have declared their acceptance of the accession.[84]

The Commission considered that the Convention fell within the EU's exclusive competence after the adoption of Council Regulation (EC) No 2201/2003 of 27 November 2003 concerning jurisdiction and the recognition and enforcement of judgments in matrimonial matters and the matters of parental responsibility.[85] Taking the view that the question of the international abduction of children fell within the exclusive external competence of the EU, the Commission adopted, on 21 December 2011, eight proposals for decisions of the Council concerning the declarations of acceptance by the Member States, in the interest of the EU, of the accession of eight third States to the 1980 Convention.[86] Within the Council most of the representatives of the Member States considered the Council to be under no legal obligation to adopt those proposals, since the EU did not, in their view, have exclusive competence in the area concerned.

After rejecting four arguments against the admissibility of the request that had been formulated by Member States, the Court dealt with the arguments on the merits. The Parliament and the Commission maintained that the adoption of the declarations of acceptance of accession fell within the exclusive external competence of the EU. They argued, first of all, that the 1980 Convention and Regulation No 2201/2003 cover the same area since they both deal with questions relating to the procedure for returning children who have been wrongfully removed, rights of access and cooperation between the central authorities in respect of parental

[82] The working of the 1980 Convention was further strengthened by the Hague Convention of 19 October 1996 on jurisdiction, applicable law, recognition, enforcement and cooperation in respect of parental responsibility and measures for the protection of children. Council Decision 2008/431/EC of 5 June 2008 authorised the Member States to ratify that convention or to accede to it in the interest of the European Community ([2008] OJ L151, 11.6.2008, pp 36–48). Unlike the 1980 Convention, the 1996 Convention also contains provisions on international jurisdiction with regard to parental responsibility, including rights of custody.

[83] The Union has also been a member of the Hague Conference since 2006. See Council Decision of 5 October 2006 on the accession of the Community to the Hague Conference on Private International Law ([2006] OJ L297, 16.10.2006, pp 1–14). The Conference's most recent conventions do include a clause allowing the accession of international organisations.

[84] Chapter VI of the Convention is entitled 'Final clauses' and contains Article 38, which provides that the Convention shall enter into force for a State acceding to it on the first day of the third calendar month after the deposit of its instrument of accession. However, '[t]he accession will have effect only as regards the relations between the acceding State and such Contracting States as will have declared their acceptance of the accession. Such a declaration will also have to be made by any Member State ratifying, accepting or approving the Convention after an accession'.

[85] [2003] OJ L338/ 1.

[86] Armenia, Albania, Seychelles, Morocco, Singapore, Gabon, Andorra and Russia. See COM(2011) 904, COM(2011) 908, COM(2011) 909, COM(2011) 911, COM(2011) 912, COM(2011) 915, COM(2011) 916 and COM(2011) 917.

responsibility. They submitted, on the basis of existing case law of the Court of Justice, that those rules form a body of rules that are inextricably linked.[87] Although the EU legislature did not consider it necessary to copy out the provisions of the Convention in that regulation, in complementing and strengthening those provisions it did in fact incorporate them. For these two Institutions, it was not possible to dissociate the competence over the Convention, and the competence to accept accessions. The later necessarily includes the former.

The Council and all intervening Member States (except Italy) maintained that the EU did not have exclusive external competence in this regard. By focusing on the declaration of acceptance of accession, they considered that such commitment is not to be capable of undermining the uniform and consistent application of Regulation No 2201/2003 because the objective of the declaration is different, the declaration relating to cooperation with the central authorities of third States, whilst the regulation governs only cooperation between the central authorities of the Member States. It was submitted that the central authorities established under the Convention cooperate with each other independently and thus the fact that a central authority of a Member State cooperates with other central authorities of third States in no way affects the cooperation between the central authorities of two Member States. Accordingly, the unilateral acceptance by a Member State of the accession of certain third States to the Convention is said to have no effect on the uniform and consistent application of EU law in the sphere of cooperation between the central authorities of the Member States.

[87] The Court of Justice had already had to interpret the Regulation and its relationship to the 1980 Convention on several occasions. In the *Rinau* case the Court held that Article 11 of the Regulation 'takes over and reinforces the provisions of Articles 12 and 13 of the 1980 Hague Convention' (Case C-195/08 PPU, *Rinau*, judgment of 11 July 2008, EU:C:2008:406, para 66). In *J McB* the Court held that: 'abductions of children from one Member State to another are now subject to a body of rules consisting of the provisions of the 1980 Hague Convention as complemented by those of Regulation No 2201/2003, though the latter take precedence on matters within the scope of that regulation' (Case C-400/10 PPU, *J McB v LE*, judgment of 5 October 2010, EU:C:2010:582, para 36). In that case the Irish courts had before them an action brought under Article 15 of the 1980 Convention, seeking a finding that the removal from Ireland of the children of the applicant in the main proceedings was 'wrongful' within the meaning of Article 3 of the Convention and Article 2 of the Regulation. In his Opinion Advocate General Jääskinen spoke of the relationship between the Convention and the Regulation. He said that Regulation No 2201/2003 reproduced 'the scope of the 1980 Hague Convention'. He went on, '[o]nly by the conjunction of Articles 60 and 62 of Regulation No 2201/2003 has the legislature reaffirmed the effects of that convention by declaring that it is, in relations between the Member States, applicable in relation to matters not governed by that regulation'. He concluded that '[t]he legislature has therefore chosen to refer to the provisions of an existing instrument of public international law rather than adopt provisions of European Union law concerning the same matters'. He recalled the debate during the progress of the Regulation through the legislature: 'The need to include in the draft of Regulation No 2201/2003 provisions dealing with the same matters as the 1980 Hague Convention was controversial at the time. Regulation No 2201/2003, as adopted, covers a plethora of situations concerning jurisdiction and the recognition and enforcement of judgments in matters of parental responsibility. According to the regulation, in cases of wrongful removal or retention of a child, the 1980 Hague Convention 'would continue to apply as complemented by the provisions of this Regulation, in particular Article 11' (para 14). He took the view that 'as regards removals from one Member State to another, the 1980 Hague Convention and Regulation No 2201/2003 are inextricably linked as far as their application is concerned' (para 42).

They also argued that, even assuming that the request for an Opinion had to be examined from the viewpoint of the 1980 Convention, an exclusive external competence cannot arise merely because the area in which the Convention applies is covered to a large extent by equivalent rules of EU law. It was argued that there is only a partial overlap between the scope of the Convention and that of Regulation No 2201/2003, both with regard to the nature of the relations governed and in relation to the persons to whom those instruments are applicable. It was also claimed that the overlaps which do exist between the Convention and Regulation No 2201/2003 are not such as to establish exclusive competence on the part of the EU since they are abstract and do not demonstrate that the Convention has any effect on the Regulation.

The Court had to decide first whether it was the Convention as a whole that should be the subject-matter of the Court's examination. It considered that the declaration of acceptance of accession and, accordingly, the international agreement of which it is a constituent part are ancillary to the 1980 Convention, 'which determines their existence and their effects and from which that declaration and agreement cannot therefore be detached'. The agreement in question is intended to ensure that the Convention applies in its entirety in bilateral relations between the two States concerned.[88]

The Court examines first 'the existence of EU competence'. The Court recalls existing case law to the effect that the EU has authority to undertake international commitments necessary for the attainment of its objective even in the absence of an express provision to that effect, case law which is now explicitly mentioned in Article 216(1) TFEU.[89] In the matter in issue, the Convention thus falls within the area of family law with cross-border implications in which the EU has internal competence under Article 81(3) TFEU. Moreover, the EU has exercised that competence by adopting Regulation No 2201/2003. In those circumstances, the EU has external competence in the area which forms the subject-matter of the Convention.

The Court then turns to the 'nature' of the competence, and therefore to the interpretation of Article 3(2) TFEU. The Opinion contains two main sections, one examining first 'the extent to which the areas concerned coincide'[90] and a second one on 'the risk that common rules may be affected'.[91]

The 1980 Convention provides, more specifically, for two procedures: on the one hand, the procedure for returning wrongfully removed children and, on the other, the procedure for securing the exercise of rights of access. The Court concludes that the provisions in Article 11 of Regulation No 2201/2003 that those provisions either (i) are based on the rules of the 1980 Convention or (ii) establish the consequences

[88] Opinion 1/13 of 14 October 2014, *pursuant to Article 218(11) TFEU—Convention on the civil aspects of international child abduction*, EU:C:2014:2303, para 65.

[89] Ibid para 67.

[90] Ibid paras 75–83.

[91] Ibid paras 84–90.

that are to follow when those rules are applied. Those two categories of provisions thus form a 'unitary body of rules' which applies to the procedures for returning children who have been wrongfully removed within the EU.

As regards, secondly, the procedure for securing the exercise of rights of access, Regulation No 2201/2003 lays down basic rules similar to those of the Convention so far as the exercise of rights of access is concerned. Finally, the 1980 Hague Convention lays down some general provisions which are common to proceedings relating to the return of a wrongfully removed child and proceedings relating to the exercise of rights of access. In turn, Regulation No 2201/2003 lays down similar rules which apply to proceedings for the return of the child and proceedings to secure the exercise of access rights.

In view of the foregoing, the Court finds that the provisions of Regulation No 2201/2003

> cover to a large extent the two procedures governed by the 1980 Hague Convention, namely the procedure concerning the return of children who have been wrongfully removed and the procedure for securing the exercise of access rights. Thus, the whole of the Convention must be regarded as covered by the EU rules.

The Court goes on, in a second part of the reasoning which is harder to grasp, as it is rather laconic.

It observes first 'that Regulation No 2201/2003 lays down uniform rules which are binding on the authorities of the Member States'. It adds that

> because of the overlap and the close connection between the provisions of Regulation 2201/2003 and those of the Convention, in particular between Article 11 of the regulation and Chapter III of the Convention, the provisions of the Convention may have an effect on the meaning, scope and effectiveness of the rules laid down in Regulation No 2201/2003.

That conclusion is not undermined by the fact that many provisions of Regulation No 2201/2003 may appear to be consonant with those of the Convention. It recalls prior case law to the effect that EU rules may be affected by international commitments even if there is no possible contradiction between those commitments and the EU rules.

The Court observes that the 'precedence' provided for in Article 60 of the regulation (which provides that the regulation is to take precedence over the Convention in so far as the matters governed by the two instruments overlap) is not an obstacle to its finding, since despite it 'the scope and effectiveness of the common rules laid down by the regulation are likely to be affected when the Member States individually make separate declarations accepting third-State accessions to the 1980 Hague Convention'. The only illustration which is given to this effect is in paragraph 89:

> as the Parliament and the Commission have submitted, if the Member States, rather than the EU, had competence to decide whether or not to accept the accession of a new third State to the 1980 Hague Convention, there would be a risk of undermining the uniform

and consistent application of Regulation No 2201/2003 and, in particular, the rules concerning cooperation between the authorities of the Member States, whenever a situation involving international child abduction involved a third State and two Member States, one of which had accepted the accession of that third State to the Convention whilst the other had not.

v. *Green Network*

The judgment in *Green Network* closes the circle.[92] The preliminary request had been made in proceedings between Green Network and the *Autorità per l'energia elettrica e il gas* (AEEG) concerning an administrative fine imposed by the latter on Green Network for its refusal to purchase green certificates in an amount corresponding to the quantity of electricity which that company imported into Italy from Switzerland. The request focused on the interpretation of Articles 3(2) TFEU and 216 TFEU, read in conjunction with Article 5 of Directive 2001/77/EC of the European Parliament and of the Council of 27 September 2001 on the promotion of electricity produced from renewable energy sources in the internal electricity market.[93]

Italian law required operators having produced or imported electricity, to feed into the national grid, during the following year, a quota of electricity produced from renewable energy sources ('green electricity') from installations that entered into service or increased their production after the entry into force of that decree. This requirement could be discharged by, inter alia, purchasing all or part of that quota from other producers, provided that the electricity fed into the national grid is green, or by purchasing green certificates from the designated national grid manager, *Gestore servizi energetici GSE SpA* (GSE), since 1 November 2005. To that end, the producers and importers concerned must either submit certificates showing that a quota of electricity produced or imported has been produced from renewable energy sources, or buy green certificates. The obligation could be performed by importing, wholly or in part, electricity generated in installations that entered into service after 1 April 1999, drawing on renewable energy sources, provided that those installations are situated in foreign countries that adopt analogous instruments for the promotion and encouragement of renewable energy, based on market mechanisms affording the same opportunity to installations situated in Italy. In the case of countries which are not members of the EU, acceptance of the application was subject to the conclusion of an agreement between the national grid manager and the equivalent local authority determining the arrangements for the necessary verifications.

[92] Case C-66/13, *Green Network SpA v Autorità per l'energia elettrica e il gas*, EU:C:2014:2399.

[93] [2001] OJ L283/33. Directive 2001/77 was repealed, from 1 January 2012, by Directive 2009/28/EC of the European Parliament and of the Council of 23 April 2009 on the promotion of the use of energy from renewable sources and amending and subsequently repealing Directives 2001/77/EC and 2003/30/EC ([2009] OJ L140/16). Nevertheless, considering the date of the facts of the dispute in the main proceedings, Directive 2001/77 was the directive applicable *ratione temporis*.

Operators which import electricity produced in other Member States of the EU could request exemption of GSE from the obligation to purchase green certificates for the proportion of electricity imported, by presenting it with a certified copy of the guarantee of origin issued in accordance with Article 5 of Directive 2001/77. In case of import of electricity produced in a third State, the exemption was conditional on the conclusion, between the Italy and the third State concerned, of an agreement requiring the electricity concerned to be produced from renewable energy sources and guaranteed as such according to the same arrangements as those provided for in Article 5 of Directive 2001/77. Such an agreement was concluded in 2007 between the competent Italian ministries and the Swiss Confederation. That agreement provided for the mutual recognition of guarantees of origin of electricity imported as from 2006, the year in which the Swiss Confederation enacted legislation in conformity with the provisions of Directive 2001/77.

The issue was whether Italy was competent at all to conclude such international agreements. Since the case concerned an obligation to purchase green certificates in respect of the year 2006, and the Lisbon Treaty did not enter into force until 1 December 2009, the Court of Justice took into consideration the rules on the exclusive external competence of the Community as laid down in the EC Treaty.

The Court recalls the main principles already recalled in its previous case law, including the *Broadcasters* case and Opinion 1/13. The Court also recalls that Directive 2001/77 was adopted on the basis of Article 175 EC, which provided for powers to be shared between the Community and its Member States.

The case had one specific feature: unlike in most previous cases, in reality no agreement had been concluded or even negotiated at the time. The Court did not find it relevant. By making the benefit of the advantage it confers on electricity importers subject to the prior conclusion of such an international agreement, Italian law sets in motion a process that could lead to such a conclusion actually being realised, which would be sufficient to affect the exclusive external competence of the Community, assuming it to have been established.

The judgment compares the areas and content of the agreements and the Directive. The Court first examines 'the area covered by the agreements whose conclusion is thus envisaged' and their content. Those agreements essentially seek to determine on what conditions and under what arrangements electricity produced in a third State and imported into a Member State must be certified as green electricity by the authorities of that third State in order for it to be recognised as such in the internal consumer electricity market of that Member State, in particular, in connection with the implementation of a national support scheme for the consumption of green energy established by that Member State.

As regards the area covered by Directive 2001/77, the Court takes into consideration, in particular, Articles 3 to 5. The Court focuses on article 5 first.[94] It concludes that an agreement of the kind provided for in Italian law was liable to

[94] Case C-66/13, *Green Network*, EU:C:2014:2399, paras 41–49.

alter the scope of the common rules contained in Article 5 of Directive 2001/77. It considers that agreements such as those whose conclusion between Italy and a third State is provided for are specifically intended to ensure that guarantees of origin issued by the authorities of that third State will—like the guarantees of origin issued in Member States pursuant to Article 5 of Directive 2001/77, and provided that conditions equivalent to those laid down by those provisions are satisfied—be recognised, on the consumer market of that Member State, as evidence of the green nature, for the purposes of that directive, of electricity imported from that third State. Accordingly, such an agreement may extend the scope of its harmonised certification mechanism established by Article 5 of Directive 2001/77 for guarantees of origin issued in the Member States, by allowing, in particular, guarantees of origin issued in third States to enjoy, on the internal consumer electricity market of the Member State concerned, a status equivalent to that enjoyed by guarantees of origin issued in the Member States.

The Courts turns to Article 4, as regards the 'national support schemes'. The Court recalls that the guarantees of origin issued by the authorities of a third State are intended in particular to be recognised in the context of a national support scheme for the consumption of green electricity, by allowing their holder to be exempted from the obligation to acquire green certificates. Directive 2001/77 allows Member States considerable latitude for the purposes of the adoption and implementation of such support schemes.

Nevertheless, the directive seeks to promote an increase in the contribution of renewable energy sources to electricity production in the internal market for electricity. Member States must, inter alia, fix national indicative targets for future consumption of green electricity, taking account, as reference values, of both 'national production' of green electricity in 1997 and the proportion, expressed as a percentage for 1997 and 2010 respectively, of green electricity in gross electricity consumption, that proportion being calculated on the basis of the 'national production' of green electricity divided by the gross national electricity consumption. It follows, in particular, that national support mechanisms for producers of electricity, which are used inter alia to help Member States achieve their respective national indicative targets, must in principle lead to an increase in national production of green electricity. The fact that a Member State concludes an agreement with a third State for the purpose of making it possible, in the operation of a national support scheme, for account to be taken of the green nature of the electricity produced in that third State could interfere, (a) with the objectives of Directive 2001/77, and (b) with the Member States' obligation to increase their production of green electricity so as to contribute to achieving the national indicative targets. The conclusion of such agreements by Member States, when Directive 2001/77 in no way authorises this, is therefore liable to affect the proper functioning of the system established by that directive and the objectives it pursues as well.

Finally the Court considers that assessing whether an area is already largely covered by Community rules requires, in particular, account to be taken, not only of

Community law as it now stands in the sphere concerned, but also of its future development, in so far as that is foreseeable at the time of that analysis. In this case the analysis of the future did not need a crystal ball. The Court took into account later developments in EU law which certainly happened during or after the events, but that were known at the time it rendered its judgment.

The Commission was required to present, not later than 27 October 2005, a report on experience gained with the application and coexistence of the different national support mechanisms, accompanied, if necessary, by a proposal for a Community framework with regard to those support schemes for electricity produced from renewable energy, specifying in that respect various criteria such a framework should meet. The Italian provision was adopted during the period in which the Commission was thus required to examine that experience with a view to the presentation of such a report and the ultimate adoption, by the Community legislature, of such a Community framework.

The Union legislature, in the framework of that new directive (Directive 2009/28), inter alia undertook to specify the conditions on which green electricity produced in a third State and imported into a Member State may, in the cooperation established between those States, be taken into account, should the case arise, by that Member State in order to achieve the binding target concerning the proportion of green energy in final energy consumption imposed on it by that directive. Having regard to all these considerations, the Court replied that the Community had exclusive external competence that precluded the provision in question.

IV. MAKING SENSE: *TUTTO BENE*?

A. External vs Internal Competence and Protocol No 25

More than 40 years after *AETR*, case law is still in a state of flux.[95] The recent case law makes a fundamental contribution to the clarification of external competences. It follows the path open in the *Lugano Opinion* and the *MOX* judgment by clearly distinguishing between the *existence* of an EU competence on the one hand and the *nature* of that competence on the other. It also draws an important distinction between the conclusion of international agreements as opposed to the adoption of national legislation, the absence of which is at the heart of certain misunderstandings. Such distinction also helps to clarify the respective fields of application of Articles 2(2) and 3(2) TFEU. Articles 2(2) and 3(2) TFEU draw a

[95] Still in 2014 Ch Timmermans can affirm that 'the Court has not developed a real doctrine, in the sense of self-standing, systematically-ordered construct, on the issue of competences and the division of competences between the EU and its Member States': see Ch Timmermans, 'ECJ Doctrines on Competences' in L Azoulai, *The Question of Competence in the European Union* (Oxford, Oxford University Press, 2014) 155.

crucial difference between external treaty-making power and internal legislative competence, which is common to many composite polities.[96]

Article 2(2) TFEU does not define competences, but explains the consequence of the exercise of one type of competence, and confirms the prohibition on Member States acting whenever the Union has adopted a legally binding act in a specific area. The characteristic of shared competences is the blocking of the exercise of national competence to the extent the Union exercises its competence.[97] This provision goes, therefore, beyond ensuring the principle of primacy. By contrast, Article 3(2) TFEU defines competences and creates a specific and independent source of competence for the EU with respect to international agreements. Obviously, it also has a comparable 'negative' effect in that the exclusivity of such competence implies that Member States are not allowed to act, unless empowered by the Union. However, unlike the prohibition in Article 2(2) TFEU, the prohibition flowing from Article 3(2) TFEU does not depend on whether or not the EU has exercised such external competence yet.

The rationale for having a provision formulated not on the basis of the subject-matter (as Article 3(1) TFEU) but on the basis of the legal instrument involved, is that international agreements are different in the way they can influence present *and future* EU action. The recent judgments contradict the contention that if EU law has left some freedom to Member States, such freedom can be exercised by way of legislation but also collectively by way of concluding an international agreement. Such position ignores the specific rule set out for international agreements in Article 3(2) TFEU. If Member States could adopt legislation or international agreements on the same basis, there would not be any difference between Articles 2(2) and 3(2) TFEU: if a Member State would not prevented from adopting a 'legally binding act' under Article 2(2) TFEU, it would not be prevented from participating in an international agreement.

It is important to explain why international agreements are different, and the rationale of Article 3(2) TFEU insofar as it 'codifies' *AETR* case law. EU law, in the form of regulations or directives, may not fully harmonise a certain area and may, therefore, not preclude all legislative action by Member States. Such action at national level may respond to different rationales or legal bases, and may be limited by EU law in different ways.[98] In certain cases such action is possible as EU law has knowingly decided not to harmonise or regulate a certain aspects. The extent of the 'coverage' by EU law will have to be then determined. However, such action can also be part of the implementation task entrusted to Member States (Articles 2(1) and 291(1) TFEU), which may also imply some degree of latitude or margin of appreciation (by choosing among different options, for example),

[96] JHH Weiler, 'Mixity and the Federal Principle: external legal relations of non-unitary actors' in H Schermers and D O'Keefe, *Mixed Agreements* (Deventer and Boston MA, Kluwer Law and Taxation, 1983).

[97] Ch Timmermans (n 95 above) 162.

[98] Ch Timmermans (n 95 above) 156 and 160.

provided that the EU legal framework is respected. Such implementing action may take legislative form at national level. For example, this is the case with exceptions or limitations which Member States may decide to introduce to a rule or right stemming from EU law, when such an option is allowed by EU law.[99] Since the right or rule is granted or established by EU law, the regulation of any such exception or limitation is necessarily a matter of EU exclusive competence. In all such cases the 'area' has been 'largely covered' even if certain choices have been left by EU law to the national level.

It was already clear from Opinion 1/03 that the mere fact that 'internally' Member States have some freedom to shape certain aspects of the law in the relevant area does not mean that 'externally' competence is not exclusive.[100] To put it differently, the external competence is not based on complete uniformity of the law internally. The case of complete harmonisation is just one of the situations where competence becomes exclusive. As rightly pointed out by Advocate-General Bot in *Green Network*, such residual action by Member States does not mean that the EU has not exercised its competence over the area in question.[101] Such action is in certain (or many) instances not the expression of 'competences retained' by Member States. The judgment in *Green Network*, already remarkable in many respects,[102] is also interesting since the outcome was not influenced by the fact, as the Court duly recognised, that Directive 2001/77 allowed Member States considerable latitude for the purposes of the adoption and implementation of such support schemes.

In terms of preserving the effectiveness of EU law, which is the principle upon which the case law is based, international agreements have a greater impact in shaping EU law (present and future) than (potentially divergent) national laws.[103] International agreements bind the contracting parties vis-à-vis third parties. National legislation becoming inconsistent with EU law can be immediately disapplied, in accordance with the principle of primacy of EU law. Although the

[99] As regards exceptions and limitation, and the exclusive nature of EU competence, see *DR, TV 2 Danmark* confirms this approach (Judgment in Case C-510/10, *DRand TV 2 Danmark A/S v Nordisk Copyright Bureau (NCB)*, EU:C:2012:244, paras 29 to 31), by considering that the Union has replaced Member States as regards the implementation of Articles 1 to 21 of the Berne Convention.

[100] Opinion 1/03 of 7 February 2006, EU:C:2006:81, paras 148–151.

[101] Opinion in Case C-66/13, *Green Network*, delivered 13 March 2014, EU:C:2014:156, para 79.

[102] This is one of the few cases where the Court finds an 'alteration' of a provision of EU law. This is done when the field of application of a certain system is extended to a third country.

[103] JV Louis explains that domestic legislative provisions do not create the same risks of consolidating a certain development of Union law, whereas international agreements, involving third countries, may constitute a political and legal obstacle to the later development of common EU rules (see JV Louis, 'la competence de la CE de conclure des accords internationaux' in JV Louis and M Donny, *Commentaire Megret—vol 12: Relations extérieures* (Brussels, Université Libre de Bruxelles, 2005) 57, 65. P Eeckhout also sees a difference between legislation and international agreements, and the exclusive competence is 'to ensure that [the EU Institutions'] internal acts are not challenged at international level in a manner which they cannot control' (n 38 above, at 628). See also L Azoulai, 'The Many Visions of Europe: Insights from the Reasoning of the European Court of Justice in External Relations Law' in M Cremona and A Thies, *The European Court of Justice and External Relations Law* (Oxford, Hart Publishing, 2014) 165, 172: 'Quite simply entering into international agreements may involve some restraints on the future exercise of powers by the Union, both externally and internally'.

same principle applies to the application of international agreements concluded by Member States, its operability will be more severely impeded, as Member States will be bound under international law. Therefore, the different needs of the internal and external policies have turned primacy and exclusivity into different principles, both aimed at settling potential conflicts.[104] Before the Treaty of Lisbon, the Court of Justice had clearly opted for exclusivity as the 'conflict rule' in the area of external relations.[105]

Although exclusive competence will prevent both individual (like in *Green Network*) and collective 'external' action by Member States, it is when Member States act collectively that the rationale of the exclusivity is easier to grasp. The *Broadcasters* judgment appears to reflect in essence the principled position that when common rules are aimed at in an area like the one at issue (which was largely covered), it is for the Union, not for Member States, to act. This was particularly evident in that case since new provisions that the Convention could contain would inevitably lead to amendments (formal or by way of interpretation) of the EU *acquis*. The same applied in the *Conditional Access Services* case. It is true that the provisions of the Convention were more specific than the general clause on enforcement in the Directive. However, if the Directive was meant to leave some freedom to Member States, the Convention was to be the vehicle through which Member States would collectively agree to be bound to use certain types of measures. To put it differently, Article 6 was the way Member States would have 'collectively' agreed to implement the 'general' obligation in Article 5 of the Directive. This being so, one wonders why such a common harmonisation effort on how to implement an EU legal obligation can be undertaken by Member States and not the Union, bearing in mind that the very same text of Article 6 of the Convention could be included in a paragraph of Article 5 of the Directive by qualified majority.

So the very same Union legislation may not preclude all national legislative action pursuant to Article 2(1) and (2) TFEU, but may at the same time be the basis for exclusive external competence of the Union. To put it differently, Article 3(2) TFEU only asserts the exclusive nature of the competence to conclude international agreements, nothing else. Article 3(2) TFEU does not cover the adoption of legislation by a Member State, which is governed by Article 2(2) TFEU.

The difference between the adoption of legislation and international agreements means that any 'authorisation' or 'empowerment' which is granted explicitly or

[104] Schütze has explained in detail how this type of exclusivity was developed in terms of conflict avoidance: 'the demarcation of mutually exclusive spheres—in which either the Community or the Member States were *sovereign*—elegantly avoided the question of the normative hierarchy of the Community over the Member States being even posed in the context of international relations' (R Schütze, 'Dual Federalism constitutionalized: the emergence of exclusive competences in the EC legal order' (2007) 32 *European Law Review* 3). See also G De Baere (n 18 above), at 33: 'while internally there is no need for the Community to prevent the Member States from legislating, as long as the primacy principle guarantees that the Community rule will prevail in case of conflict, the same cannot be said with regard to the external world, because third parties are involved'. However, Article 351 TFEU does not apply, see Case C-466/98, *Commission v United Kingdom*, EU:C:2002:624, paras 25–27, and Case T-212/02, *Commune de Champagne v Council*, EU:T:2007:194, paras 165–68.

[105] G De Baere (n 18 above) 43.

implicitly by EU law to make certain legislative choices at national level will concern exclusively the adoption of domestic laws. For the conclusion of international agreements, a specific provision to this effect is needed. This is perfectly possible and a reality in certain cases.[106] In *Green Network* the Directive in question had been amended to include an authorisation to Member States to conclude, under certain conditions, international agreements. The later authorisation somehow 'confirmed' that the competence was exclusive, but also shows that the aim of granting exclusive competence to the EU is not to 'systematically transform' the EU into the external actor which concludes the agreements, but to create order in the external relations, and preserve the EU *acquis*, present and future.

This distinction between domestic laws and international agreements is also consistent with *Pringle*. The application of Article 3(2) TFEU was opposed by some since it concerned the Union, and not Member States. But, quite logically, by defining what is the exclusive competence of the Union it also defines what Member States cannot do. The origin of the case law, the *AETR* judgment, started by setting out what Member States could not do. The fact that, because it was Member States which were party to the international agreement, it was difficult to imagine that the EU could be party to such agreement (with whom?), is irrelevant. The alternative route for the EU to act might not have been an international agreement, but an autonomous EU act. But the 'negative' *AETR* effect was deployed anyway.

The origin of the confusion is the tendency to examine issues of external competence as based on internal competence, and to put national and EU competences at the same level. The approach of examining whether Member States 'retain some competence' considers it relevant if national law may also be affected. This is, however, irrelevant. An international agreement may contain a provision which will affect both EU and, to the extent that something is not regulated by EU law, national law. Article 3(2) TFEU creates a type of 'functional' exclusive competence: the fact that national law may be affected does not give rise to a 'national competence' if EU law may also be affected.[107]

[106] On the different type of situations where Member States conclude international agreements authorised by the EU see A Rosas, 'The Status in EU Law of International Agreements concluded by EU Member States' (2011) 34 *Fordham International Law Journal* 1304–55, and M Cremona, 'Member States Agreements as Union Law' in Cannizzaro, Palchetti and Wessel (eds), *International Law as Law of the European Union* (Martinus Nijhoff, Leiden/Boston, 2012), and M Cremona (n 19 above) 74–77. The 'empowering' of Member States can take different forms. In certain cases, the Member States will act 'in the interest of the Union', so that de facto the Union agrees to be bound by the agreement. In other cases, the authorisation may have a different meaning, as the international agreement will be concluded by the Member State without the agreement being part necessarily of Union law. Yet, in all such cases, it is the EU that is originally 'in control' of the competence, and will assess whether or not there is a need for total uniformity in the external relations, or some degree of diversity (normally subject to material and procedural conditions, of course) is still compatible with the EU *acquis*. Sometimes such limited freedom is perfectly possible for a transitional period, or in order to make arrangements for the implementation of principles which the EU has already previously agreed.

[107] For example, one can imagine horizontal rules of data protection which affect both the areas where there is EU harmonisation, and areas where EU law does not yet apply. Since the provision in the international agreement cannot be 'dissociated', the provision would logically fall in the exclusive

It is the author's view that this distinction between the internal and external competence is also important to understand the debate around Protocol No 25. As regards the scope of the Union's competence, the Council in essence contended that the Treaty of Lisbon has reduced to some extent the scope of the Union's external competence, since the *AETR* case law has been 'superseded' by Protocol No 25. This position glossed over the fact that Article 3(2) TFEU contains a specific rule for international agreements, which is the result of settled case law whose rationale has been explained above. Once this difference between the scope of application of Articles 2(2) and 3(2) TFEU is adequately understood, Protocol No 25 keeps all its *effet utile*. It simply does not address the definition of the competence to conclude international agreements, but a different issue.

B. The 'Largely Covered Area' Test

Several cases have focused on whether the 'largely covered' test mentioned in several judgments prior to the Treaty of Lisbon was still applicable. It was argued by the Commission and the Parliament that if the agreement as a whole is largely covered by EU law, there is exclusive competence. It goes without saying that if the area is not largely covered, or the agreement concerns also other areas, the EU may still have exclusive competence, but probably for only parts of the agreement (which means that the Member States are not entitled to sign and conclude the agreement without prior empowerment by the EU).[108]

The application of the 'largely covered area' test, as one possible situation where competence becomes exclusive,[109] was contested by some on the basis of Protocol No 25. It was argued that Opinion 2/91 would have been superseded by that Protocol. The Court of Justice is clear in considering that the Treaty of Lisbon has not modified the landscape on this point. The test continues to apply after Lisbon, and

competence of the EU if it may affect EU law, regardless of the parallel affectation it may deploy in certain provisions of national law which are not harmonised. It is only if two different provisions or agreements regulate separately the EU and national matters that it can be held that the EU would not have exclusive competence over an agreement regulating the latter. Bearing this in mind, we can refer to an 'attractive' force of EU competence, or at least to a situation where EU and national competence are not on equal terms. The same 'attractive' force applies when discussing the relevance that the existence of 'ancillary' aspects of an international agreement. The EU may have exclusive competence over an ancillary aspect of an international agreement (Opinion 1/03, EU:C:2006:81, para131), so the agreement is not of 'national' competence just because the exclusive competence concerns an ancillary issue. The opposite is not true: if something ancillary or 'not predominant' is not yet covered by EU law, the EU exclusive competence will probably cover the whole agreement anyway (on this point see further below).

[108] This is what happened in Opinion 2/91. The EU was exclusively competent for Part III of Convention No 170 of the International Labour Organization concerning safety in the use of chemicals at work, but not for the Convention as a whole.

[109] It goes without saying that the analysis may not always involve an examination of the 'area'. If an agreement covers already a particular piece of EU legislation, competence is exclusive even if the 'area' to which the legislation belongs remains largely unregulated.

the Court does apply it in the *Broadcasters* judgment and in Opinion 1/13. The continuity is also illustrated in *Green Network*, where the Court relies on case law relating to Article 3(2) TFEU even after having previously found that the TFEU was not yet applicable to the facts of the case.[110]

The 'comprehensive and detailed analysis' to which the Court of Justice refers to is not the same as the 'atomistic' approach proposed by Member States and the Advocate-General in *Broadcasters*. The recent case law confirms that it is the 'area' ('*domaine*' in French) that counts, and not whether each and every item is specifically regulated at EU level in an exhaustive way.[111] That is why claims that the area was not fully covered or that certain EU provisions left some freedom to Member States have not been very successful in Court. The Court in *Broadcasters* defines the area as that of the 'rights of broadcasting organisations' (even if the area may be 'distributed' in several directives).[112] It also refers to the *Étang de Berre* judgment (which defined the area as that of 'water pollution') and the interaction with copyright.[113] This shows that the Court will not take a narrow view of the area of EU law which may be relevant for the analysis, contrary to what some Member States and the Council were contending.

The Court of Justice will focus on the functioning and purpose of the common rules rather than on simple comparisons of provisions: for example, in both Opinion 1/13 and *Green Network* the Court of Justice took a systemic approach of the risk 'of undermining the uniform and consistent application' of Regulation 2201/2003 and of 'the proper functioning of the system established by [Directive 2001/77] and the objectives it pursues as well'. In *Green Network*, the Court of Justice's conclusion was not influenced by the fact that the provisions only concerned guarantees of origin issued by the authorities of Member States, or that the Directive allowed Member States 'considerable latitude for the purposes of the adoption and implementation of … support schemes'.[114] The Court took into account the system and purpose of the common rules. The fact that the Directive said nothing at the time about third countries was immaterial.

This analysis in terms of 'areas' makes even more sense when the likelihood of common rules being affected or their scope altered is understood in terms of 'risks'. The judgments are based on an interpretation of Article 3(2) TFEU based on the 'risk' of common rules being affected or their scope altered, so evidentiary requirements shall focus only on the 'risk'. Although such risk cannot be a matter of simple speculation, it can be shown in different ways, including by showing risks of undermining the system in practice under certain specific scenarios.

Moreover, the examination of 'risks' also explains why the Court of Justice takes into account future developments of EU law. The concern is not only in respect

[110] Case C-66/13, *Green Network*, EU:C:2014:2399.

[111] L Azoulai refers to this phenomenon as 'arealism' (n 103 above) at 175.

[112] Case C-114/12, *Commission v Council*, EU:C:2014:2151, paras 78–83.

[113] Case C-114/12, *Commission v Council*, EU:C:2014:2151, paras 83–84 and 93.

[114] Case C-66/13, *Green Network*, EU:C:2014:2399, para 54.

of existing EU law, which the principle of primacy would anyway help to ensure, even if less effectively in case of international agreements. The concern is that the EU's freedom of action in the future in the exercise of competences conferred on it should be limited only by rules which the EU itself—and not the Member States—has shaped and consented to.[115] In *Green Network* the Court of Justice took into account that the Directive at issue was clearly a first step in the process, that there was a review clause, that the Italian law had been adopted when such review was being carried out and finally that the new Directive actually created a framework for Member States to conclude such agreements.[116] All these developments confirmed, in its view, the external exclusive competence. The Court is guided by the idea that unilateral international action of Member States could jeopardize foreseeable future development of Union law. This of course does not definitively set out the criteria to apply in other cases of rules 'in the making'.[117]

However, certain points in the case law are not without some ambiguity. In Opinion 1/03 the analysis of the Court did not stop at the simple finding that the international agreement covered also 'jurisdiction' or 'recognition and enforcement of judgments', but was based on the uniform and coherent nature of the system of rules on conflict of jurisdiction established in EU law.[118] For certain combinations of EU internal legislation and international agreements, a simple look at the 'coverage' may not be enough. Certainly, in cases of 'complete harmonisation', the analysis can just stop there since, as the Court put it in Opinion 1/03, 'any agreement in that area would necessarily affect the Community rules within the meaning of the ERTA judgment'.[119] However, since 'largely covered' is not the same thing as 'completely harmonised', the two cannot be equated. Yet, the fact

[115] On this need to preserve the future action of the Union, see n 103 above. The idea that it is for the Union to decide by which rules is to be bound, is at the heart of some key passages of Ruling 1/78 (Ruling 1/78 of 14 November 1978—*Draft Convention of the International Atomic Energy Agency on the Physical Protection of Nuclear Materials, Facilities and Transport* [1978] ECR 2151, para 32).

[116] The Union legislature, in the framework of that new directive (Directive 2009/28), inter alia undertook to specify the conditions on which green electricity produced in a third State and imported into a Member State may, in the cooperation established between those States, be taken into account, should the case arise, by that Member State in order to achieve the binding target concerning the proportion of green energy in final energy consumption imposed on it by that directive (*Green Network*, para 64).

[117] An open issue is the relevance of 'common rules' which are still in the making, i.e. where, at the moment of assessing the conditions of Article 3(2) TFEU, the area is only covered by Commission proposals or even preparatory works (communications, green papers, Council conclusions etc). This question is of particular relevance because, in practice, international and Union rules often develop in parallel. The most controversial situation is one where either the Parliament (non-legislative Resolutions) or the Commission (in communications, while or green papers etc) have taken preliminary steps towards future legislation without the Council yet having taken a political position regarding such initiatives. The position of Member States, based on Article 16(1) TEU, is that competence cannot become exclusive on the basis of the political action of the Commission or the Parliament alone.

[118] Opinion 1/03, EU:C:2006:81, paras 148–154.

[119] Ibid para 122.

that an area is 'largely covered' is normally a strong indication of the existence of a risk of common rules being affected or their scope altered.

Both in *Broadcasters* and Opinion 1/13 the Court of Justice, after recalling that the 'largely covered' test is still 'relevant'[120] adds that, since the EU has only conferred powers,

> any competence, especially where it is exclusive, must have its basis in conclusions drawn from a comprehensive and detailed analysis of the relationship between the envisaged international agreement and the EU law in force. That analysis must take into account the areas covered by the EU rules and by the provisions of the agreement envisaged, their foreseeable future development and the nature and content of those rules and those provisions, in order to determine whether the agreement is capable of undermining the uniform and consistent application of the EU rules and the proper functioning of the system which they establish.[121]

Therefore, the 'coverage' of the rules is relevant, but also their 'the nature and content'.

The fact that in *Broadcasters* the Court still examines the five points on which there was disagreement cannot be interpreted as meaning that the Court still engages in a 'point by point' analysis of whether or not a certain provision could be affected. The fact that the analysis does not simply stop after the finding of an area being 'largely covered' does not mean that the Court requires two distinct conditions, 'largely covered' and the risk of common rules being affected or their scope altered. Such interpretation does not appear to be consistent with the overall approach of the judgment. If it had been sufficient that for any of those five points the Court would have been unable to show that common rules may be affected or their scope altered in order to conclude that there was no exclusive competence, the Court would not have first defined, at paragraphs 78 to 84, what the 'area' was for the purposes of the application of the case law. Those paragraphs would be been irrelevant since whether the area was wider or narrower would not have been material for the outcome.[122]

Opinion 1/13 also confirms that the pre-Lisbon case law is alive and kicking. The Court, after having concluded that the provisions of Regulation No 2201/2003 'cover to a large extent the two procedures governed by the 1980 Hague Convention' and that 'the whole of the Convention must be regarded as covered by the EU

[120] Judgment in *Commission v Council*, EU:C:2014:2151, paras 70, 72 and 73; Opinion 1/13, EU:C:2014:2303, para 73.

[121] See Opinion 1/03, EU:C:2006:81, paras 126, 128 and 133, and judgment in *Commission v Council*, EU:C:2014:2151, para 74, and Opinion 1/13, para 74.

[122] The weight of the judgment is not diminished because certain arguments by Council and Member States are rejected for lack of evidence that the point would be negotiated. There is no indication in the judgment that should such evidence had been provided, the Court could have decided differently (paras 90–96). By relying on the lack of evidence the Court was rather stressing that it will not decide on hypothetical questions.

rules',[123] further examines if there was a 'risk that common rules may be affected', in a separate section. On closer examination, this is not surprising, as the Court proceeded in the same way in Opinion 1/03. It did not conclude that there was exclusive competence on the basis of the simple fact that the Regulation and the international agreement both concerned 'rules on conflicts of jurisdiction'. The Court recalled in Opinion 1/03 its own findings in Opinion 2/91 as regards 'minimum standards',[124] which is a situation where common rules are not affected 'even if the Community rules and the provisions of the agreement cover the same area'. That situation, where competence was shared, appears to apply only when both EU and international law limit themselves to setting out minimum standards. Opinion 2/91 was mainly about an international agreement harmonising substantive law. In cases of cooperation agreements such as those envisaged in Opinions 1/03 and 1/13, the Court may also go a step further in its analysis and examine the nature and content of the rules.[125]

In Opinion 1/13 such risk was based on two elements: the (explicit) link between Article 11 of the Regulation and Chapter III of the Convention, and the problems linked to non-homogenous acceptance of accession. One can only speculate about whether one of these two elements would have been enough (the Commission's case was based on the first one, the second not being necessary). Whereas the Court does not stop at examining the coverage of both norms (the Regulation and the Convention), the standard applied is a 'low' one, in that the Court accepts that the examples given by the Commission were enough. It is possible that this 'extra mile' was considered appropriate since the case concerned acceptance of accessions, and not only amendments of the 'pre-existing' Convention. This 'lower' level of demonstration is also seen in *Broadcasters*.

All in all the outcome in Opinion 1/13 was to be expected, since Union law in force essentially implements rights and obligations that are laid down in international law (the 1980 Convention), but attaches additional conditions and protective measures; the entire set of rights, obligations, conditions and rules is fully harmonised. The Court of Justice had accepted in preliminary rulings that the Regulation and the Convention form a 'body of rules' that are 'inextricably linked'. The additional conditions and protective measures are intended not only to expedite the proceedings and to allow the effective return of the child to the child's Member State of habitual residence (Article 11(8) of the Regulation), but also to safeguard, as a fundamental right, the right of the child and of the parties concerned to be heard. This was not the kind of reference in a regulation where a

[123] Opinion 1/13, EU:C:2014:2303, para 83.

[124] Opinion 1/03, EU:C:2006:81, para 127.

[125] If an international agreement falls within the exclusive competence of the Union, the Union has competence to determine the non-member countries with which the Union wishes to maintain relations under that agreement. The Commission took the view that the decision on the accession of a non-member country cannot be dissociated from the question of competence for the subject-matter. If the Union has exclusive competence in respect of the Convention, it has exclusive competence to accept or not to accept the accession of other countries to the Convention.

clause merely stipulates that the regulation 'shall not affect' any conventions to which the Member States are parties.[126] The Regulation went a great deal further: the procedure for the return of children in Union law is expressly based on the Convention, and the Regulation therefore necessarily presupposed the application of the Convention, in the sense that it made the substance of the Convention its own, subject to the conditions or procedures that it added.[127] If the Convention were to be renegotiated today nobody would probably contest the EU's exclusive competence. Indeed it would not even be possible for a Member State to denounce the Convention now, because it constitutes the basis of cooperation among the Member States, and it does so by virtue of Union law.[128]

Be it as it may, the judgments are important since some Member States had stressed the need to have a 'demonstrable' effect on the application of the Regulation. In reality, certain Member States were again considering that some degree of 'contradiction' was necessary. The Court rejects this view, but of course the notion of common rules being affected or their scope altered contained in the judgments may not solve all possible problems in the future. The finding of such risk is often not the result of a mechanical application of general formulae. Each piece of legislation and each international agreement may contain provisions which are different in nature and scope, and their interaction may vary. At the same time, the very content and nature of the internal piece of legislation will have an influence on the

[126] In her opinion in *TNT Express*, Advocate-General Kokott drew a distinction between the situations covered by Article 71 of Regulation No 44/2001, an article which restricts the field of application of that regulation in order to enable conventions to continue to apply as instruments to which the Member States are parties ('this does not have the effect of incorporating the provisions of those conventions into European Union law in some way'), and the situation of 'individual provisions of international conventions where the rules of European Union law refer to those provisions or where the European Union legislation was adopted in order to transpose provisions of international conventions in the European Union'. In this second situation, which AdvocateGeneral Kokott says is the situation of Article 11 of the Regulation, the Court may interpret individual provisions of international conventions (Opinion of Advocate General Kokott in Case C-533/08, *TNT Express Nederland BV v AXA Versicherung AG*, EU:C:2010:50, paras 68 and 69 and fn 36).

[127] One can see a certain illustration for this approach in some recent decisions of the Council. The Council has expressly accepted that competence to conclude the Hague Protocol of 23 November 2007 on the law applicable to maintenance obligations is 'exclusive' (fifth recital to Council Decision 2009/941/EC of 30 November 2009 on the conclusion by the European Community of the Hague Protocol of 23 November 2007 on the Law Applicable to Maintenance Obligations ([2009] OJ L331, 16.12.2009, pp 17–18). From the second recital to the Council Decision on the conclusion of that Protocol, it can be seen that the Council considered that the Union's competence was exclusive because Article 15 of Council Regulation (EC) No 4/2009 of 18 December 2008 on jurisdiction, applicable law, recognition and enforcement of decisions and cooperation in matters relating to maintenance obligations made reference to the Hague Protocol of 23 November 2007 ([2009] OJ L7, 10.1.2009, p 1), and dispensed with the exequatur requirement for judgments given in Member States that were party to that Protocol.

[128] The Council had acknowledged that for the 'proper application' of the Brussels IIa Regulation it is 'essential' that the Convention be in force between the Member States, and that Member States have an obligation to accept the accession of other Member States: 'all Member States ... need to make the necessary declarations in due course to enable the full application of the Regulation 2201/2003' (see document 10235/04, 8.6.2004, available at: register.consilium.europa.eu/pdf/en/04/st10/st10235.en04.pdf).

analysis. It may be drafted in a way that 'isolates' it from any external influence, so that any change in international agreements will by its very nature have no effect on the regulation or the directive. This may be difficult to imagine in cases where there is some degree of harmonisation of substantive laws, but it may be possible for cooperation agreements.

C. On Timing and Risks

That the test is one of 'risk' has an influence also on the 'when' to examine the issue of competence. The *Broadcasters* case was about the authorisation to negotiate. One point of contention is often whether it is appropriate to make an analysis of competence at an early stage in the process. The Commission had often argued that one must wait until the text of the agreement is final, since it is only by examining the content of the agreement that this can be decided, especially in cases of bilateral agreements which cover a wide array of areas. It is often claimed that participation of Member States does not prejudge either the identity of the final parties to the Convention or the nature of the agreement.

That the identity of the negotiating parties does not necessarily determine the identities of the parties to the agreement is in principle correct. However, it is in reality quite hard to convince Member States to sign or conclude as 'EU-only' an agreement that has been negotiated as mixed, unless this has been explicitly kept open at the early stages of the discussions in the Council.[129] Moreover, this pragmatic approach may disregard the fact that the identity of the negotiating parties will influence the content of the agreement itself.[130] That is why the Court of Justice has sometimes noted that issues of competence often need to be resolved before negotiations actually start or soon afterwards and that such early examination is perfectly possible and adequate.[131]

[129] See, for one example, Opinion 1/03, EU:C:2006:81, para 24.

[130] Even in a situation where the Union finally concluded the agreement, the fact remains that the content of the agreement will be partly determined by Member States. The outcome of a negotiation where only the Union negotiates and one where the Union must negotiate alongside Member States may not be the same. The practical problems of such negotiations, and the fact that involvement of Member States, with corresponding unanimity requirements in practice, may also affect the outcome of the negotiation as such, was well explained by Advocate-General Kokott in her Opinion in the *Vietnam* case (Opinion of Advocate-General Kokott in Case C-13/07 *Commission v Council* (*Vietnam*), delivered 26 March 2009, paras 72 and 73). It is because the definition of competences and the negotiator matters that the contested decision in *Broadcasters* deployed legal effects, which the Commission considered identical to those which led the Court of Justice to consider admissible the Commission action in *AETR* (Case 22/70, *Commission v Council* (*AETR*), EU:C:1971:32). Comparable reasons led the Court of Justice to conclude that an action against a decision of the Council on who should vote in the context of a FAO Conference should be admissible, as it was not a simple matter of procedure or protocol (Case C-25/94 *Commission v Council*, judgment of 19 March 1996, EU:C:1996:114, paras 29 to 38).

[131] Opinion 1/78, EU:C:1979:224, paras 32–35.

The important added value of two of the rulings, *Broadcasters* and *Green Network*, is that they are concerned with cases where there was no draft agreement yet, even if the broad content of any such agreement could be inferred. The key point, confirmed now by the Court, is that when it comes to defining who is competent, what matters is the subject-matter of the agreement, not the final policy options that it may contain. In *Broadcasters*, for example, the precise scope or shape of a given right or provision may be less important than the fact that it needs to be solved in advance who is competent to define such policy options.[132]

It is settled case law that even if options are later adopted that ensure consistency with EU law, this is not in itself a decisive factor in resolving the question whether the Union has exclusive competence to conclude that agreement. Any initiative seeking to avoid contradictions between Union law and the agreement envisaged does not remove the obligation to determine, prior to the conclusion of the agreement, whether it is capable of affecting the Community rules.[133] And the fact that the EU has finally ensured an outcome that renders EU law and the international agreement compatible and even explicitly independent of each other is an issue of negotiating outcomes, but not an issue of competences. The fact that no effect at all will be felt does not (and cannot) question the competence of the EU in the first place.

In most cases the simple fact that there is an on-going negotiation over largely the same area represents, by itself, a risk (and a material one) that EU law will be affected, since any future EU decision-making in the area will be influenced by the content of what has been agreed at international level.[134] That is why the 'risk' of common rules being affected or their scope altered is an operational concept more effective at defining spheres of competences, than actual influence. And that is also why the focus on the 'area' should be predominant in a meaningful analysis.

V. WHY MIXITY?

A. The Problem

The expression 'mixed agreements' is often used to cover a variety of situations, all having in common that both the EU and Member States participate in the

[132] There is one point in the *Broadcasters* case which illustrated this practical problem. Advocate-General Sharpston considered in her Opinion that, as regards one point (the protection of pre-broadcast signal), competence was dependent on the policy choice in the negotiation: to extend an existing right or to create a new one. This approach is problematic. If it is argued that option A may affect the EU *acquis*, but option B will not, who decides on such option between A and B? The EU would remain competent only if A is discussed, but not any more if A is discarded to the benefit of option B? An analysis in terms of 'areas' and 'risks' avoids this problem as the definition of the competence is not dependent on each policy choice.

[133] See, to this effect, Opinion 1/03, EU:C:2006:81, paras 129–130.

[134] The situation where EU and international levels develop in a parallel and watertight way, so that one does not influence the other, will be rare.

conclusion of the agreement. Genuine 'mixed' agreements are often bilateral (eg association or cooperation) concluded, on the one hand, by the third country or countries, and on the other—as one party—by the Union and its Member States 'together'. Prominent areas of international relations of the EU have been organised by using this technique for decades. Yet, there is still a lot of uncertainty about the nature and more specific obligations of the joint participation of the EU and its Member States. Unforeseen in the original Treaties and unprecedented in international practice, mixity has been discussed and analysed many times in the literature, but it remains an oddity ill-fitted both to the EU legal system and to the traditional concepts of international law. This chapter only intends to provide some reflections about its purpose and necessity in the light of the recent experience and case law.

In EU parlance 'shared competences' or 'non-exclusive competences' are often referred to as 'mixed competences'. However, the latter concept is not in the Treaties. This parlance appears to be premised on the principle that if competence is not exclusive, then the competence must be 'mixed', as the EU competence would have to be somehow 'completed' and therefore the agreement must also be concluded by Member States. However, before the Treaty of Lisbon the Court of Justice mentioned that certain external competences could be non-exclusive, and a distinction was also made in the literature between compulsory and optional mixity.[135]

Before the Treaty of Lisbon, the Court of Justice admittedly contributed to the ambiguity by using often the expression 'shared competence' when it simply meant that an international agreement was concluded as a mixed agreement.[136] As a result, in reality the notion of 'shared competence' was not conceptually elaborated and was given in the judgments a meaning which appeared close to that of mixity. It was assumed that if a competence is 'shared' it can be 'jointly' exercised by the EU and its Member States. The new Article 2(2) TFEU appears to change that.

The Treaties still do not have any general provision on the negotiation of mixed agreements. In the past, the Commission has insisted that the EU (or the EC as it then was) could negotiate (and conclude) agreements alone if it had competences on the matters covered: legally speaking it was not necessary that the EU has exclusive competence. Prominent examples are development cooperation agreements or agreements on cooperation in the area of science and research, which were concluded as mere Community agreements. However, this line has been confronted with great resistance. Member States have frequently requested that an agreement becomes mixed in two situations. On the one hand, parts of the agreement cover

[135] See, Ch Timmermans, 'Organising Joint Participation of EC and Member States' in A Dashwood and C Hillion, *The General Law of EC External Relations* (Butterworth, London, 2000) 239, 241.

[136] Opinion 1/94, EU:C:1994:384, paras 98, 105; Opinion 2/00 of 6 December 2001 (*Cartagena Protocol*), EU:C:2001:664, para 17; Case C-370/07, *Commission v Council*, judgment of 1 October 2009, EU:C:2009:590, para 49, and judgment of 7 October 2004 in Case C-239/03, *Commission v France* (*Étang de Berre*), EU:C:2004:598, paras 24–25.

areas in which the Community did not have competence at all (eg standard clauses on political dialogue or weapons of mass destruction, penal sanctions outside the scope of Community competence, internal institutional structure of Member States etc). On the other hand, parts of the agreement fall within the Union's shared competence.

Admittedly, when the EU does not have competence for certain parts of the agreement, mixity is legally necessary and EU-only agreements are not possible unless their scope is reduced to the limits of the competences conferred to it by the Treaty. The origin of mixity in the 1960s and 1970s was precisely the limited external competences that the Community had at the time. The Community did not have the competence to cover certain parts of the international agreement. However, subsequent Treaty amendments and in particular the Lisbon Treaty should have reduced the incidence of resort to mixity. In the first scenario, the standard clauses beyond Community competence should nowadays fall within the Union's competence (CFSP). As Article 218 TFEU allows concluding agreements with both non-CFSP and CFSP clauses, one should replace classical mixed agreements with a simple Union agreement in the future. Mixity would only continue to be imperative if an agreement contains clauses that would relate to Member States prerogatives that would fall neither under CFSP nor non-CFSP chapters of the TFEU. In the second scenario, the Union may exercise its shared competence by concluding the agreement, even if no specific EU legislation on the matter has been adopted before, as we will see that 'sharedness' does not imply 'mixity'.[137]

The impact of mixity in the EU decision-making process will escape nobody. As applied by the Council, it nullifies the procedures provided for in the Treaties. The Council considered in the *Broadcasters* case that, although qualified majority voting is the rule for international agreements, when agreements are 'mixed', this rule does not apply in practice due to an alleged requirement of 'common accord' of the Member States.

In the case concerning the agreement for accession of the EFTA States to the US-EU Air Transport Agreement (ATA) the Council had made exactly the same point. The Court of Justice annulled the decision by which the Council authorised, together with the Member States meeting within the Council (ie through a 'hybrid act'), its signature and its provisional application, on behalf of the Union.[138] The Court confirmed that the procedure of Article 218 TFEU applies to

[137] It is also irrelevant if the agreement will have to be applied by the administrative authorities of the Member States, an argument that is still often heard in Brussels. The implementation of EU law by national authorities is the normal state of affairs (see Article 291 TFEU). The Court of Justice already rejected a similar argument in Opinion 2/91, where it was argued that the agreement had to be mixed since the competent authorities referred to in certain provisions were the national authorities. The Court considered that the EU was competent to conclude agreements implying 'the attribution of certain supervisory powers to national authorities' (Opinion 2/91, EU:C:1993:106, para 34).

[138] Judgment in Case C-28/12, *Commission v Council*, EU:C:2015:282. The Court of Justice maintained the effects of the decision until the Council had adopted, in a reasonable delay, a new decision pursuant to Article 218(5) and (8) TFEU.

all international agreements of the Union, even if they were to be concluded also by the Member States (as mixed agreements).

The Court recalls two fundamental principles. First, that Member States have, by reason of their membership of the EU, accepted that relations between them as regards the matters covered by the transfer of powers from the Member States to the European Union are governed by EU law, to the exclusion, if EU law so requires, of any other law, and that the rules regarding the manner in which the EU institutions arrive at their decisions[139] are laid down in the Treaties and are not at the disposal of the Member States or of the institutions themselves.[140] The Court of Justice is very clear in stating that when a mixed agreement is negotiated and concluded, the EU and the Member States 'must act within the framework of the competences which it has while respecting the competences of any other contracting party'.[141] On the one hand, the Court finds that Member States participated in the adoption of the act although, under Article 218(5) TFEU, such an act must be adopted by the Council alone. On the other hand, the contested act was adopted under a procedure which involved without distinction elements falling within the decision-making process specific to the Council and elements of an intergovernmental nature. Accordingly, the contested decision was not compatible with Article 218(2), (5) and (8) TFEU and, therefore, also with Article 13(2) TEU.[142] Finally, it rules that the duty of cooperation, which is imposed on the EU and the Member States in the field of mixed agreements, cannot justify the Council setting itself free from compliance with the procedural rules and voting arrangements laid down in Article 218 TFEU.[143]

The judgment has wide consequences. It cannot be simply interpreted in the sense that the practice in certain areas of adopting 'hybrid acts' needs to be discontinued. Even if a parallel act (instead of a hybrid act) is adopted, the problem runs deeper. The Council practice for mixed agreements, even if no parallel act is adopted, is not to apply the majorities provided for in Article 218 TFEU, but to apply unanimity by following a procedure which has been explained in different ways in some of the more recent cases. In its latest version such procedure consists in 'verifying' first whether there is 'common accord',[144] and only then, once there is 'common accord', voting in accordance with the procedure provided for in the

[139] The French version uses a more telling expression that applies beyond the 'decisions': 'les règles relatives à *la formation de la volonté* des institutions de l'Union'.

[140] Ibid paras 40 and 42.

[141] Ibid para 47.

[142] Ibid paras 49–53.

[143] Ibid paras 54–55.

[144] On this point, see, for example, judgment in *Commission v Council*, C-377/12, EU:C:2014:1903, para 32, and Opinion of Advocate General in *Commission v Council*, C-28/12, EU:C:2015:43, para 33. The page in the Council's website explaining 'the role of the Council in international agreements' states that '[t]hroughout the procedure, the Council mostly takes its decisions using qualified majority voting'. However, it is added '[f]or agreements covering areas of shared competency decisions are taken together with the Council by common accord (agreement of all member states).' Available at: www.consilium.europa.eu/en/council-eu/international-agreements.

Treaties (qualified majority voting, if applicable). This is often presented as being in accordance with the principle of sincere cooperation, as the Union should not act before having checked whether its Member States have a problem or disagree, as the agreement also engages competences of the Member States.

This is rather strange. It is clear that the Union is bound by the principle of sincere cooperation, but any 'common accord' in the Council is meaningless since the status of such 'common accord' is just a mystery. In so far as it supposed to be the expression of the competences not exercised by the Union, it is simply a way to confer a veto right on Member States in the adoption of the act of the Union, in full contradiction with the judgment. Moreover, the fact of having a 'common accord' for competences not conferred on the Union does not mean that the Member States have agreed to sign the international agreement, for example. In the different constitutional systems of the Member States such 'common accord' is probably a non-existent or irrelevant event, or at least simply a political act without any legal consequence. Quite obviously, Member States can arrange their relations as they see fit, for the matters where the Union does not have competences. They certainly have no obligation to adopt an intergovernmental decision in matters coming under competences not conferred on the Union.[145]

If the Union and Member States, when a mixed agreement is negotiated and concluded, 'must act within the framework of the competences which it has while respecting the competences of any other contracting party', there are ways to ensure adequate cooperation while respecting the procedures in the Treaties. There can be cases where the two parts of a mixed agreement are so inextricably linked that it is not possible for the Union or its Member States to become part in isolation. However, there are still cases of 'incomplete' mixity, where not all Member States are party to the agreement besides the EU, especially in multilateral agreements, and the EU has knowingly concluded agreements even if not all Member States were yet party to it.[146] The alleged need for unanimity simply follows from the practice of depositing the instrument of ratification in coordination with that of Member States. In such cases the 'will' of the Council is shaped in accordance with Article 218 TFEU, but the implementation of such decision may be made dependent on all Member States having also agreed to go ahead (sign or conclude, for example) in accordance with their constitutional procedures. Obviously, since such obligation is reciprocal, no Member State should then go ahead before all of them have finished their constitutionally provided procedures.[147] A flow of information

[145] The Court criticised in paragraph 50 of the judgment the involvement of the Council, as an EU institution, 'in the adoption of the act concerning the provisional application of those agreements by the Member States although such an act falls within the scope of, first of all, the internal law of each of those States and, then, international law'.

[146] One prominent example is the United Nations Convention on the Rights of Persons with Disabilities, which was approved on behalf of the European Community by Council Decision 2010/48/EC of 26 November 2009 ([2010] OJ L23/35).

[147] Interestingly, it happens very often in Brussels that the same Member States that very much insist on the EU not going ahead if all Member States have not yet gone ahead or otherwise agreed by way of 'common accord' will go ahead without waiting for the EU decision on the matter.

could be organised in the Council decision. Yet, it is one thing to act in coordination, each one deciding according to its own procedures; it is another very different thing to 'mix' all the decision-making processes and apply unanimity in the Council. This would give a say (ie a veto right) to each and every Member State in the decision of the Council, even in areas of qualified majority voting.

It is often argued that mixity is not a problem, as some of these agreements, especially the bilateral cooperation agreements, can be provisionally applied. However, provisional application is not possible for certain Member States as contracting parties.[148] It follows that an intergovernmental decision on provisional application, when (and if) it is adopted, would be of a purely declaratory nature which could not guarantee the uniform provisional application of the agreement by the Member States, as it could merely contain a political expression of general willingness to accept the provisional application of the agreement with no binding effect in internal or international law.

The artificial character of mixity in many situations is well illustrated in the 'hybrid' decision judgment.[149] The agreements which were to be signed and provisionally applied by the Council decision were the Accession and the Ancillary Agreement to the ATA with the US. The provisional application on behalf of the Union therefore concerned in the first place granting to carriers from Norway or Iceland the same treatment as to Union carriers on their routes to the US. However, neither ATA nor its 2010 Amending Protocol[150] have yet entered into force—failing the conclusion of the ratification procedures in some Member States—and thus both of them are still—after almost ten years—under provisional application. In reality all these agreements are provisionally applied in full. So the Union actually exercised its competence for the entirety of the agreements. Given that certain Member States cannot provisionally apply international agreements, this means the Council had accepted as a matter of law that no parts of the agreement fell outside the competences of the Union. Otherwise it was not possible to provisionally apply such agreements. However, this shows that the participation by Member States does not add anything. The only purpose is to ensure that the agreement is to be approved by all Member States, nullifying the voting requirements in the Council while ensuring some degree of international 'visibility' to States.

[148] Whenever an international agreement contains a provision which allows for provisional application it is up to the contracting parties to implement it under the requirements of their national laws. While the great majority of Member States can only apply provisionally subject to domestic law either when the agreement does not refer to matters reserved for statutory regulation or if the requirements for parliamentary approval are respected (*Treaty making—Expression of Consent by States to be bound by a Treaty*, edited by the Council of Europe, 2001, 84–85). Following a constitutional reform in Austria in 2008, provisional application has become possible (when the international agreement does not contain rights and obligations for natural persons or when the international agreement corresponds to the existing legal situation), two Member States can certainly not apply international agreements provisionally (as is the case of Luxembourg and Portugal). In the case concerning the accession agreement of the EFTA States to the ATA, three Member States issued a statement to the Council minutes that they were not in a position to apply the accession agreement and the ancillary agreement provisionally.

[149] Judgment in Case C-28/12 *Commission v Council*, EU:C:2015:282.

[150] [2010] OJ L223/3.

B. Parallel Competences

Problems are encountered often as regards situations of so-called 'parallel' competences. They are now mentioned in Article 4 TFEU. Article 4(4) TFEU provides that:

> [i]n the areas of development cooperation and humanitarian aid, the Union shall have competence to carry out activities and conduct a common policy: however, the exercise of that competence shall not result in Member States being prevented from exercising theirs.

The respective provisions in Title III of Part Five TFEU concerning cooperation with third countries and humanitarian aid (Articles 208–214 TFEU) add that the Union's measures and those of the Member States shall complement and reinforce each other; this is set out in Article 208(1), first sentence TFEU for development cooperation and in the last sentence of Article 214(1) TFEU for humanitarian aid.[151] Article 209(2) TFEU makes it clear that the Union's competence to conclude agreements with third parties does not affect the Member States' competence to negotiate in international bodies and to conclude international agreements. The wording of this provision is similar to Article 214(4) TFEU in relation to humanitarian aid.[152]

The Union's policy neither replaces nor encroaches on the Member States' own policies in these areas.[153] By contrast to the so-called 'shared competences', which are listed in Article 4(2) TFEU, the effect pursuant to Article 2(2) TFEU does not apply to the field of parallel competences. It follows that the Union's competence in these policy fields is not exclusive, but complementary to that of the Member States.[154] The special nature of parallel competences imposes a reinforced

[151] Economic, financial and technical cooperation with third countries pursuant to Article 212 TFEU is not explicitly mentioned in Article 4(4) TFEU as an area of parallel competence. However, according to Article 212(1) TFEU 'the Union's operations and those of the Member States shall complement and reinforce each other', so that actions both by the Union and by its Member States remain possible. It should be underlined that Article 212 TFEU is subsidiary in relation to other Union policies, as it reads at the beginning 'without prejudice to the other provisions of the Treaties, and in particular Articles 208 to 211' so that this article is not designed to be a self-standing Union policy, but rather a legal basis for the financing of cooperation measures.

[152] It must, however, be recalled that situations of parallel competence may arise in other contexts too. This may be the case as regards agreements in the area of titles of intellectual property rights, where the 'EU' title coexists with national titles. See Council Decision of 27 October 2003 approving the accession of the European Community to the Protocol relating to the Madrid Agreement concerning the international registration of marks, adopted at Madrid on 27 June 1989 ([2003] OJ L296, 14.11.2003, pp 20–21) and Council Decision of 18 December 2006 approving the accession of the European Community to the Geneva Act of the Hague Agreement concerning the international registration of industrial designs, adopted in Geneva on 2 July 1999 ([2006] OJ L386, 29.12.2006, pp 28–43).

[153] One reason for treating EU's development and humanitarian aid policy differently from other areas under shared competence is the matter of cumulative spending: the Member States' own policies are financed from their own, and not from the EU's budget. As a result, more finance in total will be available for these policy areas, which results in a more intensive policy.

[154] Case C-268/94, *Portugal v Council*, EU:C:1996:461, para 36.

obligation to coordinate upon the Union and its Member States.[155] Case law has construed this competence as meaning that under the aforementioned provisions the Member States are entitled to enter into commitments themselves vis-à-vis non-member countries, either collectively or individually, or even jointly with the Union. For instance, in the *Bangladesh aid* case, Member States decided collectively outside the Union's framework, albeit meeting within the Council, to give humanitarian aid to Bangladesh.[156]

Although nobody has seriously question that mixity is not necessary in this area, and this has been confirmed in the *Portugal v Council* judgment on the agreement with India,[157] Member States still insist very often on concluding these agreements as mixed. The very cumbersome procedure which ensues is often mitigated by concluding a separate 'interim' agreement covering only trade (for which the EU has exclusive competence) or agreeing on the provisional application of certain provisions, for which the EU is competent.

One wonders why Member States would see a real need to be parties themselves to certain agreements. Article 218 TFEU allows concluding agreements with both non-CFSP and CFSP clauses, so this is not a case of the EU not having competence. The fact of the EU concluding a cooperation or partnership agreement does not affect the competence of Member States to also conclude cooperation agreements. In many cases only a few Member States have cooperation agreements with the third country, but, if the EU negotiates one, there will be an insistence on the agreement being mixed, so that all Member States will have to follow their constitutionally based provisions for concluding international agreements. Some of those Member States would have normally never thought of actually having a cooperation agreement with the third country in question; why insist on concluding this one? The conclusion of the agreement in question as mixed adds nothing in terms of competence. There is no 'gap' to be filled. The agreement will often have the same content if it is concluded as mixed or not. Therefore, the rationale of mixity in such situations of parallel competence has nothing to do with the lack of EU competence over the matter, but it is probably a way to nullify the provisions of the Treaties.

The recent *Philippines* case[158] has helped to stop a tendency to interpret too narrowly the judgment in *Portugal v Council* concerning the cooperation agreement with India, It has also helped to better define the scope of Article 209 TFEU as legal basis, even if mixity was not questioned in that case. By affirming

[155] For development policy, such a duty to coordinate is set out in Article 210 TFEU which aims at promoting the complementarity and efficiency of the action of the Union and its Member States. For humanitarian aid, a similar provision is contained in Article 214(6) TFEU. However, Member States are also bound by the principle of sincere cooperation pursuant to Article 4(3) TEU when they are acting in the area of parallel competences.

[156] Judgment in Joined cases C-181/91 and C-248/91, *European Parliament v Council and Commission*, EU:C:1993:271.

[157] Case C-268/94, *Portugal v Council*, EU:C:1996:461.

[158] Case C-377/12, *Commission v Council*, judgment of 11 June 2014, EU:C:2014:1903.

that Article 209 TFEU provided a sufficient legal basis to cover certain provisions of a sectorial nature, the Court of Justice also prevents claims of mixity based on the shared nature of the competence which other legal bases may imply.

The agreement with the Philippines belonged to a wide category of agreements ('framework', 'partnership', 'cooperation') which set out (apart from possible provisions on trade) in general terms the main areas of cooperation with the third country concerned, and the main objectives thereof. Although with varying degrees of detail, this type of framework agreement has been concluded with a number countries. The practice as to the legal basis to be used for their conclusion has not been consistent. Whereas some agreements have been concluded by the EU only and using just two legal basis (trade and development cooperation), most of them have been concluded as mixed agreements and the conclusion of a number of them has been based on several other provisions in the applicable Treaty. This addition was very often aimed at reflecting the existence of provisions covering cooperation in some specific areas. In its more recent practice the Commission has proposed to base the conclusion of these agreements on two legal bases, normally trade and development cooperation (for developing countries) or economic technical cooperation (for the other countries). The case was prompted by a review of the practice by the Council. Several legal bases were added, and the same was likely to happen from then on. The most likely scenario was that in the future the Council would not agree to only rely on two articles (trade and cooperation) in order to conclude this type of general agreement with a third country, and that the Council would systematically change the legal bases proposed in order to add a few other legal bases.

The issue of legal bases is important because they determine the procedure for concluding the agreement (voting majority and degree of participation of each institution), the nature of EU's competences to conclude and implement the agreement, and whether or not Member States may (or need to) conclude the agreement as well (mixity). Whereas development cooperation is a 'parallel' competence (Article 4(5) TFEU) and trade is an exclusive one (Article 3(1) TFEU), most of the sectorial legal bases are shared competences (Article 4(2) TFEU). The Court of Justice has added that the issue is not only of 'domestic' importance. It has held that through the choice of legal basis the Union gives an indication to the other contracting parties with regard to the extent of the Union's competence and with regard to the division of competence between the Union and its Member States.[159]

In the instant case, the Council considered that three legal basis should be added to the ones proposed (ie Articles 207 and 209 TFEU), namely, transport (Articles 91 and 100), environment (Article 192(1)) and home affairs (Article 79(3) on re-admission).

[159] Judgment in, Case C-94/03, *Commission v Council*, judgment of 10 January 2006. EU:C:2006:2, para 55.

The Court had to examine whether, among the provisions of the Framework Agreement, those relating to re-admission of nationals of the contracting parties, to transport and to the environment also fall within development cooperation policy or whether they go beyond the framework of that policy and therefore require the contested decision to be founded on additional legal bases. It considered that EU policy in the field of development cooperation is not limited to measures directly aimed at the eradication of poverty, but also pursues the objectives referred to in Article 21(2) TEU, such as the objective, set out in Article 21(2)(d), of fostering the sustainable economic, social and environmental development of developing countries, with the primary aim of eradicating poverty. The Court recalled its judgment in *Portugal v Council*, where it concluded that the fact that a development cooperation agreement contains clauses concerning various specific matters cannot alter the characterisation of the agreement, which must be determined having regard to its essential object and not in terms of individual clauses, provided that those clauses do not impose such extensive obligations concerning the specific matters referred to that those obligations in fact constitute objectives distinct from those of development cooperation.

The Court considered that even if a measure contributes to the economic and social development of developing countries, it does not fall within development cooperation policy if it has as its main purpose the implementation of another policy. Even if the word 'development' did not appear in the title of the Framework Agreement, the intention of the contracting parties to promote sustainable social and economic development, the eradication of poverty and the achievement of the Millennium Development Goals is affirmed in the preamble to the Framework Agreement. It was also apparent from the whole of the Framework Agreement that the cooperation and partnership provided for by it take account especially of the needs of a developing country and, therefore, contribute to furthering, in particular, pursuit of the objectives referred to in Articles 21(2)(d) TEU and 208(1) TFEU.

The Court concluded that the provisions of the Framework Agreement relating to re-admission of nationals of the contracting parties, to transport and to the environment, consistently with the European Consensus,[160] contribute to the pursuit of the objectives of development cooperation. As regards the extent of the obligations set out in those provisions, Article 34 relating to the environment and natural resources and Article 38 relating to transport are limited to declarations of the contracting parties on the aims that their cooperation must pursue and the subjects to which that cooperation will have to relate, and do not determine in concrete terms the manner in which the cooperation will be implemented. As regards re-admission of nationals of the contracting parties, Article 26(3) of the Framework Agreement contained specific obligations. The Philippines and the Member States undertake therein to re-admit their nationals who do not fulfil, or

[160] Joint statement by the Council and the representatives of the governments of the Member States meeting within the Council, the European Parliament and the Commission on European Union Development Policy: 'The European Consensus' ([2006] OJ C46/1).

no longer fulfil, the conditions of entry or residence in the territory of the other party, upon request by the latter and without undue delay once the nationality of those nationals has been established and due process carried out, and to provide their nationals with documents required for such purposes. They also agree to conclude an agreement governing admission and re-admission as soon as possible. However, Article 26 of the Framework Agreement does not prescribe in concrete terms the manner in which cooperation concerning re-admission of nationals of the contracting parties is to be implemented, a conclusion which is reinforced by the commitment, in Article 26(4), to conclude a re-admission agreement very soon. It concludes that the provisions of the Framework Agreement relating to re-admission of nationals of the contracting parties, to transport and to the environment do not contain obligations so extensive that they may be considered to constitute objectives distinct from those of development cooperation that are neither secondary nor indirect in relation to the latter objectives. It followed that the Council was wrong in selecting Articles 79(3), 91, 100 and 191(4) TFEU as legal bases for the contested decision.

This judgment is fully in line not only with the judgment on the agreement with India, but also with the *ECOWAS* judgment, which made it clear that the objectives of development cooperation are 'broad in the sense that it must be possible for the measures required for their pursuit to concern various specific matters'.[161] The Court held that Articles of the EC Treaty dealing with cooperation with developing countries,

> refer not only to the sustainable economic and social development of those countries, their smooth and gradual integration into the world economy and the campaign against poverty, but also to the development and consolidation of democracy and the rule of law, as well as to respect for human rights and fundamental freedoms, in compliance also with commitments in the context of the United Nations and other international organisations.[162]

While the objectives of development cooperation policy

> should therefore not be limited to measures directly related to the campaign against poverty, it is none the less necessary, if a measure is to fall within that policy, that it contributes to the pursuit of that policy's economic and social development objectives.[163]

In the light of this case law, it is obvious that individual clauses which relate to other policies do not necessarily need a distinct legal basis. This would only be necessary, if such clauses establish obligations which constitute objectives distinct from those of development cooperation.

A case apart is that of 'association' agreements. An association agreement creates 'special, privileged links with a non-member country which must, at least

[161] Case C-91/05, *Commission v Council* (*ECOWAS*), judgment of 20 May 2008, EU:C:2008:288, para 64, referring to Case C-268/94, *Portugal v Council*, EU:C:1996:461, para 37.

[162] Case C-91/05, *Commission v Council*, EU:C:2008:288, para 65.

[163] Case C-91/05, *Commission v Council*, EU:C:2008:288, para 67.

to a certain extent, take part in the Community system'.[164] Article 217 TFEU 'must necessarily empower the Community to guarantee commitments towards non-member countries in all the fields covered by the Treaty'. The Court considered in *Demirel* that if the issue was 'covered by the Treaty',

> the question whether the Court has jurisdiction to rule on the interpretation of a provision in a mixed agreement containing a commitment which only the Member States could enter into in the sphere of their own powers does not arise.[165]

Therefore, the concept of 'association' is a unique concept of EU law, which as far as this authors knows, does not exist in the laws of the Member States. The third country is associated 'to the Union', and not to Member States.[166] Association is not defined as a parallel competence, but the practice is to conclude association agreements as mixed.[167] At the time this was often justified because of the provisions on political dialogue that they included. Nowadays such reason is not enough to justify mixity. An association can only cover (partly or entirely) the areas which are covered by the Treaties.[168] If it goes beyond, it is not an association, but something different. Therefore, with hindsight, the mixity of such agreements is not only clearly unnecessary, but probably unlawful.

C. 'Shared' is not 'Mixed'

Because the issue of the nature of the competence should not be confused with the existence of the competence, it is clear that an agreement over which the EU has shared competences can also be concluded by the EU only. The existence of a competence does not depend on the prior adoption of internal rules harmonising the area concerned. It is only its nature as being exclusive which, to some extent, depends on its prior internal exercise.[169]

[164] Judgment in Case 12/86 *Demirel v Stadt Schwäbisch Gmünd* [1987] ECR 3719, EU:C:1987:400.

[165] Ibid para 9.

[166] The judgment in *Green Network* also supports the idea that 'association' can only be of exclusive competence. That case partly was about the extension of the EU rules to a third country. Quite logically the Court of Justice considered that the extension of the EU rules to a third country alters the scope of such rules and must logically be carried out by the EU, not its Member States. An association is precisely about extending EU rules to the 'associated' third country. Such extension can only be concluded by the EU.

[167] The only recent exception is the association with Kosovo, which was concluded by the Union because a few member States do not recognize Kosovo as a state. Council Decision (EU) 2016/342 of 12 February 2016 on the conclusion, on behalf of the Union, of the Stabilisation and Association Agreement between the European Union and the European Atomic Energy Community, of the one part, and Kosovo*, of the other part (OJ L 71, 16.3.2016, p 1).

[168] Judgment in Case 12/86 *Demirel v Stadt Schwäbisch Gmünd* [1987] ECR 3719, EU:C:1987:400 para 9.

[169] Still now, this basic proposition is often questioned and, in 2015, Germany (supported of France and the United Kingdom) even decided to bring a challenge to the Court. In this pending case, these Member States take the view that the Council was not empowered to adopt a decision establishing the position to be taken at a meeting of the Convention concerning International Carriage by Rail (*COTIF*) (C-600/14, pending) since the Union had not yet legislated internally on that very matter.

Although we saw before that the Court of Justice was not clear about the legal relevance of classifying one competence as shared, Article 2(2) TFEU is clearer and must be logically interpreted as pre-empting the Member States' signature (and ratification) of an agreement which is signed (and concluded) by the EU alone on the basis of its shared competences.[170] It means that when the EU exercises its (shared) competence, Member States will not exercise their competence. This is why some recent Council decisions make it clear that the Union is not exercising 'shared competence':[171] in this way, the Council paves the way for the conclusion of the agreement as a mixed one.

In her Opinion in Case C-13/07, Advocate-General Kokott further enquired about the nature of shared competence. For her, shared competence had to be understood as *concurrent* competence in the sense that 'the Member States exercise their competence in so far as the Union has not exercised its competence. However, if the Union does exercise its competence, it acts *alone*, so far as that competence is sufficient'.[172] In other words, the conclusion of an international agreement would have the same pre-emptive effect as the adoption of 'internal' EU legislation. This conclusion can be inferred also from Article 4(3) and (4) TFEU, which provides, as an exception to the general rule in Article 2(2) TFEU, that in some areas of shared competence (research, technological development, space, development cooperation and humanitarian aid) the exercise by the EU of its competences shall not result in Member States being prevented from exercising theirs.[173]

The Union may adopt 'new' common rules in a given area even if there is no prior legislation in that area, or only legislation that covers the area very partially. This adoption of common rules may take the form of a Directive or a Regulation, but also of an international agreement, which would of course be binding also on Member States (Article 216(2) TFEU). The latter situation arises, for example, if the Union, in order to harmonise the rules of Member States, chooses to simply conclude an international agreement instead of adopting a Directive. The agreement may for example already contain the set of rules which the Union legislator

[170] Ch Timmermans (n 95 above) 163–64.

[171] Council Decision of 10 June 2013 on the signing, on behalf of the European Union, of the Beijing Treaty on Audiovisual Performances ([2013] OJ L160 of 12.6.2013, p 1), recital 6: 'By signing the Beijing Treaty the Union will not be exercising shared competence, hence Member States retain their competence in the areas covered by the Beijing Treaty which do not affect common rules or alter the scope of such rules'. See similarly, recital 6 of Council Decision of 9 December 2013 on the signing, on behalf of the European Union, of the Protocol to Eliminate Illicit Trade in Tobacco Products to the World Health Organisation's Framework Convention on Tobacco Control, as regards its provisions on obligations related to judicial cooperation in criminal matters, the definition of criminal offences, and police cooperation ([2013] OJ L333, 12.12.2013, p 73).

[172] Opinion of Advocate-General Kokott in Case C-13/07 *Commission v Council*, EU:C:2009:190, para 76.

[173] The same can be said in the areas covered by the policies mentioned in Article 5 TFEU (coordination of economic, employment and social policies) and by the actions referred to in Article 6 TFEU (support, coordination or supplementing protection and improvement of human health, industry, culture, tourism, education, vocational training, youth, sport, civil protection and administrative cooperation).

considers necessary to apply internally in the Union. In other words, even if competence is not exclusive pursuant to Article 3(2) TFEU, the Union could still negotiate and conclude the agreement 'alone', as the exercise of shared competence is not based on the prior adoption of common rules.[174]

If it is clear that once the agreement at issue falls under EU competence (even as a shared competence), the participation of Member States in such agreement as contracting parties is not necessary, the next question would be whether this participation is compatible with the Treaties, and if so, whether there are any limits or conditions that must be fulfilled. In Opinion 1/76 the Court of Justice was at pains to explain why participation on the part of Member States was legally possible. The Court considered it necessary in view of the fact that they were party to an earlier Convention. Such participation was considered 'as being solely for this purpose and not as necessary for the attainment of other features of the system'.[175] Although the Opinion 1/76 never classified the competence as exclusive, this justification was partly the basis for the conclusion, later in Opinion 1/94, that this situation was one of exclusive competences. Other authors, unsatisfied with the later reinterpretation of Opinion 1/76, considered that it reflects a much sounder principle: that where an agreement 'comes entirely within the [EU's] shared competence ... mixity requires a specific justification and it is not simply optional'.[176]

Admittedly, the Council has traditionally accepted (and it did so in the *Broadcasters* case) that shared competence can be exercised by way of an international agreement, even if there is no internal *acquis*.[177] However, considering that whether or not shared competence is exercised is a matter of political discretion, it leaves in the hands of Member States whether the Council decides by 'common accord' or qualified majority. If the Council decides not to exercise the shared competence and the agreement is mixed, 'common accord' will be necessary in practice. If the Council decides to exercise shared competence, only qualified majority will be needed in most cases. And this as regards a set of provisions which may be identical in substance to the ones adopted by way of a directive, for whose adoption there is little doubt that qualified majority would suffice.

The *Broadcasters* and *Conditional Access* cases illustrated well the paradoxical results of this approach. The Union could adopt by ordinary legislative procedure

174 The exercise of the competence by an international agreement will be subject to the same material limitations as would its exercise through an 'autonomous' act. It must be borne in mind that if the legal basis excludes harmonisation, the Union will not have the competence to conclude an international agreement that entails such harmonisation: 'If an international agreement contains provisions which presume a harmonisation of legislative or regulatory measures of the Member States in an area for which the Treaty excludes such harmonisation, the Community does not have the necessary competence to conclude that agreement. Those limits of the external competence of the Community concern the very existence of that competence and not whether or not it is exclusive' (Opinion 1/03, EU:C:2006:81, para 132).

175 Opinion 1/76, EU:C:1977:63, para 7.

176 P Eeckhout (n 38 above) 216.

177 This has been done in several instances, see M Cremona (n 19 above) 78–80.

a directive that would improve the existing rights of broadcasting organisations, or an amendment to the Conditional access Directive. However, the Council's position was that if instead of adopting such internal piece of legislation, such common rules are the result of an international negotiation, Member States 'must' be party to the agreement and de facto unanimity will apply.

It is submitted that such a paradoxical result cannot be reconciled with the case law and its rationale. In certain contexts, collective action by Member States should logically be carried out by the Union. Member States have created the EU in order 'to attain objectives they have in common' (Article 1 TEU), and they cannot seek to attain those objectives by other means and procedures.[178] This principle applies in the internal as well as in the external sphere. The above reasoning seems compelling in recent cases where there is a significant body of EU legislation, and the collective action did not take place outside the Treaties. In the *Broadcasters* and *Conditional Access* cases it was the Commission that proposed to the Council to authorise it to negotiate the agreement. A collective action by Member States to agree on common rules on the few bits where the Council and Member States considers there is some 'national competence' may be also defined as an instance of harmonisation outside the framework of the Treaties. Ultimately, what the Council presents as a 'common accord' of the Member States as regards some very limited bits of the future agreement seems thus rather to be an action of the Council.[179]

The collective exercise of the shared competence by the Member States for minor pieces of the agreement implies the refusal of the possibility for the Union to exercise the shared competence. By contrast, submitting that the fact that the Council does not really have 'the option' to exercise shared competence, when the agreement is already covered for the rest by exclusive competence, explains why the EU must act alone. In view of the fact that under such circumstances the EU has no option but to exercise its competence amounts in practice to regarding the competence has having become exclusive. This 'shortcut' can be seen as part of the rationale of the 'largely covered test' for the definition of exclusive competence. The Court of Justice may not prevent Member States from concluding international agreements in areas where there is no or very little EU law, even if the EU could act under shared competence. Yet, when the regulatory centre of gravity tilts in favour of the Union, as EU law contains a set of basic rules which reflect what is considered to be the commonality that can be attained among Member States,

[178] As P Eeckhout, puts it 'where all the Member States become parties themselves, as it is the standard approach, there is no mistaking that the agreement will establish common rules for the entire EU. In that case, mixity, with all associated difficulties could, at least in some cases, be considered to violate Article 4(3) TEU' (n 38 above) 217.

[179] The Court of Justice suggests as much when it recalls that it is entitled to verify 'having regard to its content and all the circumstances in which it was adopted', whether 'the act in question is not in reality a decision of the Council' (Joined cases C-181/91 and C-248/91, *European Parliament v Council and Commission*, EU:C:1993:271).

when an international negotiation is going to strike a balance in the same area, it will be for the EU to act, not its individual Member States.[180]

On this point, the case law on competences shares the same logic as the case law on legal basis. The choice of legal basis for an EU measure must rest on objective factors that are amenable to judicial review; these include the aim and content of that measure.[181] If examination of that measure reveals that it pursues a twofold purpose or that it has a twofold component and if one of those is identifiable as the main or predominant purpose or component, whereas the other is merely incidental, that measure must be based on a single legal basis, namely that required by the main or predominant purpose or component.[182]

It has been often argued that the approach of predominant/incidental or principal and ancillary applies between legal bases, but not in the horizontal division of competences between the EU and its Member States. The recent judgments appear to defy that approach. The *Conditional Access* case is the perfect example. Provisions on confiscation were covered by the legal basis on commercial policy, as they were ancillary to the main purpose of the agreement, but the EU had (shared) competence over those provisions if examined in isolation. It is interesting to note that following similar reasoning Advocate-General Kokott had concluded that, if the legal basis was Article 114 TFEU, and the claim for exclusivity had to be based on Article 3(2) TFEU, the EU would have exclusive competence anyway, on the basis of the 'largely covered' test.

By concluding that competence is exclusive on the basis of the principal/ancillary test or the 'largely covered' test, or that shared competence is not a simple 'option', but is to be exercised in certain circumstances, the EU is not really depriving Member States of any sovereign right or 'retained competence'. More in general, there is no 'transfer of powers to Brussels' just because an international agreement is concluded in exercise of non-exclusive competences, since the EU competence is already there to be exercised. On the one hand, the EU could by qualified majority exercise the shared competence over the issues which are perceived by Member States to be within national competence (in reality shared by the EU) by

[180] The perspective of examining 'areas' justifies that a given article in the international agreement is covered by exclusive competence, since the article in question is negotiated together with other articles as a package. The 'area' which is regulated becomes crucial. For example, an article on confiscation can fall in exclusive competence when it is ancillary to other provisions. However, this does not necessarily mean that an international agreement on confiscation 'in general', covering all possible areas, will have the same effect on EU competence. In such scenario the regulatory 'area' will be confiscation as a general law enforcement measure, and the lack of any provision on confiscation in the directive may mean that the agreement will not have the same effect on EU competence. The centre of gravity will be different.

[181] Case C-137/12, *Commission v Council*, EU:C:2013:675, para 52.

[182] Ibid para 53. With regard to a measure that simultaneously pursues a number of objectives, or that has several components, which are inseparably linked without one's being incidental to the other, the Court has held that, where various provisions of the Treaty are therefore applicable, such a measure will have to be founded, exceptionally, on the various corresponding legal bases (judgment of 6 September 2012 in Case C-490/10, *Parliament v Council*, EU:C:2012:525, para 46), unless the procedures laid down for each legal basis are incompatible with each other (Ibid para 47).

adopting a directive or a regulation. The loss of sovereignty which the use of qualified majority implies is already there. It is the choice of normative instrument (EU legislation or international agreement) that is concerned, not the competence to adopt legally binding acts in the area concerned. On the other hand, Article 3(2) TFEU only refers to external competence, as its field of application is limited to the conclusion of international agreements, which means that Member States may keep whatever margin of manoeuvre EU internal *acquis* leaves them.

VI. CONCLUSIONS

Case law on external competence is forward-looking and not only backwards-looking as it was generally assumed. The Court of Justice is concerned about the future exercise of the powers of the Union, not just about contradictions with existing *acquis*. The case law also matches the tendency in composite polities to define differently external treaty-making power and internal law-making. In so doing, the judgments contain an outright rejection of certain extreme approaches, which would have led to a decrease of the competences of the EU after the Treaty of Lisbon. The Court clearly excludes the relevance of Protocol No 25, and is not impressed by arguments relying on the minimal nature of certain provisions, thereby rejecting an interpretation of prior case law to the effect that any element of minimal harmonisation would imply shared competence.

Authoritative voices wonder if the difference between exclusive and shared competence really matters.[183] In practice, it still does. Certainly there are instances where exclusivity cannot be fully operational, since the EU is not a member of an organisation, or cannot be party to an agreement because such possibility is reserved to States.[184] There can be also instances where the EU may decide to authorise Member States to act. And the EU does sometimes exercise shared competences in such a way that parallel participation of the Member States is not needed. It is not all black or white. And yet, the lack of willingness to effectively use non-exclusive competences makes it often crucial to decide first the nature of the competence. It is only if competence is exclusive that some necessary discipline in the area of external relations is (sometimes reluctantly) accepted by Member States.

Mixity implies a number of unnecessary and serious downsides. It often implies 29 separate ratification procedures, unduly delaying the EU's actions by several years; it nullifies the qualified majority, and introduces intergovernmentalism in the EU decision-making process. At the same time, unless legally required, mixity adds nothing in terms of competence, standing or effectiveness of the agreement.

[183] A Rosas, 'Exclusive, shared and national competence in the context of EU external relations: do such distinctions matter?' in S Adam, P Van Elsuwege, I Govaere, *The European Union in the World; Essays in Honour of Professor Marc Maresceau* (Oxford, Hart Publishing, 2014) 17.

[184] Yet, recent case law is a good reminder that even there the EU must follow internally the right procedure. See C-399/12, *Germany* v *Council*, EU:C:2014:2258 and Opinion 1/13, EU:C:2014:2303.

International agreements concluded by the EU within its sphere of competence bind also the Member States (Article 216(2) TFEU). In other words, national authorities will have to apply the agreements in the same way as if the agreement had been concluded by its 'own' national executives and legislatures.

The fact that Member States more easily agree to exercise shared competence through directives or regulations than through international agreements shows that that their concerns are about visibility on the international stage, nothing else. The conclusion of international agreements by the EU has a more 'existential' dimension as it shapes the identity and standing in international relations, not always easily recognised by third parties. In imposing mixity as regards international agreements which have a 'certain importance', Member States knowingly counter that process, as mixed agreements convey the message the EU is to be perceived as an appendix of Member States lacking full personality in international relations.

Time will tell what impact this recent case law will have on the EU's future practice. So far the reaction by Member States is that of surprise and denial, even if the cases were decided in the most predictable way. The next step should be the definition of the conditions of exercise and the legal consequences of shared competences. It may come sooner than expected.

Part III

International Law as Law of the EU

4

The Integration of Public International Law in EU Law: Analytical and Normative Questions

PIET EECKHOUT*

Content:

I. INTRODUCTION

THE RELATIONSHIP BETWEEN public international law and EU law continues to fascinate and to evolve. The core question of when international agreements have direct effect in EU law has long since been fully explored, and appears, at least at a level of principle, to be more or less answered.[1] But new issues have appeared on the horizon, such as the status of customary international law;[2] the relationship between UN Security Council sanctions and their implementation by the EU;[3] the role played by international treaties and conventions concluded by the Member States, but not by the EU;[4] questions of

* Professor of EU Law at University College London.

[1] See eg P Eeckhout, *EU External Relations Law*, 2nd edn (Oxford, OUP, 2011); M Mendez, *The Legal Effects of EU Agreements* (Oxford, OUP, 2013).

[2] See eg A Gianelli, 'Customary International Law in the EU' in A Cannizzaro, P Palchetti and R Wessel (eds), *International Law as Law of the EU* (Leiden, Martinus Nijhoff, 2011) 93.

[3] See eg L van den Herik, 'Peripheral hegemony in the quest to secure Security Council accountability for its individualized sanctions regimes', *Grotius Centre Working Paper* 2014/026-PSL; C Eckes, 'EU restrictive measures against natural and legal persons: from counterterrorist to third country sanctions' (2014) 51 *Common Market Law Review* 869, at 875–79.

[4] See eg A Rosas, 'The status in EU law of international agreements concluded by EU Member States' (2011) 34 *Fordham International Law Journal* 1304.

international responsibility for violations of mixed agreements;[5] and the effect of EU accession to the ECHR.[6]

It is further clear that the evolving relationship between EU law and international law cannot be dissociated from the constitutional and institutional evolution of the European Union. The Treaty of Lisbon has attempted to institutionalise the project of turning the EU into a full global actor, in particular by creating the External Action Service. It has also sought to constitutionalise this project, emphasising the need for full respect of international law (Articles 3(5) and 21 TEU). This is in line with the Normative Power Europe concept, coined by international relations scholars who emphasise the specific norm-oriented character of the EU.[7] Respect for international law is now expressly a core EU constitutional norm and value, also acknowledged by the Court of Justice.[8] These and other developments mean that it is worth revisiting the relationship between public international law and EU law, taking stock of where it stands, and reflecting on where it might be going.

Ideally this exercise should be principled, and not merely casuistic, archival, or even worse anecdotal. The *Kadi* litigation has had the fortunate effect of leading many scholars to look at the interface between EU and international law.[9] The *Kadi I* judgment of the Court of Justice was not, it is fair to say, universally acclaimed. From a theoretical perspective, many have read it as confirming legal pluralism, perhaps even in its most radical form.[10] EU law and international law were conceived of, by the Court, as wholly separate legal systems, with an unbridgeable gap between them. The Court, according to some, was even unwilling to contemplate a positive '*Solange*' principle: some read the judgment as denying *in principle*, that there could be effective judicial protection at the international level which could obviate the need for such review at EU level.[11] I have never read *Kadi I* in this way,

[5] See eg PJ Kuijper, 'International responsibility for EU mixed agreements' in C Hillion and P Koutrakos (eds), *Mixed Agreements Revisited* (Oxford, Hart Publishing, 2010) 208.

[6] See eg P Gragl, 'A giant leap for European human rights? The final Agreement on the European Union's accession to the European Convention on Human Rights' (2014) 51 *Common Market Law Review* 13.

[7] See, in the first instance, the seminal paper by I Manners, 'Normative Power Europe: A Contradiction in Terms?' (2002) 40 *Journal of Common Market Studies* 235.

[8] Case C-366/10 *Air Transport Association for America v Secretary of State for Energy and Climate Change* EU:C:2011:864, paragraph 101 and Joined Cases C-584/10 P, C-593/10 P and C-595/10 P *Commission and Others v Kadi (Kadi II)* EU:C:2013:518, paragraph 103.

[9] The literature on *Kadi* does not fit into a single footnote. Some of the notable contributions include G de Búrca, 'The European Court of Justice and the International Legal Order After *Kadi*' (2010) 51 *Harvard International Law Journal* 1; JHH Weiler, 'Editorial' (2008) 19 *European Journal of International Law* 895; D Halberstam and E Stein, 'The United Nations, the European Union, and the King of Sweden: Economic Sanctions and Individual Rights in a Plural World Order' (2009) 46 *Common Market Law Review* 13; P Eeckhout, '*Kadi and Al Barakaat*: Luxembourg is not Texas—or Washington DC' (2009) *EJIL:Talk*, available at: www.ejiltalk.org/kadi-and-al-barakaat-luxembourg-is-not-texas-or-washington-dc/. For an overview of some of the literature, see S Poli and M Tzanou, 'The *Kadi* Rulings: A Survey of the Literature' (2009) 28 *Yearbook of European Law* 533.

[10] On radical pluralism, see N Krisch, *Beyond Constitutionalism—The Pluralist Structure of Postnational Law* (Oxford, Oxford University Press, 2010).

[11] Joined Cases C-402/05 P and C-415/05 P *Kadi v Council and Commission (Kadi I)* EU:C:2008:461, paragraphs 319–322; see Weiler (above n 9); Halberstam and Stein (above n 9) at 59–61.

but have to admit that the more recent ruling in *Kadi II* does not at first sight bring us any closer to a positive '*Solange*' principle in the EU-UNSC relationship. The UN remedies are prospective—an application to the Ombudsperson may result in de-listing, but the Ombudsperson cannot judge the legality or appropriateness of the original listing—whereas the Court emphasises the need for effective judicial protection to be retrospective.[12] In those circumstances it is difficult to see the mechanism through which the Court could ever reach a finding that the UN system offers sufficient protection of fundamental rights.

The bright minds who have looked at the relationship between international law and EU law, as a result of *Kadi I*, have attempted, not just to analyse the relationship, but to move to a normative level. How should the relationship be conceived, and how should it develop? This chapter aims to further the debate, both at an analytical and a normative level. It argues that the relationship is not as pluralist as is often assumed. Instead, it takes as its starting point (and takes seriously) the Court's statement that international norms which are binding on the EU are an integral part of EU law. The basic argument is that, notwithstanding *Kadi*, the integration of international law into EU law is a more appropriate paradigm, characterising the relationship as it currently stands, and as it ought to evolve.

II. PLURALISM OR INTEGRATION?

Much of the normative reflection taking place about the relationship between international law and EU law adopts a kind of top-down approach. A particularly good example is Graínne de Búrca's article on *Kadi I*. In this impressive piece the author engages with different theoretical perspectives—strong legal pluralism, and strong constitutionalism—to put forward, in the end, her own normative position, which she calls 'soft constitutionalism'. This conception is, ultimately, derived from Immanuel Kant, and is introduced as a Kantian re-reading of cosmopolitan constitutionalism.[13] This is an immensely worthwhile intellectual project, but it is, in essence, an exercise in political philosophy, and not in legal theory. If the message is that a particular political philosophy should guide the EU Court of Justice when dealing with the relationship between EU law and international law, then frankly I disagree. It is not the role of a Court which is asked to ensure that the law is applied, to base its decisions on considerations of political philosophy which, though intellectually attractive, are too far removed from the current legal landscape.

There are other ways of engaging with the normative questions about how the relationship between international and EU law ought to evolve. Taking the law and legal developments seriously, the move to a normative level ought to be based on a prior conceptualisation of what has been taking place. Some kind of analytical

[12] *Kadi II* (above n 8), paragraph 134.

[13] De Búrca (above n 9) at 39–40.

theory is first required, which conceptualises the current state of the law. It is only on the basis of a proper conceptualisation of how the relations between legal systems *are* evolving that one can start answering normative questions. Or perhaps this needs to be put in an even more direct way: a proper conceptualisation will, of itself, yield answers to normative questions. That is not to say that the exercise is wholly value-free: the perspective of the analyst and interpreter necessarily bears on his or her findings and conceptualisation. Nor is it to say that the exercise should be de-contextualised: a complete theory on the integration of laws needs to take the political, social and economic context on board. However, none of this obviates the need for linking the 'is' and the 'ought'.

Let me put my own cards on the table. I am sceptical of the concept of legal pluralism as an appropriate characterisation of how, in a European context, legal systems relate to each other. There is, of course, a plurality of legal systems. In today's world, laws are plural and not singular. That requires not just a concept of law, but a concept of laws. However, a plurality of systems does not of necessity imply that their relationships are marked by a concept of legal pluralism. It is true that the legal pluralism literature is vast and wide-ranging,[14] and that it is difficult to cite a commonly accepted definition of the concept of legal pluralism.[15] Nevertheless, at its centre the idea appears to be that the gap between legal systems is, in essence, unbridgeable. Each system has its own supreme authority—its own rules of recognition—and conflicts between systems cannot be resolved from within the law: ultimately, each system will give precedence to its own norms over those of the other system. It is good to have dialogue—for example between supreme courts—but such dialogue is a matter of comity rather than a legal imperative; a sociological process, if you like, rather than law.

At face value, the *Kadi* judgments of the Court of Justice exemplify pluralism. The Court opted for the application of the EU's own superior norms of human rights protection, and by so doing, rejected the claim of ultimate authority embedded in Article 103 UN Charter. It limited that claim to the international legal order, which it distinguished from the EU legal order. The Charter's ultimate authority could not penetrate the EU legal order, in the sense that it could not prevail over the EU's own constitutional values.[16] This means that the gap between EU and international legal orders is unbridgeable, each containing claims to ultimate authority which, as the *Kadi* case shows, may lead to conflict.

However, this reading of the relationship between international law and EU law is open to challenge. That challenge revolves around the concept of integration of

[14] See eg N MacCormick, *Questioning Sovereignty* (Oxford, OUP, 1999) 119; N Walker, 'The Idea of Constitutional Pluralism' (2002) 65 *Modern Law Review* 317, 337; N Krisch, 'The Open Architecture of European Human Rights Law' (2008) 71 *Modern Law Review* 183, 185; *Beyond Constitutionalism—The Pluralist Structure of Postnational Law* (above n 10) at 69.

[15] N Walker, 'Constitutionalism and Pluralism in Global Context' in M Avbelj and J Komárek (eds), *Constitutional Pluralism in the European Union and Beyond* (Oxford, Hart Publishing, 2012) 17.

[16] *Kadi I* (above n 11), paragraphs 285–288.

laws, which can be contrasted with legal pluralism. In an earlier paper, I addressed the question of the protection of human rights in EU law, in light of the concept of the autonomy of EU law.[17] The paper proposed this alternative conceptualisation of legal integration. The concept may not initially come across as original, yet is arguably more novel, in theoretical terms, than it may first appear. Legal integration is not to be confused with economic, or political, or yet other forms of integration. It is a concept which points to the fact that, increasingly, legal systems, particularly in Europe, are not only building closer links, but are actually integrating each other's norms into their own system of norms. Integration *of* laws rather than integration *through* law.[18] This is a process, of course, and it has its limits: the concept of integration of laws does not remove the plurality of legal systems, and is not monism in another name. But it is, nevertheless, a process which is clearly taking place, and for many relations between legal systems in Europe the direction of travel is towards greater integration. The earlier paper focused on the most clear-cut case of increasing legal integration: that of human rights protection in Europe, for which we now have the EU Charter, which incorporates the substance of the ECHR norms;[19] the proposed accession of the EU to the ECHR, formally linking EU law and the Convention;[20] and the ever more active dialogue between the European courts and national constitutional and supreme courts on questions of human rights protection. It may be added that the EU's accession to the ECHR comes within the scope of the present chapter, as the ECHR continues to be regarded as an international law instrument, including by the ECtHR.[21] The future relationship between EU law and the Convention will therefore be a component of the broader relationship between international law and EU law.

However, it is one thing to argue that European human rights law is marked by increasing integration, but does this legal integration paradigm extend to the general relationship between EU law and international law? In the following attempt to answer that question, the focus is on the extent to which international law is integrated in EU law—not the reverse issue of how EU law is integrated into international law.[22] Clearly, that integration is not as advanced as the integration of

[17] P Eeckhout, 'Human rights and the autonomy of EU law: Pluralism or integration?' (2013) 66 *Current Legal Problems* 169.

[18] M Cappelletti, M Seccombe and J Weiler (eds), *Integration through law* (Berlin, de Gruyter, 1986–87).

[19] See further W Weiss, 'Human Rights in the EU: rethinking the role of the European Convention on Human Rights after Lisbon' (2011) 7 *European Constitutional Law Review* 65.

[20] Draft revised Agreement on the Accession of the European Union to the Convention for the Protection of Human Rights and Fundamental Freedoms, 47+1(2013)008rev2, available at: www.coe.int/t/dghl/standardsetting/hrpolicy/Accession/Working_documents_en.asp. The CJEU's negative Opinion 2/13 of 18 December 2014, EU:C:2014:2454 is considered further below.

[21] L Wildhaber, 'The European Convention on Human Rights and International Law' (2007) 56 *International Comparative Law Quarterly* 217–31.

[22] An example of the latter is the EU's practice as regards international responsibility, which has strongly influenced the ILC's work on the responsibility of international organisations. See eg F Hoffmeister, 'Litigating against the European Union and its Member States—Who responds under the ILC's Draft Articles on the Responsibility of International Organisations?' (2010) 21 *European*

EU law into national law, or of human rights law in Europe. Yet there is, also here, an ongoing process of integration, notwithstanding the *Kadi* judgments, or those denying direct effect to the WTO agreements,[23] or to the UN Convention on the Law of the Sea,[24] or those in which the Court appears hostile towards international adjudication.[25]

III. THE INTEGRATION OF INTERNATIONAL LAW INTO EU LAW

Any analysis of the extent to which international law is integrated into EU law should start with the basic principle underpinning the Court's case law on international agreements concluded by the EU: they are an 'integral part' of EU law.[26] In fact, unless this statement can be shown to be wholly disingenuous or simply untrue, it confirms the idea that one should conceive of the relationship between EU and international law as to some extent integrated. The Court further routinely states that international law is binding, including customary international law. The Treaty of Lisbon has arguably strengthened the EU's commitment towards observing international law, by referring—as already indicated, in Article 3(5) TEU—to 'the strict observance and development of international law' as one of the EU's external action objectives. Article 21(1) TEU confirms that the EU needs to *respect* international law, which goes further than the more aspirational language of Article 3(5). The Court of Justice has referred to those provisions in the *ATA* case on airline emissions (at the start of the section in which it analysed the customary international law issues),[27] and in *Kadi II*, where it referred to them when examining whether access needs to be given to all the evidence underlying a counter-terrorism listing.[28]

All of those elements point towards a degree of integration of international law into EU law. Moreover, these principles, which the Treaty and case law enunciate, are not gratuitous statements, as the practice is on the whole consistent with them. Of course the integration is, first of all, limited to those norms of international law which are binding on the EU (but see below on the issue of treaty norms binding on all the EU Member States, but not on the EU as such). However, that limitation also points towards a principle of integration, rather than pluralism: next to the EU's own action (eg the conclusion of an agreement), it is the rules of recognition

Journal of International Law 723; JM Cortes, 'European exceptionalism in international law? The European Union and the system of international responsibility' at: ssrn.com/abstract=2279276.

[23] See in particular Case C-149/96 *Portugal v Council* EU:C:1999:574.

[24] Case C-308/06 *The Queen on the application of International Association of Independent Tanker Owners (Intertanko) v Secretary of State for Transport*, EU:C:2008:312.

[25] See eg Case C-459/03 *Commission v Ireland (MOX Plant)* EU:C:2006:345 and Case C-351/04 *Ikea Wholesale Ltd v Commissioners of Customs & Excise*, EU:C:2007:547.

[26] Case 181/73 *R & V Haegeman v Belgian State*, EU:C:1974:41.

[27] *Air Transport Association for America* (above n 8) paragraph 101.

[28] *Kadi II* (above n 8).

of international law itself which determine what is binding on the EU and what is not. For example, the law of treaties determines how treaties are made binding, and how they can be suspended or terminated.[29] There is, in this respect, no radical pluralism: EU law and international law together determine which norms of international law apply, and which do not.

Looking a bit more in detail at the case law, there is indeed a great deal of respect for international law. Many international agreements concluded by the EU are recognised as having direct effect in EU law.[30] This means they can be relied upon also by private parties, as conferring rights on them; rights which are enforceable, including in the face of conflicting EU or national legislation. Particularly as regards EU legislation, direct effect is a significant enforcement tool, because a directly effective agreement prevails, independently of whether the EU legislation does or does not pre-date the conclusion of the agreement. This means that, in contrast with many 'dualist' systems, the force of an agreement does not depend on an act of transposition having the same status as 'internal' legislative acts: the norms of an international agreement concluded by the EU are hierarchically superior to EU legislation.[31] Where direct effect is not granted, the principle of consistent interpretation applies. That principle is unlimited, in the sense that it extends to all international norms binding on the EU.[32] In fact, this principle of harmonious interpretation has been further extended, in *Intertanko*, to treaties and agreements binding on the Member States—but not on the EU as such.[33] Furthermore, customary international law is binding on the EU institutions when they legislate or adopt international decisions, and may also be relied upon by private parties.[34]

All of this suggests that international law is well integrated into EU law. Moreover, next to these integration principles, there is also the substantive integration of international law. Long gone are the days when the EU concluded mainly trade agreements. The links and connections between EU and international law are now wide-ranging: international trade law, international environmental law, the law of the sea, maintenance of peace and international security, conflicts of laws, international human rights law, international labour law, and soon international investment law; they all have a presence in EU law. In that sense, too, there is a process of ongoing legal integration.

This openness of EU law towards international law is not undisputed. A critic could argue that the above overview is a formalistic and superficial way of looking at the relationship. In actual fact, the Court of Justice refuses to apply international law where it really matters, in the sense that it would interfere with

[29] On suspension in accordance with *rebus sic stantibus*, see Case C-162/96 *A Racke GmbH & Co v Hauptzollamt Mainz*, EU:C:1998:293.

[30] Eeckhout (above n 1).

[31] *Kadi I* (above n 11), paragraph 307.

[32] Case C-61/94 *Commission v Germany*, EU:C:1996:313, paragraph 10.

[33] *Intertanko* (above n 24), paragraph 52.

[34] *Air Transport Association for America* (above n 8), paragraphs 101–111.

'internal' EU norms. The Court refuses direct effect to multilateral agreements, such as the WTO agreements and UNCLOS, which are not within the EU's political control and whose norms are not as close to the EU law paradigm as those contained in many bilateral agreements which *have* been recognised to be directly effective.[35] The *Kadi* litigation, the criticism would go, is the clearest example of how autonomous EU law is, and of the extent to which ultimate authority continues to be located within and confined to EU law. Where there is a real clash with international law, such as in the case of the UN Security Council's counter-terrorism policies, the Court of Justice opts for the supremacy of EU law, even in the face of a clear and primordial international conflict norm, such as the primacy of UN Charter obligations.[36] Nothing could be as pluralist as the *Kadi* judgments. In fact, in *Kadi II* the Court does not even mention the UN attempts to improve the counter-terrorism listing system consisting of the introduction of the office of the Ombudsperson.[37] That office has worked rather well, including in the case of Mr Kadi himself, who was de-listed at the UN level as a result of his application to the Ombudsperson. However, the Court's silence does not suggest that there could be scope, at some point, for a kind of positive '*Solange*' principle: a recognition that the UN system offers comparable guarantees of effective protection of fundamental rights to those offered in EU law.

A full reply to these and other objections to the concept of legal integration, as an appropriate paradigm for the relationship between international law and EU law, is outside the scope of this chapter. Given the centrality of the *Kadi* litigation to the pluralism claim, the following is limited to that litigation saga. It is submitted that there is a clear alternative reading of *Kadi* to the one outlined above as a critique of the lack of openness of EU law, and the conflicting claims to ultimate authority.

The first point to note is that, throughout the *Kadi* litigation, there was never an actual conflict between Mr Kadi's UN listing, and the freezing of his assets by the EU. In the 2008 *Kadi I* judgment, the Court of Justice maintained the effects of the EU Regulation in issue, and gave the institutions three months to remedy the human rights violations which it had established. Those three months were used to re-list Mr Kadi, on the basis of the UN summary of reasons which identified the alleged links between Mr Kadi and Al Qaeda.[38] Therefore, the annulment of his EU listing in *Kadi I* never became operative. Mr Kadi then challenged his re-listing, and was successful before the General Court in 2010, but that annulment ruling was subject to an appeal by the EU institutions and a couple of Member States, which had the effect of suspending the annulment. At the point in time when the Court of Justice decided that appeal (2013), Mr Kadi had been de-listed by the UN Sanctions Committee, as a result of his application to the UN

[35] Compare with Mendez (above n 1) ch 3.

[36] On Art 103 as a conflict rule, see J Pauwelyn, *Conflict of Norms in Public International Law* (Cambridge, Cambridge University Press, 2003) 337–42.

[37] *Kadi II* (above n 8). On the Ombudsperson, see van den Herik (above n 3).

[38] See Case T-85/09 *Kadi II* (General Court) EU:T:2010:418, paragraphs 49–62.

Ombudsperson (2012). At the end of the day, therefore, the potential conflict was managed rather well, and was never allowed to become an actual, positive law conflict.

The second point is that the UN Security Council listened to what the Court of Justice had to say in *Kadi I*, and adjusted its policies.[39] Not only did it introduce the office of the Ombudsperson but also the latest versions of the 'Al Qaeda resolutions' go so far as to 'recognise', in the preamble, the legal challenges to the implementation of the listings, and to express the intent of continuing to ensure that procedures are fair and clear.[40] That is a far cry from a direct clash between the binding nature of UN Charter obligations and municipal judicial review of the implementation of listings, including in the EU. The Security Council's reaction to the *Kadi* litigation was not to reject the EU-level judicial review, nor was it to deny or silence it. The former UN Rapporteur on Terrorism and Human Rights, Martin Scheinin, has identified what he calls a legal fiction, capable of reconciling the authority of the Security Council with municipal judicial review. Such review is a matter of implementation, he argues, and does not challenge the powers of the Security Council.[41] Of course this can be seen as a rather artificial legal fiction. But must the binding nature of UN Resolutions of necessity translate into an absolute lack of discretion at the level of implementation, leaving no room for review of individual cases? As long as the Security Council does not introduce a full review system for listings at the international level, it will need to accept judicial review at the municipal level. The *Kadi* saga led to a hybrid review system, with the Ombudsperson capable of examining cases with a view to a prospective worldwide delisting, and with municipal courts being asked to review domestic implementation of particular listings. That hybrid system need not be seen as a challenge to the authority of the Security Council; it is better to view it as a cooperative review system which enhances the legitimacy of the Security Council's listing policies.

The third point is connected to the first one. Yes, it is true that the scope for actual conflict, in the case of UN listings, continues to be present. Mr Kadi happened to be de-listed by the UN prior to the final judgment in *Kadi II*, but what if that had not been the case? However, the integration of legal systems does not mean that there can never be any real conflict. Nevertheless, in *Kadi II* the Court of Justice made a strong effort to further limit the scope for conflict. It expressly did *not* indict the whole UN listing system. It accepted that the EU institutions must give effect to UN listings, even if they have not seen any evidence in support of those listings.[42] From a fundamental rights perspective, that is a significant

[39] van den Herik (above n 3).

[40] See eg Resolution 2161(2014).

[41] L Ginsborg and M Scheinin, 'You Can't Always Get What You Want: The Kadi II Conundrum and the Security Council 1267 Terrorist Sanctions Regime' (2011) 8 *Essex Human Rights Review* 7. Note that Strasbourg adopted the same approach, see ECtHR, *Nada v Switzerland*, Application No 10593/2008, judgment of 12 September 2012, paragraphs 175–180.

[42] *Kadi II* (above n 8), paragraphs 106–116.

limitation to a person's rights of defence and right to property. It is only where the listed person initiates judicial review that further efforts need to be undertaken to show that the listing is justified. The test which the Court developed is, at least in one sense, deferential: where five reasons are given, it suffices if just one of them can be demonstrated to the satisfaction of the judges.[43] There is a serious burden on the applicant to show that the reasons (often mere allegations) are wholly unsupported by the facts. The EU institutions are not required to hand over a complete file with evidence to either the Courts or to the applicant.[44] The bottom line is that it is sufficient for the allegations to be plausible, and to be supported by some type of evidence. The overall message of *Kadi II* is that there can be individual judicial review of UN listings, but that the UN system as a whole is fine.

This reading of the *Kadi* litigation confirms the paradigm of legal integration. The Court has been careful to be as respectful towards the UN system as the fundamental norms of EU law are capable of tolerating. It has sought to avoid a grand clash of ultimate authority, and the Security Council has done likewise. Again, that does not mean that there can never be any real conflict. There is no complete integration of international norms into EU law—there is no full monism. The process of legal integration may hint at certain limitations. The fundamental norms of a legal system cannot be simply suspended or abrogated when integrating the norms of another system. The *Kadi* litigation is indeed also about the limitations which EU law imposes when absorbing international norms. There can be hard cases to resolve, and perhaps some of them make bad law,[45] but they do make law, and there are legal principles which govern potential conflicts.

The *Kadi* litigation ultimately confirms the paradigm of legal integration, as a conceptualisation of the reception of international law into EU law. International law is increasingly integrated with EU law, and the fundamental norms of EU law—the Treaties, first and foremost—demand such integration.

IV. SOME NORMATIVE ISSUES

This chapter started off by arguing that one first needs to conceptualise the relationship between international law and EU law, before moving to a normative level. This last section offers some ideas about how the relationship can be improved, in accordance with the legal integration paradigm. There are three issues which are worth looking into. The first is what could be called the judicial review issue. The second focuses on the concept of judicial dialogue; the third, on treaties and agreements binding on the Member States, but not on the EU as such.

[43] Ibid, paragraph 130.
[44] Ibid, paragraph 137.
[45] R Dworkin, *Taking Rights Seriously* (London, Duckworth, 1977) ch 4.

There is a significant issue with the connection between EU judicial review and respect for international law. It is clear that the Court of Justice is reluctant to invalidate or annul EU legislation on the grounds of a violation of international law. The denial of direct effect to a number of multilateral agreements could well be inspired, at least partly, by the severity of the EU's judicial review system. Let us not forget that, where the Court of Justice reviews general EU legislation—in particular 'primary' legislation, ie regulations or directives adopted directly on the basis of the Treaties, under the ordinary legislative procedure involving all three EU institutions—the review is constitutional in nature. This is the EU's equivalent to *Marbury v Madison*.[46] International lawyers who are sceptical about the Court's reluctance to strike down EU legislation on international law grounds need to reflect about that constitutional dimension. It is generally rare for the Court, and rightly so, to annul primary legislation. Most instances are concerned with the limits to the EU's competences,[47] and with the protection of fundamental rights.[48] These are core constitutional issues. The annulment of primary legislation is, in effect, a 'nuclear option' for the Court of Justice. It interferes with the EU's political process which, notwithstanding legitimate concerns about a democracy deficit, is marked by its own version of checks-and-balances (called institutional balance),[49] and is based on democratic concepts.[50] Given that international law does not easily yield clear-cut and sweeping answers to complex questions, it is not surprising, and arguably is appropriate, that the Court is reluctant to deploy the 'nuclear option' in order to ensure respect for international law. This reluctance may be responsible for the Court's finding that UNCLOS does not confer rights and freedoms, which may be inspired by the desire to avoid judicial review on the basis of a UNCLOS violation.[51] It is expressly part of the Court's reasoning as regards the lack of direct effect of WTO law: the Court does not wish to interfere with the room for manoeuvre of the EU political institutions.[52]

The strict judicial review doctrine was also in issue in the *Kadi* context. In *Kadi II* the Court emphasised that effective judicial protection requires the remedy of retrospective annulment.[53] This is no more than a restatement of EU judicial review

[46] *Marbury v Madison*, 5 US 137 (1803).

[47] See eg Case C-376/98 *Germany v European Parliament and Council (Tobacco Advertising Directive Case)* EU:C:2000:544.

[48] See eg Case C-263/09 *Association Belge des Consommateurs Test-Achats and Others*, EU:C:2011:100 and Case C-293/12 *Digital Rights Ireland v Minister for Communications, Marine and Natural Resources and Others*, EU:C:2014:238.

[49] See eg K Lenaerts and A Verhoeven, 'Institutional Balance as a Guarantee for Democracy in EU Governance' in C Joerges and R Dehousse (eds), *Good Governance in Europe's Integrated Market* (Oxford, OUP, 2002) 35.

[50] Art 10 TEU.

[51] *Intertanko* (above n 24).

[52] *Portugal v Council* (above n 23), paragraphs 42–49; see further the Opinion of Maduro AG in Joined Cases C-120/06 and 121/06 P *Fabbrica italiana accumulatori motocarri Montecchio SpA (FIAMM) and Others v Council and Commission* and *Fedon & Figli SpA and Others v Council and Commission*, EU:C:2008:98, paragraphs 45 ff.

[53] *Kadi II* (above n 8), paragraph 134.

orthodoxy: in actions for the annulment of an EU act the legality of that act needs to be assessed as at the time of its adoption, and annulment therefore removes the act from the EU legal order with retrospective effect.[54] However, it is not easy to see the UN Security Council ever setting up such a system of review of its own listings, and it is perhaps also not easy to see that this is genuinely required, from a perspective of the protection of individual rights.

This tension between the current EU judicial review system, based on the action for annulment,[55] and the need to ensure respect for international law calls for further reflection on what other remedies could be conceived, which are less 'nuclear'. What appears to be missing in the EU system of remedies is something like an action for a declaration, which would work prospectively. Such an action would be useful for a range of possible conflicts with international law. In some cases it would even fit better with the international system. This would for example be the case for violations of WTO law, because the WTO review system is based on offering a prospective remedy: the WTO system is aimed at ensuring future compliance, not at remedying past wrongs.[56] It would also fit better with UN smart sanctions, such as those in issue in *Kadi*, where again the main concern is prospective: those subject to sanctions are mainly concerned with getting de-listed. In fact, the Court of Justice's approach to judicial review of listings in *Kadi II* has traces of a prospective remedy, even if the orthodoxy of retrospective annulment is not formally disturbed. The Court, by accepting that a UN listing will lawfully trigger an EU listing, and by insisting that the listed person needs to initiate review and challenge the 'summary of reasons', installed a system which is in effect geared towards de-listing rather than ex post review.

The second normative issue concerns judicial dialogue. The relationship between EU and international law, and the integration of the latter into the former, is increasingly more than an abstract question of how international law norms operate in the EU legal order. International dispute settlement systems are constantly developing and growing, and the Court of Justice will increasingly be confronted with rulings by international courts and tribunals. Its record of integrating such rulings, where relevant, into EU law is not as positive as the principle that international law is an integral part of EU law would suggest. The Court has accepted, in principle, that decisions by courts or tribunals set up pursuant to an agreement are binding on the EU institutions, including the Court itself.[57] Yet the subsequent practice has not been one of openness towards international judicial decisions.

An important segment is the case law on WTO law. It is one thing for the Court not to accept that there may be a distinction between the lack of direct

[54] K Lenaerts, I Maselis and K Gutman, *EU Procedural Law* (Oxford, OUP, 2014) 413–14.

[55] Note that the same system applies in preliminary rulings cases in which questions of validity are raised.

[56] P Eeckhout, 'Remedies and compliance' in D Bethlehem, D McRae, R Neufeld and I Van Damme (eds), *The Oxford Handbook of International Trade Law* (Oxford, OUP, 2009) 438, at 448–51.

[57] Opinion 1/91 of 14 December 1991 *re EEA Agreement*, EU:C:1991:490.

effect of WTO law and those cases in which WTO dispute settlement has reached a definitive finding that the EU is in violation of its commitments.[58] I have argued elsewhere that there ought to be a distinction here,[59] but recognise that the arguments are finely balanced.[60] What is worse is that even in cases such as *Ikea Wholesale*, in which WTO law does apply—by virtue of the principle of consistent interpretation—the Court refuses to engage, at least explicitly, with the WTO rulings.[61] This has been termed a muted dialogue,[62] but it is questionable whether the concept of a dialogue is at all apposite where courts do not even discuss other case law in their decisions. The members of courts may bear other decisions in mind, and they may meet each other and discuss their respective case law. However, a genuine *judicial* dialogue, between courts and tribunals as such, can only take place through the reasoning of their decisions. Fortunately, the tide seems to be turning, and there have been a few instances of express references to WTO case law in judgments by the EU Courts.[63]

In *Ikea Wholesale* Léger AG questioned whether the EU Courts should take WTO case law into account at all, even within the framework of EU anti-dumping law, which clearly implements the WTO Anti-Dumping Agreement.[64] His argument was that any deference to WTO dispute settlement would risk undermining the autonomy of EU law. Once the relevant WTO norms were incorporated into EU law it was solely for the Court of Justice to establish their correct interpretation. This focus on the autonomy of EU law has wider resonance, and plays an important role in case law regarding the relationship between the EU Courts and international judicial decisions.[65] This is not the place for a fuller analysis of this important principle, and the following comments are limited in scope. There is however a clear and present danger that the autonomy of EU law is extended beyond its proper remit. Where the EU concludes international agreements, incorporates the norms of those agreements into EU law, and is faced with decisions by courts or tribunals which have been given authority to interpret those agreements and settle disputes, it is difficult to see in what way the autonomy of EU law is jeopardised by respecting those international rulings, and ensuring that the incorporated norms are interpreted and applied in consonance with them.

[58] *FIAMM and Fedon* (above n 52).

[59] Eeckhout (above n 1) 365–74.

[60] See the Opinion of Maduro AG in *FIAMM and Fedon* (above n 52).

[61] *Ikea Wholesale* (above n 25).

[62] M Bronckers, 'From "Direct effect" to "Muted Dialogue"—Recent Developments in the European Courts' Case Law on the WTO and Beyond' (2008) 11 *Journal of International Economic Law* 885.

[63] See eg Case T-6/12 *Godrej Industries and Another v Council*, judgment of 6 September 2013, EU:T:2013:408, paragraph 78; Case C-414/11 *Daiichi Sankyo Co Ltd and Another v DEMO Anonymos Viomichaniki kai Emporiki Etairia Farmakon*, EU:C:2013:520, paragraph 80; Case T-304/11 *Alumina d.o.o. v Council*, 30 April 2013 EU:T:2013:224, paragraph 30; Case T-156/11 *Since Hardware (Guangzhou) Co Ltd v Commission*, judgment of 18 September 2012, EU:T:2012:431.

[64] Opinion of Léger AG in *Ikea Wholesale* (above n 25) EU:C:2006:236.

[65] See Opinion 2/13 (above n 20); Opinion 1/09 of 8 March 2011, *re Unified Patent* EU:C:2011:123; *Council v Ireland (MOX Plant)* (above n 25); Opinion 1/91 (above n 57).

The idea that such respect would undermine the autonomy of EU law comes close to an affirmation of a wholly inappropriate conception of supreme authority of EU law and of the EU Courts—superior even to binding international law.

In the earlier paper, cited above,[66] I have instead argued for a principle of limited and shared jurisdiction. That principle can be extended to the relationship between the EU Courts and international courts and tribunals. To the extent that an international agreement, with its own dispute settlement system, is an integral part of EU law, the jurisdiction to interpret that agreement is shared between the relevant international courts or tribunals (or other organs, such as WTO Panels and the Appellate Body) and the EU Courts. Moreover, the EU Courts ought to recognise that these international courts or tribunals have primary responsibility for interpreting and applying the agreement. Whether that, of necessity, translates into a strict concept of bindingness is open to further discussion, and may depend on a range of factors. However, the idea that, once incorporated into EU law, the relevant international norms have been completely domesticated, and are subject to a wholly autonomous interpretation, is not in accordance with either the Treaty-mandated observance of international law, the concept of legal integration, or the binding character of international commitments.

Unfortunately, the CJEU's very negative Opinion 2/13, regarding accession to the ECHR, has further strengthened the concept that EU law is autonomous from international law, in ways which will make it ever more difficult for the EU to participate in international dispute settlement. This chapter does not aim to offer any further analysis of Opinion 2/13, or its ramifications.[67] From the perspective of judicial dialogue, the Court's analysis of the issues it has with the draft Accession Agreement is perhaps most worrying on two counts. The first is the Court's insistence on the principle that an international court or tribunal must avoid looking at EU law as much as possible, for example EU law on the

[66] Eeckhout (above n 17).

[67] Cf P Eeckhout, 'Opinion 2/13 on EU Accession to the ECHR and Judicial Dialogue: Autonomy or Autarky?' (2015) 38 *Fordham International Law Journal* 955; and see S Øby Johansen, 'The Reinterpretation of TFEU Article 344 in Opinion 2/13 and its Potential Consequences' (2015) 16 *German Law Journal* 169; A Lazowski and RA Wessel, 'When Caveats Turn into Locks: Opinion 2/13 on Accession of the European Union to the ECHR' (2015) 16 *German Law Journal* 179; S Peers, 'The EU's Accession to the ECHR: The Dream Becomes a Nightmare' (2015) 16 *German Law Journal* 213; X, 'Editorial Comments: The EU's Accession to the ECHR—A "NO" from the ECJ!' (2015) 52 *Common Market Law Review* 1; D Halberstam, '"It's the Autonomy, Stupid!" A Modest Defense of Opinion 2/13 on EU Accession to the European Convention on Human Rights' (2015) 16 *German Law Journal* 105; C Krenn, 'Autonomy and Effectiveness as Common Concerns: A Path to ECHR Accession After Opinion 2/13' (2015) 16 *German Law Journal* 147; E Spaventa, 'A Very Fearful Court? The Protection of Fundamental Rights in the European Union after Opinion 2/13' (2015) 22 *Maastricht Journal of European & Comparative Law* 35. By way of blogs, see eg S Peers at eulawanalysis.blogspot.co.uk/2014/12/the-cjeu-and-eus-accession-to-echr.html; L Besselink at: www.verfassungsblog.de/en/acceding-echr-notwithstanding-court-justice-opinion-213/; S Douglas-Scott at: ukconstitutionallaw.org/2014/12/24/sionaidh-douglas-scott-opinion-213-on-eu-accession-to-the-echr-a-christmas-bombshell-from-the-european-court-of-justice/; PJ Kuijper at: acelg.blogactiv.eu/2015/01/06/reaction-to-leonard-besselinks's-acelg-blog/.

division of competences. The second is the emphasis on the Court's own exclusive jurisdiction, which stands in the way of systems of inter-State dispute settlement which involve the EU Member States. As I have argued elsewhere,[68] both those concerns are overrated and unjustified. They risk developing into a serious obstacle to EU participation in international dispute settlement. International courts and tribunals cannot properly judge EU acts without looking into EU law, and mixed agreements cannot be a useful object of dispute settlement if the international judge cannot determine the respective responsibilities of the EU and its Member States.

The third normative issue concerns the status of international treaties and conventions to which all the Member States are parties—but the EU is not. There are plenty of those, and in many cases the EU would be keen to sign up to them, and would have the competence to do so, but is simply precluded because it is not a State or for some other, often political, reasons. That state of affairs creates some unique problems. The EU is incapable of signing up to, for example, the Chicago Convention (air transport), or the International Maritime Organization or the International Labour Organization, even if in matters of air and maritime transport, and of labour and social policy, it has significant legislation. Indeed, the *Kadi* litigation has thrown into relief the ambivalent relationship between the EU Treaties and the UN Charter, and has shown the connections between EU policies and the Charter.

As is well known, these international treaties and conventions are not binding on the EU, unless the so-called succession principle applies: it is only where the EU Member States have transferred all their powers in relation to a particular international instrument to the EU, that the latter is bound.[69] In the absence of such a full transfer, the EU is not completely blind to these agreements, as in *Intertanko* the Court has established that EU legislation needs to be interpreted in light of these Member State commitments. However, it is questionable whether this is sufficient. As I have argued elsewhere, the requirement of a full transfer of powers effectively precludes the most significant and wide-ranging international agreements concluded by all Member States from becoming formally binding on the EU.[70] That is paradoxical, and difficult to defend from the perspective of the integration principle.

V. CONCLUDING REMARKS

The EU aspires to become a meaningful global actor—indeed, in many ways it is that already. Many international relations scholars conceive of the EU as a

[68] Ibid.

[69] See eg *Intertanko* (above n 24), in relation to the Marpol 73/78 Convention on ship pollution and Case C-366/10 *Air Transport Association for America* (above n 8), in relation to the Chicago Convention.

[70] Eeckhout (above n 1) 397–400.

Normative Power. The Treaties now clearly confirm this trajectory, and respect for international law is an essential component of being a normative power. This chapter argued that we need to conceive of the relationship between EU and international law as one of integration, rather than blind pluralism. This means that the statements by the Court of Justice on the integration of international law need to be taken seriously—including by the Court itself. There are well-known limitations to such integration, such as the lack of direct effect of important multilateral conventions and the need to respect the foundational principles of the EU legal order, even in the case of UN Security Council resolutions. However, those limitations do not, it is argued, undermine the legal integration paradigm. The latter ought to serve as the framework for analysing normative issues regarding the interrelationship between EU law and international law. This chapter has focused on three such issues, ie judicial review, dialogue between courts, and the status of Member State agreements. There are of course further questions, and there is scope for more reflection on the extent to which international law is integrated in EU law, and on the limits of such integration.

5

Customary International Law and the European Union from the Perspective of Article 3(5) TEU

ELEFTHERIA NEFRAMI[1]

Content:

I. INTRODUCTION

WHILE THE BINDING effect of customary international law in the European Union's (EU) legal order has been established in the case law of the Court of Justice,[2] the entry into force of the Lisbon Treaty shed light on a question that had not been specifically clarified: its legal basis and the

[1] Professor of European Law, University of Luxembourg.

[2] Case C-286/90, *Anklagemyndigheden v Peter Michael Poulsen and Diva Navigation Corp*, ECLI:EU:C:1992:453, para 9; Case T-115/94, *Opel Austria GmbH v Council of the European Union*, ECLI:EU:T:1997:3, para 90.; Case C-162/96, *A Racke GmbH & Co v Hauptzollamt Mainz*, ECLI:EU:C:1998:293, paras 45–46.

scope of the normative interaction.[3] In its *Air Transport Association of America* ruling,[4] the Court of Justice linked the binding effect of international law, including customary international law, to Article 3(5) of the Treaty on European Union (TEU).[5]

Article 3(5) TEU reads: 'In its relations with the wider world, the Union shall contribute to the strict observance and the development of international law, including respect for the principles of the United Nations Charter'.

This provision was explicitly considered as confirmation of the binding effect of customary international law by Advocate General Kokott in her Opinion in the *Air Transport Association* case, stating that

> It is generally recognised that the European Union is bound by customary international law as well as by the international agreements applicable to it, and this is confirmed by the second sentence of Article 3(5) TEU ('strict observance and the development of international law'). The relevant principles of customary international law form part of the EU legal order.[6]

It could thus be considered that Article 3(5) TEU fills a gap in the Treaties as it addresses the role of international law, including customary international law. Indeed, before the entry into force of the Lisbon Treaty, primary European law referred merely to the place of international agreements, stating, in what is now Article 216(2) of the Treaty on the Functioning of the European Union (TFEU), that 'Agreements concluded by the Union are binding upon the institutions of the Union and on its Member States'.

It should be noted that the introduction of Article 3(5) TEU by the Lisbon Treaty did not affect Article 216 TFEU in relation to international agreements. The obligations of the Union under conventional international law still fall under the scope of this specific provision, which has been determined to be the reception rule integrating international agreements into the EU legal order and defining their place in the hierarchy of EU law sources. By contrast, customary international law is not addressed as an autonomous source of EU law. The respect of international law in the external action of the Union covers both conventional and customary law and figures as a principle that guides the conduct of the Union in the pursuit

[3] See P-J Kuijper, 'It Shall Contribute to … the Strict Observance and Development of International Law' in *The Court of Justice and the Construction of Europe: Analysis and Perspectives on Sixty Years of Case Law* (The Hague, TCM Asser Press, 2013) 589.

[4] Case C-366/10 *Air Transport Association of America v Secretary of State for Energy and Climate Change*, ECLI:EU:C:2011:864. For a comment: B Mayer (2012) 49 *Common Market Law Review* 1113.

[5] According to paragraph 101 of the judgment, 'Under Article 3(5) TEU, the European Union is to contribute to the strict observance and the development of international law. Consequently, when it adopts an act, it is bound to observe international law in its entirety, including customary international law, which is binding upon the institutions of the European Union'.

[6] AG Kokott Opinion, *Air Transport Association of America v Secretary of State for Energy and Climate Change*, ECLI:EU:C:2011:637, para 108.

of external action objectives. Indeed, Article 21 TEU, a general provision on the Union's external action, reads in its first paragraph that

> The Union's action on the international scene shall be guided by the principles which have inspired its own creation, development and enlargement, and which it seeks to advance in the wider world: democracy, the rule of law, the universality and indivisibility of human rights and fundamental freedoms, respect for human dignity, the principles of equality and solidarity, and respect for the principles of the United Nations Charter and international law.

Furthermore, consolidation and support for principles of international law, as well as democracy, the rule of law and human rights, are referred to as objectives of the Union's external action in the list of external action objectives in Article 21(2) subparagraph (b).

The specific place of international law in the general provisions of the TEU since the entry into force of the Lisbon Treaty raises two main questions as to the integration of customary international law in the legal order of the European Union, both related to the specific status of customary law as compared to international agreements. The first question is whether the general external action provisions, and particularly Article 3(5) TEU, referred to in the Court of Justice's case law as the legal basis of the binding effect of customary law in the EU legal order, have a receptive function similar to that of Article 216 TFEU. In this sense, it should be considered whether the European Union's openness to international law is synonymous to integration of customary law into the EU's legal order. The second question depends on the answer to the first and concerns judicial review of secondary law of the European Union with regard to customary international law. In other words, the second question is whether customary law may be relied upon in order to challenge the validity of an act of the EU institutions under the same conditions and with the same effect as compared to conventional rules.

The status of customary international law in the EU legal order is not the only aspect of the normative interaction between European and international law. As results from Article 3(5) TEU, as well as Article 21 TEU, the Union shall contribute to the development of international law. However, the question of to what extent the European Union contributes, as an international actor, to the establishment of customary rules and the development of international law leads to the assessment of the efficiency of its external action from the perspective of international law.[7] This aspect will not be addressed in the present chapter, which will instead focus

[7] See F Hoffmeister, 'The Contribution of EU Practice to International Law' in M Cremona (ed), *Developments in EU External Relations Law* (Oxford, Oxford University Press, 2008) 112. A Rosas, 'The European Court of Justice and Public International Law' in J Wouters, A Nollkaemper, E de Wet (eds), *The Europeanisation of International Law* (The Hague, TMC Asser Press, 2008) 85.

on the status of customary international law in the European Union's legal order.[8] Article 3(5) TEU, although it refers to both the observance and the development of international law as objectives of the European Union's external action, will be considered, from the perspective of European Union law, as an expression of the openness of the European Union legal order to international law. Indeed, the credibility and the efficiency of the European Union's external action, on which depends its role as an international actor capable of promoting international law, presupposes respect for international law in the exercise of the Union's competences. It is thus from the perspective of European Union law that the status of customary international law raises the questions of its binding effect and of its function in the EU legal order.

However, taking European Union law as the starting point from which to assess the status of customary international law in the EU legal order leads us to analyse the basis for the autonomous development of EU law compared to international law: the question of competences, which is capable of establishing an autonomous status for customary international law (Section II). This autonomous status could explain the use of customary law by the Court of Justice of the European Union (Section III) and the limits of customary law's effects on the validity of acts adopted by the institutions (Section IV).

II. THE AUTONOMOUS STATUS OF CUSTOMARY INTERNATIONAL LAW AND THE QUESTION OF COMPETENCE

In the *Racke* ruling[9] the Court of Justice referred explicitly to customary international law as part of the legal order of the European Union.[10] The Court adopted the same approach taken in the *Haegeman* judgment,[11] where the Court ruled that international agreements are an integral part of the legal order of the Union. However, if Article 3(5) TEU implies that international law, covering both customary law and international agreements, is part of the EU legal order, the status of customary law must be distinguished from that of international agreements, the distinction being linked to the question of competence.

The Court of Justice based its consideration that customary law is part of the legal order of the Union on the ground that the European Union 'must respect

[8] For a general overview of the question, see A Gianelli, 'Customary International Law in the European Union' in E Cannizzaro, P Palchetti, R Wessel (eds), *International Law as Law of the European Union* (Boston MA/Leiden, Martinus Nijhoff Publishers, 2011) 93. R Schütze, 'On "Middle Ground". The European Community and Public International Law', *EUI Working Papers No 13* (2007). J Wouters, D Van Eeckhoutte, 'Giving Effect to Customary International law Through European Community Law', Katholieke Universiteit Leuven Faculty of Law, Institute for International Law *Working Paper No 25* (June 2002).

[9] Above n 2.

[10] According to paragraph 46 of the judgment, 'the rules of customary international law concerning the termination and the suspension of treaty relations by reason of a fundamental change of circumstances are binding upon the Community institutions and form part of the Community legal order'.

[11] Case 181-73, *R & V Haegeman v Belgian State*, ECLI:EU:C:1974:41, para 5.

international law in the exercise of its powers. It is therefore required to comply with the rules of customary international law'[12] when adopting secondary legislation. By contrast, international agreements are part of the legal order of the Union on the ground that they constitute an act of the institutions;[13] and as such are sufficient to establish the jurisdiction of the Court of Justice with regard to their interpretation, implementation and review. The consideration of an international agreement as an act of the institutions has been found to be neutral with regard to the monist or dualist approach of integration of international law into the EU legal order;[14] nevertheless, it is significant when differentiating them from customary international law.

Indeed, international agreements concluded by the Union are not only international treaties to which one contracting party is the Union, but are also a tool of the exercise of the substantive competence conferred on the Union by the Member States. A specific objective set out in the Treaties, on the basis of the conferral of a substantive competence, may or ought to be pursued through the conclusion of an international agreement. It should be noted that Article 216 TFEU addresses the question of external competence of the Union before stating the binding effect of an international agreement upon the institutions and the Member States. An international agreement is, thus, from an EU law perspective, an instrument of legislation deriving from the exercise of the competence of the Union, linked either to an external action objective or an internal one—given that external competences are not only conferred on the basis of an external action objective; such agreements may also constitute the external aspect of an internal competence, linked to an internal objective. It follows that an international agreement concluded by the Union is a source of EU law, binding on both the institutions and the Member States. The scope of the binding effect of an international agreement is also a consequence of its being seen as a tool for the attainment of a specific objective assigned to the Union. The Member States are indeed bound by the international agreement because it manifests the transfer of competence for the benefit of the Union, the Member States' competence being thereafter limited to implementation.[15] Moreover, the institutions of the Union are bound by the international agreement, as the attainment of the objective pursued by the latter presupposes the exercise of an implementing competence, subordinated to the legislative competence being exercised at the international level.

[12] ECJ, *Racke*, above n 2, para 45.

[13] ECJ, *Haegeman*, above n 11, para 4.

[14] For a general overview, see E Cannizzaro, 'The Neo-Monism of the European Legal Order' in E Cannizzaro, P Palchetti, R Wessel (eds), *International Law as Law of the European Union* (Boston MA/Leiden, Martinus Nijhoff Publishers, 2011) 35. R Wessel, 'Reconsidering the Relationship between International and EU Law: Towards an Content-Based Approach?' in E Cannizzaro, P Palchetti, R Wessel (eds), *International Law as Law of the European Union* (Boston MA/Leiden, Martinus Nijhoff Publishers, 2011) 7.

[15] One should take into consideration the specific regime of mixed agreements, which are not in their entirety the expression of the exercise of the Union competence. However, the duty of loyalty not to jeopardise the ultimate external action objective of the Union of being a credible international actor explains the consideration of the mixed agreement in its entirety as a source of EU law obligations, the Member States being under the EU law obligation to implement the provisions of the mixed agreement falling under their reserved competence.

However, the binding effect of an international agreement on the institutions of the Union is also linked to the ultimate external action objective, considered as constitutional, of being a credible international actor, which presupposes respect for international commitments. At this point, the binding effect of an international agreement meets that of customary international law. Put differently, while the conclusion of an international agreement by the Union embodies both an obligation to respect and a duty to implement, it is this latter duty that specifically stems from the exercise of a transferred competence, while the obligation to respect shows the subordination of the Union to the international law of treaties and thus to customary international law. Certainly, the duty to implement implies an obligation to respect; however the obligation to respect can be dissociated from the specific objective pursued by the agreement and be addressed in its regulatory dimension. In other words, the obligation to respect a conventional commitment is not only the consequence of the exercise of a substantive competence, but also the expression of the personification of the Union as an international actor. As such, the Union is subordinated to customary international law, as are all subjects of international law, which gives the Union the credibility needed for the attainment of the objective set out in Article 3(5) TEU.

It follows that customary international law is not a tool for the exercise of a competence of the Union and does not serve the attainment of a specific objective, but is placed beyond normative action, and acts as a regulator of the exercise of the competences of the institutions.[16] This regulatory function concerns not only the EU legislator (the implementation of an international agreement at the Union level demands, in principle, the adoption of legislative acts), but also the Court of Justice, which is called on to ensure respect for the Union's international commitments by both the institutions and the Member States according to the customary rules of the law of treaties. This regulatory function does not, however, concern the exercise of the Member States' reserved competence.

Certainly, as the conclusion of an international agreement by the Union implies a limitation of the Member States' competence and, thus, their subordination to the scope of the agreement, it could be considered that the customary principle of *pacta sunt servanda* also affects the exercise of Member States' competences. However, the differentiation between the effects of an agreement concluded by the Union and of customary international law should be highlighted. Deriving from the exercise of a transferred competence, an international agreement integrates with the legal order of the Union as a specific source of EU law. Its normative content becomes a specific source of EU law through its reception by Article 216 TFEU. An international agreement binds as such the institutions and the Member States according to the customary principle of *pacta sunt servanda*, but as this principle is also expressed in Article 216 TFEU, the content of the agreement is shaped

[16] In this sense, see A Gianelli, 'Customary International Law in the European Union' in E Cannizzaro, P Palchetti and R Wessel (eds), *International Law as Law of the European Union* (Boston MA/Leiden, Martinus Nijhoff Publishers, 2011) 93.

into an EU law obligation. The exercise of the Member States' competences is thus limited by Article 216 TFEU, because of the transfer of competences according to other provisions of the Treaties, but not customary international law. In the relations between Member States falling under the scope of EU law, the applicable rules are not international but European. In other words, while an international agreement concluded by the Union is integrated into the EU legal order and has a place between the sources of EU law, customary international law is not subject to integration, but to Europeanisation.[17]

Indeed, customary international law found its place in the relationship between Member States at the origin of the European project, on the international law foundations of the European Union.[18] Article 21 TEU suggests that international law is part of the principles having inspired the creation, development and enlargement of the Union. However, the transfer of competences with a view to attaining specific as well as ultimate objectives has led to the establishment of an autonomous legal order regulated by its own principles. Customary law principles acquired a European identity and have been adapted to the specific requirements, a consequence of the particular move towards constitutionalisation. It follows that European law applied to the Member States is different from customary international law, applied between States.[19] It also follows that when the Member States' action falls within the scope of EU law, it is subject to EU law rules, including the binding effect of international agreements concluded by the Union, expressed in Article 216 TFEU. Nevertheless, customary international law continues to regulate the exercise of reserved Member States' competence, as far as the latter is not in conflict with European law, but in this case customary international law is not the source of an EU law obligation. As to the institutions, the obligation to respect customary international law is inherent in the international law foundations and to the personification of the Union as a subject of international law. Customary rules are part of the EU legal order in the sense that they are principles that regulate the exercise of competences by the institutions, through and beyond the conclusion of an international agreement, but they are not integrated as a source of European law, because they do not correspond to a field of EU competence.

It can thus be assumed that the differentiation between customary international law and international treaties, with regard to their status in the EU legal order, lies in the question of competence. As customary international law is not linked to a specific field of competence, customary rules cannot be considered a source of European law, and their Europeanisation resulting from the establishment

[17] See, A Orakhelashvili, 'The Idea of European International Law' (2006) 17 *European Journal of International Law* 315.

[18] See, J Malenowsky, 'La contribution ambivalente de la Cour de Justice de l'Union européenne à la saga centenaire de la domestication du droit international public' in *De Rome à Lisbonne: les juridictions de l'Union européenne à la croisée des chemins, Mélanges en l'honneur de Paolo Mengozzi* (Bruxelles, Bruylant, 2013) 25.

[19] For example, specific rules of the European Treaties address the question of their revision, of their interpretation, of sanction, or of the place of Member States' agreements.

of European law principles inspired by customary rules removes their status as customary law. Nevertheless, customary international law still has a binding effect on the institutions of the Union according to EU law, but as such, in the rank of principles, and not as EU law obligation.

It follows that Article 3(5) TEU does not have the same function as Article 216(2) TFEU. The latter provision gives EU law status to international agreements, becoming sources of EU law obligations for both the institutions and the Member States. Affirming the transformation of international law commitments into EU law obligations does not confirm a dualist approach to international law. Monist or dualist concerns do not affect the receptive function of Article 216 TFEU, not addressed in Article 3(5) TEU. That provision confirms by contrast the subordination of the Union to international law, including customary international law, which produces its effects as such, by regulating the exercise of the Union's competences without being the result of such an exercise. In that sense, customary international law is placed beyond conventional obligations. It is not a question of hierarchy, but of a difference in the nature of the interaction, the place of customary law expressing merely the interaction of legal orders, while conventional obligations are the result of an exercise of external competences.

Consequently, customary international law has an autonomous status in the EU legal order, as it regulates as such the exercise of the competence of the institutions, without creating European law obligations for the Member States. In that sense, the lack of integration of customary law as such in the EU legal order is not a lack of effect. The international law foundations of the Union explain the possibility of Europeanisation of customary rules, which lose their international status if that occurs; the external action objective expressed in Article 3(5) TEU, which does not correspond to a specific competence, explains that the Union is subject to customary international law, in the fields of transferred competence. Customary international law might be viewed as having the same function as the Charter of Fundamental Rights of the European Union, in the sense that it does not correspond to specific competences, but limits their exercise and regulates the conduct of the Union.

The particular status of customary international law in the EU legal order as compared to international agreements explains its use in the case law of the Court of Justice.

III. RECOURSE TO CUSTOMARY INTERNATIONAL LAW BY THE COURT OF JUSTICE OF THE EUROPEAN UNION

The Court of Justice has recourse to customary international law as an interpretative tool insofar as *EU institutions'* action is concerned (A), while it is only one element the Court takes into account when it balances interests insofar as it relates to *Member States'* action (B).

A. Customary International Law and the Action of the Institutions: The Interpretative Function and its Limits

Article 3(5) TEU confirms the binding effect of customary international law and the openness of the legal order of the European Union to international law. If the autonomy of the EU legal order implies the Europeanisation of customary rules in relationships between the Member States in a situation falling within the scope of EU law, such a process has been legitimised through the interpretative function of customary rules in the relationships between the European Union and third countries.

In this way, if Article 216(2) TFEU establishes the binding effect of international agreements in the EU legal order, it is deprived of external effect, as it is a reception rule by which international obligations acquire the status of EU law obligations. By contrast, conventional links between the Union and third States fall within the scope of the customary international law of treaties. An international agreement concluded by the Union is an international treaty from the perspective of international law, even if it is at the same time an act serving EU objectives from the perspective of European law. From a European law perspective, one might view the content of the agreement—the *negotium*—which is Europeanised, as prevailing over the container—the *instrumentum*—subjected to international law treatment. A different approach could jeopardise the credibility of the international action of the Union and put into question its openness to international law as confirmed by Article 3(5) EU.

Consequently, it is without doubt that in the *Brita* judgment[20] the Court of Justice used the customary principles codified in the Vienna Convention on the Law of Treaties to determine the effect of the EC-Israel Association Agreement. As the Court pointed out, because the agreement had been concluded by two subjects of public international law, it was 'governed by international law and, more specifically, as regards its interpretation, by the international law of treaties'.[21] Indeed,

> the rules laid down in the Vienna Convention apply to an agreement concluded between a State and an international organization … in so far as the rules are an expression of general international customary law. Consequently, the EC-Israel Association Agreement must be interpreted in accordance with those rules

as the latter 'are binding upon the Community institutions and form part of the Community legal order'.[22] The Court concluded that the provision of the agreement defining its territorial scope had to be interpreted in a manner that was consistent with the principle of the relative effect of treaties.

[20] Case C-386/08, *Firma Brita GmbH v Hauptzollamt Hamburg-Hafen*, ECLI:EU:C:2010:91.

[21] Ibid, para 39.

[22] Ibid, paras 41–42.

The General Court confirmed this approach in the *Front Polisario* judgment,[23] concerning the annulment of Council Decision 2012/497/EU on the conclusion of an Agreement in the form of Exchange of Letters between the European Union and the Kingdom of Morocco, applied to the territory of Western Sahara. The General Court considered that, according to the *Brita* judgment, the agreement referred to in the contested decision must be interpreted in accordance with the Vienna Convention rules, expressing general international customary rules.[24]

Nevertheless, recourse to customary international law as an interpretative tool is required by Article 3(5) TEU, and before that provision's entry into force as part of the Lisbon Treaty, by the international legal personality of the Union and its international law foundations, as far as its relationship with third States is concerned, and to the extent that it is necessary in order to avoid violating international law and, thus, putting into question its credibility and legitimacy in the international sphere. The entry into force of the Lisbon Treaty did not change this approach, because Article 3(5) TEU is not a 'receptive' rule and does not transform the content of customary international rules into EU law obligations. As mentioned in the previous paragraph, customary rules produce their effect in the legal order of the European Union as principles guiding the exercise of the Union's competence in order to ensure respect for international law in Union action. Consequently, an interpretation of EU law consistent with customary rules means a non-conflicting interpretation rather than an identical interpretation. Furthermore, not every substantive European rule deriving from the exercise of the Union's competence is subject to consistent interpretation; only those concerning the exercise of the Union's competence should be subject to respecting international law. Such an assertion could be justified by the fact that customary international law is not a source of EU law obligation, could cover both conventional and unilateral action of the Union and, finally, could explain the position of the Court of Justice in the *Diakité* judgment.[25]

Indeed, in its *Diakité* ruling, the Court had been asked to interpret Council Directive 2004/83/EC of 29 April 2004 on minimum standards for the qualification and status of third country nationals or stateless persons as refugees or as persons who otherwise need international protection. More precisely, the Belgian *Conseil d'Etat* asked the Court to interpret the concept of 'internal armed conflicts' in order to determine the Directive's scope of application. The Court adopted an autonomous interpretation, independent from the meaning of 'non-international armed conflict' used in international humanitarian law arising from the Geneva conventions, which interpretation led to a greater protection for the person involved.[26] As Advocate General Mengozzi pointed out the obligation

[23] Case T-512/12, *Front Populaire pour la libération de la saguia-el-hamra et du rio de oro (Front Polisario) v Council of the European Union*, ECLI:EU:T:2015:953.

[24] Ibid, paras 92–93.

[25] Case C-285/12, *Aboubacar Diakité v Commissaire général aux réfugiés et aux apatrides*, ECLI:EU:C:2014:39.

[26] As international humanitarian law derives from the Geneva conventions, its qualification as customary international law could be questioned. However, there is no doubt that the Geneva

for the European Union to respect international law and to interpret its secondary legislation in conformity with it—a constitutional objective codified in Article 3(5) TEU—is only imposed if there is a need for '*cohérence herméneutique*' of international and European rules.[27] However, the autonomy of the objectives of the Directive when compared to international humanitarian law, specifically the internal objective of an area of freedom, security and justice ensuring the respect of fundamental rights, did not imply an interpretation of 'internal armed conflict' following international humanitarian law.[28] The Court of Justice followed the Advocate General's Opinion and took a more flexible approach, one that took into account the individual situation of the applicant. While demonstrating the difference in the scope of international humanitarian law and the EU Directive, the Court's decision emphasised respect for human rights.

One might think that the *Diakité* judgment, delivered after the entry into force of the Lisbon Treaty, did not reveal a new function for Article 3(5) TEU. Indeed, as far as the Geneva Conventions may be considered customary international law, the latter does not integrate into the EU legal order in its content. On the one hand, the scope of application of the Directive that was the subject of the Court's interpretation led to the Europeanisation of the notion of 'internal armed conflict'; on the other hand, the interpretation it gave did not contradict the values of the Union, respect for international humanitarian law included, as it was in favour of the applicant's fundamental rights.

In a similar way, one might think that the *Kadi* judgments reflect the specific status of customary international law as far as it relates to the normative interaction in question. Without pretending to draw definitive conclusions from the *Kadi* decisions as to the relationship between EU law and general international law,[29] one can note that the judicial review of the European acts implementing the United Nations' resolutions is not in contradiction to Article 3(5) TEU. More precisely, although deference to general international law is one of the values of the Union, UN Security Council's resolutions are not, as such, part of such values, because they are, in a specific case, decision-making rules deriving from an exercise of competence by the United Nations' organs. Certainly, it could be considered, as it results from the General Court's judgment of 2005, that the UN Security Council resolutions are subject to review by the European judge on the basis of customary international law relating to human rights protection, and specifically *ius cogens* rules, a position which could attenuate dualist critical arguments.[30]

conventions are universally accepted and are thus concerned by Article 3(5) TEU. See T Meron, 'The Geneva Conventions as Customary Law' (1987) 81 *American Journal of International Law* 348.

[27] Opinion of 18 July 2013, ECLI:EU:C:2013:500, para 27.

[28] Ibid para 71.

[29] See the contribution of Piet Eeckhout to this book (Chapter four).

[30] See G de Búrca, 'The ECJ and the International Legal Order: A Re-evaluation' in G de Búrca and JHH Weiler (eds), *The Worlds of European Constitutionalism* (Cambridge, Cambridge University Press, 2012) 105.

However, such a position, which has not been followed by the Court of Justice, encounters two main difficulties. UN Security Council resolutions integrate into the European order of the Union because of their content and not because of their status, as they express, in the same way as international agreements, the exercise of competence in order to attain a specific objective, such as the fight against terrorism. It follows that their content is a source of EU law obligations with a specific place in the hierarchy of sources, which is inferior to primary law and general principles. As a consequence, a European judge has jurisdiction over the UN Security Council resolution on the basis of European law, without need to have recourse to *ius cogens*. Certainly, the Court of Justice could have paid more attention to the equivalent protection argument—the *Solange* condition—but that argument only expresses a presumption of validity. It could not have changed the basis of the Court's review, which consisted of the differentiation between general international law and specific decision-making rules that conflict with the EU values in the way the exercise of competences of the institutions could do. The second, but not less important difficulty is to accept the *ius cogens* control by the European judge, who lacks jurisdiction to implement customary international law. Indeed, if customary international law is binding on EU institutions, their obligation only requires respect thereof, not implementation, as implementation presupposes interpretation, because customary international law does not have the same status as international agreements, which are considered acts of the institutions and are subject to interpretation. Certainly the argument relating to interpretative pluralism, which would create an opportunity for the Court of Justice to interpret and implement *ius cogens* rules with regard to United Nation's organs is worth analysing.[31] However, from a European law perspective, such an argument could be countered by an objection to the assimilation of customary international law with international treaties and an assertion of the limited jurisdiction of the Court of Justice. Indeed, Article 3(5) TEU refers to the obligation of the Union to respect customary international law in its external action, and to promote international law as an external action objective through the exercise of its external competences (Article 21 TEU); it does not obligate the Union to ensure respect for customary international law by all international actors at the universal level.

It should be noted that the fact that the interpretative function of customary international law in the EU legal order does not cover its own interpretation by the European judge is confirmed by the absence of the appreciation of its constitutive elements. Indeed, the existence and scope of customary international rules, which the European judge is asked to preserve by avoiding their violation through EU action, is determined by reference to international law.[32] Such a situation confirms

[31] D Halberstam, 'Local, Global and Plural Constitutionalism: Europe Meets the World' in G de Burca and JHH Weiler (eds), *The Worlds of European Constitutionalism* (Cambridge, Cambridge University Press, 2012) 150.

[32] In the *Air Transport Association of America* case, n 4 above, the Court, by reference to codification in international treaties recognises the binding force of the following principles: (a) each State has complete and exclusive sovereignty over its airspace; (b) no State may validly purport to subject any part of the high seas to its sovereignty; (c) freedom to fly over the high seas. In the *Front Polisario*

that, although customary international law is part of the EU legal order, it is not to be assimilated with a source of EU law subject to interpretation from a European law perspective.

B. Customary International Law as Part of the Member States' Sphere of Interests

The status of customary international law as part of the European Union's legal order raises a question about its function in relation to the Member States. It could be considered that, as Article 3(5) TEU expresses an external action objective of the Union, of an ultimate or constitutional nature closely linked to the integration process—the objective of being a credible international actor—the European judge should have the power to enforce respect of customary international law by the Member States. However, as has already been noted, Article 3(5) TEU reserves a particular status to customary international law, as it does not express the exercise of a competence of the Union, but regulates it as a guiding value. Consequently, customary international law is not a source of EU law obligations for the Member States and is not to be interpreted as such.

However, the openness of the EU legal order to international law, as confirmed by Article 3(5) TEU, implies that the EU institutions should take into consideration the function of customary international law in the Member States' sphere of action.

Indeed, in the *Hungary versus Slovakia* case[33] customary international law applied in the Member States' sphere of action; it determined however the application of the citizenship Directive. More precisely, the Court of Justice held that refusing to allow the Hungarian President to enter Slovakian territory was not an infringement of the citizenship Directive. It is interesting to note that, according to Advocate General Bot, the case did not fall within the scope of application of citizenship rights, which do not apply to visits by Heads of State.[34] The Advocate General pointed out that diplomatic relations between States rests within Member States' competence and are subject to their law. As international custom provides special treatment for Heads of State, it determines the scope of application of citizenship rights. In other words, according to the Opinion, the scope of application of the citizenship directive should be determined after taking into consideration

judgment, n 23 above, the General Court considers that "nothing in the arguments or evidence put forward by the applicant proves the existence of a rule of customary international law which prohibits the conclusion of an international treaty which may be applied on a disputed territory" (para 205).

[33] Case C-364/10, *Hungary v Slovak Republic*, ECLI:EU:C:2012:630. For a comment see: B Delzangles, 'Les affaires hongroises ou la disparition de la valeur "integration" dans la jurisprudence de la Cour de justice' (2013) 2 *Revue trimestrielle de droit européen* 201. M Filippin, 'A change for future intra-European relations? Case 364/100 Hungary v Slovakia, judgment of 16 October 2012 nyr' (2013) 20 *Maastricht Journal of European and Comparative Law* 120.

[34] Opinion of 6 March 2012, ECLI:EU:C:2012:124.

customary international law, which, when applied in the Member States' sphere of action, could lead to the limitation of the scope of application of EU law.

Nevertheless, the Court of Justice did not exactly follow the Opinion of the Advocate General, but took the position that customary international law applying in the Member States' sphere of action should be taken into consideration not in order to exclude the application of the EU law, but as an element in a balance of interests. The Court determined that customary international law gives grounds for derogations from EU law:

> the fact that a Union citizen performs the duties of a Head of State is such as to justify a limitation, based on international law, on the exercise of the right of free movement conferred on that person by Article 21 TFEU.[35]

In other words, Article 3(5) TEU does not obligate the Union to limit the scope of application of EU law where Member States apply international customary law in their reserved sphere of competence. As is the case with other national rules, customary rules do not preserve the Member States' reserved sphere from the impact of the scope of application of European law. If the Member States' action conflicts with EU law, the conflict and its possible justification should be assessed regardless of the reasons for such violation. Customary international law applying in the Member States' sphere of action is a valid justification of an infringement of EU law, but is not able to limit the scope of the latter.

It is to be noted that Advocate General Bot pointed out in his Opinion that

> as in the case of any competence reserved for them, the Member States should not exercise their diplomatic competence in a manner that might lead to a lasting break in diplomatic relations between two Member States. Such a break would, in fact, be incompatible with the integration process aimed at creating an ever closer union, in the words of the preamble to the EU Treaty.[36]

Consequently, customary international law in the Member States' sphere of competence does not enjoy special treatment when compared to any other legitimate national objective. The Court already took such a position in the *Rottman* case,[37] in which it recognised that the conditions of acquisition and loss of nationality are determined by customary international rules applied in the Member States' sphere of action, without however jeopardising the effective benefit of the rights derived from the European citizenship.

It follows that Article 3(5) TEU does not lead to customary international law being a source of EU law obligation for the Member States, when it applies in their sphere of retained competence. It should indeed be recalled that customary international law does not affect the conferral of competences. Article 3(5) TEU does not grant a new competence to the Union. As a consequence, the Union neither encourages respect for, nor sanctions violations of customary international

[35] ECJ, *Hungary v Slovak Republic*, above n 31, para 51.

[36] Opinion of 6 March 2012, above n 32, para 58.

[37] Case C-135/08, *Janko Rottman v Freistaat Bayern*, ECLI:EU:C:2010:104.

law within the Member States' sphere of action.[38] At the same time, it does not limit the scope of application of EU law, when Member States invoke respect for customary rules to derogate from EU law obligations. Customary international law falling within the national sphere of competence is given the same treatment at the EU level as any other national justification for derogation from EU law. Such a conclusion is in accordance with the assertion that the respect for customary international law is not an EU law obligation for the Member States beyond the scope of application of an EU competence. It follows that customary international law according to Article 3(5) TEU only creates an obligation for the EU institutions, not for the Member States themselves. The question, then, becomes the extent to which the binding effect of customary international law on the EU institutions generates a basis for challenging the validity of an act adopted by those institutions.

IV. CUSTOMARY INTERNATIONAL LAW AND THE QUESTION OF DIRECT EFFECT

It is now well-established that the binding effect of customary international law with regard to EU institutions does not have the meaning of direct effect. The circumstances under which customary international law may be relied upon in order to challenge the validity of an action of the EU institutions was first addressed in *Racke*.[39] There, the Court was asked to determine if a Community regulation suspending the trade concessions granted pursuant to a cooperation agreement concluded between the European Community and Yugoslavia was invalid because it was contrary to rules of customary international law concerning the termination and the suspension of treaty relations due to a fundamental change of circumstances.

The particularity of the *Racke* case was that the rule invoked, that of customary international law, was not the one granting rights to individuals, which were derived from the suspended agreement. The Court of Justice, after having pointed out that the Union must respect international law in the exercise of its powers, and that rules of customary international law concerning the termination and the suspension of treaty relations by reason of a fundamental change of circumstances are binding upon the Union and form part of the EU legal order, found:

> However, because of the complexity of the rules in question and the imprecision of some of the concepts to which they refer, judicial review must necessarily, and in particular in the context of a preliminary reference for an assessment of validity, be limited to the

[38] Breach of customary rules of public international law is however to be sanctioned by the Union through restrictive measures against a country, entity or individual, in the framework of the Common Foreign and Security Policy.

[39] See above n 2.

> question whether, by adopting the suspending regulation, the Council made manifest errors of assessment concerning the conditions for applying those rules.[40]

The Court of Justice thus confirmed that customary rules may be invoked, even in the absence of direct effect due to lack of precision, but the scope of the Court's review is necessarily limited to determining whether there had been a manifest error on the part on the EU institution. This Court of Justice position has been criticised as incomplete,[41] because it did not address the condition of conferring rights on individuals, which is required for direct effect of international agreements; nor did it examine the question of the suspended agreement's direct effect. Despite the confusion deriving from the fact that customary law was invoked in order to benefit from an international agreement that was not invoked as such, the *Racke* judgment did clarify the following point: the conditions for direct effect of customary rules are not the same as the conditions for direct effect of international agreements concluded by the Union.

The *Racke* Court's holdings were subsequently confirmed in *Air Transport Association*,[42] where the Court further clarified the specific conditions under which customary international rules could be relied upon in order to challenge the validity of secondary legislation. The Court pointed out that:

> The principles of customary international law mentioned in paragraph 103 of the present judgment may be relied upon by an individual for the purpose of the Court's examination of the validity of an act of the European Union in so far as, first, those principles are capable of calling into question the competence of the European Union to adopt that act ... and, second, the act in question is susceptible to affect rights which the individual derives from European Union law or to create obligations under European Union law in his regard.[43]

It is obvious that the conditions enabling private parties to invoke customary international law are not the same as those for invoking the direct effect of international agreements. The general condition for direct effect of international agreements, which requires that such agreements confer rights upon individuals on which they may rely before national courts, does not concern customary international law. Besides, the Court limits the direct effect of customary rules to those challenges questioning the competence of the Union to act and it further introduces a requirement that such act be liable to directly affect the challenger's rights or obligations under European law. Moreover, the Court reiterates the restricted scope of judicial review of the challenged act:

> since a principle of customary international law does not have the same degree of precision as a provision of an international agreement, judicial review must necessarily

[40] ECJ, *Racke*, ibid, para 52.
[41] P Eeckhout, *EU External Relations Law* (Oxford, Oxford University Press, 2012) 394.
[42] See n 4 above.
[43] *Ibid*, para 107.

> be limited to the question whether, in adopting the act in question, the institutions of the European Union made manifest errors of assessment concerning the conditions for applying those principles.[44]

The differentiation of customary international rules from international agreements, as far as the conditions of direct effect are concerned, has been subject to criticism[45] or justified by the inherent lack of precision in customary rules and the fact that such rules cannot confer rights on individuals.[46] As Advocate General Kokott observed in her Opinion in *Air Transport Association of America*, 'principles such as these are, by their very nature and broad logic, by no means capable of having an effect on the legal status of individuals'.[47]

It could however be considered that such a differentiation is in line with the specific status of customary international law in the EU legal order, as confirmed by Article 3(5) TEU. Indeed, it has been demonstrated that customary rules regulate the exercise of the competences of the Union without being integrated in the EU legal order as EU law obligations. Consequently, a customary rule can be violated, not because of the content of an act of the institutions, but because such act should not have been adopted in the first place. It is the adoption of the act that can infringe customary international law, irrespective of the question of whether the act was adopted as an exercise of external or internal competence.

With respect to the requirement that the challenged act directly affects individual rights, that requirement can also be justified by the fact that effective judicial protection is linked to the effective implementation of rights derived from European law.[48] Furthermore, it is a requirement derived from the interest to act. It should be recalled that international law is not oriented toward protection of individual rights, while the direct effect of EU law stems from the specificity of EU law to concern individuals. It follows that as the binding effect of customary international law in the EU legal order concerns only the exercise of the competence of the EU institutions, the ability to rely upon it should be linked to the effect that the exercise of that competence has on individual rights. This approach is consistent with the *Racke* Court's position, where it found that the suspended agreement conferred rights on individuals such that the act of suspension affected

[44] *Ibid*, para 110.

[45] NAJ Croquet, 'The Import of International Customary Law into the EU Legal Order: The Adequacy of a Direct Effect Analysis' (2013) 15 *Cambridge Yearbook of European Legal Studies* 47.

[46] G De Baere, C Ryngaert, 'The ECJ's Judgment in *Air Transport Association of America* and the International Legal Context of the EU's Climate Change Policy' (2013) 18 *European Foreign Affairs Review* 389.

[47] Opinion, n 6 above, para 136.

[48] See S Prechal and R Widdershoven, 'Effectiveness or Effective Judicial Protection: A Poorly Articulated Relationship' in T Baume (ed), *Today's Multi-Layered Legal Order: Current Issues and Perspectives: Liber Amicorum in Honour of Arjen WH Meij* (Paris, Zutphen, 2011) 283.

those rights. It was not the agreement that should have been relied upon, but the customary rule regulating the exercise of competence to suspend. Direct effect is linked to individual rights, which nevertheless do not necessarily stem from the rule invoked.

It can thus be considered that Article 3(5) TEU does not unify the status of conventional and customary rules in the legal order of the European Union, but rather underscores their differences, because by its nature it is a provision that regulates the exercise of competences with the view to attaining the ultimate, constitutional objective of being a credible actor in the international scene.

6

The Legal Status and Influence of Decisions of International Organisations and Other Bodies in the European Union

RAMSES A WESSEL AND STEVEN BLOCKMANS[1]

Content

I. INTRODUCTION

THE EUROPEAN UNION'S external action is not only defined by its influence on international developments, but also by its ability and the need to respond to those developments. While traditionally many have stressed the EU's 'autonomy', over the years its 'dependence' on global developments has become clearer.[2] As underlined by the preceding two chapters, international law has continued to play a key role not only in the EU's external relations, but also in the Union's own legal order.[3]

[1] RA Wessel is Professor of International and European Institutional Law, Centre for European Studies, University of Twente, The Netherlands; S Blockmans is Senior Research Fellow and Head of EU Foreign Policy, Centre for European Policy Studies (Brussels), and Professor of EU External Relations Law and Governance, University of Amsterdam. Both authors are members of the governing board of the Centre for the Law of EU External Relations (CLEER), The Hague.

[2] See RA Wessel and S Blockmans (eds), *Between Autonomy and Dependence: The EU Legal Order under the Influence of International Organizations* (The Hague, Asser Press/Springer, 2013).

[3] For a recent overview see also RA Wessel, *Close Encounters of the Third Kind: The Interface Between the EU and International Law after the Lisbon Treaty* (Stockholm, Sieps Report, 2013); as well as the

The purpose of this chapter is not to assess the role or performance of the EU in international institutions.[4] Rather it purports to reverse the picture and focus on a somewhat under-researched topic: the legal status of the decisions of international organisations in the EU's legal order.[5] While parts of the status of these decisions relate to the status of international agreements and international customary law, it can be argued that decisions of international organisations and other international bodies form a distinct category. In fact, it has been observed that 'this phenomenon has added a new layer of complexity to the already complex law of external relations of the European Union'.[6] Emerging questions relate to the possible difference between decisions of international organisations of which the EU is a member (such as the FAO) and decisions of organisations where it is not (irrespective of existing competences in that area—such as in the International Labour Organization). Questions also relate to the hierarchical status of these decisions in the EU's legal order and to the possibility of them being invoked in direct or indirect actions before the Court of Justice.

This chapter takes a broad perspective on decisions of international organisations by including decisions taken in other international institutions

contributions to E Cannizzaro, P Palchetti and RA Wessel (eds), *International Law as Law of the European Union* (Leiden/Boston MA, Martinus Nijhoff Publishers, 2012).

[4] Over the past years this topic was addressed by political scientists in particular. See for instance E Drieskens and L van Schaik (eds), *The EU and Effective Multilateralism: Internal and External Reform Practices* (London/New York, Routledge, 2014); KE Jørgensen and KV Laatikainen (eds), *Routledge Handbook on the European Union and International Institutions: Performance, Policy, Power* (London, Routledge, 2013); and S Oberthür, KE Jørgensen and J Shahin (eds), *The Performance of the EU in International Institutions* (London/New York, Routledge, 2013) (also published in (2011) 33 *Journal of European Integration, Special Issue* 599); S Blavoukos and D Bourantonis (eds), *The EU Presence in International Organizations* (London/New York, Routledge, 2011); KE Jørgensen (ed), *The European Union and International Organizations* (London/New York, Routledge, 2009). Yet lawyers have also assessed the role of the EU in international organisations: R Frid, *The Relations between the EC and International Organizations* (The Hague, Kluwer Law International, 1995); J Sack, 'The European Community's Membership of International Organizations' (1995) 32 *Common Market Law Review* 1127–256; S Marchisio, 'EU's Membership in International Organizations' in E Cannizzaro (ed), *The European Union as an Actor in International Relations* (The Hague/London/New York, Kluwer Law International, 2002) 231–60; F Hoffmeister, 'Outsider or Frontrunner? Recent Developments under International and European Law on the Status of the European Union in International Organizations and Treaty Bodies' (2007) 44 *Common Market Law Review* 41–68; RA Wessel, 'The Legal Framework for the Participation of the European Union in International Institutions' (2011) 33 *Journal of European Integration* 621–35; S Blockmans and RA Wessel (eds), *Principles and Practices of EU External Representation* (The Hague, CLEER Working Paper series, 2012); J Wouters, J Odermatt and Th Ramopoulos, 'The Status of the European Union at the United Nations General Assembly' in I Govaere et al (eds), *The European Union in the World: Essays in Honour of Marc Maresceau* (Leiden/Boston MA, Martinus Nijhoff Publishers, 2014) 211–23.

[5] With the notable exception of N Lavranos, *Legal Interaction between Decisions of International Organizations and European Law* (Groningen, Europa Law Publishing, 2004), this topic has received surprisingly little attention in academic publications. See earlier also D Bethlehem, 'International Law, EC Law, National Law: Three Systems in Search of A Framework' in M Koskenniemi (ed), *International law Aspects of the EU* (The Hague, Martinus Nijhoff Publishers, 1998) 169–96. For a specific category see also: B Martenczuk, 'EC Law-Making Through International Bodies' in V Kronenberger (ed), *The European Union and the International Legal Order: Discord or Harmony?* (The Hague, TMC Asser Press, 2001) 141–63.

[6] Martenczuk, ibid, at 162. In this citation 'Community' was replaced by 'Union'.

which do not necessarily comply with the standard definition of an international organisation,[7] be it bodies set-up by multilateral conventions or informal (transnational/regulatory) bodies. Some of these bodies are relatively close to the EU (such as the Councils established by association agreements—see further Section V below); others operate at a certain distance. Limiting the analysis to formal international organisations will not do justice to the manifold relationships between the European Union and various international bodies and to the effects of the norms produced by these bodies. The term 'international decisions' is therefore used to refer to any normative output of international institutional arrangements.

II. 'INTERNATIONAL DECISIONS': THE CHANGING ROLE OF INTERNATIONAL ORGANISATIONS

Assessing the status of decisions of international organisations as a separate category in the EU's legal order implies that these decisions can be a source of law. Whereas treaties (international agreements) and custom are undisputed as sources of international law and are as such also mentioned in Article 38 of the Statute of the International Court of Justice, the role and function of decisions of international organisations in international law is less clear. Yet by now the notion that international organisations can take decisions and that these decisions may be legally binding is well-accepted.[8] International organisations have found their place in global governance,[9] and are even considered 'autonomous actors', following an agenda that is no longer fully defined by their Member States,[10] which has caused the latter to devote much of their time and energy to responding to what has been termed the 'Frankenstein problem'.[11]

[7] International organisations can be defined in many ways. The most recent definition laid down in an international legal document may very well be the one of the International Law Commission in the 2011 Articles on the Responsibility of International Organizations (see below), which defined an international organisation as 'an organization established by a treaty or other instrument governed by international law and possessing its own international legal personality. International organizations may include as members, in addition to States, other entities'. See more extensively S Bouwhuis, 'The International law Commission's Definition of International Organizations' (2012) 9 *International Organizations Law Review* 451–65. The definition by Schermers and Blokker is also commonly used: 'international organizations are defined as forms of cooperation (1) founded on an international agreement; (2) having at least one organ with a will of its own; and (3) established under international law'—HG Schermers and NM Blokker, *International Institutional Law: Unity within Diversity* (Leiden/Boston MA, Martinus Nijhoff Publishers, 2011) at 37.

[8] Schermers and Blokker, n 7 above, at 832 et seq.

[9] IF Dekker and RA Wessel, 'Governance by International Organisations: Rethinking the Source and Normative Force of International Decisions' in IF Dekker and W Werner (eds), *Governance and International Legal Theory* (Leiden/Boston MA, Martinus Nijhoff Publishers, 2004) 215–36.

[10] ND White and R Collins (eds), *International Organizations and the Idea of Autonomy: Institutional Independence in the International Legal Order* (Abingdon, Routledge, 2011).

[11] A Guzman, 'International Organizations and the Frankenstein Problem' (2013) 24 *European Journal of International Law* 999–1025; Cf also J Klabbers, *An Introduction to International Institutional Law*, 2nd edn (Cambridge, Cambridge University Press, 2009).

There is nothing new in arguing that international organisations engage in decision-making in a sense that can even be viewed as 'law-making'.[12] Apart from the fact that states (but also the EU) may use international organisations as frameworks for *treaty*-making, it is well-accepted that also many *decisions* of international organisations can be seen as 'law'.[13] Institutional law-making has moved beyond the traditional methods and actors and is increasingly studied in a broader sense, including new actors and new regulatory activities.[14]

The role of many international institutions has developed well beyond a 'facilitation forum', underlining their autonomous position in the global legal order.[15] In those cases law-making takes place on the basis of well-defined procedures with an involvement of institutional actors other than states, but also on the basis of a sometimes dynamic interpretation of the original law-making mandate of the organisation.[16] Indeed, the outcome comes closer to a *decision* of an international organisation than to an international *agreement* concluded between states. In fact, it could be argued that this is what 'institutional law-making' is all about: it is more about law-making *by* international institutions (be it formal international organisations or other international bodies)[17] and less about law-making *through* international institutions (although the latter continues to exist in the form of, for instance, Conferences of States Parties of multilateral conventions or bodies set up by these conventions).[18] It has even become quite common to regard these types

[12] Cf A Boyle and C Chinkin, *The Making of International Law* (Oxford, Oxford University Press, 2007), at vii: 'Law-making is no longer the exclusive preserve of states'. The scope of this chapter does not allow us to address the notion of 'law' and the question of its sources. Yet obviously, using the term 'law-making' somehow implies that we accept legal effects of the norms addressed here, be it through customary law or simply because we accept the competence of the international institutions to enact legal norms.

[13] One of the most influential books may very well have been J Alvarez, *International Organizations as Law-Makers* (Oxford, Oxford University Press, 2005).

[14] J Pauwelyn, RA Wessel and J Wouters (eds), *Informal International Lawmaking* (Oxford, Oxford University Press, 2012) and A Berman, S Duquet, J Pauwelyn, RA Wessel, and J Wouters (eds), *Informal International Lawmaking: Case Studies* (Oslo, TOAEP, 2013).

[15] R Collins and ND White (eds), *International Organizations and the Idea of Autonomy: Institutional Independence in the International Legal Order* (London/New York, Routledge, 2011).

[16] J Wouters and P De Man, 'International Organizations as Law-Makers' in J Klabbers and Å Wallendahl (eds), *Research Handbook on the Law of International Organizations* (Cheltenham/Northampton, Edward Elgar Publishing, 2011) 190–224 at 192: 'It is possible … that the treaty provisions pertaining to the law-making powers of the organization will be construed in a different way than was originally intended by the drafting nations, as it proves very difficult to draft an instrument in such a manner as to effectively preclude any other possible interpretation'.

[17] Cf for instance M Fitzmaurice, 'Law-making and International Environmental Law: the legal Character of Decisions of Conference of the Parties' in R Liijova and J Petman (eds), *International Law-Making: Essays in Honour of Jan Klabbers* (London/New York, Routledge, 2014) 190–210; and in the same volume G Ulfstein, 'Law-making by Human Rights Treaty Bodies' at 249–57.

[18] See more extensively RA Wessel, 'Institutional Law-Making: The Development of a Global Normative Web' in C Bröllman and Y Radi (eds), *Research Handbook on the Theory and Practice of International Law-Making* (Cheltenham/Northampton: Edward Elgar Publishing, 2016). See on these two dimensions of international organisations, J Klabbers, 'Two Concepts of International Organization' (2005) 2 *International Organizations Law Review* 277–93; as well as his 'Contending Approaches to International Organizations: Between Functionalism and Constitutionalism' in Klabbers and Wallendahl, n 16 above, 3–30.

of acts as contributing to the development of 'world legislation'.[19] Yet, situations clearly differ. While some international organisations are well-established and display 'autonomous' powers, in other cases institutionalisation is 'light' and serves as an ad hoc vehicle for a multilateral diplomatic process. In these cases conferences are not much more that meeting points, facilitating states to conclude treaties.[20] Similar processes also take place within more permanent structures, including formal international organisations. Obvious examples include the UN General Assembly[21] and the UN specialized agencies.[22] In these cases an important function of international organisations is to reveal state practice (and *opinio juris*)[23] and to allow for a speedy creation of customary law, although one needs to remain aware of the distinction between state practice and the practice of an international organisation.[24] Furthermore, the fact that many international conventions incorporate generally accepted international rules, standards, regulations, procedures and/or practices may effectively transform a number of codes, guidelines and standards created by international organisations and bodies into binding norms. This reveals the complexity of institutional decision-making: it is not just about clearly legally binding decisions of international organisations; it may very well be about an acceptance of rules and standards because there is simply nothing else and the rules need to be followed in order for states to be able to play along. At the same time international organisations often adopt rules or standards developed in another organisation and with fewer than 200 states they are bound to run into each other in many different institutions.

'International decisions' may perhaps also take shape in the form of 'case law' rather than as decisions of an organ of an international organisation. The legal order of the European Union has largely been shaped on the basis of case law that, allegedly, went beyond what states originally (though to have) agreed on in the treaties. Less prominent examples may be found in other international

[19] See the different contributions to the forum on 'World Legislation' in (2011) 8 *International Organizations Law Review* 197–265. Cf HJ Schermers and NM Blokker, n 7 above at p 1066 (para 1657) 'It is submitted that international organizations empowered to issue Decisions have legislative capacity'.

[20] Wouters and De Man (n 16 above, at 205) have argued that in these cases International organisations 'merely act as agents, since they only propose draft conventions through gathering information and offering their expertise, which then may or may not be entered into by the member states'.

[21] Following Article 13 of the UN Charter, which refers to its responsibility for 'encouraging the progressive development of international law and its codification'.

[22] See for examples also Boyle and Chinkin, n 12 above at 124–41.

[23] Cf the ICJ's advisory opinion on the *Legality of the threat or use of nuclear weapons* [1996] ICJ Rep 226, para 70: 'General Assembly resolutions … can, in certain circumstances, provide evidence important for establishing the existence of a rule or the emergence of an opinio juris. To establish whether this is true of a given General Assembly resolution, it is necessary to look at its content and the conditions of its adoption; it is also necessary to see whether an opinio juris exists as to its normative character. Or a series of resolutions may show the gradual evolution of the opinio juris required for the establishment of a new rule'.

[24] Wouters and De Man, n 16 above, at 207–8. Once consensus has been reached within an international organisation, it will be difficult for states to deny their acceptance of a norm and to be recognised as a 'persistent objector'. See for the decision-making powers of many international organisations and other international bodies: J Alvarez, *International Organizations as Law-Makers* (Oxford, Oxford University Press, 2005).

organisations. Thus, the WTO's Dispute Settlement Body (DSB) has been said to be proof of the organisation's 'legislative' or 'adjudicative' powers.[25]

Finally, the set of international institutions encompasses not only formal international organisations, but also other international bodies, consisting of governmental representatives and/or other stakeholders. There are indications that these international decisions outnumber the traditional forms.[26] In the study of institutional decision-making it became clear that many norms originate in other international bodies or form part of a much broader international debate, including many different actors. The emerging picture is one of a broad range of international normative fora, including intergovernmental organisations with a broad mandate (see above); treaty-based conferences that do not amount to an international organisation (eg Conferences of the Parties under the main multilateral environmental agreements, such as the Framework Convention on Climate Change and the Kyoto Protocol); informal intergovernmental co-operative structures (eg the G20, the Financial Action Task Force on Money Laundering, the Basel Committee on Banking Supervision); and even private organisations that are active in the public domain (eg the International Organization for Standardization (ISO), or private regulation of the internet by the Internet Corporation for Assigned Names and Numbers (ICANN), The Internet Engineering Task Force (IETF) or the Internet Society (ISOC)).[27]

Given the EU's connection to all these different formal and informal normative processes, the question is to what extent international decisions impact on the EU's legal order. The following sections will address this question in more detail.

III. THE EU TREATIES AND INTERNATIONAL ORGANISATIONS

Apart from changes in the roles of international organisations, the relation between the EU and international organisations has also changed. From a political science perspective Jørgensen pointed to the idea that

> reactive policies have been left behind … [W]hereas the European Union in the past may have been an organization in need of learning about international affairs, the European Union now seems to master several of the disciplines of international relations.[28]

[25] See in particular N Lavranos, n. 5 above.

[26] See J Pauwelyn, J Wouters and RA Wessel, 'When Structures Become Shackles: Stagnation and Dynamics in International Lawmaking' (2014) 25 *European Journal of International Law* 733; but also Pauwelyn, Wessel and Wouters (eds), *Informal International Lawmaking*, n 14 above.

[27] More extensively on the normative activities of these bodies: RA Wessel, 'Regulating Technological Innovation through Informal International Law: The Exercise of International Public Authority by Transnational Actors' in MA Heldeweg and E Kica (eds), *Regulating Technological Innovation: A Multidisciplinary Approach* (Basingstoke, Palgrave MacMillan, 2011) 77–94.

[28] Jørgensen, *The European Union and International Organizations*, n 4 above, at 4–5.

And, as will be highlighted below: there seems to be a 'two-way flow of influence' which includes both an instrumental use by the EU of international organisations and an influence of international organisations on EU policies and policy-making.[29]

The current EU Treaties reflect this new interest in international organisations (see below). Apart from its participation in a number of actual international organisations, the institutionalisation of the role of the EU in the world is reflected in its position in international regimes in various policy fields, either as a full member or as an observer.[30] The position of the EU in international institutions is part and parcel of EU external relations law and it is at these fora that a *structural* role of the EU in global governance becomes most visible. Moreover, it is this role that has become more interesting now that it becomes clear that many EU (and national) rules find their origin in decision-making processes in other international organisations.

It is generally held that participation in a formal international organisation relates to participation in its organs; ie the right to attend the meetings, being elected for functions in the organ, and exercising voting and speaking rights. In that sense the term influence is related to the output of the international organisation (UN, ICAO, etc): decisions (often recommendations, on some occasions binding decisions) and conventions (international agreements prepared and adopted by an organ of an international organisation). In addition, the EU participates in less formal international institutions (or regimes) such as the G-20 for example. The Treaties herald an increase of the engagement of the EU in other international institutions, including its future membership of additional international organisations such as the Council of Europe (Article 6 TEU).

The absence of a clear and explicit competence means that the participation in (and the membership of) international institutions is predominantly based on implied powers, which find their source in the general competences the Union enjoys in the different policy fields. Thus, the Union's membership of the Food and Agricultural Organization (FAO) is based on Articles 43 TFEU (agriculture and fisheries), 207 TFEU (commercial policy) and 209 TFEU (development cooperation). However, as we will see below, there are specific policy areas where *cooperation* with international organisations is expressly incorporated into the TFEU.

What comes closest to a general competence-conferring provision is Article 211 TFEU: 'Within their respective spheres of competence, the Union and the Member States shall cooperate with third countries and with the competent international organisations'. That this 'cooperation' may also lead to the establishment of legal

[29] Ibid.

[30] F Hoffmeister, 'Outsider or Frontrunner? Recent Developments under International and European Law on the Status of the European Union in International Organizations and Treaty Bodies' (2007) 44 *Common Market Law Review* 41–68. Parts of this section are also dealt with more extensively in B van Vooren and RA Wessel, *EU External Relations Law: Text, Cases and Materials* (Cambridge, Cambridge University Press, 2014) chapter 8.

relationships can be derived from the provisions creating a competence for the Union to conclude international agreements. Article 216(1) TFEU also refers to international organisations:

> The Union may conclude an agreement with one or more third countries or international organisations where the Treaties so provide or where the conclusion of an agreement is necessary in order to achieve, within the framework of the Union's policies, one of the objectives referred to in the Treaties, or is provided for in a legally binding Union act or is likely to affect common rules or alter their scope.

And Article 217 TFEU adds: 'The Union may conclude with one or more third countries or international organisations agreements establishing an association involving reciprocal rights and obligations, common action and special procedure'.

The procedures to conclude these international agreements are to be found in Articles 218 and 219(3) TFEU. So-called, 'constitutive agreements' by which new international organisations are created, or accession agreements to acquire membership of an international organisation are not excluded. In fact, in *Opinion 1/76* the Court of Justice of the European Union (CJEU) has established that the EU's competences in the field of external relations included the power to create new international organisations.[31] Both the European Economic Area (EEA) and the 'associations' created by association agreements serve as examples of international organisations created by (at that time) the European Community. At the same time, in *Opinion 1/94* the Court implicitly accepted the EU's role as one of the founding members of the WTO. Although not explicitly regulated, this also seems to imply a competence of the EU to fully participate in so-called 'treaty-regimes', on the basis of a formal accession to a treaty (eg the UN Framework Convention on Climate Change and the Kyoto Protocol, which were formally ratified by the European Union in 1993 and 2002 respectively). As in formal international organisations, participation of the EU is either based on decisions by the participating states to grant the EU 'observer' or full participant status, or on the inclusion of a Regional Economic Integration Organisation (REIO) clause in international conventions.[32] For example, Article II of the FAO Constitution was specifically modified to allow for the accession of 'regional economic organizations'. A REIO is commonly defined in UN protocols and conventions as

> an organization constituted by sovereign states of a given region to which its Member States have transferred competence in respect of matters governed by … convention or its protocols and [which] has been duly authorised, in accordance with its internal procedures, to sign, ratify, accept, approve or accede to [the instruments concerned].[33]

[31] Opinion 1/76 of 26 April 1977 *Draft Agreement establishing a European laying-up fund for inland waterway vessels* [1977] ECR 741, para 5.

[32] See on the qualification of the EU as an international (integration) organisation also C Eckes and RA Wessel, 'The European Union: An International Perspective' in T Tridimas and R Schütze (eds), *The Oxford Principles of European Union Law—Volume 1: The European Union Legal Order* (Oxford, Oxford University Press, 2016; forthcoming).

[33] See for instance Articles 4.1, 4.2, 4.3 and 4.5, 21 and 22 of the Kyoto Protocol.

In the United Nations Convention on the Rights of Persons with Disabilities, the REIO clause seems to have evolved into a RIO (Regional Integration Organisation) clause, which does justice to the large scope of activities of the EU these days. In Article 44 of that Convention, a '"Regional integration organization" shall mean an organization constituted by sovereign States of a given region, to which its member States have transferred competence in respect of matters governed by this Convention'. Since Member States usually have retained certain competences, 'mixed agreements' are the appropriate instrument for the EU and its Member States to engage in international institutions in which both participate fully.

Express competences are not always needed for the EU to join an international organisation by concluding an international agreement. It is well known that, ever since the 1971 *ERTA* case, the CJEU has also acknowledged the treaty-making capacity of the Union in cases where this was not explicitly provided for by the Treaty. This means that international agreements, including the ones whereby the EU becomes a member of another international organisation or participates in a treaty-regime (*Opinion 1/94 WTO*), may also be based on the external dimension of an internal competence. This is also confirmed by Article 216(1) TFEU, which—as we have seen—explicitly refers to international organisations: 'The Union may conclude an agreement with one or more third countries or international organisations'. At least to establish membership of the EU in international organisations, this provision seems to give a broad mandate to the EU to also conclude international agreements in order to become a member of an international organisation or to join a treaty-regime.

Irrespective of these more *general* indications of a competence to engage in international institutions, the Treaties explicitly refer to a number of *specific* policy terrains or international organisations. Thus, Article 37 TEU allows for international agreements to be concluded 'with one or more States or international organisations' in the area of the Common Foreign and Security Policy (CFSP). Similar provisions may be found in relation to development for cooperation (Article 209(2) TFEU), economic, financial and technical cooperation (Article 212(3) TFEU) and humanitarian aid (Article 214(4) TFEU). In the environmental sphere, the Treaty reads that 'Within their respective spheres of competence, the Union and the Member States shall cooperate with third countries and with the competent international organisations' (Article 191(4) TFEU). In the field of humanitarian aid, the Treaty refers to 'international organisations and bodies, in particular those forming part of the United Nations system' to coordinate operations with (Article 214(7) TFEU). The United Nations (and its Charter) is also mentioned in relation to a number of other policy areas of the Union (Articles 3(5), 21(1)–(2), 34(2), 42(1) and (7) TEU; Articles 208(2), 214(7), and 220(1) TFEU) (see also below). In relation to development cooperation a number of provisions have been included explicitly to strengthen commitments of both the Union and its Member States in that area. Thus, Article 208(2) TFEU provides the following: 'The Union and the Member States shall comply with the commitments and take account of the objectives they have approved in the context of the United Nations and other competent international organisations'. Article 210(1) TFEU adds to that an obligation of coordination, which means concretely that the EU and Member States must take account of the Millennium Development Goals (MDGs) and their planned post-2015 follow-up ('Sustainable Development Goals' or SDGs), drawn up in the context of the United Nations. In addition one may come across some references in relation to the European Central Bank and the European Investment Bank (see Protocols Nos 4[34] and 5 to the Treaty (Article 14)). A somewhat more general provision, and the first one in a specific Treaty Title on 'The Union's Relations with International Organisations and Third Countries and Union Delegations' is Article 220(1) TFEU:

> The Union shall establish all appropriate forms of cooperation with the organs of the United Nations and its specialised agencies, the Council of Europe, the Organisation for Security and Cooperation in Europe and the Organisation for Economic Cooperation and Development. The Union shall also maintain such relations as are appropriate with other international organisations.

This short overview reveals that the competences of the EU in relation to international institutions are fragmented and scattered across the Treaties. Apart from these competences of the EU itself, many of the provisions relate to 'cooperation' or to the role of Member States. Thus, the idea to foster cooperation with third countries and competent international organisations returns in fields of education and sport (Article 165(3) TFEU), vocational training (Article 166(3) TFEU), culture (Article 167(3) TFEU) and public health (Article 168(3) TFEU). A similar promotion of cooperation with other international organisations is mentioned in relation to social policy (Article 156 TFEU) and cooperation in Union research, technological development and demonstration (Article 180(b) TFEU). In addition, the Union's foreign and security policy includes a number of rules on the way in which the EU wishes to present itself in international organisations, including the representation by the High Representative (Article 27(2) TEU), the cooperation between diplomatic missions of the Member States and the Union delegations (Articles 33 and 35 TEU), the coordination of Member States' actions (Article 34 TEU) and the general competence to conclude international agreements with international organisations in the area of CFSP (Article 37 TEU).

Finally, the EU Treaties present the United Nations and its Charter as the guiding legal framework for the EU in its external relations. Article 3(5) TEU mentions 'respect for the principles of the United Nations Charter' as part of the 'the strict observance and the development of international law' which are to be pursued by the EU. Similar wordings reappear in Article 21 TEU of the general provisions on the Union's external action. In fact, the promotion of 'multilateral solutions to common problems' should be done '*in particular* in the framework of the United Nations' (emphasis added). Finally, as reflected in the Preamble to the TFEU,

[34] Article 6(2): 'The ECB and, subject to its approval, the national central banks may participate in international monetary institutions'. See also Article 23 on external operations.

UN law not only guides the external relations of the Union, but also its internal relations with its overseas countries. The Member States announced that they intend to 'confirm the solidarity which binds Europe and the overseas countries and desiring to ensure the development of their prosperity, in accordance with the principles of the Charter of the United Nations'.

Article 42(1) TEU provides that the Union may use its civilian and military assets for missions outside the Union for peace-keeping, conflict prevention and strengthening international security, and again this should be done 'in accordance with the principles of the United Nations Charter'. In fact, the Treaties foresee the possibility of EU missions operating within a UN framework. The preamble of Protocol No 10 to the Treaties refers to the fact that 'the United Nations Organisation may request the Union's assistance for the urgent implementation of missions undertaken under Chapters VI and VII of the United Nations Charter'. Similarly, UN law forms the legal framework for actions in relation to the new collective defence obligation in Article 42(7) TEU:

> If a Member State is the victim of armed aggression on its territory, the other Member States shall have towards it an obligation of aid and assistance by all the means in their power, in accordance with Article 51 of the United Nations Charter [the provision on (collective) self-defence].

The attention to the United Nations and its principles in the EU treaties is thus overwhelming. In fact, the United Nations is referred to 19 times in the current EU treaties (including the Protocols and Declarations). Irrespective of the CJEU's judgment in the *Kadi* cases, which seemed to emphasise the Union's own principles,[35] the EU Member States which signed the Lisbon Treaty obviously regard many of the EU's actions as being part of a global governance programme. With a view to the legal regime governing the EU–UN relations, one may conclude that most of the provisions aim to regulate EU policy in a *substantive*, rather than an institutional manner. EU foreign policy is to take place within the limits set by UN law. This holds true for external relations in general, and for CFSP, CSDP, and development cooperation in particular. To a much lesser degree the treaties offer *institutional* improvements to allow the EU and the UN to become 'partners in multilateralism'.[36]

IV. THE INFLUENCE OF INTERNATIONAL DECISIONS ON THE EU: EMPIRICAL EVIDENCE

Given these extensive references in the EU treaties to international organisations (indicating even an occasional voluntary dependence of the EU on international

[35] Joined Cases C-402/05 P and C-415/05 P *Kadi and Al Barakaat International Foundation v Council and Commission* [2008] ECR I-6351; and Joined Cases C-584/10P, C-593/10P and C-595/10P, *Commission and Others v Yassin Abdullah Kadi*, EU:C:2013:518.

[36] J Wouters, *The United Nations and the European Union: Partners In Multilateralism* (Leuven Centre for Global Governance Studies: Working Paper No 1, 2007).

decisions), the question is to what extent decisions of these organisations actually impact on the EU. Over the years many empirical case studies revealed an influence of international organisations on the EU, including a possibility that international organisations have been 'teaching' the European Union, in particular in areas where it was a relative newcomer (such as health (the WHO), the monetary and financial system (IMF, and World Bank) or international security (NATO)).[37] Research—including a project lead by the present authors[38]—has furthermore shown that we have also witnessed a *normative* influence of international organisations on the EU legal order and that this may put the cherished 'autonomy' of that order into perspective.[39]

The influence of international norms varies considerably and reflects the constant struggle between an openness to international law and norms developed at the international level and the idea of an autonomous legal order that is there for the Court to preserve. Obviously, 'influence' is a matter of degree and here we use it to denote *the effect of norms created in or by international organisations on EU norms*. The issue can be approached from two sides: the international organisation in question should have the capacity or power to exercise its influence (there has to be an institutional and substantive link), and the EU must be willing or compelled to 'receive' the influence. Influence is not a legal concept and lawyers are not used to working with it (perhaps because it would imply the actual 'measuring' of effects—something that is also beyond the scope of the present chapter). In their recent book, Oriol Costa and Knud Erik Jørgensen reveal that 'under certain circumstances international institutions [indeed] shape both policies and policy-making processes, even in ways sometimes unintended by the EU, or undesired by some member states'.[40] They point to the fact that in International Relations (IR)-theory different 'mechanisms' to exert influence have been noticed, which may (1) provide opportunities to, or constraints on actors; (2) change their ability to influence decision-making by changing the distribution of power; (3) establish or spread norms and rules; or (4) create path dependencies. The emerging picture is a complex set of formal and (sometimes very subtle) informal ways in which international organisations (and other multilateral fora) influence the EU. The degree of influence may then also depend on the 'institutional strength' of the international organisation. Some research showed that 'international institutions embodied in toothless non-binding agreements should have less influence on the EU than fully-fledged international institutions including binding treaties and meetings of regular fora'.[41] At the same time, it is well-known that 'domestic conditions' are an important factor for the degree of influence.[42]

[37] Jørgensen, *The European Union and International Organizations*, n 4 above, at 8–9.

[38] Wessel and Blockmans, n 2 above.

[39] JW van Rossem, 'The Autonomy of EU Law: More is Less?' in Wessel and Blockmans, n 2 above, 13–46.

[40] O Costa and KE Jørgensen (eds), *The Influence of International Institutions on the EU* (London, Palgrave, 2012).

[41] As paraphrased by Costa and Jørgensen 2012 (n 40 above).

[42] Ibid.

In the end, IR-theory teaches us that the different mechanisms and degrees of influence may have different consequences. Apart from 'normative influence', it is equally possible to find elements of 'institutional consequences', including the role EU and Member State actors can play in international institutions and the way in which formal decision-making processes are used in practice. There is indeed an interaction between the EU and many international organisations, underlining the coming of age of the European Union as a polity. Whereas for an international organisation like the EU[43] stressing its autonomy is necessary to establish its position both vis-à-vis its own Member States and in the global legal order, its further development sets the limits to that autonomy. In many policy areas the EU has become a global player and everything it does cannot be disconnected from normative processes that take place in other international organisations. This process does come with the same tension that sovereign states face, ie how to square the preservation of one's institutional and constitutional values with accepting a certain dependence on the outside world.

More legally oriented research seems to support the findings of political scientists and IR-theorists: international decisions also normatively influence the creation and interpretation of EU decisions,[44] and—more generally—global, EU and domestic norms are increasingly interconnected.[45] The degree of the normative influence of international bodies on the EU and its legal order depends on a raft of factors, ranging from the binding obligations resulting from EU membership and full participation in other international organisations, to the voluntary reception or outright rejection of international norms by the EU legislator and Court of Justice. At the same time, 'domestic conditions' are also an important factor for the degree of influence. Whereas the EU is a unique and very complex legal construction, the separateness of the EU both from national and international law are still propagated by the Court of Justice's autonomous interpretation of EU law and its exclusive jurisdiction therein. In view of globalisation's growing interconnectedness between all sorts of subjects of international law, and the waning economic and financial power of the European Union on the international plane, the Court's refusal to take account of international law in order to protect the unity of the internal market becomes increasingly untenable. This is all the more so because

[43] Indeed, we consider the EU as an international organisation. See Eckes and Wessel, n 32 above.

[44] See the contributions to Wessel and Blockmans, n 2 above. That we are not only dealing with formal decisions by formal international organisations, but also with norms created in other (informal/regulatory) bodies flows from the many case studies in the 'informal international lawmaking' project: J Pauwelyn, RA Wessel and J Wouters (eds), *Informal International Lawmaking* (Oxford, Oxford University Press, 2012); and A Berman, S Duquet, J Pauwelyn, RA Wessel, and J Wouters, (eds), *Informal International Lawmaking: Case Studies* (The Hague, Torkel Opsahl Academic EPublisher, 2012).

[45] A Føllesdal, RA Wessel and J Wouters (eds), *Multilevel Regulation and the EU: The Interplay between Global, European and National Normative Processes* (Leiden/Boston, Martinus Nijhoff Publishers, 2008). Earlier see already Bethlehem, n 5 above at 195: 'Just like a web, or net is made up of numerous strands criss-crossing at various point while, at the same time, going in different directions, so is the relationship between international law, Community law and national law; interacting constantly even though the focus may be slightly different'.

the Court's recently displayed attitude towards the reception of international law in the EU legal order forms an impediment to meeting the EU's constitutional duties in its relations with the wider world, most notably full respect for international law, whether this emanates from international organisations with legal personality or less institutionalised international regimes.

There is thus empirical evidence of the intense legal interactions between the EU and a representative body of international institutions and we will mention some key examples, without attempting to be exhaustive, and mainly drawing on an earlier research project on this topic led by the present authors.[46] The influence of Security Council resolutions has been given abundant attention in relation to the *Kadi* saga. And will for that reason not be dealt with extensively here.[47] But also other rules, standards, codes of conduct, guidelines, principles, recommendations and best practices developed within a variety of international organisations and bodies influence the development of EU law, even if they are not strictly legally binding upon the Union. Thus, norms developed within several bodies—be it within the UN family such as the Food and Agriculture Organization (FAO), the *Codex Alimentarius* Commission and the World Health Organization (WHO), or the OECD, the G20 and some of the machinery this 'international regime' has brought to life, such as the Financial Stability Board (FSB), and specific bodies bringing together financial watchdogs like the Basel Committee on Banking Supervision (BCBS) and the International Organization of Securities Commissions (IOSCO)—have been dealt with within the EU legislature and/or by the judiciary. As it happens, the Union seems to have a somewhat ambivalent relationship with international bodies and the numerous norms they develop. The EU legislature demonstrates openness towards these norms and often directly refers to the international processes that led to their development. This is the case especially where the EU is represented in the international body concerned, helps to shape the rules, and where the EU has an interest in seeing them implemented. Indeed, much of the EU's recent legislation in financial governance explicitly mentions commitments made at the international level, in particular within the G20. In case law, however, the Court of Justice of the EU has rarely relied on norms emanating from these bodies in a substantive fashion. While the CJEU sometimes refers to such norms, it has often given a more autonomous meaning to the EU rules concerned.[48]

An analysis of the impact of the WTO's dispute settlement mechanism and the European Court of Human Rights (ECtHR) on the EU legal order reveals that

[46] The project 'Between Autonomy and Dependence' was initiated by the Centre for the Law of EU External Relations (CLEER) in The Hague and resulted, inter alia, in the edited volume mentioned above (Wessel and Blockmans, n 2 above). Cf also Føllesdal, Wessel and Wouters, n 45 above.

[47] See among the many publications on this issue A Gattini, 'Effects of Decisions of the UN Security Council in the EU Legal Order' in Cannizzaro et al, n 3 above, 215–27.

[48] J Wouters and J Odermatt, 'Norms Emanating from International Bodies and Their Role in the Legal Order of the European Union' in Wessel and Blockmans, n 2 above, 47–68.

the Court has so far not accepted that it must be bound by the decisions of any external (quasi-)judicial body. Yet both EU law (Article 6(3) TEU) and the status of the European Charter of Fundamental Rights (a 'constitutional instrument of European public order') can be cited in support of the argument that the decisions of the ECtHR require and deserve greater force than the decisions of other external (quasi-)judicial bodies, including the WTO dispute settlement bodies. With the Member States enjoying the convenience, the EU has taken over adjudication in the WTO. Eckes has observed that the negotiations surrounding the accession of the EU to the ECHR provide the most recent example where the EU's autonomy concern has posed and will continue to pose many questions.[49] More in general a number of Council of Europe conventions are today part of the EU's *acquis* in the field of freedom, security and justice (eg, the 2008 Council Framework Decision on Combating Terrorism, and the 2000 Convention on Mutual Assistance in Criminal Matters between the Member States of the European Union aimed at supplementing and facilitating the application, between the EU Member States, of the 1959 European Convention on Mutual Assistance in Criminal Matters).[50]

The influence of the WTO on the EU cannot be overstated. WTO primary and secondary law have had a considerable influence on EU primary and secondary law and their interpretation. Much of the EU's primary law on the free circulation of goods has been inspired by GATT 1947, and the integration of new trade subjects into the 1994 WTO Agreement triggered a constitutional process of expanding the EU's exclusive powers concerning commercial policy. Moreover, many pieces of secondary EU legislation either transpose WTO norms or have been modified to bring them into line with world trade standards after adverse WTO judicial decisions. The underlying reason for this openness may be that the EU's political institutions expect WTO rules in this area to have been largely influenced by its own practice on the matter and are thus considered to be fully legitimate.[51]

While IMF law as such has a limited influence on EU law in the sense of the IMF's power to affect EU law, it nevertheless impacts upon EU law, both directly and indirectly. First, EU jurisprudence recognises that under certain circumstances obligations under multilateral treaties, such as the IMF's Articles—to which all EU Member States are parties but the EU is not—may have a direct binding effect on the EU, to the extent that the EU assumes the Member States' competences under the TFEU related to these obligations. Secondly, the exercise of EU Member States' rights and obligations under the IMF's Articles indirectly affects the EU and EU law. This is because the EU has assumed, or shares with, EU Member States certain competences relevant to the IMF's Articles. Thirdly, the IMF and the EU also

[49] C Eckes, 'The European Court of Justice and (Quasi-)Judicial Bodies of International Organisations' in Wessel and Blockmans, n 2 above, 85–109.

[50] E Cornu, 'The Impact of Council of Europe Standards on the European Union' in Wessel and Blockmans, n 2 above, 113–29.

[51] PJ Kuijper and F Hoffmeister, 'WTO Influence on EU Law: Too Close for Comfort?' in Wessel and Blockmans, n 2 above, 131–58.

interact in other areas of common interest, thereby mutually influencing policy positions and leading to the use of similar concepts in their respective policies and laws. One example concerns the two organisations' surveillance, the IMF under Article IV of its Articles and the EU under a number of procedural frameworks, such as the Stability and Growth Pact. Similarly, IMF policy positions on collective action clauses have also impacted on EU policy decisions. The EU's legal order is thus rather open to the influence of IMF law.[52]

Another example is given by the World Intellectual Property Organization. The EU is not a member of the WIPO, whereas all its Member States are. Yet, in light of the strong link between the EU and WIPO, the autonomy of the EU in matters of intellectual property is relative. The European Union is among the most active international organisations at WIPO. The EU has been given either member or observer status by WIPO members for several internationally binding agreements and within various decision-making bodies. WIPO's norms, principles and practices are increasingly relevant to the development of intellectual property law within the EU legal order. Historically, the EU has incorporated both binding and non-binding principles created via the WIPO mechanism. Whereas the WIPO norm-making process heavily influences the body and framework of intellectual property law in the EU, WIPO norms do not have independent normative value within the EU. The EU is not bound by new or evolving intellectual property principles unless, by virtue of its own authority, it chooses to be. Yet, there is clear evidence that the EU is able to act unilaterally to accept or discard intellectual property norms in its legal order.[53]

Turning to another specialized agency of the United Nations, the Food and Agriculture Organization (FAO), it has been observed that, over time, the relationship between the two international organisations has shifted from one between equal partners to a more hierarchical one between an organisation (the FAO) and one of its members (the EU). It is exactly because the EU is a full member of the FAO that it is not wholly surprising to find that the EU legal order reveals substantial FAO influence, notably in five policy fields: fisheries, food law, animal health, international food security and forestry. Yet the extent of these effects is ultimately determined by the EU legislator and judiciary. The normative impact of the FAO on the EU legal order manifests itself chiefly in terms of the direct incorporation of FAO standards in EU secondary legislation and in references to FAO standards in both EU policy instruments and the case law of the CJEU. In food law and animal health, the influence of the FAO is strongest in internal EU rules, whereas in the fields of fisheries, international food security and forestry, FAO influence is more prominent in external EU policies and actions.[54]

[52] W Bergthaler, 'The Relationship Between International Monetary Fund Law and European Union Law: Influence, Impact, Effect, and Interaction' in Wessel and Blockmans, n 2 above, 159–98.

[53] E Kwakwa and A Talbott, 'The Influence of the World Intellectual Property Organization on the European Union' in Wessel and Blockmans, n 2 above, 199–216.

[54] F Schild, 'The Influence of the Food and Agriculture Organization (FAO) on the EU Legal Order' in Wessel and Blockmans, n 2 above, 217–41.

Notwithstanding the fact that the jurisdiction of the CJEU does not extend to Title V of the EU Treaty to the same extent as to other policy areas, it is nevertheless interesting to note that NATO's impact on the European Union's institutional design, policy-making and 'operational experience gathering' in the field of security and defence has been 'fundamental', even if only a few traces of NATO are to be found in EU primary law. It is especially on the operational side, the raison d'être of the EU's Common Security and Defence Policy, that NATO's impact has been instrumental.[55] This is evidenced most vividly by the use, however limited in number, of the so-called 'Berlin Plus' arrangements, which have enabled the European Union to borrow NATO assets and capabilities in order to launch its first-ever military mission in 2003 (EUPOL Proxima in Macedonia) and to continue its activities in Bosnia-Herzegovina (EUFOR Althea). Similarly, it has been noted that also in the Area of Freedom, Security and Justice (AFSJ) the EU is bound to respect the norms stemming from international organisations. Yet, while the EU legal order is open to external normative influences, only a couple of international organisations currently influence the development of the AFSJ. The most prominent examples are the United Nations and the Council of Europe, which muster the 1951 Geneva Convention on asylum seekers and refugees and the European Convention on Human Rights, respectively.[56]

Overall, studies over the past years have revealed the impact of many international decisions on the EU. These decisions may be taken by both formal international organisations and more 'informal' transnational, regulatory or treaty bodies.[57] Given this influence, the question is how we should assess the legal status of these decisions in the EU legal order.

V. THE LEGAL STATUS OF INTERNATIONAL DECISIONS IN THE EU LEGAL ORDER

The preceding chapters in this volume addressed the relationship between international law and EU law in more general terms. It was in the *Haegeman* case[58] that the Court presented the famous phrase that international agreements concluded by the European Union form 'an integral part of Union law'. In the more recent *American Air Transport Association* case, the Court nicely summarised the main principles related to the effect of international law in the EU legal order. First of all, the Court confirmed that the EU is in principle bound by international law.[59]

[55] S Blockmans, 'The Influence of NATO on the Development of the EU's Common Security and Defence Policy' in Wessel and Blockmans, n 2 above, 243–67.

[56] C Matera, 'The Influence of International Organisations on the EU's Area of Freedom, Security and Justice: A First Inquiry' in Wessel and Blockmans, n 2 above, 269–96.

[57] See for examples Føllesdal, Wessel and Wouters, n 45 above.

[58] Case 181/73, *R & V Haegeman v Belgian State*, EU:C:1974:41.

[59] Case C-366/10, *Air Transport Association of America and Others v Secretary of State for Energy and Climate Change* EU:C:2011:864.

This has indeed been standard case law ever since the *International Fruit Company* case in 1972.[60] Secondly, the Court can examine the validity of an act of European Union law in the light of an international treaty only where the nature and the broad logic of the latter do not preclude this.[61] Finally, where the nature and the broad logic of the treaty in question permit the validity of the act of European Union law to be reviewed in the light of the provisions of that treaty, it is also necessary that the provisions of that treaty which are relied upon for the purpose of examining the validity of the act of European Union law appear, as regards their content, to be unconditional and sufficiently precise.[62]

The question of whether this status of international law is restricted to international agreements, or also extends to decisions of international organisations, has been less frequently discussed. Yet, as rightfully stated by Martenczuk, 'international agreements … often establish a common institutional framework, including the creation of joint bodies authorized to take decisions with bring effect for the parties'.[63] Indeed, one starting point is formed by 'secondary international law' deriving from international agreements such as Association Council decisions. In *Sevince*—concerning the rights of Turkish workers under Decisions 2/76 and 1/80 of the EC-Turkey Association Council—the Court held that these decisions are also to be seen as forming part of the EU's legal order and may even have direct effect.[64] Earlier, the Court had already recognised the legal effect of decisions of the same Association Council, without being explicit on the actual legal status.[65] And, in fact in *Greece v Commission*, the Court had already used *Haegeman*-like language: 'since it is directly connected with the Association Agreement, Decision No. 2/80 forms, from the entry into force an integral part of the Community legal system'.[66]

While one could argue that association agreements and their Councils and comparable bodies are quite directly connected to the EU's legal order on the basis of their very nature, there are no reasons to limit this reasoning that they constitute international bodies (especially when seen from the perspective of the third country) to the Association regimes. In *Opinion 1/76*, in relation to the question

[60] Joined Cases 21 to 24/72 *International Fruit Company NV v Produktschap voor Groenten en Fruit* [1972] ECR 1219.

[61] See also Joined Cases C-120/06 P and C-121/06 P, *FIAMM and Others v Council and Commission*, para 110.

[62] Case C-344/04, *Queen on the application of International Air Transport Association v Department for Transport* (IATA and ELFAA), para 39, and Case C-308/06 *The Queen on the application of International Association of Independent Tanker owners (Intertanko) v Secretary of State for Transport*, EU:C:2008:312, para 45.

[63] B Martenczuk, n 5 above, at 142.

[64] Case C-192/89 *Sevince v Staatssecretaris van Justitie*. Cf also Case C-188/91, *Deutsche Shell AG v Hauptzollamt Hamburg-Harburg*, [1993] ECR I-363, para 17. Cf also N Neuwahl, 'The European Parliament and Association Council Decisions: The example of Decision 1/95 of the EC/Turkey Association Council' (1996) 33 *Common Market Law Review* 51–68.

[65] Case 204/86, *Greece v Council* [1988] ECR 5323.

[66] Case 30/88, *Greece v Commission* [1989] ECR 3711.

as to whether an agreement 'establishing a European laying-up fund for inland waterway vessels' is compatible with the provisions of the Treaty, the Court argued:

> the Community is ... not only entitled to enter into contractual relations with a third country in this connection but also has the power, while observing the provisions of the Treaty, to cooperate with that country in setting up an appropriate organism such as the public international institution which it is proposed to establish under the name of the 'European laying-up fund for inland waterway vessels'.[67]

The Court explicitly added that the 'organism' may be given 'appropriate powers of decision'.[68] In subsequent situations, such as the establishment and joining of the EU (at the time the EC) of the WTO,[69] the Court underlined this view. The current Treaties do not provide for a specific procedure for agreements to establish or join international organisations, which implies that the general rules of Article 218 TFEU apply. Indeed Article 218(1) TFEU refers to 'agreements between the Union and third countries *or international organisations* (emphasis added)' and Article 218(6)(a)(iii) TFEU mentions 'agreements establishing a specific institutional framework by organising cooperation procedures' (as one of the cases requiring the consent of the European Parliament). Examples include bilateral cooperation agreements, such as Partnership and Cooperation Agreements, but also other types of agreements which include the establishment of bodies with decision-making powers, such as the ones dealing with the mutual recognition of technical standards (concluded for instance with the US, Canada, Australia and New Zealand). Bodies are furthermore established by for instance the European Economic Area, the Energy Charter Treaty, the Energy Community Treaty and the European Common Aviation Area or on the basis of multilateral environmental agreements (MEAs).[70] The latter often use the terms Conference of Parties (COPs) or Meeting of Parties (MOPs) to refer to the bodies taking the decisions in the framework of MEAs.[71] While there is no consensus on whether COPs and MOPs could qualify as international organisations, 'the fact remains that at the same time COPs/MOPs have been endowed with the competence to adopt binding decisions'.[72] Or, as another observer stated:

> Like treaties, they compromise a specific normative framework of prescriptions that are particularly suitable to organizing internationally coordinated behaviour within a

[67] Opinion 1/76 *re draft Agreement establishing a European laying-up fund for inland waterway vessels*, n 3 above, para. 5.

[68] Ibid.

[69] Opinion 1/94 of 15 November 1994, *Competence of the Community to conclude international agreements concerning services and the protection of intellectual property* [1994] ECR I-5267 (*re WTO Agreement*).

[70] See further Martenczuk, n 5 above.

[71] See for instance T Delreux, 'The EU as an actor in global environmental politics' in A Jordan, C Adelle (eds), *Environmental Policy in the EU: Actors, Institutions and Processes* (London, Routledge, 2012) 287–305.

[72] Lavranos, n 5 above, at 81.

> limited issue-area. Like international organizations, they provide a permanent mechanism for changing these normative prescriptions.[73]

The link with 'international agreements' remains nevertheless important. In the cases on decisions by Association Councils, the Court already pointed to the need for these decisions to be 'directly connected' with the underlying international agreement. And in the absence of any specific provisions on decisions of international organisations, it would indeed be Article 218 TFEU that seems to offer the appropriate framework. The term 'international agreements' was broadly defined by the Court as to include 'any undertaking entered into by entities subject to international law which has binding force, whatever its form or designation'.[74] The Court made this assessment in the framework of an Article 218(11) TFEU procedure on the basis of which 'A Member State, the European Parliament, the Council or the Commission may obtain the opinion of the Court of Justice as to whether an agreement envisaged is compatible with the Treaties'. It would seem that in its Opinion the Court should also take into account the possible decisions to be adopted by bodies established by international agreements.[75]

Apart from the above-mentioned references to international bodies in Article 218, paragraph (9) is perhaps even more explicit:

> The Council, on a proposal from the Commission or the High Representative of the Union for Foreign Affairs and Security Policy, shall adopt a decision suspending application of an agreement and establishing the positions to be adopted on the Union's behalf in a body set up by an agreement, when that body is called upon to adopt acts having legal effects, with the exception of acts supplementing or amending the institutional framework of the agreement.

While the status of international decisions is still not clear from this provision, at least 'bodies set up by an agreement' are mentioned. More important, however, is that when introduced by the Treaty of Amsterdam, the procedure only applied to establishing the positions to be adopted on behalf of the Community in a body set up by an association agreement. The Nice Treaty extended the scope of application of the provision concerned to cover decisions, having legal effects, of bodies set up by any international agreement. It has been argued that

> the purpose of the introduction of this simplified decision-making procedure was presumably to take account of the case law of the Court of Justice according to which the status and effects, in the Union legal order, of such decisions of organs created by an

[73] T Gehring, 'International Environmental Regimes: Dynamic Sectoral Legal Systems' (1990) 1 *Yearbook of International Environmental Law* 35 at 54–55.

[74] Opinion 1/75 of 11 November 1975 *Local Cost Standard* [1975] ECR 1355, para A; Opinion 2/92 *Revised Decision of the OECD on National Treatment* [1995] ECR I-521, para II.1.

[75] Opinion 1/91 of 14 December 1991 (*European Economic Area*) [1991] ECR I-6079; Opinion 2/94 of 28 March 1996 (*European Convention on Human Rights*) [1996] ECR I-1759; Opinion 1/00 of 18 April 2002 (*European Common Aviation Area*) [2002] ECR I-3493; Opinion 1/09 of 8 March 2011, *European Patent Court*, EU:C:2011:123. Cf also Martenczuk, n 5 above, at 161.

> international agreement concluded by the Community were essentially the same as those of the agreement itself.[76]

Furthermore, there do not seem to be reasons to limit this to treaty bodies set up by multilateral conventions, in which case the provision would also apply to 'regular' international organisations. Indeed, as argued by Heliskoski, Article 218(9)'s main raison d'être may flow from the very fact 'that decisions of such bodies could have legal effects—including direct effect and primacy over secondary legislation—within the Union legal order without any subsequent act of adoption by the Union's institutions'.[77]

Yet while international organisations are (by definition) established on the basis of an international (constitutive) agreement, the EU is not always a party to that agreement, in which case the provisions in Article 218 would not apply and the source for the binding character of decisions on the Union should be found elsewhere. In the *CITES* case, for instance, the Commission sought the annulment of the decision of the Council establishing the position to be adopted on behalf of the European Community with regard to certain proposals submitted at a meeting of the Conference of the Parties to the Convention on International Trade in Endangered Species of Wild Fauna and Flora (CITES).[78] The Union is not a contracting party to CITES; it has observer status at Conferences of the Parties. However, since 1982 it has autonomously adopted measures designed to implement within the Union the obligations of the Member States deriving from CITES. For the purpose of the present chapter the CITES case is also helpful as it clarifies that the Conference of the Parties (COPs) of CITES is empowered to adopt amendments to the Appendices to the Convention, the entry into force of which is not subject to ratification, and that the decisions of the COPs are clearly capable of producing legal effects not only with regard to the Member States as parties to CITES but also within the Union's legal order. Yet the Court did not deal with the content of decisions, or their status and effect in Union law, even though it has rightfully been argued that

> the nature and effects of a decision to be taken by an international decision-making body should ... play a crucial role in determining whether the establishment of the position of the Union in such a body should be conceived of as having legal effects in the Union legal order.[79]

In a recent case, the Court had a chance to clarify the scope of Article 218(9). The case relates to decisions taken by the International Organisation of Wine and Vine (IOV), of which the EU is not a member, but several of its Member States are. Given

[76] See the case note by J Heliskoski, on Case 370/07, *Commission v Council* (2011) 48 *Common Market Law Review* 555 at 557–58.

[77] Ibid at 558.

[78] Case 370/07, *Commission v Council* [2009] I-8917.

[79] Heliskoski, n 77 above, at 364.

the EU's competences in the field, its intention is to upgrade its position in the IOV.[80] An interesting element is that Article 8 of the IOV Agreement allows international organisations to become a member of the organisation, but so far EU Council Members have not been able to reach consensus on this. On 19 June 2012, the Council, by qualified majority with Germany voting against, adopted a decision establishing an EU position to be adopted in the OIV[81] on the basis of Articles 43 and 218(9) TFEU. Germany (itself a member of the OIV) brought an action for annulment against that decision, challenging Article 218(9) TFEU as the correct legal basis for the adoption of the decision. Germany argued that Article 218(9) TFEU concerns only the adoption of positions of the Union in bodies set up by international agreements of which the Union is a member. By contrast, Article 218(9) TFEU cannot be applied in relation to the representation of the Member States in bodies of international organisations in which only the Member States participate by virtue of separate international treaties. Furthermore, Germany took the view that Article 218(9) TFEU covers only 'acts having legal effects', meaning acts binding under international law, and that OIV resolutions are not acts in that sense. Finally, Germany argued that no other legal basis for the adoption of the Council decision is apparent.[82]

On 29 April 2014 Advocate General Cruz Villalón delivered his Opinion[83] and argued that Article 218(9) TFEU can only apply to bodies established by agreements to which the Union is a party. In his final conclusion the AG holds that Article 218(9) TFEU does not provide a suitable legal basis for the decision in the present case. In its judgment of 7 October 2014 the Court reached a different conclusion.[84] It argues that there is nothing in the wording of Article 218(9) TFEU to prevent the European Union from adopting a decision establishing a position to be adopted on its behalf in a body set up by an international agreement to which it is not a party.

> Where an area of law falls within a competence of the European Union, such as the one mentioned in the preceding paragraph, the fact that the European Union did not take part in the international agreement in question does not prevent it from exercising that competence by establishing, through its institutions, a position to be adopted on its behalf in the body set up by that agreement, in particular through the Member States which are party to that agreement acting jointly in its interest (para 52).

The question then is whether we are dealing with 'acts having legal effects'. In that respect the Court argues

> that the recommendations under consideration in the present case … are capable of decisively influencing the content of the legislation adopted by the EU legislature in the area of the common organisation of the wine markets. It follows … that such

[80] G De Baere, 'EU Status in International Organizations' in Tridimas and Schütze, n 31 above.

[81] Council Document No 11436 'establishing the position to be adopted on behalf of the European Union with regard to certain resolutions to be voted in the framework of the International Organisation for Vine and Wine (OIV)'.

[82] See more extensively De Baere, n 81 above.

[83] C-399/12, *Germany v Council*, Opinion of 29 April 2014, EU:C:2014:289.

[84] C-399/12, *Germany v Council*, judgment of 1 October 2014.

> recommendations, in particular by reason of their incorporation into EU law by virtue of Articles 120f(a), 120g and 158a(1) and (2) of Regulation No 1234/2007 and the first subparagraph of Article 9(1) of Regulation No 606/2009, have legal effects in that area for the purposes of Article 218(9) TFEU and that the European Union, while not a party to the OIV Agreement, is entitled to establish a position to be adopted on its behalf with regard to those recommendations, in view of their direct impact on the European Union's acquis in that area' (paras 63–64).

What does this tell us about the status of international decisions in the EU legal order? Can we establish a link with Article 216(2) TFEU, on the basis of which 'Agreements concluded by the Union are binding upon the institutions of the Union and on its Member States'? The close connection which is visible both in the (modified) treaty provisions and in case law between 'international agreements' and 'decisions made by bodies based on international agreements' indeed points to this presumption.[85] Following Martenczuk: 'to the extent that decisions of bodies established by international law have been validly incorporated into Union law, they are part of the Union legal order' and hence their uniform interpretation and application throughout the Union's legal order is to be ensured,[86] in principle irrespective of their direct effect.[87] Allegedly this would imply the Court's jurisdiction to give preliminary rulings on the interpretation of the decisions (as was confirmed for Association Council decisions in *Sevince*).[88] While Article 267 TFEU limits the preliminary procedure to 'the validity and interpretation of acts of the institutions, bodies, offices or agencies of the Union' and 'acts of other international bodies' are not included,[89] it may be argued that the latter are a logical consequence of an earlier 'act of the institutions'. In addition, sometimes international decisions enter the EU legal order only after a decision to that end was adopted by the EU institutions.[90] Along the same lines the infringement procedure (Article 258 TFEU) applies *mutatis mutandis*.

Yet even if 'Decisions based on Agreements concluded by the Union are binding upon the institutions of the Union and on its Member States', what then about decisions by other international bodies? While in a 'CITES-situation' the Union may

[85] A similar conclusion was drawn by Lavranos, n 5 above, at 237–38: 'decisions of IOs enjoy the same legal status within the Community legal order as treaties ... and obtain Community law features such as supremacy over all domestic law of the Member States and direct effect it they meet the criteria'. See for a recent analysis of the status of international agreements M Mendez, *The Legal Effects of EU Agreements: Maximalist Treaty Enforcement and Judicial Avoidance Techniques* (Oxford, Oxford University Press, 2013).

[86] Martenczuk, n 5 above, at 161. In this quotation 'Community' was replaced by 'Union'.

[87] Cf Lavranos, n 5 above, at 83 (in relation to COPs/MOPs decisions). And at 233: 'the binding decisions are—to a varying degree—communitarized, thereby obtaining Community law features, such as supremacy over conflicting secondary EC law and all national law of the EU Member States and possible direct effect'.

[88] Above n 65, para 10.

[89] See on this point also A Peters, 'The Position of International Law within the European Community Legal Order' (1997) 40 *German Yearbook of International Law* 9 at 12–14.

[90] Martenczuk, n 5 above, at 162.

have adopted the legal effects of decisions of the COPs or another international body, it would be difficult to provide a general answer. Decisions by international organisations of which the Union is not a member, or of bodies based on international agreements to which the EU is not a party (or of international bodies not based on an international agreement at all), can have legal effects in the sense that they may 'influence' EU decision-making, but they would need to be binding on the Union to actually enjoy the hierarchically higher status comparable to international agreements in order to be able to set aside existing Union law. Conceptually speaking, it does not make any difference if an international norm that arrives at the border of the EU legal order is generated by an international organisation or whether it belongs to a less organised body of public international law. In order to have an impact on the EU legal order, all international norms will, regardless of their origins, have to be binding on the EU. Furthermore, the nature and the broad logic of these international norms should not preclude this binding force.[91]

VI. CONCLUDING OBSERVATIONS

The question of the status of decisions by international organisations and other bodies (termed 'international decisions' in this chapter) in the Union's legal order has gained importance. First of all international organisations have changed from international frameworks for cooperation to more 'autonomous' norm-creating international bodies. Secondly, there has been a proliferation of international norm-creating and/or regulatory bodies, alongside the already existing formal international governmental organisations. Thirdly, the decisions of all these international bodies are more and more influencing each other, resulting in a 'global normative web' that also impacts on the European Union.

The status of these international decisions in the EU legal order is not as clearly regulated or clarified as the status of international agreements and customary law. Yet this chapter shows that there are good reasons to follow the *Haegeman*-doctrine and start from the presumption that international decisions form 'an integral part of EU law'. In fact, the doctrinal analysis of the status of international agreements may *mutatis mutandis* be applied to international decisions, including their position 'between primary and secondary law', keeping in mind that

> [w]hilst the EU in principle automatically incorporates treaties it concludes into its legal order, it is the EU legal order that will ultimately determine the types of internal effect which such Agreements can display and, indeed, can potentially deprive them, through ex post review, of internal legal effects where they clash with EU primary law.[92]

Given the wide range of topics covered by international bodies and the diverging legal nature of their decisions, this does not make the overall question raised

[91] Cf van Rossem, n 39 above.
[92] Mendez, n 86 above, at 320.

by this chapter any easier to answer. Indeed, the question of the *reception* of the international norms seems to be decisive in establishing their status. This line of reasoning points to a more dynamic influence of international law on the EU. Where negotiations on international agreements may very well take the 'primary law' aspects of the agreement into consideration, it is much more difficult to predict any 'secondary law' based on the agreement. Yet following the interpretation of both the treaty provisions and the relevant case law it would be difficult to come to a different conclusion. Once the EU has joined an international organisation or becomes a party to an international agreement on the basis of which international decisions can be taken, these decisions not only influence the EU legal order, but—when binding—also become an integral part of that order. The presumption suggested above would at least hold for decisions of Association Councils (and similar bodies) and for decisions of bodies (and Conferences of States Parties) based on agreements to which the Union is a party or where it has accepted the legal effects through internal legislation. As such, these decisions may also obtain EU law features such as supremacy and possible direct effect—features that they previously did not necessarily possess.[93] This may even be possible in cases where the EU itself is not a member of the particular international organisation (such as in the case of the ICAO) or treaty regime (CITES). In cases where Member States are not a member of an international organisation, but the EU is (for instance the regional fisheries organisations), the international decisions reach the Member States as (supreme) EU law and not as international law of which the status is determined by their national constitutions.[94] The possible impact of international decisions on fundamental rights, the principles of democracy and rule of law, have been analysed extensively, in particular in the context of the *Kadi* saga.

The fact remains that, unlike international agreements, international decisions usually do not require ratification to enter into force. This may be particularly problematic when the notion of 'international decisions as integral part of EU law' is combined with majority decision-making at the international level, potentially allowing non-EU members to create supreme EU law. Again, this issue became apparent in many of the anti-terrorism cases. At the same time it is clear that in most cases international bodies work on the basis of consensus or offer a way to opt out.

Decisions by international organisations or other international bodies can have legal effects in the sense that they may 'influence' EU decision-making, but

[93] Cf Lavranos, n 5 above, at 238.

[94] Lavranos, n 5 above., noted an interesting correlation between the instruments used for implementation of decisions of international organisations and the EU scope of competence: 'In the case of exclusive competence of the EC (Fisheries, SC, GATT), the EC uses Regulations as the main instrument, whereas in the cases of concurrent competences, the EC appears to prefer Directives as the main instrument for the implementation of decisions of IOs—although sometimes also Regulations or Council Decisions are used. Also in the case where the EC is not a member of the IO (ICAO), the EC used Directives when it implements Annexes adopted by the ICAO Council'.

they would need to be binding on the Union to actually enjoy the hierarchically higher status comparable to international agreements in order to be able to set aside existing EU law. Conceptually speaking therefore, it does not make any difference if an international norm that arrives at the border of the EU legal order is generated by an international organisation or whether it belongs to a less organised body of public international law. In order to have an impact on the EU legal order, all international norms will, regardless of their origins, have to be binding on the EU.

7

The Relationship of the Member States' International Agreements with the EU

JAVIER ROLDÁN BARBERO[1]

Content

I. INTRODUCTORY REMARKS

TRADITIONALLY, *IUS AD tractatum* has been considered as a State policy solely or mainly exercised by the executive branch of a country. But times are changing as regards international agreements and their contracting parties, public or private. Logically, this circumstance raises the issue of the legality, consistency and coordination of the different conventional activities.

In the domestic field, and speaking of the Spanish case, this situation is one of the main reasons for a Law of Treaties, drafted but blocked for many years and

[1] Professor of Public International Law, University of Granada.

finally passed in 2014.[2] Both in the Spanish and in the European arena, federalism is evoked and there are calls both for unity and for diversity in international conventional action.

Having said this, it is obvious that the 'cohabitation' of the treaty-making power of the EU and that of its individual Member States (hereafter MS) is particularly intricate, multifaceted and very different from the solely national perspective. In fact, complexity is to be found also when we compare the peculiarities brought together in the internal cohabitation of the EU and the MS in the European legal order. This is so for a variety of reasons: the special use and consequences of subsidiarity and of two-speed integration, with particular opposition from the States to losing their international presence; the special directories of MS in these matters;[3] the intrinsic transversal essence of external relations and the necessity for a holistic approach towards the partners; and of course, the very particular instrument of the Common Foreign and Security Policy. Although the CFSP is generally outside the jurisdiction of the European Court of Justice (hereafter ECJ), there have been many judgments devoted to relating, and at the same time distinguishing, the external domains of the CFSP and of the rest of the external relations of the EU.[4]

[2] In 2014 too, another law of international character, and also devoted to the coordination of different sectors of the administration, has been adopted: Law 2/2014, 25 March, on External Action and Service of the State. *Boletín Oficial del Estado* (Official State Gazette), 26 March 2014 (BOE-A-2014-3248).

[3] In this sense, it is interesting to consult the European Foreign Policy Scorecard 2014, a project launched by the European Council of Foreign Relations that 'assesses the performance of the 28 MS and the EU institutions on 66 policy areas arranged around six key themes': www.ecfr.eu/scorecard/2014.

[4] The aspiration to separate 'external economic relations' from 'political foreign relations' has nonetheless a great deal of artificiality, taking into account the interdisciplinary conception of international relations. On these complex 'interpillar' relations, see C Martínez Capdevila, 'Sobre el reparto horizontal de competencias entre la CE y la UE (Comentario a la Sentencia del TJCE, de 20 de mayo de 2008, as. Comisión c. Consejo—Lucha contra la proliferación de armas ligeras C-91/05). (2009) 29 *Revista Española de Derecho Europeo* 101. The EU, in the framework of the previous second pillar, still differently regulated in the current primary law, has been concluding international agreements for many years. See for example Council Decision 2009/88/CFSP of 22 December 2008 concerning the conclusion of the Agreement between the European Union and the Republic of Djibouti on the status of the European Union-led forces in the Republic of Djibouti in the framework of the EU military operation Atalanta [2009] OJ L33/41. Sometimes the agreement is formally accepted through a unilateral decision: Political and Security Committee Decision ATALANTA/2/2009 of 21 April 2009 on the acceptance of third States' contributions to the European Union military operation to contribute to the deterrence, prevention and repression of acts of piracy and armed robbery off the Somali coast (Atalanta) (2009/356/CFSP) [2009] OJ L109/52). Besides, the mixed agreements usually contain rules devoted to political dialogue aimed at achieving a concerted diplomacy between the EU and its partners. The external dimension of the former third pillar, focused on Justice and Home Affairs, would also merit a separate analysis. The first example of agreement concluded in this field was the Agreements on Extradition and Mutual Legal Assistance, signed on 25 June 2003 between the EU and the United States [2003] OJ L181/27. See C Martínez Capdevila, 'Los acuerdos internacionales del tercer pilar de la UE' in A Remiro Brotóns, I Blázquez Navarro (eds), *El futuro de la acción exterior de la Unión Europea* (Valencia, Tirant lo Blanch, 2006). Occasionally, a particular agreement has affected both the second and third former pillars. For instance, Council Decision 2007/551/CFSP/JHA of 23 July 2007 on the signing, on behalf of the European Union, of an Agreement between the European Union and the United States of America on the processing and transfer of Passenger Name Record (PNR) data by air carriers to the United States Department of Homeland Security (DHS) (2007 PNR Agreement) [2007] OJ L204.

The fractures and weaknesses within European foreign policy are frequently propagated and deplored, even—paradoxically and cynically—by the European Council, whose task it is to take the main and strategic external decisions aimed at reinforcing Europe as an international actor and power. The lack of appropriate coordination encompasses the institutional field, the relations between internal and international activities of the EU and the interaction of different European competences.

Of course, the shadow of the State is omnipresent in European integration, as well as in the institutional equilibrium[5] and in the exclusive European competences[6] (Common Commercial Policy or Common Fisheries Policy). The 'joint venture' of the EU-MS is at the centre of the construction of Europe, its objective being to compound two principles drawn from the Treaties: on the one hand, the respect shown towards national identity and its international subjectivity and, on the other hand, the recognition and promotion of the European personality and its visibility in the international community. The principle, usually invoked by the ECJ, of international cooperation between the EU and its MS with a view to achieving unity in international representation is so vague and unspecific that it is not always enough to ensure the proper synergies. The improvements and elucidations inserted in the Lisbon Treaty in terms of institutions and competences in foreign affairs have not been sufficient to delimit and consolidate the international personality of the EU or to establish a definitive vertical list of the EU capabilities in the international field.[7]

Admittedly, the external action deployed by a State is quite different from the external action deployed by the EU, so it is inappropriate to extrapolate from the national parameters to the European domain. It also goes without saying that the present moment of crisis has revealed the EU to be more an international problem than an international pattern, involved as it is in a process of decay with perhaps consequently less capacity and less responsibility in international affairs, fewer normative powers, more introspection in order to resolve first of all its internal problems, and more nationalist temptations among the States. But the

[5] See Case C-36/98 *Kingdom of Spain v Council* [2001] ECR I-810. In this case, the legal basis for the ratification of the Convention on cooperation for the protection and sustainable use of the river Danube, signed in 1994 was contested. For internal reasons, Spain was interested in the use of unanimity for the conclusion of this convention. The ECJ dismissed the action. Another significant case in this field is Case C-327/91 *France v Commission* [1994] ECR I-976. The ECJ upheld the action, declaring that the Commission is not competent to conclude an international agreement in the sphere of competition law. This power is vested in the Council, the intergovernmental institution.

[6] Regarding the common fisheries policy, the particular Spanish interest over the agreements signed with Morocco and Mauritania is quite notorious. Regarding the common commercial policy, the Council Decisions authorising extension or tacit renewal of certain trade agreements concluded between Member States and third countries has been traditional. See for example Decision 87/391/EEC [2004] OJ L202/62.

[7] F Esteve García, 'Alcance de las competencias externas de la Unión Europea en el Tratado de Lisboa' (2008) 16 *Revista General de Derecho Europeo* 1; J Roldán Barbero, 'La delimitación de competencias en las relaciones exteriores de la UE' in DJ Liñán Nogueras and C López-Jurado (eds), *La reforma de la delimitación competencial en la futura Unión Europea* (Granada, University of Granada, 2003) 115–31.

solution to the crisis must be more, not less, Europe, even if some of the Community instruments and measures agreed are essentially intergovernmental. Autarchy is an undesirable and impossible way out for the MS and for the EU as well, and the EU must act not just as a mere sum of its 28 MS but with a supplementary strength.

The present study traces a map of the legal connections linking the international agreements concluded by the States of the EU with the European legal order. The political liaisons would be infinite. From the juridical point of view, the general rule is the relative effect of the treaties: these MS agreements do not bind the EU, even though the contrary happens: the agreements made by the EU bind the MS, at the very least, internally. However, the MS should in certain circumstances extend the rights drawn from their bilateral agreements to other citizens of the EU, as a Judgment given on 15 January 2002 confirms.[8]

Logically, the international conventional activity of the MS is subject to the judicial control of the ECJ through the infringement procedure, as the 'Open Skies' case exemplified. Obviously too, a MS must be charged through the same procedure for violating an international agreement concluded by the EU.[9] In any case, beyond the relative effects of the treaties, many MS international agreements have legal links with the European legal order and for many reasons, as we shall see.

II. AGREEMENTS LINKED TO THE ENLARGEMENT

A. Before Accession

In spite of its internal crisis, the EU preserves its magnetism vis-à-vis third European countries, attracting them to be associated to it through a mixed agreement, or even to fully join the Union. Some of these States, however, cannot or simply do not want to be a member; in this case, the clause 'everything but institutions' marks the ceiling of their aspirations. The EU invokes the 'more for more' slogan to boost the political and social reforms of the partner with a view to closer cooperation and participation in the *acquis communautaire*.[10] For the candidates, it

[8] Case C-55/00 *Gottardo v Istituto nazionale della previdenza sociale (INPS)* judgment of 15 January 2002, [2002] ECR I-433: 'when a Member State concludes a bilateral international convention on social security with a non-member country which provides for account to be taken of periods of insurance completed in that non-member country for acquisition of entitlement to old-age benefits, the fundamental principle of equal treatment requires that that the Member State grant nationals of other Member States the same advantages as those which its own nationals enjoy under that convention unless it can provide objective justification for refusing to do so'. In other circumstances, as those described in the Judgment Case C-376/03 given on 5 July 2005, the content of the bilateral agreement is not extended necessarily to other Member States [2005] ECR I-5821: 'Articles 56 EC and 58 EC do not preclude a rule laid down by a bilateral convention for the avoidance of double taxation such as the rule at issue in the main proceedings from not being extended, in a situation and in circumstances such as those in the main proceedings, to residents of a Member State which is not party to that convention'.

[9] Case C-204/86 *Commission v Greece* [1988] ECR I-1835.

[10] An illustrative example is that of the Stabilisation and Association Agreement between the European Communities and its Member States, on the one hand, and Republic of Serbia, on the other, in force as a whole since 1 September [2013] OJ L278.

is a way to shorten the negotiations and, after accession, to reduce the transitory periods pending full integration. These circumstances help to ease the division between Member and non-Member States.

In the process leading to accession, the candidate frequently has the conclusion of some international agreements imposed upon it as part of its path towards finally joining the EU, which often brokers the accord. This was the case in the border deals between Croatia and Slovenia, and it is currently the example of the process of mutual understanding and recognition between Serbia and Kosovo.[11] However, the European attempt to seal a reunification agreement for the island of Cyprus in parallel to the 2004 enlargement unfortunately failed.

It is much more unusual for a Member State to be given the legal obligation, derived from an international agreement signed by both the EU and its Member States, to adhere to another treaty. This was the case, resolved by ECJ Judgment of 19 March 2002, in which the Court decided that Ireland had failed to fulfil its obligation inserted in the EEA Agreement to adhere, within the prescribed period, to the Berne Convention for the Protection of Literary and Artistic Works.[12]

B. After Accession

i. Concerning the Previous Agreements of the EU and Member States

Logically, the accession of new States, compounding institutional and interstate elements from the EU's point of view, entails the import and export of a series of opportunities and challenges for the EU as a whole in an external policy that becomes, on the one hand, more ambitious and heterogeneous but, on the other hand, more difficult to handle and develop in some aspects.

The Treaty of Accession, and more specifically its Act of Accession, specifies in similar, but not identical, terms in the successive enlargements, the position of the new Member State regarding the international agreements of the EU, including those of mixed character.[13] To sum up, for some agreements, like the Cotonou partnership with the ACP countries, accession is automatic from the same date of the entry into force of the Treaty of Accession. On the other hand, for some other agreements, the new Member States 'undertake[s] to accede, under the conditions

[11] The SAA with Serbia contains in its Article 15, 1 a *pactum de contrahendo* under which Serbia shall start negotiations with the countries that have already signed an SAA with a view to concluding bilateral conventions on regional cooperation. In fact, negotiations bound to an Stabilisation and Association Agreement have already been concluded with Kosovo too, despite the continuing non-recognition of this country as a State by five Member States of the EU.

[12] Case C-13/00 *Commission v Republic of Ireland* [2002] ECR I-393. The obligation was set out in Article 5 of Protocol 28 to the EEA Agreement.

[13] C Hillion, 'The European Union is dead. Long live the European Union ... A commentary on the Treaty of Accession 2003' (2004) 29 *European Law Review* 583; E Lannon, 'Le traité d'adhésion d'Athènes: les négociations, les conditions de l'admission et les principales adaptations des traités résultant de l'élargissement de l'UE à vingt cinq états members' (2004) 40 *Cahiers de droit européen* 15, 47.

laid down in the Act', eg the EEA.[14] Evidently, in these processes, the consent of the third country is indispensable, and not always easy to attain in order to approve the necessary amendments when the simple extension of the agreement would entail an unbalanced system, notably in commercial matters.

ii. Concerning the Previous Agreements of the New Member States

These agreements are subject to rethinking as well. The Act of Accession expressly mentions the fisheries agreements that first of all are submitted to the Union's management and, later on, undergo a process of *communautarisation*. The experience of Spain and Portugal's accession to the European Communities in 1986 reveals that this process can be hindered by a third State: in fact, the Fisheries Agreement concluded by Spain and Portugal with South Africa has been renewed by the Council's authorisation despite the exclusive nature of the Common Fisheries Policy.

In more general terms, the Treaty on the Functioning of the European Union has contained a clause since the origin of European integration, now established in its Article 351, that compels new Member States, without prejudice to the immediate *pacta sunt servanda* principle, to 'take all appropriate steps' with a view to aligning their international agreements to the EU's commitments. This clause has generated an abundant jurisprudence from the ECJ with different judgments on the compatibility of the former international agreement with this article and with the general *acquis*. In 2009, the ECJ declared that the three States that joined in 1995 (Austria, Finland and Sweden) had failed to adopt appropriate measures to eliminate the incompatibilities with the EC Treaty—as implemented by the directives restricting free movement of capital—of the bilateral investment treaties entered into with third countries prior to accession to the EU.[15] Contrary to this, a later judgment focusing also on a bilateral investment treaty, dated 2011 and concerning Slovakia, deemed that this country did not infringe the European legal order by fulfilling the obligations derived from the agreement (in accordance with Article 307.1) and consequently not complying with the obligations set out in a European Directive.[16] In any case, even if Article 351.1 is binding upon European institutions, this kind of agreement is not considered in any way binding upon the EU itself.

This obligation to gradually align international agreements to the European principles applies to all the Member States when the EU assumes a new competence,

[14] See, ultimately, the Treaty concerning the Accession of Croatia to the EU [2012] OJ L112. In particular, Article 6.

[15] Cases C-205/06 and C-249/06, and C-118/09. See J Díez-Hochleitner, 'El incierto futuro de los acuerdos bilaterales sobre protección de inversiones celebrados por los Estados Miembros de la Unión Europea' (2010) 33 *Revista Española de Derecho Europeo* 5.

[16] Case C-264/09 *Commission v Republic of Slovakia* [2011] ECR I-1075.

which is occurring now with the investments treaties, as we will examine in a later section.[17]

III. MIXED AGREEMENTS

Only provided for expressly in the Treaty concerning the Euratom, and still without explicit recognition in the primary law of the EU, the agreements (co-) concluded by the EU and its Member States are a common and well-known category of European external relations.

The effects of mixed agreements on European identity and visibility are normally criticised and their management from the European perspective raises perplexity both inside and outside this legal order,[18] so it is a fertile source of juridical research even today.[19] However, the existence of mixed agreements is effectively inevitable due to the presence in many bilateral or multilateral treaties of shared or separated competencies between both kinds of international subjects. In this sense, environmental policy constitutes a constant source for this type of agreement and of subsequent jurisprudence.[20] More doubtful is the use of mixed agreements solely on the grounds of the financing system, as Opinion 1/78 established. The ACP-EU (plus its MS) Association has an additional reason for the mixity of its agreements, to be found in the traditional interstate financing of its development fund, at least until 2020. In any case, it is a commonplace to state that practice has abused this instrument: false or artificial mixed agreements, which could be concluded exclusively by the EU at its political will, have proliferated. The goal of avoiding scrutiny or dispute over the accurate delimitation of competences—and international responsibility—has necessarily been a factor in fostering and generalising mixed agreements. Yet the EU and its MS are more and more frequently compelled to elucidate vis-à-vis their partners their respective spheres of

[17] P Manzini, 'The Priority of Pre-Existing Treaties of EC Member States within the Framework of International Law' (2001) 12 *European Journal of International Law* 781. Also J Klabbers, *Treaty Conflict and the European Union* (Cambridge, Cambridge University Press, 2009).

[18] Despite the legal problems raised by its mixity, some third States may prefer this formula as the example of the African, Caribbean, Pacific (ACP) States, which consider the association with the MS as formal contracting parties financially and politically more secure.

[19] C Hillion (ed), *Mixed Agreements Revisited: The EU and its Member States in the World* (Oxford, Hart Publishing Oxford, 2011). More distant in time, JHJ Bourgeois J-L Dewost and M-A Gaiffe (eds), *La Communauté Européenne et les accords mixtes* (Brussels, Bruylant, 1997). Even in a determined sector, like air transport, we find mixed agreements along with exclusive State agreements. See the Agreement between the Kingdom of Spain and Australia relating to Air Services, concluded 24 June 2009. *Boletín Oficial del Estado* 28.04.2011 (BOE-A-2011-7532). As an example of a mixed agreement concerning air transport, with three different partners, see the Agreement between the United States, on the one hand, the EU and its MS, on the other hand, Iceland, on another, and Norway on another, made in 2011.

[20] A Roger: *L'action environnementale extérieure de l'UE: Les accords mixtes* (Paris, LGDJ, 2010); T Fajardo del Castillo, 'Avances y retrocesos en materia de acuerdos mixtos y de acceso a la justicia para la protección del medio ambiente a la luz de la sentencia del Tribunal de Justicia de 8 de marzo de 2011 en el asunto Oso Pardo' (2013) 29 *Revista General de Derecho Europeo* 1.

competence, which are no longer considered, as the ECJ wrongfully did in 1978, an internal matter.[21] The official confirmation by the EU of the United Nations Convention on the Rights of Persons with Disabilities illustrates this international obligation, set out in Article 44.1 of this Treaty.[22] This declaration, however, does not offer definitive and dogmatic answers, among other reasons, because the apportionment of competences is an evolving process. Besides this international commitment to clarifying the powers possessed by the EU and/or its MS, a judgment given by the ECJ in 2002 confirms that this list of competences is subject to judicial control, and eventually to annulment, on merely domestic grounds, by the Luxembourg Court of Justice.[23]

It is both true and clear, as has been confirmed by the ECJ,[24] that, putting aside the indefinite material scope of the European Common Foreign and Security Policy, the principle of attribution of competences is applied to the external field as well, but obstacles set up by International Law and by the MS themselves, reluctant to lose importance in this arena, explain how external competences possessed by the EU are not always effectively implemented and that the role of the MS overshadows the EU's practical foreign policy as far as conventional activity is concerned.

The example of the association agreement, contemplated in the foundational European Economic Community Treaty, and today enshrined in the Treaty on the Functioning of the European Union with almost identical wording,[25] is very eloquent. This is a kind of agreement which is useful not only as pre-accession training, but also for the preferential partners from abroad as a means towards their socio-economic development. Its ambiguous and imprecise wording necessarily justifies the changing ideas and hesitations in doctrine and jurisprudence concerning the scope of these kinds of agreement and their capacity to encompass the arrangements of the EU with or without the company of their MS. In fact, only two of these Association agreements have been ratified solely by the European Community (as the predecessor of the EU) and they happen to be no longer in force.

[21] Ruling 1/78 of 14 November 1978, *Draft Convention of the International Atomic Energy Agency on the Physical Protection of Nuclear Materials, Facilities and Transports* [1978] ECR 2151.

[22] Council Decision of 26 November 2009 concerning the conclusion, by the European Community, of the United Nations Convention on the Rights of Persons with Disabilities [2010] OJ L23.

[23] Case C-29/99 *Commission v Council* [2002] I-11221. It is useful to note that some domestic European acts point out that the act does not alter the sharing of competences as regards a particular treaty. See, in relation to the 1982 UN Convention on the Law of the Sea, Council Decision of 26 April 2010 supplementing the Schengen Borders Code as regards the surveillance of the maritime external borders in the context of operational cooperation coordinated by the European Agency for the Management of Operational Cooperation at the External Borders of the Member States of the European Union [2010] OJ L111/20.

[24] Opinion 2/94 of 28 March 1996, *Accession of the Community to the European Convention for the Protection on Human Rights and Fundamental Freedoms*, [1996] ECR I-1759.

[25] Article 217 TFEU.

Admittedly, the ECJ declared that this association can cover all the policies included in the treaties.[26] In fact, many provisions of this kind of agreement literally incorporate measures contained in the primary law, but the European Court does not always declare that the interpretation of these identical clauses must be the same. The latest decision so far, that of the *Demirkan* case, overrules the thesis that the regime of association set up with Turkey has the same political and legal scope as the EU's treaties. Therefore, it rejects the suggestion that passive free movement of services can be applied to that country.[27]

It is evident that the mixity formula allows, besides double publicity in the respective official journals, an even more heterogeneous and ambitious cooperation with the partner, and reflects a more realistic image of the current structure of European integration, in which Member States play a dominant role. But, at the same time, the artificial agreements diminish the legal and political autonomous personality of the European Union. In the case of the association agreement, MS retain a double means of control: unanimity at the Council and joint ratification, irrespective of whether the rules set out in the agreement are implemented domestically or at the European level. Moreover, we must take into account that every MS, separately, can conclude with the same partner a cooperation agreement of similar character, possibility foreseen in the so-called *Canada* clause, contained for the first time in the 1974 EC-Canada cooperation agreement. This kind of arrangement is supposed to promote the EU's purposes.[28] Furthermore, Opinion 2/92 said that the provision now enshrined in Article 352 TFEU, modifying the scope of the principle of attribution of competences, cannot be the basis for an exclusive EU competence, even if it is the exclusive legal basis from the Community point of view.

Another drawback for mixed agreements is the long time needed for the national ratifications and their subsequent entry into force. In the case of the Cotonou agreement, despite its 20 years' validity, every five years a revision is undertaken, which entails a real feeling of practical encroachment between the entry into force of the modifications and the negotiations for a new revision.[29] This long process is complemented by internal agreements signed by the MS in order to develop their own competences and establish their financial contributions to the partnership,[30]

[26] Case 12/86 *Demirel v Stadt Schwäbisch Gmünd* [1987] ECR 1573.

[27] Case C-221/11 *Demirkan v Germany* judgment of 24 September 2013, EU:C:2013:583. It is important to add that the identical wording (and possible different interpretation) of provisions in primary and conventional European law is not only limited within the Association agreements.

[28] This is the case of the agreement establishing a Strategic Agreement between Spain and Kazakhstan, whose preamble expresses the wish to support the establishment of a new association between the EU and Central Asia. *Boletín Oficial del Estado* 27 September 2010 (BOE-A-2010-14715).

[29] The Cotonou Partnership ACP-EU Agreement, signed in 2000, was last revised in 2010. [2010] OJ L287.

[30] Internal Agreement between the Representatives of the Governments of the Member States, meeting within the Council, on the financing of Community aid under the multiannual financial framework for the period 2008 to 2013 in accordance with the ACP-EC Partnership Agreement.

and it is softened by the provisional application of the commercial clauses, which come under the EU's competence.

The ECJ is right when it affirms that practical problems of management of the mixed agreements do not constitute a reason to alter the EU-MS distribution of competences.[31] But these problems are aggravated in the case of common membership in international organisations like the FAO, where the guiding method is the alternative exercise of competences between the EU and its MS. The ECJ stresses in these circumstances the principle of cooperation with a view to safeguarding the unity of representation.[32] Actually, this two-way principle lacks a legal basis in primary and secondary law and it is resolved in a pragmatic and casuistic way in every international organisation (the WTO offers another good example of these ad hoc *modus vivendi* formulas).[33] Let us note that MS, according to primary law, are linked to the general duty of loyalty relating to the EU; and, more specifically, according to the CFSP, must coordinate their positions in international institutions and conferences.

Another element of complexity is given by the incomplete mixed agreements, ie the agreements not ratified by all MS, in some cases because of the very nature of the agreements, circumscribed to some geographic areas.[34] But more often, the incompletion stems from a separate decision by certain MS, which is sometimes definitely contrary to the aforementioned principle of international cooperation and gives rise to an anomalous legal *situationism* for both the EU and its MS. Admittedly, a mixed agreement links MS twice: as members of the EU[35] and as separate contracting parties. Therefore, these undue, incomplete, mixed agreements sometimes give rise to hidden, de facto, irregular reservations, as in the 1982 UN Convention on the Law of the Sea,[36] against the general prohibition on reservations to the treaty. In fact, the MS that refrains from national ratification participates selectively, through EU membership and, to the extent of its competences, in the regime set up by the international agreement. Consequently, we can wonder, taking into account also the ECJ's Opinion 2/13, if, regarding the EU's joining the

[31] Opinion 2/00 of 6 December 2001, [2002] ECR I-9713.

[32] See Judgment given by ECJ 19 January 1996. Case C-25/94 *Commission v Council*. Right to vote to adopt the FAO Agreement to Promote Compliance with International Conservation and Management Measures by Fishing Vessels on the High Seas.

[33] Specifically Opinion 1/94 by the ECJ recognises, even in a dominating exclusive EU competency, the participation of MS in the agreements concluded at the Uruguay Round and instituting of the WTO. This Opinion was criticised by a some scholars for reducing the scope of the AETR principle. See Jacqueline Dutheil de la Rochère, 'L'ère des compétences partagées. À propos de l'étendue des compétences extérieures de la Communauté européenne' (1995) 390 *Revue du Marché Commun et de l'Union européenne* 461.

[34] It is the case of the Alpine Convention, an international agreement seeking the protection and sustainable development of the region signed in 1991 between eight European States and the European Union [2013] OJ L177.

[35] Article 216.2, TFEU.

[36] J Roldán Barbero, 'La CEE y el Convenio sobre Derecho del Mar de 1982: Consideraciones sobre la relación entre el derecho comunitario y el derecho internacional' (1991) 18 *Revista de Instituciones Europeas* 551.

European Convention on Human Rights, a MS could be kept out of a particular protocol whilst the EU is bound by it, or the contrary. (We must remember that accession is contemplated by primary EU law as an imperative mandate for the EU, and MS are supposed to help towards this goal within the framework of the Council and as part of a mixed agreement).[37] In the case of Kosovo, whose statehood has been rejected so far by five MS, the Association agreement could be ultimately hindered due to this cause. A final remark about this issue: in other cases, both the EU and MS, on their own, are authorised to pose legal reservations: see the example of the United Nations Convention on the Rights of Persons with Disabilities, of which so far 26 MS, alongside the EU, are contracting parties, even if the 28 are signatories.[38]

In spite of the confusion over the legal and political identity of the EU, mixed agreements go through a process of *communautarisation* through the control and case-law implemented by the ECJ. First of all, this Court implements the general control of the distribution of competences as far as external relations are concerned. Once the agreement is concluded, it is incorporated into the European legal order, according to the early *Haegeman* judgment, irrespective of the mixed nature of the agreement.[39] Furthermore, a State must be condemned by the ECJ for infringing a mixed agreement after breaching the principle of unity at the international representation of the EU when it makes an individual proposal disregarding the concerted position, even if it is not yet proposed, within the EU at an international institution.[40] From the *Hermès* case it is inferred that the ECJ guarantees the uniform interpretation of the mixed agreements:

> where a provision can apply both to situations falling within the scope of national law and to situations falling within the scope of Community law, it is clearly in the Community interest that, in order to forestall future differences of interpretation, that provision should be interpreted uniformly.[41]

In the more recent *Zoskupenie* judgment, the ECJ has admitted that national tribunals are competent and free to interpret the MS' competences in the agreement, but, in respect of the Habitat Directive, it has determined the EU's competence even if the EU accepted in the declaration of competences linked to the Aarhus Convention that there was no absolute coverage of European legislation in that matter. Besides, even without direct effect, a provision must be interpreted by the

[37] See R Marín Aís, *La Unión Europea y el Derecho internacional de los derechos humanos* (Madrid, Tecnos, 2013).

[38] [2010] OJ L23/35. The reservation posed by the EU is related to the right enjoyed by MS, according to Directive 2000/78/CE, not to apply the non-discrimination principle on the ground of disability with respect to employment in the armed forces. From the MS' point of view, we can mention the objection put by Slovakia to the reservation posed by Iran to this Convention.

[39] Case 181/73 *R & V Haegeman v Belgian State* [1974] ECR 449.

[40] Case C-246/07 *Commission v Sweden* [2010] ECR I-3045.

[41] Case C-53/96 *Hermès International v FHT Marketing Choice BV* [1998] ECR I-3638. See too Cases 300/98 and 392/98, *Parfums Christian Dior SA v TUK Consultancy BV and Assco Gerüste GmbH and van Dijk v Wilhelm Layher GmbH*, [2000] ECR I-11307.

national judge in a way respectful to European law in accordance with Article 9 of the Aarhus Convention.[42]

IV. COMMUNAUTARISATION OF THE INTERNATIONAL AGREEMENTS CONCLUDED BY MEMBER STATES

A. The Mention in the EU's Primary Law

The current treaties on the EU and its functioning contain some references to international agreements held by MS, not by the EU itself. Such is the case of the 1961 European Social Charter and the 1951 Geneva Convention on the Status of Refugees and its New York Protocol.[43] They are, in fact, two domains in which the EU is usually criticised for not meeting these international standards.

More far-reaching is the invocation of the UN system in different provisions, which reveals a major engagement by the EU regarding multilateralism and general international law, an engagement also reflected in the new qualified-observer status achieved by the EU at the General Assembly.[44] As is well known, the 'saga' of the *Kadi* case has analysed, sometimes with contradictory approaches, the controversial relationship between UN law—in particular its secondary law adopted by the Security Council—and the obligation assumed by the EU to comply with this mandate even at the expense of the protection of human rights.

Focusing more on the object of our research, in 1997, the *Centre-Com* ECJ Judgment wrongfully considered the United Nations Charter just as a treaty concluded by the MS before the creation of European integration.[45] Logically, as the several mentions in the current primary law confirm, the UN system is not a treaty external to European law, not just a 'pre-existing' agreement, but, as an embodiment of international general law, an inescapable part of both the national and the European structure; it is what Krajewski called the 'Secondary Constitution'.[46] Even with the prior silence of the foundational law, this assertion seemed indubitable, in spite of the inherent uncertainty, manipulation and misapplication of the structural principles—the material constitution—of the international community and its main incarnation: the United Nations framework.

[42] Convention on Access to Information, Public Participation in Decision-Making and Access to Justice in Environmental Matters. Case C-240/09 *Lesoochranárske zoskupenie VLK v Ministerstvo životného prostredia Slovenskej republiky* [2011] ECR I-1255.

[43] A judicial application of the 1951 Convention is given in Cases C-57/09 and C-101/09, *Germany v B and D*, judgment of November 2010, [2010] I-10979.

[44] In general, A Blanc Altemir (dir), *Las relaciones entre las Naciones Unidas y la Unión Europea. Seguridad, cooperación y derechos humanos* (Madrid, Tecnos, 2013).

[45] Case C-124/95, *The Queen, ex parte Centro-Com Srl v HM Treasury and Bank of England* [1997] ECR I-81.

[46] M Krajewski, 'Foreign Policy and the European Constitution' (2003) 22 *Yearbook of European Law* 435, 454.

B. International State Agreements as Customary Law

The legal value of the UN Charter and the rest of the juridical system of the world organisation takes us to the application of agreements celebrated by MS that acquire a customary nature, and consequently bind the EU. It is obvious that the customary process may be created outside a conventional manifestation and as such be taken into consideration by the ECJ, as the *ATAA* judgment reveals.[47] But the customary process may be interconnected as well with a conventional phenomenon. The ECJ's *Brita* judgment[48] recalls the circumstance that the 1969 Vienna Convention on the Law of Treaties (applicable among States) provides for in its article 3(b). In fact, the treaty on treaties has been implemented by the Luxembourg Court in various cases related always to the international stage, not with intra-community relations, and usually concerning the interpretation of treaties (articles 31–33). In the *Racke* case, the *rebus sic stantibus* clause, established in article 62 of the 1969 Convention, is used as a customary norm, for this Convention is strictly reserved for States, and consequently not open to the EU. The 1986 Vienna Convention on the Law of Treaties between States and International Organizations or between International Organizations has never been used by the ECJ, this Convention has not yet entered into force and the EU itself has rejected the applicability of its provisions, taking into account its exceptional nature in the field of these international subjects. We must add that in the application of the 1969 Convention as evidence of the custom, no attention is paid to the ratification of this treaty by the MS as a whole. As a matter of fact, France has refused to be bound by this Treaty.

In some other cases, and concerning other treaties, the ECJ has also matched the conventional provision with the customary one, as has happened with the notion of 'damage' inherent in International General Law and in the Montreal Convention for the Unification of Certain Rules for International Carriage by Air.[49] But this convention had previously been concluded by the European Community.[50]

C. Succession by the EU to the International Agreements of the Member States

This last idea leads us to the possibility that an international agreement concluded by all the MS is assumed by the EU if the issues set out in the agreements belong to the European competences. This possibility was confirmed in relation to the GATT 1947 in the framework of an exclusive competence: the common commercial policy.[51]

[47] Case C-366/10, *Air Transport Association of America and Others v Secretary of State for Energy and Climate Change* [2011] ECR I-13755.

[48] C-386/08 *Firma Brita GmbH v Hauptzollamt Hamburg-Hafen* of 25 February 2010.

[49] Case C-63/09 *Axel Walz v Clickair SA* [2010] ECR I-4239.

[50] Council Decision 2001/539/EC [2001] OJ L194.

[51] Joined Cases 21–24/72 *International Fruit Company NV and others v Produktschap voor Groenten en Fruit* [1972] ECR 1219.

From then on, no more agreements have been recognised as being substituted by the EU: certainly not the European Convention on Human Rights. As is well known, the formal accession by the EU to this far-reaching treaty is now pending, an accession that is mandatory according to the new primary law and which Member States must, consequently, facilitate, even if the specific terms of the EU's accession seem quite difficult to fulfil after ECJ Opinion 2/13. The EU will therefore be attached to the mechanism of control set up by the Rome Convention and it will no longer be linked to this Convention only through general principles of law, but through a conventional instrument of mixed nature.

In the *Commune de Mesquer* case the ECJ established the conditions for a functional succession: namely, that every MS is a contracting party and the subject of the agreement has been handed over completely to the EU.[52]

The hypothesis of 'succession' has also been evoked, but finally rejected, by the Court, with regard to the Marpol Convention (International Convention for the Prevention of Pollution from Ships, adopted in 1973), in the *Intertanko* case,[53] and with regard to the Chicago Convention on International Civil Aviation, in the *ATAA* case. In the former judgment, the ECJ admits that a directive sought to implement the Marpol rules within the EU system, but this single goal is not sufficient to qualify this link as succession, for the EU does not assume, unlike the GATT case, the competences attributed by the MS in this treaty, despite the fact that all MS are contracting parties. The *ATAA* case, in this respect, is clearer because the Chicago Convention, ratified alike by all MS, has been incorporated into the EU's legal order only partially and concerning a competence that is not at all exclusive.

An alternative choice is that followed in respect of the 1989 United Nations Convention on the Rights of the Child, of which every Member State is a contracting party, and whose content has been incorporated, and surpassed, by the EU through institutional domestic acts.

In any case, it is out of the question that the formal conventional link will entail much more legal certainty than the doubts and discrepancies raised by the theory of succession.

D. Assumption of State External Competences by the EU

The succession previously dealt with is, in effect, an exceptional and unsatisfactory way of substitution, also for third States that discover without their prior formal approval a new de facto partnership. More transparent and legally reassuring is the method of the formal and nominal substitution of the MS' agreement signed

[52] Case C-188/07, *Commune de Mesquer v Total France SA and Total International Ltd* [2008] ECR I-4501.

[53] Case C-308/06 *The Queen, on the application of International Association of Independent Tanker Owners (Intertanko) and Others v Secretary of State for Transport* [2008] ECR I-4057.

by the EU as long as the subject-matter becomes a European competence. This phenomenon occurs nowadays, for example, with the agreements on readmission of people found in an irregular situation, a kind of arrangement until recently concluded exclusively by the MS. Occasionally, the so-called Community clause (or 'substitution clause') introduced by a MS reminds third States of the possibility that the EU could assume the competence of the international agreement and, therefore, the formal condition of contracting party.[54]

The competences assigned to the EU are dynamic, like the process of European integration itself, and as the EU likes to remind its partners. Sometimes, the very nature of the competence is evolving, as happens in relation to international trade. But more often, primary law itself is formally modified through an always complex process of amendment of its provisions. The Common Commercial Policy offers an example of this explicit expansion with the trade-related aspects of intellectual property[55] and foreign direct investment.

Currently, the agreements concerning foreign direct investment are concluded by MS, and the EU and other MS can provide only collateral and political support and pressure. However, as the ECJ recognised, even the provisions relating to free movement of capital could be infringed by these bilateral agreements.[56] With the Lisbon Treaty, the literal scope of the Common Commercial Policy has been expanded with a view to inserting expressly foreign investment and, consequently, to launch a process of gradual substitution of the current MS agreements by the EU. This process, as far as the internal European perspective is concerned, has been initiated by a Commission proposal in 2010[57] and has been continued through a Regulation adopted in 2012.[58] In the international sphere, negotiations have been started with third States in this sector, as is the case of China. This process of replacement of the partner for third States will also entail the convenient consequence of simplifying the legal traffic: with China all the MS but Ireland have now signed a foreign investment treaty, so 27 international agreements will hopefully become a single one.[59]

Let us recall the possibilities, but also the limits, provided for by Article 352 TFEU as a sweeping clause designed to conclude new EU agreements without altering the wording of the primary law. In its Opinion 2/94, the ECJ considered

[54] Besides, the 'disconnection clause' also included in some international agreement means that the European acts, possibly more advanced, could be applicable in the *inter se* relations among MS instead of the international agreement.

[55] See Case C-414/11 *Daiichi Sankyo Co Ltd and Sanofi-Aventis Deutschland GmbH v DEMO Anonimos Viomikhaniki kai Emporiki Etairia Farmakon*. EU:C:2013:520. In this judgment, the Court declares that the TRIPs adopted in the framework of the World Trade Organization fall within the exclusive competence of the EU.

[56] See n 15 above.

[57] FJ Pascual Vives, 'Los acuerdos sobre promoción y protección recíproca de las inversiones extranjeras y el Derecho de la Unión Europea' (2011) 40 *Revista Española de Derecho Europeo* 441.

[58] A Pastor Palomar, 'La aplicación práctica del Reglamento 1219/2012 sobre los acuerdos bilaterales de inversión entre Estados miembros y terceros países' (2013) 31 *Revista General de Derecho Europeo*.

[59] In general, see the Policy Brief by ECFR by Jonas Parello-Plesner, Elena Ortiz de Solórzano, *A Comprehensive Approach to Investment Protection*. 26 June 2013.

that the EU's adhesion to the ECHR would not be possible without a prior amendment of the original law, which has actually been implemented in the 2007 Lisbon Treaty. The express reforms inserted in the EU treaties have reduced the application of this sweeping clause, as many domains, for instance economic and technical cooperation with third countries, have been explicitly included in the list of EU competences.

Yet the accurate scope of the EU's external competences must be determined also by scrutinising the nature and depth of the secondary law, which is derived, of course, from and subordinate to primary law, but whose exact scope cannot be entirely established by the treaties. This assertion is confirmed by the principle of parallelism of internal and external competences (*in foro interno, in foro externo*). It is not possible to split up the regime of internal and external measures, said the ECJ in its pioneer *ERTA* judgment, given in 1971.[60] Consequently, the adoption by the EU of an autonomous act entails the assumption by the EU of the competence to adopt international agreements in the same matter, exerting an effect of pre-emption. Unlike Article 352 TFEU, where there is no allocation of competences at all, in this case the EU possesses a tacit competence, pending implementation.

One more recent judicial application of the parallelism principle is the 2002 *Open Skies* judgments, in which it is considered that European approval of certain acts concerning aerial transport prevents MS from signing international agreements in this area because otherwise the internal market would be distorted.[61] Actually, it is a commonplace that the single European market suffers from the lack of unity and coherence of European international relations.

The same pre-emption has just occurred with the illicit manufacturing and trafficking of firearms, because there is already an internal directive on this issue which permits European ratification of the 2001 United Nations Protocol.[62] More notorious is the case of the automatic exchange of fiscal data, subject to a European directive revised in 2014 and needed urgently, in order to reach the real goals, of international agreements with third States in accordance with the OECD model.[63] The consequences of the *in foro interno, in foro externo* adagio are communicated to third States, an instance being the EU's official confirmation of the Convention on the Rights of Persons with Disabilities.

However, we must point out that practice has not always been consistent with the identity of the internal and external spheres, partly because of the self-restraint exercised by MS with a view to retaining international powers, and partly

[60] Case 22/71 *Commission v Council* (*ERTA*) [1971] ECR 263.

[61] See for instance C-476/98 *Commission v Germany* [2002] ECR I-9855.

[62] The main EU instrument is Directive 2008/51/EC on Control of Acquisition and Possession of Weapons [2008] OJ L179/5, and the later Regulation (EU) No 258/2012.

[63] Another issue that is experiencing this process of gradual substitution of the MS' agreements by EU agreements is the readmission of persons residing without authorisation. Some of these agreements are of a profound political significance, like the one signed with Turkey on 16 December 2013. See a published agreement of this kind, signed with Albania, in [2005] OJ L304.

due to the interstate structure dominating International Law. Case law itself has evolved and shaped the scope or the principle, occasionally to restrict its ambition, as the doctrine emphasised in relation to the 1/94 Opinion regarding WTO membership.[64]

Finally, the parallelism principle has been codified in European primary law (Article 216.1 TFEU), but the proper interpretation of the provision continues to show a certain opacity, and discrepancies exist among scholars and among the MS themselves, who are often inclined to reduce its effective scope. As we said, the international structure also helps to consolidate State powers, because in many opportunities the international rules stop the EU from executing its internal competences on the external stage.[65]

E. Other links of Member States' International Agreements with EU Law

The map of the rest of the connections is highly heterogeneous and almost endless. Sometimes, the EU or one of its institutions and organs signs an agreement with some or all of the MS, especially when the MS[66] or one of its particular zones is excluded from that policy.[67] The legal nature of these arrangements is not always the same, nor is it clear.[68] As is well known, far-reaching in effect and controversial, some MS, shocked by the crisis, have signed a Memorandum of Understanding with the so-called *troika* (formed by the European Commission, European Central Bank and IMF) in order to receive financial assistance.

The conventional external activity of a MS must be dominated by the loyal cooperation principle, which is applicable even when the EU does not belong to a particular international agreement or institution, as the *International Maritime Organisation-Greece* Case confirmed.[69] The general principles of the EU's foreign

[64] T Flory and F-P Martin, 'Remarques à propos des avis 1/94 et 2/92 de la Cour de Justice des Communautés Européennes au regard de l'évolution de la notion de politique commerciale commune' (1996) 32 *Cahiers de droit européen* 379.

[65] See, above all, Opinion 2/91 of 19 March 1993, concerning the ratification of a convention adopted under the auspices of the ILO, whose constitutional rules prohibit the accession of a subject like the EU [1993] ECR I-1061.

[66] Agreement between the European Community and the Kingdom of Denmark on jurisdiction and the recognition and enforcement of judgments in civil and commercial matters [2005] OJ L299/62.

[67] Agreement on Fisheries between the European Economic Community, on the one hand, and the Government of Denmark and the Home Government of the Faroe Islands, on the other, [1980] OJ L226/12.

[68] See for instance the Agreement among Defence Ministers from France, Italy, United Kingdom and Spain with the High Representative of the Common Foreign Security Policy (CFSP) concerning the transfer to the EU of the images from HELIOS I, done in 2007 and published in the *Boletín Oficial del Estado* of 11 February 2011.

[69] Case C-45/07, *Commission v Greece* [2009] ECR I-4376. The unilateral proposal from a Member State is a fortiori reprehensible when the agreement is mixed. See Case C-246/07, *Commission v Sweden* [2011] ECR I-2870.

policy compel MS to coordinate their positions in the framework of international organisms with or without the EU's membership. If this procedural coordination works properly, the question of whether the EU itself is a member of the organisation or not is not so important. The TFEU sets out explicitly the required cooperation of the EU with certain international organisations like the WTO or OECD, apart from the UN. We could say that every treaty concluded by a MS could either hamper or foster the EU's objectives: we can think of environmental or human rights agreements aiming to improve the ecological and humanitarian purposes of the EU's treaties. Therefore, the EU factor is always present.

European primary law itself provides for some MS' international agreements with a view to completing European policies or goals. This is the case of the agreements designed to facilitate the diplomatic and consular mutual assistance as a part of the citizenship status. Cooperation for development, whose general rules are described in a politically mixed Consensus,[70] offers another example of this intricate connection. As a shared and transversal competence, this matter is the object of mixed agreements, but moreover, the TFEU expressly admits the capacity of MS to sign individually international agreements, which are theoretically subject to the subsidiarity principle. Furthermore, these agreements must be coordinated by the EU and interlinked with the EU's action. Consequently, the MS' international agreements are an indispensable and express element of the EU's activity in this field.

A possible systematisation of these other ways of political/legal connection between MS' international agreements and EU law could be the following one: the EU may compel or recommend the State's ratification along with its own[71] or instead or on behalf of it when the EU itself is not enabled to conclude the treaty[72] or as a convenient complement for a European rule.[73] The EU's position vis-à-vis MS may also be of authorisation (sometimes, under certain conditions),[74] incitement,[75]

[70] Joint declaration by the Council and the representatives of the governments of the Member States meeting within the Council, the European Parliament and the Commission on the development policy of the European Union entitled 'The European Consensus' [2006] OJ C46.

[71] It is the case of the 1995 UN Convention on straddling and highly migratory fish stocks.

[72] See above Opinion 2/91. More recently, and regarding as well an ILO Convention on working in fisheries, the European Parliament has invited the MS to ratify this treaty, related to the EU's competences.

[73] See the Spain-Andorra agreement, made in 2000, based upon Council Regulation No 259/93 on the supervision and control of shipment of waste within, into and out of the European Community [1993] OJ L30. The bilateral agreement is published in the *Boletín Oficial del Estado* (BOE-2004-221).

[74] Interesting on this issue is Case C-355/87, *Commission v Council* [1989] ECR 1517. This judgment concerns the authorisation given by the Council to Italy to be a contracting party in a convention on maritime transport with Algeria. Noteworthy also is Regulation No 454/79 concerning the requirements that MS had to fulfil when ratifying the UN Convention on a Code of Conduct for Liner Conferences, or when acceding thereto [1979] OJ L21.

[75] In this sense, many calls have been made from the EU for the national ratifications of the 1990 UN International Convention on the Protection of the Rights of All Migrant Workers and Members of their Families. The situation is paradoxical because not one MS has so far ratified this treaty, ratified already by 47 States. An analogous situation occurs in relation to the ILO Convention concerning Decent Work for Domestic Workers.

prohibition[76] or obligation to withdraw,[77] termination,[78] necessity to adapt,[79] duty to provide proper information,[80] permission for the posterior ratification by the EU,[81] or use of the MS' agreement in anticipation of later internal or international European legal development.[82] The interstate international agreement may also be an instrument for spreading to other countries some of the achievements of European domestic law.[83]

It is interesting to note as well that sometimes the EU's position alludes to the stance of third States respecting international agreements: hailing[84] or encouraging their ratification or deploring their lack of it.[85]

V. *INTER SE* MEMBER STATES' AGREEMENTS

European integration itself is grounded in and reformed by international treaties subject to the MS' ratification in a long and winding process. The Budgetary Pact and the Stability Mechanism have otherwise been formed in parallel with the validation given by the ECJ, to exempt from the draconian rule of

[76] The same Code of Conduct for Liner Conferences cited in n 74 above provides us with an example of prohibition because Regulation 1490/2007 [2007] OJ L339 repealed the 1979 Regulation and prevents MS from fulfilling the obligations falling within this Convention.

[77] For instance, Spain was forced in 2007 to denounce its agreement with Bolivia concerning the exemption of visas between the two countries after the modification of the pertinent Regulation on this issue. *Boletín Oficial del Estado* (7 June 2007) 136 (BOE-A-2007-11206).

[78] The Western European Union, an organisation born in 1948 and centred on security issues, has finally been terminated mainly because of the advances experienced by the EU on the same subject.

[79] This is the case with the agreements on extradition and mutual legal assistance between the United States of America and the European Union, which have forced an adaptation of the previously-signed bilateral agreements on this issue by MS. See the Spanish case in the *Boletín Oficial del Estado* of 26 January 2010 (BOE-A-2010-1172 & 1173): Instruments provided for in Article 3(2) of the USA-EU's agreement on extradition.

[80] In the field of energy, the EU has just created a mechanism designed to obtain information from the bilateral agreements made between MS and third States.

[81] The Patent Law Treaty, adopted in 2000, sets out in Article 20(2): 'Any intergovernmental organization may become party to this Treaty if at least one Member State of that intergovernmental organization is party to the Paris Convention'.

[82] Nine MS have signed with Morocco an agreement concerning mobility for a better management of immigration. It is the first one with a country from the region, a model to be repeated. The text of the agreement says that the goal is, amongst others, to foster free movement of citizens in the framework of the application of the EU's provisions. Similarly, five MS signed agreements with the United States according to the FATCA model (Foreign Account Tax Compliance Act). This type of arrangement will be imitated by the EU itself in order to complete the free exchange of fiscal data in all the developed and emerging countries.

[83] See the Iberoamerican Agreement concerning the mutual protection on Social Security matters, the original objective of the famous 1408/71 Regulation, many times modified. *Boletín Oficial del Estado* (2011).

[84] Council Action 2008/858/CFSP of 10 November 2008 in support of the Biological and Toxin Weapons Convention (BTWC), in the framework of the implementation of the EU Strategy against the Proliferation of Weapons of Mass Destruction [2008] OJ L302.

[85] In this sense, both the EU and its MS have been encouraging Japan's ratification of the 1980 Hague Convention on Civil Aspects of International Child Abduction.

unanimity any progress for the European law,[86] underlining the complex relationship in European integration between international and the institutional acts.[87]

The founding EEC treaty also envisaged the development of certain issues through MS' *inter se* agreements, as the 1968 Brussels Convention on jurisdiction and the enforcement of judgments in civil and commercial matters illustrates. The formula was chosen in other cases, bypassing the possibilities offered by the subsidiary clause now inserted in Article 352 of the TFUE. The European University Institute in Florence was created this way.

Many years later, the former third pillar of the EU, devoted to Home and Justice Affairs, used this instrument for its legal progress, encouraging MS to join it, but respecting the autonomy of every single MS to ratify or not the international agreement.[88]

This kind of agreement has gradually been substituted by EU institutional acts, which entail a more supranational and rapid tool of legal development, above all, when it is a regulation adopted by a qualified majority and not by unanimity. This way, the previous 1968 Convention has become Brussels I Regulation, whose modification seems much easier.[89]

Yet agreements concluded by all MS for EU purposes continue in practice, for instance, for adopting measures linked to the Cotonou agreement and its modifications, and measures taken by the Representatives of the Governments of MS meeting within the Council as a consequence of the mixed nature of the agreement. The European construction also fosters deals among regions from different MS bound to reinforce this kind of infra-state cooperation.[90]

[86] Case C-370/12 *Pringle v Government of Ireland, Ireland and The Attorney General*, judgment of 27 November 2012, upholds the Council Decision 2011/199/EU amending Article 136 TFEU with regard to a stability mechanism for MS whose currency is the euro. For this purpose, therefore, the simplified revision procedure is used. The agreements amongst MS regarding both the Stability Mechanism and the Stability, Coordination and Governance agreements were concluded without demanding the unanimous ratification of all MS. 12 ratifications from States adopting the euro as the single currency were sufficient. There is the prospect of inserting these two agreements in Community law over a 5-year period.

[87] Very useful are the reflections on this issue of P Andrés Sáenz de Santa María, 'El tiempo de las cooperaciones reforzadas y los acuerdos inter se en la Unión Europea: ¿Todos los instrumentos llevan a la integración?' (2013) 10 *La Ley Unión Europea* 5–28.

[88] For example, Council Act of 26 July 1995, drawing up the Convention establishing the European Police Office (Europol Convention) [1995] OJ C316.

[89] The Regulation 'Brussels I' is No 44/2001 [2001] OJ L12. Articles 71 and 72 of this regulation expressly respect the compatible international agreements signed on this issue by the Member States. The Convention establishing Europol has also taken the form of Decisions, 'since such Decisions are more easily adaptable to changing circumstances and emerging political priorities'. Explanatory memorandum of the Council Decisions of 6 April 2009 establishing Europol [2009] OJ L/121. See also the termination of the Austria and Spain Agreement on Custom Administrative Assistance (2015) *Boletín Oficial del Estado*, 15 July 2015 (BOE-A-2015-7900).

[90] This is the case of the Convention on Trans-boundary Cooperation establishing the Alentejo-Algarve-Andalucía Euroregion, published in the *Boletín Oficial del Estado* of 9 July 2010 (BOE-A-2010-10942).

Separately, countless agreements signed between two MS are directly[91] or indirectly[92] linked to European objectives and policies, sometimes with a view to advancing European rule and properly implementing it. Some of these agreements may have the same content as those concluded by the EU with third countries.[93] Some others are concluded indistinctly between MS or between MS and third States.[94]

[91] Agreement between the Competent Authorities of Belgium and Spain on the reimbursement of expenditures in accordance with CEE Regulations 1408/71 and 574/72, done in 1999. (2001) *Boletín Oficial del Estado* 93.

[92] For example, the agreements regarding the creation and development of the Airbus Programme. This programme has been adopted and promoted by the governments of Belgium, France, Germany, the United Kingdom and Spain.

[93] See, concerning the readmission of persons residing without authorisation, the agreement between France and Spain, made in 2002. *Boletín Oficial del Estado* of 26 December 2003 (BOE-A-2003-23647).

[94] In 'Fighting against Criminality', for example, Spain has concluded cooperation agreements with a MS like Cyprus and a third State like Israel. These agreements are published in the *Boletín Oficial del Estado*, respectively, of 12 June 2007 and 14 February 2009.

8

The Contribution of the EU to the Development of Customary Norms in the Field of Human Rights Protection

JOSÉ RAFAEL MARÍN AÍS[1]

Content

I. A BRIEF LEGAL OVERVIEW OF THE PROMOTION OF HUMAN RIGHTS ACROSS EU'S EXTERNAL ACTION

THE ROOT OF the intergovernmental coordination of the positions of the Member States in face of situations of mass violation of human rights in third countries is found in the second half of the 1970s with the new-born European Political Cooperation.[2] Those questions were dealt with despite the initial absence of any explicit reference to human rights and democracy in the Founding Treaties of the European Communities. On their part, the institutions showed their interest from the early stages: the European Parliament since the early 1980s

[1] Lecturer in Public International Law and EU Law at the University of Granada. Contact e-mail: marinais@ugr.es.

[2] Member States established the practical pattern of consulting each other within the framework of the European Political Cooperation in order to coordinate the measures to be adopted. That happened primarily when the United Nations Security Council had previously adopted a resolution condemning a situation as particularly serious from the point of view of human rights protection. See Ms Candela Soriano, *Los Derechos Humanos, la Democracia y el Estado de Derecho en la Acción Exterior de la Unión Europea. Evolución, Actores, Instrumentos y Ejecución* (Madrid, Dykinson, 2006) 75–79.

called attention to the necessity to build a European Communities' foreign policy for human rights; in the 1990s, the European Commission defended the introduction of the promotion of human rights and democracy as a critical orientation for the development of cooperation policies; the Council, on its behalf, declared itself in favour of the universality and indivisibility of human rights, and hence, of the interdependence between those principles, and democracy and development, respectively.[3]

The Treaty of the European Union (TEU), adopted in Maastricht in 1992, for the first time introduced at the level of primary law the objective of the development and consolidation of democracy, rule of law, and respect of human rights and fundamental freedoms[4] as a target for the Common Foreign and Security Policy (CFSP, which was in fact the successor of the European Political Cooperation).

Therefore, since the 1990s, it can be assured that the promotion of human rights, democracy and rule of law[5] in EU's international relations has evolved into a transversal goal of the praxis of Member States and Community Institutions, in the same way for the community pillar as for the intergovernmental pillar. This objective, following the suppression of the pillar structure operated by the Lisbon Treaty, has been reflected in articles 3.5 and 21.1 of the TEU.[6]

Since the beginning of the '90s, the introduction of the so called *human rights and democracy clause* has been widespread in the EU's practice concerning different types of international agreements: for instance, in the agreements concluded with the candidates prior to their accession,[7] in its commercial agreements,[8] and

[3] Ibid 79–82.

[4] See, P Koutrakos, *EU International Relations Law* (Oxford, Hart Publishing, 2006) 383–413.

[5] The European Union acts with the conviction of their *universality and indivisibility*.

[6] Article 21 TEU concerns the complete scope of the EU's external action: that is, Title V of the TEU – including CFSP—and the Fifth Part of the Treaty on the Functioning of the European Union (TFEU) which encompasses the Common Commercial Policy, the Development Cooperation, the Economic, Financial and Technical Cooperation and Humanitarian Aid.

[7] See M Nowak, 'Human Rights "Conditionality" in Relation to Entry to, and Full Participation in, the EU' in P Alston, MR Bustelo and J Heenan (eds), *The EU and Human Rights* (Oxford, OUP, 1999) 687–98. The political criteria for the accession of countries from Central and Eastern Europe were stipulated at the European Council of Copenhagen, which took place during 21 and 22 June 1993.

[8] Further analysis of the utilisation of the human rights clause in the scope of commercial relations can be found in DJ Liñán Nogueras and LM Hinojosa Martínez, 'Human Rights Conditionality in the external trade of the European Union; legal and legitimacy problems' (2001) 7 *Columbia Journal of European Law* 307–36. See also, B Brandtner and A Rosas, 'Trade Preferences and Human Rights' in P Alston, MR Bustelo and J Heenan (eds), *The EU and Human Rights* (Oxford, OUP, 1999) 699–722. Alston warns about the risk that the conditionality discourse entails subordinating the logic of International Human Rights Law to WTO Law and broadly to Economic Policy goals, in that sense: P Alston, 'Resisting the Merger and Acquisition of Human Rights by Trade Law: A Reply to Pettersmann' (2002) 13 *European Journal of International Law* 815–44. It has been said that the European Union has lost its momentum to speak with one voice in the discussion on correlation between trade and labour standards, which was at an impasse within the WTO framework when the single voice was reached by the European Union. The future of social rights conditionality seems to be in bilateral and regional agreements, in cooperation with international organisations, such as the ILO, the World Bank and UNCTAD (more so than in WTO). As has been brilliantly illustrated: 'The EU, as the world's largest trading bloc, still maintains a powerful tool in its conduct of external trade to enhance the convergence between internationally recognized labour standards and the implications of globalization': Tamara

finally, its many association and development cooperation agreements—including in this last category the agreements concluded with the ACP countries. By means of these ACP agreements a preferential access to the Union internal market is granted to a group of developing countries from the African, Caribbean and Pacific regions, most of them being former colonies of the EU's Member States.[9]

Until the present moment the EU has succeeded in including the *human rights and democracy clause* in international agreements with more than 120 States.

It has to be borne in mind that accession agreements are formally negotiated and concluded by Member States; therefore there are no restrictions on the EU's competencies regarding the conditionality on human rights issues that can be exercised toward the third countries which are candidates to accession.

The Court of Justice of the European Union (ECJ) recognised in 1996 the competence of the, at that time, European Community to negotiate and conclude international agreements with third countries in the field of development cooperation, including the above-mentioned *human rights and democracy clause* as an essential element.[10] Thus the Court admitted the possibility for the Community unilaterally to terminate or suspend the application of the international agreement when it considers that the third country has violated substantially the human rights obligations:[11] this reasoning seems to be in accordance with paragraphs 1 and 3(b) of article 60 of the Vienna Convention on the Law of the Treaties of 1969,[12] concerning the serious violation of an essential element of a bilateral treaty.[13]

Takacs, 'Human rights in trade: the EU's experience with labour standards conditionality and its role in promoting labour standards in the WTO' in JE Wetzel (ed), *The EU as a 'Global Player' in Human Rights?* (London, Routledge, 2011) 97–112. In that sense, J Kenner, 'Economic Partnership Agreements: Enhancing the Labour Dimension of Global Governance? in B Van Vooren, S Blockmans and J Wouters (eds), *The EU's Role in Global Governance. The Legal Dimension* (Oxford, OUP, 2013) 306–22.

[9] The text of the agreement can be found in (EC) 2000/483 Partnership agreement between the members of the African, Caribbean and Pacific Group of States of the one part, and the European Community and its Member States, of the other part, signed in Cotonou on 23 June 2000—Protocols—Final Act—Declarations [2000] OJ L317/3; the agreement was modified for the first time by Council Decision (EC) 2005/599 of 21 June 2005, signed in Cotonou on 23 June 2000 [2005] OJ L209/26; and it was reviewed for the second time by Council Decision (EU) 2010/648 of 14 May 2010, signed in Cotonou on 23 June 2000, as first amended in Luxembourg on 25 June 2005 [2010] OJ L287/1. The former Yaounde Conventions only included a brief mention to the United Nations principles in their Preambles. For their part, the Lomé III (1985) and Lomé IV (1990) Conventions only referred in a broad manner to the obligation to respect human rights, but they did not provide for a legal basis which allowed the suspension or termination or those international agreements. See H Cuyckens, 'Human Rights Clauses in Agreements between the Community and Third Countries. The Case of the Cotonou Agreement', Katholieke Universiteit Leuven, *Institute for International Law Working Paper No 147* (March 2010).

[10] See E Riedel and M Will, 'Human Rights Clauses in External Agreements of the EC' in P Alston, M R Bustelo and J Heenan (eds), *The EU and Human Rights* (Oxford, OUP, 1999) 723–54.

[11] Case C-268/94 *Portugal v Council* [1996] ECR I-6177, para 27.

[12] The same applies to the identical articles of the Vienna Convention on the Law of Treaties between States and International Organizations or between International Organizations, 21 March 1986.

[13] It is not the object of the present research to analyse the practical application of the *human rights and democracy clause* throughout the external action, for that purpose: E Fierro, *The EU's Approach to Human Rights Conditionality in Practice* (Leiden, Martinus Nijhoff, 2003); also A Rosas and B Brandtner, 'Human Rights and the External Relations of the European Community: An Analysis of Doctrine and Practice' (1998) 9 *European Journal of International Law* 468–90.

Nowadays we find the use of *human rights and democracy clauses* not only in the above-mentioned cases,[14] but also in the context of the European Neighbourhood Policy and the Stabilisation and Association agreements concluded in the framework of the enlargement towards the Western Balkans:[15] both cases constituted, even before the entry into force of the Lisbon Treaty, examples where the separation between pillars blurs and the political and economic conditionalities overlap.[16] In respect of the European Neighbourhood Policy,[17] it comprises both cooperation agreements concluded with former Soviet Union countries[18] and the association agreements concluded within the framework of the Strategic Partnership with the Mediterranean and the Middle East, which was launched with the Barcelona Declaration in 1995.[19]

[14] The European Union has used the *human rights and democracy clauses* both in international agreements concluded only by the European Union and in international mixed agreements concluded by the Member States and the Union itself, A Rosas, 'Mixed Union—Mixed Agreements' in M Koskenniemi (ed), *International Law Aspects of the European Union* (TheHague, Kluwer, 1998) 144–45.

[15] As an example we find the Stabilisation and Association Agreement between the European Communities and their Member States, of the one part, and the Republic of Albania, of the other part—Protocols—Declarations [2009] OJ L107/166. This agreement considers Albania as a 'potential candidate' for accession to the EU; for this reason it stipulates in its article 2 a *human rights clause* more stringent than those contained in commercial or association agreements: 'Respect for the democratic principles and human rights as proclaimed in the Universal Declaration of Human Rights and as defined in the European Convention on Human Rights, in the Helsinki Final Act and the Charter of Paris for a New Europe, respect for international law principles and the rule of law as well as the principles of market economy as reflected in the Document of the CSCE Bonn Conference on Economic Cooperation, shall form the basis of the domestic and external policies of the Parties and constitute essential elements of this Agreement'.

[16] M Cremona, C Hillion, 'L'Union fait la force? Potential and Limitations of the European Neighbourhood Policy as an Integrated EU Foreign and Security Policy', *EUI Working Papers Law No 39* (2006).

[17] See the Communication from the Commission, *European Neighbourhood Policy*, Strategic Paper, COM(2004) 373 final; the Joint Communication of the European Commission and of the High Representative of Foreign Affairs and Security Policy to the European Parliament, the Council, the European Economic and Social Committee and the Committee of the Regions, *A new response to a changing Neighbourhood*, COM(2011) 303; and finally the Joint Communication of the European Commission and of the High Representative of Foreign Affairs and Security Policy to the European Parliament, the Council, the European Economic and Social Committee and the Committee of the Regions, *European Neighbourhood Policy: Working towards a Stronger Partnership*, JOIN(2013) 4 final.

[18] The regime of these agreements is studied in C Hillion, 'The EU's Neighbourhood Policy towards Eastern Europe' in A Dashwood, M Maresceau, *Law and Practice of EU External Relations* (Cambridge, Cambridge University Press, 2008) 309–33; also, P Koutrakos, *EU International Relations Law*, n 4 above, 363–65. Article 2 of the agreement with Georgia could be taken as a reference: 'Respect for democracy, principles of international law and human rights as defined in particular in the United Nations Charter, the Helsinki Final Act and the Charter of Paris for a New Europe, as well as the principles of market economy, including those enunciated in the documents of the CSCE Bonn Conference, underpin the internal and external policies of the Parties and constitute essential elements of Partnership and of this Agreement'—Partnership and Cooperation Agreement between the European Communities and their Member States, of the one part, and Georgia, of the other part [1999] OJ L205/3. This clause is contained as well in the cooperation agreements concluded by the European Union and its Member States with Armenia, Azerbaijan, Moldavia and Ukraine, but not with Belarus. This case, compared with the clause in the agreement with Albania, reflects a tangential and less strict mention of human rights obligations.

[19] Barcelona Declaration, adopted at the Euro-Mediterranean Conference of Foreign Affairs Ministers, celebrated in Barcelona during 27 and 28 November of 1995, and by virtue of which the Euro-Mediterranean Partnership was created. In this sense, see A Blanc Altemir, 'El proceso

An example of a democracy clause in the Euro-Mediterranean agreements is found in Article 2 of the agreement with Algeria: 'Respect for the democratic principles and fundamental human rights established by the Universal Declaration of Human Rights [UDHR] shall inspire the domestic and international policies of the Parties and shall constitute an essential element of this Agreement'.[20] This clause mentions explicitly and places in a central position in the agreement respect for the rules enshrined in the UDHR, in clear contrast with what has been revealed regarding the collaboration and cooperation agreements concluded with former Soviet Union States, where an *in abstracto* reference to human rights or a simple invocation of instruments adopted within the framework of the OSCE is formulated. A clause similar to the one included in the agreement with Algeria is contained in the Euro-Mediterranean agreements concluded with Egypt, Israel, Jordan, the Palestinian Occupied Territories, Lebanon, Morocco and Tunisia. However this kind of clause has not been possible in the relationship between the EU and Libya or Syria.

Concerning the Eastern dimension of the Neighbourhood Policy, it has been said that the experience and rules of the Council of Europe in the field of human rights can be utilised, and that the EU could benefit from this synergy and that, besides, it has the legitimacy to guide by means of political and financial mechanisms their Eastern partners towards respect for international agreements and obligations that have been assumed by itself in the framework of the Council of Europe.[21]

The EU has shown its preference for positive conditionality[22] instead of negative conditionality,[23] which remains as an *ultima ratio*, because of both the greater

euromediterráneo: una década de luces y sombras' (2005) 21 *Anuario de Derecho Internacional* 185–225; also, Erwan Lannon, 'The EU's Strategic Partnership with the Mediterranean and the Middle East: a new geopolitical dimension of the EU's proximity strategies' in A Dashwood, M Maresceau, *Law and Practice of EU External Relations* (Cambridge, Cambridge University Press, 2008) 360–75; and R Rhattat, *La politique européenne de voisinage dans les pays de l'aire méditerranéenne* (Brussels, Bruylant, 2011). Taking into account the development of the so called '*Arab Springs*' in some of the countries on the South Shore of the Mediterranean it is evident that neither the Neigbourhood Policy nor the association agreements concluded have supposed a sufficient incentive in order to improve substantially the situation of human rights in Algeria, Egypt, Israel, the Palestinian Occupied Territories, Syria or Tunisia, for instance.

[20] Euro-Mediterranean Agreement establishing an Association between the European Community and its Member States, of the one part, and the People's Democratic Republic of Algeria, of the other part [2005] OJ L265/2.

[21] Barbara Schumacher, 'The Influence of the Council of Europe on the European Union: Resource Exchange and Domain Restriction as Venues for Inter-Institutional Influence' in O Costa and K Jørgensen (eds), *The Influence of International Institutions on the EU: When Multilateralism hits Brussels* (Basingtoke, Palgrave MacMillan, 2012) 186–206.

[22] For instance, Council Decision 2011/106/CFSP of 15 February 2011 on adapting and extending the period of application of the measures in Decision 2002/148/EC concluding consultations with Zimbabwe under Article 96 of the ACP-EC Partnership Agreement [2011] OJ L43/31.

[23] M Candela Soriano, *Los Derechos Humanos, la Democracia y el Estado de Derecho en la Acción Exterior de la Unión Europea. Evolución, Actores, Instrumentos y Ejecución*, n 2 above, 249–51. However, the negative measures are not negligible. This is the case in respect of sanctions adopted even without a contractual link with the third country. They constitute a selective and decentralised enforcement of human rights towards third countries, as for instance Syria, Iran, Libya, Ivory Coast, etc. See in that respect, A Pellet, 'Les sanctions de l'Union européenne' in M Benlolo-Carabot, U Candas and E Cujo (eds), *Union européenne et droit international. En l'honneur de Patrick Daillier* (Paris, Pedone, 2012) 431–55.

efficacy of positive measures and the problems of international legality that the doctrine has emphasised regarding sanctions in face of violations of human rights obligations committed by third countries within their own territories.[24]

Moreover, this criticism is sharpened by the fact that has been suggested brilliantly by De Waele:

> there is an ample proof that the Union does not treat all its partners alike, and that some countries are seen as patently more equal than others. Quite often, such blatant inconsistencies can be explained by the overriding commercial interests, which 'necessitate' turning a blind eye to a partner's fundamental rights record. In the past, this has particularly held true for relations with many African and Middle Eastern nations. Vivid examples can also be found in Europe itself, especially in the run-up to the most recent rounds of EU enlargement. Officially, the admittance of new members is conditional upon an unqualified respect for fundamental rights, as the Copenhagen Criteria make clear. Yet, in 2004 as well as 2007, the EU consciously eroded its own precepts, contenting itself instead with empty promises and paper realities, so as to avoid political feuds and humiliation when the timetables for accession would prove impossible to meet.[25]

Concerning the positive measures, the special regime of tariff preferences aimed at sustainable development and good governance constitutes an interesting example: this regime is offered to developing countries, classified as vulnerable, which voluntarily demand its application. It consists of the suppression of custom tariffs for certain products, which is made conditional upon the ratification of certain United Nations and ILO Conventions related to human rights and labour rights. Within the first group of treaties upon which these preferences are made conditional we find: the two United Nations Covenants adopted in 1966 (Civil and Political Rights, and Economic, Social and Cultural Rights, respectively), the Covenant on the Elimination of Racial Discrimination, the International Covenant on the Suppression and Punishment of the Crime of Apartheid, the Covenant on the Elimination of All Forms of Discrimination against Women, the Convention against Torture and Other Cruel, Inhuman or Degrading Treatment or Punishment, the Convention on the Rights of the Child, and finally, the Convention on the Prevention and Punishment of the Crime of Genocide. Among the second group of ILO Conventions whose ratification is required in order to obtain the commercial preferences, we find those relating to: the minimum legal age of admission to employment, the prohibition of the worse forms of child labour, the

[24] In this regard, DJ Liñán Nogueras, 'Límites del discurso de la condicionalidad en la acción exterior de la Unión Europea' in F Mariño Menéndez (ed), *Acción Exterior de la Unión Europea y Comunidad Internacional* (Instituto de Estudios Internacionales y Europeos 'Francisco de Vitoria', Universidad Carlos III de Madrid, 1998) 433–34. Detractors of all forms of political conditionality could be classified in two groups: those who consider the subordination of external aid to the fulfilment of western patterns as a return to paternalist models with ambitions of neo-colonialist domination; and those who are opposed to the link between aid and political values, being simply partisans of the apparently 'aseptic' market economy from an axiological point of view, see MC Muñoz Rodríguez, *Democracia y derechos humanos en la acción exterior de la Unión Europea* (Madrid, Reus, 2011) 26.

[25] H de Waele, *Layered Global Player. Legal Dynamics of EU External Relations* (Berlin, Springer, 2011) 103–4.

abolishment of forced labour, equal remuneration for men and women workers for work of equal value, the prohibition of discrimination in the field of employment, and freedom of association and collective bargaining. Besides these international treaties relating to the protection of fundamental and worker's rights, this preferential regime is also conditional upon the ratification of other treaties concerning environmental protection, the fight against the trafficking of drugs and psychotropic substances and the fight against corruption.[26]

Concerning the negative measures, the EU has applied the *human rights and democracy clause* suspending partially and temporarily some of the international agreements with the ACP countries.[27] It also withdrew the tariff preferences from Burma because of its infraction of the ILO Convention no 29 (forced labour) and from Belarus due to the violation of ILO Conventions no 87 and 98 (referring to freedom of association and to collective bargaining, respectively). In 2010, the EU suspended temporarily the application of special tariff preferences to Sri Lanka, because it failed to apply effectively the provisions of the International Covenant on Civil and Political Rights, the Convention against Torture and Other Cruel, Inhuman or Degrading Treatment or Punishment, and finally the Convention on the Rights of the Child.[28]

[26] Council Regulation (EC) 732/2008 of 22 July 2008 applying a scheme of generalised tariff preferences for the period from 1 January 2009 to 31 December 2011 and amending Regulations (EC) 552/97, (EC) 1933/2006 and Commission Regulations (EC) No 1100/2006 and (EC) No 964/2007, [2008] OJ L211/ 1. The EU has decided to extend the application of this regulation until the end of 2013, see Regulation (EU) 512/2011 of the European Parliament and of the Council of 11 May 2011 amending Council Regulation (EC) 732/2008, [2011] OJ L145/28. Since the beginning of 2014, the new Generalised Scheme of Preferences granted to countries which ratify and implement such international conventions relating to human and labour rights, environment and good governance (called GSP +) has replaced the above-mentioned schemes: see in that sense Regulation (EU) 978/2012 of the European Parliament and of the Council of 25 October 2012 applying a scheme of generalised tariff preferences and repealing Council Regulation (EC) 732/2008 [2012] OJ L303/1; and finally the Commission Delegated Regulation (EU) 155/2013 of 18 December 2012 establishing rules related to the procedure for granting the special incentive arrangement for sustainable development and good governance under Regulation (EU) 978/2012, [2013] OJ L48/5. This unilateral fight by the EU against social and environmental dumping is often perceived by the developing countries as a hidden protectionism, see C López-Jurado, 'La oferta comercial preferencial de la Unión Europea a los Países en Vías de Desarrollo: modalidades e interacciones' (2011) 39 *Revista de Derecho Comunitario Europeo* 443, 461; or, more concretely, about social conditionality and the importance of fundamental labour rights, LM Hinojosa Martínez and T Fajardo del Castillo, 'Los nuevos problemas del comercio internacional y la Ronda de Doha' in LM Hinojosa Martínez and J Roldán Barbero (coord), *Derecho Internacional Económico* (Madrid, Marcial Pons, 2010) 223; and also Luis Miguel Hinojosa Martínez, *Comercio justo y derechos sociales*, (Madrid, Tecnos, 2002). Obviously the fight against dumping at a multilateral level can lose its credibility due to the fact that companies legally based in the European Union's internal market profit by the lower labour standards in third countries by means of delocalisation. The exigency of a corporate social responsibility to European companies which operate in third countries is of utmost importance in order to break the natural trend to a race to the bottom concerning labour standards and in order to promote the realisation of a universal respect to the fundamental social and labour rights.

[27] See, B De Witte, 'The EU and International Legal Order: The Case of Human Rights' in M Evans and P Koutrakos (eds), *Beyond the Established Legal Orders: Policy Interconnections between the EU and the Rest of the World* (Oxford, Hart Publishing, 2011) 142; and also K Del Biondo, 'EU Aid Conditionality in ACP Countries: Explaining Inconsistency in EU Sanctions Practice' (2011) 7 *Journal of Contemporary European Research* 380–95.

[28] The measures adopted in respect of Sri Lanka have had little success both from a geostrategic point of view and from the perspective of human rights and democracy improvement: C Castillejo,

II. THE CONTRIBUTION OF THE EU TO THE CREATION AND DEVELOPMENT OF INTERNATIONAL CUSTOMARY NORMS IN THE FIELD OF HUMAN RIGHTS PROTECTION

From the above-mentioned practice, can we infer that the EU has conviction about the obligatory character of the main international normative instruments for the protection of human rights, besides any conventional link to them?[29] Notwithstanding all the diversity and complexity of the activity of promoting human rights that the EU carries out in its external action and despite criticism of double standards, the answer should be unambiguously in the affirmative: there is a category of international instruments for the protection of human rights that the EU has permanently invoked in its external relations. This is the case of instruments belonging to the International Bill of Human Rights,[30] the remaining international conventions for human rights protection adopted within the United Nations' framework, the European Convention on Human Rights, and finally some instruments from the OSCE which are not international treaties, such as for instance the Helsinki Final Act of 1975, or the Charter of Paris for a New Europe of 1990.[31]

The EU is not formally bound as an International Law subject by any of the above-mentioned international conventions for the protection of human rights. Therefore, this constitutes a fracture in the conditionality carried out by the EU in its external action that can only be solved by considering that the European Union is indeed bound by those instruments in the guise of General International Law, that is, as International customary law.[32]

The international instruments from the Council of Europe or OSCE framework belong to a customary heritage of regional character (not only European, but Western States in the case of the latter). In the case of international instruments of universal scope adopted within the framework of United Nations,

'Sri Lanka: The failure of EU human rights sanctions' (2011) 63 *FRIDE Policy Brief*. In the case of Venezuela the application of the 2009 preferential regime was suspended due to the lack of ratification of the United Nations Convention against corruption: see C López-Jurado, 'La oferta comercial preferencial de la Unión Europea a los Países en Vías de Desarrollo: modalidades e interacciones', n 26 above, 443, 468. The doctrine has raised problems of compatibility with WTO Law of those commercial sanctions put in place without the existence of a *human rights and democracy clause*, see RL Howse and JM Genser, 'Are EU Trade Sanctions on Burma Compatible with WTO Law?' (2008) 29 *Michigan Journal of International Law* 165–96; in this line, see B Wardhaugh, 'GSP+ and Human Rights: Is the EU's Approach the Right One?' (2013) 16 *Journal of International Economic Law* 827–46.

[29] T Meron, *Human Rights and Humanitarian Norms as Customary Law* (Oxford, Clarendon Press, 1991).

[30] This is to say the ensemble composed of: the Universal Declaration of Human Rights of 1948, the International Covenant on Civil and Political Rights of 1966, the International Covenant on Economic, Social and Cultural Rights, and the Optional Protocols to both.

[31] Both constitute examples of non-normative acts, following the expression used by P Weil, 'Towards Relative Normativity in International Law?' (1983) 77 *American Journal of International Law* 413, 414.

[32] A Rosas, 'The European Union and Fundamental rights/Human rights' in C Krause and M Scheinin (eds), *International Protection of Human Rights: A Textbook* (Turku/Âbo, Institute for Human Rights of the Âbo Akademi University, 2009) 466.

the EU has acted under the internal assumption that those instruments reflect General International Law, be it in terms of international custom or as general principles of International Law.[33] As the judge Rosas of the Court of Justice of the European Union puts it:

> The human rights clause seems to be based on the understanding that the principles contained in the Universal Declaration reflect existing general international law, whether seen as customary law or as general principles of law recognised by civilized nations. While this does not necessarily mean that each word of the Universal Declaration has become legally binding, the EU's treaty practice contributes to the reaffirmation of the status of the Declaration as an expression of general international law binding on all States.[34]

Obviously, problems might appear when the question of identifying which of the articles of the UDHR benefit from such general acceptance is faced.[35]

The muddle in search of international legality and legitimacy for political conditionality would be solved if the EU became a party to most of the international agreements concerning human rights protection that it constantly invokes in its relations with third countries: being tied by international agreements in this field could bring legal certainty, as opposed to the enigmatic and mysterious character of international custom. In a certain way, the question of legality is already clarified with the Lisbon Treaty, which introduces explicitly among the objectives of the European Union in its relations with the wider world the protection of human rights and the strict respect and development of International Law, with a particular emphasis on the principles of the United Nations Charter (article 3.5 TEU).[36] Thus this reference in European Union primary law finds accommodation in General International Law, in line with the United Nations Human Rights Committee's view: every State which is party to the International Covenant on

[33] A Rosas, 'The Role of the Universal Declaration of Human Rights in the Treaty Relations of the European Union' in P Baehr, et al (eds), *Innovation and Inspiration: Fifty Years of the Universal Declaration of Human Rights* (Koninklijke Nederlandse Akademie van Wetenschappen, 1999) 201–9.

[34] A Rosas, 'The European Union and International Human Rights Instruments' in V Kronenberger (ed), *The EU and the International Legal Order: Discord or Harmony?* (Amsterdam, Asser Press, 2001) 61.

[35] The practice of judicial and quasi-judicial bodies suggest that the recognition through customary law is essentially referred to civil and political rights, at a doctrinal level more doubts seems to cast the inclusion of economic, social and cultural rights within the body of customary international human rights law, see J Bonet Pérez, 'Aproximación al tratamiento jurídico de las crisis de naturaleza económica en el ámbito del Derecho Internacional de los Derechos Humanos' in J Bonet Pérez and J Saura Estapà (eds), *El Derecho internacional de los derechos humanos en períodos de crisis. Estudios desde la perspectiva de su aplicabilidad* (Madrid, Marcial Pons, 2013) 181. Beyond legal analysis, it has been assessed that the hegemony of neo-liberalism in the process of globalisation clearly undermines socioeconomic rights reducing their emancipatory potential by presenting them as mere aspirations and market outcomes, see J Wills, 'The World Turned Upside Down? Neo-Liberalism, Socioeconomic Rights, and Hegemony' (2014) 27 *Leiden Journal of International Law* 11–35.

[36] See J Larik, 'Shaping the international order as an EU objective' in D Kochenov and F Amtenbrink (eds), *The European Union's Shaping of the International Legal Order* (Cambridge, Cambridge University Press, 2014) 62–86.

Civil and Political Rights has an interest in its due compliance, especially in the respect towards the basic rights of the human person which constitute *erga omnes* obligations.[37] Therefore beyond the contractual dimension, 'there is a United Nations Charter obligation to promote universal respect for, and observance of, human rights and fundamental freedoms'.[38] International human rights treaties impose integral obligations which go beyond the bilateralist or synallagmatic logic of traditional international law.

The EU has therefore incorporated the provisions of the UDHR as an essential element of many of its international agreements with third countries. The EU has also encouraged third countries to ratify a large number of international treaties for human rights protection adopted under the auspices of United Nations, and also some of the fundamental ILO Conventions,[39] and it has done so both through its development cooperation and through its purely commercial relations. This behaviour of the EU constitutes an expression of its internal conviction that the above-mentioned instruments are generally binding beyond State consent, and it also has shown the conviction that those international treaties together with the UDHR form a *corpus* of general customary norms which the EU itself feels obliged and engaged to respect.[40] In that way some of the provisions enshrined in those instruments invoked in the EU's external relations become legally binding for third States, overcoming the relative effect of those treaties as article 38 of the Vienna Convention on the Law of the Treaties stipulates: thus

[37] International Court of Justice (ICJ), *Barcelona Traction, Light and Power Co Ltd (Belgium v Spain)*, Judgment of 5 February, ICJ Reports 1970, p 32, paras 33–34.

[38] Human Rights Committee, General Comment No 31, *The Nature of the General Legal Obligation Imposed on States Parties to the Covenant* (2004) CCPR/C/21/Rev.1/Add.13, para 2. Indeed, due to the *erga omnes* nature of the obligations arising from International Human Rights Law a large number of treaties have foreseen interstate complaint mechanisms. These mechanisms reflect the legitimate interest which every single State of the international community has in respect for human rights obligations. The activation of such control mechanisms is possible because every contracting State has locus standi to denounce other States for the violation of human rights obligations.

[39] ILO is a specialised organism which integrates the family of the United Nations in a broad sense.

[40] Evidence of this internal conviction is the adoption by the Council of the European Union on 25 June 2012 of the EU Strategic Framework and Action Plan on Human Rights and Democracy, 11855/12, as well as the designation of a European Union Special Representative for Human Rights, Mr Stavros Lambrinidis. In the former document the European Union expresses its commitment to the Universal Periodic Review mechanism by the United Nations Human Rights Council: 'The EU underlines the leading role of the UN Human Rights Council in addressing urgent cases of human rights violations and will contribute vigorously to the effective functioning of the Council; the EU stands ready to cooperate with countries from all regions to this end. The EU calls on all members of the Human Rights Council to uphold the highest standards of human rights and to live up to their pledges made before election. Welcoming the establishment of Universal Periodic Review (UPR), the EU and its Member States are committed to raising UPR recommendations which have been accepted, as well as recommendations of treaty monitoring bodies and UN Special Procedures, in bilateral relations with all third countries; the Member States are equally determined to ensure implementation of such recommendations within their own frontiers. In forthcoming UPR rounds, the EU will pay close attention to the degree of implementation by third countries of UPR commitments which they have accepted and will endeavour to provide support for their implementation'.

it can be said that an exception to the general rule *pacta tertiis nec nocent nec prosunt* arises.[41]

The suitability of custom as a way of creation of norms concerning the international protection of human rights is beyond any reasonable doubt in the case of negative obligations, that is, the obligation to refrain from actively infringing those norms which may have acquired a customary legal value. On the other hand, the potentiality and utility of custom are clearly lower in the field of positive obligations, which are destined to establish authentic subjective rights that entail a correlative duty to act. Moreover, the suitability of custom comes from the fact that the international instruments concerning the protection of human rights aim at establishing a permanent and stable regime.[42] Customary international law, as is well known, presents particular difficulties when it comes to the delimitation between the *ascending* phase, concerning its formation and creation, and the *descendent* phase, regarding its application and reception. It could be said that both phases are practically simultaneous: the EU's legal order consecrates the automatic reception of customary international law.[43] It is possible that the existence of customary norms of general scope concerning the protection of the fundamental rights of human beings preceded the practice of political conditionality carried out first by the European Community, and later the EU, since the '90s. This idea seems to appear from the following words expressed at that time by Schermers: 'Public international law offers a strong legal obligation to respect the most fundamental human rights. This obligation is addressed to all subjects of international law and therefore also to the European Community'.[44] Nowadays, responsibility

[41] The harsher questions could be on the one hand, the identification of the concrete norms which have become *erga omnes*, and on the other hand, how to establish if such norms are legally binding for other international organisations. It is abundantly evident that the EU in the same way that identifies norms as binding for third countries remains itself bound by them. But even third party international organisations could be bound by such norms concerning human rights protection, that possibility is feasible by means of an analogical application of article 38 of the Vienna Convention on the Law of Treaties between States and International Organizations or between International Organizations, adopted in 1986. This possibility was recognised by the ICJ, *North Sea Continental Shelf cases*, Judgment of 20 February 1969, ICJ Reports 1969, p 3.

[42] The contribution to the development of international law by judicial and quasi-judicial human rights monitoring bodies shall not be underestimated: 'There is no doubt, in fact, that, starting with the Universal Declaration of 1948, and then with the entry into force of the various conventions on human rights and the institution of the above-mentioned organs, not only has the system of protection of human rights constituted a revolutionary development in itself, but it has also produced an innovative effect on various institutions of a general nature disciplined by customary law, as well as affecting the discipline of other specific international actors': see Benedetto Conforti, 'The specificity of human rights and international law' in Ulrich Fastenrath, et al (eds), *From Bilateralism to Community Interest. Essays in Honour of Judge Bruno Simma* (Oxford, OUP, 2011) 440.

[43] See among other judgments of the ECJ: Case C-162/96 *A Racke GmbH & Co v Hauptzollamt Mainz* [1998] ECR I-3655; Case C-366/10 *Air Transport Association of America and others v Secretary of State for Energy and Climate Change*, EU:C:2011:864; and finally Case C-286/12 *Commission v Hungary*, EU:C:2012:687.

[44] Henry G Schermers, 'The European Communities bound by Fundamental Human Rights' (1990) 27 *Common Market Law Review* 249, 251.

to protect in the light of recent experiences in Libya, for instance, can be seen as an emerging area where a general obligation of customary law might one day crystallise, but this does not impair the EU's pursuit of the development of international law and the definitive emergence of customary law in this field through its fragmented Common Foreign and Security Policy, according to the objectives of articles 3.5 and 21.1 of the TEU.[45]

An additional issue for reflection could be the unilateral initiative of the EU of introducing as an essential element of its international agreements with third countries the *human rights and democracy clause*; to what extent does the EU become bound by its own acts according to the *estoppel* doctrine, and to what extent does it contribute to the creation of customary law with the exercise of political conditionality?[46] In order to answer these questions it is convenient not to neglect the fact that when the EU introduces respect for human rights as an essential element of an international agreement it is giving to its counterpart a clear message: the EU respects and feels itself obliged by those international standards of human rights protection for which it demands respect by third countries. Any change of that state of assumptions can never be detrimental to the third country, consequently, it can be inferred that the EU, being a subject of international law, is obligated by the same international standards concerning human rights protection which the third country is required to respect. As it was put by the Vice-President of the ICJ Alfaro in his Separate Opinion in the *Temple of Preah Vihear* case:

> Whatever term or terms be employed to designate this principle such as it has been applied in the international sphere, its substance is always the same: inconsistency between claims or allegations put forward by a State, and its previous conduct in connection therewith, is not admissible (*allegans contraria non audiendus est*). Its purpose

[45] G De Baere, 'The EU and the Responsibility to Protect' in B Van Vooren, S Blockmans and J Wouters (eds), *The EU's Role in Global Governance. The Legal Dimension* (Oxford, OUP, 2013) 95–109. A critical appraisal of the EU's role in the Libyan armed conflict raised in 2011 from the perspective of human rights and democracy in J Ferrer Lloret, 'La Unión Europea ante la crisis Libia ¿Derecho Internacional, Democracia y Derechos Humanos en las Relaciones Euromediterráneas?' (2012) 41 *Revista de Derecho Comunitario Europeo* 13–56.

[46] The *human rights and democracy clause*, once incorporated into an international agreement, is transformed into a bilateral act. To the extent that it receives consent by both parties it becomes reciprocal and its infraction would enable either of them to terminate or suspend the application of the international agreement according to articles 60.1 and 60.3(b) of the Vienna Convention on the Law of Treaties between States and International Organizations or between International Organizations, adopted in 1986. However, the original gestation of this clause has to be attributed to the EU, adding that its respective counterparts have accepted it—with a few exceptions—in an uncritical and unconditional way which means in practice adhering to it as a non-negotiable element. It is in this sense that the doctrine of the own acts and *estoppel* is brought. The practical application until the present moment of the clause reaffirms this approach to the extent that it has only been wielded by the EU and not against it. This reasoning could be illustrated by Australia's reluctance to include the above-mentioned clause. In that case, negotiations could be released only when political conditionality was substituted by a declaration merely mentioning in abstract terms the compromise with democratic values, see J Roldán Barbero, 'Les relations extérieures de l'Union européenne: quelques faiblesses et incertitudes juridiques' in *Jean-Victor Louis*, et al, *Mélanges en Hommage à Jean-Victor Louis*, vol II (Brussels, Éditions de l'Université Libre de Bruxelles, 2003) 182.

> is always the same: a State must not be permitted to benefit by its own inconsistency to the prejudice of another State (*nemo potest mutare consilium suum in alterius injuriam*). *A fortiori*, the State must not be allowed to benefit by its inconsistency when it is through its own wrong or illegal act that the other party has been deprived of its right or prevented from exercising it. (*Nullus commodum capere de sua injuria propria*). Finally, the legal effect of the principle is always the same: the party which by its recognition, its representation, its declaration, its conduct or its silence has maintained an attitude manifestly contrary to the right it is claiming before an international tribunal is precluded from claiming that right (*venire contra factum proprium non valet*).[47]

Moreover, according to the ICJ jurisprudence on the *North Sea Continental Shelf* cases, the body of customary law could be integrated with the norms enshrined in international treaties to which a large number (*widespread and representative participation*) of States of the International Community have become parties, and that is undoubtedly the case of the United Nations' core human rights conventions[48] which are constantly wielded by the EU throughout its external action.[49] Additional elements which support this idea can be found in the ICJ's jurisprudence

[47] See the Separate Opinion of Judge Alfaro in the *Temple of Preah Vihear (Cambodia v Thailand) case*, Judgment of 15 June 1962, ICJ Reports 1962, p 40.

[48] We consider that a reasonable threshold in order to have a large and representative number of States of the International Community which are parties to an international treaty could be a two-thirds majority of the 193 States which are members of the United Nations. Therefore, a majority of 128 States which are parties to a human rights multilateral convention will enable us to think that its rules may have a customary nature and be binding as general international law. This is the case with the seven following human rights conventions adopted under the auspices of United Nations: the International Covenant on Civil and Political Rights of 16 December 1966; the International Covenant on Economic, Social and Cultural Rights of 16 December 1966; the International Convention on the Elimination of All Forms of Racial Discrimination of 7 March 1966; the Convention on the Elimination of All Forms of Discrimination against Women of 18 December 1979; the Convention against Torture and Other Cruel, Inhuman or Degrading Treatment or Punishment of 10 December 1984; the Convention on the Rights of the Child of 20 November 1989; and finally the Convention on the Rights of Persons with Disabilities of 13 December 2006. However, two of the considered *core* conventions have not reached such a threshold of ratifications: namely the International Convention on the Protection of the Rights of All Migrant Workers and Members of their Families, of 18 December 1990 and the more recently adopted International Convention for the Protection of All Persons from Enforced Disappearance, of 20 December 2006. Even if it is not considered one of the *core* human rights conventions the Convention on the Prevention and Punishment of the Crime of Genocide of 9 December 1948, has also reached the above-mentioned threshold for accession. Among the optional protocols to the conventions previously referred to only two of them have reached the two-thirds majority of State parties: the Optional Protocol to the Convention on the Rights of the Child on the involvement of children in armed conflict of 25 May 2000 and the Optional Protocol to the Convention on the Rights of the Child on the sale of children, child prostitution and child pornography of 25 May 2000. States are verbally more engaged with the idea of recognising and protecting human rights at the universal level than with real support to the mechanisms established for their guarantee at the international level.

[49] ICJ, *North Sea Continental Shelf cases*, Judgment, n 41 above, para 73. The ECJ has invoked this jurisprudence in Case C-37/00 *Herbert Weber v Universal Ogden Services Ltd* [2002] ECR I-2013, para 34. Notable as well is the *Legality of the Threat or Use of Nuclear Weapons*, Advisory Opinion, ICJ Reports 1996, p 257, para 79: 'It is undoubtedly because a great many rules of humanitarian law applicable in armed conflict are so fundamental to the respect of the human person and "elementary considerations of humanity" as the Court put it in its Judgment of 9 April 1949 in the *Corfu Channel* case (*ICJ Reports 1949*, p 22), that the Hague and Geneva Conventions have enjoyed a broad accession. Further these fundamental rules are to be observed by all States whether or not they have ratified

where it affirms the customary nature of some basic human rights[50] that the EU has tried to promote through its external action with third States, namely: the prohibition of genocide,[51] the prohibition of racial discrimination, including apartheid, and the prohibition of slavery,[52] the right to physical integrity,[53] the right of protection against arbitrary denial of justice,[54] and more recently the prohibition of torture.[55] Nowadays, there is not, concerning the customary nature of those rights, any State which openly characterises itself as an official *persistent objector*.[56]

Therefore, the EU has promoted respect for the international norms concerning human rights protection that it considers to have customary nature and to be of universal scope. Therefore, the spiritual element in the creation of custom (*opinio iuris sive necessitatis*) appears to be without difficulties. More objections could affect the health of the objective element of custom in this case: despite hesitations and vacillations[57] and despite the examples of double standards it

the conventions that contain them, because they constitute intransgressible principles of international customary law'. See D Momtaz and A Ghanbari Amirhandeh, 'The interaction between international humanitarian law and human rights law and the contribution of the ICJ' in K Bannelier, T Christakis and S Heathcote (eds), *The ICJ and the Evolution of International Law. The enduring impact of the Corfu Channel Case* (London, Routledge, 2012) 256–63.

[50] See, B Simma, 'Mainstreaming Human Rights: The Contribution of the International Court of Justice' (2012) 3 *Journal of International Dispute Settlement* 7–20. An article which draws a comparison between the contribution to human rights of the ICJ jurisprudence and the specialist courts and bodies suggests that the ICJ has a potential *ripple effect* when it comes to interpretation of fundamental issues rather than enforcement of individual rights, see R Wilde, 'Human Rights Beyond Borders at the World Court: The Significance of the International Court of Justice's Jurisprudence on the Extraterritorial Application of International Human Rights Law Treaties' (2013) 12 *Chinese Journal of International Law* 639–77.

[51] *Reservations to the Convention on the Prevention and Punishment of the Crime of Genocide*, Advisory Opinion, ICJ Reports 1951, p 23. The judgment which has contributed definitively to the explanation of the regime of international liability arising from genocide is the *Application of the Convention on the Prevention and Punishment of the Crime of Genocide (Bosnia and Herzegovina v Serbia and Montenegro)*, Judgment of 26 February, ICJ Reports 2007, p 43.

[52] *Barcelona Traction, Light and Power Co Ltd (Belgium v Spain)*, Judgment, n 37 above, paras 33–34; see also *Legal Consequences for States of the Continued Presence of South Africa in Namibia (South West Africa) notwithstanding Security Council Resolution 276 (1970)*, Advisory Opinion, ICJ Reports 1971, p 57.

[53] *United States Diplomatic and Consular Staff in Tehran*, Judgment of 24 May, ICJ Reports 1980, 42, para 91. The Court cited the fundamental principles enshrined in the UDHR to support the illegality of wrongful deprivation of a person's freedom.

[54] *Barcelona Traction, Light and Power Co Ltd (Belgium v Spain)*, Judgment, n 37 above, 47, para 91.

[55] *Questions relating to the Obligation to Prosecute or Extradite (Belgium v Senegal)*, Judgment of 20 July 2012, ICJ Reports 2012, 457, para 99: 'In the Court's opinion, the prohibition of torture is part of customary international law and it has become a peremptory norm (*jus cogens*)'.

[56] It should be borne in mind that it is not welcomed that the persistent objector status might be used concerning matters of a general interest, which the international norms relating to human rights or environmental protection are. South Africa was in fact an active objector to the apartheid prohibition for decades, but that conduct has not released that State from the international liability which is a consequence of the infraction of the prohibition. See Y Dinstein, 'The Interaction between Customary International Law and Treaties', *Collected Courses of the Hague Academy of International Law* vol 322 (Leiden, Brill/Nijhoff, 2007) 243, 285–87.

[57] Beyond the scope of the present study remain the fractures and ruptures which often appear in the framework of the CFSP and the dissonances that also happen between the latter and the respective foreign policies of every single Member State.

cannot be denied that the EU has a uniform and reiterated practice of utilisation and invocation, vis-à-vis third countries, of international human rights instruments. From this *usus*, from this voluntary repetition of precedents it is possible to infer the juridical obligation for the EU itself. Before giving lessons one must first lead by example; however, an excessive degree of self-criticism is also dangerous as eloquently has been enunciated: 'If the passionate demand for self-scrutiny leads to paralysis, we should perhaps begin to wonder if we have not gone too far in our denunciations of those who appeal to the universal'.[58]

Even though the material element is weaker than the spiritual one in order to ascertain the EU's contribution to the creation of customary international law in the field of human rights, it is appropriate to point out that international jurisprudence has granted an increasing importance to the subjective element for the emergence of international custom.[59] It is worthwhile to note the ICJ's position on the *Nicaragua v United States* case, where it took the view that *opinio iuris* should prevail over practice in order to affirm and determine the existence of a customary norm:

> The Court does not consider that, for a rule to be established as customary, the corresponding practice must be in absolutely rigorous conformity with the rule. In order to deduce the existence of customary rules, the Court deems it sufficient that the conduct of States should, in general, be consistent with such rules, and that instances of State conduct inconsistent with a given rule should generally have been treated as breaches of that rule, not as indications of the recognition of a new rule. If a State acts in a way prima facie incompatible with a recognized rule, but defends its conduct by appealing to exceptions or justifications contained within the rule itself, then whether or not the State's conduct is in fact justifiable on that basis, the significance of that attitude is to confirm rather than to weaken the rule.[60]

According to that reasoning, whereas in the field of human rights dissonances between practice and juridical belief are frequent, those discordances are not strong enough to constitute the denial of the customary norm in the field; nor do they propose an alternative customary norm: they suppose examples of deviation from the norm, infraction of international customary norms concerning human rights protection, which simply entail violations within the general framework

[58] P-M Dupuy, 'Some Reflections on Contemporary International Law and the Appeal to Universal Values: A Response to Martti Koskenniemi' (2005) 16 *European Journal of International Law* 136.

[59] See in that respect among others, G Abi-Saab, 'La coutume dans tous ses états ou le dilemma du développement du droit international général dans un monde éclaté' in *Le droit international à l'heure de sa codification. Études en l'honneur de R Ago*, vol I (Milan, Giuffrè 1987) 53–65; M Mendelson, 'The Subjective Element in Customary International Law' (1995) 66 *British Yearbook of International Law* 177–208; and finally, it has been maintained that *opinio iuris* cannot be distinguished, at least, functionally, from State consent: O Elias, 'The Nature of the Subjective Element in Customary International Law' (1995) 44 *International and Comparative Law Quarterly* 501–23. Domestic courts may face problems due to the primacy of the subjective element in the formation of custom, which may lead to antagonistic international norms being raised, RB Baker, 'Customary International Law in the 21st Century: Old Challenges and New Debates' (2010) 21 *European Journal of International Law* 173–204.

[60] *Military and Paramilitary Activities in and against Nicaragua (Nicaragua v United States of America)*, Judgment of 27 June 1986, Merits, ICJ Reports 1986, p 98, para 186.

of subsistence, acceptance and observance of the norm.[61] This dilution of the material element for the identification of customary norms is not an exclusive phenomenon of the International Human Rights Law field, it also appears within the scope of International Humanitarian Law, as has been shown by the International Criminal Court for the Former Yugoslavia, which has put a prevailing attention on the psychological element in order to determine the existence of the customary norm.[62]

[61] See in that sense, J Roldán Barbero, 'El valor jurídico de las Resoluciones de la Asamblea General de la ONU en la Sentencia Nicaragua contra Estados Unidos de 27-6-86' (1990) XLII *Revista Española de Derecho Internacional* 81, 88–91. It has been argued by human rights-oriented lawyers that the method of customary law in the field of human rights and international humanitarian law differs structurally from the classical positivist customary law method of formation. Giving a greater role to *opinio iuris* than to State practice allows one to ascertain more easily a customary norm in the field of human rights protection through what has been called *the Nicaragua method*, see J Wouters and C Ryngaert, 'The Impact of Human Rights and International Humanitarian Law on the Process of the Formation of Customary International Law', Katholieke Universiteit Leuven, *Institute for International Law Working Paper No 121* (2008). This method not only emphasizes *opinio iuris* over State practice, it also gives a greater role to verbal State practice over physical State practice. According to verbal practice of the States in the field of basic human rights it is difficult to find examples of a *persistent objector*: even States which formulate reservations prima facie contrary to the object and purpose of human rights conventions try to defend the compatibility of their domestic legislation with the standards of the international treaty; for instance, the United Nations Committee on the Elimination of Discrimination against Women has found that Saudi Arabia, despite its general reservation to the Convention, is bound to implement all the provisions of the Convention in its legal order. Moreover, the delegation of Saudi Arabia, even if it has not withdrawn the reservation which undermines the effective application of the Convention, has assured that there is no contradiction in substance between the Convention and Islamic Sharia. See 'Concluding comments of the Committee on the Elimination of Discrimination against Women' (2008) CEDAW/C/SAU/CO/2, paras 8–10. About this topic in a broad perspective see A Pellet, 'Reservations to Treaties and the Integrity of Human Rights' in S Sheeran and Sir N Rodley (eds), *Routledge Handbook of International Human Right Law* (Abingdon, Routledge, 2013) 323–38.

[62] See for instance, Case no IT-95-16-T *Kupreškić et al*, International Criminal Court for the Former Yugoslavia, Judgment of 14 January 2000, para 527: 'As for reprisals against civilians, under customary international law they are prohibited as long as civilians find themselves in the hands of the adversary. With regard to civilians in combat zones, reprisals against them are prohibited by Article 51(6) of the First Additional Protocol of 1977, whereas reprisals against civilian objects are outlawed by Article 52(1) of the same instrument. The question nevertheless arises as to whether these provisions, assuming that they were not declaratory of customary international law, have subsequently been transformed into general rules of international law. In other words, are those States which have not ratified the First Protocol (which include such countries as the U.S., France, India, Indonesia, Israel, Japan, Pakistan and Turkey), nevertheless bound by general rules having the same purport as those two provisions? Admittedly, there does not seem to have emerged recently a body of State practice consistently supporting the proposition that one of the elements of custom, namely *usus or diuturnitas* has taken shape. This is however an area where *opinio iuris sive necessitatis* may play a much greater role than *usus*, as a result of the aforementioned Martens Clause. In the light of the way States and courts have implemented it, this Clause clearly shows that principles of international humanitarian law may emerge through a customary process under the pressure of the demands of humanity or the dictates of public conscience, even where State practice is scant or inconsistent. The other element, in the form of *opinio necessitatis*, crystallising as a result of the imperatives of humanity or public conscience, may turn out to be the decisive element heralding the emergence of a general rule or principle of humanitarian law'. Some authors had pointed out some time before the major role of *opinion iuris* and the minor relevance of State practice for the emergence of customary norms in the field of human rights protection. See in that respect: B Simma, 'International Human Rights and General International Law: a Comparative Analysis' in *Collected Courses of the Academy of European Law (vol IV, Book 2)* (Florence, 1994) 226; also R Huesa Vinaixa, 'El impacto de los regímenes especiales en las fuentes del Derecho internacional' in

Henceforth, it is not ludicrous nor unrealistic to affirm that the EU's juridical conscience—previously analysed throughout its practice in external action—constitutes a valuable argument to support its contribution and impulse as an international organisation for the emergence and creation of legally binding norms in the field of human rights protection of a customary nature. Normativity as brilliantly was exposed by Weil is above all 'a matter of degree', and a rule enshrined in an international treaty for human rights protection, as vague as it might be, does not cease to be a legal norm with extra-conventional effects when it has already crystallised into the *corpus* of customary law.[63] Thus, the obligatory character of most of the rules enshrined in the core United Nations human rights treaties[64] and more precisely their binding nature for the EU—as a subject of international law[65]—are not undermined by the fact that in the face of comparable violations of human rights committed by third countries, the EU has adopted different responses and positions through its external action according to its political margin of appreciation: be it on the scope of CFSP, be it through the suspension or not of trade preferences, the continuation or termination of development cooperation international agreements, or the maintenance of financial assistance in some cases and not in others, etc.[66]

ÁJ Rodrigo and C García Segura (eds), *Unidad y Pluralismo en el Derecho internacional Público y en la Comunidad internacional, Coloquio en Homenaje a Oriol Casanovas, Barcelona, 21–22 de mayo de 2009* (Madrid, Tecnos, 2011) 184–85.

[63] Prosper Weil, 'Towards Relative Normativity in International Law?' n 31 above, 413, 414–16. The author explains the process described as a *veritable revolution in the theory of custom* at p 439: 'Once the conventional norm had been absorbed into the customary norm and deprived of its specificity, all that remained to be done, in the second place, was to submit it to that increasing indeterminacy of the subjects of international obligations which we have seen affecting the customary norm. Thus, through the relay of the customary norm—itself qualified as a general rule or rule of general international law—the conventional norm, too, comes to be imposed on all states, including those who never became parties to the convention in question or never even signed it'. And more precisely at p 440: 'In sum, the intention manifested by a state in regard to a given convention is henceforth of little account: whether it signs or not, becomes party to it or not, enters reservations to such and such a clause or not, it will in any case be bound by any provisions of the convention that are recognized to possess the character of rules of customary or general international law. Thus, while nearly all the distinctions established by the classic law of treaties have finally been more or less blurred, it has at the same time become necessary to differentiate, within each conventional instrument, between those provisions which are subject to the diluted regime of the customary norm and those remaining subject to the strict traditional discipline of classic conventional norms'.

[64] See A D'Amato, 'The Concept of Human Rights in International Law' (1982) 82 *Columbia Law Review* 1110, 1137–38.

[65] *Interpretation of the Agreement of 25 March 1951 between the WHO and Egypt*, Advisory Opinion, ICJ Reports 1980, pp 89–90, para 37: 'International organizations are subjects of international law and, as such, are bound by any obligations incumbent upon them under general rules of international law, under their constitutions or under international agreements to which they are parties'.

[66] The following words may illustrate the aforementioned statement: 'The degree to which new customary rules may be imposed on recalcitrant States will depend, and should depend, on the whole set of relevant circumstances. It would be unwise, as well as futile, to prescribe a categorical rule for so complex and delicate issue': O Schachter, *International Law in Theory and Practice* (Leiden, Martinus Nijhoff, 1991) 14, quoted in J Roldán Barbero, *Ensayo sobre el Derecho Internacional Público* (Almería, Universidad de Almería, 1996) 82.

Fluctuations and inconsistencies that happen within the different instruments of the EU's external action practice, as well as recourse in some cases to measures of negative conditionality while it employs positive measures in others according to a political margin of appreciation, are all factors which do not impair the *opinio iuris* that the EU has shown when identifying as compulsory the basic norms which integrate the human rights *acquis*. This affirmation is perfectly plausible if the scopes of the existence and the efficacy of legal norms are conceptually separated and thereby, the customary norm resists both the political discretion which might exist in its effective application and its open texture which brings it closer to the notion of general principles of international law.

The real motivation behind measures of retaliation or sanctions adopted against a third State responsible for a violation of the international norms protecting human rights is not always legal; frequently legal reasoning is the mask which conceals economic or political reasons.[67] Admittedly, real reasons could remain more or less hidden or visible; the difference in intensity of the reaction of the EU in the face of violations of the international norms concerning human rights protection clearly depends on priorities and interests of every Member State's own foreign policy. Therefore, even if the *opinio iuris* should be analysed in the light of the practice of the EU, a possible subordination of its function to promote human rights protection in the wider world to other goals and less altruistic finalities does not per se deny the EU's contribution to the development of norms of general International Law of a customary character concerning human rights protection.

III. FINAL QUESTIONS: AN *ETERNAL RECURRENCE* OVER THE OLD QUESTIONS OF LEGITIMACY AND EFFICACY. FROM PARTICULARISM TO UNIVERSALISM?

According to Koskenniemi, facing the material inexistence of a representative who embodies the universal, it is not outrageous that the EU, as a regional actor and a particular element of the international system, proclaims itself as a leader and defender of universal values:[68] the EU, from its particular perception and interpretation of general international law, approaches the former with the intention to identify international norms of a customary nature and to promote respect for them by third countries through its external relations. In other words, from its internal conviction and belief that respect for human rights and their *universality and indivisibility* constitute norms of general international law of a customary nature, the EU has dared to pursue a practice which prima facie is consequent

[67] J Ferrer Lloret, *Responsabilidad internacional del Estado y Derechos Humanos* (Madrid, Tecnos, 1998) 152–53 and 177–97.

[68] M Koskenniemi, 'International Law in Europe: Between Tradition and Renewal' (2005) 16 *European Journal of International Law* 113–24.

upon its own perception of the international legal order, a practice which is not exempt from controversy nor from valid grounds.[69]

This desired leadership of the EU as an exponent of the universal reflects its own belief in international law with all its strengths and weaknesses, and is inevitably influenced by its own values and particular vision. Prima facie it seems legitimate that the EU tries to universalise its own tradition of pluralistic democracy and respect for human rights, a tradition that might achieve a global dimension if it succeeds in proving itself as the more satisfactory in competition with the other traditions. This objective clearly entails several risks and responsibilities, the promotion of human rights cannot be an argument used to impose one's own convictions or preferences, with an ethnocentric or solipsistic vision which hides an instrumental and economic vision oriented at generating relations of dependence and domination with third countries. On the opposite side, it is also possible to incur what has been described as *kitsch*,[70] that is, an excessively sentimental vision which may turn the promotion of human rights and democracy into a simply aesthetic trend. It has to be rejected that the EU's external action concerning human rights obeys mainly to altruist motivations. *Realpolitik*, geostrategy, casuistic pragmatism and politicisation are always present. However, it can be maintained that through its external action the EU contributes to reinforcing and identifying respect for human rights and their universality, indivisibility and interdependence as a general principle of international law or even as an emerging or emerged international customary norm. From the most optimistic point of view, the EU's position can be said to be aimed at establishing the pillars of an international legal order which goes beyond the statist function of regulating bilateral rights and obligations of States, creating the multilateral Public International Law of an International Community which locates the human being at the centre of its construction. In the also enthusiastic words of Simma, the establishment of a universal public order with human rights at its centre would entail more profound transformations of the nature of current Public International Law:

> The concept implies the expansion of international law beyond the inter-state sphere, particularly by endowing individuals with international personality, establishing a hierarchy of norms, a value-oriented approach, a certain 'verticalization' of international law, de-emphasizing consent in law-making, introducing international criminal law, by the existence of institutions and procedures for the enforcement of collective interests at the international level—ultimately, the emergence of an international community, perceived as a legal community.[71]

[69] A brief analysis of the ideological split *North-South* and the criticism of *eurocentrism* which faces the discourse and practice of political conditionality can be found in J Roldán Barbero, *Democracia y Derecho Internacional* (Madrid, Civitas, 1994) 77–91.

[70] This expression used by Koskenniemi is borrowed from the Czech writer Milan Kundera from one of the passages of its famous novel *The Unbearable Lightness of Being*, see M Koskenniemi, 'International Law in Europe: Between Tradition and Renewal', 113, 121–24.

[71] B Simma, 'Universality of International Law from the Perspective of a Practitioner' (2009) 20 *European Journal of International Law* 265, 268. This view received sharp criticism by the traditional

This contribution of the EU and its own subordination to International Human Rights Law is a step, incipient as it may be, toward the reaffirmation of the legal and normative element, regarding Public International Law as more than a simple instrument of foreign policy. Not in vain has the EU been characterised as an international player which demands and promotes on the multilateral plane the establishment and consolidation of normative standards that it is prepared to guarantee at a domestic level; while the United States, is often figured as a hard power (not a mere 'herbivore' as the EU is) which is able to venture in a unilateralist manner where Public International Law is a tool at its own service, entailing a weak inner compromise, but for which the United States is able to demand respect with rigorous and coercive mechanisms toward third countries (this characterisation could be at stake after the Syrian episode).[72] Nowadays, neither realist hypothesis nor a naïve altruistic approach suffices to explain the EU's position: its defence of the universality, indivisibility and interdependence of human rights starts with the assumption that their enjoyment is inextricably linked to the establishment of a pluralist democracy with a social dimension. Both of them, human rights and democracy, depend on the stability, security and development in third countries. These factors are widely believed to condition the stability, security and well-being of the EU itself and its Member States, this belief being particularly deep-rooted concerning the immediately neighbouring countries.[73]

This *civilizing* mission of regenerating, reincarnating, and developing democracy, rule of law and human rights on a planetary scale has both an altruist and an egoist component, but the predominance of the latter, as has been pointed out by Morin, is highly likely.[74] Inclination for the universality, indivisibility and interdependence of human rights has its formal justification in the Vienna Declaration

scholarship, because in their view, an attempt to establish a content-based or value-based hierarchy of international norms rather than attending to the process by which international obligations are created could be a misleading appreciation towards what international law is, see P Weil, 'Towards Relative Normativity in International Law?', 413, 425–26.

[72] B de Witte, 'International Law as a Tool for the European Union' (2009) 5 *European Constitutional Law Review* 265–283. The situation of *impasse* Syria is facing since the beginning of 2011, which has turned into a bloody civil war, illustrates what has been described as a *G-Zero World*, a multipolar world where the balance of powers leads to a paralysis of multilateral action or even unilateral action in order, for instance, to stop crimes against humanity: inaction is a consequence of the fact that no single State or coalition of States has the real capacity to provide effectively global goods: see I Bremmer, *Every Nation for Itself, Winners and Losers in a G-Zero World* (Portfolio, Penguin, 2012).

[73] A description of the different means by which the EU tries to promote its holistic view of the so-called *human rights–democracy–rule of law trinity* is found in L Pech, 'Promoting the rule of law abroad: the EU's limited contribution to the shaping of an international understanding of the rule of law' in D Kochenov and F Amtenbrink (eds), *The European Union's Shaping of the International Legal Order* (Cambridge, Cambridge University Press, 2014) 108–29.

[74] E Morin, *Penser l'Europe* (Paris, Gallimard, 1990) 235. The EU's fisheries agreements with Morocco have been argued as illustrations of the primacy of economic interests over human rights in practice, due to the fact that they include the Western Sahara's waters without a clear respect for the right to self-determination of the Saharawi people: see J Soroeta Liceras, 'La posición de la Unión Europea en el conflicto del Sahara Occidental, una muestra palpable (más) de la primacía de sus intereses económicos y políticos sobre la promoción de la democracia y de los derechos humanos' (2009) 34 *Revista de Derecho Comunitario Europeo* 823–64.

and Programme of Action adopted at the World Conference on Human Rights on 5 June 1993, by consensus of the representatives of 171 States: its text reflects the link between democracy and human rights upon which security and development seem also to depend.[75] In consequence, the EU when it identifies International Human Rights Law as customary international law of a general nature, acting with a clear preference for a concrete conception of democracy, contributes to a certain degree to eroding the traditional neutrality of Public International Law regarding the political system of States.[76] In fact, the whole of the UDHR is influenced by the notion of democracy. In particular, its articles 21 and 29.2 illustrate that requirements of a democratic society could be validly wielded as a legitimate objective capable of restrict the scope of some basic human rights.[77] It has been argued that a 'rule of law and pluralistic democracy based system' is not the unique and exclusive model capable of being compatible with International Human Rights Law. Chinese authoritarianism has been described as an appropriate model for shaping international law despite Western scholars' apparent *phobia* of it; according to some scholars it could be an alternative reading of International Human Rights Law which puts more emphasis on local self-goverment and cultural rights with an absence of freedom of expression and in spite of the hegemony of the Communist Party.[78] The EU has a long way to go if it aims at persuading the rest of the world (or at least the vast majority of it) of the self-conviction that its own social model and values are the ones which ensure the higher degree of individual freedom, social justice and equity.

[75] This connection between pluralistic democracy and human rights can be also found in the United Nations General Assembly Resolution 55/2 *United Nations Millennium Declaration* [2002] A/RES/55/2, and in the Report of the Secretary-General Kofi Annan, *In larger freedom: towards development, security and human rights for all* [2005] A/59/2005/Add.3.

[76] European Parliament and Council Regulation (EC) 1889/2006 on establishing a financing instrument for the promotion of democracy and human rights worldwide [2006] OJ L386/1. See J Roldán Barbero, 'Democracia y Derecho Europeo' (1993) 20 *Revista de Instituciones Europeas* 101, 131.

[77] It is often argued that a pluralistic democracy with periodical multiparty elections is not explicitly required in International Human Rights Law, in spite of the fact that it permeates the European public order. As a matter of fact, it is notable that the European Court of Human Rights, when interpreting the provisions of the European Convention on Human Rights, defends a substantial conception of democracy not limited to the formal organisation of periodical elections. Even though the invocation of pluralistic democracy in the framework of the United Nations is more frequent since the end of the Cold War, it has been maintained that a more explicit link between International Human Rights Law and a pluralistic conception of democracy is required. Some objections to the universalisation of the conception of democracy enshrined in the jurisprudence of the European Court of Human Rights are revealed by J Vidmar, 'Multiparty Democracy: International and European Human Rights Law Perspectives' (2010) 23 *Leiden Journal of International Law* 209–40. Its main objection resides in the inexistence of a customary norm of general scope in favour of a concrete model of political participation. However, article 25(b) of the International Covenant on Civil and Political Rights concedes to the EU enough legitimacy and a wide margin of appreciation to promote on a multilateral level its particular conception of democracy: 'Every citizen shall have the right and the opportunity, without any of the distinctions mentioned in article 2 and without unreasonable restrictions:… (b) To vote and to be elected at genuine periodic elections which shall be by universal and equal suffrage and shall be held by secret ballot, guaranteeing the free expression of the will of the electors'.

[78] PCW Chan, 'Human Rights and Democracy with Chinese Characteristics?' (2013) 13 *Human Rights Law Review* 645–89.

Nowadays, the EU's institutions and the traditional democratic institutions of its Member States are facing a serious loss of confidence from European citizens. Xenophobic, populist, nationalist and Europhobic feelings are spreading throughout the Member States, contributing to the erosion of the axiological heritage that liberal democracy does undeniably constitute for Western Europe. This situation, due partially to the various financial and sovereign-debt crises which the Euro Zone has experienced uninterruptedly since 2008, undermines both the credibility and the legitimacy of the EU's discourse on the promotion of human rights and democracy in the wider world, which is underpinned by its external policies. A good start could be the introduction of a more preventive, proactive and effective mechanism to govern Member States' internal situation that the one foreseen in article 7 TEU.[79] Further reflection is also required in order to determine if the EU should accede, not only to the European Convention on Human Rights, but to the main human rights multilateral conventions adopted under the auspices of the United Nations.[80] Following the example of the United Nations Convention on the Rights of Persons with Disabilities to which the EU has already become a party,[81] if this line were to be followed with other international treaties, the EU could perhaps increase the level of credibility of its *civilizing* role towards third countries (and why not its efficacy?), and it would in all likelihood have higher

[79] For instance, Hungarian Prime Minister Mr Viktor Orban has defended openly the possibility of reinstating the death penalty in Hungary during a debate at the plenary session of the European Parliament held on 19 May 2015. The abolition of the capital punishment is precisely one of the main goals that the European Union pursues throughout its external action, see *Bulletin Quotidien Agence Europe*, 11317, 20 May 2015.

[80] Dinstein, following the opinion of the *Institut de droit international* has proposed an interesting method to ascertain the existence and consolidation of a communal *opinio iuris*: successive treaties may imply it through repetition. He finds that a model of successive law-making treaties that reaffirm the customary nature of the initially non-binding UDHR is the *plethora* of treaties that has been concluded both on the global and regional plane in the realm of human rights. Thus, *a contrario* when a particular human right has been included in some treaties while deliberately excluded from others doubts about the existence of a communal *opinio iuris* emerge. As a subject of international law which the EU is, it is undoubtedly bound by the norms which have acquired customary status in the field of human rights and through their reaffirmation in its external relations it contributes to the progressive development of international law, notwithstanding inconsistencies or double standards. This reasoning does not undermine EU's suitability to be subject and explicitly committed beyond customary law to the external mechanisms of supervision of human rights performance existing on the global plane. See Y Dinstein, 'The Interaction between Customary International Law and Treaties' n 56 above*loc. cit.*, 243, 299–303. Of course, the customary nature of each one of the particular provisions of the human rights treaties has to be assessed individually and proved independently on its own merits, as the same author states at p 372.

[81] See Council Decision (EC) 2010/48 concerning the conclusion, by the European Community, of the United Nations Convention on the Rights of Persons with Disabilities [2010] OJ 23/35. In more detail, G De Búrca, 'The EU in the Negotiation of the UN Disability Convention' (2010) 35 *European Law Review* 174–96. An overview about possible motivations of the EU to conclude international agreements in the field of human rights in T Stiegler, 'Reaching for a Calculator or a Mirror? Why the EU Joins International Human Rights Treaties', *EU Diplomacy Papers* 2013/1, College of Europe, Bruges.

legitimacy from an international law point of view if it were subject to the scrutiny of those conventional mechanisms for human rights protection.

Human rights rules enshrined in multilateral global conventions are thus nearer to *jus cogens* than to *jus dispositivum*. However, a severe setback to the envisaged process of the EU's accession to the European Convention on Human Rights has been given by the recent Opinion 2/13 of the European Court of Justice, where the Court has found the draft agreement on the accession to be incompatible with primary law. None of the obstacles raised by the ECJ in this opinion are insurmountable but they oblige the EU to reopen a complex set of negotiations which have already taken more than three years to reach the rejected draft agreement involving the European Union and the Council of Europe Member States.[82]

The EU's role as a promoter of worldwide human rights respect has made it worthy of characterisation as a *normative power*, a *rule generator* and even as a *norm entrepreneur*.[83] Even so the temptation to exaggerate the EU's role as guardian of the universal morality shall be avoided. It shall not be ignored that the influence of the positions of the EU and its Member States in multilateral fora is nowadays clearly decreasing:[84] in the General Assembly of the United Nations during the 1997–98 period the most influential positions concerning human rights issues were those of the United States followed by the EU as a bloc. By contrast, during the 2010–11 period China and Russia have had the main voting coincidence percentage regarding human rights matters. Nowadays, the EU can be said to be the third diplomatic power in that sense, with about a 44 per cent of voting coincidence on their opinions, overcoming the United States influence.[85] Within the

[82] See Opinion 2/13 of 18 December 2014, EU:C:2014:2454. Further comments on this opinion can be read in: Steve Peers, 'The CJEU and the EU's accession to the ECHR: a clear and present danger to human rights protection' (*EU Law Analysis*, 18 December 2014): eulawanalysis.blogspot.com.es/2014/12/the-cjeu-and-eus-accession-to-echr.html; J-P Jacqué, 'Non à l'adhésion à la Convention européenne des droits de l'homme?' (*Droit de l'Union Européenne*, 23 December 2014): www.droit-union-europeenne.be/412337458; L Besselink, 'Acceding to the ECHR notwithstanding the Court of Justice Opinion 2/13' (*Amsterdam Centre for European Law and Governance (ACELG)*, 24 December 2014) acelg.blogactiv.eu/2014/12/24/acceding-to-the-echr-notwithstanding-the-court-of-justice-opinion-213/; and finally, PJ Kuijper, 'Reaction to Leonard Besselink's ACELG Blog' (*ACELG*, 6 January 2015) acelg.blogactiv.eu/2015/01/06/reaction-to-leonard-besselinks%E2%80%99s-acelg-blog/.

[83] See I Manners, 'Normative Power Europe: A contradiction in terms?' (2002) 40 *Journal of Common Market Studies* 235–58; M Cremona, 'The Union as a Global Actor: Roles, Models and Identity' (2004) 41 *Common Market Law Review* 553, 557; and E Herlin-Karnell, 'EU values and the shaping of the international legal context' in D Kochenov and F Amtenbrink (eds), *The European Union's Shaping of the International Legal Order* (Cambridge, Cambridge University Press, 2014) 103–6, respectively. The description of the EU as a *rule generator* reflects its efforts to actively export its own normative *acquis* to the domestic law of third countries.

[84] A broader perspective of analysis about the European Union and Human Rights at the United Nations is contained in Chapter 10 of the present volume by C Pérez Bernárdez, where the EU in the Third Committee of the General Assembly of the United Nations and the EU in the Human Rights Council are examined.

[85] A different question is the internal voting consistency and cohesion of the Member States which has increased clearly in positive terms concerning human rights issues. Nowadays, cohesion of the Member States regarding its positions on human rights matters is about 85 per cent.

United Nations Council of Human Rights the influence of the EU and its Member States can be said to be suffering a similar trajectory. In both cases, the questions which more often divide the sense of the votes of the Member States are related to the conflict between Israel and Palestine.[86] The process of adoption of the Resolution 26/9 of the Human Rights Council could be illustrative of this trend: this resolution on the elaboration of an international instrument, legally binding on transnational corporations and other business enterprises with respect to human rights was adopted with a recorded vote of 20 to 14, with 13 abstentions, the EU Member States being among those who voted against.[87]

An opportunity to correct this trend toward the permanent loss of influence comes with the new enhanced observer status which the EU has recently acquired in the United Nations General Assembly.[88] The EU will need to work to forge new strategic diplomatic partnerships in order to reach general consensus on new human rights problems. Nowadays, besides Russia and China, African and Arab countries are the States which clearly differ more frequently from the EU's Member States in voting.[89] The potential of the Resolutions adopted by consensus in the United Nations General Assembly or within the Human Rights Council should

[86] See inter alia: KE Smith, 'The European Union at the Human Rights Council: Speaking with One Voice but Having Little Influence' (2010) 17 *Journal of European Public Policy* 224–41; R Gowan and F Brantner, *The EU and Human Rights at the UN* (European Council of Foreign Relations, 2011); J Ferrer Lloret, 'La acción exterior de la Unión Europea en el Consejo de Derechos Humanos de Naciones Unidas: luces y sombras de la Política Exterior europea' in A Blanc Altemir, *Las relaciones entre las Naciones Unidas y la Unión Europea: seguridad, cooperación y derechos humanos* (Madrid, Tecnos, 2013) 414–35; and finally in the same collective work, see the contribution of S Salinas Acelga, 'La acción de la Unión Europea en la Asamblea General de las Naciones Unidas: un test de su condición de actor global en materia de derechos humanos' at 436–63.

[87] Human Rights Council Resolution 26/9 *Elaboration of an international legally binding instrument on transnational corporations and other business enterprises with respect to human rights* [2014] A/HRC/RES/26/L.22/Rev.1. The voting results were the following: *In favour:* Algeria, Benin, Burkina Faso, China, Congo, Côte d'Ivoire, Cuba, Ethiopia, India, Indonesia, Kazakhstan, Kenya, Morocco, Namibia, Pakistan, Philippines, Russian Federation, South Africa, Venezuela (Bolivarian Republic of), Vietnam; *Against*: Austria, Czech Republic, Estonia, France, Germany, Ireland, Italy, Japan, Montenegro, Republic of Korea, Romania, the former Yugoslav Republic of Macedonia, United Kingdom, United States of America; *Abstaining:* Argentina, Botswana, Brazil, Chile, Costa Rica, Gabon, Kuwait, Maldives, Mexico, Peru, Saudi Arabia, Sierra Leone, United Arab Emirates.

[88] See United Nations General Assembly Resolution 65/276 *Participation of the European Union in the work of the United Nations* [2011] A/RES/65/276. In that respect, see J Wouters, J Odermatt and T Ramopoulos, 'The Status of the European Union at the United Nations After the General Assembly Resolution of 3 May 2011' (2011) *Global Governance Opinions*, Leuven Centre for Global Governance Studies. As stated in this paper one of the main handicaps the EU shall overcome is that: 'The international community apparently does not conceive the EU as a powerful actor capable of pursuing and achieving its central goals without bending to pressure', p 8.

[89] Sergio Salinas Acelga, 'La acción de la Unión Europea en la Asamblea General de las Naciones Unidas: un test de su condición de actor global en materia de derechos humanos', n 86 above, 449–450.

not be underestimated.[90] Even though to date the EU has not succeeded as an autonomous international actor due mainly to its ties with its own Member States, human rights in the external relations constitute an excellent opportunity (as only a few others, like environment, common trade policy, and monetary policy) where co-existence and complementarity between the Union and its Member States is fundamental. The rising EU prominence due to the increasing external competence it has in this area can only be beneficial and synergic for the Member States, because it is the only way in which their accelerated road to invisibility in human rights matters can be reversed in the global scene.

[90] They constitute a reflection of the attitude of the States,which can provide certain evidence of the existence of *opinio iuris*, essential for the establishment of custom. In further detail, Y Dinstein, 'The Interaction between Customary International Law and Treaties' n 56 above, 243, 303–12.

Part IV

Membership, Representation and Performance of the European Union in International Organisations

9

Brussels Meets Westphalia: The European Union and the United Nations

JAN WOUTERS AND ANNA-LUISE CHANÉ*

Content:

I. INTRODUCTION: THE UN AS A 'EUROPEAN PRIORITY'

AS 'THE WORLD'S most successful case of multilateralism'[1] the European Union (EU or Union) has demonstrated since its early beginnings a commitment to multilateralism as the preferred form of global governance.[2] Yet, it was only with the European Security Strategy (ESS), adopted by the

* Respectively, Full Professor and Jean Monnet Chair *ad personam*, Director, Leuven Centre for Global Governance Studies—Institute for International Law, KU Leuven, Adjunct Professor, Columbia University, Visiting Professor, College of Europe (Bruges), Sciences Po (Paris) and Luiss (Rome); Research Fellow and PhD Candidate, Leuven Centre for Global Governance Studies—Institute for International Law, KU Leuven. The research leading to these results has received funding from the European Commission's Seventh Framework Programme (FP7/2007–2013) under the grant agreement FRAME (project no 320000).

[1] KV Laatikainen and KE Smith (eds), *The European Union at the United Nations: Intersecting Multilateralisms* (Basingstoke, Palgrave Macmillan, 2006) 2.

[2] J Wouters, S de Jong and P De Man, 'The EU's Commitment to Effective Multilateralism in the Field of Security: Theory and Practice' (2010) 29 *Yearbook of European Law* 164, 170.

European Council in December 2003, that the EU endorsed its idiosyncratic concept of 'effective multilateralism' as the central guiding principle of its external action.[3] Recognising that global problems require global solutions, the ESS states that European 'security and prosperity increasingly depend on an effective multilateral system' and proclaims the 'development of a stronger international society, well-functioning international institutions and a rule-based international order' as a European objective.[4] Importantly, the ESS highlights the pivotal role of the United Nations (UN) in the global multilateral order. Recognising the UN Security Council's (UNSC) 'primary responsibility' in the area of international peace and security and the status of the UN Charter as the 'fundamental framework for international relations', the ESS states that '[s]trengthening the United Nations, equipping it to fulfil its responsibilities and to act effectively, is a European priority'.[5] 2003 also saw the publication of a Commission Communication on 'The European Union and the United Nations: The choice of multilateralism'[6] which set out a general strategy for EU-UN cooperation. Again, the Union's commitment to multilateralism as a 'defining principle' of its external action was reiterated, as was the importance of the UN as the 'pivot of the multilateral system'.[7] EU commitment to multilateralism in general and to the UN as its principal forum was taken a step further in the 2008 Report on the implementation of the ESS.[8] By declaring that 'Europe must lead a renewal of the multilateral order', the Union set itself apart from other actors in the multilateral system and took on additional responsibilities, committing itself to the aspiration of assuming a leadership role.[9]

While EU official statements and policy documents have since then contained an abundance of references to the concept of 'effective multilateralism',[10] it was with the entry into force of the Lisbon Treaty that the Union's commitment to multilateralism was considerably strengthened. Through multiple references to the UN and the UN Charter,[11] the Treaty on European Union (TEU), the Treaty on the Functioning of the European Union (TFEU) and the accompanying Protocols

[3] European Council, 'European Security Strategy: A Secure Europe in a Better World', Brussels, 12 December 2003.

[4] Ibid 9.

[5] Ibid.

[6] Communication from the Commission to the Council and the European Parliament, 'The European Union and the United Nations: The choice of multilateralism', COM(2003) 526 final, 10 September 2003.

[7] Ibid 3.

[8] European Council, 'Report on the Implementation of the European Security Strategy—Providing Security in a Changing World', Brussels, 11 December 2008, S407/08.

[9] Ibid 2.

[10] See for an analysis of the 'effectiveness' component of the concept Wouters, de Jong and De Man (n 2 above).

[11] TEU arts 3(5), 21(1) and(2)(c), 34(2), 42(1) and (7) TEU, 7th recital of the preamble of the TFEU, TFEU arts 208(2), 214(7), 220(1), 3rd and 8th recital of the preamble, as well as Art 1(b) of Protocol No 10 on permanent structured cooperation, Declaration No 13 concerning CFSP, Declaration No 14 concerning CFSP; cf J Wouters, A-L Chané, J Odermatt and T Ramopoulos, 'Improving the EU's Status in the UN and the UN System: An Objective Without a Strategy?' in C Kaddous (ed), *The European Union in International Organisations and Global Governance* (Oxford, Hart Publishing, 2015).

and Declarations elevated the principle of multilateralism to the rank of primary law and enshrined the UN framework as the guide and benchmark of EU external action. Of particular relevance is Article 3(5) TEU which defines the 'respect for the principles of the United Nations Charter' as one of the foreign policy goals of the EU. Article 21 TEU provides additional detail, stating that the Union 'shall promote multilateral solutions to common problems, in particular in the framework of the United Nations' and affirming the promotion of an 'international system based on stronger multilateral cooperation and good global governance' as an objective of the Union's foreign policy. Other TEU and TFEU provisions oblige the EU institutions to comply with the commitments taken on in the UN system when implementing EU policies, and to cooperate with relevant UN bodies.[12]

Although the UN, as the paramount institution of multilateral global governance, has been recognised as an organisation which the EU seeks to support, with which it aspires to cooperate and through which it intends to pursue its policy objectives,[13] the Union's engagement with the UN has in practice been fraught with difficulties. The EU, as a regional international organisation with strong supranational features, has been faced with the challenges of multilateral diplomacy in a predominantly state-centric global institution. The acquisition of participatory rights in various UN bodies required an investment of considerable diplomatic and political capital, and the implementation of the obtained rights frequently led to additional controversies. Despite its considerable economic and political clout, the EU has not—yet—been able to assume a leadership role in the UN framework. It frequently finds itself in a minority position, failing not only to build cross-regional coalitions but also to garner support among its close allies for its positions and initiatives. Among the culprits identified in recent scholarship are a lack of cohesion, the unclear division of external competences, as well as the time-consuming and inflexible internal coordination process.

The Lisbon Treaty attempted to remedy some of these shortcomings through extensive institutional reforms, including in particular the creation of the office of the multi-hatted High Representative of the Union for Foreign Affairs and Security Policy and Vice-President of the European Commission (HR/VP) and the establishment of the European External Action Service (EEAS), but also by creating the office of a permanent President of the European Council and by limiting the role of the rotating Council Presidency. While the new external relations architecture of the EU has led to noticeable improvements in terms of continuity and effectiveness of the Union's engagement with the UN, considerable challenges still remain.

This chapter seeks to provide an overview of the legal basis for EU participation at the UN and the various forms that this participation can take. It addresses issues of EU internal coordination and external representation at the UN, takes a closer

[12] See eg TFEU arts 208(2), 214(7), 220(1).

[13] Cf the three chapters of the Commission Communication 'The European Union and the United Nations: The choice of multilateralism' (n 6 above).

look at the practical EU-UN cooperation on the ground, and highlights the ensuing challenges and opportunities.

II. LEGAL BASIS FOR EU ENGAGEMENT WITH THE UN

The status of the EU in the UN and the UN system is determined by both the Union's internal division of powers with the Member States, as incorporated in the TEU and the TFEU, and by the constituent treaties (including the UN Charter), resolutions, rules of procedure and other instruments that form the legal framework of the UN and the UN system. EU participation is conditioned on (1) the existence of a legal instrument (eg resolution, exchange of letters or regional economic integration organisation (REIO) clause)[14] allowing for the participation of the EU in (2) a UN body whose mandate falls into an area of EU competence. The legal framework of the respective UN body additionally determines the specific arrangement of EU participation and the associated rights and duties.

A. EU Legal Framework

The TFEU devotes a separate title to the 'Union's relations with international organisations'.[15] Article 220(1) TFEU provides that the 'Union shall establish all appropriate forms of cooperation with the organs of the United Nations and its specialised agencies'. From the perspective of its own constitutional framework, the Union thus has the power and obligation to establish and maintain contacts with the UN and the UN system and to participate in their work. Similar provisions on cooperation with international organisations exist for a variety of different policy areas, eg Article 191(4) TFEU (environment), Article 211 TFEU (development cooperation) and Article 212(3) TFEU (economic, financial and technical cooperation). With regard to the cooperation with the UN and the UN system, however, Article 220(1) TFEU may be said to constitute a *lex specialis*.[16] It should be noted that 'cooperation' within the meaning of these provisions does

[14] EU participation in UN bodies can be governed by a variety of legal instruments, see only UNGA Res 65/276 (3 May 2011) UN Doc A/RES/65/276 granting the EU enhanced observer rights in the UNGA and certain subsidiary bodies; Exchange of letters of 21 22 December 1989 between the European Commission and the International Labour Organization [1989] OJ C 24/8, renewed by an exchange of letters of 14 May 2001 [2001] OJ C165/23, concerning the EU's observer status in the ILO; or FAO Constitution art II(3) which contains a so-called REIO clause, allowing for the membership of an international organisation.

[15] TFEU, Title VI, arts 220–221.

[16] Kirsten Schmalenbach in Christian Calliess and Matthias Ruffert (eds), *EUV/AEUV: Das Verfassungsrecht der Europäischen Union mit Europäischer Grundrechtecharta*, 4th edn (München, Beck, 2011) TFEU art 211 (para 3), art 212 (para 13); Rudolf Streinz and Tobias Kruis in Rudolf Streinz (ed), *EUV/AEUV: Vertrag über die Europäische Union und Vertrag über die Arbeitsweise der Europäischen Union*, 2nd edn (München, Beck, 2012) TFEU art 211 (para 2), art 212 (para 22).

not necessarily include the right to obtain or even request membership of a UN body, given that this would presuppose the conclusion of an international agreement in accordance with the requirements and the procedure of Articles 216 and 218 TFEU.[17]

While EU primary law does not contain a provision explicitly granting the Union a general competence to acquire membership of an international organisation,[18] such a competence is widely recognised, based on an opinion of the European Court of Justice (ECJ or Court). In Opinion 1/76 the ECJ affirmed the Community's power to set up an international institution and to provide it with decision-making power.[19] This reasoning was implicitly confirmed almost two decades later in the ECJ's Opinion 1/94, which dealt with the Communities' participation in the World Trade Organization (WTO), of which the EU is a founding member. As the Court expressly recognised the Union's power to establish a new international organisation, it has been concluded *a majore ad minus* that the EU also has the power to accede to an already existing organisation. Membership in an international organisation requires the conclusion of an international agreement according to the requirements and procedure outlined in Articles 216 and 218 TFEU. Article 216(1) TFEU provides that the Union may conclude agreements with international organisations in four cases: (1) where the Treaties so provide, (2) where the conclusion of an agreement is necessary in order to achieve an objective referred to in the Treaties, (3) where this is provided for in a legally binding Union act or (4) where this is likely to affect common rules or alter their scope.[20] While numbers one and three refer to cases in which an express competence exists, numbers two and four refer to implied competences. The EU may thus conclude international agreements whenever this is necessary to attain a Treaty objective, as well as in all those areas where it holds exclusive or shared internal competences.

As Hoffmeister has stated, '[f]rom a legal perspective, the case for a formal status of the European Union in multilateral fora is strongest in policy areas subject to exclusive competence of the European Community'.[21] But also in those areas of

[17] Schmalenbach (n 16 above) art 220 (para 7); Juliane Kokott in Rudolf Streinz (ed), *EUV/AEUV: Vertrag über die Europäische Union und Vertrag über die Arbeitsweise der Europäischen Union*, 2nd edn (München, Beck, 2012) TFEU art 220 (para 35).

[18] P Eeckhout, *EU External Relations Law*, 2nd edn (Oxford, OUP, 2011) 222.

[19] Opinion 1/76 of 26 April 1977 (*Draft Agreement establishing a European laying-up fund for inland waterway vessels*) [1987] ECR 741, para 5; implicitly confirmed by Opinion 1/94 of 15 November 1994 (*World Trade Organization*) [1994] ECR I-5267.

[20] Note that principles 2 and 4 were developed in ECJ case law and only later codified in TFEU art 216(1), see Case 22/70 *Commission v Council* (*European Agreement on Road Transport*) [1971] ECR 263; Opinion 1/76 *Draft Agreement establishing a European laying-up fund for inland waterway vessels* [1977] ECR 741.

[21] F Hoffmeister, 'Outsider or Frontrunner? Recent Developments Under International and European Law on the Status of the European Union in International Organizations and Treaty Bodies' (2007) 44 *Common Market Law Review* 41, 42; see also M Emerson, R Balfour, T Corthaut, J Wouters, P Kaczynski and T Renard, '*Upgrading the EU's Role as Global Actor: Institutions, Law and the Restructuring of European Diplomacy*', Centre for European Policy Studies (CEPS), Egmont—The Royal Institute for International Relations, European Policy Centre (EPC), Leuven Centre for Global Governance

shared EU-Member States competences, in which the EU has made extensive use of its competences, a strong argument for EU participation in an international organisation can be made. The Union's membership in the Food and Agriculture Organization (FAO) and in the Codex Alimentarius Commission, for example, corresponds to the extensive use of its shared competences in the field of agricultural policy (Article 4(2)(d) TFEU). Its full participant status in Conferences concerning the issues of fisheries and development cooperation are in line with the corresponding shared and 'parallel' competences provided for in Article 4(2)(d) and 4(4) TFEU.[22] Nevertheless, strong internal competences do not necessarily correspond to strong participatory rights. The International Labour Organization (ILO) is considered as one of the examples where the Union's weak (observer) status is insufficient to ensure the effective exercise of its wide-reaching competences with regard to employment policy. Similarly, the European Commission (not even the EU as such) only has observer status in the International Maritime Organization (IMO) and the EU only has an ad hoc observer status in the International Civil Aviation Organization (ICAO) despite its considerable competences in the field of both maritime and air transport (Article 4(2)(g) TFEU) and the extensive use thereof.

While EU law thus grants the Union the competence to obtain observer or even full member status in the UN system, depending on whether the field of activity of a given UN body corresponds to the Union's internal division of competences with its Member States, the actual acquisition of such a status depends on the institutional framework of the respective UN forum.

B. UN Legal Framework

The UN legal framework is the second decisive factor which determines the possibility and extent of EU engagement in the organisation. The UN remains a predominantly state-oriented institution, and therefore a challenging environment for EU foreign policy and diplomacy. Only a small minority of UN bodies allow other international organisations to join as full members. The vast majority either limit their participation to narrow observer rights or exclude any formal participation at all. In line with its commitment to effective multilateralism and in order

Studies, University of Leuven, 2011, p 4; and J Wouters, J Odermatt and T Ramopoulos, 'The EU in the World of International Organizations: Diplomatic Aspirations, Legal Hurdles and Political Realities' in M Smith, S Keukeleire and S Vanhoonacker (eds), *The Diplomatic System of the European Union: Evolution, Change and Challenges* (London, Routledge, 2015).

[22] See for example the EU's full participant status at the 1992 UN Conference on Environment and Development (Rio Conference), the 1994 International Conference on Population and Development, the 1995 World Summit for Social Development, the 2001 Third UN Conference on the Least Developed Countries, the 2002 World Summit on Sustainable Development or the 1995 UN Conference on Straddling Fish Stocks and Highly Migratory Fish Stocks: J Wouters, F Hoffmeister and T Ruys (eds), *The United Nations and the European Union: An Ever Stronger Partnership* (The Hague, TMC Asser Press, 2006) annex.

to safeguard the exercise of its competences at the international level, the Union has continuously sought to ensure a strong presence in the UN. In its 2003 Communication 'The European Union and the United Nations: The Choice of Multilateralism', the Commission declared that the Community 'should be given the possibility to participate fully in the work of UN bodies where matters of Community competence are concerned, and Member States should contribute effectively towards this'.[23] Full membership was regarded as the preferred status and ultimate goal. However, in reality the EU's efforts for status enhancement have only yielded slow and partial successes, and have met considerable obstacles, both external and with the EU's own Member States. European Commission President Barroso and Vice-President Ashton proposed a far less ambitious policy in their 2012 'Strategy for the progressive improvement of the EU status in international organisations and other fora in line with the objectives of the Treaty of Lisbon'.[24] While this strategy still held onto the aim of an 'improvement of the EU status and its alignment with the objectives of the EU Treaties', it avoided any endorsement of concrete negotiation goals.[25] So far, as far as the UN system is concerned, the EU only holds member status in the FAO and in the Codex Alimentarius Commission. It has observer status in most UN bodies, and acquired enhanced participation rights in the UNGA in 2011. In a number of bodies the EU is nevertheless still not formally represented, most importantly in the UNSC.

i. Member Status

Article 4(1) UN Charter, which states that '[m]embership in the United Nations is open to all other peace-loving *states*' (emphasis added) is generally understood to limit membership in the main organisation to states only, thereby prohibiting the accession of other international actors, such as the EU.[26] However, it does obviously not bar the multitude of bodies and fora in the UN system from including provisions in their respective governing instruments which allow for membership.

The FAO was the first and is so far the only UN Specialised Agency that has amended its Constitution in order to allow for the accession of the EU (then still the European Economic Community, EEC). In light of the EEC's wide-reaching agricultural competences, first contacts between both organisations were established as early as the 1950s.[27] The EEC started to participate as an observer in the meetings of the FAO, acquired enhanced participation rights in 1970 and finally

[23] Communication from the Commission to the Council and the European Parliament—The European Union and the United Nations: The choice of multilateralism, COM(2003) 526 final, 23.

[24] Communication to the Commission from the President in Agreement with Vice-President Ashton—Strategy for the progressive improvement of the EU status in international organisations and other fora in line with the objectives of the Treaty of Lisbon, C(2012) 9420 final, 20 December 2012, on file with the authors.

[25] See for a detailed analysis of the Barroso-Ashton Strategy, Wouters, Chané, Odermatt and Ramopoulos (n 11 above).

[26] Hoffmeister (n 21 above) 41.

[27] Wouters, Chané, Odermatt and Ramopoulos (n 11 above).

obtained membership status in 1991, after the FAO Conference had amended the FAO Constitution to include a REIO clause.[28] As a 'Member Organization',[29] the EU enjoys largely the same participation rights as Member States, including the right to submit proposals and to vote. Nevertheless, there remain a few important exceptions, which render its status inferior to that held by states. In particular, the EU does not have the right to participate in certain restricted committees[30] and the committees responsible for the internal working of the conference; it does not have voting rights for elective places[31] and budget matters;[32] and it may not hold office in the Conference, the Council and their subsidiary bodies.[33]

In 2003 the EC also gained member status in the Codex Alimentarius Commission, a subsidiary body of the FAO and the World Health Organization (WHO). The Union's participation rights there are even weaker than in the FAO, given that the determination of a quorum, and thereby the Union's voting power, depends on the number of EU Member States which are present.[34] The EU may therefore not vote on behalf of all its Member States but only on behalf of those which attend the session. As Hoffmeister has noted, this is a 'legally unsatisfactory arrangement … because Member States vested competence in the Community by concluding the EC Treaty: they do not grant ad hoc "empowerments" through their presence'.[35]

Although the 1991 amendment of the FAO Constitution was at that time expected to prompt other UN bodies to follow suit, so far there have been no similar developments in the UN framework, with the exception of the Codex Alimentarius Commission (see below).

ii. Observer Status

The EU has observer status in a considerable number of UN bodies. Among them are the UNGA[36] and its programmes and funds, the Economic and Social Council (ECOSOC) and its functional and regional commissions,[37] specialised agencies, such as the ILO,[38] the United Nations Educational, Scientific and Cultural Organization (UNESCO), the WHO, as well as other bodies such as the International

[28] Ibid.

[29] FAO Constitution art II(3).

[30] Programme Committee, Finance Committee, Committee on Constitutional and Legal Matters, FAO Constitution art II(9), FAO General Rules, r XLVI.

[31] FAO General Rules, r XLV(2).

[32] FAO Constitution art XVIII(6).

[33] FAO Constitution art II(9); FAO General Rules, rr XLIII(3), XLIV.

[34] Rules of Procedure of the Codex Alimentarius Commission, r II(8).

[35] Hoffmeister (n 21 above) 44.

[36] The EU has held observer status in the UNGA since 1974, see UNGA Res 3208 (XXIX) (11 October 1974).

[37] With regard to the regional commissions the Union's observer status is subject to invitation, Wouters, Hoffmeister and Ruys (n 22 above) 403.

[38] Exchange of letters of 21 and 22 December 1989 between the European Commission and the International Labour Organization [1989] OJ C24/8, renewed by an exchange of letters of 14 May 2001 [2001] OJ C165/23.

Atomic Energy Agency (IAEA).[39] While the participation rights of observers can vary, they usually include the right to attend (formal) meetings and the right to speak. They generally exclude the right to vote, to raise points of order and to submit candidates. Observers are usually seated apart from the Member States. They may typically speak only after all the Member States have spoken and are allocated shorter speaking time slots than the Member States.[40]

Given that these limited participation rights may conflict with the Union's effective exercise of those competences that have been conferred on it by its Member States, the EU has sought to improve its observer status by turning it into a full membership or by enhancing it with additional rights. One of the most notable examples is the 2011 'upgrade' of the Union's observer status in the UNGA, which aimed to align the Union's representation in the UNGA with its changed system of external representation after the entry into force of the Lisbon Treaty. In particular, the EU sought the opportunity to participate in its own right instead of having to rely on the rotating Council Presidency. A first draft resolution was introduced in the UNGA in September 2010 but it failed to be adopted.[41] Even some of the Union's traditional allies, such as Australia, Canada and New Zealand, did not support the Union's proposal, thus contributing to the EU's 'shambolic defeat'.[42] After increased outreach and substantive amendments, UNGA Resolution 65/276 was eventually adopted on 3 May 2011. Although the final Resolution had been watered down, the EU achieved its core goal, the right to be represented through its own officials. Its enhanced participation rights include:

1. To be inscribed on the list of speakers among representatives of major groups, in order to make interventions;
2. To participate in the general debate of the UNGA;
3. To have its relevant communications circulated directly, and without intermediary, as documents of the Assembly, meeting or conference;
4. To present proposals and amendments orally;
5. To exercise the right of reply.[43]

[39] Wouters, Hoffmeister and Ruys (n 22 above) annex.

[40] Cf the speaking time arrangements of the HRC, where observers are allocated 1-2 minutes less speaking time than Member States, depending on the type of discussion, HRC, 'Information note for ease of reference on speaking time arrangements', 24th session, 9–27 September 2013.

[41] The Union's diplomatic debacle around its UNGA status upgrade has received considerable scholarly attention, see for example E Brewer, 'The Participation of the European Union in the Work of the United Nations: Evolving to Reflect the New Realities of Regional Organizations' (2012) 9 *International Organizations Law Review* 181; G De Baere and E Paasivirta, 'Identity and Difference: The EU and the UN as Part of Each Other' in H De Waele and J-J Kuipers (eds), *The Emergence of the European Union's International Identity—Views from the Global Arena* (Leiden, Brill, 2013) 21–42; J Wouters, J Odermatt and T Ramopoulos, 'The Status of the European Union at the United Nations General Assembly' in I Govaere, E Lannon, P Van Elsuwege and S Adam (eds), *The European Union in the World: Liber Amicorum Professor Marc Maresceau* (Leiden, Brill, 2014) 211–23.

[42] P Luif, quoted in J Dempsey, 'For Europe, a Challenge to Make Its Voice Resonate' (*The New York Times*, 13 October 2010): www.nytimes.com/2010/10/14/world/europe/14iht-letter.html?_r=3&, accessed 24 June 2014.

[43] UNGA Res 65/276 (3 May 2011) UN Doc A/RES/65/276 para 1.

The EU explicitly does not have the right to vote, to co-sponsor draft resolutions or decisions, or to submit candidates.[44]

The practical implementation of these rights subsequently entailed considerable and unexpected difficulties.[45] Some UN Member States, most vocally the CARICOM group, advocated a narrow interpretation of UNGA Resolution 65/276, fearing an erosion of the intergovernmental character of the body and the principle of sovereign equality of the UN Member States. In particular the right 'to be inscribed on the list of speakers *among representatives of major groups*' (emphasis added) triggered controversies about whether major groups represented by states should take preference. Another dispute focused on the right to deliver an explanation of vote, which some considered to be only assigned to those actors that also had a right to vote. Most of those issues have been resolved in subsequent sessions.[46] Nevertheless, the realisation that the successful implementation of formally obtained rights cannot be taken for granted prompted President Barroso and Vice-President Ashton to call for continued efforts to ensure the full implementation of the Resolution.[47]

iii. No Formal Status

The UN Security Council (UNSC) is one of the few UN bodies in which the EU holds no formal status. Instead, the EU has to rely on those of its Member States that have either a permanent seat (France and the United Kingdom) or have been elected as temporary Council members (on average two other EU Member States).[48] Aiming to safeguard EU representation even in the absence of formal presence, Article 34(2) TEU provides that the EU Member States have the duty to represent the positions and the interests of the Union.[49] The Treaty also strengthened the role of the HR/VP in the UNSC, obliging Member States to request that the HR/VP be invited to a meeting whenever a Union position on a UNSC agenda item exists.[50] Even in the absence of membership or observer status, the HR/VP—in most cases, the EU Ambassador—has regularly been able to represent the EU's position in the UNSC.[51] Nevertheless, there is still no 'strong collective

[44] Ibid, annex para 3.

[45] See for more detail Wouters, Chané, Odermatt and Ramopoulos (n 11 above).

[46] J Wouters and others, 'Organisation and Functioning of the European External Action Service: Achievements, Challenges and Opportunities', Study for the European Parliament, Directorate-General for External Policies of the Union, EXPO/B/AFET/2012/07, February 2013, p 79.

[47] Communication to the Commission from the President in Agreement with Vice-President Ashton—Strategy for the progressive improvement of the EU status in international organisations and other fora in line with the objectives of the Treaty of Lisbon, C(2012) 9420 final, 20 December 2012.

[48] S Gstoehl, '"Patchwork Power" Europe: The EU's Representation in International Institutions' (2009) 14 *European Foreign Affairs Review* 385, 400.

[49] TEU art 34(2).

[50] Ibid.

[51] See for a list of statements: European Union Delegation to the United Nations—New York, 'EU Statements at the UN Security Council': http://eu-un.europa.eu/security-council/, accessed 5 May 2016.

EU presence' in the UNSC.[52] Proposals for a single EU seat on the UNSC have so far not found sufficient political support to present a realistic alternative. While they have been endorsed by various EU institutions and actors, in particular the EP, the former High Representative Javier Solana and the former Commissioner for External Relations and the European Neighbourhood Policy, Benita Ferrero-Waldner, the United Kingdom and France have been concerned to maintain their strong position at the UNSC.[53]

Similarly, neither the EU nor the Eurozone hold formal status in the International Monetary Fund (IMF). Despite the Union's wide-ranging exclusive and shared competences on matters covered by the mandate of the IMF (with regard to those EU Member States that are also members of the Eurozone), it has to rely on representation through its Member States. Against this background, and in line with Article 138(2) TFEU the Commission presented a proposal for a Council Decision aiming to establish unified representation of the Eurozone in the IMF in October 2015.[54] The proposal foresees a number of steps in order to align the Union's internal competences with its participation rights, including the attainment of observer rights for the Eurozone and the strengthening of the internal coordination process.

III. EXTERNAL REPRESENTATION AND INTERNAL COORDINATION

As a Union of 28 Member States the EU requires sophisticated internal coordination mechanisms in order to ensure that all EU and Member States representatives at the UN 'speak with one voice'. In addition, a complex framework of Treaty provisions and internal arrangements governs the external representation of the EU in the various UN bodies.

A. External Representation

Before the entry into force of the Lisbon Treaty, the external representation of the Union was ensured by the European Commission concerning 'first pillar' (ie Community) issues, and by the Member State holding the rotating Council Presidency concerning all other issues. The advantage of this solution was that the Council Presidency as a UN Member State easily fitted within the state-centric structure of the UN. It could smoothly and prominently deliver presidential statements for the EU in speaking slots reserved for states, circulate documents and negotiate

[52] S Blavoukos and D Bourantonis, 'The EU's Performance in the United Nations Security Council' (2011) 33 *Journal of European Integration* 731, 733.

[53] Ibid 737 et seq.

[54] European Commission, 'Proposal for a Council Decision laying down measures in view of progressively establishing unified representation of the euro area in the International Monetary Fund', 21 October 2015, COM(2015) 603 final.

with third countries. The downside was, however, a lack of stability due to the six-monthly rotation. Third states criticised the lack of transparency of the external representation, due to the ever changing 'hats'. Moreover, logistical issues ensued and EU representation appeared chaotic when Commission and Presidency representatives had to switch seats during meetings depending on the agenda item.[55]

The Lisbon Treaty not only abolished the three-pillar structure of the EU, it also sought to increase the coherence and unity of the Union's external representation through a series of institutional reforms. In areas of EU competence—which includes the CFSP as a special competence as well as non-CFSP matters where the Union has exclusive competence or exercised its shared competences—the Union is now solely represented through its own officials. Depending on the subject-matter and on the level of the meeting, the responsibility for the Union's external representation falls either upon the Commission, the President of the European Council, the HR/VP or the EEAS. Member States remain competent to conduct their own foreign policy, albeit in line with the principle of sincere cooperation (Article 4(3) TEU). Their competences comprise both areas in which no powers have been conferred to the EU, as well as those areas of shared EU-Member States competences where the EU has not exercised its competences. Whenever an issue falls within both an area of EU and of national competence, the responsible representative will be determined based on whether or not the 'thrust'[56] or the 'preponderance'[57] of the issue lies within an area of EU competence.

The Commission represents the Union in all areas of EU competence that do not fall under the CFSP,[58] with the President of the Commission assuming the role of EU representative at summit level.[59] Concerning issues that fall under the

[55] De Baere and Paasivirta (n 41 above) 25.

[56] Cf Arrangement concerning preparation for the meetings of the FAO as well as interventions and voting, 18 December 1991, unpublished, reproduced in R Frid, *The Relations between the EC and international organizations—Legal Theory and Practice* (The Hague, Kluwer, 1995) annex VI, art 2.3. The 1991 Arrangement was updated in 1992 and 1995. In 2013 the Commission proposed to revise the existing Arrangements. The Draft Arrangement provides that an 'entrusted Member State' will deliver common statements whenever the 'common position primarily contains elements not covered by an EU position', the assessment of which will be based on 'the main expected impact of the policy pursued within the FAO on the EU or on its Member States', COM(2013) 333 final, annex 2, para 3.3. This proposal was met with criticism in the Council, where a majority of delegations opted for maintaining the current division of competences, Presidency Non-Paper, Doc No 5337/14.

[57] Cf Code of Conduct between the Council, the Member States and the Commission on the UNESCO negotiations on the draft Convention on the protection of the diversity of cultural contents and artistic expressions, Doc No 5768/05, para 3; Code of Conduct between the Council, the Member States and the Commission for the participation of the Community and its Member States in meetings regarding the implementation of the Convention on the Protection and Promotion of the Diversity of Cultural Expressions, Doc No 5914/07, para 4; Code of Conduct between the Council, the Member States and the Commission setting out internal arrangements for the implementation by and representation of the European Union relating to the United Nations Convention on the Rights of Persons with Disabilities [2010] OJ C340/11, art 8.

[58] TEU art 17(1), which also makes exception for 'other cases provided for in the Treaties', by which external representation in monetary matters seems to be meant.

[59] S Gstoehl, 'EU Diplomacy After Lisbon: More Effective Multilateralism?' (2011) 17 *Brown Journal of World Affairs* 181, 186.

CFSP, the tasks of external representation are divided between the HR/VP and the President of the European Council.[60] The latter only plays a limited role in this context. As Article 15(6) TEU provides, the President of the European Council ensures the external representation 'at his level and in that capacity' and 'without prejudice to the powers of the High Representative'. His tasks are therefore mainly reduced to representing the Union at the level of Heads of State or Government, for example during the 'High Level' General Debate at the beginning of each year's ordinary session of the UNGA.[61] The HR/VP on the other hand bears the main responsibility of conducting the CFSP. This includes not only the responsibility to drive forward the development of this policy, but also to lead the political dialogue with third countries and to represent the Union in international organisations and at international conferences. Nevertheless, the division of work between the President of the European Council and the HR/VP is not clearly determined.[62] Article 15(6) TEU deliberately contains a vague formulation. The respective roles will therefore be flexibly shaped through both cooperation and coordination, but potentially also through power plays and turf battles between the respective office-holders. The Union Delegations are responsible for the representation of the Union at the UN.[63] EU Delegations to UN bodies exist in Geneva (established in 1961), New York (1964), Paris (1964), Nairobi (1976), Vienna (1979) and Rome (1993).[64] They cover CFSP and non-CFSP matters[65] and lend assistance to the HR/VP, the President of the European Council, the President of the Commission, and the Commission at the summit level as well as in other settings.[66] The EEAS also supports and cooperates with the diplomatic services of the EU Member States in order to ensure the consistency of the Union's external action.[67] The EU Member States are lastly responsible for representing Union positions whenever the EU's participatory rights are weak.[68] While the rotating Council Presidency lost its formal role as an external representative of the Union under the Lisbon Treaty, it is in practice still frequently relied upon to speak 'on behalf of the EU'.[69]

[60] TEU arts 15(6), 27(2).

[61] G Edwards, 'The EU's foreign policy and the search for effect' (2013) 27 *International Relations* 276, 281; Gstoehl (n 59 above) 186; the President of the European Union has addressed the UNGA during each session since 2011, cf for the most recent address 'Address by President Donald Tusk at the 70th UN General Assembly debate', New York, 29 September 2015: www.consilium.europa.eu/press-releases-pdf/2015/9/40802202963_en.pdf, accessed 23 June 2016.

[62] X Jin and M O Hosli, 'Pre- and Post-Lisbon: European Union Voting in the United Nations General Assembly' (2013) 36 *West European Politics* 1274, 1278.

[63] TFEU art 221(1).

[64] E Drieskens, 'What's in a Name? Challenges to the Creation of EU Delegations' (2012) 7 *The Hague Journal of Diplomacy* 51, 53.

[65] Gstoehl (n 59 above) 186.

[66] Council Decision 2010/427/EU of 26 July 2010 establishing the organisation and functioning of the European External Action Service [2010] OJ L201/30, art 2.

[67] Ibid art 3(1).

[68] Cf ECJ, Opinion 2/91 of 19 March 1993 (*Internation Labour Organization*) [1993] ECR I-1061 para 5; ECJ, Case C-45/07 *Commission v Greece* [2009] ECR I-701 para 31.

[69] See only the HRC, where the rotating Council Presidency still frequently speaks on behalf of the EU: J Wouters and K Meuwissen, 'The European Union at the UN Human Rights Council: Multilateral Human Rights Protection Coming of Age?' (2014) 2 *European Journal of Human Rights* 135, 161.

B. Internal Coordination

Internal coordination of the Union's positions in UN fora serves a variety of purposes, all of which contribute to the larger goal of increasing the effectiveness and the impact of the external action of the EU. Primarily, coordination between the various EU Member States and EU institutions is necessary to ensure that all actors 'speak with one voice' and vote consistently. Secondly, in those fora where the EU has no official status, coordination takes place in order to ensure that the positions taken by Member States are not only consistent, but also in line with existing EU positions. In addition, whenever both the EU and its Member States have member status in a UN body (mixity), coordination is necessary to determine who will exercise the voting and speaking rights with regard to each individual agenda item.[70]

Article 4(3) TEU commits the EU Member States to the principle of sincere cooperation, which, as one of the fundamental principles of EU law, permeates all policy areas and all state functions. In the area of external action, it binds the Member States to refrain from any act that might weaken the negotiating position of the Union.[71] In the area of CFSP, Article 24(3) TEU provides more specifically that the 'Member States shall support the Union's external and security policy actively and unreservedly in a spirit of loyalty and mutual solidarity and shall comply with the Union's action in this area'. The commitment to a coherent Union policy limits the freedom of the EU Member States to take unilateral action and presupposes some degree of internal coordination. This duty of coordination is elevated to a legal obligation through Article 34(1) TEU, which states that 'Member States shall coordinate their action in international organisations and at international conferences. They shall uphold the Union's positions in such forums'. With regard to the UNSC, where the EU has no formal status and not all EU Member States are present, Article 34(2) TEU obliges the participating Member States to 'concert', to 'defend the positions and the interests of the Union' and to keep the other EU Member States and the HR/VP 'fully informed'.

In practice these legal obligations are translated into a complex coordination process, spread over multiple venues, bodies and channels. Generally, the process can be divided into the formulation of the general strategies in Brussels, and the fine-tuning of those positions on the ground in New York, Geneva, Rome or other meeting places of UN bodies. In Brussels, the Council of the European Union develops the priorities and positions of the Union at the UN. It is assisted by the Political and Security Committee (PSC), which serves as the main contact point for the EU Delegation in New York with regard to CFSP and CSDP

[70] In case of mixity, member rights can generally only be exercised on an alternative basis by either the EU or its Member States, see eg FAO Constitution art II(8).

[71] W Kahl in C Calliess and M Ruffert (eds), *EUV/AEUV: Das Verfassungsrecht der Europäischen Union mit Europäischer Grundrechtecharta*, 4th edn (München, Beck, 2011) TEU art 4 (para 100).

issues.[72] Nevertheless, by far the largest part of the work is done in the Council's multiple working groups and committees, many of which have direct relevance for EU participation in the UN.[73] Of primary importance is the United Nations Working Party (CONUN) whose responsibilities include, among others, monitoring the work of the UN, coordinating candidatures for high-level UN posts and leading the coordination process with regard to UN conferences.[74] CONUN plays a 'supervising role'[75] with regard to UN matters dealt with by the various thematic and geographic Council working parties. For example, several working parties under the Agriculture and Fisheries Council (AGR) deal with the Union's participation in the FAO[76] and the Working Party on International Environment Issues coordinates the Union's policy with regard to negotiations taking place in the United Nations Environment Programme (UNEP) and the High-level Political Forum on Sustainable Development. The Union's human rights policy at the UN—in particular at the UNGA's Third Committee and the Human Rights Council (HRC)—falls under the responsibility of the Working Party on Human Rights (COHOM), whereas issues of development cooperation, disarmament and arms control are dealt with in the Working Party on Development Cooperation and in the Working Party on Global Disarmament and Arms Control, respectively. Usually working parties meet no more than once per month, generally in a closed setting, convening delegates from the 28 Member States' capitals. Since the entry into force of the Lisbon Treaty, the chairmanship of many of the Council's preparatory bodies has been taken over by EEAS officials, thereby replacing the six-monthly rotating Presidency.[77]

The strategies developed in Brussels require further refinement through 'on the ground' negotiations at the various UN bodies. As with the chairmanship of many Council working parties, the EEAS has succeeded the rotating Council Presidency as the leader of the local coordination process. EU Delegations accredited to multilateral organisations, including the UN organisations in Geneva, Paris, Nairobi, New York, Rome, and Vienna, were supposed to 'assume as soon as possible the role and functions … performed by the rotating Presidency in terms of local coordination'[78] upon the entry into force of the Lisbon Treaty, which

[72] MB Rasch, *The European Union at the United Nations: The Functioning and Coherence of EU External Representation in a State-centric Environment* (Leiden, Brill, 2008) 126.

[73] Degrand-Guillaud estimates that approximately 70 per cent of Council texts are agreed in working groups, A Degrand-Guillaud, 'Actors and Mechanisms of EU Coordination at the UN' (2009) 14 *European Foreign Affairs Review* 405, 416.

[74] Rasch (n 72 above) 130; Degrand-Guillaud (n 73 above) 416.

[75] Rasch (n 72 above) 130.

[76] In particular the Coordination Working Party, the Codex Alimentarius Working Party, the Working Party on External Fisheries Policy and the Working Party on Forestry.

[77] Council Decision 2009/908/EU of 1 December 2009 laying down measures for the implementation of the European Council Decision on the exercise of the Presidency of the Council, and on the chairmanship of preparatory bodies of the Council [2009] OJ L322/28.

[78] Council of the European Union, 'Presidency report to the European Council on the European External Action Service' (14930/09) 23 October 2009, para 31.

presented them with no small challenge in terms of expertise and manpower.[79] An estimated 1300 coordination meetings are held in New York each year, another 1000 meetings in Geneva.[80]

It is the task of the HR/VP to ensure coherence between the CFSP and the non-CFSP areas of EU external action at the UN (Articles 18(4) and 21(3) TEU). Commentators initially noticed the HR/VP's 'lop-sided persona'[81] with its extensive competences in the field of CFSP and considerably lesser powers as a member of the Commission. This situation has changed under the Juncker Commission, which saw a revival of the Commissioners' Group on External Action (CGEA) chaired by the HR/VP,[82] and a generally higher degree of cohesiveness of the HR/VPs multiple 'hats'.[83]

IV. EU-UN COOPERATION ON THE GROUND

Any analysis of EU-UN relations would be incomplete if it focused only on the institutional aspects of the partnership and ignored the actual practical cooperation between both organisations. Whereas the former remains fraught with difficulties, the latter is generally perceived more favourably. Recent years have witnessed increasing consultations between the UN and the EU, as evidenced through the conclusion of numerous strategic partnerships, memoranda of understanding and other agreements which aim to make the cooperation between both bodies more strategic and efficient.[84] The dialogue between EU and UN actors has intensified with frequent meetings between high-level officials of both organisations. Today, the UN operates 26 liaison offices in Brussels, while six EU Delegations represent the Union in the major UN bodies.

EU-UN cooperation has been assigned particular importance by EU primary law in the areas of development cooperation, humanitarian aid and peacekeeping/conflict prevention. In the area of development cooperation,

[79] See for more detail Wouters and others (n 46 above) 77.

[80] Gstoehl (n 59 above) 183.

[81] S Blockmans and M Spernbauer, 'Legal Obstacles to Comprehensive EU External Security Action' (2013) 18 *European Foreign Affairs Review* 7, 13.

[82] A Rettman, 'EU commission creates new foreign policy cell', EU Observer, 11 September 2014, https://euobserver.com/institutional/125567, accessed 5 May 2016.

[83] S Blockmans and S Russack, 'The Commissioners' Group on External Action—Key political facilitator', CEPS Special Report No 125, December 2015.

[84] Eg Memorandum of Understanding concerning the establishment of a strategic partnership between the European Commission and the United Nations Development Programme, 28 June 2004; Memorandum of Understanding between the European Union and the United Nations entity for Gender Equality and the Empowerment of Women (UN Women), 16 April 2012; Memorandum of Understanding concerning the establishment of a partnership between the United Nations Educational, Scientific and Cultural Organisation Secretariat and its subsidiary bodies and the European Union, 8 October 2012; the Financial and Administrative Framework Agreement between the European Community, represented by the Commission of the European Communities and the United Nations (FAFA), 29 April 2003, and Addendum No 1, 21–26 February 2014.

Article 208(2) TFEU commits the Union and its Member States to 'comply with the commitments and take account of the objectives they have approved in the context of the United Nations and other competent international organisations', thereby not only presupposing a collaboration between the EU and the UN in the field of development aid, but also creating a legal obligation to adhere to those commitments and objectives that fall otherwise in the category of 'soft law'.[85] Article 214(7) TFEU goes even further, stipulating that the 'Union shall ensure that its humanitarian aid operations are coordinated and consistent with those of international organisations and bodies, in particular those forming part of the United Nations system', thereby creating a legal obligation to achieve coherence between EU and UN actions. Finally, Article 42(1) TEU enshrines the status of the UN Charter as the guiding legal framework for EU missions in the areas of peace-keeping, conflict prevention and international security.

The EU holds the top rank among the world's biggest development aid donors.[86] Together with its Member States it accounts for more than 50 per cent of the total official development assistance. Part of these funds is channelled through the various UN organisations which are active in the area of development cooperation, among them most importantly the FAO and the UN Development Programme (UNDP). Cooperation between the EU and the FAO is particularly close, as evidenced by the fact that the FAO is the only UN agency that granted the EU membership status. The FAO and EU concluded a Strategic Partnership Agreement in 2004, aiming to further increase their strategic cooperation in selected policy areas.[87] While the EU does not contribute to the FAO's regular budget, it has developed into the organisation's largest extra-budgetary donor through its voluntary contributions, currently funding over 150 FAO projects world-wide.[88] Going beyond EU-FAO cooperation, the EU furthermore concluded a 'Strategic Programmatic Framework on Food Security and Nutrition', bringing together the three Rome-based agencies, FAO, World Food Programme (WFP) and International Fund for Agricultural Development (IFAD) in June 2011, aiming 'to harmonize and coordinate the implementation of … food security and humanitarian food assistance goals'.[89] The top beneficiary of the financial contributions of EuropeAid

[85] Streinz and Kruis (n 16 above) TFEU art 208 para 37.

[86] European Commission, 'EU Official Development Assistance reaches highest-ever share of Gross National Income', 13 April 2016, http://europa.eu/rapid/press-release_IP-16-1362_en.htm?locale=en, accessed 5 May 2016.

[87] European Commission/FAO, 'Memorandum of Understanding concerning the establishment of a Strategic Partnership between the Food and Agriculture Organization of the United Nations and the Commission of the European Communities in the field of development and humanitarian affairs', 13 September 2004.

[88] FAO Technical Cooperation Department, Field Programme Management Information System (FPMIS), 'List of EU-Funded Projects': https://extranet.fao.org/fpmis/FPMISReportServlet.jsp?type=PRJ_EU, accessed 5 May 2016.

[89] European Commission/Rome based United Nations Agencies, Statement of Intent: Programmatic Cooperation on Food Security and Nutrition, 27 June 2011.

to the UN is, however, the UNDP,[90] with whom the EU has cooperated for the past 15 years.[91] As with the FAO, the EU sealed its cooperation with the UNDP through the conclusion of a Strategic Partnership Agreement in 2004,[92] which was again endorsed by UNDP Administrator Clark and EU Commissioner for Development Piebalgs in a joint statement in 2012.[93] Other UN institutions working in the development field that rank among the main beneficiaries of EU funding are the United Nations Children's Fund (UNICEF) and the United Nations Relief and Works Agency for Palestine Refugees in the Near East (UNRWA).[94]

The EU is equally active in the field of humanitarian aid and has endorsed the 'central and overall coordinating role of the United Nations, particularly the Office for the Coordination of Humanitarian Affairs (OCHA), in promoting a coherent international response to humanitarian crises'.[95] In line with this commitment and the obligation of Article 214(7) TFEU, the EU strives to closely cooperate with the UN's humanitarian aid organisations, in particular OCHA, the UN High Commissioner for Refugees (UNHCR), the WHO and UNICEF. Notably, between July 2013 and June 2014 the EU held for the first time the chairmanship of the OCHA Donor Support Group (ODSG),[96] an informal forum which acts as a '"sounding board" and a source of advice on policy, management, budgetary and financial questions'.[97] As with OCHA, the EU and its Member States are among the top donors in UNHCR.[98] The EU and UNHCR cooperate not only on matters outside of the Union's borders but have also worked on setting up a Common European Asylum System (CEAS).[99]

[90] See European Commission, 'EuropeAid Financial Contributions to the United Nations—2014-2014': https://ec.europa.eu/europeaid/sites/devco/files/europeaid-un-statistics-for-2014_en.pdf, accessed 5 May 2016.

[91] UNDP Representation Office in Brussels, 'UNDP and the European Union': www.undp.org/content/brussels/en/home/partnerships_initiatives/overview/, accessed 26 June 2014.

[92] See above n 84.

[93] UNDP, 'Joint Statement by EU Commissioner Andris Piebalgs and UNDP Administrator Helen Clark', 8 May 2012: www.undp.org/content/undp/en/home/presscenter/speeches/2012/05/08/joint-statement-by-eu-commissioner-andris-piebalgs-and-undp-administrator-helen-clark/, accessed 26 June 2014.

[94] See above n 90.

[95] Joint Statement by the Council and the Representatives of the Governments of the Member States meeting within the Council, the European Parliament and the European Commission, 'The European Consensus on Humanitarian Aid' (2008/C 25/01) para 25.

[96] Permanent delegation of the European Union to the UN Office and other international organisations in Geneva, 'EU takes chairmanship of OCHA Donor Support Group (17/07/2013)': eeas.europa.eu/delegations/un_geneva/press_corner/all_news/news/2013/ocha_donor_support_group_en.htm, accessed 26 June 2014.

[97] OCHA, 'How OCHA is funded': www.unocha.org/about-us/ocha-funded, accessed 26 June 2014.

[98] OCHA, 'OCHA Donor Ranking': https://oct.unocha.org/mobile/Donor/DonorRanking, accessed 5 May 2016; Permanent delegation of the European Union to the UN Office and other international organisations in Geneva, 'Working with UNHCR': eeas.europa.eu/delegations/un_geneva/eu_un_geneva/humanitarian_affairs/unhcr/index_en.htm, accessed 26 June 2014.

[99] See for more detail European Commission, 'Common European Asylum System': ec.europa.eu/dgs/home-affairs/what-we-do/policies/asylum/index_en.htm, accessed 26 June 2014.

In 2003, the EU and the UN concluded a Financial and Administrative Framework Agreement (FAFA),[100] which turns the requirements of the Union's Financial Regulation[101] into contractual obligations for funding agreements between both organisations.[102] The FAFA governs the procedural side of EU contributions to the UN, including reporting requirements and issues of visibility. It provides a uniform set of rules for a large number of EU-UN projects[103] and is intended to increase the efficiency of the cooperation.[104] In light of concerns about a lack of visibility of EU contributions to UN projects, the European Commission and the UN additionally agreed on a Joint Action Plan on Visibility in 2006.[105] The Action Plan aims to ensure the implementation of the visibility provisions included in the FAFA in order to 'communicate the positive results of [EU-UN] partnership more effectively to beneficiaries and other stakeholders'.[106]

Lastly, peace-keeping, conflict prevention and international security are among those policy areas where EU-UN cooperation has gained particular momentum in the past decade. EU-UN partnership in the field was prominently affirmed by the 2003 Joint Declaration on UN-EU Cooperation in Crisis Management, which established a joint consultative mechanism—the Steering Committee—in order to strengthen the inter-institutional cooperation in the areas of planning, training, communication and best-practices.[107] As indicated before, the ESS, adopted by the European Council only a few months later, recognised the supremacy of the UNSC for the maintenance of international peace and security and placed EU operations within the legal framework of the UN Charter.[108] Since then, the Union has participated in an increasing number of military and police operations,

[100] Above, n 84.

[101] Regulation (EU, Euratom) No 966/2012 of the European Parliament and of the Council of 25 October 2012 on the financial rules applicable to the general budget of the Union and repealing Council Regulation (EC, Euratom) No 1605/2002 [2012] OJ L298/1.

[102] European Court of Auditors, 'The Efficiency and Effectiveness of EU Contributions Channelled Through United Nations Organisations in Conflict-Affected Countries', Special Report No 3, 2011, p 10.

[103] In particular it applies to the UN bodies listed in fn 1 of the FAFA, as well as to those bodies that individually acceded in line with art 15.3 of the FAFA, namely CTBTO, FAO, IAEA, ICAO, IFAD, ILO, ITU, UNCDF, UNESCO, UNIDO, UNOPS, UN-Women, WHO and WMO, see: https://ec.europa.eu/europeaid/un-specialised-agencies-covered-financial-and-administrative-framework-agreement_en, accessed 5 May 2016. On the EU side, the FAFA applies to the Commission, as well as to the European Agency for Reconstruction in Kosovo, Euratom and the European Environment Agency, which have acceded to the FAFA in 2003, 2004 and 2010 respectively, see: http://ec.europa.eu/europeaid/sites/devco/files/adhesion-of-the-ear-to-the-fafa-2003_en.pdf; http://ec.europa.eu/europeaid/sites/devco/files/adhesion-of-the-eaec-to-the-fafa-2003_en.pdf; and http://ec.europa.eu/europeaid/sites/devco/files/adhesion-of-the-eea-to-the-fafa-2003_en.pdf, all accessed 5 May 2016.

[104] J Wouters, 'The United Nations and the European Union: Partners in Multilateralism', *Leuven Centre for Global Governance Studies, Working Paper No 1*, May 2007, p 12.

[105] European Commission/United Nations, 'Joint Action Plan on Visibility', 22 September 2006.

[106] Ibid 2.

[107] EU/UN, 'Joint Declaration on UN-EU Co-operation in Crisis Management', 24 September 2003, available at: europa.eu/rapid/press-release_PRES-03-266_en.pdf, accessed 5 May 2016.

[108] European Security Strategy (n 3 above) 9.

maintaining a geographical focus on Europe and Africa. While the 28 EU Member States today contribute more than two-fifths of the UN peacekeeping operations,[109] EU military personnel (including police, observers and troops) only amount to 5 per cent of the personnel deployed in all UN peacekeeping operations.[110] Most of the EU's civilian and military crisis management missions so far have taken place in the context of a UN operation, while others aimed to prepare or to continue UN engagement.[111] In 2003, for example, the EU Police Mission (EUPM) replaced the UN Mission in Bosnia-Herzegovina (UNMIBH), and, equally in 2003, the EU supported the UN Mission in the Democratic Republic of the Congo (MONUC) through its rapid deployment of 'Operation Artemis'. Currently, the EU supports the International Support Mission to the Central African Republic (MISCA) and the African Union's (AU) mission in Somalia (AMISOM), two peacekeeping missions led by the AU with the approval of the UNSC. The UNSC has explicitly recognised the Union's 'significant contribution' to international peace and security in a Presidential Statement of 14 February 2014.[112] The Statement highlights various areas of EU action, both independent and in cooperation with the UN. The three mentioned examples of 'extensive' EU-UN cooperation include the Union's support of the OPCW/UN Joint Mission for the elimination of the Syrian chemical weapons programme, the Union's role in the Middle East Quartet, and its contribution in Afghanistan, in particular through EUPOL Afghanistan and the European Gendarmerie Force (EGF). Lastly, the UNSC calls for further strengthening of EU-UN cooperation and invites the HR/VP to submit regular briefings to the UNSC. While EU-UN cooperation in the field has thus significantly increased over the past decade, room for improvement remains, particularly with regard to the planning of mandates, training coordination and the contribution of military capabilities.[113] Both organisations are currently undertaking steps to address these challenges. The EU has adopted a set of priorities aimed at strengthening its partnership with the UN in 2015[114] and is currently preparing a new 'Global Strategy'.[115] On the UN side a High-Level

[109] Permanent delegation of the European Union to the UN Office and other international organisations in Geneva, 'The EU and the UN': eeas.europa.eu/delegations/un_geneva/eu_un_geneva/index_en.htm, accessed 27 June 2014.

[110] UN, 'Monthly Summary of Contributions (Police, UN Military Experts on Mission and Troops) As of 31 March 2016': www.un.org/en/peacekeeping/contributors/2016/mar16_1.pdf, accessed 5 May 2016.

[111] R Gowan, 'The UN and European Strategy' in S Biscop and R Whitman (eds), *The Routledge Handbook of European Security* (London, Routledge, 2013) 270.

[112] UNSC, Statement by the President of the Security Council (14 February 2014) S/PRST/2014/4.

[113] European Parliament Research Service, 'EU-UN cooperation in peacekeeping and crisis management', Briefing November 2015, p 10-11; W Hummel and T Pietz, 'Partnering for Peace: Lessons and Next Steps for EU-UN Cooperation on Peace Operations', Center for International Peace Operations, Policy Briefing, February 2015, p 4.

[114] Council of the European Union, 'Strengthening the UN-EU Strategic Partnership on Peacekeeping and Crisis Management: Priorities 2015-2018', 27 March 2015, Doc No 7632/15.

[115] EU, 'A Global Strategy on Foreign and Security Policy for the European Union': https://europa.eu/globalstrategy/en, accessed 5 May 2016.

Independent Panel on UN Peace Operations was established in October 2014 as part of the ongoing review process.[116] In its 2015 report, the High-Level Panel recognized the contribution of the EU to UN-AU missions and recommended standby arrangements with regional rapid-response capabilities, namely the European Union Battlegroups.[117] Overall, the partnership between the UN and the EU on peacekeeping activities has grown continuously stronger over the past years, prompting the UNSG to anticipate an 'era of "partnership peacekeeping"'.[118]

V. CHALLENGES AND OPPORTUNITIES

There are a number of factors which could turn the EU's engagement with the UN into a success story. These include above all the Union's reformed institutional external relations architecture, which, by creating continuity, holds the potential to considerably increase the effectiveness and coherence of EU action within the UN framework. The creation of the posts of President of the European Council and HR/VP as well as the establishment of the EEAS not only buffer the Union's external action from the six-monthly changes entailed by the rotation of the Council Presidency, they also allow for the creation of an institutional memory and provide third countries with the necessary 'European phone number'. EU Delegations at the various UN bodies have successfully assumed their new responsibilities,[119] even though the transition period after the entry into force of the Lisbon Treaty was not without difficulties.[120] The fact that the coordination in both settings—in Brussels and on the ground—is now largely chaired by EEAS officials, may contribute to lessening the often perceived distance between the decision-makers in the capital and the diplomats in the Delegations.[121] An analysis of the Union's voting records in recent UN sessions shows that voting cohesion is generally quite high, thus indicating the success of the internal coordination mechanisms. Split votes have become rare and are usually limited to very sensitive issues, eg the Israel/Palestine

[116] See UNSG, 'Secretary-General's statement on appointment of High-Level Independent Panel on Peace Operations', 31 October 2014.

[117] Report of the High-level Independent Panel on Peace Operations on uniting our strengths for peace: politics, partnership and people, 17 June 2015, UN Doc A/70/95 and S/2015/446.

[118] UNSG, 'Partnering for peace: moving towards partnership peacekeeping', 1 April 2015, UN Doc S/2015/229, para 57. Note also that the Advisory Group of Experts on the 2015 Review of the United Nations Peacebuilding Architecture recognized the importance of the EU-UN partnership with regard to peacebuilding, 'The Challenge of Sustaining Peace: Report of the Advisory Group of Experts on the 2015 Review of the United Nations Peacebuilding Architecture', 29 June 2015, para 94.

[119] Wouters and others (n 46 above) 78.

[120] Experiences at the various EU Delegations were mixed. The EU Delegation at the UN in New York achieved a relatively smooth transition owing to its extensive preparations, whereas the UN Delegation in Geneva encountered more difficulties, amongst other things due to the Union's fragmented participation rights in the various Geneva-based UN bodies and the ensuing complex legal and political environment, see Wouters and others (n 46 above) 79.

[121] Cf Rasch (n 72 above) 131.

conflict or the use of drones.[122] The realisation that intensive internal coordination should not come at the expense of external outreach has prompted a number of EU actors to rethink the coordination process, aiming to make it more efficient and to ensure a more strategic planning of EU action in UN fora. COHOM, for example, has launched a new practice to hold a meeting with the ambassadors of the EU Member States in Geneva in the beginning of each calendar year, in order to formulate the Union's annual priorities in the UN human rights fora and to thus allow for a more coordinated and proactive outreach. Apart from these institutional aspects, it is the multilateral nature of the EU that might prove to be an advantage in the UN framework after all. Not only do the EU's 'multiple voices' come with the benefit of the extensive expertise, capacities and third country networks of the 28 Union Member States, but the EU, as a prime example of peace and stability through regional integration, may itself serve as a model and leader of successful multilateralism.

This assessment should not, however, distract from the fact that the Union is still far off from realising its full potential in the UN and the UN system. One of the main issues is the EU's frequent inability to translate its high degree of voting cohesion into actual impact. A number of studies in recent years have demonstrated that the EU often fails to garner sufficient support for its initiatives in UN bodies and to prevent initiatives by third countries which run counter to its policy preferences.[123] Although the Union is frequently in a numerical minority position in the UN setting and therefore has to rely on forming strong cross-regional, coalitions, its capacities are still primarily bound by the time-consuming internal coordination process. As a negotiator the EU is widely perceived as a slow and inflexible 'bloc', which comes to the table with painstakingly elaborated and hardly amendable positions. It has also been commented that the Union rarely takes strong and confrontational stances, given that it has to represent a compromise of 28 views. EU positions tend to aim for the lowest common denominator in order to avoid a voting defeat.[124] It is possible that these issues will partially be resolved

[122] See eg HRC Res A/HRC/22/L.41 (19 March 2013) concerning the 'Follow-up to the Report of the UN Independent International Fact-Finding Mission on the Gaza Conflict', where the Czech Republic abstained while all other EU Member States voted in favour, or the recent HRC Res A/HRC/25/L.32 (24 March 2014) on 'Ensuring use of remotely piloted aircraft or armed drones in counter-terrorism and military operations in accordance with international law, including international human rights and humanitarian law', which caused a three-way split among EU Member States, with Ireland voting in favour, France and the United Kingdom voting against and Austria, the Czech Republic, Estonia, Germany, Italy and Romania abstaining.

[123] See only S Gstoehl (n 59 above); D Panke, 'Regional Power Revisited: How to Explain Differences in Coherency and Success of Regional Organizations in the United Nations' (2013) 18 *International Negotiation* 265; KE Smith, 'The European Union at the Human Rights Council: speaking with one voice but having little influence' (2010) 17 *Journal of European Public Policy* 224; KE Smith, 'The European Union and the Politics of Legitimization at the United Nations' (2013) 18 *European Foreign Affairs Review* 63; DC Thomas, 'Still Punching below Its Weight? Coherence and Effectiveness in European Union Foreign Policy' (2012) 50 *Journal of Common Market Studies* 457.

[124] A prominent example is the Union's support of HRC Res 7/20, which terminated the expert mandate for the DR Congo, even though it had previously argued for a renewal, HRC Res 7/20

once the Union's post-Lisbon institutional architecture is fully implemented. A number of developments indicate that the relevant EU actors are well aware of the problem and are looking for solutions. COHOM's initiative to develop clear priorities covering the entire calendar year and all UN human rights bodies is a step in the right direction, allowing, for example, EU Delegations in third countries to start lobbying for Union policies well in advance of the respective session. In addition, the Commission has addressed the internal negotiation process at the FAO, where the mixed membership of the EU and its Member States and the ensuing need to coordinate the alternative exercise of membership rights causes an additional burden. In its 2013 Communication on 'The role of the European Union in the Food and Agriculture Organisation (FAO) after the Treaty of Lisbon' (FAO Communication)[125] the Commission proposes a more flexible coordination process in which the elaboration of full statements would be the exception, and the drafting of 'lines to take', the rule. The proposed new 'Arrangements between the Council and the Commission regarding the Exercise of Membership Rights of the European Union and its Member States in the Food and Agriculture Organisation (FAO)'[126] (FAO Arrangements) are currently under revision in the Council.

It is the lingering fear of some Member States of a silent 'competence creep'[127] and of a loss of standing in international fora that frequently stands in the way of a stronger EU presence at the UN. Not only have they often been reluctant to support the Union's quest for stronger participation rights in UN fora,[128] they have fought over the use of nameplates,[129] the phrasing of declarations of competence[130] and the introductory clauses of statements. A prominent example is

(27 March 2008); cf S Basu, 'The European Union in the Human Rights Council' in J Wouters, H Bruyninckx, S Basu and S Schunz (eds), *The European Union and Multilateral Governance: Assessing EU Participation in United Nations Human Rights and Environmental Fora* (Basingstoke, Palgrave Macmillan, 2012) 91 et seq.

[125] Communication from the Commission to the Council, 'The role of the European Union in the Food and Agriculture Organisation (FAO) after the Treaty of Lisbon: Updated Declaration of Competences and new arrangements between the Council and the Commission for the exercise of membership rights of the EU and its Member States', COM(2013) 333.

[126] Ibid annex 2.

[127] FD Schild, 'The Influence of the Food and Agriculture Organization (FAO) on the EU Legal Order' in RA Wessel and S Blockmans (eds), *Between Autonomy and Dependence: The EU Legal Order Under the Influence of International Organisations* (The Hague, Asser Press, 2013) 228.

[128] Eg with regard to EU attempts to obtain enhanced participation rights in ICAO, cf RA Wessel and B Van Vooren, 'The EEAS's diplomatic dreams and the reality of European and international law' (2013) 20 *Journal of European Public Policy* 1350, 1354 et seq.; or with regard to the IMO, cf Wouters, Chané, Odermatt and Ramopoulos (n 11 above).

[129] See the United Kingdom's insistence that Member States should have the right to 'intervene in support of an agreed EU statement from behind their national nameplate' in the context of the negotiations on the new FAO Arrangements: United Kingdom, Department for International Development, Explanatory Memorandum on COM(2013) 333 final, Doc No 10368-13, 27 June 2013, para 17.

[130] The United Kingdom criticised the Commission's proposal for an updated Declaration of Competences to be submitted to the FAO, alleging that it lacked 'any recognition of the extent to which the EU has not exercised its competence under shared competence areas': United Kingdom, Department for International Development, Explanatory Memorandum on COM(2013) 333 final, Doc No 10368-13, 27 June 2013, para 3.

the United Kingdom's 2011 blockage of a considerable number of EU statements, in the context of a dispute over whether statements on matters of shared EU/Member States competences should be delivered 'on behalf of the EU' or 'on behalf of the EU and its Member States'.[131] While a set of arrangements adopted in October 2011 was able to preliminarily settle the conflict, no final solution appears yet to have been found.[132] Nevertheless, it is not only an internal but also an external lack of support that hinders the Union's effective participation at the UN. Third states have in the past been reluctant to grant the EU participation rights in UN fora, based on a mix of concerns about endangering the state-centric system of the UN and the principle of sovereign equality of states, as well as on a lack of sufficient knowledge about the exact nature and workings of the EU and other regional integration organisations. These problems became particularly apparent during the Union's quest for enhanced participation rights in the UNGA,[133] but also when the EU tried to obtain negotiation rights with regard to the 2005 Convention on the Protection and Promotion of the Diversity of Cultural Expressions.[134] Despite recent attempts to push for a stronger status of the EU in the UN,[135] the prospects for status upgrades are generally dim. The gap between internal EU competences and external participation rights that exists in a number of UN bodies will therefore most likely persist for the foreseeable future.

This has consequences for EU-UN cooperation on the ground. The disconnection between the Union's significant financial contribution and its lack of participation rights at the policy level raises the question whether the EU is 'a payer or a player' in its relationship with the UN. The Union contributes actively to the UN's work in the areas of development cooperation and humanitarian aid, but it only has a modest observer status in the UNDP, the WFP, UNRWA, UNFPA, UNICEF and other competent UN bodies. Nevertheless, while a weak status hinders the EU from actively shaping the policy formulation in the UN, a strong status is no panacea either.[136] Even if the EU acquires the strongest participatory rights, its

[131] J Borger, 'EU Anger over British Stance on UN Statements' (*The Guardian*, 20 October 2011): www.guardian.co.uk/world/2011/oct/20/uk-eu-un-statements-wording, accessed 25 June 2014.

[132] Council of the European Union, 'EU Statements in Multilateral Organisations—General Arrangements', Doc No 15901/11, 24 October 2011; for more detail see C Flaesch-Mougin, 'Représentation externe et compétences de l'Union européenne: quelques réflexions à propos des arrangements généraux du Conseil relatifs aux déclarations de l'UE dans les organisations multilatérales' in C Boutayeb (ed), *La Constitution, l'Europe et le droit—Mélanges en l'honneur de Jean-Claude Masclet* (Paris, Publications de l'Université Paris-Sorbonne, 2013) 571–92.

[133] See above, section II.B.(ii).

[134] For more detail see Wouters, Chané, Odermatt and Ramopoulos (n 11 above).

[135] See eg above, section II.B, the 2012 'Strategy for the progressive improvement of the EU status in international organisations and other fora in line with the objectives of the Treaty of Lisbon'.

[136] See H Bruyninckx, J Wouters, S Basu and S Schunz, 'The Position(s) of the EU in the UN System: The Examples of Human Rights and Environmental Governance' in H Bruyninckx, J Wouters, S Basu and S Schunz (eds), *The European Union and Multilateral Governance: Assessing EU Participation in United Nations Human Rights and Environmental Fora* (Basingstoke, Palgrave Macmillan, 2012) 253, 267, who conclude that 'possessing competence and a highly developed legal status does not guarantee the EU a central position, while having a low status does not exclude it from playing a significant role in or impact on a UN governance process or forum'.

actual impact depends on how it fills them with life. For example, in the FAO the EU sought to establish a 'more policy-oriented type of cooperation',[137] but commentators disagree on whether there is really a 'true partnership' between both organisations,[138] or whether the FAO sees its cooperation with the EU 'mostly about securing EU funding'.[139] The EU should not let itself be relegated to the 'payer' role but should play an active part in the agenda-setting and strategy development in line with its own policy preferences and values. This means not only that the Union must actively seek to bring its status in UN bodies in line with its scope of competences and actions, but also that it must make the most of those rights that it has been granted.

VI. CONCLUSIONS

The EU's commitment to 'effective multilateralism' has found expression in an ever stronger partnership with the UN. Development cooperation, humanitarian aid and crisis management are only three of the policy areas where EU-UN cooperation has developed into a stable alliance of common objectives and values. Nevertheless, a lot of potential is still lost due to inconsistencies between the EU and the UN legal framework, the organisational challenges associated with a Union of 28 Member States and fears of both EU and non-EU states about a loss of status and influence. The Union's status in the UN still far too often differs from its actual competences. The unwieldy coordination process continues to bind valuable resources on the internal front, limiting the EU's capacity for proactive outreach and coalition-building. Disputes over the allocation of powers and external representation reduce the Union's impact in UN bodies by focusing the attention of the involved EU actors often too much on the process rather than on the substance. The Lisbon Treaty reforms have provided a number of tools to address some of the most pressing issues. It still remains to be seen whether all involved actors—EU institutions and Member States alike—will muster the degree of constructive cooperation that is necessary for their successful implementation.[140]

[137] Schild (n 127 above) 223.

[138] JM Pedersen, 'FAO-EU Cooperation: An Ever Stronger Partnership' in J Wouters, F Hoffmeister and T Ruys (eds), *The United Nations and the European Union: An Ever Stronger Partnership* (The Hague, TMC Asser Press, 2006) 65.

[139] Schild (n 127 above) 223.

[140] See J Wouters and T Ramopoulos, 'Revisiting the Lisbon Treaty's Constitutional Design of EU External Relations' in L S Rossi and F Casolari (eds) *The EU after Lisbon: Amending or Coping with the Existing Treaties*? (Dordrecht, Springer, 2014) 215, 235 et seq.

10

The Consistency of the European Union's Human Rights Policy at the United Nations

CARMELA PÉREZ BERNÁRDEZ*

Contents:

I. INTRODUCTION

THE PURPOSE OF this chapter is to assess the current degree of cohesion of the European Union and its Member States in the field of human rights and their influence within the United Nations. In this sense, an

* Senior Lecturer in Public International Law and EU Law. University of Granada.

evolutionary analysis, taking into account the changes in the external representation of the European Union introduced by the Lisbon Treaty, is required to rule on the possible causal relationship between the internal cohesion and effectiveness of the EU and to indicate the progress, setbacks or status quo in the post-Lisbon era.[1]

This study also proposes improvements for greater EU efficiency at the United Nations in human rights matters. Previously, certain parameters will be established to delimit the scope of the research.

First, (the parties involved). This research analyses the behaviour of the European Union (EU or Union hereafter) as well as its Member States, acting within the United Nations. This obliges us to examine not only the behaviour of the EU States that have the status of 'full membership' of the UN, but also those EU States with 'observer', generally 'privileged', status in certain UN organs. From the UN perspective, the set of EU Member States acting in UN organs is perceived as a regional group, solid and consistent in various fields, such as human rights. From the EU perspective, it is necessary to act as a 'Regional Integration Organization' within the United Nations system and other international organisations, although it has caused the Union itself and its Member States many problems.[2]

Conjugating the EU with the United Nations is not a new issue. Institutionally, from 1974 this non-State European entity had a very limited observer status in the General Assembly of the United Nations, which was de facto strengthened and became official in 2011.[3] The EU's privileged and varied participation as a Regional Integration Organisation at the United Nations and its large system of specialised bodies and agencies is one of the consequences of the growing number of areas in which the United Nations operates (security, humanitarian aid, poverty eradication, sustainable development of the planet and human rights), which are non-exclusive EU competences. Harmonising their respective competences and the growing interest among both institutions explains, for example, a more palpable EU physical presence at the United Nations, and vice versa, as shown in the 2010 decision to establish an EU delegation in Geneva accredited and differentiated at the United Nations, and another EU representation at the World Trade Organization (WTO)—resuming the former tasks of the Delegation

[1] See on the tandem cohesion-efficacy, KE Smith, 'Speaking with One Voice? European Union Co-ordination on Human Rights Issues at the United Nations' (2006) 44 *Journal of Common Market Studies* 113–37; DC Thomas, 'Still Punching below its Weight ? Coherence and Effectiveness in EU Foreign Policy' (2012) 50 *Journal of Common Market Studies* 457–74; LG Van Schaik, *The EU's Effectiveness in Multilateral Negotiations: More than the Sum of its Parts* (Basingstoke, Palgrave Macmillan, 2013).

[2] Small island States in development in the Caribbean, through the Caribbean Community (CARICOM), among others, have forcefully expressed the need for the UN to be an international organisation of 'States', not admitting regional bodies such as the European Union, and question the basic intergovernmental character of the UN. See below on this issue in relation to the adoption of UNGA Res 65/276 (10 May 2011) Doc A/RES/65/276/2011 on the 'Participation of the EU in the work of United Nations', which expressly attributed reinforced observer status to the EU in the UNGA.

[3] See UNGA Res 3208 (XXIX) (11 October 1974) and UNGA Res 65/276 (n 2 above).

of the European Commission and the Liaison Office of the General Secretariat of the Council of the Union.[4]

In this context the numerous references made by the primary law of the EU to the United Nations is understandable, given that the EU itself is a dynamic example of multilateralism. It needs to project its activities linking itself to and creating 'partnerships with third countries and regional or global organisations' with which it shares basic principles, including universality and the indivisibility of human rights and fundamental freedoms and others set out in the Charter of the United Nations and international law (see Article 21.1 of the Treaty of the European Union—(TEU)—as the general provision dedicated exclusively to the external action of the EU). The mandate, therefore, to facilitate 'multilateral solutions to common problems, in particular in the framework of the United Nations',[5] is logical, since it promotes 'an international system based on stronger multilateral cooperation and good global governance' (Article 21.2(h) TEU).[6] Thus, the EU's support for international organisations or institutions is the most solid way for collective management of globalisation, highlighting the United Nations.[7]

[4] This will allow a European Ambassador at the highest level to represent the EU at the UN, without the problems of overlap frequent before the adoption of this measure by representations in other international forums in which the EU has very strong powers, as in the case of the WTO. See C Pérez Bernárdez, 'Una visión desde el Derecho de la puesta en marcha de las nuevas Delegaciones de la Unión Europea' in F Aldecoa Luzárraga (ed), *La Diplomacia Común Europea: El Servicio Europeo de Acción Exterior* (Madrid, Marcial Pons, 2011) 85, 94. Due to its multifaceted approach, see the contributions in A Altermir Blanc (ed), *Las relaciones entre las Naciones Unidas y la Unión Europea. Seguridad, cooperación y derechos humanos* (Madrid, Tecnos, 2013); LN Alonso González (ed), A Garrido Muñoz (coor), *La Unión Europea y el Multilateralismo Eficaz. ¿Un compromiso consistente con Naciones Unidas?* (Madrid, Iustel, 2011).

[5] See Treaty on European Union (Lisbon) art 21.

[6] Here are some examples of references to the United Nations in primary law, although there are many such provisions, such as the current Art 220 of the Treaty on the Functioning of the EU (TFEU) that reproduces, in updated form, the reference already included in the 1950s in the former Treaty establishing the European Economic Community (EEC), now stating that 'the EU will establish all appropriate forms of cooperation' with the UN in the broadest sense. Other references can be found in Art 3.5 TEU—in a clear external projection (n 13 below); Art 34.2 TEU referring to the concert of EU Member States in the Security Council of the United Nations; Art 42.1 TEU indicating that the EU's operational capability will be in accordance with the principles of the Charter of the United Nations; Art 42.7 TEU that on establishing a self-defence collective between EU Member States it will be in accordance with Art 51 of the Charter of the United Nations; also Art 208.2 TFEU, in the context of cooperation to development, indicates that 'the Union and its Member States shall comply with the commitments and take account of the objectives they have approved in the context of the United Nations and other competent international organisations'; and the recent Art 214.7 TFEU, indicating that EU humanitarian aid operations will be coordinated and consistent with that of other international organisations, including the United Nations system.

[7] To this end, the coordination of the activities of the Member States is fundamental. Arts 32 and 34 TEU refer to this, the latter in the broader context of international organisations. Multilateral cooperation is not exclusive, and can be combined with bilateral cooperation, which may in turn be associated with effective multilateralism through linkages with strategic partners: see E Barbé Izuel, 'La UE en el contexto internacional, a la hora de las potencias emergentes' in *Cambio Mundial y Gobernanza Global. La interacción entre la Unión Europea y las instituciones internacionales* (Madrid, Tecnos, 2012) 62.

The financial contribution of the EU as a major contributor to the United Nations confirms this support.[8]

Secondly, (the subject-matter). The material selected for this study area is human rights, which both the UN and the EU have developed as a flagship activity, despite the discreet treatment that both institutions gave to this area in their early years. The United Nations, on the one hand, is the cornerstone with a broad policy and organisational system and diversified promotion and protection of human rights at the universal level. This system has evolved intensely, branching out and including conventional and extra-conventional guarantee mechanisms.[9] The EU, on the other hand, strives to promote and protect human rights, which thus constitute a 'leading thread of performance both inside and outside',[10] functioning as the EU's leitmotiv, principle and at the same time, aim. And so, regardless of whether the UN as the universal international organisation is the leader in this matter, the Council of Europe remains the protagonist in the Greater Europe, with its mechanism of protection of human rights based on the European Convention for the Protection of Human Rights and Fundamental Freedoms and therefore in the European Court of Human Rights in Strasbourg.

If we look back at the process of European integration, we see it had to wait until the Maastricht Treaty in 1992 for 'some formalization of the issue of fundamental

[8] Through the regular contributions of EU Member States the EU has funded 38 per cent of the ordinary budget of the United Nations; in addition, the EU provides more than two-fifths of the cost of the maintenance of peace-keeping operations, reaching half of the contributions of all members of the United Nations for UN funds and programmes. See: ec.europa.eu/europaid.

[9] Although the Charter of the United Nations in June 1945 did not include a specific chapter or section systematically devoted to human rights, it is necessary, to understand the legal and institutional functioning of the current complex system of promotion and protection of human rights, to know the network that has been developed at the United Nations with such a function.

[10] See the Joint Communication of the High Representative of the Union for Foreign Affairs and Security Policy and the Commission to the European Council, the European Parliament and the Council of 12 December 2011, 'Human Rights and Democracy at the heart of the EU external action—towards a more effective approach', COM(2011) 886 final 4. Similarly, the medium-term priorities of the EU regarding the United Nations (2012–15) indicate that human rights are at the core of the EU's external action: 'European Union Medium-term Priorities at the United Nations (2012–2015)', Ref GA12-001 EN, 23 May 2012. Whether the European Union itself is based, 'on respect for human rights' (Article 2 TEU), the primary law, and the seat of external action, exposes clearly—distilling a necessary utopianism and a controversial and sensitive messianism—that the EU's action on the international scene, is based on the 'principles which have inspired its own creation, development and enlargement, and which it seeks to advance in the wider world: democracy, the rule of law, *the universality and indivisibility of human rights and fundamental freedoms, respect for human dignity, the principles of equality and solidarity, and respect for the principles of the Charter of the United Nations and international law*' (Article 21 TEU) (emphasis added). In this sense, it seems clear that 'the interest of the EU for the promotion of human rights beyond the borders of its member states does not respond exclusively to pure altruism'; thus, the aim of promoting human rights abroad indirectly guarantees the security of the EU itself through improving the welfare of other states; and this despite the difficulties of the promotional task, since there is a clear conviction of the Union itself and its members that their common political values shape a more just and equitable system of legal and social organisation that must serve such an end. See S Salinas Alcega, 'La acción de la Unión Europea en la Asamblea General de las Naciones Unidas: Un test de su condición de actor global en materia de derechos humanos' in A Blanc Altemir (ed) (n 4 above) 436–63.

rights in the EU in the Treaties'.[11] The Lisbon Treaty has made fundamental rights more positive. There are various developments in both the internal dimension in its own Member States and the external, with third parties, other international organisations, various entities or States with which it interacts. The primary law of the EU is now crystal clear in the relevance it gives to the area of human rights, as expressly shown in its provisions,[12] but also in the case law developed by the EU Court of Justice, the existence of an ad hoc list of rights, freedoms and principles with the 'Charter of Fundamental Rights of the EU'—which is legally binding since the entry into force of the Lisbon Treaty[13]—and the creation of an increasingly ambitious 'Fundamental Rights Agency of the EU' (FRA),[14] to name just a few of these developments as the tip of the iceberg.

Thirdly, (the institutions). In the framework of the United Nations, this analysis focuses on two intergovernmental bodies, the General Assembly (UNGA) and the Human Rights Council (HRC). The first is selected for its high degree of representation—the 193 Member States of the UN belong to it—and because various issues relating to human rights are examined in it. Therefore, the UNGA is a privileged place in which to take the true pulse of international society.[15] In particular, we shall pay attention to the Third Committee of the UNGA on 'social, humanitarian and cultural affairs', in whose agenda the issue of human rights captures most of the work.[16] The Human Rights Council, as a second forum for

[11] See DJ Liñán Nogueras in A Mangas Martin and D J Liñán Nogueras, *Instituciones y Derecho de la Unión Europea*, 8th edn (Madrid, Tecnos, 2014) 121. The Union shall respect the fundamental rights such as are guaranteed by the European Convention for the Protection of Human Rights and Fundamental Freedoms signed in Rome on 4 November 1950—developed within the Council of Europe—and which are common to the constitutional traditions of the Member States, very similar to the current Art 6.3 TEU, pointing out that they 'shall constitute general principles of the Union's law'.

[12] See TEU arts 2, 3.5 and 21. Article 2, acting as a driving force in primary law states: 'The Union is founded on the values '*of respect for human dignity*, freedom, democracy, equality, the rule of law and respect for human rights, *including the rights of persons belonging to minorities*'. That same provision goes on to state that 'these values are common to the Member States in a society in which *pluralism, non-discrimination, tolerance, justice, solidarity and equality between women and men prevail*' (emphasis added). Going into it more deeply, Article 3.5 TEU indicates specifically that in its relations with the wider world, the EU upholds and promote those values, contributing, amongst others, to 'the protection of human rights, in particular the rights of the child, as well as to the strict observance and development of international law, including respect for the principles of the United Nations Charter'. More specifically, Article 21 TEU asserts that the EU shall define and pursue common policies and actions, and 'will strive to achieve a high degree of cooperation in all fields of international relations in order to: … (b) consolidate and support democracy, the rule of law, *human rights* and the principles of international law' (21.2(b) TEU) (emphasis added).

[13] See TEU art 6.1, which refers to the Charter of Fundamental Rights of the EU promulgated on 7 December 2000 in Nice.

[14] Cf Council Regulation (EC) 168/2007 of 15 February 2007 establishing an Agency for Fundamental Rights of the European Union [2007] OJ L53/13.

[15] Gowan and Branter corroborate the importance of the UNGA by analysing the effectiveness of the external action of the EU in the field of human rights, noting that its resolutions are a useful barometer of the collective climate of the members of the United Nations. They take into account the large number of votes that this plenary body records and the fact that it elects the members of the HRC and UNSC; see R Gowan and F Brantner, *A Global Force for Human Rights? An Audit of European power at the UN* (European Council of Foreign Relations, 2008) 18.

[16] The Third Committee of the UNGA, in addition to human rights questions, examines other issues such as those related to social development, crime prevention and international drug control. In

analysis, consists of 47 Member States of the United Nations—with, for example, eight EU Member States in 2015. The HRC is the current UNGA subsidiary body specifically for the promotion and protection of human rights, building on the extra-conventional mechanisms that prior to 2006, the former Commission on Human Rights had been developing, which have now been replaced and updated.

Fourthly, (the time period). As more than five years have passed at the time of writing since the entry into force of the last major reform of primary law of the European Union, the Treaty of Lisbon in December 2009, sufficient time has passed to create an analytical perspective from which to assess the situation on human rights at the United Nations and the role the EU has played in it. In a period marked by the economic and financial crisis, which began in late 2007,[17] changes have been introduced in the external representation—which before the Lisbon Treaty was preferably undertaken by the Member State of the Union holding the rotating Presidency of the EU Council—now more actively relying on different institutional representatives as expressly set out in Resolution 276 of the UNGA on 'Participation of the EU in the work of the UN' adopted in 2011. That resolution notes that the representatives who take on the role of acting on behalf of the EU in this universal body are: 'the President of the European Council, the High Representative of the Union for Foreign Affairs and Security Policy, the European Commission and the EU delegations'. This function, at least partially, moves prominence to the Member State which holds the rotating presidency of the EU, as we shall see later.[18]

II. THE EU IN THE THIRD COMMITTEE OF THE GENERAL ASSEMBLY OF THE UNITED NATIONS

One of the salient features of the performance of the EU and its Member States in the UNGA is consensus, including in the field of human rights. Indeed, examination of the resolutions corresponding to the work of its Third Committee in the eight periods of the most recent sessions (61st to 68th) shows no significant variations in the strong consensus among the EU Member States in this plenary body of the United Nations (see Table 1 below). No substantial changes were observed from session 65th (2010–11), in which the EU set in motion changes in external representation with the entry into force of the Lisbon Treaty or, from

this chapter we focus on the issue of human rights, taking into account that its material scope can be extended to many issues, including universal jurisdiction and the International Criminal Court, and others that will be treated tangentially in this chapter.

[17] It was precisely on 13 December 2007 when the Lisbon Treaty was signed. After its entry into force on 1 December 2009, the crisis continued over time, with slight signs of improvement from 2014.

[18] Cf UNGA Res 65/276 (10 May 2011) (n 2 above). The change mentioned is not absolute, since for example, although the accommodations made after the entry into force of the Lisbon Treaty, in the Human Rights Council the EU coordination is led by representatives of the Delegation of the European Union, the modest representation of the EU, with observer status in this body continues using the State presiding over the Council of the European Union every six months to present the formal statements of the EU, as will be analysed in paragraph three below.

66th (2011–12), during which the EU already enjoyed enhanced observer status at UNGA, compared to the previous situation.[19] Let us consider the situation more concretely:

A. Promotion of Human Rights

The Third Committee spends much of its efforts in the field of 'promotion of human rights' generally encompassed in points 64 to 69 of the list of topics under the programmes of the sessions of the General Assembly, whether or not it deals with other areas. Thus, along with social development, drug control, crime prevention and combating international terrorism, it treated issues of the advancement of women and the effective coordination of humanitarian assistance, among others. However, the bulk of the Third Committee is specifically dedicated to the *promotion* of human rights, exceeding more than half of the resolutions that deal with other issues in the various sessions analysed (see Table 1).

B. EU Priorities within UNGA

EU activity has been more strongly developed in a number of areas which have been established as priorities within the UNGA and deal with particular subjects or countries. Among the most important are the following: to preserve the universality of the International Law of Human Rights and the independence of the United Nations System of Human Rights; freedom of expression, including internet; the abolition of the death penalty and establishing its moratorium; freedom of religion or belief; collective rights of lesbian, gay, bisexual or transgender (LGBT) people, as well as other sectors of the population;[20] fighting against gender discrimination and violence;[21] and the elimination of all forms of racism, racial discrimination, xenophobia and intolerance, paying particular attention to monitoring the so-called *Durban process against racism*.

The special concern of the EU on these issues, included in its priorities, justifies the repetitive content of the Resolutions that it sponsors at the UNGA in different sessions (see the spheres in Table 2).[22]

By *countries*, among others, the attention paid by the EU to human rights in nearby Belarus, Myanmar, Iran, the Democratic People's Republic of Korea

[19] Table 1 shows that the General Assembly of the United Nations maintains a similar number of resolutions adopted at different periods in its Third Committee, at about 55, although their reduction in the 61st period is notable (2006–07). This number was easily exceeded in the 66th period (2011–12).

[20] Especially children, youth, disabled persons and activists and human rights defenders in different States.

[21] Including female genital mutilation, early marriage, forced labour and sexual violence.

[22] Cf EU Priorities for the 68th General Session of the Assembly of the United Nations, Council of the European Union, 24 June 2013; EU Medium-term Priorities at the United Nations (2012–15), IV. Human Rights, Ref: GA12-001EN, 23 May 2012.

(DPRK), Palestine and, more recently, Syria is most prominent; as it shows the adoption of ad hoc decisions by the UNGA.[23]

From a horizontal perspective, the EU is particularly concerned about strengthening its pulling power in order to attract a larger number of third countries to align their positions with it; although this is already considerable, more are needed to reinforce its active diplomacy and to obtain new supports that are key.[24] Other areas of particular interest to the EU are increasing *complementarity* and collaborative work between the Third Committee of the UNGA and the Council of Human Rights, avoiding duplication between them in order to streamline the growing workload of the latter and to strengthen the conventional system of human rights protection.

C. The Increase of Consensus

From a general perspective, there has been a progressive increase in the number of resolutions adopted by consensus by the General Assembly from the 61st period of sessions (2006–07),[25] reducing therefore the number of resolutions brought to a vote. In the subsequent years there has been even greater consensus among the Member States of the United Nations. In this context, we examine the behaviour of EU Member States in the Third Committee of the UNGA and the resolutions taken to a vote in this area that reflect continuity in the virtually insignificant and anecdotal number of resolutions in which there has been split vote.[26] This very small number has not increased after the entry into force of the Treaty of Lisbon in the 65th session, and did not exceed two resolutions in the 66th to 68th periods of sessions (see Table 1).

[23] In North Africa, in the context of the Arab Spring revolutions—Libya, Tunisia and Egypt—and other States in this continent such as Ivory Coast, Somalia, Eritrea, Mali and Yemen as well as Bahrain and Sri Lanka in Asia.

[24] In this connection may be mentioned, among the EU strong traditional allies, the *candidates* for membership of the EU: Croatia, before it joined the EU; Turkey; the Former Yugoslav Republic of Macedonia; Montenegro; Serbia; and Iceland, member country of the European Free Trade Association (EFTA); and Albania and Bosnia & Herzegovina—*potential candidate* states and members of the Association and Stabilization Process. To this list are usually added some Member States who are part of the *European Neighbourhood Policy*, such as Georgia, Armenia, Moldova and Ukraine. Cf, for example, the Declaration of the EU and its Member States on the rights of the child (Case 65), presented by P Köhler, in which those countries joined; EU Delegation to the United Nations, Third Committee of the UNGA, 17 October 2013, *Overview of the 68th Session of the United Nations General Assembly, Third Committee 2013—Delegation of the European Union to the United Nations*, New York, February 2014, p 54; Statement of the EU on the promotion and protection of human rights, (Case 69), presented by F Tschampa, EU Delegation to the United Nations Third Committee of the UNGA, 22 October 2013, ibid p 77. See on this issue, section V of this chapter.

[25] Thus, the number of resolutions adopted without a vote—that is, by consensus—in sessions 61 (2006–07), 62 (2007–08) and 63 (2008–09) already exceeded more than half the total.

[26] Prior to the 65th period of sessions (2010–11), the most serious disagreement came with two resolutions in the 64th period (2009–10). In the previous period, the 63rd (2008–09) there was only one resolution where the vote was split among Member States of the EU with none in the 61st and 62nd periods.

D. No Incidence of EU Enlargement

One thing to keep in mind is that the good results of the coordination of EU Member States in the General Assembly in this subject have not been altered by successive enlargements of the EU, from that in 2004 (10 States) and 2007 (2 more).[27] Indeed the division of votes does not show relevant incidents in the 59th period of sessions (2004–05) with the great enlargement of the EU by 10 new Member States, nor in the 61st period (2006–07) or the next, despite an anecdotal dissenting opinion in the Czech Republic in one resolution, which did not use to happen before its incorporation as a member of the EU. As a candidate it adhered to and participated in the positions agreed by EU Member States.[28]

E. Limited and Specific Dissent

A more detailed analysis of the 10 resolutions that did not obtain a unified vote of the EU Member States between the 61st (2006–07) and 68th (2013–14) sessions of UNGA is interesting for various reasons. First, their content shows that the topics where there has been dissent are specific and limited, repeated and dragging over successive years for lack of agreement, in the three specific areas discussed below; and, secondly, the lack of agreement between EU Member States manifested itself through abstentions rather than votes for or against, radical dissent—ie opposing views being expressed within the voting and thus representing genuine lack of agreement—being exceptional. The three areas of concern for such resolutions are:

i. Durban Process/Racism

In relation to the *Durban process/racism,* or on 'Global efforts for the total elimination of racism, racial discrimination, xenophobia and related intolerance and the comprehensive implementation of and follow-up of the Declaration and

[27] The European Commission itself is aware both of the positive consequences of the enlargement process as well as its 'serious challenges' posed internally to the EU action in the UNGA; cf *Communication from the Commission to the Council and the European Parliament*'. European Union and the United Nations: The choice of multilateralism', 10 September 2003, COM(2003) 526 final. See The Treaty of Accession of the Czech Republic, Estonia, Cyprus, Latvia, Lithuania, Hungary, Malta, Poland, Slovenia and Slovakia [2003] OJ L236, 23 September 2003 and Treaty of Accession of the Republic of Bulgaria and Romania [2005] OJ L157 21 June 2005.

[28] In February 2013 on the Resolution on the *Durban process*, the Czech Republic alone voted against, while the rest of the then 26 Member States voted in favour, which is an exception to the dynamics of the EU at the UNGA. In fact, it was the only time concerning the resolutions adopted in the framework of this process in which the lack of agreement of EU Member States has been radical. See UNGA Res 67/155 (11 February) UN Doc A/RES/67/155, 'Global efforts for the total elimination of racism, racial discrimination, xenophobia and related intolerance and the comprehensive implementation of and follow-up to the Declaration and Programme of Action'. The result of the vote was 133 in favour, 7 against and 48 abstentions.

Programme of Action of Durban'[29]—there have been five periods of sessions in which unanimous consensus among EU Member States was not found. In the 68th period of sessions (2013–14) the Group of 77 (G-77) which presented the draft resolution on this subject did not appear receptive to the proposals of the EU, although involved in the same, and finally the resolution included language that did not comply with EU positions.[30]

In adopting these resolutions there underlay the commitment to defend the *universal application* of human rights by most EU Member States and others of the Western group or developed countries, which on occasion has been put in doubt. These States have maintained a contrary position or abstained on the resolutions adopted under the *Durban process*, on the grounds that such decisions do not adequately combat racism, intolerance and anti-Semitism, encouraging, on the contrary, the erosion of freedom of expression.[31]

However, only once in the five sessions in which EU Member States failed to act in unison on this matter—with the sole dissenting vote of the Czech Republic in February 2013—has there been a clear division of votes between them, as in the other four cases there were abstentions rather than votes against or in favour of these controversial decisions. Even in the December 2013 vote, there were four EU Member States who voted against, three more than in the past, while the rest abstained.

ii. Fuelling Contemporary forms of Racism

Another issue, connected to the former, which did not obtain the full agreement of the EU Member States was the 'inadmissibility of certain *practices* that contribute to *fuelling contemporary forms of racism*, racial discrimination, xenophobia and related intolerance' (emphasis added). Specifically, a group of countries—

[29] UNGA Res 63/242 (22 January 2009) UN Doc A/RES/63/242, with 6 EU Member States voting against (including the Czech Republic, Poland, Romania and the Netherlands) and 21 abstentions. The resolution was adopted by 109 votes in favour, 13 against and 35 abstentions. UNGA Res 64/148 (26 March 2010) UN Doc A/RES/64/148, examined the same issue in the following period of sessions, with 22 EU Member States voting in favour and 5 abstentions (the Czech Republic, Germany, Italy, Poland and Romania). The result of the vote was 166 in favour, 7 against and 9 abstentions. UNGA Res 65/240 (5 April 2011) UN Doc A/RES/65/240, received 13 votes against from the EU Member States (including the Czech Republic, Germany, Bulgaria, Italy and the Netherlands) and 14 abstentions. The result of the vote was 104 in favour, 22 against and 33 abstentions. UNGA Res 67/155 (11 February 2013) UN Doc A/RES/67/155, above n 28. In UNGA Res 68/151 (18 December 2013) UN Doc A/RES/68/151, the vast majority of EU Member States abstained (24) and 4 voted against; there was a total of 134 votes in favour, 11 against and 46 abstentions.

[30] With references to complementary standards or the revitalisation of the Group of Eminent Experts; cf Overview of the 68th Session of the United Nations General Assembly, Third Committee 2013 (n 24 above) 17.

[31] Cf *EU General Statement—United Nations 3rd Committee: Durban Declaration and Programme of Action*, 24 November 2010 EUUN10-161EN, accessible through: www.eu-un.europa.eu/. A year earlier, in 2009, some EU Member States (Czech Republic, Germany, Italy, Netherlands and Poland) boycotted the UN Conference on Racism (Durban II) held in Geneva in protest at the anti-Israel implications of its final document. Cf R Gowan and F Brantner, *The EU and Human Rights at the UN: 2010 Review* (European Council on Foreign Relations, 2010) 6.

including most of the EU and others of the Western group—have argued in respect of different resolutions in 2012 and previous years on this subject, that they do not adequately reflect the distinction between some actions and statements that are certainly offensive (such as some on the glorification of Nazism), but which should be protected under the *freedom of expression* in the rule of law, and other criminal actions that should be banned.[32]

iii. The Right to Development

The right to development as an integral part of human rights is another area of annual consideration in the General Assembly of the United Nations where the EU has not found consensus in four different periods of sessions in the years 2010, 2012, 2013 and 2014.[33] In its explanation of its vote in 2010, for example, the EU emphasised that the lack of economic development may not be invoked by States to justify weakening of or infringing internationally recognised human rights. The EU recalled that it had been the largest provider of development assistance to third countries, but stressed that it is the primary responsibility of the States to create the conditions for the realisation of this right. It also believed that as the right to development was changing, it did not think it proper to adopt a process of binding international law in this area.[34]

From the above, it can be seen that the number of resolutions with a split vote among EU Member States from 2006 to 2014 is very low, 10 in human rights in three areas over different periods of sessions, reflecting the continued work of internal coordination in the plenary organ of the United Nations. In

[32] UNGA Res 66/143 (29 March 2012) UN Doc A/RES/66/143. 17 EU Member States voted against (including Belgium, Denmark, Hungary and Spain), while the remaining 10 abstained. The vote gave a result of 134 votes in favour, 24 against and 32 abstentions.

[33] UNGA Res 64/172 (25 March 2010) UN Doc A/RES/64/172, proposed by Cuba; cf para 24 therein. 13 EU countries voted against (including Belgium, Bulgaria, the Czech Republic, Denmark and Poland) while 14 others abstained. The result of the vote was 133 in favour, 22 against and 30 abstentions (among the latter was Spain). In UNGA Res 66/155 (20 March 2012) UN Doc A/RES/66/155, the vote showed exceptional division in the distribution of votes among the Member States, including the three possible positions, since 10 voted in favour, with only the United Kingdom voting against while 16 EU countries abstained. The result of the vote was 154 in favour, 6 against and 29 abstentions. In UNGA Res 67/171 (22 March 2013) UN Doc A/RES/67/171, 10 EU countries voted in favour (including Spain), while the United Kingdom voted against and 15 States abstained (including the Czech Republic). Belgium was absent. The result of the vote was 154 in favour, 4 against and 28 abstentions. For UNGA Res 68/158 (18 December 2013) UN Doc A/RES/68/158 18, sponsored by Cuba and the Non-Aligned Movement, there were 158 votes in favour, 4 against and 28 abstentions. The Member States of the EU were divided into three, the majority (16) abstained, 11 were in favour and there was only one vote against, the United Kingdom. The Resolutions on the 'right to development' include, among other matters, the sensitive reference to the contributions of 0.7 per cent of gross national product of developed countries for official development assistance to developing countries, and 0.15 per cent and 0.2 per cent to the least developed—cf section 26 in different resolutions on the subject. These resolutions use the verb 'urge' to refer to appealing to countries to 'make concrete efforts towards meeting these targets', an admittedly weak expression, particularly bearing in mind the non-legally binding nature of UNGA resolutions.

[34] *European Union Explanation of Vote at the United Nations General Assembly Third Committee resolution on 'The right to development'*, EUUN10-167EN, 22 November 2010, New York.

2008 there were 1,000 coordination meetings in New York alone between the various representatives of the EU overall; and, for issues of the Third Committee alone in 2013, 60 meetings took place daily in two different groups during the 68th session.[35] Hence, even without their votes being totally in the same direction and with radical dissension being exceptional between Member States, the EU explained its positions within the UNGA in the three areas discussed above (Durban process/racism, exacerbation of contemporary forms of racism and right to development), which is fundamental to understanding its position against third parties (see Table 2).

We see, therefore, that EU Member States maintained a cohesive policy on human rights in the post-Lisbon era, similar to the previous situation in the Third Committee of the General Assembly of the United Nations. Quantitatively and qualitatively, the declarations adopted by the EU, the explanations of its votes, positions, speeches and resolutions presented in its name or co-sponsored by it show the high degree of internal coordination achieved: the result of its efforts in seeking synergies between the Member States and the EU. The coordination mechanism used is certainly *exhausting*, since it is necessary to deploy powerful diplomatic energies with third States and, more specifically, toward emerging non-Western powers,[36] in order to achieve a more effective action of the Union.[37] However, this process becomes a *multiplier of influence* within and from each Member State and of the Union itself, enabling monitoring of and reaction to each Resolution.[38] This is regardless of the various effects of the economic and financial crisis or the process of EU enlargement. Therefore, the work of the EU in the Third Committee of the UNGA can be considered as positive, despite the difficulties it has had to confront.

[35] See *Overview of the 68th Session of the United Nations General Assembly, Third Committee 2013* (n 24 above).

[36] Already in 2006 Professor Karen Smith put the emphasis on the extensive time spent on coordination between EU Member States and its negative impact, preventing the key work of searching for support and negotiating with third States or groups of States from United Nations, but also from Brussels and the capitals of the Member States; see Karen E Smith, at n 1 above, (2006) 44 *Journal of Common Market Studies* 113, 133; R Gowan and F Brantner, *The EU and Human Rights at the UN: 2011 Review* (European Council on Foreign Relations, Policy Memo, 2011)10; R Gowan and F Brantner, *A Global Force for Human Rights? An Audit of European Power at the UN* (European Council on Foreign Relations, 2008) 58.

[37] In this sense, we agree with S Salinas when, in addition to finding a 'progressive advance in coordination among Member States' on human rights, he put the emphasis on the need to seek external support through a dialogue with third parties who support EU initiatives. However, we would disagree with his assertion that EU's loss of credibility as an international actor is particularly serious for human rights. Consulting the work of academic authors prior to 2008 does not reveal a momentum in recent years in the field. See *La acción de la Unión Europea en la Asamblea General de las Naciones Unidas: Un test de su condición de actor global en materia de derechos humanos*, A Blanc Altemir (n 10 above) 445, 462.

[38] See E Giaufret, 'The EU in the UNGA Third Committee' in J Wouters, H Bruyninckx, S Basu and S Schunz (eds), *The European Union and Multilateral Governance. Assessing EU Participation in United Nations Human Rights and Environmental Fora* (Basingstoke, Palgrave MacMillan, 2012) 75.

Table 1: United Nations General Assembly—Third Committee on Social, Humanitarian and Cultural Affairs—Resolutions

PERIOD OF SESSIONS	YEAR	RESOLUTIONS (RES) 3RD UNGA COMMITTEE	RES NOT VOTED ON (CONSENSUS)	RES VOTED ON	RES 'PROMOTION OF HUMAN RIGHTS'	AGENDA SUBJECTS 'PROMOTION OF HUMAN RIGHTS'	RES WITH DIVISION OF VOTES AMONG EU MEMBER STATES
61	2006–2007	48	26	22	30	63 to 67	0
62	2007–2008	59	38	21	37	65 to 70	0
63	2008–2009	57	38	19	38	58 to 64	1
64	**2009–2010**	**58**	**43**	**15**	**37**	**64 to 69**	**2**
65	**2010–2011**	**55**	**39**	**16**	**33**	**64 to 69**	**1**
66	***2011–2012***	***66***	***51***	***15***	***46***	***65 to 70***	**2**
67	***2012–2013***	***58***	***43***	***15***	***33***	***64 to 69***	**2**
68	***2013–2014***	***71***	***57***	***14***	***44***	***64 to 69***	**2**

Sources: Resolutions of UNGA www.un.org/es/ga/sessions/, accessed June 2015 (Author's compilation).

— The data highlighted in bold indicate the activity of the UNGA Third Committee subsequent to the entry into force of the Lisbon Treaty on 1 December 2009.

— Italics indicate the period from which the EU strengthened its observer status in the UN under A/RES/65/276 (10 May 2011).

Table 2: United Nations General Assembly—Third Committee on Social, Humanitarian and Cultural Affairs—European Union

YEAR	EU STATEMENTS *(1)*	EXPLANATIONS OF EU VOTING OR POSITIONS	EU INTERVENTIONS	SUBJECTS
2006	18	11 (10 voting and 1 position)	0	Belarus—USA—Iran—Myanmar—PDR Korea & UNHCR—Combat defamation of religions—Right of Self-determination—Social Development—Elimination of all forms of discrimination and intolerance based on religion or belief—Globalisation and effect on human rights—Report of Human Rights Committee—Immigrants and indigenous peoples of Canada—Women—Children—Crime Prevention and Criminal Justice and International drug control—Democratic and equitable International Legal Order—Indigenous people—Palestinian people—Taking hostages
2007 *(2)*	14	4 (3 voting and 1 position)	0	Belarus—Iran—PDR Korea—Myanmar & UNHCR Combat defamation of religions—Human Rights Council—Right to development—Rights of the child—Human rights and cultural diversity—Social development Durban/racism*—Fuelling contemporary forms of racism, racial discrimination, xenophobia and connected forms of intolerance—Moratorium on the use of the death penalty—Promotion and protection of human rights—Crime Prevention and Criminal Justice and International drug control

(continued)

Table 2: *(Continued)*

YEAR	EU STATEMENTS *(1)*	EXPLANATIONS OF EU VOTING OR POSITIONS	EU INTERVENTIONS	SUBJECTS
2009 *(3)*	8	16 (8 voting and 8 positions)		Afro descendants—Combat defamation of religions—Cooperation against drugs—Right to food—Right to development—Rights of the child—Human rights and cultural diversity—Social development—Family—Indigenous peoples –Free determination—Women—Situation of human rights and examination of reports of special representatives—Trafficking in persons—Mercenaries—Protection of Migrants—Durban Declaration follow up—Human rights treaty bodies—Crime Prevention and Criminal Justice and International drug control
2010 *(4)*	**18 (2 additional questions)**	**8 (4 voting and 4 positions)**	22	**Myanmar & UNHCR—Water—Human Rights Council—Defenders of human rights—Right to food—Right to education—Right to development—Freedom of expression—Rights of migrants—Rights of the child—Social development—Durban/racism*—Extrajudicial executions—Businesses and human rights—Standard of physical and mental health—Standard of life—Elimination of racism, xenophobia and other forms of intolerance—Aging—Globalisation and human rights—Independence of judges and lawyers—Indigenous peoples—Freedom of religion and belief—Women—Minorities—Democratic and equitable International Legal Order—Internally displaced persons—Crime Prevention and Criminal Justice and International drug control—Promotion of peace—Prevention of Torture—Durban process follow up—Palestinian Territory—Trafficking of human beings—Sale of children, Child prostitution and child pornography—UNICEF**

(continued)

Table 2: ***(Continued)***

YEAR	EU STATEMENTS (1)	EXPLANATIONS OF EU VOTING OR POSITIONS	EU INTERVENTIONS	SUBJECTS
2011	***5***	***0***	***7***	***Iran & UNHCR—Defenders of human rights—Rights of the child—Fight against terrorism and promotion and protection of human rights—Extreme poverty—Promotion and protection of human rights—Indigenous peoples—Torture—Racism***
2012 (5)	***9***	**-**	**-**	***UNHCR—Rights of the child—Social development—Durban/ racism*—Women—Crime Prevention and Criminal Justice and International drug control—Indigenous peoples***
2013	***11 (6)***	***17 (8 voting and 9 positions)***	***27 (7)***	***Iran—Myanmar—PDR Korea– Syria & UNHCR—Combat intolerance—Combat the glorification of Nazism—Defenders of Women's Human rights—Rights of the child—Social development—Girls' Infancy—Infancy, forced and early marriage—Report of HRC—Durban/racism*—Freedom of religion and belief—Women (Rural)—Crime Prevention and Criminal Justice and International drug control—Promotion and protection of human rights—Indigenous peoples—Racism—Strengthening of treaty monitoring system—Strengthening of coordination system of UN protection of childhood—Aging***

Sources: EU Statements at the UN Third Committee of the General Assembly of the United Nations: www.eu-un.europa.eu, accessed June 2015 (Author's Compilation).

— The data highlighted in bold indicate the activity of the UNGA after the entry into force of the Lisbon Treaty on 1 December 2009.
— Italics indicate the period from which the EU strengthened its observer status in the UN under A/RES/65/276 (10 May 2011).

** The sphere called Durban/racism refers to 'global activities for the total elimination of racism, racial discrimination, xenophobia and related intolerance', known as the Durban process.*

(1) In EU Statements we include various types such as general declarations, statements of the EU Presidency—that is, of the Presidency of the EU Council—opening statements or reintroduced statements. In most cases these formal statements are presented by the Permanent Representative accredited to the UN or his Deputy.

(2) The compilation of information about the activities of the EU in the UNGA has been a complex task due to the lack of rigour in its publication of free access via the internet and the failure to use consistent methods in different years. For example, in 2008 during the French Presidency of the EU Council no information was published on the EU Statements or explanations of votes, among other matters, due to coordination failures. Nor has the Office of the Permanent Representative of France to the United Nations in New York seen fit to provide such information for this study.

(3) Since 2009, the specific statements of the Third Committee on the situation of human rights in certain countries have been reduced or discontinued to be encompassed by the examinations in Joint Declarations; see, for example, the extensive and detailed EU Declaration on the Promotion and Protection of Human Rights, 30 October 2013, examining the Sahel region, the Arab Spring and a total of 16 countries—Iran, Sudan, South Sudan, PDR Korea, China, Russia, Egypt, Bahrain, Central African Republic, Myanmar, Eritrea, Belarus, Sri Lanka, Mali, Democratic Republic of the Congo and Syria.

(4) From 2010 the 'Statements by the Presidency of the EU' have been renamed 'EU Statements' taking into account the explicit attribution of international legal personality with the EU's Lisbon Treaty (Article 47). Of the 18 statements adopted by the EU, seven included 'questions', the Union formulating two additional ones.

(5) From 2012, there were only 'EU Statements', not including explanations of votes, positions or other interventions.

(6) In 2013, during the 68th UNGA session, the EU Delegation presented statements on agenda items, 10 in the Third Committee and one in the Plenary at the level of Permanent Representative or Deputy accredited to the United Nations.

(7) The EU Delegation to the UN has intervened on 45 occasions during the interactive dialogues in line with the special procedures on human rights and high UN officials. Similarly, the State chairing the Council of the Union in the second half of 2013—Lithuania—made 26 interventions relating to the introduction and adoption of resolutions, a situation reflecting the existence still of a 'two-headed' EU.

III. THE EU IN THE HUMAN RIGHTS COUNCIL

Following the approach taken by the UNGA, as a starting point for assessing the cohesion and effectiveness of the EU's human rights policy, we must analyse the activity of the Union acting by itself and through its Member States as a regional group in the Human Rights Council (HRC). This body is the key to the extra-conventional mechanisms to protect human rights at the universal level, replacing and updating the work—not without shadows—done by the former Commission on Human Rights.[39]

The General Assembly of the United Nations established the Human Rights Council in 2006 as a subsidiary body maintaining the intergovernmental composition and location of its predecessor at the United Nations in Geneva. However, it reduced the number of State representatives from 53 to 47.[40] The current 47 States which enjoy this full status in the HRC are elected directly and individually by secret ballot by the majority of members of the UNGA. It chooses a 'fair' geographical distribution set at five different groups of States, although the contribution of candidates to the promotion and protection of human rights and the voluntary pledges and commitments made should be taken into account.[41] Consistent with the status of members, the States represented at the HRC enjoy the right to vote to adopt resolutions.

The EU, for its part, is involved in the HRC with observer status, a condition that due to its restricted nature does not allow it to intervene directly in the process of adopting resolutions by voting. Membership of the HRC is reserved for members of the United Nations, so that in 2013 and 2014, for example, nine of the 47 representatives in the HRC were part of the EU. In 2015, eight EU States hold the membership status, a slightly lower EU representation than in 2014 and 2013, similar to previous years (2012 and before) (See Tables 3 and 4).[42] This is important, because each of the EU Member States in the HRC, consistent with their competences, does not renounce its own national initiatives, but tries to harmonise them with the EU.[43]

[39] The Commission on Human Rights, established by ECOSOC in 1967, played a very active role in human rights until it was replaced by the Human Rights Council almost 40 years later. The Commission's activity can be measured by its significant achievements and successes, but its work was marred by, among other things, the election of certain States with dubious credentials for human rights, as members.

[40] The members of the Human Rights Council serve for a period of three years and cannot qualify for re-election for the next two consecutive terms: see its founding resolution UNGA Res 60/251 (15 March 2006) UN Doc A/RES/60/251, sections 7 and 8. The Institutional construction of the HRC was agreed in Resolution A/HRC/5/21 (18 June 2007), establishing the novel mechanism of Universal Periodic Review (UPR) and resuming and updating the Special and Complaints Procedures.

[41] The distribution of the 47 positions is made among the five regional groups as follows: 13 for the Group of African States; 13 for the Group of Asian and Pacific States; six for the Group of Eastern European States; eight for the Group of Latin American and Caribbean States, and seven for the group of Western European and other States.

[42] The current 28 Member States of the EU are divided among three separate regional groups: there are 16 States that belong to the Group of Western Europeanand other States, 11 in the Eastern European Group and just one—Cyprus—in the Asian Group. For example, in 2015, six are integrated into the Group of Western European and other States and the other four in the Eastern European Group.

[43] As derived from the Treaty on European Union (Lisbon) art 34.1. However, in practice not all EU Member States are equally committed to boosting EU influence in the HRC. National sensitivities clearly influence their projection and consequently in the EU.

Table 3: EU Member States in the Human Rights Council (HRC) and in the former Commission on Human Rights

PERIOD	TOTAL OF MEMBER STATES OF HRC AND OF THE FORMER COMMISSION ON HUMAN RIGHTS *(1)*	NUMBER OF EU MEMBER STATES *(2)*	EU MEMBER STATES
HUMAN RIGHTS COMMISSION 2003	53	7	Austria—Belgium—France—Germany—Ireland—Sweden—United Kingdom
HUMAN RIGHTS COMMISSION 2004	53	9	Austria—France—Germany—Ireland—Italy—Holland—Sweden—United Kingdom & Hungary
HUMAN RIGHTS COMMISSION 2005	53	8	Germany—Finland—France—Ireland—Italy—Holland –United Kingdom & Hungary
HUMAN RIGHTS COMMISSION 2006	53	8	Germany—Austria—Finland—France—Italy—Holland—United Kingdom & Hungary
HRC 19 June 2006—18 June 2007	47	8	Germany—Finland—France—Holland—United Kingdom & Czech Republic—Romania—Poland
HRC 19 June 2007—18 June 2008	47	7	Germany—France—Italy—Holland—United Kingdom & Slovenia—Romania
HRC 19 June 2008—18 June 2009	**47**	**7**	**Germany—France—Italy—Holland—United Kingdom & Slovakia—Slovenia**
HRC 19 June 2009—18 June 2010	***47***	***8***	***Belgium—France—Italy—Holland—United Kingdom & Hungary—Slovenia—Slovakia***
HRC 19 June 2010—18 June 2011	***47***	***7***	***Belgium—France—Spain—United Kingdom & Slovakia—Hungary—Poland***
HRC 19 June 2011—31 December 2012	***47***	***8***	***Austria—Belgium—Italy—Spain & Hungary—Poland—Romania—Czech Republic***

(continued)

Table 3: ***(Continued)***

PERIOD	TOTAL OF MEMBER STATES OF HRC AND OF THE FORMER COMMISSION ON HUMAN RIGHTS *(1)*	NUMBER OF EU MEMBER STATES *(2)*	EU MEMBER STATES
HRC 1 January 2013—31 December 2013 (3)	***47***	***9***	***Germany—Austria—Spain—Ireland—Italy & Estonia—Czech Republic—Poland—Romania***
HRC 1 January 2014—31 December 2014 (4)	***47***	***9***	***Germany—Austria—France—Ireland—Italy—United Kingdom) & Estonia—Rumania—Czech Republic***
HRC 1 January 2015—31 December 2015	***47***	***8***	***Germany (2015)—France (2016)—Ireland (2015)—Netherlands (2017)—Portugal (2017)—United Kingdom (2016) & Estonia (2015)—Latvia (2017)***

Sources: Documents from the website of the Office of the High Commissioner for Human Rights—Human Rights Council: www.ohchr.org, and former Commission on Human Rights: www2.ohchr.org/english/bodies/chr/index.htm, accessed June 2015 (Author's Compilation).

— The data highlighted in bold indicate the activity of the HRC after the entry into force of the Lisbon Treaty on 1 December 2009.
— Italics indicate the period from which the EU's observer status was strengthened at the United Nations pursuant to A/RES/65/276 (10 May 2011).
— The symbol '&' distinguishes between EU Member States belonging to the Western European Group and others—most of which are included in the Eastern European Group.

(1) The Commission on Human Rights worked from its inception in 1946 until 27 March 2006, ending its activity in the 62nd session. The Human Rights Council (HRC) was created on 15 March 2006 with the UNGA resolution A/60/251, establishing its operational framework. Its first ordinary session extended from 19 June 2006 to 18 June 2007.
(2) The number of Member States of the EU with representation before the Human Rights Council and the former Commission on Human Rights has been affected by the successive enlargements of the EU, such as the fifth and most ambitious, with 10 new States on 1 May 2004, another two—Romania and Bulgaria—on 1 January 2007 and, finally, Croatia on 1 July 2013, all included in the Eastern European Group, except Malta and Cyprus.
(3) From 1 January 2013 the beginning of the cycle of composition of the HRC has been modified; cf A/RES/65/281 (20 July 2011) 'Review of HRC' section 4.
(4) In the corresponding period in 2015 the date of expiry of the mandate of the EU Member States, which are in turn members of the HRC, is shown in parentheses.

Table 4: Comparative number of States in regional groups—Human Rights Council (HRC) and in the former Commission on Human Rights

REGIONAL GROUPS OF STATES	FORMER COMMISSION ON HUMAN RIGHTS (53 Members)	6 FEWER REPRESENTATIVES	CDH (47 Members)	MEMBER STATES OF HUMAN RIGHTS COUNCIL 2015 *(1)(2)*
AFRICA	15	-2	13	Algeria (2016)—Botswana (2017)—Congo (2017)—Côte d'Ivoire (2015)—Ethiopia (2015)—Gabon (2015)—Ghana (2017)—Kenya (2015)—Morroco (2016)—Namibia (2016)—Nigeria (2017)—Sierra Leone (2015)—South Africa (2016)
ASIA AND PACIFIC	12	+1	13	Bangladesh (2017)—China (2016)—India (2014)—Indonesia (2017)—Japan (2015)—Kazakhstan (2015)—Maldives (2016)—Pakistan (2015)—Qatar (2017)—Republic of Korea (2015)—Saudi Arabia (2015)—United Arab Emirates (2015)—Vietnam (2016)
LATIN AMERICA AND CARRIBEAN	11	-3	8	Argentina (2015)—Bolivia (2017)—Brazil (2015)—Cuba (2016)—El Salvador (2017)—Mexico (2016)—Paraguay (2017)—Venezuela (2015)
EASTERN EUROPE	5	+1	6	Albania (2017)—Estonia (2015)—Latvia (2017)—Montenegro (2015)—Russian Federation (2016)—The Former Yugoslav Republic of Macedonia (2016)
WESTERN EUROPE AND OTHERS	10	-3	7	France (2016)—Germany (2015)—Ireland (2015)—Netherlands (2017)—Portugal (2017)—United States of America (2015)—United Kingdom (2016)

Sources: Documents from the website of the Office of the High Commissioner for Human Rights—Human Rights Council: www.ohchr.org, accessed June 2015 (Author's compilation).

(1) In the column on the appointment of the members of the Human Rights Council the year in which the term expires is included in parentheses.

(2) The final composition of the HRC with the choice of countries like China, Cuba, Algeria and Cuba, whose mandates expire in 2016, presents new challenges for the EU in the work of that body.

We shall now examine retrospectively the activity of the EU in the Human Rights Council, distinguishing two stages, in order to discern its impact in the field of human rights:

A. From 2006 to 2009

When considering the activity of the EU in the Human Rights Council during its first years of operation—from 2006 to 2009—compared to the previous situation in the Commission on Human Rights, on occasions the European States have been in the minority, with reduced support for EU positions. This activity has failed to live up to the expectations generated by establishing the HRC, for example, by maintaining a secondary role with little receptivity and openness to cooperation on priority issues for some States.[44] This has been justified, in part, by the fact that the EU lost some structural influence within the Human Rights Council, compared to the situation in the former Commission on Human Rights; having to make the necessary accommodations by the reduction in the new human rights body from 53 to 47 representatives, thereby losing six State representatives from across the five regional groups. In particular the African groups, and above all, the Asian countries obtained a better, albeit discreet, representation in the new HRC at the expense of the 'Western European and others group' (see Table 4).[45] In fact, during the years 2006 and 2007, the Organization for the Islamic Conference (OIC), whose States are split between African and other Arab States, has been regarded as the most influential in the HRC, both in its agenda and in the debates held there.[46]

[44] Cf Gowan and Brantner, *A Global Force for Human Rights? An Audit of European Power at the UN, 2008* (n 15 above) 37, 39; J Laso Perez, 'La participación de la Unión Europea y sus Estados miembros en el Consejo de Derechos Humanos de Naciones Unidas', *La Unión Europea y el Multilateralismo Eficaz* (n 4 above) 346–47; J Wouters and K Meuwissen, 'European Union at the UN Human Rights Council. Multilateral Human Rights Protection Coming of Age' (*Leuven Centre for Global Governance Studies, Working Paper No 126*, December 2013) 7.

[45] The former Human Rights Commission divided its 53 members into the following regional groups: African States 15, 12 for Asia, five for Eastern Europe, 11 for Latin America and the Caribbean and 10 for Western Europe and others. This group's number was reduced from 19 per cent in the former Commission on Human Rights to 15 per cent in the HRC. See KE Smith, 'The European Union at the Human Rights Council: Speaking with One Voice but Having Little Influence' (2010) 17 *Journal of European Public Policy* 224–41.

[46] The OIC—since 2011 the Organisation of Islamic Cooperation—is an international organisation composed of 57 regional States spread across different continents. Some members are part of the UN African Group, which is the largest with 54 States, and some the Non-Aligned Movement, with 20. The existence of these forces requires the EU to negotiate with other groups of States, given that the two majority groups, the African and the Asian-Pacific, together have a majority in the HRC of 26 votes out of a total of 47 (See Table 4).

This structural readjustment for EU Member States in the HRC is in line with the claims of third countries other than those of the Union, in groups or regional bodies which have raised critical voices about the *overrepresentation* of Europe (and thus, the EU) at the United Nations and in the whole international institutional system.[47]

However, even at this early stage, the EU has actively influenced the HRC on occasions; for example, successfully negotiating and strengthening the functioning of the HRC, supporting the active participation of NGOs, national human rights institutions, the High Commissioner for Human Rights (HCHR) and other civil society actors in the key context of the mandate on the Special Procedure therein developed.[48]

B. From 2010 Onwards

Five years after the creation of the HRC, from the Fourteenth period (May–June 2010 onwards), greater cohesion of the EU Member States in the Human Rights Council is found, with a more active and constructive attitude becoming visible through its involvement in the review of the work and functioning of this body,[49] as well as sponsoring of resolutions in subject areas (such as children's rights or freedom of religion or belief) or countries (on the situation of human rights in

[47] See on this subject, E Barbé Izuel, 'La UE en el contexto internacional, a la hora de las potencias emergentes' in *Cambio Mundial y Gobernanza Global* (n 7 above) 46–65; S Gstöhl points out in this respect: 'In fact, Europe's weight in the global institutions (in terms of seats and/or votes) usually exceeds the relative share in population, and often also in gross domestic product, which it represents' in 'Patchwork Power Europe: The EU's Representation in International Institutions' (2009) 14 *European Foreign Affairs Review* 385; A Hamonic, *L'Union Européenne à l'ONU. Perpectives ouvertes par le Traité constitutionnel* (Paris, Éditions Apogée, 2007) 77; C Pérez Bernárdez, 'Respuestas del sistema diplomático ante el Servicio Europeo de Acción Exterior (SEAE): El caso de la Unión Europea ante la Asamblea General de las Naciones Unidas' (2011) 44 *Cuadernos Europeos de Deusto* 139–40. This claim was made clear during the dynamic process by which the General Assembly of the United Nations granted the EU enhanced observer status within it through UNGA Res 65/276 (10 May 2011) Doc A/RES/65/276/2011 (n 2 above). It is interesting to compare it with the failed draft resolution on the 'Participation of the EU in the work of the United Nations', UNGA Res 64/L.67 (8 August 2010) Doc A/64/L.67, proposed nine months before being approved with a somewhat weaker content than the initial claims of the European Union.

[48] On promoting the opening of special sessions on the situation of human rights in Myanmar (5th session in 2007), in the Democratic Republic of Congo (8th session 2008) and Sri Lanka (11th in 2009) see Wouters and Meuwissen (2013) (n 44 above) 7. We should bear in mind that the special meetings are convened to address human rights violations or emergencies, as long as they are requested by at least one third of the Member States. Regular meetings take place at least 3 times a year, in March, June and September. Since the creation of HRC 23 special sessions have been held (until June 2015) and 28 regular sessions (until 14 June 2015). On these see www.ohchr.org.

[49] However, the EU failed to establish, under the mandate of the Universal Periodic Review (UPR), one of the basic aspects defended by the Group of Western European States, namely, that the submission to the HRC of updated information midterm on the follow-up that a State in question gives to

Myanmar or in the DPR of Korea).[50] A progressive trend in which the EU has managed to impose its priorities and views on the agenda and resolutions of the HRC more effectively is seen in this second stage. In 2011, for example, the EU reacted more flexibly to different crises, drawing on the formation of coalitions, where a climate of diplomatically fluid alliances dominated which favoured the protection of human rights.[51] The work done by the EU in the HRC has strengthened and defended the priority areas of the Union, such as the most recent list compiled for the period 2012–15, which largely coincided with the EU priorities for the 68th session of UNGA (2013–14).[52] The EU has developed these lines from different angles and through various qualitative and quantitative means, as can be seen from the large number of areas on which the EU has expressed its views in the HRC and the different instruments used (see Table 5). In this way the EU has selected key areas in which it was already working and where it needed to continue its activities. However, it also introduced new aspects in thematic initiatives and countries, in constant collaboration with other States outside the European Union, achieving a greater impact in the HRC from 2011 in the international context governed by the events of the Arab Spring.[53]

The EU expresses its positions and concerns through statements, speeches, interactive discussions and questions raised, for example, with United Nations officials or relators, among others, under special procedures that are substantiated in the HRC. Of the instruments used by the EU to present its positions, the

the recommendations of that body, should be legally binding. This process continues being a mere recommendation; see paragraph 18 of Annex, UNGA Res 65/281 (25 July 2011) UN Doc A/RES/65/281 on the 'Review of the Human Rights Council'; A/HRC/RES/16/21 (25 March 2011). Other aspects maintained by the EU relating to the greater involvement of civil society actors were accepted, eg the ability of NGOs and National Human Rights Institutions to make statements by video, which has happened since the period of 19th HRC in 2011. The EU has strongly criticised some States that do not adequately follow up the recommendations of the UPR in the national field with the consequent waste of human and material resources for the HRC. See *EU Statement—UN Human Rights Council, Universal Periodic Review*, Item 6, Ref EUUNG10-026EN, 11 June 2010. In this sense we can say that the proposals made by the EU tend to be the most progressive and committed to the policies being examined here.

[50] Thus, although in 2009 the EU had sponsored two resolutions at the HRC on the situation of human rights in Myanmar and PDR Korea, in 2012 the EU increased its sponsorship to five resolutions, for the cases of Belarus, again PDR Korea and Syria, as well as the rights and freedom of religion and belief. In 2013, there were four resolutions sponsored by the Union, in particular on the situation of human rights in Myanmar and, as in the previous year, again resolutions on PDR Korea, freedom of religion and belief and rights of the child—priority areas for the EU (See Table 5).

[51] In this sense, for the years 2011 and 2012, see J Ferrer Lloret, 'La acción exterior de la Unión Europea en el Consejo de Derechos Humanos de Naciones Unidas: Luces y sombras de la política exterior europea' in A Blanc Altemir (ed) (n 4 above) 426–30. However, that author indicates that there are areas where it was expected that the EU would show greater strength for the human rights violations in the occupied territory of Western Sahara. Cf also Wouters and Meuwissen (n 44 above) 12.

[52] Cf *European Union Medium-term Priorities at the United Nations (2012–2015)* (n 10 above).

[53] For example, in 2011 the EU urged the suspension of Libya's membership of the HRC, approving the establishment of a commission of inquiry to report on the field of human rights violations and a possible prosecution before the International Criminal Court, UNGA Res 65/265 (1 March 2011) UN Doc A/RES/ 65/265. The creation of another commission of inquiry on Syria and the commissioning of a special public procedure with Iran was also approved.

statements made within the HRC are the most formal.[54] Given the restricted status of EU involvement in the HRC, EU statements are still presented by the Permanent Representative of the State accredited to the United Nations in Geneva chairing the Council of the EU during that semester of the Union—generally at the highest level of Ambassador—and regardless of whether that State is a member of the HRC during this mandate, which is perhaps surprising.[55] However, these positions have been worked out with the Delegation of the Union accredited to the United Nations in Geneva, according to the amendments introduced by the Lisbon Treaty.[56] The coordination is done with the national representatives of the current 28 Member States, especially with the State holding the Presidency of the Council. This takes into account the priorities and strategic guidelines established by the *Working Group on Human Rights of the Council of the Union* (COHOM).[57] This complex internal coordination, as occurs in the Third Committee of the UNGA, means that the EU is not characterised by its speed in taking positions, rather the opposite.[58] This has not prevented the EU from significantly increasing the statements presented since 2012 as reflected in its active intervention, indicating that it is more involved in the work of the HRC in various fields and countries (see Table 5).

[54] The EU interventions have a more informal character than the Statements and exceptionally, include comments, contributions or discussions about the issues discussed in the HRC. The number of procedures increased substantially in 2013 and 2014, although in the vast majority of cases interventions occur in the context of an interactive dialogue, which earlier, in 2012 already showed a significant increase. In 2014 46 interactive dialogues (39 in 2013) were maintained, 32 of which were developed in the process of EU interventions (24 in 2013) (See Table 5).

[55] Given that although he is a State representative, that State is not part of the composition of the HRC. If we look back, we see a variety of situations, eg Spain and Belgium, respectively, in the first and second half of 2010, undertook to submit Statements to the HRC on behalf of the EU; Hungary and Poland presented this same pattern in 2011. In these four cases holding the Presidency of the EU coincided with that State's membership in the HRC. However in 2012 this did not occur with Denmark and Cyprus, which nevertheless did not prevent the permanent representatives of the two States accredited to the UN undertaking to present EU Statements in the HRC on behalf of the EU. In 2013, Ireland, who presided over the Council in the first half of the year, was a member of the HRC, but not Lithuania, during the second half. In 2014, the Greek Presidency of the Council did not coincide with its membership in the HRC, while Italy, President of the Council of the Union in the second half, was a member of the HRC.

[56] TFEU (Lisbon) art 221.1.

[57] The COHOM was created in 1987 by the EU Council and is responsible for human rights issues in the external relations of the EU. Its staff are drawn mainly from Member States, together with Commission staff, and the European External Action Service (EEAS). The agenda of COHOM meetings addresses aspects of EU human rights policy action in international forums, dialogues with third countries, thematic issues and other current issues considered urgent. Regular meetings of COHOM have increased in recent years, being particularly frequent in periods of great activity that coincide with the sessions of the Third Committee and UNHRC. This is a change in the terms of the original mandate; initially, it envisaged at least two meetings a year, before the sessions of the former Commission on Human Rights in Geneva and the plenary of the UNGA.

[58] From the perspective of competences, this combination of participating subjects is explained by considering that the promotion and protection of human rights are not exclusive competences of the EU, but shared—coexisting in this area with the external policies developed by each of the 28 Member States. This means that in the context of EU coordination in Geneva when the HRC is in session, up to 3 or 4 meetings per day are held, to which is added abundant electronic correspondence. Cf Wouters and Meuwissen (n 44) 6.

Table 5: UN Human Rights Council (HRC)—European Union

YEAR	EU STATEMENTS	EU INTER-VENTIONS	QUESTIONS / INTERACTIVE DIALOGUES *(1)*	PRIORITY COUNTRIES FOR THE EU	SUBJECTS
2009	14		9	Afghanistan—Burundi Cambodia—China—Cuba—Iran—Liberia—Myanmar*—DR Congo—PDR Korea*—Somalia—Sudan—Zimbawe	Death penalty—Defenders of human rights/civil society—Durban/racism—Freedom of expression and association—Fight against terrorism—Migrants/detention centre—Sexual Orientation—Technical assistance and reconstruction—Transnational Justice—Palestine—Special procedures—Women—UN High Commissioner for Human Rights (UNHCR)—Universality and indivisibility of human rights—Universal Periodic Review (UPR)
2010	**24**	**8**		**Afghanistan—Guinea Conakry—Myanmar—Nepal—DR Congo—PDR Korea**	**Administration of justice and vulnerable groups—Civilians and armed conflict—Children /Sexual Violence –Combat intolerance against persons for religion or belief—Defenders of human rights—Incapacity—Durban/racism—Education—Freedom of expression—Freedom of religion and belief—Fight against terrorism—Global economy and the financial crisis—Impunity—Journalists—LGBT—Maternal mortality—Migrants—Palestine—Special procedures—Technical assistance and reconstruction—Transnational businesses—Trafficking of Women/Children—Women—UN High Commissioner for Human Rights (UNHCR) — Universality and indivisibility of human rights—Universal Periodic Review (UPR)**

(continued)

Table 5: *(Continued)*

YEAR	EU STATEMENTS	EU INTER-VENTIONS	QUESTIONS / INTERACTIVE DIALOGUES (1)	PRIORITY COUNTRIES FOR THE EU	SUBJECTS
2011	*9*	*1*		*Bahrain -Belarus—Cambodia—Iran—Egypt—Eritrea—Syria—Somalia—Sri Lanka—DR Congo—Libya—Tunisia -Yemen*	*Children/Child labour—Civil society—Defenders of human rights—Freedom of expression and association—Impunity—Journalists—Migrants—Near east and North Africa –Racism, racial discrimination, xenophobia and intolerance—Special procedures—Technical assistance and reconstruction—UNHCR—Universality and individuality of human rights—UPR*
2012 (2)	*35*	*9*	*34*	*Belarus*—Cambodia—Côte d'Ivoire—Guinea—Eritrea Haití—Iran—Libya—Syria*—Mali—Myanmar*–Palestine—Somalia—DR Congo—PDR Korea*—Sudan—South Sudan—Yemen*	*Afro-descendants—Arbitrary, summary or extrajudicial executions—Defenders of human rights/Women—Disabilities—Displaced persons—Detentions—Durban/racism—Education –- Health and education—Slavery—Technical assistance and reconstruction—Rights of the child*—Transnational businesses –- Independence of judges and lawyers—Indigenous peoples—Trafficking of persons—Torture—Freedom of religion and belief –* Fight against terrorism—Mercenaries—Migrants—Women—Democratic and equable legal order—Sexual orientation—Human rights monitoring bodies– Poverty—UPR*

(continued)

Table 5: *(Continued)*

YEAR	EU STATEMENTS	EU INTER-VENTIONS	QUESTIONS / INTERACTIVE DIALOGUES *(1)*	PRIORITY COUNTRIES FOR THE EU	SUBJECTS
2013	*30*	*36*	*39*	*Bahrein—Belarus—Cambodia—China—Egypt Eritrea—Iran—Mali—Myanmar*–Palestine—CAR DR Congo—PDR Korea*– Syria—Sri Lanka -Somalia -Sudan—Yemen*	*Business and human rights—Civil society and cooperation with UN—Drinking water—Durban/racism—Forced marriage of Minors—Economic, social and cultural rights—Female genital Mutilation—Freedom of religion and belief*—Indigenous peoples—Minorities—The elderly—Technical assistance and Reconstruction—Right to health—Rights of the child*—Women/empowerment*
2014	*27*	*61*	*46*	*Cambodia—Côte d'Ivoire—China—Eritrea—Haiti—Iraq—Mali—Myanmar—Palestine—PDR Korea—CAR—Somalia—South Sudan—Sudan—Syria—Thailand Ukraine*	*Arbitrary, summary or extrajudicial executions—Death penalty—Defenders of human rights—Democratic and equable legal order Detentions—Displaced persons—Durban/racism—Indigenous peoples—Sexual orientation—Female genital Mutilation—Freedom of religion and belief Freedom of religion and belief—Indigenous peoples—Rights of the child—Sexual orientation—Technical assistance and reconstruction—Trafficking of persons—The elderly—Women/Human rights monitoring bodies—UPR*

Sources: EU Statements at the UN Human Rights Council, available through www.eu-un.europa.eu.

Permanent Delegation of the EU to the United Nations Office and other International Organisations in Geneva, available through: eeas.europa.eu/delegations/un_geneva/eu_statements, accessed June 2015 (Author's Compilation).

— The data highlighted in bold indicate the activity of the HRC after the entry into force of the Lisbon Treaty on 1 December 2009.
— Italics indicate the period from which the EU's observer status was strengthened at the United Nations pursuant to A/RES/65/276 (10 May 2011).
— The asterisk * indicates that the EU has been the sponsor or co-sponsor of resolutions on a particular country or a material subject. Eg, in 2012 the resolution on human rights in the PDRK was introduced in the HRC jointly by the EU and Japan; and the resolution relative to the situation of human rights in Syria was introduced by the EU on behalf of more than 70 co-sponsors or on children's rights with the support of the Group of Latin American and Caribbean States (GRULAC).

(1) The interactive dialogues that the EU maintains usually develop the thread of interventions concerning special procedures on human rights and with high UN officials on the matter.

(2) Starting in 2012 the documentary information about the EU's activities in the Human Rights Council included in: www.eu-un.europa.eu is systematised in a couple of summaries of the type: UN Human Rights Council closes with successful results for the European Union, 22.03.2013, Ref EUUNG13-500EN, Human Rights Council, European Union. The weight of the systematisation and publication of materials has passed from the EU delegations to the European External Action Service (EEAS), cf www.eeas.europa.eu.

In 2012 the renewed role of the EU Delegation to the United Nations in Geneva became involved, housing 'virtually' statements, speeches and interactive dialogues made, among others, on behalf of the EU to the Human Rights Council at: www.eeas.europa.eu, accessed June 2015.

In the calculation of 2012 EU Statements we include those made by the High Representative of the EU for Foreign Affairs and Security Policy, on the occasion of the completion of the HRC, A 431/12, Brussels, (28 September 2012).

IV. PRIORITY AREAS FOR EU ACTION

The activity of the EU and its members in the Third Committee of the UNGA and the HRC has been developed in a number of areas that reflect their main concerns and goals in the matter. The EU has pronounced on them through statements, sponsored or co-sponsored initiatives, and interacted through dialogues or proposed panel discussions—as mentioned above, and set out on an annual basis in Tables 2 and 5, respectively, for the UNGA and HRC. The contents of these tables show that the topics have been repeated and delayed; for example, in relation to the situation of certain groups such as the rights of the child,[59] the rights of women, or more recently, advocates of human rights,[60] the situation of journalists, racism or xenophobia, the latter of which the EU and its members have been working on for decades. Without being exhaustive, certain key areas have been selected that illustrate some of the EU priorities developed in the UNGA and the HRC which indicate a positive and efficient trend in recent years:

A. Freedom of Religion or Belief

The defence of *freedom of religion or belief* is one of these priorities. The EU has often successfully introduced into the UNGA a resolution on the subject of *elimination of all forms of intolerance and discrimination based on religion or belief*, supported by several countries. In the HRC the EU has maintained a very active role in the review of the special procedure mandates, with the Special Rapporteur on freedom of religion or belief, thanks to the numerous informal consultations during the special session of 2007.[61] In line with recent EU directives and conclusions of COHOM, the EU has decided to reinforce certain aspects linked to the defence of this freedom, such as equality between men and women and the right of each individual to change their religion or belief. Thus, in 2014 the EU has managed to introduce more direct and explicit language on the subject in a resolution before the UN General Assembly in session 68, despite meeting strong opposition from most States of the Organisation of the Islamic Cooperation (OIC). The resolution on freedom of religion or belief was adopted without a vote being taken, with 68 co-sponsors together with the 28 Member States of the EU.[62]

One of the touchstones for the EU in this area, linked to the freedom of expression, is the adoption of resolutions on *combating defamation of religions* carried by both the UNGA and the HRC and generally introduced by OIC member

[59] In this sphere, the EU has emphasised including in its agenda discussion of early and forced marriages.

[60] Specifically, women activists or the issue of female genital mutilation.

[61] Cf J Wouters, S Basu and N Bernaz, 'The Role of the European Union in the Human Rights Council' (*Study for the European Parliament Policy Department External Policies*, EXPO/B/DROI/2007/41, November 2008) 14.

[62] UNGA Res 68/170 (21 January 2014) UN Doc A/RES/68/170.

countries.[63] The EU has made its opposition to these resolutions clear, considering that the International Law on Human Rights protects primarily *individuals* in the exercise of their freedom of religion or confession, rather than the religions themselves.[64] As an example, in the HRC the then seven Member States of the EU unanimously voted against the resolutions submitted in 2008 and 2009 on this issue.[65] Thereafter, coinciding with more robust examples of EU actions within the HRC, the OIC failed to present the controversial resolution on defamation of religion—for the first time in nearly a decade in the HRC and the former Commission on Human Rights.[66] The loss of support for the OIC in this area was also reflected in the UNGA, as demonstrated in the voting that took place on *combating defamation of religions*.[67]

B. Defending the Rights of the LGBT Communities

Defending the rights of LGBT communities (lesbian, gay, bisexual and transgender people) is one of the priority areas of EU activity in the United Nations through which the universality of human rights is defended.[68] That LGBT people have the same rights as other people is a vindication of the EU in the United Nations and other international forums, so this area is closely linked to European diplomacy. The Union has led campaigns at various levels to defend the rights of this collective,[69] aligning itself with third countries in order to get key support. In this

[63] UNGA Res 62/154 (18 December 2007) UN Doc A/RES/62/154. This resolution on 'combating defamation of religions' was approved with 108 votes in favour, 51 against and 25 abstentions. The result shows the lack of agreement between the members of the international community in this regard.

[64] Specifically, in order that legislation that undermined freedom of expression should not be adopted the EU has argued that defamation of Islam is not a racist backlash against Muslims. The terrorist attack on the French satirical weekly magazine 'Charlie Hebdo', where 12 people were killed in 2015, shows the extreme difficulties of understanding in a consistent manner freedom of expression and freedom of religion.

[65] UNHRC Res 7/19 (2008) and Res 10/22 (2009). A/HRC/7/L.11, 27 March 2008. The result of the vote was 21 in favour, 10 against and 14 abstentions.

[66] Cf UNGA Res 66/168 (19 December 2011) UN Doc A/66/168. From 2012 the resolutions on this subject were called more shortly *freedom of religion and belief*.

[67] Talks between the US and Pakistan were instrumental in paving the way and preventing the OIC from submitting its resolution on defamation of religion. UNGA Res 65/224 (21 December 2010) UN Doc A/RES/65/224 was adopted with 76 votes in favour, 64 against and 42 abstentions. The EU explained its vote against, specifically requesting that the resolution be put to the vote. Again the results show the lack of consensus of the international community on this issue, projected in the General Assembly. It was a breakthrough since in the following sessions no resolution was presented at the UNGA, but in 2012 and 2013 one was presented relating to '*Combating intolerance, negative stereotyping, stigmatization, discrimination, incitement to violence and violence against persons based on religion or belief*, cf UNGA Res 67/178 (20 December 2012) UN Doc A/RES/67/178 and UNGA Res 68/169 (18 December 2013) UN Doc A/RES/68/169.

[68] Cf, among EU Statements within the HRC in 2010, one dedicated to protecting the rights of LGBT, *Statement EU—UN Human Rights Council, Thematic reports of UN High Commissioner for Human Rights and Secretary-General*, Item 2/3, Ref EUUNG10-025EN, 9 June 2010.

[69] Within the United Nations the 'Statement on Human Rights and Sexual Identity and Gender Orientation' of 2008, put forward by France is striking.

sphere, the role of NGOs in the work of the HRC is of great value for this body, its members and the EU.[70] The EU and the US formed a coalition to react with a counter-offensive, to vote in favour on the protection of individuals, regardless of sexual orientation, within the UNGA, which finally obtained 93 votes in favour and 53 against.[71]

Also in that same year, EU activity in the HRC was intense in relation to the need to promote the universality of these human rights in order to protect the rights of LGBT people.[72] In 2011 the EU, through Hungary, urged international consensus on the responsibility to ensure non-discrimination and protection from violence of LGBT people. With the support of other regional groups, a total of 85 States including non-members of the HRC supported this declaration that requested an end to acts of violence, criminal sanctions and human rights violations against individuals based on their sexual orientation or gender.[73] The support of Western European countries was crucial to the adoption of a resolution of the HRC in 2011 to commission the UN High Commissioner for Human Rights to investigate acts of violence and discrimination against people because of their sexual orientation and gender identity.[74] This issue, however, still finds opposition from many States of the OIC and the African Group, so the EU has difficulties in finding the necessary support to reintroduce once again the resolution on LGBT rights in the HRC.[75]

[70] See general comments of Amnesty International or COC Nederland to certain countries on the failed recommendations intended to decriminalise sexual activity between consenting adults of the same sex and combat discrimination based on sexual orientation and gender identity in A/HRC/17/2, 24 May 2011.

[71] The EU strongly supported an amendment by USA (A/65/L.53) which sought to recognise that all people have the right not to be victims of extrajudicial execution, including those who have been attacked because of their 'sexual orientation'. As against this, a coalition of African and Muslim-majority States expressed their rejection to include obligations of States to protect LGBT people as part of a resolution on extrajudicial, summary or arbitrary executions. Cf UNGA Res 65/208 (30 March 2011) UN Doc A/RES/65/208. This coalition argued that the amendment reinterpreted international law instruments on human rights that had been agreed, equating discrimination based on an undefined notion of 'sexual orientation' to other forms of discrimination universally recognised and codified in international human rights instruments, such as race, colour, gender, ethnicity, nationality, religion and language. Cf UNGA Res A/65/PV.71 (21 December 2010).

[72] *EU Statement—UN Human Rights Council, Thematic reports of UN High Commissioner for Human Rights and Secretary—General,* Item 2/3, Ref EUUNG10-025EN, 9 June 2010.

[73] *Human Rights Council holds general debate follow-up and Implementation of the Vienna Declaration and Programme of Action,* 22 March 2011, Press Releases, News and Events, Press Release Archives: www.ohchr.org.

[74] The study was aimed at documenting laws, discriminatory practices and violence against LGBT people in all regions of the world, and analysing how international human rights law can be applied to stop these acts; cf A/HRC/17/L.9/Rev.1 (15 June 2011), *Human rights, sexual orientation and gender identity*. Most African and Asian countries opposed it. However, South Africa took a strong position relative to other non-Western States, being one of the members of the coalition that led the resolution. This was passed by 23 votes for and 19 against (China abstained).

[75] For this reason, the Guidelines adopted on the promotion and protection of the rights of this group have been widely developed to serve as an instrument for the EU, its organs, institutions and officials. Cf *Guidelines to promote and protect the enjoyment of all human rights by lesbian, gay, bisexual, transgender and intersex persons* (LGBTI), Union Council, 24 June 2013, 11492/13, COHOM 134.

C. Abolition of the Death Penalty

Abolition of the death penalty and the moratorium on executions is another priority of the EU, as well as one of its flagship actions. The results are due to the intensive coordination work that the EU and its Member States have carried out at different levels, including bilateral dialogues with countries that maintain the death penalty in their legislation; consciousness-raising campaigns, with the support of the UN High Commissioner on Human Rights,[76] using a time-limited campaigns approach; as well as the action of NGOs that also participate as observers in the HRC.[77] The worldwide support in favour of the moratorium on the death penalty is one of the most remarkable achievements brought about by the essential drive of the EU in the Third Committee of the UNGA and the HRC.[78]

D. Universality of the International Law of Human Rights

A priority and cross-cutting issue for the EU is the defence of the *universality of the International Law of Human Rights*, generating considerable tension with certain countries. The universality of human rights as a guiding principle appears solidly defended by numerous declarations made 'on behalf of the EU' in the UNGA and the HRC. In the Human Rights Council, these declarations have included open criticism of certain States, for example, requesting clarification of concepts such as 'cultural diversity', 'traditional values' or 'regional particularities', the EU considering that sometimes they are used in order to accommodate interpretations not consistent with the obligations of those States in the field of human rights, and this is so irrespective of whether they are committed to them legally

[76] Among activities organised with other agencies, a recent one has been the discussion panel conducted by the Office of the High Commission of Human Rights with the support of the EU Delegation at the UN in Geneva on 'Moving away from the death penalty—Wrongful Convictions', 27 June 2013.

[77] Eg, Amnesty International, in its general observations on the Report of the HRC in its 17th session, examines countries that did not support the HRC's recommendations on the abolition of the death penalty, urging these governments to repeal these provisions and declare a moratorium on executions. A/HRC/17/2 (24 May 2011) para 536. Noting this fact, the EU *Strategic Framework on Human Rights and Democracy*, 25 June 2012, emphasises that the EU will raise Universal Periodic Review recommendations in bilateral dialogues with third countries, as well as the conventional security mechanisms of guarantee and the Special Procedures of the United Nations; cf in COHOM 163, 11855/12, p 8. In another development, a reflection of the pressure from the EU in this area is found in its comments on the shortages suffered by US prisons of drugs for the lethal injection protocol, which had tragic consequences for the implementation of the death penalty for two inmates in 2014 that the UN has assimilated to cruel and inhumane treatment amounting to torture.

[78] The EU stated that 'the abolition of the death penalty is one of the main objectives of the EU external human rights policy', taking into account the atrocities committed by ISIS/Daesh or by terrorist groups in different parts of the world: EU Intervention, HRC res 26/2, 4 March 2015, Biennial High-level Panel on the question of the Death Penalty and on the moratorium on the use of the death penalty, adopted by a record number of 117 yes votes and 95 countries co-sponsoring the initiative, where the EU has been extremely active. Regarding the United Nations General Assembly, see R Kissack, 'The EU in Negotiations of a UN General Assembly Resolution on a Moratorium on the Use of the Death Penalty' in Wouters et al (eds), *The European Union and Multilateral Governance* (n 38 above) 103.

under international treaties.[79] The block vote of the seven EU Member States participating in the HRC, opposing an HRC resolution on the *promotion of human rights and fundamental freedoms through a better understanding of the traditional values of humankind* reflects the clear EU position on the matter.[80] Another particular example shows the determination of the EU High Representative for Foreign Affairs and Security Policy to deny the charge sometimes made that the EU is 'exporting' so-called 'European values' to other countries, indicating that the rights of freedom of speech, assembly, judicial protection and equality, among others, are not only European rights, but universal.[81]

E. Belarus, PDR Korea and Myanmar

The EU has paid special attention to certain countries, some of which are relatively close, like Belarus, as well as Asian countries such as PDR Korea and Myanmar. Developments driven by the EU on Myanmar (Burma) have been very positive, with a clear reflection in the most recent decisions. This can be seen in the review of domestic legislation in this State that was done to ensure compatibility with international standards on human rights and, more specifically, in the progress on the release of political prisoners. The resolution on the situation of human rights in Myanmar by the EU, through Lithuania as the State presiding over the Council of the Union, in session 68 of UNGA (2013–14) had a greater number of sponsors than in previous years, 49 in total. Previous EU contacts with the OIC as well as both agencies with Myanmar were key to negotiating the content of the resolution.[82] Also in the ordinary session 22 (in 2013) of the HRC, the EU tabled a resolution on Myanmar, which was adopted unanimously, concerning

[79] Cf *Statement* by the Spanish Ambassador, on behalf of the EU, as Permanent Representative of the Member State which held the Council presidency of the EU in the first half of 2010, that is, with the Treaty of Lisbon newly entered into force, *EU—UN Human Rights Council, Vienna Declaration and Programme of Action*, Item 8 General Debate, Ref EUUNG10-028EN, 15 June 2010. The reflections on the imposition of a model of human rights by the EU to respond to a Western conception of neocolonial spirit against which other States are positioned are interesting. See eg those not aligned with the EU proposal in the UNGA: C Leben, 'Is there a European Approach to Human Rights?' in P Alston (ed), *The EU and Human* Rights (Oxford, Oxford University Press, 1999) 69–97.

[80] Cf A/HRC/RES/16/3 (8 April 2011), which refers to 'better understanding of the traditional values of humankind underpinning the international human rights norms and standards (para 1) or 'the important role of family, community, society and educational institutions in upholding and transmitting these values' (para 5). This resolution was approved with 24 votes in favour, 14 against and 7 abstentions. The *EU Strategic Framework on Human Rights and Democracy*, 25 June 2012 is clear about this, when it states in regard to human rights, that their 'universal nature is questioned on grounds of cultural differences' (n 77 above) 3.

[81] The first High Representative of the Union stated 'we must never fall into the trap of believing people in other parts of the world are any less passionate about their rights too'. In this sense, she recalls the 2005 report of the Secretary-General Kofi Annan when he stated, in relation to the broad concept of freedom that 'Human rights are as fundamental to the poor as to the rich, and their protection is as important to the security and prosperity of the developed world as it is to that of the developing world'. Speech by EU High Representative for Foreign Affairs and Security Policy Catherine Ashton before the Human Rights Council, Ref SP11-018EN, 28 February 2011.

[82] The most complex aspects of consensus referred to the situation of human rights of Muslim minorities such as the Rohingyas, primarily in the Rakhine area of Myanmar, as well as delays in the opening of an UNHCR office; cf UNGA Res 68/242 (27 December 2013) UN Doc A/RES/68/242.

the continuation of the above-mentioned reforms and, in particular, the delicate situation of minorities reflecting the positive developments in this country.[83] Even in the EU's least active period in the HRC in 2007, it managed to put forward an initiative on Myanmar in the extraordinary Fifth period of sessions.

The EU, through the State chairing the Council, has submitted a resolution on the situation of human rights in North Korea to session 68 (2013–14) of UNGA, which did not need to lead to a vote. However, in contrast to Myanmar, that State linked a possible dialogue with the EU to the withdrawal of the draft resolution. The EU did not accede to this request, receiving significant support from Japan and the US, with a total of 59 sponsors for the resolution, exceeding that of the previous year.[84] Progress has been made towards greater cohesion between the States of different regional groups, as shown by the consensus reached at the HRC to submit a joint proposal by the EU and Japan to establish an International Commission of Inquiry. Nevertheless, the PDR Korea has not yet accepted its creation. In relation to this country, there is more widespread dissatisfaction than in the period before 2013, which the EU shares, about the process that has developed, eg, in relation to the situation in prison camps.

Finally, the EU interest in the situation of human rights in Belarus is clearly reflected in the UNGA and HRC.[85] At the 20th session of the HRC in 2012, the EU and its Member States submitted a resolution on the establishment of a *Special Rapporteur on the situation of human rights in Belarus*, which was adopted by a wider majority than the previous year.[86] This success contrasts with the abolition of the mandate to Belarus at the HRC, which was a defeat for the EU and its Member States.

These areas include, like a shop window, a sample of EU activity in the field of human rights in the General Assembly of the United Nations and the Human Rights Council.

V. THE THIRD STATES AND THEIR BROAD SUPPORT FOR THE EU

The EU has spent decades developing an intense and active coordination with third countries and groups of countries in order to combine positions and promote joint actions—with significant economic support—which has gained in intensity in recent years.[87] Such collaboration is clearly reflected in the work

[83] This achievement is another part of the process, since in the 20th regular session of the HRC held in 2012, the EU introduced a resolution on the establishment of a Special Rapporteur on human rights in Belarus, which was approved by a bigger majority than in the previous year.

[84] UNGA Res 68/183 (18 December 2014) UN Doc A/RES/68183. *Overview of the 68th Session of the United Nations General Assembly, Third Committee 2013* (n 24 above) 13, 120.

[85] In 2011, the HRC paid attention to the complaints relating to the detention of human rights defenders and the precarious situation of the media.

[86] In the debates, the EU highlighted the deteriorating human rights in this European country since the presidential elections of December 2010, the only country applying the death penalty in Europe.

[87] For the 2014–20 multiannual financial framework the Commission proposed increasing funding for the European Instrument for Democracy and Human Rights worldwide to €1.5 million, with €1.1 million for the previous multi-year period (2007–13); cf Council and European Parliament Regulation (EC) 1889/2006 of 20 December 2006 [2006] OJ L386/1; the Joint Communication of the High Representative of the Union for Foreign Affairs and Security Policy and the Commission to the European

carried out in both the UNGA, and specifically in its Third Committee, as well as in the Human Rights Council, as shown in the previous sections of this chapter.

Formal EU statements made in the context of the work of the Third Committee of the UNGA and HRC are made through, respectively, the Head of the EU Delegation to the UN and the Permanent Representatives of the State or those who on attachment that semester hold the Presidency of the Council of the Union, accredited to the UN. Such statements usually include an opening paragraph that indicates the alignment or accession to that statement of other countries linked in various ways to the EU—candidates or potential candidates, certain States integrated in the association and stabilisation,[88] of the EU Neighbourhood Policy (ENP)[89] or the European Free Trade Association (EFTA).[90]

Most EU statements not only reflect the consensus of its Member States, but also include, on ad hoc basis, a large number of States, that on average, in recent years, range from eight to eleven in number.[91] That seems common—apparently reached on the basis of continuous work—on issues related to human rights, and is a reflection of a broad global consensus on the adoption of resolutions. In the Third Committee of UNGA there is a regular exchange of information among the countries aligned with the EU, through meetings prior to each session, in which the priorities and positions to be adopted by the Union during the session are addressed. Most countries co-sponsoring the EU initiatives vote in a similar way and adhere to their declarations and positions. In this broad group are the States with values similar to those of the EU principles.[92] Visually (see Table 6) the consensus in the adoption of resolutions brought to a vote during the work of the 68th session (2013–14) of the Third Committee of the UNGA can be easily checked showing the position of the EU—with its 28 Member States—and of the above States, belonging to the process of stabilisation and association with the EU, with EFTA, and including candidates.

Council, the European Parliament and the Council of 12 December 2011, 'Human Rights and Democracy at the centre of EU external action' (n 10 above) 10. Other financial instruments of EU external action affecting the field of human rights for 2014–20 are The Development Cooperation Instrument with €23.3 million, the Pre-accession Instrument of 14.11 million Euros, the European Neighbourhood Instrument of €18.1 million and the Association Instrument of €1.1 million.

[88] In the Association and Stability Process, the EU has a special relationship with the following candidate countries: Turkey, Montenegro, Serbia, the Former Yugoslav Republic of Macedonia, as well as with Bosnia & Herzegovina and Albania, as potential candidates.

[89] The countries with which the EU develops its ENP are Tunisia, Armenia, Azerbaijan, Belarus, Georgia, Moldova, Ukraine, Algeria, Egypt, Israel, Jordan, Lebanon, Morocco and Syria.

[90] Members States of EFTA are Switzerland, Liechtenstein, Norway and Iceland, the latter as a candidate for the EU.

[91] Eg in the 68th session (2013–14), Turkey, a candidate State, did not align itself to EU Statements so assiduously, however, Liechtenstein did. cf EU Statement, UN Human Rights Council: Universal Periodic Review, 11 June 2011, Ref EUUNG10-026EN. Eight States aligned to the EU appear in the EU Statement—General Debate Item 6, Universal Periodic Review, UN Human Rights Council, 21 March 2014, 25th Session (3–28 March 2014), in which the EU reiterates its strong commitment to the UPR as a mechanism that encompasses all human rights and all UN Member States, and in which civil society organisations develop an essential role.

[92] For a detailed analysis and consultation of tables comparing voting patterns of the UN States grouped with those of the EU in the UNGA Third Committee, cf Overview of the 68th Session of the United Nations General Assembly, Third Committee 2013 (n 24 above) 20–21, 155–62.

Table 6: United Nations General Assembly—Third Committee on Social, Humanitarian and Cultural Affairs—68th period of sessions—Voting patterns of EU, candidates, Association and Stabilisation Process and EFTA countries

EFTA CANDIDATES											
RES A/C.3/68	**EU 28**	**Switzerland**	**Liechtenstein**	**Norway**	**Montenegro**	**Serbia**	**Turkey**	**Iceland**	**Former Yugoslav Republic of Macedonia**	**Bosnia and Hezegovina**	**Albania**
Right to development (A/RES/158)	11Y/ 16A/ 1N	Y	Y	A	Y	Y	Y	A	Y	Y	A
Cultural Diversity (A/RES/159)	N	N	N	N	N	N	N	N	N	N	N
Equitable Geographically Distribution in human rights treaty bodies (A/RES/68/161)	N	N	N	N	N	N	N	N	N	N	N
Unilateral coercive measures and human rights (A/RES/68/162)	N	N	N	N	N	N	N	N	N	N	N

(continued)

Table 6: *(Continued)*

RES A/C.3/68	EU 28	Switzerland	Liechtenstein	Norway	Montenegro	Serbia	Turkey	Iceland	Former Yugoslav Republic of Macedonia	Bosnia and Hezegovina	Albania
Human rights situation in Syria (A/RES/68/182)	Y	Y	Y	Y	Y	Y	Y	Y	Y	Y	Y
Globalisation and its impact on human rights (A/RES/68/168)	N	N	N	N	N	N	N	N	N	N	N
Centre for South-East Asia and the Arab Region for training in human rights (A/RES/68/241)	Y	Y	Y	Y	Y	Y	Y	Y	Y	Y	Y
Situation of human rights in Iran (A/RES/68/184)	Y	Y	Y	Y	Y	Y	Y	Y	Y	Y	Y

(continued)

Table 6: *(Continued)*

RES A/C.3/68	EU 28	Switzerland	Liechtenstein	Norway	Montenegro	Serbia	Turkey	Iceland	Former Yugoslav Republic of Macedonia	Bosnia and Hezegovina	Albania
Promotion of international democratic and equitable order (A/RES/68/175)	N	N	N	N	N	N	N	N	N	N	N
Combating glorification of Nazism (A/RES/68/152)	A	A	A	A	A	Y	Y	A	Y	A	A
Use of Mercenaries as a means to violating human rights (A/RES/68/152)	N	A	N	N	N	N	N	N	N	N	N
Universal realisation of right to self-determination (A/RES/68/153)	Y	Y	Y	Y	Y	Y	Y	Y	Y	Y	Y

(continued)

Table 6: ***(Continued)***

RES A/C.3/68	EU 28	Switzerland	Liechtenstein	Norway	Montenegro	Serbia	Turkey	Iceland	Former Yugoslav Republic of Macedonia	Bosnia and Hezegovina	Albania
Durban/Racism Process (A/ RES/68/151)	24 A/ 4N	N	N	N	N	N	N	N	N	N	N
Report of HRC (A/RES/68/144)	N	N	N	N	N	N	N	N	N	N	N

Source: *Overview of the 68th Session of the United Nations General Assembly, Third Committee 2013—Delegation of the European Union to the United Nations*, New York, February 2014, pp 155–62.

— 'Y' corresponds to Yes as a vote in favour; 'A' corresponds to Abstention and 'N' to No as a vote against.

Together with the States which regularly align their positions to that of the EU in the UNGA and HRC as examined above, are other members of the United Nations. Many of them are key actors in building interregional coalitions with whom the EU has relations to achieve their mutual goals and priorities in the field of human rights. We can contrast an interesting classification showing the support obtained by the EU in the UNGA for the period 2006–08,[93] with a more recent one that reflects the current status of relationships between the EU and other States in the human rights field, usually acting as a regional group:

a) With Japan, the US, Canada, Australia and New Zealand (JUSCANZ), the EU has maintained close relationships and exchanged information prior to the beginning of the sessions of the Third Committee of the UNGA for some years now. Among them the close cooperation between the EU and Japan has notably intensified in recent times.[94] In the HRC, the adhesion of the US as a member since June 2009 has strengthened the group initiatives of the Western and other States, where the majority of the Member States of the EU are found, benefiting from the activity and support network of US power. The EU and the US, with the Obama administration enjoying the second year of its first term, have voted identically on one-third of the occasions since the latter country obtained membership status in 2009, both trying to maintain a constructive dialogue with other countries on human rights. However, there are some specific and critical areas on which there is no convergence and which affects their joint work.[95]

[93] Gowan and Brantner classified different groups, showing voting coincidence between UN Member States and the EU: 1. 'Wider Europe' which includes the current 28 Member States and other European countries generally aligned with the EU, that is, generally voting with it. This group has been strengthened and increased in number over the last decade. It brings together 44 States, 23 per cent of the members of the United Nations. 2. 'Liberal Internationalist', which brings together the countries that voted with the EU on more than half of the occasions. In sessions 61 and 62 (2006 to 2008) there were 44 States, 23 per cent of the members of the UN. It includes three sub-groups: the US and Israel; non-European advanced economies like Canada or the Republic of Korea (South), and finally Latin American democracies. 3. The largest group in the UNGA is the 'swing voters' with between 36 per cent and 50 per cent of UN members and includes, for example, most of the G-77. Notable sub-groups are: India and South Africa as representatives of Alienated Emerging Powers; members of the OIC; and other African and Asian States. 4. The final group, 'Axis of Sovereighnty', is the smallest and includes 19 States representing 10 per cent of the members of the United Nations. They are characterised by voting against EU human rights positions. The influence of the 'Axis of Sovereignty' is greater because of its special membership. For example, China and Russia possess greater influence because of their status in the United Nations, while Egypt hold greater influence on the basis of being a regional power. Also belonging to this group are the former Soviet republics of Kazakhstan and Uzbekistan, as well as Algeria, Azerbaijan, Bangladesh, Belarus, PDR Korea, Cuba, Egypt, Equatorial Guinea, India, Iran, Indonesia, Libya, Russia, Tunisia, Venezuela and Vietnam. See Gowan and Brantner (n 15 above) 2–3.

[94] The partnership between the EU and the countries of JUSCANZ was essential in relation to the resolution on the report of the HRC (A/RES/68/144, 18 December 2013). Specifically, Japan worked jointly with the EU in proposing the amendment. With Japan, the EU developed advocacy campaigns in order to take specific decisions on countries such as the joint initiative on the Resolution on PDR Korea (A/RES/68/183), Myanmar (Resolution sponsored by Japan, A/RES/68/242), Resolutions on freedom of religion or belief (A/RES/68/170) and on the rights of the child (A/RES/68/147, also co-sponsored by Japan and the EU) (see Table 5 above on the key areas).

[95] The death penalty, the International Criminal Court, the Guantanamo detention centre, and more recently, the protection of personal data. Moreover, the EU and the US still maintain differences

b) Cooperation with Latin American and Caribbean States (GRULAC) can generally be classified as very good. The Union works closely with Mexico, Argentina, Uruguay, Chile, Peru, Guatemala, Costa Rica and, to some extent, El Salvador. There have appeared, however, tensions in the dynamics in consultations on the resolution on the rights of the child, in which the EU has been working intensively with other States from an integrative perspective on the problem, for example, with Uruguay. Within GRULAC, the relations with Cuba, as well as Venezuela, Ecuador and Nicaragua, remain complex and show clear dissension.

c) Within the African group the EU has had traditional partners on key issues, including gender. Nevertheless, the 68th period of sessions, mainly developed in late 2013, has revealed clear differences, eg, resolution on defenders of human rights of women, or the EU's own resolution on the report of the HRC, with delegations from Cameroon, Djibouti and Nigeria, and even, to some extent, South Africa, being particularly active. Negotiating the resolution on the Durban Process/racism has been more complex than in previous years.

d) Member States of the Organisation of the Islamic Cooperation (OIC) have played an active role in the work in the Third Committee of the UNGA, due, among other reasons, to its sponsoring the resolution on combating intolerance and the involvement of some of the countries of the Arab group regarding the situation in Syria. As in other years, this group has a proactive approach in relation to the situation of the minority Rohingya people in Myanmar. In general, the EU believes that the work with the States of the OIC, despite its complexity and some disagreements, is constructive for a better mutual understanding, as has been shown with Egypt or Djibouti, and in pursuit of a complex consensus on the resolution on freedom of religion or belief.

e) The different sensitivities and approaches to human rights between the EU and China are evident in the development of their work, eg, on issues such as the moratorium on the death penalty, freedom of assembly and the rights of the child. However, relations between the two countries through regular consultations at the Third Committee of the UNGA have been constructive, as shown in bringing about the resolution on children's rights to which China presented no amendments, or the resolutions on PDR Korea or Myanmar.

f) Prior to the events in Crimea and eastern Ukraine, relations between the EU and the Russian Federation had progressed in certain respects in the course of the work

with other non-European States on various generic issues, some relating to basic principles such as religious freedom and other issues relating to the internal nature of the UN, such as the geographical distribution of the members of the treaty bodies for the protection of rights. See Gowan and Brantner, *The EU and Human Rights at the UN: 2010 Review* (n 31 above) 3.

of the Third Committee. There had been a better understanding, for example, in terms of the resolution on combating the glorification of Nazism. However, in other relevant areas differences remain, eg, the stubborn defence of traditional family values (in contrast to LGBT rights or non-parental sex education) in relation to the resolution of the HRC report, which the Russian Federation co-sponsored in conjunction with the African group.

g) A State with which disagreements and tensions continue is Belarus, despite its geographical proximity to the EU, having no conciliatory positions with those of the EU, either in informal discussions or in the Third Committee, including the set of ad hoc resolutions on countries. Belarus maintains, with the Russian Federation and with the support of the Holy See, the radical defence of traditional family values, expressed by questioning the EU Special Representative for Human Rights' position in the subjects listed above.[96]

h) With India and Indonesia, the EU is making greater efforts than in the past to achieve consensus; for example, with the latter, its work on the negotiation of the resolution on Myanmar remains extremely collaborative.

i) Finally, the relations of the EU and CARICOM States have not been notable for their harmony in the Third Committee of the UNGA, maintaining on occasions a certain tension, eg, in negotiations on the resolution on the rights of the child, cited above.[97]

In short, the EU uses its strong position with third States in the Third Committee of the UNGA and the HRC. This activity is key to achieving the priority objectives of the EU's human rights policy and, in particular, to promoting the creation or extension of extra-conventional procedures to protect human rights. Therefore, the EU and its Member States have to use the common bases and tools established at other levels,[98] from political dialogues to development to cooperation,

[96] The new figure of the EU Special Representative for Human Rights completed his first term from 1 September 2012 until the end of 2014, Stavros Lambrinidis having been appointed to that post. In his role he 'shall act and speak on behalf of the Union, reflecting the shared and indivisible responsibility of all EU institutions and Member States to protect and promote human rights worldwide', emphasising visibility, effectiveness, coherence and accountability of EU policy on human rights, cf European Parliament recommendation to the Council of 13 June 2012, P7_TA (2012) 0250; Council Decision 2012/440/PESC July 25, 2012, appointing the EU Special Representative for Human Rights, (27 July 2012) [2012] OJ L200/21.

[97] Member States of CARICOM are Antigua and Barbuda, Bahamas, Barbados, Belize, Dominica, Granada, Guyana, Haiti, Jamaica, St Lucia, St Kitts and Nevis, St Vincent and the Grenadines, Suriname and Trinidad and Tobago. CARICOM's strong stance regarding the strengthening of EU observer status in the UNGA is interesting; see (n 1 above).

[98] In this regard, numerous international agreements between the EU and third countries and with international organisations at bilateral and multilateral level are of extraordinary value, which may include, among other things, various forms of economic cooperation by the EU, development of joint projects, supplemented with information exchanges and political dialogue or other multi-level contacts.

in order to promote a stronger cohesion between States and groups from different continents, which may, in turn, generate a carry-over effect for the sake of greater commitment and efficiency in this area given to parochial interpretations and applications.[99]

VI. CONCLUSIONS

1. In the post-Lisbon era, we find the cohesion of the EU Member States is similar to the previous situation (2006 to 2009) at the Third Committee of the UN General Assembly (devoted mainly to human rights), despite the difficulties associated with the more complex internal coordination following the EU enlargements of 2004 and 2007. It is precisely the enormous effort of internal coordination in search of synergies between the Member States of the EU that has produced an erosion in the diplomatic energies that need to be deployed, above all, with third countries, with the negative effect of reducing the EU's capacity and time to project itself.

2. From mid-2010 the situation of internal cohesion in the UNGA has also been seen among the EU Member States participating in the Human Rights Council,[100] defending the most progressive and ambitious proposals on promotion and protection of human rights. However, the status of observer and member, respectively, of the EU and its Member States (eight in 2015 and 2016) in the HRC should be used even more effectively to plan their strategies and conduct their activities in accordance with their priority lines, weaving with care a network of interregional support. To this end, campaigns to promote certain candidates for election in the HRC, both from EU countries and third parties, which the EU deems appropriate to foster human rights, might help.[101] To do this it would be desirable for the EU to mobilise its resources in order to strengthen its observer status at the HRC, with experience acquired in the UNGA. For example, this would enable the Permanent Representative of the EU Delegation accredited to the UN in Geneva, not only to direct the coordination with the indispensable support of Member States and

[99] See KV Laatikainen and KE Smith, 'Introduction—The European Union at the United Nations: Leader, Partner of Failure?' in KV Laatikainen and KE Smith (eds), *The European Union at the United Nations, Intersecting Multilateralisms* (Basingstoke, Palgrave, 2006) 9; Salinas (n 4 above), 454.

[100] Some authors analyse the behaviour of the EU in human right matters in the United Nations as making unrealistic proposals bearing in mind its limited powers. By considering itself as a State, and comparing itself with third countries (the USA, China, Russia, and others) it is demanding a degree of cohesion and activity that the EU does not and will not have unless its 28 members as such disappear and are absorbed in a new, solid supranational entity in international society. Given the current situation of the Member States this seems very implausible in the near future, almost science fiction. See in that sense, Gowan and Brantner, 2008 (n 15 above) 8–10.

[101] In this sense, the EU and its Member States in the HRC are presented with the challenge of dealing with the latest batch of elected countries, including States that are characterised by their excessive zeal for sovereignty and little commitment to multilateralism, such as China, Cuba, the Russian Federation and Algeria; cf GA/11454, 12 November 2013, 68th General Assembly Plenary, 51st meeting.

their embassies, but also to take the floor on behalf of the Union in the Palais des Nations, instead of the State chairing the EU Council doing so, in line with the provisions of the Lisbon Treaty.

3. In maintaining and strengthening the internal cohesion of the EU in the promotion and protection of human rights, the work of the Third Committee of the UNGA and the HRC has been largely matched by the efficient progression of EU activity projected outwards. The greater visibility of the EU, appreciable since 2010, through increased interventions, interactive dialogues or statements, with positive dynamics of cohesion enhance the carry-over effect which it produces for third countries.[102]

The adoption of resolutions in the Third Committee of the UNGA and the HRC, as well as the statements and actions of the EU in response to them, present the positions and interpretations of a group of European States—bearing in mind the intergovernmental nature of those bodies—as well as a regional organisation. In almost all cases these positions and interpretations are unified and cohesive, which contributes greatly to a better understanding of the content and application of freedoms and rights between the EU, on the one hand, and other States, on the other. This exercise in understanding and homogenisation of sensitivities on the rights that States seek to promote and protect helps to bring about the conclusion of international agreements, in whose negotiation the EU can participate and to which it can then express its consent—eg the United Nations Convention on the Rights of Persons with Disabilities.[103] A similar function is played in their amendment, in accepting reservations made by other States and consequent objections to reservations that are incompatible with the object and purpose of the treaty.[104]

[102] Thus, the annual comparative assessment of 2013 carried out by the European Council on Foreign Relations on the European policy in the UN, including the UNGA and UNHRC, among others, is valued more positively than in previous years, with a B-; 2012 had a C-; and 2011 a C+. See on this study and the method of valuation in the European Council, *European Foreign Policy Scorecard 2014*, (London, January 2014), especially at 101, available from: www.ecfr.eu/. This does not exclude that in 2013, for example, relations with some third countries were more problematic than in previous years, as with Turkey regarding the situation of human rights, or with Russia.

[103] See Council Decision (EC) 48/2010 concerning the conclusion by the European Community of the UN Convention on the Rights of Persons with Disabilities [2009] OJ L23/35. The EU already participated in the development of other related conventions linked in the broadest sense to human rights, including the 1998 Statute of the International Criminal Court or the 1997 Convention on the Prohibition of the Use, Stockpiling, Production and Transfer of Anti-Personnel Mines and on their Destruction. Cf on the possible accession of the EU to other international human rights conventions and their effects, R Marín Aís, *La participación de la UE en tratados internacionales para la protección de los derechos humanos* (Madrid, Tecnos 2013) 100–115.

[104] See the repeated objections of certain EU Member States with regard to the reservations made upon accession by some predominantly Muslim countries (Oman and UAE, among others) regarding the interpretation of the treaties on human rights in accordance with *sharia* law. In such objections European States question the will of those countries to 'honour' the obligations accepted as object and purpose of the treaty, although in most cases the objections to the reservations have no radical effect to prevent the entry into force of the treaty between the reserving and objecting State, in accordance with the provisions of Art. 21.3 of the Vienna Convention on the Law of Treaties of 1969.

Regardless of the non-legally binding nature of the content of resolutions or acts of the UNGA and HRC, their worth should not be underestimated. First for the legal effects which occur in relation to the principle of good faith that the Charter of the United Nations includes, linked, eg, to international cooperation and the peaceful settlement of disputes; secondly, for the political pressure generated in the States which are marked out as non-compliant with the recommendations in the matter. This is because the decisions of these organs play an interesting 'amplification and repetition' role of the obligations of States included in international customary or treaty norms, such as the Universal Declaration of Human Rights and international conventions, such as the New York International Covenant of 1966 and others with regional scope.[105]

In this sense, the EU has developed a normative role in silence or at least sotto voce.[106] Hence, the cohesion in the adoption of resolutions within other international organisations with competences for human rights[107]—thanks to the membership of the Member States of the EU itself or with restricted status as an observer or similar in other International Organisations, such as the OAS—gives an indirect or channellised effectiveness and utility to the work of the General Assembly and the HRC. This effect is sometimes underestimated by virtue of the fact of working in bodies with competences of cooperation rather than integrated in the United Nations.

The EU should prioritise the improvement of the internal coordination process with its Member States in order to make it more agile and dynamic, and so foster a stronger position and enjoy greater leadership on human rights at the UN. To do this it should build upon the established structures and avoid creating new mechanisms that make the system more complex. This proposal can be

[105] First, the Universal Declaration of Human Rights of 10 December 1948, despite having the form of a UNGA resolution (UNGA Res217 (III)), maintains the legally binding obligation of its content by its interaction with international custom. Secondly, they are binding under the Vienna Convention on the Law of Treaties of 23 May 1969, eg, the International Covenant on Civil and Political Rights and the International Covenant on Economic, Social and Cultural Rights, both of 16 December 1966 and their various optional protocols, as well as the European Convention for the Protection of Human Rights and Fundamental Freedoms of 4 November 1950.

[106] That the first permanent President of the European Council, Herman Van Rompuy directed the plenary session of UNGA at its inaugural meeting in September 2011, after the reinforcement of the observer status of the EU, has an important symbolic value, reflecting the achievement of a regional integration body in an institution created 'by and for' States, diminishing the clear intergovernmental nature of the UN.

[107] Regional organisations such as the Council of Europe or more open ones such as the Organization for Security and Cooperation in Europe (OSCE), in which the EU has been 'at the forefront in building strong standards and mechanisms for the promotion and protection of human rights.' See Joint Communication of the High Representative of the Union for Foreign Affairs and Security Policy and the Commission to the European Council, the European Parliament and the Council of 12 June 2011 (n 10) 5, 18.

extrapolated to other areas in the United Nations and, with appropriate adjustments, to forums or other international organisations. In this sense, the new work routines established in the framework of the European External Action Service (EEAS), as a permanent coordination structure, should be consolidated optimally at different levels in the overall context of relationships, with the support of the European institutions in Brussels and the capitals of Member States. The work developed from the New York and Geneva headquarters of the EU delegations to the UN, with greater capacities in human rights, is essential.[108] That is why a clear political will is an essential element to precede any external action of the EU in this area. The appointment of a Special Representative of the Union for Human Rights since 2012 and the designation of a 'focal point' in this area of every single EU delegation are positive measures in order to achieve better internal coordination. Also, the creation in the EEAS of the Director of Human Rights and Democracy, and the optimisation of the work performed by the Human Rights Working Group of the Council of the Union (COHOM), affects the human rights strategies prepared by the EU with over 150 countries from 2011—and with the intention of expanding them to all States in international society.[109]

4. Third States have occasionally expressed concern about the situation of certain human rights infringements within the borders of EU Member States, with a negative impact on the activities in the UNGA and the HRC, so questioning the credibility of the EU and its members and even invoking the existence of an internal/external double-standard. Of course, the solid work of the EU Agency for Fundamental Rights (FRA), and above all, the advanced European monitoring system on the topic of natural justice—the EU Court of Justice and the European Court of Human Rights (to be reinforced in the medium or long term with the expected accession of the EU to the ECHR)[110]—is a sound starting

[108] This approach would be consistent with the pragmatic, reactive and even unthinking form that the EU has had in introducing human rights in this action, which has occurred in a 'late, fragmented and complex form'; see D J Liñán Nogueras, *Institutions and Law in the European Union* (n 11 above) 139.

[109] The allocation of permanent COHOM capabilities with physical headquarters in Brussels that lighten the workload would be another positive step. Thus it would intensify its cooperation with other working groups of the Council of the Union dedicated to fundamental rights, such as the Working Party on 'Fundamental Rights, Citizens' Rights and Free Movement of Persons' (known as FREMP); cf EU *Strategic Framework and Action Plan on Human Rights and Democracy*, 25 June 2012 (n 77 above) 12; Joint Communication of the High Representative of the Union for Foreign Affairs and Security Policy and the Commission to the European Council, the European Parliament and the Council of 12 December 2011, (n 10 above) 19.

[110] A more difficult accession due to the problems with regards to its compatibility with EU Law as stated by the EU Court of Justice at Opinion 2/13, 18 December 2014, EU:C:2014:2454.

point to answer the arguments used.[111] However, the EU should be vigilant and adopt even more proactive conduct on human rights within the Union itself, improving its actions to implement mechanisms to prevent and respond to human rights violations.

5. Thus, for all we have noted, we are critical of the generalisation made in some studies extrapolating to other areas—such as human rights—the loss of the EU's influence in international institutions, based on the mismatch between coherence and effectiveness. According to the so-called paradox of influence defended by some authors, the post-Lisbon reality shows that the unique voice of the EU has not necessarily led to a greater ability to influence.[112] However, these works—certainly interesting –are limited to specific areas to which the application

[111] This does not mean, obviously, that no human rights violations deserving of attention and recrimination by third parties occur within the EU. A review of press releases of the HUDOC database of cases decided by the European Court of Human Rights in Strasbourg condemning the Member States of the 'Great Europe' is very enlightening in this regard. Cf hudoc.echr.coe.int. Following these considerations about human rights violations in European territory, at the Spanish national level, the unfortunately infamous situation of migrants trying to jump the border fence in Melilla, with the authorities using razor wire, and the police firing rubber bullets into boundary waters near Ceuta are two alarming examples close at hand. However, as the main competence for border control is that of the Member State and not of the EU, this should not lead to a thoughtless 'lynching' of the EU. On the other hand, other formulas that would enable the EU to be subject to 'scrutiny and supervision of control mechanisms associated with human rights treaties of universal scope, or even the extra-conventional mechanisms' such as HRC and Universal Periodic Review are interesting. This includes transparently debating the status of certain human rights and their application to specific groups within the EU, especially the reports submitted by the Member States under the Universal Periodic Review at the HRC. The EU and its Member States could jointly analyse the reasons why none of them has ratified the UN Convention on the Protection of the Rights of All Migrant Workers and Members of Their Families (adopted 18 December 1990), proposing alternatives; see status of ratifications in 2220 UNTS 3, available through: treaties.un.org. Regarding the EU and its States' effort in this sense from an internal perspective, see Communication from the Commission to the European Parliament and the Council, *A new EU Framework to Strengthen the Rule of Law*, COM(2014) 158 final/2, 19.3.2014 and its application to Poland.

[112] Thus, the work directed by Prof Barbé Izuel in various fields maintains there has been a marked loss of EU influence in international institutions, that is, those which the EU has supported over its strategy of 'effective multilateralism and are the most genuinely European management proposal collective of globalization'. One study shows that European institutions face the 'paradox of influence', that is, that '[just] when the Union has finally been endowed with the legal and institutional foundations necessary to raise and implement a common foreign policy, achieving a significant advance in the integration process, is just when a steeper loss in its international influence is recognized'. This approach is supported in other studies such as that of Prof Thomas. However, that author, in order to know whether the argument 'coherence-effectiveness' is valid, tests his hypothesis by examining the extent and consequences of the EU's coherence on a specific issue that the EU itself has considered as essential in foreign policy, that is, the promotion of international criminal justice through supporting the International Criminal Court, concluding that coherence is not enough. The issue that we criticise is that this result is extrapolated to many areas of EU action with weak legal and political reasoning. In this regard, we believe that we must be wary of introducing other areas, such as human rights, into the group of sectors in which the EU has suffered a loss of influence in international bodies. See E Barbé Izuel, 'La Unión Europea en las instituciones de gobernanza global: Marco analítico y preguntas de investigación' in *Cambio Mundial y Gobernanza Global. La interacción entre la Unión Europea y las instituciones internacionales?* (n 7 above) 11–25; Thomas (n 1 above) 457–74.

of their results is logical and obvious. Dysfunction occurs when, in some cases, their findings, translated into other areas, in turn become a cliché, without being justified and without testing this apparent decline of the EU, which the evidence produced has not proved.

6. One author states that we shall require a 'new rationale for why Europe will be needed in the next 50 years'.[113] Without over-emphasising the EU competences in this regard, we believe that this justification—if it has to be sought—would find itself strongly reinforced by the privileged position of the EU to influence the promotion and development of human rights in third countries, using its various tools and capacities for action, including international organisations, and specifically from its status and that of its Member States in the UNGA and the HRC. In this task the EU, with confidence and eliminating any hint of neo-colonial arrogance, must be aware of its vast potential, use it wisely, and do so, whether or not its idea of itself in the future is defined.

[113] F Steinberg, 'La Gran Recesión en la Economía Internacional' in the Seminar 'Las nuevas crisis políticas económicas: Nuevos escenarios internacionales', DJ Liñán Nogueras (ed), 22 May 2013, Faculty of Law, University of Granada. Comment made in the context of *Índice Elcano de Presencia Global 2012* which, for the first time included the EU as if it were a political and economic union with its own identity; available in: www.realinstitutoelcano.org/, accessed June 2015.

11

The European Union in the International Monetary and Financial System

DOMINIQUE CARREAU[1]

Content

I. INTRODUCTION

IF THERE IS a noticeable trend in the European construction, it is clearly a 'benign neglect' approach to monetary and financial issues. The original Treaty of Rome of 1957 is typical in this respect: it contained a broad and undefined statement according to which 'each State shall treat its policy with regard to rate of exchange as a matter of common concern' (Article 107)—nothing more than a platitude—while it handled with extreme caution the key freedom of capital movement, not placing it on a par with the other 'fundamental' freedoms (persons, services and goods) for fear of its 'lever' effect and attributing to it a subordinated role by providing only that all restrictions on movement of capital will be abolished at the end of the transitional period 'to the extent necessary to ensure the proper functioning of the common market' (Article 67); and all that accompanied by a vague mechanism of financial cooperation under the name of 'mutual assistance' which could take the form of 'limited credit' granted by Member States (Article 119). In sum, from a monetary and financial viewpoint, the Rome common market was an institution for 'happy' times.

When the first monetary crises erupted at the end of the 1960s to culminate in 1971 with the collapse of the key 'par value system'—established at Bretton-Woods

[1] Professor Emeritus of International Law, Université Paris-I Panthéon-Sorbonne.

in 1944 with the aim of ensuring exchange rate stability—and, subsequently, when the crucial 1978 amendment to the IMF articles of agreement formally legalised the free floating of currencies, the European Community response proved entirely inadequate. Worse, during the 1980s and the early 1990s, the continuing existence of the EEC (as it was then called) could seriously be questioned due to the disruptive effect on the 'single market' of the marked instability affecting most Member States' currencies.

Obviously, the Maastricht Treaty of 1992, launching an 'Economic and Monetary Union' (EMU) of participating countries, represented a great leap forward based on the idea that a 'single currency' was inherent in the proper functioning of a 'single market'. However grand the design inspired by the US template, it still remains far from being completed. True, the systemic financial crisis that detonated in 2008 highlighted the risk of implosion not only of the eurozone but of the EU itself without any further improvement and integration. Thus, during the last couple of years significant loopholes have been plugged thanks in particular to two 'side treaties'—the Treaty on Stability, Coordination and Governance in the EMU of 2 March 2012 (currently known as the 'fiscal compact') and the treaty establishing the European Stability Mechanism (ESM) of 2 February 2012—both now in force. Here, it is to be noted that although the 'fiscal compact' is EU-wide, the Czech Republic and the UK have refused (up to now) to sign it, while Croatia joined the Union only on 1 January 2013, so that it is only binding on 25 out of the 28 Member States. The ESM treaty, for its part, is reserved to the financial assistance for the 19 Euro-area participating States. But several significant links are still missing, frustrating the objective of creating a real and effective banking union in order to break the 'vicious circle between banks and sovereigns', to quote the eurozone summit statement of 29 June 2012.

That being said, at this stage of its development, how should one assess the role of the EU in the international monetary and financial system? Before proceeding further, two terminological remarks should be made. First, the term 'system' to qualify the present level of organisation of international monetary and financial relations appears to be a misnomer—albeit a convenient simplification—analogous to the former Holy Roman Empire which never corresponded to its title; in effect, it consists of a mix, a hodgepodge, of treaty norms, unilateral acts of international organisations and transnational actors as well as central banks' practices, altogether far from constituting a coherent whole. Secondly, for the sake of clarity, monetary and financial aspects will be differentiated while they are clearly closely intertwined. In addition, it should be noted that the EU itself—in contrast to the 'eurozone'—has a very limited existence of its own in the international monetary and financial sphere due to a lack of fully-fledged legal personality, as is the case in the trade law area for example; consequently, under the heading 'EU', it is the eurozone that will be primarily concerned.

II. THE EU IN THE INTERNATIONAL MONETARY SYSTEM

The euro, now, constitutes a big—if not the most significant—dividing line between EU Member States and, in particular, for all that regards monetary matters. Hence, the logical consequence of that divide: the EU as such only possesses a specific and limited legal existence through the conclusion of international agreements under the terms and conditions laid down by Article 219 Treaty on the Functioning of the European Union (TFEU), which introduces a key distinction between conventions affecting the euro itself and those involving all the EU member currencies.

The first category relates to the conclusion of 'formal agreements on an exchange rate system for the euro in relation to the currencies of third States' (Article 219.1). Contrary to the ordinary treaty-making procedure prescribed under Article 218 TFEU, the Council has full and exclusive authority to conclude such agreements (for instance, the Parliament has merely to be consulted) but only after a recommendation from either the Commission or the European Central Bank (ECB)—which means it has no right of initiative; furthermore, it must act 'unanimously' and strive to 'reach a consensus consistent with the objective of price stability'—the only cardinal mission of the ECB (see Article 282.2 TFEU) as well as one of the key aspects of the 'internal market' (see Article 3.3 European Treaty (TEU)).

This procedure has to be followed when the central rate of the euro is modified (or abandoned) within the long-established exchange rate mechanism (ERM)—which has never been the case to the present—and when third States would like to adopt the euro as their legal currency (currently referred to as 'euro-isation'—see also below). In this last respect, in the early 2000s, Article 219.1 was relied on when several agreements were made between the EU and four European 'micro-States' (Andorra, Monaco, San Marino and the Vatican) which, although remaining outside both the EU and the eurozone, were eager to adopt the euro as their currency as a solution of continuity after the passing of the Spanish peseta, the French franc and the Italian lira, which had traditionally enjoyed legal tender status in their respective territories.

In the same vein but with a slightly different procedure, the Council enjoys full power to negotiate and conclude 'agreements concerning monetary or foreign exchange regime matters' with third States or international organisations (Article 219.3 TFEU). That may be the case for instance—and probably this example was very present in the minds of the Maastricht Treaty negotiators—should the International Monetary Fund (IMF) decide to activate the stricter exchange rate legal discipline incorporated into and annexed to the 1978 amendment to its Articles of Agreement (see Article IV, sections 1, 3, 4, 5 and particularly Annex C). In other terms, the EU Council would have a decisive say if the present system of freely floating exchange rates were to be replaced by a binding agreement founded on stable currencies authorised to oscillate within a mutually agreed and limited band of fluctuation. Needless to say such an evolution remains a remote option.

If the sum total of these powers is nevertheless far from making the EU a force to be reckoned with in international monetary matters, the same cannot be said of the smaller and more concentrated eurozone.

From a legal point of view, the euro is a fully-fledged currency issued by a central bank (the ECB) common to now 19 Member States, which enjoys legal personality (Article 282.3 TFEU) in the conduct of the monetary policy of the euro-zone members (Articles 127–133 TFEU), thus becoming in modern history the first conventional and institutional currency.

Translated into the international sphere and leaving aside its advisory role, this means that the ECB is empowered to conclude appropriate agreements for the fulfilment of its objectives—but naturally within the limits of its jurisdiction. For instance, it can enter into 'swap' transactions with other central banks, consisting of the extension of reciprocal credit lines on which participants can draw in case of need to support their respective currencies on foreign exchange markets; it has done so with its opposite numbers in Canada, China, Switzerland, the UK and the US, albeit on a more limited scale than the American Federal Reserve System (FED).

Moreover, the euro, as substitute for the Deutsche mark and the French franc which have disappeared as national currencies, has been included *pro tanto* in the composition of the Special Drawing Right (SDR), itself a 'basket currency' issued by the IMF, to represent 30.93 per cent of its weight as at 1 October 2016 pursuant to the latest definition decided by the Fund Managing Board of November 2015 following the inclusion of the Chinese Renminbi.

However, the international jurisdiction of the ECB appears limited by international monetary law constraints as well as by the specificity of the EU monetary law itself.

At the highest level of the IMF, the official recognition of the euro as a currency of full exercise has had limited, if not paradoxical, consequences considering the fact that the Fund's Articles of Agreement—its binding constitutive charter, signed in 1944—expressly reserve membership to national 'States' (Article II), a traditional solution indeed though not adopted later by the GATT in 1947 and the World Trade Organization (WTO) in 1994. Both the GATT and the WTO opened to 'separate customs territor(ies) possessing full autonomy in the conduct of (their) commercial relations' (WTO article XII.1), thus enabling first the EC and afterwards the EU to become full members of these organisations. Thus, EU Member States participating in the eurozone and having the euro as their common and 'single' currency retain full IMF membership with all its attributes though no longer having a 'national' money of their own, while the ECB as issuer of the euro has no official role, being absent from the Fund decision-making process. This is an awkward situation that will have to be sorted out in the future through an appropriate revision of the IMF statutes, which should take into consideration the existence of 'monetary unions' particularly because they have tended to proliferate during the last couple of years. Thus, because of this loophole in the IMF constitutive charter, Article 138.2 of the TFEU envisaging for the eurozone countries a 'unified representation within the international financial institutions' has remained a dead letter.

In addition, as indicated earlier, at the EU level, the international monetary power belongs primarily to the Council, which has a decisive say, while the ECB is relegated to an advisory function. If we leave aside the case of EU members, which have quite naturally to follow the multilateral process laid down by the Maastricht Treaty with a view to adopting the euro, what about the situation of third States which, for exclusively economic and financial reasons, would like to adopt the European currency as their own by making it legal tender in their territory? Are they entitled to do so and under what type of procedure?

To the question of principle—'are States free to adopt the currency of third countries as their own'?—there are clearly different answers from each side of the Atlantic. The US, following a pragmatic approach, has traditionally recognised the possibility for third States and at their own initiative to adopt the dollar as their national currency if they so wish. Needless to say such a choice implies the close collaboration of the issuing country that has to supply the 'borrowing' one with an adequate amount of bank notes and coins and, in this respect, the US via its Treasury and the FED has been pleased to oblige, sensitive to seignioriage gains inherent in that type of operation (namely the difference between the cost of production and the face value of such notes and coins). This lenient view of the so-called 'dollar-isation' phenomenon has lead several countries, at their own risk and peril, to adopt the US dollar as their only national monetary vehicle (eg Costa Rica, Equador, Panama) or as a parallel currency (eg Cambodia, Vietnam, Liberia or Zimbabwe—not to mention Argentina until its financial crisis of 2001–02).

The European official position has always been the complete opposite, based on the prevailing 'State definition' of money according to which the issuance of a currency is an attribute and exclusive privilege of States as sovereigns; consequently, each currency being legally national by definition, cannot be adopted by any given third State without the formal approval of the issuing country. Clearly, such a 'State' conception of money was transposed at the EU/Euro level, the European competent institutions being vested with such 'sovereign' monetary powers. Formally, the ECB enunciated the official EU position on the occasion of an opinion it rendered on 1 April 2004 concerning the monetary relations between the Community and the Principality of Andorra, when it affirmed that 'a third country should only introduce the euro following agreement with the Community' (point No 4, [2004] OJ C88/18, 8.4.2004); hence the various agreements referred to earlier concluded between the Community and a few European micro States.

This official European policy was put to the test of unilateral 'euro-isation' in the early 2000s—in 2002 to be precise—when two Balkan States—Kosovo and Montenegro—embarked in that direction, a limited experience indeed but which confirmed, at least in theory, the EU doctrine. In the case of Kosovo, the European Central Bank proved actually very cooperative in supplying an adequate amount of fiduciary currency since the switch to the euro was merely the continuation of the previous legal tender status of the German mark, which disappeared officially as a monetary unit from 1 January 2002. In contrast, in the case of Montenegro, European institutions (to begin with the Commission and the Central Bank) expressed criticisms of this unilateral euro-isation process but did not go as far as they would have been entitled to in asking for the withdrawal of the euro's legal tender status there. Moreover, considering the potential EU membership ambitions of these two European States, it was sensible to wait for their application negotiations to resolve those monetary issues. Thus, the real litmus test was not there, as it would have been the case if non-European States had been involved.

However, from the point of view of international law, one can but side with the above-mentioned ECB statement according to which no State has the right to unilaterally adopt as its own a currency issued by a third State (or by an international institution like the EU as the case may be); for in doing so, it has to obtain the formal (preferably) or at least the informal agreement of the issuing State/institution—which is, by the way, a practical necessity if only to obtain an adequate amount of fiduciary money.

If the identity within the international monetary system of the European Union and even (to a lesser extent) of the eurozone rests on weak legal foundations, this drawback has not prevented the euro from playing a major role on the world stage. Rapidly, the ECB-issued euro has become an international currency second only to the US dollar, in spite of the deficiencies of the Frankfurt-based institution which lacks two big advantages of its American opposite number—namely a role limited to ensuring price stability and not also covering growth or employment, and the absence of backing by a euro Treasury. The euro now accounts for something like 26 per cent of international monetary reserves, thus placing a significant overhang on the ECB policy options. As the evolution of the US dollar has clearly demonstrated, the more non-residents who hold a given currency, the smaller the margin for manoeuvre for the issuing institution.

III. THE EU IN THE INTERNATIONAL FINANCIAL SYSTEM

The present international financial 'architecture' (as it is now currently known) consists in a highly diversified aggregate of institutions (or emanations thereof), assistance mechanisms and norm-setting bodies, all far from constituting a coherent whole—not to speak of a 'system'– and within which participate primarily the European Central Bank and, to a lesser extent, the EU through the Commission.

On the institutional plane, the key player happens to be the Bank for International Settlements (BIS) with its seat in Basel, Switzerland, a unique and weird organisation founded on international law (its creation is due to a formal treaty) but operating under Swiss commercial law. Over the last 40 years, it has become the hub of the international financial architecture in the sense that it has given birth to a score of subsidiary organs (eg the Basel Committee on Banking Supervision and the Committee on the Global Financial System) with direct reporting links to it, while it has also hosted independent organs, such as the central and new Financial Stability Board (FSB) established in 2009 by and reporting to none other than the G-20, and the International Association of Insurance Supervisors.

Thus, in contrast to the international monetary system which is organised vertically, with the IMF and the World Bank on top, the international financial architecture is built on a horizontal basis made of central banks (primarily) and intergovernmental cooperation. Accordingly, while the ECB quite naturally participates in every bank-related institution beginning with the BIS itself, the EU is only present in the FSB through the Commission. In addition, when the IMF or the World Bank are involved either in the standard-setting operation or in the granting of financial assistance, the European institutions as such have no voice and have then to rely on their Member States, hoping that they will present a common front and position.

All the above-mentioned international bodies contribute to the determination of standards applicable to the financial field. Here, two remarks have to be made regarding the content and nature of such standards. From a material viewpoint, these standards appear as the best practices that have been detected on a comparative analysis by learned observers (regulatory authorities, intergovernmental organisations such as the OECD, or professional associations) in a given financial area. In short, they originate both in national legislation/regulation (primarily) and market usages (accessorily). From a legal perspective, such standards have commonly been described as having the nature of 'soft law', meaning by that that they are non-binding. However, beyond this useful simplification, their legal characterisation needs to be deepened.

While it remains true that the various standard-setting bodies in the financial sphere have no formal legislative power, as their recommendations possess no legal force on their own and then have to be implemented at the national level to become legally binding rules, this should not be the end of the diagnosis. Such standards, as representing the best available practices, enjoy a potent persuasive power by themselves, sufficient for States to formally adopt them and the more so recently since, due to the globalisation movement, countries are placed in a situation of international competition. It is to be reasonably assumed that no State, without compelling reasons, will be willing to appear isolated, sticking to antiquated national rules that would place its economic agents at a disadvantage on the world stage. And, as a matter of fact and law, this has been the practice commonly followed by States which, over the years, have given full effect in their domestic legal order to a raft of international financial standards. No better example of that trend can be given than the evolution of the banking sector framework. Since 1975, the afore-mentioned 'Basel Committee' has periodically recommended a complete set of standards (known as Basel I, Basel II and Basel III) regarding the capital of banks (amount and composition, via the famous 'tiers'), the assessment of risks thorough their weighting and the determination of a solvency ratio. Far from remaining pious vows, these recommendations have been progressively implemented by most economically significant States (the process is not over yet for Basel III); the EU for instance has transcribed them into its own legal order through several banking directives. In other terms, the EU has been of the opinion that such standards, although formally devoid of any legal force on their own, deserved to be adopted for their intrinsic value.

Now, if we turn to the cooperative aspect of international financial relations, the EU presence and influence through the eurozone appear better delineated and identified in light of the most recent developments. But, to begin with, a key distinction has to be introduced between the financially-affected States asking for international assistance, belonging to the EU, and in particular to the eurozone itself, and those which do not.

In case of a financial crisis hitting non-EU countries, the traditional course of action will be to get in touch with the IMF with a view to obtaining its assistance, itself traditionally subject to observing a vast array of conditions formalised in a Fund-approved programme. In that process, the EU as such will be conspicuously absent for want of power and specific representation while its Member States are left free to act as they see fit and according to their own interests and policy goals.

However, since the early 1990s, the Community has developed a so-called 'Macro-Financial Assistance' (MFA) policy, a financial instrument aimed at helping third countries to face short-term balance of payments or budget difficulties, usually combined with IMF-supported programmes. It is granted on the basis of the observance of economic and financial conditions contained in the Memorandum of Understanding (MoU) agreed between the Commission and the beneficiary country (usually its central bank). Its main recipients have been Central and Eastern European countries, the Western Balkans and Mediterranean States. Although the amounts involved have fluctuated markedly over the years, the global trend is clearly on the decline, the disbursed MFA funds having barely exceeded the €100 million mark in 2010.

When EU members are concerned by a financial crisis, two situations have to be singled out depending on their participation or not in the euro area.

EU countries 'in difficulties or … seriously threatened with difficulties as regards [their] balance of payments' according to the terms of Article 143.1 TFEU, can benefit from a 'mutual assistance' mechanism granted by the Council which can take the form of 'limited credits' from other Member States, 'subject to their agreement' (Article 143.2.(c) TFEU). In the recent past, three EU members—Hungary and Latvia in 2008 and Romania in 2011—have received that type of assistance to ease their external financing constraints. Such relief presents a number of common features. First, it is of a medium-term nature as it extends normally over a three-year period. Secondly, it is conditional as it is accompanied by a programme of structural reforms that the recipient State is committed to undertake pursuant to a MoU entered into with the Commission. Thirdly, its progressive implementation is overseen by a surveillance mechanism effectively guaranteed by a gradual and conditional disbursement of funds. Finally, but only as a point of fact, this EU 'mutual assistance' has been extended in combination and cooperation with IMF-supported programmes.

Another and much more disturbing situation arises when eurozone countries have to face severe financial difficulties due to their excessive indebtedness, making it hard for them to tap financial markets at affordable cost. The Maastricht Treaty is silent on this issue, which is understandable since, in theory at least, EU Member States having the euro as their single currency should never have to be confronted with that type of problem provided that they live up to their legal obligations concerning 'excessive deficits' (see Article 126 TFEU and Protocol No 12 implemented by Council Regulation (EC) 1466/97 as amended, most recently by Council Regulations (EU) Nos 472/2103 and 473/2013).

But, as we all know, these rules were eagerly flouted by France and Germany as early as 2003, soon to be followed by most euro area countries. However, the sovereign bond markets were not affected during the subsequent years, as spreads remained in close proximity to each other. In other words, sovereign risks were under-priced on financial markets which failed to take into consideration profound cross-country differences in underlying fiscal and structural positions. When the systemic financial crisis struck in full during the autumn of 2008, it led to an abrupt and disorderly re-pricing of the sovereign risk, thus threatening several financially-unbalanced countries (eg Greece, Ireland and Portugal) with of loss of access to market financing for their huge public deficits.

When in 2010 it became clear that such was to be the case of Greece, euro area Members decided in a hurry to extend a series of bilateral intergovernmental loans to that country. In addition and simultaneously, two new institutions were established—the European Financial Stabilisation Mechanism (EFSM)—an EU-wide safety net created by Council Regulation 407/2010—and the European Financial Stability Facility (EFSF)—a special purpose vehicle owned by eurozone countries and incorporated under Luxemburg law. But these were to be temporary solutions only aimed at addressing the absence in the Maastricht Treaty of any specific mechanism of financial assistance and management crisis. That serious loophole was to be plugged by the recent European Stability Mechanism (ESM).

The decision to set up a permanent crisis management mechanism to safeguard financial stability in the euro area as a whole was adopted by the European Council at its 28–29 October 2010 meeting. Soon thereafter, the same European Council reached political consensus on 16–17 December to add a new paragraph to Article 136 TFEU via the limited and simplified amendment procedure under Article 48.6 TEU introduced by the Lisbon Treaty. Accordingly, on 25 March 2011, the European Council adopted Decision 2011/199 /EU amending Article 136 TFEU by adding a new paragraph (3) stating that:

> The Member States whose currency is the euro may establish a stability mechanism to be activated if indispensable to safeguard the stability of the euro area as a whole. The granting of any required financial assistance under the mechanism will be made subject to strict conditionality.

Following far-reaching discussions, euro area Member States concluded the treaty giving birth to the ESM on 2 February 2012 and, as required, submitted it to their respective constitutional ratification procedures—which process was rapidly carried out so as to allow the inauguration on 8 October 2012 of the new institution in Luxembourg—its statutory seat.

While the analysis of the ESM from an EU law angle is clearly beyond the scope of this chapter, some remarks deserve to be made, since several criticisms had been voiced from various quarters regarding the compatibility both of the creating process and key characteristics of this new rescue mechanism with substantive provisions contained in the TEU and TFEU—all of which objections were rejected by the full Court of Justice of the European Union in its landmark judgment *Pringle v Ireland* of 7 November 2012 (Case C-370/12). First, the Court validated the 'side' establishment of the ESM by a specific treaty concluded among eurozone Member States, since it 'clearly does not fall within monetary policy'—a domain within the exclusive competence of the Union for the euro area—but rather belongs to the 'economic policy'—a domain where the role of the Union is restricted to the adoption of 'coordinating measures'. Secondly, on issues of substance, the Court had to decide whether the ESM Treaty was intended to circumvent two emblematic prohibitions contained in the TFEU—namely the granting of credit or overdraft facilities (Article 123) and the famous 'no bail-out clause' (Article 125). Regarding Article 123, the Court had no difficulty in putting that objection aside since the prohibition at stake is only addressed to the ECB and the Central Banks of Member States. Regarding Article 125, the Court rightly noted that this provision was 'not intended to prohibit either the Union or the Member States from granting any form of financial assistance whatever to another Member State'. Interestingly, and based on the preparatory work relating to the Maastricht Treaty, the Court mentioned that the objective pursued by that article was to ensure 'that the Member States remain subject to the logic of the market when they enter into debt, since that ought to prompt them to maintain budgetary discipline' which is precisely the basic purpose of the ESM Treaty; in other words, the only type of prohibited financial assistance under Article 125 would be one that would result in a 'diminished incentive' for the recipient Member State to 'conduct a sound budgetary policy'. In addition, the Court examined whether the instruments of stability support listed under Articles 14 to 18 of the ESM Treaty (credit lines, loans, purchase of bond issues on the primary or/and secondary markets) ran afoul of this 'no-bail out clause', to conclude its analysis negatively by stressing that 'the ESM will not act as guarantor of the debts of the recipient State (who) … will remain responsible to its creditors for its financial commitments' while 'ESM members do not act as guarantors of the debt of the defaulting ESM Member'. To summarise, a mechanism such as the ESM and the Member States who participate in it are not liable for the commitments of a Member State which receives stability support nor do they assume those commitments, within the meaning of Article 125 TFEU.

That being said, the creation of the ESM presents a major contribution to international financial law and its underlying 'system'—if only from a regional point of view. First, until now, it constitutes the only comprehensive financial crisis management framework ever set up in the world, presently limited to the 19 eurozone countries but with a view to potentially being extended to the entire EU membership. Compared to the worldwide IMF for instance, it is all-encompassing, as it includes the creation of an intergovernmental organisation enjoying full legal personality, specifically dedicated to dealing with financial crises, having an impressive total subscribed capital of €700 billion (of which €80 will be paid-in and €620 call-able) with the capacity of raising funds by issuing financial instruments on the markets (which the IMF is not entitled to do) or entering into 'financial or other agreements or arrangements with ESM members, financial institutions or other third parties' (Articles 3 and 21) and possessing a vast panoply (which the IMF does not have) of instruments of financial assistance 'subject to strict conditionality' (Article 12.1).

Secondly, while the ESM shares with the IMF some traditional instruments of financial assistance to member countries experiencing or threatened by severe financial problems, such as loans (Article 16) or precautionary credit lines (Article 14), it can go further through bond purchases of an ESM member in the secondary (Article 18) or even in the primary debt market (Article 17). In addition, the ESM is empowered to grant loans to members for the purpose of recapitalisation of financial institutions (as it is doing in Spain)—although, and this is presently a controversial issue, it cannot recapitalise banks directly (Article 15). In order to minimise 'moral hazard', the pricing structure of ESM loans is in line with IMF financing policy, which is to make the provision of financial assistance unattractive by charging interest rates at a minimum level corresponding to a notch above the historical average markets rate under 'normal conditions' (Article 20). Moreover, it is of interest to note that, pursuant to an opinion rendered by the Committee on Monetary Financial and Balance of Payments Statistics (CMFB), Eurostat decided to assimilate the statistical treatment of loans from the ESM to those from similar international financial organisations such as the IMF, which means that loans from the ESM to a euro area member will only increase the gross government debt of the recipient country and will not affect the gross government debt of other euro area members—a marked and welcome difference from the previous temporary mechanisms of assistance of 2010–12 (bilateral loans and operations of the EFSF) which produced such a cumulative effect.

Thirdly and most important, the ESM Treaty officialises a very close type of cooperation with the IMF 'in providing stability support' (Recital no 8)—which was far from a foregone conclusion. As a matter of fact, at the time of the eruption of the debt crisis in Greece, when asked by a journalist whether the intervention of the IMF was to be envisaged, the then ECB Governor, Jean-Claude Trichet, icily answered:

> I do not want to enter into some kind of fantasy scenario ...We are, in a way, in a system which is very different from the usual environment. When you are inside the euro area, you are helped by the very fact of belonging to the euro area, and you are helped considerably ... I do not believe that it would be appropriate to introduce the IMF as a supplier of help through standby arrangements or through any kind of help (Press conference of 4 March 2010).

For its part, the *initial* position of the IMF proved to be identical, as the Director in charge of the External Relations Department expressed the view that 'we have often said that we expect the EU and the Eurozone countries to want to and to plan to resolve this question (of mutual financial assistance) by themselves' (Press briefing of 18 March 2010). But, as we all know, this 'stand-alone' policy was set aside by the German Chancellor, Angela Merkel, who insisted on and eventually obtained the inclusion of the IMF in the euro area financial assistance process, for both political (ie sharing the blame for unpopular measures) and technical (the IMF's proven expertise) reasons. Thus, the triumvirate made up of the European Commission, the ECB and the IMF which was formed on the occasion of the financial rescue operations in favour of Greece, Ireland or Portugal has now received a seal of formal approval; in other words, the so-called 'Troika' has been officialised by the ESM Treaty.

This involvement of the IMF (albeit merely potential, since it depends upon its eventual consent) entails far-reaching consequences for euro area countries in need of financial assistance. Thus, if a euro area Member State requests financial assistance from the ESM, it is also 'expected to address, wherever possible, a similar request to the IMF' (Recital no 8).

The Fund will be encouraged to play, if it has so decided according to its own procedures and mandate, a key role in all phases of the activation and monitoring processes. Following a request from a eurozone country, the IMF will be associated with the European Commission and the ECB to assess whether the conditions for granting stability support are met (Article 13)—namely that there is a risk 'to the financial stability of the euro area as a whole' and to the 'sustainability' of the public debt of the concerned Member State. If this last 'sustainability analysis' demonstrates that the public debt can be restored to a supportable level pursuant to a macroeconomic adjustment programme, that same troika will assess 'the actual or potential financing needs of the ESM Member concerned' (ibid). Here, it is noteworthy that this first phase of analysis closely follows the Fund's approach to debt sustainability assessments (see *Staff guidance note on debt sustainability analysis for market-access countries*, IMF, Washington DC, July 2008).

On the basis of this assessment, the Commission, duly mandated by the ESM Board of Governors, will negotiate with the concerned State a macroeconomic adjustment programme to be included in an MoU 'detailing the conditionality attached to the financial assistance facility' and that together with the IMF and in liaison with the ECB (Article 13.3). Here, it is to be remarked that the ESM MoU procedure closely reproduces the IMF practice of the so-called 'Letter of Intent'—a document signed by the Fund member concerned and containing the list of its negotiated commitments establishing the level of 'conditionality'. This is obviously the crux of the matter for that type of financial rescue operation: the 'assisted' Member State—should it belong to the ESM or the IMF—comes to be deprived of significant 'sovereignty' attributes, as it is being placed under some form of 'trusteeship' exercised by the international institutions disbursing the funds. In view of the EU's lack of experience in this type of financial rescue, the ESM had to rely heavily on a long and well-established IMF practice and expertise, which it has officially endorsed and made its own (see Recital nos 8 and 12). In consequence, the IMF- and ESM- supported macroeconomic adjustment programmes will be largely similar; in particular, on the critical issue of 'private sector involvement' the ESM has followed the IMF guidance to make its assistance conditional upon the conclusion of a comprehensive debt restructuring plan if the above-mentioned 'debt sustainability analysis' has led to the conclusion that an affordable debt level was impossible to achieve through traditional policy adjustment measures (Recital no 12). In the same vein, following an initial Euro Group statement of 28 November 2010, the ESM Treaty decided to include standardised and identical 'collective action clauses' (CAC) in all euro area government bonds (Recital no 11)—a practice long advocated by the IMF for its positive role in facilitating an orderly restructuring of international sovereign bond contracts.

The formal recognition and endorsement by the ESM Treaty of the role and practice of the IMF are further exemplified at the compliance level. The European Commission, 'in liaison with the ECB and, wherever possible, together with the IMF' will 'monitor compliance with the conditionality attached to the financial assistance facility', to use the terms of the ESM treaty itself (Article 13.7)—which is another officialisation of the troika procedure. The ESM beneficiary Member State is obliged to provide the troika with all the information necessary for monitoring the policy conditionality of the programme as agreed in the MoU; this overall 'ex-post' surveillance includes periodic visits of troika experts who will report to their respective dispatching institutions on the implementation of the macroeconomic adjustment programme. Since 'loans' are provided in tranches themselves disbursed periodically, if monitoring processes highlight substantial deviations showing that the beneficiary ESM member is not complying with the policy requirements, the disbursement of tranches may be delayed or suspended—a very powerful means of pressure indeed. This post-programme surveillance mechanism coupled with potential financial sanctions is directly borrowed from the IMF practice as it has evolved over the years.

Finally, considering the close links with the IMF advocated by the ESM Treaty, it was necessary to settle the delicate legal issue regarding the respective 'rankings' of their loans. While there is no formal legal basis for granting the IMF 'preferred creditor status' there is, however, common agreement (and for bilateral 'public' creditors this is evidenced by the so-called Paris Club's constant policy of excluding the Fund from its restructuring process) that priority should be given to repayment of obligations to the Fund, as it is essential to preserve and guarantee its financing role. The ESM Treaty includes a very interesting compromise: if, quite naturally, it claims 'preferred creditor status' for its own loans (Recital no 13), it also recognises and accepts 'preferred creditor status of the IMF over the ESM' (ibid).

In 2012, the only financial facility provided by the ESM was the Financial Stability Agreement signed with Spain on 29 November 2012, which includes a Financial Institution Recapitalisation Facility for a total amount of €100 billion with a maximum maturity of 15 years; this first programme to recapitalise the

Spanish banking sector replaces, under the same financial and commercial terms, and transfers to the ESM the initial facility signed with Spain on 24 July 2012 under the now defunct EFSF. Up to now, two disbursements of respectively €39.348 billion on 11 December 2012 and €1.865 billion on 5 February 2013 have been made through the delivery of an identical number of ESM bonds provided to the Bank of Spain.

Following a request by the Cyprus government presented to the Euro Group on 25 June 2012 for stability support and after extensive negotiations, the ESM Board of Governors approved on 8 May 2013 a more traditional Financial Facility Agreement in favour of that country—its first to a euro area Member State. It naturally followed the road map laid down in the ESM Treaty for granting stability support 'together with the IMF' (Article 13) and 'under the form of a loan to an ESM Member' (Article 16). In concrete terms, that meant an initial phase of assessment of the existence of a risk to the 'euro area as a whole', of the sustainability of the country's public debt and ('together with the IMF') of the financial needs of Cyprus; in a second step and here again 'together with the IMF' a MoU containing a 'macroeconomic adjustment programme' representing the 'conditionality attached to the financial assistance' had to be negotiated (and it included an appropriate downsizing of the financial sector, fiscal consolidation, structural reforms and privatisations); finally, a package of financial assistance to Cyprus of up to €10 billion was decided, with the ESM providing up to €9 billion and the IMF expected to contribute around €1 billion. The ESM loan facility has a maximum maturity of 15 years and the first tranche of €3 billion was disbursed in two instalments in May and June 2013. In parallel, on 15 May 2013, the IMF Executive Board duly approved a €1 billion loan to Cyprus over three years. On 7 November 2013, the European Commission, the ECB and the IMF published a common statement on their second quarterly review mission on the Cyprus economic programme jointly supported by their respective financial assistance, indicating that this programme was 'on track' and would justify further disbursements. This short summary of the recent financial assistance to Cyprus clearly illustrates the critical role and modus operandi of the formally officialised troika in times of crises affecting euro area countries.

A comparable scenario developed in the case of Greece which had to face a new and severe financial crisis at the beginning of 2015 that culminated on 30 June in an unprecedented default towards the IMF for an amount of 1,5 billion euros. This dramatic event led many to express doubts not only on the possible continuing presence of this country within the single currency, if not the EU itself (hence the expression 'Grexit', which characterises that option), but also on the very survival of the eurozone itself (both issues that were conspicuously absent from the previous rescue operations). After tough and often bitter discussions between the Greek government and the 'Troika', a final agreement was reached on 19 August to activate the ESM for a third time. It was the most comprehensive in its scope ever, as it implied a financial assistance of 86 billion euros and conditions covering more than 30 pages.

Going to the essentials, a number of points should be highlighted as they confirm past practices while evidencing obvious problems of coordination between the EU Commission and the IMF and thus the proper functioning of the much-heralded Troika.

Firstly, the official process between the initial Greek request to the ESM for a loan facility was launched on 8 July to be finalised by all participants by 19 August, with the passing of appropriate Greek legislation occurring in between. The analyses was to be conducted by the Commission under article 13 of the ESM Treaty along with, most importantly, the negotiation between the Greek government and the Troika of the required Memorandum of Understanding detailing the *conditionality* for a financial assistance facility covering the period 2015-2018. The first disbursement of funds took place almost immediately on 20 August which proves that the institutional machinery, albeit heavy on paper, could work in a smooth and efficient way in practice.

Secondly, this new eurozone financial rescue operation fully endorses the traditional IMF approach in similar circumstances which is based on a triptych: a given level of conditionality, a tranche distribution of funds and periodic monitoring. Here, in the case of Greece, the negotiated conditions constitute a true program of government which is both broad (it contains many structural reforms including that of the State) and corresponding to the so-called 'Washington consensus' with a reduction of the public perimeter and lower taxes. If many observers have characterised these conditions as 'draconian', they only point to the fact that a over-indebted State such as Greece, which is under the financial respiratory assistance of its creditors, is 'sovereign' but in name having lost the free conduct of its policies; under another name, it is a real international 'trusteeship' situation.

Thirdly, this Greek template illustrates the awkward nature of a Troika-like mechanism within the eurozone. While Greece also lodged a separate request of financial assistance to the IMF on 23 July 2015, it received no positive answer as yet since the Washington institution holds views that differ from those of the eurozone governing bodies, particularly with regard to the 'debt relief' issue. Although the 19 August MoU with Greece formally mentions the 'IMF input' recognising the Fund involvement, the Fund has until now abstained from supporting the Greek program not only because it already holds claims on this country above the 20 billion dollar mark but also because it insists—and this is part and parcel of its traditional policy—on a 'significant' debt reduction. Up to now, the Eurozone institutions have been more than reluctant to go in that direction since the debt at stake is of a 'public' nature—ie it is owed to national States or EU institutions such as the Central Bank—so that any reduction would not only constitute a bad precedent but would also affect public finances and then taxpayers money—obviously not the right message to send at a time of European construction questioning. This Greek example unsurprisingly evidences the different agenda of the IMF and the Eurozone institutions and puts into question the wisdom of their official association under the aegis of the ESM Treaty.

IV. CONCLUSION

Aside from the troika approach to the solution of financial crises actually limited to eurozone countries, two general lessons can be drawn from the new European Stability Mechanism recently set up as they place the rescue operations launched under the auspices of the IMF on an enhanced legal footing. First and foremost, the concept of 'conditionality' as well as its transcription into Fund-supported macroeconomic adjustment programmes have been vindicated in their entirety in spite of the controversies that have never ceased to surround them over the years; this is more than a simple encouragement for the IMF and its staff since it demonstrates a frequently forgotten message valid for any state in dire financial straits—be it developing or developed—according to which no assistance can be expected if the needy country does not put its house in order at the same time. In other words, the long-standing practice of the IMF in terms of 'conditionality' and of its implementation, which as such enjoys the simple status of unilateral acts of an intergovernmental organisation, is here recognised as having a conventional mandatory value—a strong endorsement indeed that goes far beyond the sphere of the European states involved.

Secondly, and more 'lawyers' law' the ESM Treaty endorses and contributes to the recognition of the IMF's 'preferred creditor' status—a primacy de facto recognised, albeit never formally officialised conventionally. This is particularly important for securing the lending activities of the IMF, as its outstanding claims will have to be met and will not be subject to the general and prevailing *pari passu* clause—obviously a legal encouragement for the Fund to provide financial assistance and guarantee the 'revolving' nature of its resources; it is also important for the protection of the reserve assets that creditor countries may place in the Fund's custody.

In brief, from the point of view of the international financial system, the EU (via the eurozone) can easily be seen as having 'flexed its muscles' by acquiring a specific personality through the creation of the ESM—a complete intergovernmental organisation—and by formally validating and adopting the IMF role and practice for its own rescue operations in favour of euro area Member States.

In the monetary field, the role and influence of the EU have been felt through the Maastricht Treaty of 1992, giving birth to a comprehensive 'zone' with a new currency issued by a central bank. If, for want of adequate powers, the ECB pales in comparison with the Federal Reserve System in America, this has not prevented the euro from rapidly becoming a major reserve currency—second only to the US dollar.

However, when monetary and financial issues have to be dealt with on a worldwide basis under the auspices of the IMF, the EU's clout is significantly affected by an absence of autonomous representation which would make its voice heard within the Fund's decision-making process—an avenue followed by the more recent World Trade Organization charter but unknown in 1944 when the Fund's Articles of Agreements were drafted. Clearly, at least from an EU perspective, a new amendment to the IMF's constitutive charter, allowing for the full membership of 'monetary zones', would be more than welcome.

12

EU-IMF Relations: The Long Way to a Single EU Chair in the IMF

MANUEL LOPEZ-ESCUDERO[1]

Content

I. PRELIMINARY REMARKS

THE MAASTRICHT TREATY and then the Lisbon Treaty thoroughly regulate the internal aspects of the Economic and Monetary Union (EMU). In contrast, external representation was extremely complex, and its regulation was very limited in the Maastricht Treaty (Article 111 EC) and the Treaty

[1] Professor of Public International Law and European Union Law, University of Granada Law School (Spain). Legal Secretary at the Court of Justice of the European Union, Luxembourg. Research made within the Research Project DER2010-21083.

of Lisbon maintains this line with small modifications in Articles 138 and 219 TFEU. Consequently, the external elements of the EMU are less developed than the internal framework. It would be logical to equilibrate these two sides of the EMU. Obviously, EU relations with the most relevant and powerful international economic organisation, the International Monetary Fund (IMF), are an essential part of these EMU external relations.

Due to the current fragmentation of its representation in international financial institutions and forums, the EU and the Eurozone do not have an influence or a leadership role in monetary and economic international relations commensurate with their economic weight and the position of the euro as the second international currency after the US dollar.[2] The best way to understand the unsatisfactory development of the EMU's external relations is to analyse the EU's weak and unsatisfactory position in the IMF, the centre of the international monetary system built at Bretton Woods. This position has become more complicated, because the IMF is reforming its legal framework to maintain its representational equality and legitimacy in a changing economic world with the increasing power of the emerging economies. The EU countries have strong, cumulated quotas and voting shares in the IMF and are also overrepresented on the Executive Board. The big countries with emerging economies and the US are pressing the EU to consolidate its representation at the Fund in a single chair, and this seems to be a key point in continuing the IMF governance and quota reform. However, the way to an EU centralised representation in the IMF is complicated, and there are legal and political obstacles due to IMF rules and barriers related to the EMU legal framework and the political wills of the EU countries. The 2010 IMF reform can eliminate some of these obstacles from IMF law, and the reinforcement of the internal EU economic governance in response to the global crisis could also facilitate an improvement in the EMU external governance.

The financial crisis due to the so-called Great Recession has accelerated the rebalancing of the global economy towards emerging economies, and the global financial architecture is adapting to these developments. This situation strengthens the case for a common EU/Eurozone voice in a world in which individual EU Member States have less influence and are most likely in any event to lose the

[2] R Smits, 'International Representation of Europe in the Area of Economic and Monetary Union: Legal Issues and Practice in the First Ten Years of the Euro' (2009) *Euredia, European Banking and Financial Law Journal* 297–333. There is abundant literature about the international role of the euro. See generally M Angeloni, A Benassy-Quéré, M Carton, Z Darvas, N Phedestais, J Pisani-Ferry, *Global Currencies for Tomorrow: A European Perspective* (Brussels, Bruegel, 2011); D Cohen, *The Future of Global Currency. The Euro versus the Dollar* (New York, Routledge, 2011), European Central Bank, *International Role of the Euro* (Frankfurt, 2013); M López-Escudero, *El Euro en el Sistema Monetario International* (Madrid, Tecnos, 2005); M Papaioannou and R Portes, *The International Role of the Euro: A Status Report*, Euro Economic Papers 317 (2008); J Pisan-Ferry and A Posen (eds), *The Euro at 10: The Next Global Currency?* (Brussels, Bruegel, 2009).

formidable positions they used to have. A better representation of the EU/Eurozone in key international economic institutions and forums seems to be the only way for EU member nations to maintain a relevant and strong influence in this new, multipolar economic world.

First, I intend to explain the obstacles in both IMF and EU law which have prevented a more appropriate EU representation in the IMF and I will analyse both the minimalist approach applied to IMF-EU relations since the introduction of the single currency in 1999 and the pragmatic solutions put into practice by the IMF to take into account the euro reality. Secondly, I will review the consequences for EU-IMF relations of the 2010 IMF reform, which is pending US Congressional approval, before coming into force. Thirdly, I will consider the new arguments for a big change in the representation of the EU in the IMF, and I will review the legal possibilities for a single EU chair at the IMF. Finally, I will present some conclusions for developing better EU-IMF relations, useful also for better international economic and financial governance.

II. OBSTACLES TO THE EU-IMF RELATIONSHIP AND THE APPLICATION OF A PRAGMATIC APPROACH

The EU-IMF relations were and continue to be a field full of obstacles. Some of these barriers come from IMF law and IMF institutional dynamics, and most of them have their origin in the EMU legal framework and in the EU Member States' attitudes towards the IMF.

There are two main barriers due to IMF law and IMF functioning: the country-based character of the IMF and the institutional complexity of the IMF Executive Board. All EU Member States are IMF members, but only individual countries are eligible for IMF membership, and the Fund's Articles do not contain a provision that allows for the membership of monetary unions or regional organisations.

The Executive Board is the heart of the IMF, and its complex composition is a relevant obstacle to improving EU representation at the Fund. In effect, the Executive Board consists of 24 executive directors[3] but there is no EU, Eurozone, or EU Member States constituency. The EU Member States' representation is spread among 10 executive directors. While Germany, the United Kingdom, and France each appoint one executive director and an alternate, all other EU Member States participate in the election of seven different executive directors and form mixed constituencies, together with other non-EU Member States. Seven of the 24 executive directors are from the EU Member States (FR, DE, UK, NL, IT, ES) and two from close-by advanced European economies (Switzerland, Norway).

[3] The current Executive Board composition is in the IMF, 'IMF's Executive Directors and Voting Power', available at: www.imf.org/external/np/sec/memdir/eds.aspx.

Depending on the rotating arrangements in the constituencies, Austria, Nordic/ Baltic EU Member States, and in the near future Poland will nominate executive directors. In my opinion, this panorama of the EU presence in the IMF shows two contradictory situations. On one hand, the EU and even the Eurozone are overrepresented on the IMF Executive Board, in particular when compared with their declining share of the global economy and the position of the emerging and developing countries.[4] On the other hand, the spread of many EU Member States in mixed constituencies dominated by third countries (Poland in the Central Asian constituency, Ireland in the Canadian and the Caribbean constituency, Spain in the Central American constituency) is a clear handicap for coordination among EU countries. It is important to take into account that elected executive directors may not split their votes but must cast as a unit. This requires them to reconcile their constituents' views before voting.[5] Coming to a common EU position on any issue would require countries in mixed constituencies (be they non-European or consisting of both developed and developing countries) to persuade other members in their constituency to vote along European lines.[6] There is a contradiction between the EU's overrepresentation in the Executive Board and the more limited influence of the Europeans on IMF policy. This overrepresentation (one-third of the Executive Board) and the high voting share (more than 30 per cent) are not fruitful and the EU is seen as less influential there than the US, which has, however, a quota about half the size of the EU's aggregate quota.[7]

[4] E Virmani, 'Global Economic Governance: IMF Quota Reform', (2011) *IMF Working Papers* WP/11/208, at 24.

[5] W Bergthaler, 'The Relationship between International Monetary Fund Law and European Union Law: Influence, Impact, Effect, and Interaction' in R Wessel and S Blockmans, *Between Autonomy and Dependence* (Berlin, Springer Verlag, 2012) at 176; A Martinez-Diaz, 'Executive Boards in International Organizations: Lessons for Strengthening IMF Governance', (2008) IMF, Independent Evaluation Office, *Background Paper* no BP/08/08, at 49.

[6] L Bini-Smaghi has said that the current constituency system also gives European representatives a 'perverse' incentive to differentiate their preferences artificially when speaking at the Executive Board, drawing out small and generally insignificant differences for the sake of justifying holding different votes L Bini Smaghi, 'A Single EU Seat in the IMF?' (2005) 42 *Journal of Common Market Studies* 229 at 242.

[7] The clearest way to explain this contradiction is to use power index analysis, which political scientists use to measure the power of an institution's member by taking into account not only its voting share but also its real possibilities to influence the final outcome of the voting process. Applying the Banzhaf Index, the Coleman's Power Index, and the Shapley and Shubik Index, some economists have analysed the voting power of the EU and the Eurozone in the IMF. These analyses show that the U.S. has more real voting power in the current IMF decision-making process than its voting share would suggest. See A Giovannini et al, *External Representation of the Euro Area*, Study for European Parliament, IP/A/ECON/FWC/2010 (19 May 2012), at 45. See also Leech and Leech, 'Power versus Weight in IMF Governance: the Possible Beneficial Implications of a United European Bloc Vote' in A Buira (ed), *Reforming the Governance of the IMF and the World Bank* (Anthem Press, 2005); Brandner and Grech, 'Unifying EU Representation at the IMF—A Voting Power Analysis' (2009) *Austrian Federal Ministry of Finance Working Paper* no 2/2009; Brandner, Grech, and Paterson, 'Unifying EU Representation at the IMF Executive Board A Voting and Veto Power Analysis', *Economics Series*, no 245 (Vienna, Institute for Advanced Studies, 2009).

The EU law has generated also some barriers to the development of EU-IMF relations and the most relevant are: the asymmetric character of the EMU, the dichotomy between the EU and the Eurozone and, the lack of use of the EU treaties' legal basis for EMU external representation. A more political obstacle from inside the EU is the reluctance of some EU Member States and their bureaucracies to lose privileged positions at the IMF, in particular some Euro area holding the chair or the alternate executive director position of their constituencies.[8]

The EMU has been characterised by a specific combination of monetary transfer of competences from the Member States to the EU institutions, basically the ECB, and the weak economic coordination of national economic policies at the EU level. The asymmetry between the 'M' of EMU and the 'E' is one of the dominant features of the EMU[9] and it determines much of the EMU's external relations.[10] Taking into account the logic of Articles 3(2) and 216(1) TFEU and the ECJ case law on the parallelism of internal and external competences,[11] I consider an

[8] This argument was mentioned by European Commission, 'EMU@10:The Evolution of Economic Governance in EMU', (June 2008) *Economic Papers* no 328, at 46. See the strong criticism of the former Executive Board member of the ECB, L Bini Smaghi, 'Powerless Europe: Why is the Euro Area Still a Political Dwarf?' (2006) 9 *International Finance* 261 at 276 'The real obstacle to stronger [Euro area] representation does not reside in the aversion of its citizens but rather in its national institutions and policy makers' reluctance to leave their seats at the table ... Unless national representatives are particularly gifted in understanding the little power that they have in their current role, they will tend to use all possible arguments to oppose a single Euro area representation. The ultimate argument is "the political conditions are not yet ripe", which means in plain words "I don't like it"'. See also C Padoan, 'Europe and Global Economic Governance', *EU Diplomacy Papers* 2008/2, College of Europe, Bruges, at 7.

[9] RM Lastra and J-V Louis, 'European Economic and Monetary Union: History, Trends, and Prospects' (2013) 32 *Yearbook of European Law* 1 at 4–5.

[10] ECB, 'The External Representation of the EU and EMU' (May 2011) *ECB Monthly Bulletin* at 96–97; Dutzler, 'EMU and the Representation of the Community in International Organizations' in S Griller and B Weidel (eds), *External Economic Relations and Foreign Policy in the European Union* (Wien, Springer, 2002), 449; CW Herrmann, 'Monetary Sovereignty of the Euro and External Relations of the Euro Area: Competences, Procedures and Practices' (2002) 7 *European Foreign Affairs Review* 1; M López-Escudero, 'La politique de taux de change de l'euro vis-à-vis des monnaies de pays tires' in *Mélanges en hommage à Jean-Victor Louis*, vol II (Brussels, Bruylant, 2003) 282–300; J-V Louis, 'Les relations extérieures de l'Union économique et monétaire' in E Cannizzaro (ed), *The European Union as an Actor in International Relations* (The Hague, Deventer/Kluwer, 2002), 77; C Zilioli and M Selmayr, 'The External Relations of the Euro Area: Legal Aspects' (1999) 36 *Common Market Law Review* 273.

[11] Case 22/70 *Commission v Council* ('*European Road Transport Agreement*') [1971] ECR 263; Opinion 1/76 *re Inland Waterways* [1977] ECR 741; Opinion 1/94 *re the WTO Agreements* [1994] ECR I-5267; Case C-519/03 *Commission v Luxemburg* [2005] ECR I-3067 and Case C-433/03 *Commission v Germany* [2005] ECR I-6985; Opinion 1/03 *Lugano Convention* [2006] ECR I-1145, paras 114–133; Case C-523/04 *Commission v Netherlands* [2007] ECR I-3267. After the Lisbon Treaty, see Case C-114/12, *Commission v Council*, EU:C:2014:2151; Case C-137/12, *Commission v Council*, EU:C:2013:441; Opinion 1/13, EU:C:2014:2303. About this doctrine see, among others, P Eeckhout, *EU External Relations Law*, 2nd edn (Oxford, OUP, 2011); P Eeckhout, 'Exclusive External Competences: Constructing the EU as an International Actor' in ECJ, *The Court of Justice and the Construction of Europe: Analyses and Perspectives on Sixty Years of Case-law* (Berlin, Springer Verlag, 2013) 613–26; C Hillion and P Koutrakos (eds), *Mixed Agreements Revisited* (Oxford, Hart Publishing, 2011); G De Baere and P Koutrakos, 'The interactions between the legislature and the judiciary in EU external relations' in Syrpis (ed), *The Judiciary, the Legislature and the EU Internal Market* (Cambridge, Cambridge University Press, 2012); R Gosalbo-Bono, 'Insuficiencias jurídicas e institucionales de la acción exterior de la Unión Europea'

exclusive EU external competence in monetary and exchange rate matters to be logical. Because the EU has an exclusive internal competence on monetary and exchange rate policy, the EU alone must be responsible for the external representation of that competence. In contrast, the EU is not able to exercise an exclusive external competence on economic matters due to the persistent internal competences of EU Member States on economic policy. It is an area of shared competence, and a mixed representation at the IMF (Member States and EU) would seem to be a consistent way for the EU to proceed.[12]

The dichotomy between the EU and the Eurozone seems also an inconvenience for the EU-IMF relationship. Nowadays, only 19 EU Member States make up the Eurozone, and nine Member States have not yet made the leap to the common currency. The EU cannot expect to substitute for the EU members outside the Eurozone in international organisations and forums like the IMF, because these countries maintain their monetary sovereignty.[13]

In relation to the lack of use of the EU treaties' legal basis for EMU external representation, it is interesting to note that the original EU primary law did not include express references to the IMF, but in the EC Treaty as reformed by the Maastricht Treaty, there was a provision that could have been used as the legal basis for EU participation in the IMF.[14] This was Article 111(4) EC, which after the Lisbon Treaty became Article 138 TFEU. It is divided into three paragraphs, dedicated respectively to EU participation, EU representation in international economic institution and forums, and the decision-making powers of EU institutions in these matters. It is the Council which, acting on a proposal of the Commission and after consulting the ECB, will decide on the Eurozone's participation and representation in international financial institutions and conferences, based on a qualified majority of the Member States which have adopted the euro. Nowadays there is no decision based in Article 138, but in 1998 the Commission submitted a

(2015) 50 *Revista de Derecho Comunitario Europeo* 242–56; and specially the excellent analysis of F Castillo de la Torre, 'The Court of Justice and external competences after Lisbon: some reflections on the latest case law', Chapter 3 in this book.

[12] For a different view, see J-V Louis, *L'Union Européenne et sa monnaie*, Commentaire J Mégret (Brussels, Bruylant, 2009) at 162; and S Cafaro, *Il Governo delle Organizzazioni di Bretton Woods. Analisi critica, processi di revisione in atto e proposte di reforma* (Bari, Giapichelli, 2012) at 162.

[13] In that sense, Art 139 TFEU excludes the application of the following provisions of the Treaties to the Member States 'with a derogation: (g) monetary agreements and other measures relating to exchange-rate policy (Article 219); … (i) decisions establishing common positions on issues of particular relevance for economic and monetary union within the competent international financial institutions and conferences (Article 138(1)); (j) measures to ensure unified representation within the international financial institutions and conferences (Article 138(2))'. The rules related to the external representation of the EMU bind Eurozone countries but not EU Member States outside the euro. I can only note that Art 142 TFEU requests that a Member State with a derogation which in principle maintains that state's autonomy in the field of monetary policy treat its exchange policy as a matter of common interest.

[14] See J-V Louis, 'The International Projection of the Euro and the International Monetary System' in M Telò (ed), *The European Union and Global Governance* (London, Routledge, 2009) at 74.

modest proposal for a Council decision on external representation[15] calling for the Council, along with the Commission and the ECB, to represent the Community at the international level in the context of EMU. The Council could not agree on this proposal, and, instead, it submitted a report to the Vienna European Council, which adopted it, considering that a pragmatic approach would be the most successful to minimise the adaptation of the international rules and practices.[16] The EU Member States decided not to use the legal basis for EMU external representation and opted for a low profile based on pragmatic arrangements.

In spite of these barriers, the adoption of the euro has had a profound impact on the EU-IMF relationship. In particular, the transfer of competence to the EU institutions with respect to the conduct of both exchange rate and monetary policy has had an important impact on how EU members exercise these rights and fulfil these obligations under IMF law.[17] The clearest examples of the interactions between IMF law and EU law are as follows:[18]

1. The IMF conducts surveillance over its members' exchange rate policies under Article IV of the IMF's Articles of Agreement, in respect of all IMF members including Euro area Member States, even though they no longer have competences related to monetary and exchange rate policy, as they have transferred those to the European institutions;
2. In the context of the EU sovereign debt crisis, EU Member States have turned to the IMF to request the use of its financial resources, and the new European Stability Mechanism frequently refers to IMF terminology and practices and even encourages IMF involvement in national rescues;
3. In its financial operations the IMF continues to interact with EU Member States' institutions such as national central banks, and EU law takes into account this interaction; and
4. To represent joint positions on IMF-related matters, the EU needs to coordinate positions with EU Member States because only they may exercise their voting rights at the IMF's governance bodies, and EU institutions merely have observer status.

Logically, the need for coordination between EU countries at the IMF organs is higher in these matters, and some pragmatic arrangements have been developed at the IMF in relation to those IMF matters transferred by the EU countries to the EU.

[15] COM(1998) 637 final, 'Proposal for a Council Decision on the Representation and Position Taking of the Community at International Level in the context of Economic and Monetary Union'.

[16] *Presidency Conclusions*, European Council, Vienna, 11 and 12 December 1998. See the comments from S Cafaro, 'The missing voice of the Euro. Legal, technical and political obstacles to the external representation of the Euro area' (2011) *Il Diritto dell'Unione Europea* 895 at 901–2; B Steinki, 'Competencies of the European Community on International Monetary Fund matters: an overview of the key legal issues' in IMF, *Current Developments in Monetary and Financial Law*, vol 2 (IMF, 2003) at 120.

[17] S Hagan, '10 Years of the Euro: A perspective from the IMF', speech at the EC in Frankfurt, 29 January 2009. Available at: www.imf.org/external/np/speeches/2009/012909.htm.

[18] See, W Bergthaler, n 5 above, at 161 and also B Steinki, n 16 above, 109–47.

The most relevant manifestations of this pragmatism in the EU-IMF relations are institutional (limited presence of EU institutions in IMF organs and coordination mechanisms of EU countries at the IMF) and substantive (IMF surveillance of the Euro area economic policy and EU countries' economic policies, incorporation of the euro in the composition of the Special Drawing Rights (SDR) basket, and IMF financial assistance to EU countries).

A. Coordination of the EU Member States at the IMF: The SCIMF and the EURIMF

EU leaders have called for enhanced cooperation on economic and financial matters related to the IMF since the Vienna Council in 1998. Following this, EU Member States set up a multi-layered structure of coordination, composed of two bodies that allow for a certain level of coordination among EU Member States at the IMF: the EURIMF and the SCIMF.[19]

The SCIMF is a sub-committee on IMF matters and related issues, linked to the Economic and Financial Committee (EFC).[20] The SCIMF comprises one representative of each country's finance ministry and central bank plus two from the Directorate General for Economic and Financial Affairs of the European Commission (DG Ecfin) and two from the ECB. The Commission acts as the SCIMF's secretariat, preparing agendas and minutes, although it does not take an active part in discussions. The two members of DG Ecfin speak in meetings on behalf of the Commission but do not vote. The European executive director at the IMF chairing EURIMF also attends these meetings to ensure consistency with what goes on in Washington, DC. The SCIMF meets eight to 10 times a year in Brussels, depending on its chairman, and is a consensus-based body (although simple majority voting is the legal rule). Due to its intergovernmental nature, SCIMF is dominated by a culture of diplomacy and compromise building.[21] The President of SCIMF is chosen by consensus amongst high-ranking officials belonging to the EFC.

The SCIMF drafts the text of the EU Council President's speech at the spring and autumn meetings of the International Monetary and Financial Committee

[19] J Aubrechtová, W Coussens and G Pineau, 'How to Reconcile EU Integration with the Governance of the International Monetary Fund' (2010) 18 *Banking Journal* at 7–8.

[20] The EFC also meets in a Euro area configuration, the so called Eurogroup Working Group (EWG), in which only the Euro area Member States, the Commission and the European Central Bank are represented. In this configuration, the Committee prepares the work of the Eurogroup and usually meets once a month ahead of Eurogroup meetings. The Eurogroup Working Group members elect a President for a period of four years, which may be extended by a further two years. It is a full-time role, in line with the agreement by the heads of state or government of the Euro area of 26 October 2011, and is based in Brussels in the General Secretariat of the Council of the EU. See Eurozone Portal: eurozone.europa.eu/eurogroup/eurogroup-working-group/.

[21] EURODAD, *European Coordination at the World Bank and International Monetary Fund: A Question of Harmony?* 2006, at 11. Available at: www.eurodad.org/uploadedfiles/whats_new/reports/eurodad%20euifigovernance.pdf.

of the IMF, which is usually broad enough to be consensual. In addition to this speech, each Member State represented at the Board makes additional statements, as does the European Commissioner on Economic and Financial Affairs, who also gives a speech on behalf of the Commission, which has observer status at the International Monetary and Financial Committee of the IMF. Another task of the SCIMF is to prepare the Article IV review of the Eurozone, and, on an ad hoc basis, the SCIMF may draft common policy papers known as 'common understandings' about key subjects of IMF activity.[22]

The second body, the EURIMF, is an informal body based in Washington, DC, composed of representatives of EU Member States at the IMF and a representative from both the EU Delegation in Washington, DC, and from the ECB. Interestingly, the presidency of this group is chosen for two years, and therefore does not always reflect the EU presidency, which rotates more frequently. The EURIMF so-called permanent President is in charge of presenting the views of the EU and the Euro area to the IMF Executive Board in the form of written statements.[23] An additional and more reduced group ('mini EURIMF'), which convenes on an ad hoc basis, is the one-per-chair or one-per-office meeting. It is composed of envoys of European countries represented on the Executive Board.

The EURIMF meets once to three times a week in Washington, and its activities consist primarily of day-to-day coordination and informal exchange of views and information on Member States' positions, especially on IMF economic surveillance activities. The reports are periodically prepared by the IMF staff on the general economic situation of the EU, each EU Member State, and some of the most important IMF member countries. Moreover, for the Euro area Article IV discussions in the IMF Executive Board, the Euro area speaks with one voice and issues a written statement, which includes a distinct section on monetary policy prepared by the ECB. Apart from these Article IV review exercises, EURIMF discusses almost all important political or economic topics that are on the agenda of the IMF Executive Board. It is interesting to note that the strongest coordination occurs when the Executive Board is discussing policies where competence has been transferred to the EU institutions. For example, when discussing exchange rate policies of the Euro area, there is a single written statement by the President of the EURIMF, representing all euro members, and the ECB also makes a statement during the Board meeting. The EURIMF tries to coordinate as closely as

[22] In reality, SCIMF only provides useful information to Member States; its decisions are not binding. SCIMF can put forward proposals for common decisions, but thus far this mechanism has not been effective due to the divergent national interests which have impeded unity. Also, due to the different pace of meetings between the IMF Executive Board and the SCIMF, the latter is unable to feed the day-to-day debates (A Giovanini, M Gros, G Ivan, M Maciejkaczyński and D Valiante, *External Representation of the Euro Area* (Brussels, European Parliament, 2012) at 36.

[23] J Aubrechtová, W Coussens, G Pineau, n 19 above, at 5–9; D Hodson, *The Paradox of EMU's External Representation: The Case of the G20 and the IMF* (2011) at 13. Available at: www.euce.org/eusa/2011/papers/6e_hodson.pdf.

possible with EU representatives on the IMF Executive Board on those matters which involve national or shared competencies.[24]

The EU Member States' coordination has evolved in recent years through EURIMF and SCIMF activities. However, there are limits to the ability of the EU members to forge common positions.

B. Restricted Presence of the EU Institutions in the IMF Organs

The IMF opened a little window for the direct representation of EU institutions in the IMF. In particular, since 1999 the IMF granted the ECB observer status by a decision of the Board of Governors.[25] The ECB sends a representative to meetings of the Executive Board which deal with Euro area policies in the context of the Article IV consultations with member countries, Fund surveillance under Article IV over the policies of individual Euro area members, the role of the euro in the international monetary system, the World Economic Outlook, global financial stability reports, and world economic and market developments. Provided that there is no objection from the member concerned, the ECB is invited to send a representative to meetings of the Executive Board on Fund surveillance over the United States and Japan under Article IV, Fund surveillance under Article IV over and on use of Fund resources by the non-Euro area member countries of the EU, and Fund surveillance over the policies of and on the use of Fund resources by members which have been placed by the European Commission on the list of countries that are candidates for entry into the EU. In addition, the ECB could be invited to send a representative to meetings of the Executive Board on agenda items recognised by the ECB and the Fund to be of mutual interest for the performance of their respective mandates.

[24] The most common and formalized coordination method is the EU Presidency 'grey' mechanism. Indeed, before each Board meeting, each constituency prepares its own position paper on IMF staff reports known in IMF jargon as 'grey'. These are presented to the Executive Board. Basically, the EU presidency prepares a European grey to be discussed at EURIMF before the Board meeting. The strongest form of coordination is the so-called common written statement (also known as grey), which precludes other EU chairs from issuing separate written statements. This is normally used for issues exclusively related to Euro area common policy such as Article IV consultations on the Euro area, multilateral consultations on global imbalances, and exchange rate issues. Other weaker forms of coordination are the EURIMF presidency statement (used, for example, for Article IV consultations on EU Member States), which allows other EU chairs to issue separate statements, provided that they do not contradict the common elements of the presidency statement, and joint statements, which are co-signed only by the EU chairs wishing to do so. The EURIMF is a deliberative body dedicated simply to exchanging views and opinions with a high degree of frankness and openness without taking binding decisions. The European executive directors are linked to their capitals. See ECB, 'The External Representation of the EU and EMU', May 2011 *ECB Monthly Bulletin*, at 92.

[25] Decision No 12925-(03/1), 27 December 2002, as amended by Decision Nos 13414-(05/01), 23 December 2004, 13612-(05/108), 22 December 2005, and 14517-(10/1), 5 January 2010, IMF, *Selected decisions and selected documents of the International Monetary Fund*, As updated as of 31 December 2011 (IMF, 2011). Available at: www.imf.org/external/pubs/ft/sd/index.asp?decision=12925-(03/1).

The observer status means that the ECB representative at Executive Board meetings will be able to address the Board with the permission of the Chairman on matters within the responsibility of the ECB and may circulate written statements in advance of Board meetings to which the ECB has been invited. Logically, the Fund communicates the agenda and documentation for the Board meetings to the ECB.

Finally, it is interesting to note that, for the IMF's first multilateral consultation on the topic of global imbalances in 2006, the Euro area as an entity (rather than individual Member States) was invited to participate together with China, Japan, Saudi Arabia, and the United States. The aim was to select economies which either were directly part of the imbalances through their current account deficits or surpluses, or which represented a very large share of global output and could thus contribute to sustaining world growth as demand and savings/investment patterns adjusted.[26]

C. Incorporation of the Euro in the Composition of the SDR Basket

The Special Drawing Right (SDR) is the unit of account for the IMF. Before the appearance of the euro, the SDR basket was composed of the US dollar, the pound sterling, the Japanese yen, the French franc, and the German mark. The IMF took into account the euro and changed the composition of the SDR basket by three Board of Governors' decisions on September 1998. Taking effect on 1 January 1999, these decisions replaced references in the SDR basket to the German mark and the French franc with references to the euro as the currency of Germany and France, respectively. Also, the currency amounts of the German mark and the French franc in the SDR valuation basket have been automatically replaced by the euro as the currency of Germany and France.[27]

After the regular five-yearly review in 2010, the value of the SDR continues to be based on a weighted average of the values of a basket of currencies comprising the US dollar (41.9 per cent compared with 44 per cent at the 2005 review), euro (37.4 per cent compared with 34 per cent), pound sterling (11.3 per cent compared with 11 per cent), and Japanese yen (9.4 per cent compared with 11 per cent). The currencies included in the SDR are the four currencies issued by Fund members or by monetary unions that include Fund members whose exports of goods and services during the five-year period ending 12 months before the effective date of the revision had the largest value and which have been determined by the Fund to be freely usable currencies in accordance with Article XXX(f) of the Fund's

[26] IMF Staff, 'The Multilateral Consultation on Global Imbalances', (2007) *IMF Issues Brief* 07/03.

[27] Decision No 11801-(98/101) G/S, Decision No 11802-(98/101) G/S and Decision No 11803-(98/101) G/S, 21 September 1998. See IMF, *Selected decisions and selected documents of the International Monetary Fund*, as updated as of 31 December 2011 (IMF, 2011).

Articles of Agreement. The weights assigned to these currencies continue to be based on the value of the exports of goods and services by the member (or by members included in a monetary union) issuing the currency and the amount of reserves denominated in the respective currencies that are held by other members of the IMF.[28] This choice of the euro for the SDR basket highlights the relevance of the euro as the second international currency, the increase of the utilisation of the euro, and also the fact that the IMF takes into account the euro as the currency of the European monetary union. This is an interesting precedent for changing the nature of the IMF to a currency-based organisation in lieu of a State-based one in the future.

D. IMF Surveillance of Euro Area Policies under Article IV Consultations

Under Article IV, Section 3 of the IMF Articles of Agreement the Fund oversees the international monetary system in order to ensure its effective operation, and oversees the compliance of each member with its obligations. This is the legal basis for the surveillance activity of the IMF over the national economies of all member countries and over the world economy, and the Board of Governors have adopted decisions to regulate this core activity of the Fund. A new Decision on Bilateral and Multilateral Surveillance (Integrated Surveillance Decision) to strengthen the underlying legal framework for supervision came into effect on 18 January 2013.[29]

In the EMU the competences on monetary policy and exchange rate policy have been transferred to the EU institutions, and the IMF members which are also members of the Euro area do not have monetary and exchange rate policy. To remedy this situation, the solution was that bilateral Article IV consultations are conducted with all Euro area Member States and are supplemented by discussions with EU institutions responsible for common policies in the areas examined by the IMF. The Executive Board adopted decisions in 1998 and 2002[30] to extend IMF surveillance to the Euro area, maintaining at the same time the individual supervision of the Euro area countries. There are twice-yearly staff discussions with EU institutions responsible for common policies in the Euro area (ECB, European Commission, and Eurogroup). These discussions are held separately from the discussions

[28] IMF, 'IMF Determines New Currency Weights for SDR Valuation Basket', *IMF Press Release* No 10/434 (24 November 2010). Available at: www.imf.org/external/np/sec/pr/2010/pr10434.htm.

[29] IMF, *Modernizing the Legal Framework for Surveillance—An Integrated Surveillance Decision* (26 June 2012). Available at: www.imf.org/external/np/pp/eng/2012/062612.pdf.

[30] Decision No 11846-(98/125), 9 December 1998, on modalities for conducting surveillance over the monetary and exchange rate policies of the members of the euro area, as set out in SM/98/257 (11/25/98), effective 11 December 1998; Decision No 12899-(02/119), 4 December 2002, on Modalities for surveillance over Euro area policies in context of Article IV consultations with member countries, as amended by Decision No 14062-(08/15) 12 February 2008. See IMF, *Selected decisions and selected documents of the International Monetary Fund*, as updated as of 31 December 2013 (IMF, 2013). Available at: www.imf.org/external/pubs/ft/sd/index.asp?decision=11846-(98/125).

with individual Euro area countries, but they are considered an integral part of the Article IV process for each member. The discussions with individual Euro area countries are clustered, to the extent possible, around the discussions with the relevant EU institutions. There is an annual staff report prepared by a staff team from the IMF. This occurs following discussions with the officials of the Euro area on economic developments and policies. A Public Information Notice (PIN) is published summarising the views of the Executive Board and a 'Buff' statement on the Article IV consultation with the Euro area by the President of EURIMF that reflects the common view of the Member States of the Euro area and the EU in their respective fields of competence.[31] It is interesting to note that the EU speaks here with a single voice, manifested in the statement of the EURIMF President.

The new Decision on Bilateral and Multilateral Surveillance regulates the application of surveillance procedure to the currency unions and has thus completed the specific decisions on the Euro area. Its paragraph 8 says that members of currency unions remain subject to all of their obligations under Article IV, Section 1, and, accordingly, each member is accountable for those policies that are conducted by union-level institutions on its behalf. In its surveillance over the policies of members of a currency union, the Fund will assess whether relevant policies implemented—at the level of the currency union (including exchange rate and monetary policies) and at the level of members—are promoting the balance of payments and domestic stability of the union and will advise on policy adjustments necessary for this purpose. Because exchange rate policies in a currency union are implemented at the level of the union, the principles for the guidance of members' exchange rate policies and the associated indicators set out in paragraph 21 of this Decision only apply at the level of the currency union. In my opinion, it is another relevant precedent for an EU membership at the IMF, taking into account the currency and not the home country of that currency.[32]

[31] In 2015, all the documents related to the Article IV consultation on Euro area are published in the same IMF document, 'Euro Area Policies: 2015 Article IV Consultation Press Release; Staff Report; and Statement by the Executive Director', *IMF Country Report* 15/204; 10 July 2015.

[32] A deep study of the IMF surveillance practice in the Euro area has revealed that the Eurozone surveillance and the surveillance of individual euro countries by the Fund were not integrated. The focus of the Euro area surveillance was ECB policy and discussions with the European Commission on broad economic policies, including areas of macroeconomics, trade, and competition policy, and on issues related to the Stability and Growth Pact and the financial supervisory framework. The Euro area Article IV documents rarely discuss national problems that could have significant implications for the Eurozone in aggregate, as national discussions are part of the national Article IV process. At the same time, monetary and exchange rate developments ceased to be part of the national Article IV surveillance. In effect, surveillance was split into two parts: one addressing policies conducted by Eurozone authorities and one addressing national policies. This study shows more defects in the IMF surveillance of the Euro area due to the unique character of this monetary union and proposes some improvements in the IMF surveillance procedure in the Euro area. See Pisani-Ferry, Sapir and Wolff, *An evaluation of IMF surveillance of the Euro Area* (Brussels, Bruegel Blueprint 14 2011). See also Task Force on IMF Issues of the International Relations Committee of the European System of Central Banks, 'IMF Surveillance in Europe', *Occasional Paper Series*, No 158 (ECB, Frankfurt am Main, January 2015) and ECB, 'IMF surveillance of the Euro Area and its member countries' (2015) *ECB Economic Bulletin* 78–85.

The Eurozone was also considered directly by the IMF in the Financial Sector Assessment Program (FSAP). In April 2010 the IMF's Executive Board agreed to consider making stability assessments under the FSAP a mandatory part of bilateral surveillance. In September 2010 this agreement took concrete shape when the IMF made it mandatory for 25 jurisdictions with systemically important financial sectors to undergo financial stability assessments under the FSAP every five years. The Euro area is one of these jurisdictions with a systemically important financial sector, and the first EU-wide FSAP was concluded in March 2013.[33]

E. IMF Financial Assistance for EU Member States

The 2008 Great Recession precipitated a European sovereign debt crisis, and some EU members needed economic assistance from abroad to address their economic problems. EU Member States outside and inside the Eurozone required financial assistance, and in this context the IMF and the EU have cooperated closely to assist those EU countries with balance of payments problems. The IMF secured EU countries, and about 60 per cent of the IMF's total disbursement and precautionary commitments were made during the crisis to EU Member States, a situation which some non-European IMF member states have criticised. The pragmatic approach was applied one more time, the IMF and the EU cooperate seriously, and today the EU is the biggest user of IMF resources.

Article V, Section 3 of the IMF Articles of Agreement allow the IMF to finance member states with balance of payments problems. Any member country, whether rich, middle-income, or poor, can turn to the IMF for financing if it has a balance of payments need, that is, if it cannot find sufficient financing on affordable terms in the capital markets to make its international payments and maintain a safe level of reserves. The states in economic trouble develop a quantitative and structural macroeconomic programme; a lending arrangement in consultation with the IMF which stipulates specific economic policies and determines that the borrowing country has agreed to resolve its balance of payments problem.

From the IMF law perspective, EU Member States have access to Fund facilities in the same way that all IMF members do, and being part of a currency union is irrelevant. The EU primary law does not preclude an EU Member State from requesting the use of IMF resources, but some requirements must be fulfilled which differ from those laid down for Eurozone members. The EU Member States outside the Eurozone which face difficulties can be helped by the EU using the medium-term financial assistance facility, for which the legal basis is Article 143 TFEU developed by Council Regulation (EC) No 332/2002.[34] Article 143(2)(a)

[33] IMF, 'European Union: Financial System Stability Assessment', *IMF Country Report No 13/75*, March 2013.

[34] Council Regulation (EC) 332/2002 of 18 February 2002 establishing a facility providing medium-term financial assistance for Member States' balances of payments, [2002] OJ L53/1.

TFEU enables the EU Member State to request aid from 'any other international organisation to which such a member may have recourse'. The use of the EU's medium-term financial assistance facility was combined with IMF loans to help Hungary and Latvia in 2008 and Romania in 2009, 2011 and 2013.[35]

The legal framework for Eurozone countries under EU laws was different, and the assistance of the IMF to these states was more complicated. In spite of Article 125 TFEU, which prohibits EU Member States from assuming the commitments of other EU Member States (the 'no bail-out' clause), the EU Council in May 2010 used Article 122(2) as the legal basis for establishing an assistance mechanism for Euro area states in crisis and built the European Stabilisation Mechanism with two legs. The EU leg was the European Financial Stabilisation Mechanism (EFSM), established by Council Regulation (EU) No 407/2010[36] and reproducing for the Eurozone countries the medium-term financial assistance facility for non-Euro area countries. The intergovernmental leg was the European Financial Stability Facility (EFSF), created outside EU law by Euro area Member States on a temporary basis until June 2013. In December 2010 the European Council decided to enact a permanent crisis resolution mechanism, and it was adopted as a simplified reform of the TFEU by European Council Decision 2011/199/EU.[37] The Treaty Establishing the European Stability Mechanism (ESM) was signed in Brussels on 2 February 2012. The ESM was inaugurated on 8 October 2012 and is now fully operational, using the staff and buildings of the EFSF, which has substituted for the ESM. The ESM is an intergovernmental organisation under public international law and a permanent crisis resolution mechanism for the countries of the Euro area.

These Eurozone resolution mechanisms have been activated in the context of the EU sovereign debt crisis, and in many cases the IMF has supported the Eurozone area countries: Greece in 2010 and 2012, Ireland in 2010, Portugal in 2011 and, Cyprus in 2013.[38] On 3 December 2012 the Spanish government formally requested the disbursement of close to €39.5 billion in funds. The IMF did not agree to provide any loan to Spain, but it did agree to monitor European financial assistance for Spain's bank recapitalisation programme under technical assistance, which ended in January 2014. Ireland and Portugal concluded their programmes

[35] All the information is on the EU website at: ec.europa.eu/economy_finance/assistance_eu_ms/index_en.htm.

[36] Council Regulation (EU) 407/2010 establishing a European financial stabilization mechanism, [2010] OJ L118/1.

[37] European Council Decision 2011/199/EU amending Article 136 of the Treaty on the Functioning of the European Union with regard to a stability mechanism for Member States whose currency is the euro, [2011] OJ L91/1. The validity of this decision and the ESM Treaty was confirmed by the ECJ in the famous full Court judgment of 27 November 2012 in Case C-370/12, *Pringle v Government of Ireland, Ireland and The Attorney General*, EU:C:2012:756.

[38] All the information is on the EU website at: ec.europa.eu/economy_finance/assistance_eu_ms/index_en.htm.

in December 2013 and June 2014, respectively, and they then entered into Post-Programme Monitoring. On 19 August, the European Commission signed a Memorandum of Understanding (MoU) with Greece following approval by the European Stability Mechanism Board of Governors for further stability support accompanied by a third economic adjustment programme. This paves the way for mobilising up to €86 billion in financial assistance to Greece over three years (2015–18).[39] The IMF did not agree at the moment to lend more money to Greece but the IMF has confirmed that it has assisted in preparing the programme and it continues to support the process.

From an economic and political perspective, the IMF's involvement in the assistance to EU countries during the sovereign debt crisis was colossal. The three biggest borrowers of IMF resources were Greece, Portugal, and Ireland. About 60 per cent of the IMF's total disbursements and precautionary commitments were to Europe as a whole.[40] Even though the EU is not a member of the IMF, the EU countries have been assisted by the Fund, and the Fund has collaborated extensively with the EU to prepare the European crisis resolution mechanisms.

Besides the IMF's participation in EU Member State rescues, the IMF law and practice has impacted on the legal framework of the EU financial assistance mechanisms in several ways.[41] In particular, the surveillance of the EU Member States' fulfilment of the economic programme has been assumed by a troika composed of agents from the European Commission, the ECB, and the IMF. The EU institutions were little experienced in the surveillance of economic programmes, and they needed the expertise of the IMF, which has more than 60 years of experience in lending money and encouraging reforms to help countries with balance-of-payments problems or in financial crisis. The ESM Treaty tries to reduce this EU dependence on IMF expertise, and it will be the European Commission—in liaison with the ECB and, wherever possible, together with the IMF—which is the institution in charge of monitoring compliance with the conditionality attached to the financial assistance facility (Article 13(7) ESM Treaty). The IMF expertise will be used only 'where possible' by the Commission and the ECB to negotiate with the country the memorandum of understanding detailing the conditionality attached to the financial assistance facility. The reluctance about the troika is perceived also in the European Parliament which opened an enquiry into the role and operations of the troika.[42]

[39] See the information on the EU web site at: ec.europa.eu/economy_finance/assistance_eu_ms/greek_loan_facility/index_en.htm.

[40] IMF, *The IMF and Europe*, Factsheet (30 September 2013).

[41] See W Bergthaler, n 5 above, 183–86. For a deep analysis of the IMF assistance to the EU countries, see J Pisani-Ferry, A Sapir and M Wolff, *EU-IMF assistance to euro-area countries: an early assessment* (Blueprint 19, Bruegel (2013). See also Seitz and Jost, The Role of the IMF in the European Debt Crisis', *HAW im Dialog—Weidener Diskussionpapiere* No 32 (January 2012) at 10–11.

[42] All the documents about this enquiry, including the European Parliament draft Report, are available in: www.europarl.europa.eu/oeil/popups/ficheprocedure.do?reference=2013/2277%28INI%29&l=en.

III. THE 2010 IMF REFORM IMPLEMENTATION: CONSEQUENCES FOR THE EU

The 2008 IMF reform, which became effective on 3 March 2011, had a limited impact on the EU position in the IMF.[43] A more ambitious IMF reform package was agreed to by the G-20 leaders in Seoul in November 2010. It was implemented by the Board of Governors of the IMF, which approved a package of relevant reforms of the Fund's quotas and governance on 15 December 2010, completing the Fourteenth General Review of Quotas.[44]

The 2010 reform fixed an unprecedented 100 per cent increase in total quotas and a reallocation of quota and voting shares in the IMF to better reflect the changing relative weights of the IMF's member countries in the global economy. The reform also restructures the composition of the IMF's Executive Board, paving the way for an increase in the representation of emerging markets and developing economies (EMDCs) in the day-to-day decision-making at the IMF. There will be two fewer Board members from advanced European countries, and all executive directors will be elected rather than appointed, as some are now.

The package of IMF governance reforms was intended to be in place by November 2012, in time for the biennial election of executive directors at that time. That deadline was not met, because the United States had not given its approval.[45] The budgetary technicalities in the US and some voices in Congress criticising both the IMF intervention in the EU debt crisis and even the utility of the Fund itself are complicating the approval of the 2010 IMF reform.[46] The Obama administration

[43] The 2008 reforms were approved by the Board of Governors in April 2008 and came into effect on 3 March 2011, with the acceptance of the 'Voice and Participation' amendment to the Articles of Agreement. See IMF, *IMF Governance—Summary of Issues and Reform*, 2009; B Eichengreen, 'Out of the Box Thoughts about the International Financial Architecture', 2009 *IMF Working Papers* 09/116.

[44] IMF Resolution 66-2 on Fourteenth General Review of Quotas and Reform of the Executive Board, 15 December 2010, in IMF, *Selected Decisions and Selected Documents of the IMF, Thirty-Sixth Issue*, updated as of 31 December 2011, at 9. The content of the 2010 reform is well explained in IMF, *IMF Quota and Governance Reform: Elements of an Agreement*, 2010. For a general overview, see S Hagan, 'Reforming the IMF' in M Giovanoli and D Devos (eds), *International Monetary and Financial Law. The Global Crisis* (Oxford, OUP, 2010) at 40–68; W Bergthaler and G Bossu, 'Recent legal developments in the International Monetary Fund' (2010) 1 *European Yearbook of International Economic Law* 391.

[45] At this moment, the 2010 IMF reform will enter into force if the US Congress approves it, because all the requirements are fulfilled except that the requirement for 85 per cent of member countries' votes cannot be met, as the US, with 16.75 per cent of the vote, has a veto power. Consents to the quota increase and acceptances of the Executive Board reform amendment are recorded online here: www.imf.org/external/np/sec/misc/consents.htm, last updated: 23 January 2014.

[46] Nelson & Weiss, *IMF Reforms: Issues for Congress*, 1 February 2013. Available at: www.fas.org/sgp/crs/misc/R42844.pdf. For many commentators, the IMF reflects US economic policy preferences more faithfully than perhaps any other international organisation and consequently the United States has played a prominent role in the 2010 reform pushing for responsible change to make the voices and votes in the IMF better reflect the new international economic and political landscape. This reform will strengthen the central role of the IMF in stabilising the global economy and financial system and it is crucial to maintain the legitimacy of the IMF. A failure to enact the pending IMF legislation due to rejection in Congress would undermine US leadership without justification and would decrease US standing with key emerging market and developing countries, which are the principal beneficiaries

will therefore seek the necessary congressional approvals at its earliest opportunity, but the US Congress rejected again in January 2014 and 2015 the approval.[47] This is ironic since the United States was the principal architect of the 2010 agreement.[48]

The 2010 IMF reform is relevant for the EU position in the IMF in two ways. First, it marks a clear tendency to reduce the EU Member States' quotas in the IMF and promote the rise of the EMDCs linked to the increase in the influence of the emerging countries in the global economy. The subsequent modifications in IMF quotas will erode the EU's relative position. Secondly, it introduces some legal changes in the composition and functioning of the Executive Board that would facilitate the joint EU/Euro area representation.

A. New Quotas Assignments and the EU

Each member country of the IMF is assigned a quota, based broadly on its relative position in the world economy, and this quota determines a member's maximum financial commitment to the IMF and its voting power. The distribution of IMF quotas is the key to explaining the balance of power in the IMF, and the formula to calculate quotas was always a highly controversial matter.

The current quotas and voting shares of the EU Member States are based on the application of the 2008 quota formula that is a weighted average of GDP (weight of 50 per cent), openness (30 per cent), economic variability (15 per cent), and international reserves (5 per cent). For this purpose, GDP is measured through a blend of GDP based on market exchange rates (weight of 60 per cent), and on purchasing power parity (PPP) (40 per cent). The formula also includes a 'compression factor' that reduces the dispersion in calculated quota shares across members.[49] The EU Member States together have 31.9 per cent of the quota shares and 30.9 per cent of the voting shares, which is more than the US (17.7 and 16.7 per cent respectively) which is the single biggest shareholder in the IMF.

The Executive Board uses the 2008 quota formula as a basis for calculating the new quotas, but using many highly technical and complex corrections to attain the agreed-upon results. The 2010 package of reforms doubled the overall IMF quotas

of the package. R Henning, 'U.S. Interests and the International Monetary Fund' *Policy Brief no 09-12* (2009), Peterson Institute for International Economics; G Lavelle, *Legislating International Organization: the US Congress, the IMF and the World Bank* (Oxford, OUP, 2011).

[47] 130 scholars, former government officials, and policy-makers sent a letter to the Congress urging passage of this reform, because it is in the interest of the US and it is crucial to maintaining the legitimacy of the IMF. See 'US fails to approve IMF Reform', *Financial Times*, 14 January 2014; 'Pressure mounts on US over IMF reform', *Financial Times*, 11 March 2013.

[48] T Truman, 'What Next for the IMF?' *Policy Brief 15-1*, 2015, Peterson Institute for International Economics, Washington DC available at: piie.com/publications/interstitial.cfm?ResearchID=2742.

[49] The documentation about the IMF studies on quota formula can be found in IMF, *IMF Quota and Governance Publications* (Last Updated: 9 October 2012).

to about US$ 755 billion and shifted voting power to dynamic emerging market economies. In fact, the Fourteenth General Review of Quotas will: (i) double quotas from approximately SDR 238.5 billion to approximately SDR 477 billion, (about US$ 715 billion at current exchange rates); (ii) shift more than six per cent of quota shares from over-represented to under-represented member countries, a quota shift made possible mainly by reducing the shares of a number of advanced economies and oil-producing countries; (iii) shift more than six per cent of quota shares to dynamic EMDCs; (iv) preserve the quota and voting share of the poorest member countries, and (v) significantly realign quota shares. As a result of these modifications, the 10 Fund members with the largest voting shares will consist of the United States, Japan, the so-called BRICs (Brazil, the Russian Federation, India, China), and four of the more prominent European countries (France, Germany, Italy, the United Kingdom).[50]

The 2010 quota reform will only reduce the EU quotas by 1.616 per cent. There will be some EU Member States that will sacrifice a significant voting share (Belgium, 43 per cent; the Netherlands, 18 per cent; and Bulgaria 37 per cent); the current biggest states (Germany, France, United Kingdom, and Italy) lose between 5 and 7 per cent. Most of the Central and Eastern states will increase their voting shares by 5 to 17 per cent), and Spain, Ireland, and Luxembourg will capture significant additional voting shares. Clearly, the 2008 quota formula was fruitful for the EU Member States, and the adjustments applied in 2010 do not modify those results. The EU decline in the world economy in favour of emerging economies is insufficiently reflected in the IMF quota and voting shares.

Although the implementation of the 2010 quota reform is pending, it is a transitory modification, because the 66-2 Resolution required the Executive Board to complete a comprehensive review of the formula by January 2013 and to apply it to the Fifteenth General Review of Quotas in January 2014. The Executive Board has discussed the new formula without success and has decided that consensus on a new quota formula will best be done in the context of the Fifteenth Review rather than on a stand-alone basis.[51]

In any case, the negotiation of a new quota formula will be a challenge for the EU Member States, and their quotas and voting shares in the IMF will be reduced

[50] All the calculations by IMF Staff are available in IMF, *Quota and governance reform elements of an agreement* (2010). See also P Moreno, *Metamorfosis del FMI* (Madrid, Tecnos, 2011) 174–96; New Rules for Global Governments, *Impact of 2010 IMF Quota Reform: Winners, Losers and Realignments* (24 July 2012). Available at: www.new-rules.org/storage/documents/imf_reform/impact%20of%202010%20 imf%20reforms.pdf.

[51] Nevertheless, there is a lack of agreement on the relative weight of GDP at market prices and exchange rates and purchasing power parity GDP, on what variables other than GDP should be included in the formula, and on how the variables should be constructed. See IMF, *Executive Board Reports on the Quota Formula Review,* Press Release No 13/30 (30 January 2013); See IMF, *IMF Executive Board Discusses Quota Formula Review—October 2012* (9 October 2012) and Truman, 'The Congress Should Support IMF Governance Reform to Help Stabilize the World Economy', Peterson Institute for International Economics *Policy Brief PB2013-7* (2013), at 10.

in line with the decrease in their relative weights in the world economy.[52] This is a good argument for going to a single EU or Eurozone chair at the IMF and thus compensating for the loss of individual quotas by unifying the national quotas.

B. The Executive Board's Reforms and Representation of the EU Member States

Some legal conditions of the current legal framework constrain joint EU/Eurozone representation at the IMF Executive Board. First, members having the five largest quotas (currently the US, Japan, Germany, the United Kingdom, and France) have the right but also the obligation to appoint an executive director to the Executive Board.[53] Accordingly, Germany, the UK, and France do not participate in the biannual regular elections of executive directors and thus no other EU member could join a German, British, or French chair. It would thus be impossible for all of the EU or Eurozone members to form a single constituency and elect a single executive director.[54] Secondly, the rules under which executive directors are elected biannually prescribe that, in order to achieve an equitable distribution of voting power among executive directors, there is an upper limit of nine per cent of voting power imposed on the constitution of any constituency. Consequently, EU Member States (currently representing together about 30.8 per cent of the IMF's total voting power)—minus the UK, Germany, and France, who together represent about 14.4 per cent of the IMF's total voting power—represent about 16.4 per cent of the total voting power of which the Euro area accounts for 12.2 per cent and thus both groups would exceed the current upper limit of nine per cent. Finally, the formation of constituencies is voluntary, and no IMF member can be compelled to be part of a constituency.

The 2010 IMF reform introduces relevant changes in these legal conditions to improve the governance of the IMF,[55] and some of them would facilitate the consolidation of the European representation on the Executive Board. In particular, five aspects must be emphasised: (i) the elimination of the category of appointed directors at the IMF Executive Board thereby enabling European consolidation on the Board (ie, members with the five largest voting powers would no longer appoint one executive director each) would mean that all of the Executive Board will be elected; (ii) the election rules contained in Schedule E of the Articles of Agreements will be deleted, and, going forward, the IMF Board of Governors will set the upper and lower limits for the regular election of executive directors for

[52] Un update analysis is available in R Mohan and M Kapur, 'Emerging Powers and Global Governance: Whither the IMF?', *IMF Working Paper 15/219*, 2015.

[53] Article XII, Section 3 of the IMF's Articles.

[54] S Hagan, '10 Years of the Euro …', n 17 above, at 8.

[55] W Bergthaler, 'The Relationship between International Monetary Fund Law and European Union Law: Influence, Impact, Effect, and Interaction' in R Wessel and S Blockmans (eds), *Between Autonomy and Dependence* (Berlin, Springer Verlag, 2012) at 179.

each biannual election (ie, making a Euro area chair pooling more than nine per cent of the votes possible); (iii) under Article XII, Section 3(e) of the IMF's Articles together with the Board of Governors Resolution 66-2, executive directors representing seven or more members in a constituency may appoint a second 'alternate' following the 2012 regular elections of executive directors (ie, a Euro area chair would be an executive director as well as two Euro area alternate executive directors, which would be an interesting way to distribute the responsibilities between Eurozone countries); (iv) the commitment to 24 executive directors at the IMF Executive Board would remain in place for the time being;[56] and (v) the IMF Board of Governors noted the commitment to reduce 'advanced European country representation' at the IMF Executive Board by two executive directors leading to a greater integration and consolidation of European representation.[57]

It was argued that the overrepresentation of the EU on the Executive Board was denying emerging countries the opportunity to play a bigger role in the IMF, which was seen as vital for the Fund's effectiveness and legitimacy.[58]

The first step towards Board realignment was taken in November 2012 for the Executive Board of 2012–14.[59] The Netherlands and its constituency partners, Belgium and Luxembourg, decided to create a new constituency as of first November 2012.[60] After the EU accession of Croatia, the constituency will comprise seven states, or a full quarter of all EU members (three Eurozone countries), alongside a number of (potential) EU candidate countries and close European neighbours (15 members). This new constituency is represented by the fifth largest chair, and it is the largest multi-country constituency on the Executive Board in terms of quota (6.57 per cent of votes). Belgium and the Netherlands designate the executive director for this group on a rotating basis. Currently, the executive director is Dutch; the alternate executive director is Belgian. Except for Luxembourg and Montenegro, most of the countries in the new constituency will be adversely affected by the 2010 IMF reform and will lose quota and voting shares (almost 22 per cent). Therefore, this realignment is particularly advantageous for these medium and small European countries.

[56] Article XII, Section 3(b) of the IMF's Articles (currently, and as proposed to be amended by Board of Governors Resolution 66-2) sets the number of executive directors at 20, which may be increased or decreased by the Board of Governors with a majority of 85 per cent of the total voting power, for the purposes of each regular election of executive directors.

[57] This political agreement was adopted at the G-20 Ministerial Meeting in Korea in 2010. See IMF, *G-20 Ministers Agree 'Historic' Reforms in IMF Governance*, News Release, 23 October 2010. Available at: www.imf.org/external/pubs/ft/survey/so/2010/NEW102310A.htm.

[58] K Gnath, 'The Reform of the IMF: Europe's Short-Term Arithmetic and Long-Term Choices', American Institute for Contemporary German Studies, *Transatlantic Perspectives* (November 2010), at 4; T Truman, 'The Congress Should Support IMF Governance Reform to Help Stabilize the World Economy' (2013) *Peterson Institute for International Economics Policy Brief PB2013-7*, at 4.

[59] See IMF, 'New IMF Executive Board Begins Two-Year Term', (1 November 2012) *Press Release No 12/409*.

[60] Nederland Central Bank, 'IMF Governance reform: Open economies have a place at the table', (October 2012) *DN Bulletin*.

The eight left-over countries from the old Belgian chair have constituted a new Central and Eastern European IMF Constituency. The Constituency Agreement was signed in Vienna on 11 July 2012,[61] and includes five EU Member States and three Eurozone countries. As result of the Constituency Agreement, the current executive director is from Austria and the alternate executive directors rotate between Turkey, the Czech Republic, and Hungary. The first alternate executive director will be from Austria in 2014-2022 and the second Alternate Director will rotate between Turkey, Czech Republic, and Hungary. Through this complex rotation scheme, one seat on the IMF's Executive Board will be redistributed from the advanced European countries to the emerging market countries.

The Executive Board is undergoing the biggest reshuffle in two decades,[62] but the emerging economies consider it cosmetic.[63] These changes are a realignment of some European constituencies taking into account the character of non-advanced economies of some of the EU Member States and their neighbours.

IV. PROPOSALS FOR A RENOVATION OF EU-IMF RELATIONS

A. New Elements in the EU-IMF Relationship and the Positions of the EU Institutions

There are new elements in the EU and from the IMF side that nowadays are creating better conditions for an evolution of EU-IMF relations. I will highlight in particular two new elements for a renovated EU-IMF relationship: the major improvements of the EU internal economic governance and the decline of Europe's share in the global economy.

As I pointed out before, the structural weakness of the economic leg of the EMU was an obstacle to the development of EMU external relations. The EU Member States maintained the core competences in economic policy, and the EU institutions could not try to represent or to substitute for them in international institutions and forums like the IMF or G-20. As a result of the Great Recession

[61] The agreement is available at: www.rokovania.sk/File.aspx/Index/Mater-Dokum-146426.

[62] In the 2012 Tokyo meeting of the IMF, other decisions related to the functioning of the Executive Board were taken. It has also been reported that the grouping of Nordic countries will permit all the Baltic members of the group to rotate serving as the executive director and that the Swiss executive director will rotate with Poland in a few years. It is interesting to note that Colombia left the Brazilian chair to join the Spain, Mexico, Venezuela, and Central American countries' constituency, and also that Nicaragua, Cape Verde, and East Timor moved to Brazil's constituency. See S Rastelloo, *IMF Board Sees Biggest Power Shift Reshuffle in Two Decades*, Bloomberg, 14 October 2012.

[63] See also about the opinion of EMDCs the *Intergovernmental Group of Twenty-Four on International Monetary Affairs and Development Communiqué* (18 April 2013), 'We regret that the recent Board realignment did not go far enough towards meeting the goal of enhancing the voice and representation of EMDCs. We call on advanced European countries to fulfil their commitment towards the consolidation of chairs'.

and the subsequent European debt crisis, the EU has started reforming its internal economic governance. It is necessary to determine if the transfer of economic competences from EU Member States to the EU institutions is so great that it will allow or induce a change in the external EMU governance and open the opportunity for a centralised representation of the Eurozone.[64] The economic leg of the EMU was established in the TFEU, and the Stability and Growth Pact (SGP) was adopted to reinforce the prohibition of excessive public deficit, which was the most relevant rule of budgetary discipline. Articles 120–126 TFEU and the SPG were insufficient to prevent the increase of the public deficits and public debts of EU countries as a consequence of the Great Recession and the subsequent sovereign debt crisis. The economic crisis revealed the weakness of the economic union. Since 2010, EU institutions have adopted many new EU secondary law rules and even intergovernmental treaties outside EU law to reinforce the internal governance of the economic leg of the EMU. These new measures are the strengthening of the EU mechanism to coordinate the national economic policies and the tightening of sanctions in case Member States breach EU disciplines; the introduction of crisis resolution mechanisms to assist Member States in crisis; and the transfer of responsibilities in banking supervision to the EU institutions in order to achieve a banking union progressively.[65]

In relation to the Europe position in the global economy, the rapid growth rates witnessed in many emerging markets during recent years are changing the economic balance of power. EU countries need to realise that the world economy is evolving and that this very rapid evolution seems unlikely to grind to a halt in the coming years and decades. The Union's successive enlargements have added economic weight to the EU and enabled it to maintain its pre-eminent position in the world economy, world trade, and many key sectors. Nevertheless, its share of the world economy has diminished as other actors have grown more quickly. Most of the economic analyses predict a relative decline of the developed economies (the EU, the US, and Japan) from now until 2050.[66]

[64] D Schwarzer; F Steinberg, D Valiante, *Towards a common external representation for the Eurozone?* (Madrid, Real Instituto Elcano, March 2013) at 5, put the question: 'A so far unexplored question is the extent to which internal governance reform holds consequences or opens up opportunities for a better external representation of interests'. See also R Chemain, 'L'UE dans le système monétaire international' in C Benlolo-Carabot, U Candas, S Cujo, *Union européenne et droit international* (Paris, Pedone, 2012) at 503.

[65] About the reforms in the European economic governance after the crisis, see generally F Allemand and F Martucci, 'La nouvelle gouvernance économique européenne' (2012) 48 *Cahiers de droit européen* 17–99, 409–57; O Clerc, *La gouvernance économique de l'Union européenne. Recherches sur l'intégration par la différenciation* (Brussels, Bruylant, 2012); D Hodson, *Governing the Euro Area in Good Times & Bad* (Oxford, OUP, 2011); M López-Escudero, 'La Unión Europea ante la crisis económica y financiera' (2011) 39 *Revista de Derecho Comunitario Europeo* 353–66; F Martucci, 'Union économique' (2011) *Jurisclasseur Europe*; M Ruffert, 'The European debt crisis and European Union Law' (2011) 48 *CML Rev* 1777–806.

[66] At constant relative prices, the US would account for only 17 per cent of the world economy in 2050, compared to 27 per cent in 2010. By 2050 China would account for 20 per cent of global GDP (compared to 7 per cent in 2008), and India would have a 7 per cent share (compared to 2 per cent in

A decline in economic weight and the loss of normative power will weaken the EU's capacity to influence global governance of the international economy. The EU will only be able to secure its place among the major players if it combines a sound economic base with an effective representation of its interests on a global scale. It will also have to retain stable alliances, in particular with the US, which itself wants the EU to improve the coherence of its external representation.[67] This evolution provides an additional argument for the amalgamation of EU representation in the IMF as a way of maintaining influence and power.

These new elements are influencing the opinion and positions of the EU institutions related to the EU-IMF relations. In spite of the academic literature[68] which voiced the inadequacy of the EU position in the IMF and proposed several approaches to a more unified EU representation or even a single chair for the EU at the IMF, the EU institutions have remained silent since 1998, apparently comfortable with the pragmatic approach that was chosen for EU-IMF relations. Nonetheless, the European Parliament in 2006[69] and the European Commission in 2008[70] started to denounce the minimalist approach imposed by Member States in the Council.

The Great Recession contributed to a louder call from the European authorities for a unified external representation of the Euro area and a single chair at the IMF. The Eurogroup President, Jean-Claude Juncker,[71] was quite clear, as was the European Commissioner for Economic and Monetary Affairs, Joaquin Almunia.[72] The European Parliament also pressed for such action, the Feio Report re-launched

2008). The shares of the EU (27 per cent in 2010, 23 per cent in 2025, and 17 per cent in 2050) would also fall dramatically during this period. See, J Fouré, A Bénassy-Quéré and L Fontagné, '*The Great Shift: Macroeconomic Projections for the World Economy at the 2050 Horizon*' *CEPII Working Paper 2012-03* (2012), at 52–56; Hawksworth and Tiwari, *The world in 2050—The accelerating shift of global economic power: challenges and opportunities*, January 2012: www.pwc.com/en_GX/gx/world-2050/pdf/world-in-2050-jan-2011.pdf; Ward, 'The world in 2050: quantifying the shift in global economy', *HSBC Global Economics* (January 2011).

[67] D Schwarzer et al, n 64 above, at 5; Van den Noord, Döhring, Langedijk, Nogueira Martins, L Pench, D Temprano-Arroyo and M Thiel, 'The evolution of economic governance in EMU' (June 2008) *European Economy. Economic Papers No 328*, at 46.

[68] A Ahearne and B Eichengreen, 'External monetary and financial policy: a review and a proposal' in A Sapir (ed), *Fragmented power: Europe and the global economy* (Brussels, Bruegel, 2007) at 142; S Cafaro, *Il governo delle organizzazioni di Bretton Woods. Analisi critica, processi di revisione in atto e proposte di reforma* (Bari, Giappichelli, 2012) 141–77; J-V Louis, *L'Union Européenne et sa monnaie*, n 12 above, para 418–24; L Bini Smaghi, 'A Single EU Seat in the IMF?' (2004) 42 *Journal of Common Market Studies* at 229; M López-Escudero, 'Crisis y reforma del Fondo Monetario Internacional' (2007) *Revista Española de Derecho Internacional*, at 435; de Larosière et al, *Report of the High-Level Group on Financial Supervisions in the EU*, 2009, para 256.

[69] Resolution on the strategic review of the International Monetary Fund adopted on 14 March 2006: www.europarl.europa.eu/sides/getDoc.do?type=TA&reference=P6-TA-2006-0076&language=BG.

[70] European Commission, 'EMU@10: Successes and challenges after 10 years of Economic and Monetary Union' (2008) *European Economy. Economic Papers No 142*.

[71] Mr Juncker said: 'It is absurd for those 15 countries not to agree to have a single representation at the IMF. It makes us look absolutely ridiculous. We are regarded as buffoons on the international scene', declaration of the Eurogroup President Mr Junckers in April 2008: euobserver.com/9/25984.

[72] Speech by Mr Almunia, *Laying the Foundations of a European Foreign Economic Policy*, 6 April 2009, europa.eu/rapid/press-release_SPEECH-09-175_en.htm. He clearly stated that 'The Commission has long called for a consolidation of European representation on the boards of the IFIs. In the case of the IMF, the argument for a single consolidated Euro-area chair is quite obvious'.

the debate and more recently, on 25 October 2011 a non-legislative resolution on Global Economic Governance was adopted by the European Parliament—the Hökmark Report—recalling 'that, under Article 138 of the Lisbon Treaty, the euro area is supposed to introduce unified external representation; [the Parliament] urges the Commission to put forward a legislative proposal to that effect'.[73]

Now, after some delays, new expectations have been opened by the European Commission with a very important 2012 Communication about the development of the EMU in the coming years,[74] which included a serious compromise to activate Article 138 TFEU. The European Commission wants to take into account the progress achieved in the internal economic governance of the Euro area in response to the crisis to strengthen and consolidate its external representation on the basis of the current Treaties (Article 17 TEU and Article 138 TFEU). The Commission considers that the Euro area has become the natural counterpart of major economic powers when global growth, financial assistance, or financial regulations are discussed. However, because of the current fragmentation of its representation in international financial institutions and forums, the Euro area does not have influence and leadership commensurate with its economic weight. The focus of the coming proposal will be on EU representation in the IMF, and no reference is made to the EU's participation in other international economic organisations (World Bank, OECD, BIS) and forums (G-20, G-8, Financial Stability Board, and financial standard-setting bodies). The pragmatic approach was deemed unsatisfactory, and the Commission will propose a two-stage process to enhance the Euro area representation in the IMF. In a first stage, the Commission will design a rearrangement of the country constituencies in the IMF so as to re-group countries into Eurozone constituencies which could also include future Euro area Member States. In parallel, observer status at the IMF Executive Board should be sought for the Eurozone. At a second stage, a single seat in the IMF bodies is planned with a few specifications.

The Commission will in due course make formal proposals under Article 138(2) TFEU to establish a unified position to achieve an observer status for the Eurozone at the IMF Executive Board, and subsequently for a single seat. The Commission will also put forward proposals for improving the coordination among Member States on IMF issues related to the EMU. Leaving the IMF to one side, the Commission will consider making use of Article 138(1) TFEU to propose common positions on EMU-related matters in competent international financial institutions and conferences (G-20, G-8, and international financial standard-setting bodies). Logically, the Commission considers itself the appropriate institution to represent the Euro area in the IMF in accordance with Article 138 TFEU, with the ECB being

[73] European Parliament, Committee on Economic and Monetary Affairs, Rapporteur Diego Feio; A7-0282/2010, *Report with recommendations to the Commission on improving the economic governance and stability framework of the Union, in particular in the euro area*, October 11, 2010; European Parliament, Committee on Economic and Monetary Affairs, Rapporteur: Gunnar Hökmark A7-0323/2011, *Report on Global Economic Governance, European Parliament*, 25 October 2011.

[74] COM(2012) 777 final/2, 'Communication from the Commission: A blueprint for a deep and genuine economic and monetary union. Launching a European debate'.

associated in the area of monetary policy. I suppose that the Council, the Eurogroup, and the European Council will disagree and will demand a leading role in EU-IMF relations. The Barroso Commission did not submit this proposal. The new Juncker Commission had not been adopted yet, even though it is announced as a measure included in the reform of EMU after the five Presidents' Report.[75]

B. Scenarios for the Relations Between the EU and the IMF

An overrepresentation (one-third of the Executive Board) and the high voting share (more than 30 per cent) are strong arguments for defending the status quo, and it is easy to understand the reluctance of the EU Member States to modify this situation. Nevertheless, it seems to me it will be extremely difficult to maintain and justify this situation in the future due to the decreasing prospects for the EU's share in the global economy and the under-influence of the EU on the IMF policy in spite of its overrepresentation.[76]

Rejecting the status quo as a solution for EU-IMF relations,[77] I believe that some scenarios could be suggested to improve this complex relationship. The easiest but limited scenario is an improvement of EU Member States' coordination at the IMF. A more ambitious scenario may be the progressive consolidation of the EU representation at the IMF and, the ideal situation will be a single EU chair or two chairs for the EU/Euro area.

i. Improvement of the Current EU Coordination Mechanisms related to IMF Activity

To counterbalance the loss of power with the same EU representation in the IMF, the EU must improve and reinforce its coordination mechanism in IMF matters and, more importantly, agree on a common position among all EU countries on IMF decisions.

[75] J-C Juncker et al, *Completing Europe's Economic and Monetary Union* (2015): ec.europa.eu/priorities/economic-monetary-union/docs/5-presidents-report_en.pdf, p 15.

[76] Some EU Member States are reluctant to change the status quo, arguing that it is illogical to renounce such a privileged situation in quota shares, voting shares, and executive director slots. Some commentators have analysed the EU member countries' performances in the IMF during the economic crisis, and they have found that EU Member States have exercised considerable collective influence within the IMF. The manner in which such funding was secured provides evidence of the EU influence within the Fund. Hodson spokes about a paradox in the external representation of the EMU: When Member States agree on international economic priorities, there is little point in establishing a more unified system of external representation, but, when Member States fundamentally disagree about what to do on the world stage, there is little hope that a more unified system of external representation could fare any better (D Hodson, 'The Paradox …', n 23 above, at 4).

[77] 'The EU approach to the IMF governance reform is a "wait-and-delay" tactic. Now is time for the EU to move towards a proactive strategy vis-à-vis IMF. For doing so, the Eurozone needs a seat at the IMF table' said J O'Neill and D Lombardi, *Financial Times*, 17 April 2012.

The current mechanism is based on the work of two committees, the Brussels-based SCIMF and the Washington-based EURIMF. The SCIMF has demonstrated little ability to steer the EURIMF due to a number of deficiencies. First, the SCIMF is hindered by its composition, which includes too many officials, some of whom are too junior to speak with authority on sensitive policy issues. Secondly, the SCIMF meets on a monthly basis, whereas the EURIMF meets as many as three times per week when there are urgent matters to discuss. Thirdly, the SCIMF devotes most of its attention to horizontal policy issues such as the development of common views on exchange rate policy and the international economic situation, whereas the EURIMF spends most of its time trying to reach a common view on country-specific issues in the context of IMF Article IV consultations.[78] Also, the Eurozone economic coordination has become more intensive, and the relation between the SCIMF and the Eurogroup Working Group (EWG) must be stronger. Perhaps it will be possible to create a Eurozone SCIMF, linked to the EWG, and maintain the current SCIMF dependence on the European Financial Committee, similarly to the way the relations between the Eurogroup and the Ecofin Council are organised. This is a way to gain more involvement in IMF matters for the Eurogroup, due to its increasing relevance in the EMU internal governance and its participation representing the EU in other international forums.[79] The SCIMF function might be reformed using as a model the EU Trade Committee (previously known as the Article 133 committee), which closely monitors the Commission involvement in international trade talks through weekly meetings at the level of deputies and monthly meetings at the level of full members. As one commentator has proposed,[80] the SCIMF performance could be strengthened by the commitment of Member States not to vote within the IMF Executive Board if no common position can be agreed upon in this committee beforehand. However, there is no legal basis for this procedure, and it can weaken the EU position in the IMF in case of disagreement among EU countries. Also, the reverse majority procedure now accepted within the new EU economic governance framework could be applied in the decision-making process of the SCIMF.

Certainly the EU Member States' coordination has evolved in recent years through EURIMF and SCIMF activities.[81] However, there are limits to the ability of the EU members to forge common positions that result in reduced EU-country

[78] See D Hodson, n 23 above, at 24–25.

[79] See the bilateral dialogue with China on macroeconomic and exchange rate issues, in which the EU delegation was composed of the Commissioner of Economic and Monetary Affairs, the President of the Eurogroup and the President of the ECB.

[80] A Giovannini, et al, n 7 above, at 39.

[81] Another gap to close in the current EU coordination mechanism is the weak position of the European Commission. The representative from the Delegation of the EU to the United States in Washington, DC, is a member of the EURIMF but has merely observer status and does not have an effective coordination role. That role must increase in line with the relevance of Commission involvement in IMF matters and its participation in the troika which supervises the fulfilment of the adjustment of economic programmes by EU countries which are beneficiaries of combined loans from the EU and the IMF.

influence in the IMF despite the high European quotas and votes.[82] First of all, some EU countries have difficulties or have no possibility of respecting the agreed position when they are in mixed constituencies where the majority is against the EU common position. Secondly, EU coordination becomes difficult when discussions take place regarding surveillance or provision of financial assistance to countries outside the EU, where the differing geopolitical priorities of EU members may surface. In any case the improvement of the current EU coordination mechanisms is a scenario feasible with the current legal framework but it misses the possibilities opened up by Article 138 TFEU.

It is interesting to note that the European Court of Justice in a recent case has clarified the scope of Article 218, paragraph (9),[83] in a way that could be useful to strengthen the EU coordination in the IMF. In effect, the case relates to decisions taken by the International Organisation of Wine and Vine (IOV), of which the EU is not a member, but several of its Member States are. On 19 June 2012, the Council by qualified majority with Germany voting against, adopted a decision establishing an EU position to be adopted in the OIV[84] on the basis of Articles 43 and 218(9) TFEU. Germany (itself a member of the OIV) brought an action for annulment against that decision, challenging Article 218(9) TFEU as the correct legal basis for the adoption of the decision and arguing that Article 218(9) TFEU concerns only the adoption of the positions of the Union in bodies set up by international agreements of which the Union is a member. On 29 April 2014 Advocate General Cruz Villalón delivered his Opinion[85] to the effect that Article 218(9) TFEU can only apply to bodies established by agreements to which the Union is a party. In his final conclusion the AG holds that Article 218(9) TFEU does not provide a suitable legal basis for the decision in the present case. In its judgment of 7 October 2014 the Court reached a different conclusion.[86] It argues that there is nothing in the wording of Article 218(9) TFEU to prevent the European Union from adopting a decision establishing a position to be adopted on its behalf in a body set up by an international agreement to which it is not a party.

> Where an area of law falls within a competence of the European Union, such as the one mentioned in the preceding paragraph, the fact that the European Union did not

[82] S Hagan, n 17 above, at 7; J Wouters and S van Kerchoven, 'The International Monetary Fund' in Jorgensen and Laatikainen (eds), *Routledge Handbook on the European Union and International Institutions* (Routledge, 2013), at 225.

[83] Article 218, paragraph (9), provides: 'The Council, on a proposal from the Commission or the High Representative of the Union for Foreign Affairs and Security Policy, shall adopt a decision suspending application of an agreement and establishing the positions to be adopted on the Union's behalf in a body set up by an agreement, when that body is called upon to adopt acts having legal effects, with the exception of acts supplementing or amending the institutional framework of the agreement'.

[84] Council Document No 11436 'establishing the position to be adopted on behalf of the European Union with regard to certain resolutions to be voted in the framework of the International Organisation for Vine and Wine (OIV)'.

[85] C-399/12 *Germany v Council*, Opinion of AG Cruz Villalón delivered 29 April 2014, EU:C:2014:289.

[86] C-399/12, *Germany v Council*, judgment of 1 October 2014.

take part in the international agreement in question does not prevent it from exercising that competence by establishing, through its institutions, a position to be adopted on its behalf in the body set up by that agreement, in particular through the Member States which are party to that agreement acting jointly in its interest. (paragraph 52).

ii. Progressive Consolidation of EU Representation by Reshuffling EU Constituencies

It is possible to envisage a more ambitious step that regroups Euro area countries into a few constituencies. This would make EU coordination easier and unable the Union to speak with a single voice at the IMF.

The implementation of the 2010 IMF reform after US approval could open the door to a significant reshuffling of the EU constituencies on the IMF Executive Board. With the move to an all-elected Executive Board, it would become legally possible for executive directors who were formerly appointed by single-seat countries such as France, Germany, and the United Kingdom to be elected by other Member States and to represent them in the future. Also, the limit of nine per cent of the quotas on countries merging in a constituency will go out, and it will be possible for big EU countries to come together and with other medium-size and small EU countries.

As I pointed out before, a first reshuffling was decided for some EU countries in November 2012. A new Benelux constituency and a Central and Eastern European constituency have been created, in order to accomplish the commitment to reduce 'advanced European country representation' at the IMF Executive Board by two executive directors, a move included in the still-unimplemented 2010 reform. The European Commission announced in its November 2012 Communication a two-stage process to enhance the Euro area representation in the IMF, activating the Article 138(2) TFEU legal basis. Before a single Euro area chair comes about, the Commission will design a rearrangement of the country constituencies in the IMF as a first step and re-group countries into Euro area constituencies which could also include future Eurozone Member States.

There are many possibilities for reshuffling EU constituencies, and some proposals have been proffered.[87] After the 2010 IMF reform becomes reality, a wide variety of possibilities is open for EU countries in the next election of executive directors. It is possible to speculate about potential new EU-country constituencies, but it is always necessary to take into account the logic applied

[87] In 1998 Dominique Strauss-Kahn, then Finance Minister of France, suggested forming a common chair with Germany at the IMF, something not allowed by IMF law at that time. Truman, for example, has proposed a consolidation of EU representation in three stages: As a first step, non-EU countries in EU-led constituencies would join different constituencies, and EU countries in non-EU majority constituencies would join EU-led constituencies. In subsequent steps, EU constituencies could be consolidated gradually, until a single EU constituency was formed. T Truman, 'Rearranging IMF Chairs and Shares: The Sine Qua Non of IMF Reform' in Truman (ed), *Reforming the IMF for the 21st Century* (Washington DC, Institute for International Economics, 2005) 201–32.

when IMF member states create and join constituencies. The practice shows that the motivation to join a constituency is often linked to the distribution of power within that constituency and to the 'upgrade' one country would get by joining. Such calculations, of course, always take into account the effectiveness of the constituency as well as the capacity to build coalitions, because the individual members have a very small influence on decisions.[88] Following the rationale to create constituencies in the IMF, explained by Woods and Lombardi,[89] only external pressure or a clear agreement to go to a single EU chair can encourage the EU countries to join in new IMF constituencies.

Perhaps, the easiest reshuffle would be for Spain to leave its current Central American constituency and join the Italian constituency with an agreement between these two states to rotate the posts of executive director and alternate. However, Italy is reluctant to share its privileged position with Spain. Poland could migrate to the Central and Eastern European constituency and Ireland could leave the Canadian constituency and join either the Nordic/Baltic or the Benelux constituencies. It is also possible to envisage[90] a Mediterranean chair that could encompass France, Italy, Spain, Portugal, Greece, Malta, and Cyprus; a British/Nordic/Baltic chair which would add the United Kingdom and Ireland to the current Nordic/Baltic constituency; a German-Benelux constituency that would encompass Germany, the Benelux countries, and Austria; and a Central and Eastern European constituency comprising Poland, Hungary, the Czech Republic, Slovakia, Slovenia, Romania, Croatia, and Bulgaria. It will be interesting to see whether to increase their voting power, these EU constituencies attract European candidates for future accession to the EU (Balkan states, Iceland) and other European countries like Norway, Switzerland, Ukraine, Moldova, Belarus, and even Turkey.

The reshuffle of the EU constituencies needs the entry into force of the 2010 IMF reform and a clear political will from EU Member States. No legal change is needed in EU law to bring this about.

iii. A EU Single Chair vs Two EU Chairs for EU/Euro Area

After the reshuffle of the EU constituencies, the next step should be the centralisation of the EU representation in the IMF. To do that, there are different possibilities: (i) two EU chairs (Eurozone countries and the remaining EU Member

[88] EURODAD, n 21 above, at 22–23.

[89] For Woods and Lombardi an effective constituency has four features: Maximization of voting powers, a shared agenda, unity within the constituency beyond shared interests, and lobbying capacity and technical support. Applying these features to the creation of constituencies by EU countries, the panorama is discouraging. In spite of the fact that EU countries share a similar agenda, have shared interests in IMF matters, and have lobbying capacity and technical means to build new IMF constituencies, they will not maximise the voting power of each EU country in the IMF (N Noods and D Lombardi, 'Uneven patterns of governance: how developing countries are represented in the IMF' (2006) 13 *Review of International Political Economy* 480–515).

[90] See also C Gnath, n 58 above, at 4.

States) without EU membership in the IMF; (ii) EU membership in the IMF and mixed representation (both EU institutions and EU Member States) with two EU chairs or a single chair; and (iii) substitution of EU countries by an EU representation and a single EU chair.

The first question to address in order to apply these solutions is whether the EU can become an IMF member.[91] As now constituted, the IMF is strictly a country-based organisation due to the formalistic interpretation of the word *countries* included in Article II, Section 2 of the IMF's Articles of Agreement. Nevertheless, some scholars have proposed a more open and updated interpretation of this word that would allow the inclusion of States and also international organisations which benefit from an attribution of states' powers in the monetary and exchange rate fields. In the case of the EU, the responsibility for monetary matters, an essential characteristic of statehood and a condition for compliance with the obligations resulting from membership of the IMF, no longer lies with the Member States; it is in the hands of the EU institutions. Under these circumstances, the Euro area has arguably already assumed the characteristics of a country for the purposes of the Articles of Agreement.[92]

The modification of the BIS statute to open up membership in the BIS to the ECB[93] is a relevant precedent to support this broad interpretation of the word *country* in Article II, Section 2 of the IMF's Articles of Agreement. Another way for the EU to become an IMF member could be the inclusion of a Regional Economic Integration Organization (REIO)[94] clause in the Articles of Agreements.[95]

[91] In the UN system the EU only holds member status in the FAO and in the Codex Alimentarius Commission. It has observer status in most UN bodies, and acquired enhanced participation rights in the UN General Assembly in 2011. In a number of bodies, the EU is nevertheless still not formally represented, most importantly in the UN Security Council. See J Wouters and A-L Chané, 'Brussels Meets Westphalia: The European Union and the United Nations', Chapter 9 in this book.

[92] E Denters, 'Representation of the EEC in the IMF' in M Giovanoli (ed), *International Monetary Law. Issues for the New Millenium* (Oxford, OUP, 2000) 221–24; E Denters, 'The IMF' in J Wouters (ed), *International Encyclopaedia of Laws*, vol 3, *Intergovernmental Organizations* (Deventer, Kluwer, 2010), para 23; D-C Horng, 'The ECB's membership in the IMF: Legal approaches to constitutional challenges' (2005) 11 *European Law Journal* 802; R Smits, *The European Central Bank in the European Constitutional Order* (Utrecht, Eleven International Publishing, 2003) at 443; Ligue Europeenne de Cooperation Economique, 'European Economic Governance Revisited' (2004) 11 *Cahiers Comte Boël* at 21; J Wouters, S Van Kerchoven and M Ramopoulos, 'The EU and the euro area in international economic governance: the case of the IMF' in D Kochenov and F Amtenbrink (eds), *The European's Union shaping of the International Legal Order* (Cambridge, Cambridge University Press, 2013) at 321–26.

[93] Article 56 of the Statutes of the Bank for International Settlements (20 January 1930; text as amended on 27 June 2005), available at: www.bis.org/about/statutes-en.pdf.

[94] A REIO is commonly defined in UN protocols and conventions as 'an organization constituted by sovereign states of a given region to which its Member States have transferred competence in respect of matters governed by … convention or its protocols and [which] has been duly authorised, in accordance with its internal procedures, to sign, ratify, accept, approve or accede to it [the instruments concerned]'. On the qualification of the EU as an international (integration) organisation also C Eckes and RA Wessel, 'The European Union: An International Perspective' in T Tridimas and R Schütze (eds), *The Oxford Principles of European Union Law – Volume 1: The European Union Legal Order* (Oxford, Oxford University Press, 2014).

[95] See for instance Articles 4.1, 4.2, 4.3 and 4.5, 21 and 22 of the Kyoto Protocol. Article II of the FAO Constitution was specifically modified to allow for the accession of 'regional economic organizations'.

However, a less controversial way to open IMF membership to international organisations with competence in monetary matters is to introduce a specific clause in Article II to open the IMF to monetary unions with specific conditions. Articles XI and XII of the Agreement Establishing the World Trade Organization could be a model, and I think that the new Section 3 in Article II of the IMF's Articles of Agreement could be 'Membership shall be open to international organizations with full competences in monetary matters at such times and in accordance with such terms as may be prescribed by the Board of Governors'.[96] The membership of the EU in the IMF raises the question of whether there should be a new quota to the EU that simply amasses the current EU member quotas or a new quota excluding the intercommunity trade and subsequently its effect on a member's role in the IMF's governance.

The last two possibilities to unify the EU representation in the IMF (EU membership in the IMF and mixed representation and substitution of EU countries by an EU representation and single EU chair) need the membership of the EU in the Fund, and the modification of the IMF Articles of Agreement is *conditio sine qua non* to do that and requires an 85 per cent renovation of EU-IMF relations majority of the votes of the IMF members. The interest of the EMDC countries in EU unification in the IMF, supported by the US opens up possibilities for this step. However, a strong political will in the EU countries is required to encourage this relevant IMF reform, and nowadays that does not yet exist.

In any case, the EU is a regional organisation with legal personality (Article 47 TFEU), and it will be the EU that joins the IMF. The Euro area has no international legal personality as an international organisation and thus could not be an IMF member[97] even it were possible to organise two EU constituencies in the IMF, one for the Euro area countries and the other for the EU countries outside the Eurozone with less intervention by EU institutions. It is clear, however, that a strong coordination between these two EU constituencies could be desirable and easy to establish.

The last option is the substitution of a single EU representation, and a single EU chair for EU countries is neither legally founded, nor politically workable, because the EU could not substitute for the EU countries outside the Eurozone, which continue to have their own currencies and national economic and monetary policies. On the other hand, the IMF has competences related to the surveillance of economic and fiscal policies, and even the Euro area Member States continue to keep competences in this field. In my opinion, the IMF's Articles of Agreement do not fulfil the ECJ conditions, and the functional succession doctrine applied to the GATT is excluded in this case, because the matters covered by IMF activity are partially shared competences in EU law. Moreover, the other IMF members

[96] In that sense, see R Henning, *Regional Arrangements and the IMF*, Seminar of the Institute for International Economics on IMF Reform (Washington DC, Institute for International Economics, 2005).

[97] See the reasoning in that sense of J Wouters, S Van Kerchoven and M Ramopoulos, n 92 above, at 317–19.

did not accept the EU institutions in substitution for EU countries in the Fund.[98] Consequently, an EU membership in the IMF could be a mixed representation and will not affect the IMF membership of the EU countries. This conclusion[99] is in line with the EU membership in other international organisations such as the WTO, the (FAO), or the (EBRD).

In my opinion, a mixed representation of both EU Member States and EU membership in the IMF is the most adequate way to improve EU participation in the IMF in the middle and long term.[100] There will be many years during which some of the EU countries will remain outside the Eurozone. This factor counsels the EU to order its representation in the Fund into two constituencies, one Eurozone countries' constituency and the other made up of the remaining EU countries, with a close coordination between them. This scenario will be very close to a single EU voice at the Fund. In the short term and while the EU cannot become an IMF member today, I think that the best way to articulate EU participation at the IMF is by merging the EU countries into these two constituencies and strengthening

[98] This functional succession doctrine has been constructed by the ECJ in, among others, Joined Cases 21–24/72 *International Fruit Company NV et al v Produktschap voor Groenten en Fruit* [1972] ECR 1219; Case C-308/06 *Intertanko et al v Secretary of State for Transport* [2009] ECR 4057, para 48; Case C-366/10 *Air Transport Association of America and Others v Secretary of State for Energy and Climate Change* [2011] ECR I-13755, paras 61–63. The ECJ recognised that multilateral agreements to which the EU is not a party may be binding upon the EU, provided that a five conditions are satisfied: (i) All EU Member States are parties to the multilateral agreement; (ii) Member States intend to continue to be bound by such multilateral agreement as evidenced by their statements or in provisions of the TFEU; (iii) the multilateral agreement has been entered into prior to 1 January 1958 or before the accession of the country to the EU; (iv) the matter of the multilateral agreement has later been fully and exclusively assumed by the EU; and (v) the other contracting parties to the multilateral agreement have recognised such a shift in competence from the Member States to the EU. The only international agreement that the ECJ considers as fulfilling these conditions was the GATT. However, the Court recently considered these conditions were missing in the Chicago Convention on Civil Aviation and the MARPOL Convention on marine pollution. On this cases, see J Kuiper, 'It Shall Contribute to … the Strict Observance and Development of International Law' in ECJ, *The Court of Justice and the Construction of Europe: Analyses and Perspectives on Sixty Years of Case-law* (Berlin, Springer Verlag, 2013) 593–94; A Rosas, 'The status in EU Law of International Agreements concluded by the Member States' (2011) 24 *Fordham International Law* 1304–45; S Van Rossem, 'Interaction between EU law and international law in the light of *Intertanko* and *Kadi*: the dilemma of norms binding the Member States but not the Community' (Amsterdam, Asser Institute, 2009), available at: www.asser.nl/upload/documents/11172009_42019clee09-4comb.pdf; R Wessel, 'Reconsidering the relationship between international and EU law: towards a content-based approach' in E Cannizzaro, P Palchetti and R Wessel (eds), *International law as law of the European Union* (Leiden, Martinus Nijhoff, 2011) 7–33.

[99] Louis rejects this interpretation because he said that 'the economic perspective in the Fund is limited by the main objective of monetary and financial stability that, in turn, has to contribute to growth and jobs. On the other hand, the joint participation of the EU and its Member States raises problems due to IMF is a very specific financial institution based on quotas that are intended to express, by the use of objective data, the relative ranking of any country in the world economy. Nothing similar is to be found in other international institutions' (J-V Louis, The International Projection …', n 14 above, at 80).

[100] A good example of how a unified external representation would enhance the euro area's external clout is the EU's common trade policy and its representation in the WTO. See C Mcnamara and S Meunier, 'Between National Sovereignty and International Power: What External Voice for the Euro' (2002) 78 *International Affairs* at 852; G Glöcker and Z Truchlewski, 'From polyphony to harmony? The external representation of EMU' in J Lieb, N Von Ondarza and D Schwarzer (eds), *The European Union in International Fora. Lessons for the Union's External Representation after Lisbon* (Baden-Baden, Nomos, 2011) at 135.

the coordination between the EU institutions and the EU Member States in IMF matters.

This scenario (EU and EU Member States membership in the IMF and mixed representation with two EU chairs) is a development in accordance with the spirit and letter of Article 138 TFEU and it holds the promise of solving the overrepresentation of the European countries in the IMF Executive Board and their reduced effectiveness in the IMF.[101] This EU consolidation could liberate quota shares and voting shares for EMDCs in the IMF, because the quota and voting shares of the EU or Eurozone will be higher than the US quota if this re-calculation is done, removing intra-EU flows from the calculation of the quota (around 21 per cent, while the US quota is around 17 per cent).[102] These two seats would also fit better with the image of the EU as a single entity in international economic relations[103] and could provide important economies of scale against the expected decline of EU shares in the world economy during the next decades.[104] The Eurozone seat would have an executive director designated by the Eurogroup and two alternate EDs, one from the European Commission and the other from the ECB, to take into account the distribution of powers in the internal side of the EMU. The constituency of the EU remaining states could be an ED from the UK and the alternate ED rotating asymmetrically among the more powerful states in IMF quotas.

V. CONCLUSIONS

The changing international environment and the new dynamics in the European integration process provide a strong rationale for the EU and Eurozone to reassess the external representation of the EU in EMU issues, including the

[101] J Wouters and S Van Kerchoven, n 82 above, at 227.

[102] C Garnier, D Daco and F Di Mauro, 'UN-EU cooperation on financial issues: The role of the European Union at the International Monetary Fund and the World Bank' in J Wouters, F Hoffmeister and M Ruys (eds), *The United Nations and the European Union: An ever stronger partnership* (The Hague, TMC Asser Press, 2006) at 133.

[103] A Ahearne and B Eichengreen, n 68 above, at 142; C Mcnamara and S Meunier, n 100 above, at 855; L Frieden, 'EU Representation and the Governance of the International Monetary Fund' (2005) 6 *European Union Politics* 493–510.

[104] In a study ordered by the European Parliament, its authors proposed that, in the longer term, the Euro area could achieve a single membership through the ESM as an institution with its own legal personality representing the fiscal authorities of the Euro area. The unified representation of the Eurozone in the IMF could be achieved by using the ESM as the legal instrument to merge Member State quotas at the IMF into a single Euro area quota. (M Giovannini et al, n 7 above, at 40). I disagree with this proposal, and articulating it in legal terms is difficult. The ESM is an international organisation different from the EU but composed of Euro area countries. Nevertheless, the ESM is the permanent crisis resolution mechanism for the Eurozone countries and has competences only to furnish economic assistance to Euro area countries upon request and conditioned by the application of an economic programme. But the ESM has no other powers, and it is not able to represent the fiscal authority of the Euro area countries in other international institutions and forums. In a similar way see Louis, 'The Euro Area and Multilateral Financial Institutions and Bodies. An update' in I Govaere, E Lannon, P Van Elsuwege and E Adam (eds), *The European Union in the World: Essays in Honour of Marc Maresceau* (Amsterdam, Brill, 2014) at 200.

participation in international institutions and forums and, in particular, in the IMF. The distribution of power in the global economy is changing, and the EU share in it is expected to decline in the coming years and decades due to the rise of EMDCs like China, India, and Brazil. The EU Member States' power in the international institution must also decline in a similar way, and the best measure to counterbalance this tendency is joint representation and speaking with one voice. In the IMF, the way to a single EU voice is long and complex, but the current dispersion of European representation is not only sub-optimal from an effectiveness and efficiency perspective when trying to pursue EU and EMU interests, but it is also increasingly at odds with the expectations of the international partners.

After more than a decade of inactivity, the time is coming to rearrange the EU-IMF relationship. The implementation of the 2010 IMF reform after the US congressional approval will eliminate legal obstacles to a consolidation of the EU Member State constituencies in the IMF. The economic crisis and the subsequent sovereign debt crisis in Europe have forced more transfers of competences from the EU countries to the EU institutions in the economic policy field, and these changes must be reflected in the EMU's external relations, including at first the EU's participation in the IMF. To this end and to develop Article 138(2) TFEU, the European Commission has announced a proposal to enhance the Euro area representation in the IMF in a two-stage process.

I propose a reshuffling of the current IMF constituencies with EU Member States and the strengthening of the EU coordination mechanism in IMF matters in the short term. In the long term, I propose an EU mixed representation in the IMF, the EU member countries must continue to be IMF members, and the EU must also become an IMF member, after changing the IMF's Articles of Agreement or using a broad interpretation of Article II, Section 2. In this scenario, the EU representation at the IMF Executive Board could be structured into two constituencies, one including the Euro area countries and controlled by EU representatives and the other including the remaining EU countries outside the Eurozone with a candidate to join the EU in the future. These two EU chairs would be maintained until all the EU countries adopt the common currency, and the coordination between the two EU constituencies must be strong so that they speak with one voice.

The challenge to articulate a single voice at the IMF is a test for the external action of the EU in the coming years and will be decisive for the EU's position in the new economic world governance.

Note:

During the publication process of this contribution, the European Commission adopted a Proposal for a Council Decision in order to unify progressively the euro area representation in the IMF that followed our recommendations to strength the EU participation in the IMF. Furthermore, the approval by US Congress in December 2015 of the 2010 IMF reform has enabled the entry into force of this reform and its implementation opens new possibilities for EU representation in the IMF as indicated in our contribution.

The Five Presidents' Report of June 2015 on completing EMU indicates as EMU evolves towards Economic, Financial and Fiscal Union, its external representation should be increasingly unified'. This Report proposes in the first stage of the completion on EMU to "take steps towards a consolidated external representation of the euro area".

Taking into account Article 138 TFEU and the Five Presidents' Report mandates, the European Commission published in October 2015 a Communication designing a road map for a more consistent external representation of the euro area and a Proposal for a Council Decision in order to unify progressively the euro area representation in the IMF. This proposal suggests moving to a unified representation for the euro area in the IMF with the President of the Eurogroup as the representative for the euro area. It proposes a gradual approach for achieving this goal involving intermediate transitional steps for representation in the International Monetary and Financial Committee (IMFC) and the IMF Executive Board. Such transitional steps would involve granting observer rights to the euro area represented by a representative of a euro area Member State already member of the Board, in association with the Commission and the European Central Bank. Furthermore, the coordination process for establishing common positions should be strengthened in order to have systematic common statements on all IMF policy, country and surveillance issues that are of relevance to the euro area. Finally, these steps should also aim to strengthen cooperation of the euro area with non-euro area Member States regarding IMF issues.

Part V

Substantive Areas of the EU External Action

13

The Transformation of the EU Common Commercial Policy

CHRISTINE KADDOUS*

I. INTRODUCTION

THE COMMON COMMERCIAL Policy (CCP) has been at the heart of the European integration process since the entry into force of the EEC Treaty in 1958. With its internal and external dimensions, it plays a crucial role in the economic development of the European Union (EU). Trade policy is also the most important field of EU external relations in practical terms. It notably allowed the European Union to become one of the key actors of the global trading system, competing with other economic powers like the USA or China.[1]

* Christine Kaddous, Professor, LLM (Cambridge), Geneva University, Jean Monnet Chair *Ad personam*, Director of the Centre d'études juridiques européennes, Jean Monnet Centre of Excellence of the University of Geneva, www.ceje.ch.

[1] See European Commission, *Global Europe—Competing in the World, A contribution to the EU's Growth and Jobs Strategy*, COM(2006) 567 final.

CCP has been fundamentally transformed since its inception, in relation to its scope and to the nature of the EU competence; in relation also to the objectives to be achieved in that policy as well as to the roles of the EU institutions in the definition and implementation of that policy. The content of CCP has been adapted to the needs of the economy and to the realities of international trade. The transformation occurred stepwise. It was sometimes carried out on the basis of teleological interpretations in the case law rendered by the Court of Justice of the European Union and sometimes, when extensive interpretations were not possible, through modifications of treaty provisions.

This chapter analyses this transformation five years after the entry into force of the Lisbon Treaty. It assesses first the successive steps which led to the extension of the CCP scope and to the recognition of the exclusive nature of the EU competence first through case law and then through codification in the primary law of the European Union (Section II). The adaptation to the needs of the economy brought new challenges for the European Union and its institutions.

The recognition of the exclusivity of EU competence in the CCP had impacts on the definition of this policy internally in the adoption of autonomous rules, and externally in the conclusion of international agreements. The CCP includes today fields such as trade in services, commercial aspects of intellectual property rights and foreign direct investment.

The general principles and objectives called on to guide the EU action on the international scene must also be respected and pursued in the CCP. This obligation affects the design of the CCP and may give rise to problems when these general principles and objectives conflict with the trade objectives of the CCP. The characteristics and the legal value of each of these sets of principles and objectives will be examined in order to determine the rules applicable in cases of conflict (Section III).

Finally, the transformation of the CCP is also related to the change brought by the Lisbon Treaty to the distribution of powers between the institutions of the European Union and to the roles attributed to each of them in the design and implementation of the CCP (Section IV). The main actors in trade issues are today the Council, the European Parliament and the Commission, even if the European Council has become involved in the external action of the European Union in identifying the EU strategic interests and objectives (including the commercial ones), and even though the High Representative of the Union for Foreign Affairs and Security Policy was assigned responsibility to assist the Council and the Commission in their task to ensure consistency between the different areas of external action and between these and the other policies of the Union. The increased participation of the European Parliament in the adoption of internal legislation and in the conclusion of international trade agreements is the most striking element in the institutional transformation of the CCP.

II. EVOLUTION IN THE SCOPE AND NATURE OF THE CCP

Originally, the CCP was seen as the external side of the internal market, in particular as far as trade in goods was concerned. The former Article 114 TEEC indeed focused on the liberalisation of trade in goods. At that time, there was no debate on the liberalisation of services within the external dimension of the CCP. The exclusive nature of the trade competence was immediately recognised by the Court of Justice, whereas the extension of the scope of the CCP occurred by stages, which will be examined hereafter. In the mid and late 1970s, the scope and nature of the competence in this policy were not determined in the Treaty and progress was brought about through case law.

A. Case Law Developments

The exclusivity of the competence has been recognised by the Court of Justice in *Opinion 1/75*.[2] The Court considered it 'cannot … be accepted that, in a field … governed by the common commercial policy, the Member States should exercise a power concurrent to that of the Community, in the Community sphere and in the international sphere'. The exclusivity of the Community competence did not allow concurrent powers of the Member States and constituted then the basis for the application of the uniformity principle in CCP, which has been largely debated in the case law of the Court related to the import and export of goods.[3] Nowadays, common regimes regulate the import and export of goods,[4] allowing however the Member States to take restrictive measures on the basis of non-economic grounds such as public morality, public policy or public security, protection of health and life of humans, animals or plants, or on the basis of the protection of national treasures possessing artistic, historic or archaeological value, or also on the ground of the protection of industrial and commercial property.[5] Despite this wide margin of manoeuvre left to the national authorities, the two regimes of importation and exportation of goods are considered uniform overall.

[2] ECJ, Opinion 1/75 of 11 Novmber 1975, *OECD Understanding on a local cost standard*, [1975] ECR 1355.

[3] ECJ, Case 41/76, *Criel, née Donckerwolcke and Schou v Procureur de la République au tribunal de grande instance de Lille and Director General of Customs*, [1976] ECR 1921; Case 174/84, *Bulk Oil v Sun International*, [1986] ECR 559; Case 50/84, *Tezi v Commission*, [1986] ECR 887; Case 242/84, *Tezi v Minister for Economic Affairs*, [1986] ECR 933.

[4] Regulation 2015/478 of the European Parliament and of the Council of 11 March 2015 on common rules for imports, [2015] OJ L83, 27.3.2015, p 16. Regulation 2015/479 of the European Parliament and of the Council of 11 March 2015 on common rules for exports, [2015] OJ L83, 27.3.2015, p 34.

[5] Article 24 (2) of Regulation 2015/478 on common rules for imports, and Article 10 of Regulation 2015/479 on common rules for exports.

After the assertion of the exclusivity of the EU competence in common commercial policy, the debate between the Union and the Member States has been focused on the scope of this policy, particularly because the Treaty did not give a general definition of the CCP content, but only referred to specific fields covered by this policy, such as changes in tariff rates, conclusion of tariff and trade agreements, achievement of uniformity in measures of liberalisation, export policy and measures to protect trade such as those to be taken in the event of dumping or subsidies (former Article 113(1) TEEC). Therefore the exact content of the CCP was disputed between the Union and its Member States, but also between the institutions, mainly the Commission and Council. The latter two gave definitions of the very notion of CCP according to opposing doctrines; an instrumentalist approach was developed by the Commission and a finalist one developed by the Council. The Commission's position was in favour of an extension of the commercial policy,[6] whereas the Council defended rather a reduction of the scope of this policy.[7] Interestingly enough, the Court of Justice never took a general position in the debate in favour or against one of the two theses, preferring a case-by-case approach.

In *Opinion 1/78*, the Commission considered that the draft agreement on natural rubber, which was negotiated within the United Nations Conference on Trade and Development, came entirely or at least in its essentials, within the context of Article 113 TEEC and therefore the negotiation and conclusion of the agreement came within the Community's exclusive competence.[8] According to the Council, the subject-matter of the agreement fell outside the framework of commercial policy and thus called for a division of powers between the Community and the Member States so that the agreement had to be concluded according to the 'technique of the so-called mixed type agreement'.[9] One would have expected a restrictive interpretation of the CCP's scope by the Court of Justice, given the recognition in *Opinion 1/75* of the exclusivity of the Community's competence in that field. Paradoxically the Court did not construe the scope of the CCP narrowly. It referred in *Opinion 1/78* to the complex objectives pursued by the commodity agreements and to their increasing number, opining it would not be possible to carry on a worthwhile common commercial policy if the Community were not in a position to avail itself also of more elaborate means devised with a view to furthering the development of international trade.[10]

[6] According to the instrumentalist thesis, the former Article 113 TEEC applies to every 'instrument regulating international trade', see an expression of this thesis in ECJ, *Opinion 1/78 re International Agreement on Natural Rubber*, [1979] ECR 2871, para 38.

[7] According to the finalist thesis, the former Article 113 TEEC applies to 'any measure the aim of which is to influence the volume or flow of trade', see an expression of this thesis in ECJ, *Opinion 1/78*, [1979] ECR 2871, para 39.

[8] ECJ, *Opinion 1/78*, [1979] ECR 2871, para 2.

[9] ECJ, *Opinion 1/78*, [1979] ECR 2871, para 2.

[10] ECJ, *Opinion 1/78*, [1979] ECR 2871, para 44.

The Court admitted in 1978 an extensive interpretation of the main provision in the CCP field in order not to restrict the common commercial policy to the use of instruments intended to have an effect on the traditional aspects of external trade and to extend it to more highly developed mechanisms such as the ones provided for in the agreement on natural rubber.[11]

From this perspective, commodities and international agreements have been considered as part of the concept of trade policy under the provisions of the treaty. Furthermore, *Opinion 1/78* allowed the Court to state that Article 113 empowered the Community to formulate a commercial policy based on 'uniform principles' in order to avoid disturbances in intra-Community trade by reason of the disparities which would then exist in specific sectors of economic relations with non-member countries.[12] This mid and late 1970 case law shows that 'external trade' had to be understood in a wide perspective and covered topics which go far beyond the simple administration of customs or quantitative restrictions.

B. Limits of Case law Developments and Treaty Modifications

Since the two early *Opinions 1/75* and *1/78*, the Court has had the opportunity to decide on many different issues in relation to CCP. It was undisputed that this policy covers trade in all goods falling under the Treaty. Some special cases, such as ECSC, Euratom, agricultural or dual-use goods, were submitted to the Court and have been the subject of particular case law.[13] Progressively, trade in services and commercial aspects of intellectual property rights were included in the common commercial policy. However, the acceptance of this extension has not been achieved without resistance, due to the original 'silence' of the Treaty on the precise content of this policy and to the exclusive nature of the competence recognised by the Court. Different positions emerged between the European institutions in that respect.

The potential extension of the CCP's scope to new fields was first analysed by the Court in *Opinion 1/94* on the accession of the European Communities to the WTO. In this Opinion, the Court considered on the one hand that the EC had an exclusive competence with regard to trade in goods. On the other hand it rejected the Commission's view that GATS and TRIPs fell in their entirety under the scope of CCP, or that they were covered by implied exclusive powers.[14] The competence to conclude the WTO agreements was shared between the EC and the Member

[11] ECJ, *Opinion 1/78*, [1979] ECR 2871, para 44. The opinion raised the more general issue of the link between trade and development, this last field not being envisaged as such in the EEC treaty at the time the Court rendered its Opinion.

[12] ECJ, *Opinion 1/78*, [1979] ECR 2871, para 45.

[13] For ECSC, Euratom and agricultural goods, see *Opinion 1/94 on the competence of the EU to conclude the WTO agreements*, [1994] ECR I-5267. For dual-use goods, see notably ECJ, Case C-83/94, *Criminal Proceedings against Leifer and others*, [1995] ECR I-3231.

[14] ECJ, Opinion 1/94, [1994] ECR I-5267, paras 35–105.

States. This meant that the dynamic character of the CCP, which was at the heart of *Opinion 1/78*, was no longer sufficient in 1994 to assess the inclusion of trade in services and trade-related intellectual property rights as within the exclusive competence of the EC. Despite the economic importance of these sectors on a global level, the transformation of the CCP on the basis of case law rendered by the Court had limits. It became clear that if changes in the CCP are politically and economically desired, they have to be envisaged through a modification of the Treaty. This is what happened. Following *Opinion 1/94*, the EEC Treaty was modified in 1997 by the Treaty of Amsterdam, and in 2000 by the Treaty of Nice.

The Amsterdam Treaty added a paragraph (5) to Article 133 TEC. This addition allowed the Council, acting unanimously, to extend the competence of the Community to negotiations and international agreements on services and intellectual property rights. The condition of the unanimity rule resulted in the fact that the provision has never been applied, because of a lack of consensus within the Council to submit these fields to the general rules applicable in the CCP. The Treaty of Nice took this important step forward and included in the CCP the fields of trade in services and trade-related aspects of intellectual property rights. Besides this important modification, two paragraphs ((6) and (7)) formulated in a complex manner were added to Article 133. These were not easy to apply[15] and they have been subsequently modified by the Lisbon Treaty.

The approach developed for the extensive interpretation of Article 133 as to the scope of the CCP, including the fields of services and trade-related aspects of intellectual property rights, has been consolidated in Article 207 TFEU with the entry into force of the Lisbon Treaty.

C. Consolidation of the *Acquis* and Modernisation of the CCP

The modifications brought about by the Lisbon Treaty give the current state of the developments in the CCP. Article 207 TFEU entrusts the European Union with full powers in trade in services, commercial aspects of intellectual property rights and 'foreign direct investment'. The issues covered by commercial policy in this post-Lisbon period are conceived in a non-exhaustive list which keeps the door open to new matters related to external trade. Sensitivities of the Member States are integrated into Article 207(4), which provides for the Council to act unanimously for the conclusion of agreements in the above mentioned fields, where such agreements include provisions for which unanimity is required, or for the adoption of internal rules.

[15] On these two paragraphs, see Opinion of Advocate General Kokott delivered on 26 March 2009, Case C-13/07, *Commission v Council*, case removed from the register by Order of the President of the Court 10 June 2010.

Furthermore agreements on cultural and audio-visual services fall under unanimity voting where they risk prejudicing the Union's cultural and linguistic diversity. The same applies to agreements in the field of social, education and health services, when they risk disturbing the national organisation of such services and creating difficulties for the Member States to deliver them. It is worth noting that agreements in all these fields do not have to be concluded anymore as 'mixed agreements', but as 'EU-only' agreements. The exclusivity of the EU competence has now been expressly anchored in primary law in Article 3 TEU. However the issue of the scope and the nature of the EU competence in the CCP are so interrelated that they still raise important questions, as evidenced by the recent case law in matters of TRIPs (*Daiichi Sankyo*)[16] and services (*Commission v Council*)[17] and by the debate on the notion of 'foreign direct investments'.

i. Concept of Commercial Aspects of Intellectual Property Rights and Services

The scope of the CCP concerning the 'commercial aspects of intellectual property rights' has been disputed in the *Daiichi Sankyo* case. On the one hand, the Member States argued that the TRIPs agreement was concluded in 1994 by the Community and its Member States by virtue of shared competence[18] and that it must therefore rely on the case law on mixed agreements, which establishes the dividing line between the obligations which the Union assumes and those which remain the responsibility of the Member States, in order to determine whether in the field covered by Article 27 of the TRIPs, the EU has exercised its powers in the field of patents. On the other hand, the European Commission submitted that the classical case law was no longer relevant for the TRIPs agreement, since it applies only to agreements which fall within the shared competence of the EU and the Member States, not to those for which the Union has sole competence. For the Commission, the TRIPs agreement as a whole relates to 'commercial aspects of intellectual property rights' within the meaning of Article 207(1) TFEU and consequently the agreement in its entirety now falls within the field of the common commercial policy.

The Court of Justice recognised the significant development of primary law brought about by the Lisbon Treaty and underlined the noticeable differences in Article 207 TFEU compared with Article 113 which it replaced, and which was in force when the TRIPs agreement was concluded.[19] The question of distribution

[16] ECJ, Case C-414/11, *Daiichi Sankyo Co Ltd and Sanofi-Aventis Deutschland GmbH v DEMO Anonimos Viomikhaniki kai Emporiki Etairia Farmakon*, ECLI:EU:C:2013:520.

[17] ECJ, Case C-137/12, *Commission v Council*, ECLI:EU:C:2013:675.

[18] ECJ, Joined Cases C-300/98 and C-392/98, *Parfums Christian Dior SA v TUK Consultancy BV and Assco Gerüste GmbH and van Dijk v Wilhelm Layher GmbH*, [2000] ECR I-11307, para 33; Case C-431/05, *Merck Genericos Produtos Farmacêuticos Lda v Merck & Co Inc and Merck Sharp & Dohme Lda*, [2007] ECR I-7001, para 33.

[19] ECJ, *Daiichi Sankyo*, n 16 above, paras 46 and 47.

of competences between the EU and the Member States had to be examined on the basis of the treaty now in force[20] and Article 207 with its 'new' content had to be applied. As far as intellectual property is concerned, the Court stated that, of the rules adopted by the EU in the field of intellectual property, only those with a specific link to international trade were capable of falling within the concept of 'commercial aspects of intellectual property rights', and hence within the field of CCP.[21]

The link with international trade was decisive for the Court in order to admit that the primary objective of the TRIPs agreement is to strengthen and harmonise the protection of intellectual property on a worldwide scale. The TRIPs agreement clearly has the aim of reducing distortions of international trade by ensuring the effective and adequate protection of intellectual property rights. It was therefore obvious that Article 27 of the TRIPs agreement, which relates to the rules on patentable subject-matter, fell within the field of CCP and not, as the Member States tried to allege, in the field of the internal market. There is no doubt that the context of those rules was the liberalisation of international trade, and not the harmonisation of the laws of the Member States of the Union.

The other case worth mentioning in the post-Lisbon period relates to the field of services. It demonstrates, as in *Daiichi Sankyo* case, the tension between trade policy and the internal market. The choice of the legal basis for the adoption of a Council Decision on the signature, on behalf of the Union, of the European Convention on the legal protection of services based on, or consisting of, conditional access, was at stake.[22] The contested decision was adopted on the basis of Article 114 TFEU, and not of Article 207(4) as proposed by the Commission. The latter, supported by the Parliament, submitted that the aim and content of the Convention concern primarily the common commercial policy and only incidentally the internal market policy. By contrast, the Council and the Member States, intervening in its support, submitted that the Convention and the contested decision were essentially linked to the internal market policy and only incidentally linked to the common commercial policy.[23] After an examination of the aim and content of the Convention, the Court highlighted that the primary objective of the Convention was not to improve the functioning of the internal market, but to extend legal protection of the relevant services beyond the territory of the EU and thereby to promote international trade in those services.[24] The Convention and the contested decision had been considered as pursuing primarily an objective that had a specific connection to the common commercial policy. Article 207(4) had therefore to be cited as the legal basis for the signing of the Convention, on behalf of the EU, which fell within the exclusive competence of the Union.[25]

[20] ECJ, *Daiichi Sankyo*, para 48.
[21] ECJ, *Daiichi Sankyo*, para 52.
[22] ECJ, Case C-137/12, *Commission v Council*, (*conditional access services*), EU:C:2013:675.
[23] ECJ, Case C-137/12, *Commission v Council*, para 54.
[24] ECJ, Case C-137/12, *Commission v Council*, para 67.
[25] ECJ, Case C-137/12, *Commission v Council*, para 76.

These two judgments show that the debate on the scope and nature of CCP is not complete and that future developments are expected to be decided by the Court of Justice. Case law will also provide clarifications on the definition of the notion 'foreign direct investment' and on the distribution of powers between the Union and the Member States in that field.

ii. Concept of Foreign Direct Investment and Distribution of Competences

The first fundamental issue to be examined relates to the meaning of the term 'foreign direct investment' in Article 207. In the absence of a definition in the CCP provision, one may refer to the case law rendered by the Court of Justice in relation to the concept of 'direct investment' under the field of free movement of capital. These terms have been interpreted as including

> investments of any kind undertaken by natural or legal persons and which serve to establish or maintain lasting and direct links between the persons providing the capital and the undertakings to which that capital is made available in order to carry out an economic activity.[26]

This definition has been given in the context of the application of Directive 88/361,[27] which sets out in its Annex I a nomenclature of movements of capital. It also appears from this case law relating to the free movement of capital that a distinction has to be made

> between 'direct' investments, namely investments in the form of participation in an undertaking through the holding of shares which confers the possibility of effectively participating in its management and control, and 'portfolio' investments, namely investments in the form of the acquisition of shares on the capital market solely with the intention of making a financial investment without any intention to influence the management and control of the undertaking.[28]

This distinction could and should be applied to the notion of investment in the CCP in order to assess the limits of EU external competence in relation to 'foreign direct investment'.

However the European Commission considers that the EU has an exclusive competence for foreign direct investments as part of the CCP, which also includes portfolio investments. It also argues that, in case this approach is not accepted by the Court, the EU competence under Article 207 is, according to the ERTA principle,[29] complemented by an implied competence as far as portfolio investments are concerned, which derives from the internal market chapter on free

[26] ECJ, Case C-446/04, *Test Claimants in the FII Group Litigation*, [2006] ECR I-11753, para 181.

[27] Council Directive 88/361, of 24 June 1988, for the implementation of Article 67 of the [EC] Treaty (article repealed by the Treaty of Amsterdam), [1988] OJ L178, 8.7.1988, p 5.

[28] Notably, ECJ, *Commission v Portugal,* Case C-171/08, [2010] ECR I-6817, para 49.

[29] ECJ, Case 22/70, *Commission v Council* (*European Road Transport Agreement*), [1971] ECR 263.

movement of capital (Articles 63–66 TFEU).[30] The European Parliament shares the Commission's view that EU investment policy includes both foreign direct investments and portfolio investments.[31] The Council acknowledged the importance of a comprehensive approach to shaping the future EU international investment policy—that does not discriminate between different types of investors and their investments—and supported the definition of a broad scope for the new EU policy in this field as suggested by the Commission. It stressed, however, that this policy has to be further elaborated with full respect to the respective competences of the Union and its Member States as defined by the Treaties,[32] a position which tends to be understood as a restrictive one.

The debate on the definition of 'foreign direct investment' in Article 207 TFEU, being not agreed upon by the Commission and the Member States, has been put before the Court of Justice,[33] which is asked to decide on whether the Union has the requisite competence to sign and conclude alone the Free Trade Agreement with Singapore. The Court will also have to determine which provisions of the agreement fall within the Union's exclusive competence and which ones fall within the Union's shared competence. The Commission also asked the Court to indicate whether there is any provision of the agreement that falls within the exclusive competence of the Member States. In other words, the Court will have to decide on whether the concept of foreign direct investment of Article 207 TFEU includes portfolio investments or not. On the other hand, it will have to determine whether the harmonisation achieved at the European level in the field of capital markets is comprehensive enough to deduce an EU implied exclusive competence with regard to this specific form of investment.[34] Generally speaking, if the court considers that not all aspects of foreign investment fall under the exclusive competence of the Union, the role of the Member States will remain essential when it comes to the conclusion and ratification of future EU investment agreements, which will then be concluded as mixed agreements.[35]

Two other important issues in the field of investment relate to the fate of the bilateral investment treaties (BITs) concluded by the Member States of the

[30] See European Commission Communication of 7 July 2010: *Towards a Comprehensive European International Investment Policy*, COM(2010) 343 final, p 8.

[31] European Parliament Resolution of 6 April 2011 on European International investment policy, para 11.

[32] Conclusions of the Council on a *Comprehensive European International Investment Policy*, of 25 October 2010, para 7.

[33] ECJ, *Opinion 2/15* concerning the issue of the competence to sign and conclude the Free Trade Agreement with Singapore, pending.

[34] On the scope of harmonisation of capital markets law, see J Schwarze (ed), *EU Kommentar* 2012, *Art. 63 AEUV* (Baden-Baden, Nomos, 2012) 920–50; A Dimopoulos, *EU Foreign Investment Law* (Oxford, Oxford University Press, 2011) 104–5.

[35] The European Commission had decided to request an opinion of the Court of Justice on the EU competence to sign and ratify the free trade agreement with Singapore. Press Release of 4 March 2015: trade.ec.europa.eu/doclib/press/index.cfm?id=1269.

EU with third countries, and of those concluded between Member States (intra-EU BITs). The compatibility of the first mentioned category of agreements with EU law was considered by the Court of Justice in three infringement procedures introduced by the Commission against Austria, Finland and Sweden.[36] The judgments rendered in 2009 revealed the incompatibility of these agreements with EU law, due to the fact that the agreements at issue did not contain any provision reserving the possibility for the Community to restrict the free movement of capital connected with investments and allowing the Member States to give effect to the restrictive measures which could be adopted by the Council against third parties in connection with investments. Therefore, the Court declared that the Member States in not having taken appropriate steps to eliminate the incompatibilities with EU law have failed to fulfil their obligations under Article 307(2) TFEU. Following this important case law a regulation was adopted, in 2012, by the Council and the European Parliament to establish transitional arrangements for bilateral investment agreements concluded between the Member States and third countries.[37] In that sensitive context, the European Union decided to maintain in force, at least transitionally, these bilateral investment treaties for legal certainty reasons. However the Commission is empowered to conduct an evaluation of these agreements, in cooperation with the Member States, in order to assess whether the provisions of these agreements constitute a serious obstacle to the negotiation and conclusion by the European Union of bilateral investment treaties with third countries, in view of the gradual replacement of the existing agreements[38] due to the EU competence. The regulation also foresees an authorisation procedure when a Member State intends to conclude a new agreement with a third country or wishes to amend an existing one, and attributes to the Commission a potential right of participation in the negotiations with the third country.[39]

This regulation clearly strengthens legal certainty as to the existing bilateral investment treaties concluded between Member States and third countries, even if these agreements are to be replaced over time by others concluded by the Union alone or jointly by the Union and its Member States. However this fundamental text does not make any reference to the bilateral agreements concluded between Member States of the European Union (intra-EU BITs) whose fate seems still difficult to determine. The Commission communication of July 2010, which describes the main directions of EU investment policy for the future, does not address this sensitive and controversial issue. For a specific period of time, the EU

[36] ECJ, Case C-205/06, *Commission v Austria*, [2009] ECR I-1301; ECJ, Case C-249/06, *Commission v Sweden*, [2009] ECR I-1335; ECJ, Case C-118/07, *Commission v Finland*, [2009] ECR I-10889.

[37] Regulation No 1219/2012, of the European Parliament and the Council, of 12 December 2012, establishing transitional arrangements for bilateral investment agreements between the Member States and third countries, [2012] OJ L351, 20.12.2012, p 40.

[38] Articles 5 and 6 of Regulation No 1219/2012.

[39] Articles 7 to 11 of Regulation No 1219/2012.

institutions left the question in the hands of arbitral tribunals and national courts.[40] However this is not true anymore. The European Commission has initiated infringement proceedings against five Member States (Austria, the Netherlands, Romania, Slovakia and Sweden) on 18 June 2015 requesting them to terminate intra-EU bilateral investment treaties between them (intra-EU BITs). Two Member States (Ireland and Italy) have already ended their intra-EU BITs in 2012 and 2013. As for the 21 remaining Member States which still have intra-EU BITs in place, the Commission announced that it is requesting information from and initiating an administrative dialogue with them.[41]

Parallel to these developments, the Union has to design the new investment policy. Broad trade negotiations are taking place with the USA, Canada, India and Japan with investment protection chapters. Negotiations for the conclusion of Deep and Comprehensive Free Trade Agreements (DCFTAs) are ongoing with four southern Mediterranean countries: Egypt, Tunisia, Morocco and Jordan. The EU has also entered into negotiations with Malaysia, Vietnam and Thailand. A specific approach has been chosen for the free trade agreement negotiations with China and Myanmar in the sense that the outcome will possibly be stand-alone investment agreements.[42] Moreover in October 2015, the Commission adopted a communication proposing a new trade and investment strategy for the European Union, entitled 'Trade for All: Towards a more responsible trade and investment policy'. This new strategy is given as a response to the current intense debate on trade in the EU—including the debate on the Transatlantic Trade and Investment Partnership (TTIP) that is being negotiated with the USA. It is based on the idea that trade policy must become more effective, more transparent and more in tune with our values.[43]

III. BALANCE BETWEEN THE GENERAL OBJECTIVES OF ARTICLE 21 TEU AND THE CCP OBJECTIVES

The transformation of the CCP is also linked to the general objectives introduced by the Lisbon Treaty in the whole field of EU external action. CCP is concretely subject to two categories of objectives. The specific policy objectives around liberalisation and open markets continue to be fostered. Article 206 TFEU reflects, however, the extension of the scope of the CCP to foreign direct investment and

[40] C Kaddous, 'Arbitrage, Union européenne et accords bilatéraux d'investissement' (2013) 23 *Revue suisse de droit international et européen* 1, 3.

[41] Press Release of 18 June 2015, available at: europa.eu/rapid/press-release_IP-15-5198_en.htm.

[42] See Report from the Commission to the European Council Trade and Investment Barriers Report 2015, COM(2015) 127 final.

[43] Trade for All: Towards a more responsible trade and investment policy', http://trade.ec.europa.eu/doclib/docs/2015/october/tradoc_153846.pdf. On this communication, see our comments in C Kaddous/E Ruiz Cairo/M Bierme, *Politique commerciale commune*, in Annuaire de droit européen 2015, Editions Panthéon Assas, forthcoming.

refers to the harmonious development of world trade. This includes the progressive abolition of restrictions on international trade and foreign direct investment, as well as the lowering of customs and other barriers.

These specific economic objectives are supplemented, since the entry into force of the Lisbon Treaty, by a number of general principles and objectives that have to be respected and pursued in the whole field of EU external action. This more comprehensive legal framework results from the text of Article 207(1) TFEU, according to which the CCP shall be conducted in the context of these general principles and objectives which are listed in Article 21(1) TEU in an exhaustive manner. These principles and objectives, which relate to 'democracy', 'rule of law', 'universality and indivisibility of human rights and fundamental freedoms', 'respect for human dignity', 'principles of equality and solidarity' and 'respect for the principles of the UN Charter and international law' are among the founding values and principles of the Union and are to guide the Union's action on the international scene.

In addition to this set of principles, the Union 'shall' also define and pursue common policies and actions according to Article 21(2),[44] and work for a high degree of cooperation in all fields of international relations in order to 'safeguard its values', 'consolidate and support' democracy, the rule of law and human rights, to 'foster' sustainable development, to 'help' develop environmental protection measures, and to 'encourage' integration of all countries into the world economy. Some of these objectives have been introduced by the Lisbon Treaty, such as the promotion of an international system based on an enhanced multilateral cooperation and good worldwide governance. Others resume partially the objectives mentioned in the common foreign and security policy (CFSP), development cooperation, common commercial policy or environment matters. Whereas most of these objectives appear familiar, the fact of putting them together in one single provision, at the heading of the title devoted to the general provisions on EU external action, constitutes a major 'innovation' in the foreign policy of the Union.

The general framework of Article 21 shall apply to the whole range of EU external action and is to constitute the basis for operating choices in the development of this action. This set of common principles and objectives must be considered as constituting the 'spinal column' of EU action on the international scene.

As far as the CCP is concerned, the link between Article 21 and the TFEU is established through Article 205 TFEU. Therefore the entry into force of the Lisbon Treaty implies changes in the definition of the CCP, insofar as measures taken by the Union in that field should be based upon the general principles and objectives (Article 21 TEU) and comply with the specific objectives of the CCP (Article 206 TFEU).

The pursuance of the general goals results in the integration of trade and non-trade objectives in the formulation of the CCP. The integration of the general

[44] The provision uses the verb 'shall' which in the text of the Treaties relates to an obligation for the Union.

trade objectives in the CCP does not lead a priori to difficulties.[45] However, the integration of the non-trade objectives may require potential re-orientations. Two examples to illustrate the phenomenon: the reference to the principles of democracy, rule of law, the respect for human rights which the EU shall 'consolidate and support' is of fundamental significance for the application of trade conditionality.[46] In the same way, the reference to 'help and develop international measures to preserve and improve the quality of the environment and the sustainable management of global natural resources' ensures that environmental protection is integrated into the CCP, although it has anyway to be part of all Union policies according to Article 11 TEU.

The core issue here is to reconcile the Article 21 non-trade objectives with the CCP specific objectives, when these two sets of objectives are in conflict. In that regard a decision to maintain trade relations with third countries which openly violate democracy or human rights principles, should in principle require from the EU institutions detailed explanations and strong motivation in order to explain how and why the pursuance of the EU economic goals should prevail over the fundamental principles.[47] The link created between the CCP and the general provisions of Article 21 has been considered in doctrine as leading to a 'politicisation' of trade policy. This is true. However trade policy was never 'apolitical', as demonstrated by the integration of human rights considerations as incentives for trade concessions in the EU's system of generalised preferences for developing countries.[48]

Hence trade policy has to be defined to meet the objectives and respect the principles of Articles 21 TEU, 206 and 207 TFEU. In that context, it must be stressed that all—trade and non-trade—objectives are of equal value.[49] Furthermore, the pursuance of the general principles and objectives in all fields of the EU external action is of a binding nature, as is the achievement of the trade objectives in the

[45] See however the discussion on the concept of 'free and fair trade' mentioned in Article 3(5) TEU and the objective 'to encourage the integration of all countries into the world economy, including through the progressive abolition of restrictions on international trade' enshrined in Article 21(2)(e) TEU. The concept of 'fair trade' is linked with social and labour goals, see on this point the European Commission Communication on '*Fair Trade*', COM(1999) 619 final, 19 November 1999, p 4.

[46] L Bartels, *Human Rights Conditionality in the EU's International Agreements* (Oxford, Oxford University Press, 2005).

[47] M Krajewski, 'The Reform of the Common Commercial Policy' in A Biondi and P Eeckhout (eds), *EU Law After Lisbon* (Oxford, Oxford University Press, 2012) 297.

[48] Council Regulation No 732/2008, of 22 July 2008, applying a scheme of generalised tariff preferences from 1 January 2009 and amending Regulations No 552/97, No 1933/2006 and Commission Regulations No 1100/2006 and No 964/2007, [2008] OJ L211, 6.8.2008, p 1, as lastly amended by Commission Implementing Regulation No 496/2013, of 29 May 2013, amending Annex I to Council Regulation No 732/2008 applying a scheme of generalised tariff preferences, [2013] OJ L143, 30.5.2013, p 11.

[49] In the same sense, see A Dimopoulos, 'The Effects of the Lisbon Treaty on the Principles and Objectives of the Common Commercial Policy' (2010) 15 *European Foreign Affairs Review* 153–70, 165; M Krajewski, 'The Reform of the Common Commercial Policy' in A Biondi and P Eeckhout (eds), *EU Law After Lisbon* (Oxford, Oxford University Press, 2012) 298.

CCP. Article 21 TEU uses the word 'shall' when it refers to the principles that have to guide the Union in its international action, and when it lists the objectives to be pursued by it. The same word appears in Article 207(1) TFEU for their application in the CCP.[50] Therefore it is for the EU institutions to consider respect for Article 21 in the formulation and implementation of EU's trade policy.[51] In accomplishing that mission the Council and the European Parliament, but also the Commission when exercising its initiative's right, benefit from a large political discretion, given the fact that the general objectives (Article 21(2) TEU) are broadly formulated. If for example the institutions consider that trade liberalisation is an adequate tool to promote human rights, nothing in the Treaty opposes such a position. However there might be situations where the conflict between the general objectives on the one hand, and the specific objectives of the CCP, on the other hand, is obvious and cannot be resolved by 'simple' interpretations. In such cases there is a need to 'arbitrate'. This kind of arbitration may be performed on the basis of the application of the proportionality principle. Being developed by the Court of Justice in its case law operating a balance between the objectives in the EU of free movement and of human rights,[52] this approach could be applied to resolve conflicts between EU external action general objectives and trade policy objectives. Consequently, the cases of conflicts which cannot be sorted out by the EU political institutions should or could be submitted to the appreciation of the Court of Justice in order for it to assess whether the pursuance of a particular trade policy objective violates or not the principles and objectives enshrined in Article 21.

Although the application of Article 21 TEU raises many difficulties, the general framework given by this provision is to be considered as a positive development brought about by the Lisbon Treaty in the definition of EU external relations. It aims at strengthening the global coherence of the EU external action as well as the consistency between the internal and external policies of the Union. The common list of principles and objectives helps to achieve this better consistency, even if it

[50] According to Article 207(1), 'The common commercial policy *shall be conducted* in the context of the principles and objectives of the Union's external action'.

[51] C Kaddous, 'External Action under the Lisbon Treaty' in I Pernice, E Tanchev (eds), *Ceci n'est pas une Constitution—Constitutionalisation without a Constitution?* (Baden-Baden, Nomos, 2007) 172–87; M Cremona, 'A Constitutional Basis for Effective External Action? An assessment of the provisions on EU External Action in the Constitutional Treaty', *EUI Working paper Law 30* (2006) p 30, para 52; C Vedder, 'Ziele der Gemeinsamen Handelspolitik une Ziele des auswärtigen Handelns' in Herrmann/Krenzler/Streinz (eds), *Die Aussenwirtschaftspolitik der Europäischen Union nach des Verfassungsvertrag* (Baden-Baden, Nomos, 2005) 43 ff, 47.

[52] The first two cases on that topic were ECJ, Case C-112/00, *Schmidberger, Internationale Transporte und Planzüge v Österreich*, [2003] ECR I-5659 and ECJ, Case C-36/02, *Omega Spielhallen- und Automatenaufstellungs-GmbH v Oberbürgermeisterin der Bundesstadt Bonn*, [2004] ECR I-9609. On this very interesting case law where human rights come into conflict with the fundamental freedoms of the internal market, see notably Ce Kaddous, 'Droits de l'homme et libertés de circulation: complémentarité ou contradiction?' in *Promenades au sein du droit européen, Essays in the Honour of Georges Vandersanden* (Brussels, Bruylant, 2008) 563–91.

is evidently not sufficient to guarantee it alone.[53] The recourse to the Court of Justice could be envisaged, as a last resort, in order to promote legal certainty in the international relations of the Union, in cases where the EU political institutions did not manage to cope with the conflicts.

IV. CHANGES IN THE PARTICIPATION OF THE INSTITUTIONS IN THE CCP

The Lisbon Treaty transformed significantly the institutional balance in the field of CCP. The European Parliament has become a co-legislator for the adoption of autonomous instruments in the CCP and participates fully in the conclusion of EU international agreements. In addition, some voting requirements within the Council have been modified.

The EU Treaty assigned responsibility to the Council and Commission, assisted by the High Representative of the Union for Foreign Affairs and Security Policy, in order to ensure consistency between the different areas of the external action and between these and its other policies (Article 21(3)). The participation of the High Representative in this search for coherence in the field of EU external action on the one hand, and between this field and the other policies of the Union on the other hand, is due to his/her double hat and multiple functions.[54]

The European Council has become expressly involved in the external action of the Union. According to Article 22 TEU, it shall identify the strategic interests and objectives of the Union. The decisions taken by the European Council shall relate to the common foreign and security policy (CFSP) and to the other areas of external action, including naturally the CCP. However, in the following section, only the transformation related to the role of the main actors in the definition and implementation of the CCP, ie the European Parliament, the Council and the Commission, will be examined.

A. Promotion of the European Parliament

The institution has long been kept away from EU's trade policy. The Lisbon Treaty has provided the European Parliament with significant powers. The ordinary legislative procedure enshrined in Article 294 TFEU henceforth applies for the adoption of 'measures defining the framework for implementing the common commercial policy'. As a co-legislator, the Parliament is able to amend the proposals made by the Commission, and has a veto right with regard to the adoption of

[53] M Cremona, 'The Draft constitutional Treaty: External Relations and External Action' (2003) 40 *Common Market Law Review* 1347, 1349.

[54] C Kaddous, 'Role and Position of the High Representative of the Union for Foreign Affairs and Security Policy under the Lisbon Treaty' in S Griller and J Ziller (eds), *The Lisbon Treaty. EU Constitutionalism without a Constitution Treaty?* (Berlin, Springer Verlag, 2008) 205–23.

internal measures. However, the ordinary legislative procedure is not supposed to be applied for the adoption of individual commercial policy measures.[55] It is aimed to be used to adopt the basic regulations on imports, exports or framework regulations for the trade defence instruments. The ordinary legislative procedure was notably applied in 2012 for the adoption of the regulation on the future of Member States' bilateral investment agreements with third countries.[56] The regulation establishing a framework for managing financial responsibility linked to investor-to-state dispute settlement tribunals established by international agreements to which the European Union is party,[57] as well as the two new regimes for the import and export of goods[58] were also adopted on the basis of this procedure. It is, however, questionable if this procedure will be applied in the future to modify or adopt new specific regimes, such as for example the one on the export of cultural goods.[59]

The role of the European Parliament has also been modified regarding the negotiations, conclusion and implementation of international trade agreements. Til the entry into force of the Lisbon Treaty, such agreements were negotiated by the Commission on the basis of a mandate issued by the Council in consultation with a special committee of the Council.[60] The European Parliament did not formally participate in the negotiations, but was kept informed of progress in the negotiation of the international agreements with third countries or international organisations on the basis of an informal arrangement.[61] Today, according to Article 207(3) TFEU, the Commission shall conduct the negotiations in consultation with a special Committee of the Council (the Trade Policy Committee)[62] and shall report regularly to this Committee and to the European Parliament on the progress of negotiations. Concretely, the reports are made to the Parliament's

[55] M Krajewski, 'New Functions and New Powers for the European Parliament: Assessing the Changes of the Common Commercial Policy from the Perspective of Democratic Legitimacy' in M Bungenberg, C Herrmann (eds), *Common commercial Policy after Lisbon*, special issue of *European Yearbook of International Economic Law* (Heidelberg, Springer, 2013) 67–87, 71.

[56] Regulation No 1219/2012, of the European Parliament and the Council, of 12 December 2012, establishing transitional arrangements for bilateral investment agreements between the Member States and third countries, [2012] OJ L351, 20.12.2012, p 40.

[57] Regulation No 912/2014, of the European Parliament and the Council, of 23 July 2014, establishing a framework for managing financial responsibility linked to investor-to-state dispute settlement tribunals established by international agreements to which the European Union is party, [2014] OJ L257, 28.8.2014, p 121.

[58] Regulation No 2015/478 of the European Parliament and of the Council of 11 March 2015 on common rules for imports, [2015] OJ L83, 27.3.2015, p 16; Regulation No 2015/479 of the European Parliament and of the Council of 11 March 2015 on common rules for exports, [2015] OJ L83, 27.3.2015, p 34.

[59] Regulation No 116/2009, of the Council, of 18 December 2008, on the export of cultural goods, [2009] OJ L39, 10.2.2009, p 1.

[60] It was the so-called '133 Committee'.

[61] It was the so-called *Luns-Westerterp* procedure.

[62] It is the successor of the '133 Committee'.

International Trade Committee (INTA committee).[63] The right of the Parliament to be regularly informed on the state of the negotiations has become legally binding, which thus contributes to the strengthening of its role in trade policy.

In addition, due to Article 207 TFEU the Council and the European Parliament are to be treated equally with regard to the information right. The non-respect of this rule may be considered as a violation of the Treaty. However the equality between the two institutions is specific to the right to information and does not apply to the involvement in the process of negotiations. The Commission still conducts the negotiations in consultation with the Trade Policy Committee of the Council, and not with the INTA Committee of the Parliament. This difference which is of a political nature is closely linked to the current state of development of foreign policy within the European Union. This specific institutional imbalance is 'partially' compensated for by the role attributed to the European Parliament in the conclusion phase of trade agreements.

No specific rules are provided for in Article 207 TFEU as to the conclusion of international agreements. The general provision of Article 218 TFEU applies with the two forms possible of European Parliament's participation. In principle the Parliament is consulted before the Council concludes an international agreement,[64] the only exception being the agreements related exclusively to CFSP, on which the Parliament is not even consulted.[65] The other form of Parliament's participation requires its consent to the conclusion of an international agreement. Among the five cases expressly stipulated in Article 218(6), the most important one in practice relates to the agreements covering fields to which the ordinary legislative procedure applies,[66] ie the adoption of 'measures defining the framework for implementing the common commercial policy'. Hence the consent of the Parliament is required for the conclusion of international agreements in the field of CCP. It has therefore the power to give or withhold its consent for the conclusion of trade agreements with third countries.

[63] See the Framework Agreement between the European Parliament and the European Commission, [2010] OJ L304, 20.10.2010, p 47, p 50, paragraphs 23–32 on 'International Agreements and Enlargement'.

[64] Article 218(6) 2 b TFEU.

[65] Article 218(6) 2 TFEU; ECJ, Case C-658/11, *Parliament v Council*, ECLI: EU:C: 2014:2025. See the comments made by C Kaddous on this judgment in F Picod (ed), *Jurisprudence de la CJUE 2014. Décisions et commentaires*, Collection 'Droit de l'Union européenne', série 'Grands arrêts' (Brussels, Bruylant, 2015) 600–606.

[66] Article 218(6)(a)(v) TFEU. The other cases cover: association agreements, agreement on Union accession to the European Convention for the Protection of Human Rights and Fundamental Freedoms; agreements establishing a specific institutional framework by organising cooperation procedures; agreements with important budgetary implications for the Union; and the agreements covering fields to which the special legislative procedure applies where consent by the European Parliament is required.

The first international agreement for which this provision has been applied is the Free Trade Agreement with Korea.[67] The agreement was signed on 6 October 2010 and has been provisionally applied since 1 July 2011.[68] According to Article 218(5) TFEU, the provisional application of an international agreement may be taken by the Council on a proposal made by the Commission without the prior consent of the Parliament. This rule is based on the need to act quickly in some situations[69] and is accepted as an international practice under Article 25 of the Vienna Convention on the law of Treaties. However it is worth noting that the Council's decision on signature and provisional application of this agreement considered that the positive vote of the European Parliament on conclusion was a precondition for the provisional application to start as of 1 July 2011.[70] In that way, it is interesting to note that the consent requirement of the European Parliament for the conclusion of a trade agreement may impact on the decision regarding the provisional application of the said agreement, a field in which the European Parliament has no specific competence according to the Treaty.

The consent requirement for the conclusion of trade agreements constitutes clearly one of the key aspects of the changes brought about by the Lisbon Treaty in the institutional reform of the CCP.[71] The role given to the European Parliament in this field responds to the old critique concerning the lack of democratic accountability in trade policy.[72] Since December 2009, the Parliament has taken its

[67] Council Decision, of 16 September 2010, on the signing, on behalf of the European Union, and provisional application of the Free Trade Agreement between the European Union and its Member States, of the one part, and the Republic of Korea, of the other part, [2011] OJ L127, 14.5.2011, p 1.

[68] Notice concerning the provisional application of the Free Trade Agreement between the European Union and its Member States, of the one part, and the Republic of Korea, of the other part, [2011] OJ L168, 28.6.2011, p 1. The process of ratification is still ongoing. See also CM Brow, 'Changes in the Common Commercial Policy of the European Union After the Entry into Force of the Treaty of Lisbon: a Practioner's Perspective' in M Bungenberg and C Herrmann (eds), *Common commercial Policy after Lisbon, special issue of European Yearbook of International Economic Law* (Berlin, Springer, 2013) 163–83, 165–67.

[69] F Hoffmeister, 'The European Union's Common Commercial Policy a year after Lisbon—sea change or business as usual?', *CLEER Working Papers* 2011/13, pp 83–95, 92.

[70] Press Release of the Council of the European Union of 16 September 2010, ST 13670/10, states that: 'The Council agreed that provisional application of the agreement will start on 1 July 2011, provided that the European Parliament has given its consent to the agreement and that a regulation implementing an EU-South Korea safeguard clause is in force' available at: www.consilium.europa.eu/uedocs/cms_Data/docs/pressdata/EN/foraff/116545.pdf.

[71] The consent procedure has also been applied for the conclusion of the free trade agreement with Peru and Colombia, see Council Decision 2012/735 of 31 May 2012 on the signing, on behalf of the Union, and provisional application of the Trade Agreement between the European Union and its Member States, of the one part, and Colombia and Peru, of the other part, [2012] OJ L354, 21.12.2012, p 1. The agreement was signed in June 2012 and has been provisionally applied to Peru since 10 March 2013 and to Colombia since August 2013, press release at: europa.eu/rapid/press-release_IP-13-749_en.htm.

[72] M Krajewski, 'External Trade Law and the Constitution Treaty: Towards a Federal and More Democratic Common Commercial Policy?' (2005) 42 *Common Market Law Review* 91.

new powers seriously. It even started to adopt resolutions to express its intention as to the conclusion of specific international agreements before the entry into force of the Lisbon Treaty. It stated for example in 2006 that it would give its consent only to agreements containing human rights clauses.[73] In the same way, the Parliament declared in 2008 that it would give its consent to the conclusion of an international agreement with the Gulf Cooperation Council only if the objectives of Article 21 TEU are sufficiently taken into consideration.[74]

The internal and external dimensions of the CCP are now largely influenced by the role given to the European Parliament. The modifications brought by the Lisbon Treaty put the Parliament at the same level as the Council for the adoption of secondary legislation in the essential fields of trade, such as anti-dumping, anti-subsidies, trade barriers, rules of origin, investment and conclusion of international trade agreements. To that respect the institutional balance has been adjusted in allowing the parliamentary institution to take part in the political decision-making process in a field where the EU has to compete with strong partners at the international level.

B. Stabilisation of the Council of the European Union

The main actor in the CCP remains, however, the Council. This institution has the power to decide on the opening of negotiations with a third country or an international organisation (Article 207(3) TFEU). It decides as well on the signature, the provisional application and the conclusion of trade agreements (Article 207 and 218 TFEU). The Council also plays an important role during the negotiation phase of an international agreement through the consultation of the Member States within the Trade Policy Committee, which acts in a certain way as an advisory body.

For the negotiation and conclusion of trade agreements, the Council acts by a qualified majority vote. The decision-making rule is applicable, except for the agreements in the fields of trade in services, commercial aspects of intellectual property and foreign direct investment, for which the Council acts unanimously where such agreements include provisions for which unanimity is required for the adoption of internal rules. It is worth noting that a potential veto right may be exercised by every Member State in the decision-making process for the opening of negotiations or for the conclusion of agreements with third countries in the above-mentioned situations.

[73] Resolution of the European Parliament of 14 December 2006, EP Doc A6-4/2006.

[74] Resolution of the European Parliament, of 24 April 2008, on the free trade agreement between the EC and the Gulf Cooperation Council (GCC), [2009] OJ C259 E, 29.10.2009, p 83. The negotiations on a free trade agreement with the six countries of the Gulf Cooperation Council were suspended by the GCC in 2008. However, informal contacts are taking place regularly.

Furthermore, the Council must decide unanimously for the negotiation and conclusion of agreements in the field of trade in cultural and audio-visual services, when these risk prejudicing the Union's 'cultural and linguistic diversity', and in the field of trade in 'social, education and health services', when these agreements risk seriously disturbing the national organisation of such services and prejudicing the responsibility of Member States to deliver them. All these notions are not defined in the Treaty. Being broadly formulated they leave a wide margin of manoeuvre for interpretations by the EU political institutions and, in case of conflicts, by the Court of Justice.

C. Increase in the Implementing Powers of the European Commission

The powers of the European Commission under CCP are kept largely identical to the ones prior to the entry into force of the Lisbon Treaty. The Commission shall make recommendations to the Council for the opening of negotiations with third countries or international organisations. It shall conduct the negotiations in consultation with the Trade Policy Committee appointed by the Council. It has to report regularly to this special Committee and to the European Parliament on the progress of negotiations in the terms described above. The Commission shall also be responsible with the Council for ensuring that the agreements negotiated are compatible with the internal policies and rules of the Union (Article 207(3) TFEU).

Internally, the ordinary legislative procedure is applicable for the adoption, by the Council and the European Parliament, of the basic regulations on imports, exports or framework regulations for the trade defence instruments. However the Commission has implementing powers in trade policy. In January 2014, two regulations were adopted to amend specific regulations relating to the common commercial policy as regards the procedure for the adoption of certain measures[75] and as regards the attribution of delegated and implementing powers for the adoption of certain measures.[76] The aim of these changes is to ensure consistency with the provisions introduced by the Lisbon Treaty in granting the Commission, where appropriate, delegated powers and in applying certain procedures as set out in the regulation laying down the rules and principles concerning the mechanisms for control by the Member States of the Commission's exercise of implementing powers.[77] The Commission has made use of this implementing power in adopting

[75] Regulation No 37/2014, of the European Parliament and of the Council, of 15 January 2014, amending certain regulations relating to the common commercial policy as regards the procedures for the adoption of certain measures, [2014] OJ L18, 21.1.2014, p 1.

[76] Regulation No 38/2014, of the European Parliament and of the Council, of 15 January 2014, amending certain regulations relating to the common commercial policy as regards the granting of delegated and implementing powers for the adoption of certain measures, [2014] OJ L18, 21.1.2014, p 52.

[77] Regulation No 182/2011, of the European Parliament and of the Council, of 16 February 2011, laying down the rules and general principles concerning mechanisms for control by Member States of the Commission's exercise of implementing powers, [2011] OJ L55, 28.2.2011, p 13.

a regulation in July 2014 concerning trade in certain goods which could be used for capital punishment, torture or other cruel, inhuman or degrading treatment or punishment.[78]

Apart from these changes in the implementing powers, the Commission continues to be the main initiator and negotiator in trade policy. It carries out seriously its missions as guardian of the Treaties, illustrated notably by the infringement procedures introduced against Member States for violations of EU law. This kind of procedure is rather rare in the EU external relations. However in the field of investment the Commission brought cases against Austria, Sweden and Finland which resulted in a finding of violations of Article 351 TFEU.[79] At the political level these judgments led to the adoption in 2012 of the regulation on the transitional arrangements for the bilateral investment treaties concluded by Member States with third countries.[80] On 18 June 2015, the Commission also decided to initiate procedures against five Member States requesting them to terminate their intra-EU BITs.[81]

Taking part in the institutional balance which governs the functioning of the EU, the Commission introduces cases for annulment, such as *Commission v Council* already referred to[82] or introduces requests for advisory opinions according to Article 218(11) in situations where the distribution of powers between the Union and the Member States is unclear as to the conclusion of comprehensive trade agreements.[83]

V. CONCLUDING REMARKS

The CCP has been transformed in many ways. It takes into account ever more fields in trade policy leading to a continuously more comprehensive scope of no comparison with the one which existed at the time of the foundation of the European Communities. The transformation occurred through case law, through Treaty modifications, depending on the one hand on the internal requirements of the Union, whether of legal, political or economic nature, and on the other hand on the external challenges the Union had to face in the global trading system. Trade policy covers nowadays topics which go far beyond the progressive abolition of customs tariffs and quantitative restrictions and includes trade in all goods, trade in services, commercial aspects of intellectual property rights as well as foreign

[78] Commission Implementing Regulation no 775/2014, of 16 July 2014, amending Council Regulation no 1236/2005 concerning trade in certain goods which could be used for capital punishment, torture or other cruel, inhuman or degrading treatment or punishment, [2014] OJ L210, 17.7.2014, p 1.

[79] ECJ, C-205/06, *Commission v Austria*, [2009] ECR I-1301; Case C-249/06, *Commission v Sweden*, [2009] ECR I-1335; Case C-118/07, *Commission v Finland*, [2009] ECR I-10889.

[80] See above (n 56).

[81] See above (n 41).

[82] See above (n 17).

[83] See above (n 35).

direct investment. The non-exhaustive character of the list in Article 207 TFEU keeps the door open to future developments. In order to respond to these different challenges, the European Union is designing the main streams of its investment policy with the adoption of detailed internal rules and the negotiation of comprehensive trade agreements with third countries including investment chapters.

The current period of transformation of the CCP brings into consideration the double set of objectives and principles that have to be pursued and respected by the European Union in the definition of its trade policy. In addition to the specific objectives aiming at trade liberalisation, the non-trade objectives and general principles of Article 21 TEU are to be integrated into the design and implementation of the CCP. As previously observed, this obligation may lead to some politicisation of the policy, whereas the original objective in Article 113 was mainly economical, ie the achievement of trade liberalisation in avoiding obstacles created by politics at the national or international levels. The politicisation of the policy, required by the Treaty, was criticised by many scholars but is today a consequence of the globalisation and of the interdependence of diverse objectives and interests which cannot anymore be ignored whether on the European or the WTO level. On the contrary, not admitting the politicisation of the CCP would constitute in my view an incorrect assessment of the reality and an inadequate design of the EU trade policy.

The Lisbon Treaty brought about a significant modification of the institutional balance in the field of CCP. The European Parliament has become a co-legislator for the adoption of internal legislation and participates in the conclusion of trade agreements. Its increased role has democratised the CCP in bringing more legitimacy to this policy. This change responds to the criticism often made of a lack of democratic accountability in trade policy. This phenomenon is accompanied by a loss—which can't be stressed enough—of powers for the national parliaments in the ratification process of trade agreements when these fall within the exclusive competence of the Union. The modification in the balance between the European and the national parliaments may favour the political approach of promoting the conclusion of a greater number of mixed agreements in the future.

The Council of the European Union remains the main actor in the CCP, with its co-legislative powers in internal matters and its power to decide on the opening of negotiations with third countries as well on the signing, provisional application and conclusion of trade agreements. The competences of the European Commission have been kept largely identical to the pre-Lisbon period, except for the implementing powers linked to the granting of delegated powers concerning the adoption of certain measures, which result in an increase of its margin of manoeuvre in the CCP field.

The Lisbon Treaty modernised the CCP and repaired some of the institutional imbalance with respect to the role of the European Parliament. It introduced into the debate new sensitive issues, such as the definition of 'foreign direct investment' or the achievement of non-trade objectives in the design of CCP, which may trigger fundamental problems and revive the tensions between the Union and its Member States in EU foreign policy.

14

The European Union Facing Investment Arbitration

JAVIER DIEZ-HOCHLEITNER[1]

I. INTRODUCTION

As is well known, the conclusion and entry into force of the Treaty of Lisbon sparked an intense debate on the scope of the competence on foreign investment, conferred upon the Union by Article 207 TFEU. The future of more than 1,300 Bilateral Investment Treaties (BITs) previously concluded by Member States is also

[1] Professor of Public International Law, Autónoma University of Madrid.

at stake.[2] The compatibility of intra-EU BITs (190 approximately) with EU law has concurrently been questioned.[3]

A significant part of the literature considers that the new EU competence does not cover certain aspects of the BITs to which Member States are parties, and neither does it cover all types of foreign investment.[4] Hence, it has been argued that the reference to 'direct' investment in Article 207 excludes portfolio investment, the protection of which is ensured in most BITs concluded by Member States. Furthermore, the competence in the field of investment allegedly only includes trade-related aspects and not investment protection. In this regard, however, it is not always easy to distinguish between the pre- and post-establishment phases, since the effective implementation of the investment is actually determined by the treatment and legal certainty afforded to the investor. It is worth recalling,

[2] See J Díez-Hochleitner, 'El incierto futuro de los acuerdos bilaterales sobre protección de inversiones celebrados por los Estados miembros de la Unión Europea' (2000) 33 *Revista Española de Derecho Europeo* 5, 10 ff, in which I discuss the compatibility of extra-EU BITs concluded by Member States in accordance with EU Law, as well as ECJ decisions in this regard. See also A Gouri, *Interaction and Conflict of Treaties in Investment Arbitration* (International Arbitration Law Library, vol 32) (Deventer, Kluwer Law International, 2015) 149 ff, and E Böhm and M-C Motaabbed, ch IV Investment Arbitration: 'The European Union and the Unloved BITs of its Member States', *Austrian Yearbook of International Arbitration 2014*, 371.

[3] See Díez-Hochleitner (ibid,35 ff), Gouri (ibid, 149) and Böhm and Motaabbed (ibid, 371), also cited above. The European Commission initiated on June 2015 infringement proceedings against five Member States (Austria, the Netherlands, Romania, Slovakia and Sweden) requesting them to terminate intra-EU BITs between them. The European Commission argues that those BITs are contrary to the principle of non-discrimination based on nationality as they confer rights on some EU investors on a bilateral basis. The Commission is also requesting information from and initiating an administrative dialogue with the remaining Member States who still have intra-EU BITs in place (Ireland and Italy have already ended all their intra-EU BITs). See europa.eu/rapid/press-release_IP-15-5198_en.htm.

[4] Among the abundant literature on the subject, see Díez-Hochleitner, 'El incierto…', n 2 above, 30, JA Bischoff, 'Just a Little Bit of "Mixity"? The EU's Role in the Field of International Investment Protection Law' (2001) 48 *Common Market Law Review* 1527, 1534; M Bungenberg, 'The Division of Competences between the EU and Its Member States in the Area of Investment Politics' in Bungenberg, Griebel and Hindelang (eds), *European Yearbook of International Economic Law* (*Special Issue: International Investment Law and EU Law*) (Heidelberg, Springer, 2011) 29, 35; J Chaisse, 'Promises and Pitfalls of the European Union Policy on Foreign Investment—How will the new EU Competence on FDI affect the Emerging Global Regime?' (2012) 15 *Journal of International Economic* Law 51, 57; A Dimopoulos, *EU Foreign Investment Law* (Oxford, OUP, 2011) 122; by the same author: 'The Common Commercial Policy after Lisbon: Establishing Parallelism between Internal and external Economic Relations' (2008) 4 *Croatian Yearbook of European Law and Policy* 102, 112; Th Eilmansberger, 'Bilateral Investment Treaties and EU Law' (2009) 46 *Common Market Law Review* 383; A Emch, 'News from Luxembourg—Is the New EU Investment Law Taking Shape?' (2008) 9 *Journal of World Investment and Trade* 497; M Krajewski, 'External Trade Law and the Constitution Treaty: Towards a Federal and More Democratic Common Commercial Policy?' (2005) 42 *Common Market Law Review* 91, 114; PJ Kujper, 'Foreign Direct Investment: The First Test of the Lisbon Improvements in the Domain of Trade Polity' (2010) 37 *Legal Issues of Economic Integration* 261; A Reinisch, 'The Division of Powers between the EU and its Member States "after Lisbon"' *European Yearbook of International Economic Law* (Special Issue, n 4 above) 43; A Reinisch, 'The EU on the Investment Path—*Quo Vadis* Europe? The Future of EU BITs and other Investments Agreements', *Social Science Research, Working Papers Series*, 2013 (papers.ssrn.com/sol3/papers.cfm?abstract_id=2236192); S Woolcock and J Kleinheisterkamp, 'The EU Approach to International Investment Policy After the Lisbon Treaty', *Study for the European Parliament's Committees on International Trade* (INTA), 2010, at p 9).

in this context, that former Article 57.2 TCE (now Article 64.2 TFEU) already conferred an implicit external competence on the Union to conclude agreements in the field of free movement of capital, thus affecting the post-establishment stage. The 'Minimum Platform on Investment for EU FTAs', adopted by the Council of the European Union in 2006,[5] clearly illustrates this point. Its provisions relating to the establishment of free trade agreements not only cover market access, but also include the National and Most-Favoured-Nation Treatment.

The Commission rejected a narrow interpretation of Article 207 TFEU in its Communication entitled 'Towards a comprehensive European international investment policy'.[6] Rather, it advocated an exclusive EU competence to conclude agreements covering all investment-related aspects, including the establishment of investor-state dispute settlement mechanisms. Moreover, with regard to investment arbitration, the Commission stated that the EU should be the sole defendant even in cases concerning 'any measure taken by a Member State which affects investments by third country nationals or companies falling within the scope of the agreement concerned'.[7] Furthermore, the Commission makes the case for an exclusive implicit competence in respect of portfolio investments, provided by Articles 63 to 66 TFEU.[8]

In its Regulation Proposal on financial responsibility linked to investor-state dispute settlement tribunals established by agreements to which the EU is party (which led to the adoption of the current Regulation (EU) 912/2014)[9], the Commission insisted on the Union's exclusive competence to conclude agreements covering all matters relating to foreign investment.[10] However, the proposed system with regards to the defendant status leads to mixed agreements at all events (as we will see latter).

The Council, of course, advocates the negotiation and conclusion of investment agreements by the EU in the line of Member States BITs, therefore providing for a wide protection, including the investors' right to submit any dispute with the host State to international arbitration.[11] This is especially reflected in the Negotiating Mandates approved by the General Affairs Council for investment

[5] Document 15375/06, 27 November 2006.

[6] COM(2010) 343 final, 7 July 2010.

[7] Ibid at 11.

[8] Ibid at 8–9.

[9] Regulation (EU) 912/2014 of the European Parliament and of the Council, of 23 July 2014, establishing a framework for managing financial responsibility linked to investor-state dispute settlement tribunals established by international agreements to which the European Union is party ([2014] OJ L257, 28.8.2014).

[10] COM(2012) 335 final, 21 June 2012, at p 3.

[11] See Council of the EU, 'Conclusions on a comprehensive European international investment policy', 3041st Foreign Affairs Council meeting, 25 October 2010; conclusion No 7 states that the Council 'supports the definition of a broad scope for the new EU policy in this field as suggested by the Commission, to be further elaborated in full respect of the respective competences of the Union and its Member States as defined by the Treaties'.

protection chapters in Free Trade Agreements.[12] Nonetheless, when it comes to aspects such as portfolio investment, dispute settlement, property and expropriation, the Council holds these agreements to affect shared competence areas.[13] Accordingly, it supports the widely held view that EU agreements in the field of investment should be concluded as 'mixed agreements'. That is also the position taken by the German Federal Constitutional Court in its ruling on the Treaty of Lisbon.[14]

The European Parliament seems also to favour a wide definition of the Union policy in the field of investment and, in any case, an 'integrated and coherent investment policy'. However, it also acknowledges that 'negotiating a broad variety of investments would lead to mixing exclusive and shared competences'. In fact, in its Legislative Resolution of 16 April 2014 on the Regulation Proposal on financial responsibility, the European Parliament proposed to provide in Article 1.1 of the Regulation that

> the adoption and application of this Regulation shall not affect the delimitation of competences established by the Treaties, including in relation to the treatment afforded by the Member States or the Union and challenged by a claimant in investor-to-state dispute settlement conducted pursuant to an agreement,[15]

a wording that *was* finally included in it.

The progressive definition of the European international investment policy has been accompanied by transitional arrangements in order to maintain Member States' BITS in force. Such transitional scheme has been set up by Regulation No 1219/2012,[16] adopted precisely on the basis of Article 207 TFEU. The said

[12] See, for example, Negotiating Mandates approved by the General Affairs Council for investment protection chapters in free trade agreements with Canada, India and Singapore (12 September 2011), with China and the Association of South East Asian Nations (ASEAN) member countries (Brunei Darussalam, Myanmar/Burma, Cambodia, Indonesia, Laos, Malaysia, Philippines, Singapore, Thailand, and Vietnam) (18 October 2013) and in the *EU-US Transatlantic Trade and Investment Partnership* (*TTIP*) (14 June 2013; see doc 11103/13, DCL 1, WTO 139, SERVICES 26, FDI 17, USA, 9 October 2014).

[13] Ibid (see para 22 of the TTIP Mandate).

[14] Judgment of 30 June 2009 (BVERFG, 2 BE 2/08), in para 379: 'The extension of the common commercial policy to 'foreign direct investment' (Article 207.1 TFEU) confers exclusive competence on the European Union also in this area. Much, however, argues in favour of assuming that the term 'foreign direct investment only encompasses investment which serves to obtain a controlling interest in an enterprise … The consequence of this would be that exclusive competence only exists for investment of this type whereas investment protection agreements that go beyond this would have to be concluded as mixed agreements'. See JP Terhechte, '(National) Constitutional Law Limitations on the Advancement of the EU's Common Commercial Policy' in M Bungenberg and C Hermann (eds), *Common Commercial Policy after Lisbon, European Yearbook of International Economic Law* (Berlin/Heidelberg, Springer, 2013) 19, 25.

[15] European Parliament Legislative Resolution of 16 April 2014 (P7_TA-PROV(2014)0419).

[16] Regulation (EU) No 1219/2012 of the European Parliament and of the Council of 12 December 2012 establishing transitional arrangements for bilateral investment agreements between Member States and third countries ([2012] OJ L351, 20.12.2012). See A Pastor Palomar, 'La aplicación práctica del Reglamento (UE) núm 1219/2012 sobre los Acuerdos bilaterales de inversión entre Estados miembros y terceros países' (2013) 31 *Revista General de Derecho Europeo* (www.iustel.com/v2/revistas/detalle_revista.asp?id=13&numero=31).

Regulation empowers Member States to keep in force such previous agreements until replaced by investment treaties concluded by the EU—or an FTA including chapters on investment protection, such as the agreement with Singapore or the Comprehensive Economic and Trade Agreement (CETA) with Canada—on the condition that Member States notify the Commission about these replacements.[17] Moreover, the Regulation provides for the possibility that Member States may amend their BITs and even conclude new ones, subject to the Commission's authorisation granted under the current advisory procedure of the 'comitology' Regulation.[18] The authorisation may only be refused in certain specific cases, which include the incompatibility of the envisaged treaty with EU law or if the treaty constitutes a serious obstacle to the negotiation or conclusion of investment agreements by the Union.[19]

This chapter does not aim at reassessing once again the scope of the EU's competences in the field of investment, nor at analysing the aforementioned transitional scheme. Our objective is to analyse the role that investor-State arbitration should play in future EU investment agreements (2), and to address the problems posed by the irruption of the EU onto the investment arbitration arena (3).

II. THE ROLE OF ARBITRATION IN FUTURE EU INVESTMENT AGREEMENTS

A. The Key Role of Investor-State Arbitration

The effectiveness of the current investment protection system depends on the investor-State dispute settlement mechanisms (ISDS) provided by almost all BITs in force, and other agreements covering investment protection such as the Energy Charter Treaty or North American Free Trade Agreement (NAFTA). The direct recourse to arbitration granted to investors when they consider that any of their rights enshrined in investment agreements has been breached explains the key role generally attributed to the latter in the promotion of international investment. In short, access to arbitration strengthens investors' trust, since disputes with the host State are no longer subject to national courts or to the discretion of the State of nationality in the exercise of diplomatic protection.

[17] Art 3 of the Regulation. The Regulation reduces considerably the Commission's self-attributed powers in its proposal regarding the possible maintenance of the BITs in force. See Proposal for a Regulation of the European Parliament and of the Council establishing transitional arrangements for bilateral investment agreements between Member States and third countries (COM(2010)344 final, of 7.7.2010). See List of the bilateral investment agreements referred to in Art 4(1) of Regulation (EU) No 1219/2012 of the European Parliament and of the Council establishing transitional arrangements for bilateral investment agreements between Member States and third countries ([2013] OJ C131, 8.5.2013, and [2014] OJ C169, 5.6.2014).

[18] Art 4 of Regulation (EU) No 182/2011 of the European Parliament and of the Council, of 16 February 2011, laying down the rules and general principles concerning mechanisms for control by Member States of the Commission's exercise of implementing powers ([2011] OJ L55, 28.2.2011).

[19] Arts 7 to 9 of Regulation No 1219/2012.

It is widely known that most investment protection agreements follow three models regarding investor-State dispute settlement. According to the first one, known as 'fork-in-the-road', when a dispute arises the investor has to choose between two mutually exclusive options after the expiration of the period allowed for a friendly settlement: to refer to the host State's national courts or to submit an arbitration claim to an arbitration procedure. Under the second model, the investor must not only pursue a friendly settlement, but also refer to the host State's courts and wait for a certain period of time (usually 18 months) before applying for arbitration. The third model permits the foreign investor to submit its claim to arbitration at any time under the condition that the notice of arbitration is accompanied by a written waiver of any right to initiate or continue proceedings before any administrative tribunal or court under the law of the host State ('no u-turn'). Moreover, most investment protection agreements grant the investor the possibility to choose among various arbitration forums, generally including the International Centre for Settlement of Investment Disputes (ICSID) and ad hoc arbitration under United Nations Commission for International Trade Law (UNCITRAL) rules.

Nevertheless, recent years have witnessed the emergence of some criticism towards investor-State arbitration based on different reasons, among them, the alleged pro-investor bias of most arbitration tribunals, the system's lack of predictability due to the inconsistencies between arbitration awards and above all, the way some awards impinge on the host States' regulatory powers. The denunciation of some BITs and the ICSID Convention by Bolivia, Ecuador and Venezuela should be framed in this context.[20]

Also in the EU voices have been raised against investment arbitration as we know it. Hence, the European Parliament claimed in its 2011 resolution on the future European international investment policy that:

> changes must be made to the present dispute settlement regime, in order to include greater transparency, the opportunity for parties to appeal, the obligation to exhaust local judicial remedies where they are reliable enough to guarantee due process, the possibility to use amicus curiae briefs and the obligation to select one single place of investor-state arbitration.[21]

Furthermore, in the first reading of the Regulation Proposal on financial responsibility linked to investor-state dispute settlement tribunals, the Parliament initially advocated leaving investor-State dispute settlement mechanisms out of EU agreements, including them solely 'in the cases where it is justifiable'.[22]

[20] Denunciation of the ICSID Convention by Bolivia in 2007, by Ecuador in 2009 and Venezuela in 2012. See LT Wells, 'Backlash to Investment Arbitration: Three Causes' in Waibel, Kaushal, Chung and Balchin (eds), *The Backlash Against Investment Arbitration: Perceptions and Reality* (Leiden, Kluwer Law International, 2010) 341; see also C Schreuer, 'Denunciation of the ICSID Convention and Consent to Arbitration', ibid p 455.

[21] Resolution of 6 April 2011 on the future European international investment policy (2010/2203(INI)), para 31.

[22] Amendments adopted by the European Parliament on 23 May 2013 on the proposal for a regulation establishing a framework for managing financial responsibility linked to investor-state dispute set-

The European Parliament raises two major concerns regarding investment arbitration. On the one hand, 'the level of discretion of international arbitrators to make a broad interpretation of investor protection clauses, thereby leading to the ruling out of legitimate public regulations';[23] on the other, that future EU investment agreements could provide for more protection to foreign investors than European investors are granted under EU law.[24]

Nonetheless, investment protection agreements are based upon reciprocal treatment. Consequently, as has been noted by some authors, a 'no greater rights' position on both sides 'would lead to rendering international investment protection provisions ad absurdum: the whole point of establishing such legal provisions is to grant foreign investors rights that are different from those in the host country'.[25]

Taken to its logical conclusions, the 'no greater rights' approach would lead EU agreements to provide exclusively for the submission of investor-State disputes to the host country's courts, allowing for dispute settlement mechanisms only between the States parties. This solution may make sense as regards investment agreements with third countries that offer protection standards similar to those granted by the EU and its Member States. In this regard, it should be recalled that Chapter 11 of the Australia-US Free Trade Agreement 2004, on investment protection, does not provide for investor-State arbitration.[26] However, if applied on a general basis, this solution would mean a step back in the protection and legal certainty now enjoyed by European investors under BITs in force and would therefore be

tlement tribunals (P7_TA(2013)0219); amendment No 3 to recital (2) of the Regulation Proposal, adopted by unanimity, on the basis of a INTA proposal also unanimously adopted (INTA Report A7-0124/2013, of 26 March 2013); the matter was referred back to the committee responsible for reconsideration pursuant to Rule 57(2), second subparagraph, of the European Parliament's Rules of Procedure. However, in its Legislative Resolution of 16 April 2014, n 15 above, the European Parliament softened its position by agreeing to the following wording (finally included in recital 2 of Regulation 912/2014): 'Agreements providing for investment protection may include an investor-to-state dispute settlement mechanism' . See also European Parliament Resolution of 9 October 20013 on EU-China negotiations for a bilateral investment agreement (P7_TA-PROV(2013)0411), para 43.

[23] Resolution of 6 April 2011, n 21 above, para 24. See also Resolution of 9 October 2013 on EU–China negotiations for a bilateral investment agreement, cited above, para. 41.

[24] In its Legislative Resolution of 16 April 2014, the European Parliament proposed to include the following new recital (4): 'Union agreements should afford foreign investors the same high level of protection as Union law and the general principles common to the laws of the Member States grant to investors from within the Union, but not a higher level of protection. Union agreements should ensure that the Union's legislative powers and right to regulate are respected and safeguarded'. The new recital was finally included in Regulation (EU) 912/2014.

[25] J Kleinheisterkamp, *Financial Responsibility in the European International Investment Policy*, LSE Law, Society and Economic Working Papers 15/2013, p 22 and pp 25–26;

[26] Agreement of 18 May 2004, Art 11.16 of which provides as follows: 'If a Party considers that there has been a change in circumstances affecting the settlement of disputes on matters within the scope of this Chapter and that, in light of such change, the Parties should consider allowing an investor of a Party to submit to arbitration with the other Party a claim regarding a matter within the scope of this Chapter, the Party may request consultations with the other Party on the subject, including the development of procedures that may be appropriate. On such a request, the Parties shall promptly enter into consultations with a view towards allowing such a claim and establishing such procedures'.

contrary to the position expressed by both the Commission and the Council.[27] Moreover, the exclusion of investment arbitration in certain agreements that could deserve such a solution (as the EU-US Transatlantic Trade and Investment Partnership—TTIP) would hinder the inclusion of such an ISDS mechanism with other countries.

However, investment arbitration is the subject of a lively debate within the framework of TTIP negotiations both within the European Parliament and public opinion. Suffice it to recall a Parliament resolution concerning the TTIP adopted on July 2015. Although accepting the possible inclusion of an arbitration mechanism to resolve investor-State disputes, it recommended:

> to replace the ISDS system with a new system for resolving disputes between investors and states which is subject to democratic principles and scrutiny, where potential cases are treated in a transparent manner by publicly appointed, independent professional judges in public hearings and which includes an appellate mechanism, where consistency of judicial decisions is ensured, the jurisdiction of courts of the EU and of the Member States is respected, and where private interests cannot undermine public policy objective.[28]

The approach towards some of the concerns raised by the European Parliament and their content in future EU agreements is a distinct question. The issues related to this approach will be discussed below.

B. Compatibility of Investor-State Arbitration with EU Law

The inclusion of investor-State arbitration mechanisms in future investment agreements evidently assumes that an arbitration tribunal could consider an EU law measure to be contrary to the protection standards enshrined in such agreements. In our view, those mechanisms would not undermine the autonomy of EU law, nor the exclusive jurisdiction of the ECJ in order to ensure such autonomy.[29] As the ECJ itself pointed out in its Opinion 1/91, an international agreement providing

[27] In its Communication 'Towards a comprehensive European international investment policy', n 6 above, the European Commission states that the investor-State dispute settlement 'forms a key part of the inheritance that the Union receives from Member State BITs' (COM(2010) 343 final) at p 9; see also the memorandum of its Proposal for a Regulation establishing a framework for managing financial responsibility linked to investor-state dispute settlement tribunals, n 10 above (COM(2012) 335 final, p 3). As regards the Council of the EU, in its 'Conclusions on a comprehensive European international investment policy', n 11 above, it considers equally necessary 'an effective investor-to-state dispute settlement mechanism in the EU investment agreements' (para 18) and claims that 'the creation of a common EU international investment policy should increase the current level of protection and legal security for the European investor abroad' (para 8).

[28] European Parliament resolution of 8 July 2015 containing the European Parliament's recommendations to the European Commission on the negotiations for the Transatlantic Trade and Investment Partnership (TTIP) (2014/2228(INI)), para (d).(xv).

[29] A summary of this discussion is found in I Pernice, 'Study on International Investment Protection Agreements and EU Law' in *Investor-State Dispute Settlement (ISDS) Provisions in the EU's International Investments Agreements*, vol 2, part III (European Parliament, Directorate-General for External Relations, 2014) 132, 145 ff.

for its own system of courts, 'including a court with jurisdiction to settle disputes between the Contracting Parties to the agreement, and, as a result, to interpret its provisions' is in principle compatible with Community law.[30] Albeit true that the ECJ sets a limit, ie that the system of courts 'will not have the effect of binding the Community and its institutions, in the exercise of their internal powers, to a particular interpretation of the rules of Community law referred to in that agreement'.[31] Naturally, the ECJ also rejects the possibility that a tribunal established by an international agreement could affect its exclusive jurisdiction to review the legality of the acts of the institutions.[32]

I do not see how investment arbitration could interfere with the autonomy of EU law.[33] It is true that most BITs designate as applicable law for investor-State dispute settlement not only the provisions of the agreement itself and the relevant international law rules, but also the law of the host State.[34] But the national law of the respondent (host country) only applies in order to establish the facts or to interpret, where relevant, the domestic rules contested by the investor.[35] Let us think, for example, of a claim based on discriminatory treatment with respect to nationals.[36]

[30] Opinion 1/91, of 14 December 1991, *relating to the creation of the European Economic Area*, paras 39 and 40.

[31] Opinion 1/00, of 18 April 2002, *on the establishment of a European Common Aviation Area*, para 13. See also Opinion 1/91, n 30 above, paras 41 ff; Opinion 1/92, of 10 April 1992, also *relating to the creation of the European Economic Area*, para 41; Opinion 1/09, of 8 March 2011, *relating to the creation of a Unified patent litigation system*, paras 78 ff; and Opinion 2/13, of 18 December 2014, *on the accession of the EU to the ECHR*, para 184.

[32] Opinion 1/09, n 31 above, para 78.

[33] See in this regard A Dimopoulos, 'The Involvement of the EU in Investor-State Dispute Settlement: a Question of Responsibilities' (2014) 51 *Common Market Law Review* 1671, 1697 ff.

[34] See in this respect Reinisch, 'The Division of powers…', n 4 above, at p 37.

[35] However, Hindelang points to the 'factual effects' that the interpretation of the EU Law by arbitral tribunals could have, noting that such effects could also be deemed contrary to the principle of autonomy of EU law; likewise, he considers that the fact that they could call into question the compatibility of an act of the EU with the relevant agreement might go against the monopoly of the ECJ to review the legality of acts and measures of other EU institutions. See S Hindelang, 'The Autonomy of the European Legal Order. EU Constitutional Limits to Investor-State Arbitration on the Basis of the Future EU Investment-Related Agreement' in *Common Commercial Policy after Lisbon, European Yearbook of International Economic Law* (n 14 above) 187, 194. See also N Lavranos, 'Designing an International Investor-to-State Arbitration System After Opinion 1/09', ibid, 199, 215; M Burgstaller, 'Investor-State Arbitration in EU International Investment Agreements with Third States' (2012) 39 *Legal Issues of Economic Integration* 207; M Parish, 'International Courts and the European Legal Order' (2012) 23 *European Journal of International Law* 141; S Schill, 'Luxembourg Limits: Conditions for Investor-State Dispute Settlement under Future EU Investment Agreements' in (Bungenberg, Reinisch and Tietje (eds), *EU and investment agreements* (Baden-Baden, Nomos, 2013) 37; and FJ Pascual Vives, 'Shaping the EU Investment regime: Choice of *Forum* and Applicable Law in International Investment Agreements?' (2014) 6 *Cuadernos de Derecho Transnacional* 269, 287.

[36] See, inter alia, the decision by the Annulment Committee of 5 February 2002 in *Wena v Egypt* (ICISID No ARB/98/4, paras 26 ff; in (2002) 41 *ILM* 933). In any case, there is no doubt that in the event of conflict, the provisions of the BIT and the rules of international law prevail over the municipal law of the State of the investor. Therefore, as Prosper Weil has pointed out, efforts to define the respective roles of domestic and international law are ultimately useless: see 'The State, the Foreign Investor and International Law: The No Longer Stormy Relationship of a *Ménage à Trois*'(2000) 15 *ICSID Review* 401, 409. See also in this regard the decision of the Annulment Committee in *Wena v Egypt*, above. In spite of attributing in principle a merely supplementary role to International Law with respect to municipal law of the host state, the annulment decision of 16 May 1986 in *Amco Asia v*

Thus, the interpretation of a Union measure by an arbitration tribunal in order to determine its compatibility with the relevant investment agreement would not have a binding effect on the Union and its institutions in the exercise of their internal powers.

It would be different if the role of arbitration tribunals were to attribute international responsibility for the treaty violation either to the EU or to its Member States. This possibility must be sternly rejected.[37] It should so be foreseen both in investment agreements and in EU dispositions on the subject (ie the Regulation on financial responsibility proposed by the Commission).

On a different note, it should be taken into account that according to the system enshrined in Member States' BITs, arbitration tribunals could end up rendering awards declaring EU legislative acts incompatible with the relevant agreement, which involves choices of economic policy. That could be considered contrary to the ECJ case law, which establishes that the EU does not incur liability on account of such a legislative measure unless a sufficiently serious breach of a superior rule of law for the protection of the individual has occurred.[38]

The European Parliament has gone further to advocate in this respect that the Regulation Proposal on financial responsibility should include a new recital stating that future investment agreements to be concluded by the Union 'should respect those safeguards to the Union's legislative powers and should not establish stricter standards of liability allowing a circumvention of the standards defined by the Court of Justice'.[39]

Nevertheless, this issue is already arising with regards to BITs concluded by Member States. All of them grant considerable discretion to arbitration tribunals in order to rule on the compatibility with the agreement of any regulatory measure adopted by the host State, regardless of their connection with economic policy or of their goal to protect public goods such as the environment. Moreover, nothing

Indonesia (ICSID No ARB/81/1; see in (1986) 25 *ILM* 1439) also recognises its precedence over the latter in case of conflict: 'where the rules of the applicable domestic law are in collision with such norms [of International Law]' (para 20). The award of 5 June 1990 later rendered on that case recognises that 'international law is fully applicable and to classify its role as "only" "supplemental and corrective" seems a distinction without a difference' (partially reproduced in (1992) 17 *Yearbook of Commercial Arbitration* 73, at 75). The situation is different for arbitrations under BITs between EU Member States. Thus, in its decision of 30 November 2012 on jurisdiction, applicable law and liability in the *Electrabel SA v Hungary* case (ICSID No ARB/07/19), the arbitral Tribunal concluded that 'EU law (not limited to EU Treaties) forms part of the rules and principles of international law applicable to the Parties' dispute under Article 26(6) ECT' and that 'EU law, as part of the Respondent's national law, is also to be taken into account as a fact relevant to the Parties' dispute' (para 4.195).

[37] See Opinion 1/91, n 30 above, paras 34–35.

[38] See, for all, Judgment of the ECJ (Grand Chamber) of 9 September 2008 in Case C-120/06 and C-121/06 *Fabbrica italiana accumulatori motocarri Montecchio SpA (FIAMM) and Others v Council and Commission*, para 172, and Case C-119/88 *AERPO and others v Commission* judgment of the ECJ (First Chamber) of 6 June 1990, para 18.

[39] Amendment No 5 on the Proposal for a Regulation establishing a framework for managing financial responsibility linked to investor-state dispute settlement tribunals adopted by the European Parliament on 23 May 2013 (P7_TA(2013)0219, cited above), quoting the Judgment of the CJ in the *FIAMM case*.

within the framework of current BITs prevents a foreign investor from submitting an arbitration claim challenging national measures that simply enforce Union measures without leaving Member States with any room for discretion. We may think of European Commission decisions requiring the recovery of illegal state aid granted by Member States and the possible qualification of the implementing measures adopted by national authorities as contrary to the principle of fair and equitable treatment, for violating the investor's legitimate expectations.[40]

It is curious anyway that EU institutions should show such concern about the 'regulatory chill' risks associated with investment arbitration now that there is much internal debate on the potential responsibility of the EU itself under agreements to be concluded. However, many awards have already been rendered against third countries as a result of European investors' claims that challenge States' regulatory powers, even in situations of serious economic crisis. Some of the ICSID awards rendered against Argentina in recent years illustrate this point.

Be that as it may, the underlying debate is directly linked to the investment agreement model that should be promoted by the EU.[41] This issue will be addressed in the following section, although briefly, since it exceeds the scope of this work.

[40] See the Decision of 30 November 2012 on jurisdiction, applicable law and liability in the *Electrabel SA v Hungary* case, n 36 above, which arises from Hungary's alleged infringement of the ECT by withdrawing from a long-term power purchase agreement after the adoption in 2008 of a Decision by the European Commission, considering that such agreement entailed state aid contrary to the TFEU and required both the suspension of such aid and the recovery of the aid unduly received. In its decision, the Tribunal affirmed its jurisdiction on the grounds that: 'the Claimant is not here impugning the validity of the European Commission's Final Decision of 4 June 2008 under EU law or the ECT; nor is the Claimant attacking any act of the Commission (or other EU institution), whether by alleging any liability against the European Union (including the Commission) or by seeking to attribute liability to the Respondent for any act of the European Union' (para 5.34). The Tribunal pointed out in this respect that 'the Claimant's claim is limited to whether the Respondent's own acts in terminating the PPA violated the ECT' (ibid), on the understanding that, in its opinion, the Commission's decision did not necessarily imply the termination of the agreement.

The *Micula v Romania* case (ICSID No ARB/05/20), concerned a BIT concluded between Sweden and Romania. The defendant claimed that the suppression of incentives subject of the dispute was due to the obligation to comply with the EU State aid regime. Nevertheless, the Tribunal concluded in its decision of 11 December 2013 that EU Law was not applicable to the case because the facts were prior to the incorporation of Romania into the EU (paras 318 ff). According to Romania's claim – supported by the European Commission that took part in the proceedings as *amicus curiae* – should it be condemned, the enforcement of the award would imply a State aid contrary to the TFEU. The Tribunal limited itself to state that it would be 'inappropriate for the Tribunal to base its decisions in this case on matters of EU law that may come to apply after the Award has been rendered' (para 340). Following the issuance of the award, the European Commission has opposed its implementation by Romania as being contrary to Community rules on state aid (see European Commission, C(2014)6848 final, 1 October 2014). It is also worth mentioning the UNCITRAL arbitration in the *Binder v Czech Republic* case, where the arbitration tribunal rendered an award on jurisdiction (unpublished) on 6 June 2007 and an award on the merits (unpublished too) on June 2011.

For an analysis of these and other possible tensions between EU law and investment arbitration, see GA Bermann, 'Navigating EU Law and the Law of International Arbitration' (2012) 28 *Arbitration International* 397.

[41] See, *per omnia*, I Pernice, 'Study on International Investment Protection…', n 29 above, at 155 ff.

C. Towards a New Model of Investment Protection Agreements

Whilst both the Commission and the Council have called for keeping a high level of protection for European investors abroad, they agree with the European Parliament on the need to achieve in future treaties a balance between investor protection and the protection of the right to regulate. They also insist on the importance of BITs agreements being consistent with the different EU policies.[42]

The European Parliament underlines the regulatory capacity in fields such as the protection of national security, the environment, public health, workers' and consumers' rights, industrial policy and cultural diversity. It has even suggested deciding on a case-by-case basis on sectors not to be covered by future agreements.[43] It has also insisted on including in such agreements the needs of developing countries, especially regarding public services, and the requirement to be consistent with the principles guiding the EU's external action, including the promotion of human rights and sustainable development.[44]

New US and Canada Model BITs adopted in 2004[45] could serve as a source of inspiration.[46] In contrast to the BITs concluded by EU Member States, new US and Canada agreements offer a detailed and precise regulation that seek such balance between the need to protect investors and to preserve the host State's regulatory powers in the public interest.[47] The inclusion in these agreements of provisions setting a protection level similar to that granted by their own national tribunals deserves to be mentioned apart.[48] It is in this spirit that some authors have advocated the elaboration of detailed principles of investor protection

> not on the basis of existing BITs but on the basis of the rich experience with, and the detailed rules on, state liability in the legal systems of the countries with the highest level of investment protection and the most sophisticated balancing of private and public interest.[49]

[42] COM(2010) 343 final, n 6 above (pp 9–10). See also, inter alia, the Negotiating Mandates for investment protection chapters in free trade agreements with Canada, India and Singapore, cited above (Title 3A). See in this respect L Markert, 'The Crucial Question of the Future Investment Treaties: Balancing Investor's Rights and Regulatory Interests of Host States', *European Yearbook of International Economic Law* (*Special Issue: International Investment Law and EU Law*) n 4 above, 145.

[43] Resolution of 6 April 2011, n 21 above, paras 25–26.

[44] Ibid, paras 26, 27 and 37. See Woolcock and Kleinheisterkamp, 'The EU Approach…', n 4 above, at p 49.

[45] See US Model Bilateral Investment Treaty of 2004 revised in 2012 (www.state.gov/documents/organization/188371.pdfxxx); the US BIT model was revised in 2004 following several awards that put into question its regulatory power (see, for example, UNCITRAL Award of 3 August 2005 in the *Methanex Corporation v USA* case, rendered under NAFTA).

[46] The European Parliament took this view in its Resolution of 6 April 2011, n 21 above (recital H).

[47] See MA Clodfelter, 'The Future Direction of Investment Agreements in the European Union' (2014) 12 *Santa Clara Journal of International Law* 159, 165.

[48] See Kleinheisterkamp, *Financial Responsibility…*, n 25 above, at p 19.

[49] Ibid, p 24.

CETA and the Agreement with Singapore clearly respond to this approach.[50] Thus, in CETA, after stating in the preamble that the agreement preserves the right of the parties to regulate, several provisions considerably reduce the discretion of arbitral tribunals in determining the existence of a violation of the main standards of protection.

A special mention should be made to the CETA provisions regarding the obligation of fair and equitable treatment. Unlike most BITs in force, its investment chapter establishes a closed list of behaviours attributable to the host State (or EU) that can be considered as contrary to the said obligation (denial of justice, fundamental breach of due process, manifest arbitrariness, targeted discrimination on manifestly wrongful grounds, such as gender, race or religious belief), while strongly limiting the possibility of a successful claim based on an alleged violation of the legitimate expectations of the investor. In this respect CETA provides that:

> when applying the above fair and equitable treatment obligation, a tribunal may take into account whether a Party made a *specific representation* to an investor to induce a covered investment, that created a legitimate expectation, and upon which the investor relied in deciding to make or maintain the covered investment, but that the Party subsequently frustrated (emphasis added).[51]

As regards cases of 'indirect expropriation'—which require, as in the case of direct expropriation, the payment of a prompt, adequate and effective compensation—the provisions of CETA are based on the need to safeguard the regulatory power of the investment State (EU). Thus, in addition to requiring—in line with current arbitral 'case law'—that the measure or measures considered, 'substantially deprives the investor of the fundamental attributes of property in its investment, *including the right to use, enjoy and dispose of its investment, without formal transfer of title or outright seizure*' (emphasis added), CETA states that:

> except in the rare circumstance where the impact of the measure or series of measures is so severe in light of its purpose that it appears manifestly excessive, non-discriminatory measures of a Party that are designed and applied to protect legitimate public welfare objectives, such as health, safety and the environment, do not constitute indirect expropriations.[52]

In addition, following the example of the BITs concluded by the United States and Canada in recent years,[53] CETA contains a detailed account of measures taken

[50] See CETA consolidated text, dated 26 September 2014 (trade.ec.europa.eu/doclib/docs/2014/september/tradoc_152806.pdf) and Singapore Agreement, text dated May 2015 (trade.ec.europa.eu/doclib/press/index.cfm?id=961).

[51] CETA, Art X.9 of the consolidated text.

[52] Annex X.11 of the consolidated text.

[53] See, for instance, the BITS between US and Uruguay of 4 November 2005 and between Canada and Serbia of 1 September 2014.

by each of the parties prior to its conclusion, as well as sectors that are partially outside the scope of protection afforded to investors of the other party.[54]

On the other hand, CETA includes specific provisions regarding the possible restructuring of public debt. Specifically, it excludes the possibility that investors of the other party may have recourse to arbitration in the event that the restructuring has been negotiated in accordance with the provisions of the instrument of issuance, or that the restructuring has been accepted by holders representing the 75 per cent of the total amount, imposing in any case a cooling period (for consultation) of 270 days.[55] It is also important to consider the provision contained in CETA—that the Commission wishes to extend to other agreements concluded by the EU—by which the parties can adopt interpretations of the Agreement binding on the Arbitral Tribunals.[56] Besides this provision—based on Article 1131 of NAFTA and on BIT models the model of US and Canada, cited before[57]—CETA also envisages the creation of an appellate mechanism, as explained in the next section.

As we have seen, the changes that the EU may introduce in the scope of protection granted to investors by current BITs are certainly very relevant. But no less important is the revision of the current investment arbitration system that may arise from EU agreements.

D. A New Model of Investment Arbitration?

As noted above, the debate within the European Parliament and the public on the future European policy on investment protection is not limited to the substantive protection that should grant agreements concluded by the EU but also relates the current configuration of investment arbitration.[58]

The European Commission itself has not been immune to this debate but, on the contrary, has taken over some of the proposals made in Parliament and elsewhere. This is reflected in its document entitled 'Concept Paper. Investment in TTIP and beyond—the path for reform',[59] released in May 2015.

The 'Concept Paper' takes into account the results of the public consultation launched by the Commission in 2014 on the protection of investments in the framework of the TTIP[60] and the subsequent report made from the results of

[54] See Art X.14 of the consolidated text.

[55] Annex X of the consolidated text.

[56] See Art X.27 of the consolidated text.

[57] See NAFTA, Notes of Interpretation of Certain Chapter 11 Provisions, *NAFTA Free Trade Commission*, 31 July 2001 (www.sice.oas.org/tpd/nafta/Commission/CH11understanding_e.asp).

[58] See, for example, S Hindelang, 'Study on Investor-State Dispute Settlement ("ISDS") and Alternatives of Dispute Resolution in International Investment Law' in *Investor-State Dispute Settlement (ISDS) Provisions in the EU's International Investments Agreements*, vol 2, n 29 above, at pp 46 ff.

[59] European Commission, Concept Paper. 'Investment in TTIP and beyond—the path for reform' (May 2015).

[60] trade.ec.europa.eu/consultations/index.cfm?consul_id=179.

the survey.[61] In this report the Commission identified three areas of reforms for investment arbitration: (i) the establishment and functioning of arbitral tribunals; (ii) the relationship between domestic judicial systems and ISDS; and (iii) the review of awards through an appellate mechanism.

Regarding the first point, the main reforms advocated by the Commission are the following:

— That all arbitrators shall be chosen from a roster list pre-established by the parties and that they all be qualified to hold judicial office in their home jurisdiction and experts in international law.
— That the president of the Arbitral Tribunal shall be chosen by the disputing parties (not by the arbitrators appointed by the parties) or, failing agreement, by an external actor (as the Secretary General of ICSID) among the members of the roster.[62]
— That arbitrators comply with the rules of the International Bar Association (IBA) on Conflict of Interest[63] or with a similar code of conduct, corresponding to the appointing authority (and not to rest of arbitrators) to decide whether here has been a conflict.[64] In this regard, the Commission questions the possibility of appointing arbitrators to persons acting as lawyers in other investment arbitrations. This possibility would be in practice excluded if the arbitrators were to be appointed from the aforementioned roster list.
— That the arbitral procedure is governed by the principle of full transparency, so that all pleadings and decisions, as well as the hearings are public. The Commission proposes in this regard to assume the UNCITRAL rules on Transparency in Investment Arbitrations.[65]
— In addition to the possibility for the Arbitral Tribunal to accept amicus curiae briefs—foreseen in the UNCITRAL rules on Transparency—the Commission proposes to confer the right on third parties 'with a direct and existing interest' to intervene in the proceedings.

As regards the relationship between judicial systems and the ISDS, the Commission focuses on two aspects: (i) the possibility of parallel proceedings undertaken before the courts of the investment State and an Arbitral Tribunal; and (ii) that the Arbitral Tribunals respect the autonomy of EU law.

The 'Concept Paper' supports the 'fork-in-the-road' model but also welcomes the approach called 'no u-turn' (both explained above). The Commission seems

[61] Doc SWD(2015), of 31 January 2015, p 30.

[62] CETA provides that the 'roster list' only obliges the Secretary General of ICSID as appointing authority in the absence of agreement between the parties, and excludes Canadians and nationals of Member States from being President. However, it requires all members of Arbitral Tribunals to be experts in International Law; see Art X.25 of the consolidated text.

[63] IBA Guidelines on Conflict of Interest in International Arbitration of 2014. See Art X.25 of CETA consolidated text.

[64] See in this sense Art X.25 of CETA consolidated text, n 62 above above.

[65] UNCITRAL Rules on Transparency in Treaty-based Investor-State Arbitration of 2014.

to even show a preference for the latter formula—envisaged both in CETA and the Agreement with Singapore[66]—insofar as it favours the investor's recourse to national courts.

As for the fear—in my opinion unfounded—that the awards may interfere with the autonomy of EU law, the Commission proposes that the agreements concluded by the EU explicitly rule out the jurisdiction of the Arbitral Tribunals to apply the law of the investment State (or EU). It also advocates the inclusion therein of a provision clarifying that the EU Law should only be taken into account when establishing the facts giving rise to the dispute, and that any interpretation of an internal rule by an Arbitral Tribunal would not be binding on the courts of the parties.[67] In the case of CETA and the Agreement with Singapore, the formula has been to delete any reference to the domestic laws of the parties as the law applicable to the resolution of disputes.[68]

Along with the above proposals, it is important to mention another one aimed at preventing investors from abusing the system. In this regard, the 'Concept Paper' refers to the need to combat 'forum shopping', a practice followed by some multinational companies seeking to channel their complaints through the most favourable BIT. This objective can be achieved in various ways currently, such as through corporate restructurings or claiming intermediary companies that are simple vehicles for an investment and do not develop any real economic activity ('mail box companies'). For this purpose, CETA includes a provision limiting the scope of protection to companies of one party that have substantial activity in the territory of the other party.[69]

It is also worth mentioning the idea of introducing in the EU agreement mechanisms to combat unfounded or 'frivolous' claims. In this sense, CETA includes an 'early dismissal' mechanism regarding claims that are both 'manifestly without legal merit' and 'unfounded as a matter of law', namely the possibility that the defendant may raise an objection (within a period of 30 days from the constitution of the tribunal if it considers the request for arbitration 'without legal merit', or before the deadline fixed to file the statement of defence in the second case).[70] CETA also introduces the principle of 'loser pays', under which the plaintiff should bear the costs of arbitration if claim was rejected in its entirety.[71]

The possible introduction of a mechanism to review awards—already supported by the Commission in 2010, as well as by the European Parliament in 2011—is by far one of the most ambitious and controversial proposals referred to in the 'Concept Paper'.

There is no doubt that the creation of an appellate mechanism would introduce greater predictability in the system for both investors and the investment States

[66] Art X.22 of CETA consolidated text and Art 9.17 of the Agreement with Singapore.

[67] See above section II.B of this chapter.

[68] See Art 10.27 of CETA and Art 9.19 of the Agreement with Singapore.

[69] Art X.10 of the consolidated text.

[70] Arts X.29 and X.20 of the consolidated text.

[71] Art X.36 of the consolidated text.

and greater coherence in the arbitral 'case law'. Indeed, a permanent body would be competent to review awards as regards any error of law and manifest errors in the assessment of the facts. These reasons largely explain the broad support for the proposal in the public consultation organised by the Commission, referred to before, both by the business sector (a part of it) and NGOs. But the most compelling reason is the desire of many sectors of civil society and some States to give greater legitimacy to investment arbitration.[72] The 'Concept Paper' indicates in this regard that 'the right of appeal must be part of any legal or quasi-legal system … where issues pertaining to public policy may be at stake' and emphasises the mechanism of appointment of its members and their qualifications, suggesting that the model of the Appellate Body of the World Trade Organization be followed.

The creation of an appeal mechanism, like many of the other proposals of the Commission, seeks the judicialisation of the system (moving away from international commercial arbitration). There are strong reasons in favour of this option, but it risks reducing the incentives that the system currently provides for undertaking investment abroad. It seems that in the design of the European investment policy that is being carried out by the European Commission—under pressure from the European Parliament and of very active sectors of civil society—the EU perspective as a possible defendant prevails over the interests of European investors. The claim in recent years against some EU Member States (such as Germany or Spain)[73] plays against the interests of the latter.

In any case, the emergence of an appellate mechanism—to which States parties in the agreement (and the EU) would resort systematically in the event of unfavourable awards—could make investment arbitration less attractive for investors. First, there is the issue of time. Note that, in the case of ICSID, the average length of arbitral proceedings has fallen currently to three and a half years,[74] not considering the possibility of an annulment action. Secondly, there are cost-related concerns. As regards costs for investment States (and the EU), it should be noted that it is difficult to imagine the creation of a multilateral appeal body that serves the entire system. Consequently, the Commission favours the creation of bilateral bodies under the various agreements entered into by the Union. In its 'Concept Paper', the Commission refers to bodies composed of seven permanent members, of which two would be nationals of each party and three non-nationals.

The difficulties in the implementation of an appeal mechanism explain why the agreements with Canada and Singapore only include 'rendez-vous' clauses, in

[72] See N Hachez and J Wouters, 'International Investment Dispute Settlement in The 21st Century: Does the Preservation of the Public Interest Require an Alternative to the Arbitral Model?', Leuven Center for Global Governance Studies, Working Paper No 81, February 2012.

[73] In consideration of the *Vattenfall* cases against Germany (ICSID No ARB/09/6, settled by agreement embodied in an award by consent of 11 March 2011, and No ARB/12/12), and the numerous arbitral claims against Spain as a consequence of the regulatory changes in the field of renewable energy.

[74] ICSID, 2014 Annual Report (Washington DC, August 2014) at p 30.

which the parties agree to continue negotiations on this issue.[75] In the case of TTIP, despite the fact that the negotiating mandate approved by the EU Council in 2013 provides for the possible inclusion in the agreement of such a mechanism,[76] We can not anticipate if negotiators will be able to go further.

III. PROBLEMS POSED BY THE PARTICIPATION OF THE EU IN INVESTOR-STATE ARBITRATION

A. Who Should be Held Internationally Responsible for the Violation of Future Investment Protection Agreements?

i. The Commission's Position

Inasmuch as future investment agreements were only concluded by the EU (and not as 'mixed agreements'), there is no doubt that international liability would lie with the EU at all events. It is a different issue altogether that, in accordance with relevant ECJ case law, the Member States are obliged to comply with its provisions as part of EU law. As pointed out by the ECJ in the *Demirel* case,

> in ensuring compliance with commitments arising from an agreement concluded by the Community institutions, the Member States fulfil, within the Community system, an obligation in relation to the Community, which has assumed responsibility for the due performance of the agreement.[77]

Consequently, the Commission could start an infringement procedure against a Member State as a result of any measure taken in violation of the mentioned agreements.[78]

However, the issue at stake is whether the future agreements should be purely EU agreements, as we have already discussed. Even admitting that the external competence of the EU under article 207 TFEU covers the whole of its contents (not being the case in our understanding), the presence of investor-State arbitration mechanisms entails configuring the agreements as mixed agreements. It should be noted that the majority of claims that could be brought by foreign

[75] See Art X.42 of CETA consolidated text and Art 9.30 of the Agreement with Singapore.

[76] Negotiating Mandate approved by the General Affairs Council of 14 June 2013, n 12 above.

[77] Judgment of the ECJ of 30 September 1987 in Case 12/86 *Demirel v Stadt Schwäbisch-Mundt* [1987] ECR 3719 (para 11). See also judgments of the ECJ of 19 March 2002 in Case C-13/00 *Commission v Ireland* [2002] ECR I-2943 (para 15) and of 7 October 2004 in Case C-239/03 *Commission v France* [2004] ECR I-9325 (para 26). In its judgment of 26 October 1982 in Case 104/81 *Hauptzollamt Mainz v CA Kupferberg & Cie KG aA* [1982] ECR 3641, the Tribunal was a less accurate when stating that: 'In ensuring respect for commitments arising from an agreement concluded by the Community institutions the Member States fulfil an obligation not only in relation to the non-member country concerned but also and above all in relation to the Community which has assumed responsibility for the due performance of the agreement' (para 13).

[78] See again judgment of 7 October 2004 in the *Commission v France* case, n 77 above, paras 22 ff.

investors would arise from measures taken by Member States, given the internal allocation of competences that governs the Union's competence system.

The above considerations do not seem to have shaped the view of the Commission. In its Regulation Proposal on financial responsibility it considers that international responsibility for the breach of a future investment agreement concluded by the European Union 'has to be decided not by the author of the act, but on the basis of the competence for the subject matter of the international rules in question, as set down in the Treaty', underlining that in this regard 'it is immaterial that a Member State has competence under the rules on the internal market allowing it to legislate in its domestic sphere'.[79] The Commission's starting point regarding investments is that Article 207 decouples the external and internal competences of the EU in a way that those competences would cover every aspect relative to investment protection in the external sphere. This is a stance that I do not share, but the issue will not be analysed further in this paper.

Notwithstanding the foregoing, in its Proposal the Commission understands that 'it would be appropriate that each Member State bears financial responsibility for its own acts, unless such acts are required by Union law',[80] favouring the separation between international responsibility and internal responsibility. This approach is followed by Regulation No 912/2014, the content of which essentially reproduces the Commission proposal. We will refer to it in section 3.1.4.

ii. The International Law Perspective

The possibility of decoupling international and internal liability is not strange to those States with a complex structure. For instance, Article 104a(6) of the German Constitution provides that the Federation and the Länder shall bear the costs entailed by a violation of obligations incumbent on Germany under supranational or International Law in accord with the internal allocation of competencies and responsibilities.[81]

[79] COM(2012) 335 final, n 10 above, p 4. In support of its position, the Commission cites Opinion 1/91 of the ECJ, n 30 above, which in para 33 states that: 'The expression "Contracting Parties" is defined in Article 2(c) of the agreement. As far as the Community and its Member States are concerned, it covers the Community and the Member States, or the Community, or the Member States, depending on the case. Which of the three possibilities is to be chosen is to be deduced in each case from the relevant provisions of the agreement and from the respective competences of the Community and the Member States as they follow from the EEC Treaty and the ECSC Treaty'. As has been pointed out by C Tietje, E Sipiorski and G Töpfer (in *Responsibility in Investor-State Arbitration in the EU*, Study requested by the European Parliament's Committee on International Trade (PE 457.126), 2012 (p 16): 'although the European Court of Justice (ECJ) has indicated that international responsibility follows the division of competences between the EU and MS, it is questionable whether this will always lead to a clear situation in which the EU is always comprehensively externally responsible under public international law, whereas MS only internally might have financial responsibility'.

[80] The Commission specifies (COM(2012) 335 final, n 10 above, p 5).that: 'while, for the reasons set out above, the Union bears, in principle, international responsibility for the breach of any provision within the Union's competence, it is possible, as a matter of Union law, to provide for the allocation of financial responsibility between the Union and the Member States'.

[81] See Tietje, Sipiorski and Töpfer, *Responsibility in Investor-State-Arbitration*..., n 79 above, at pp 11–12.

In the same vein, Spain has introduced a mechanism in virtue of which the State can charge Autonomous Regions and local authorities for the amounts of the financial penalties that may be imposed by the EU related to their performance.[82]

However, what is far from settled is the assertion that the international liability for the breach of future investment agreements should rest upon the Union at all events. The 2011 ILC Draft Articles on the Responsibility of International Organizations might be instructive in this regard.[83] In accordance with Article 4, there is no doubt that the EU should be held liable for its agents' and bodies' behaviours found to be contrary to international law. However, if a Member State acts in a manner required by EU law, the Draft Articles opt for a possible joint responsibility.

Article 17(1) states that

> *an international organization incurs international responsibility* if it circumvents one of its international obligations by adopting a decision binding member States or international organizations to commit an act that would be internationally wrongful if committed by the former organization (emphasis added).

Nevertheless, paragraph (3) of the above-mentioned provision clarifies that this is the case regardless of whether the act in question is internationally wrongful for the Member States to which the decision is addressed.[84]

[82] See *Real Decreto* 515/2013, of 5 July 2013, *por el que se regulan los criterios y el procedimiento para determinar y repercutir las responsabilidades por incumplimiento del Derecho de la Unión Europea* (Bolet n Oficial del Estado of 6 July 2013).

[83] Draft Articles on the Responsibility of International Organizations, with Commentaries, adopted by the International Law Commission of the UN at its sixty-third session in second reading in 2011, A/66/10 (paras 77 ff) (published in *Yearbook of the ILC*, 2011, vol II, Part Two).

[84] See in this respect F Hoffmeister, 'Litigating against the European Union and Its Member States—Who Responds under the ILC's Draft Articles on International Responsibility of International Organizations?' (2010) 21 *European Journal of International Law* 723. See also commentary to Art 17 of the ILC Draft Articles on the Responsibility of International Organizations, n 83 above, from which we quote the following paragraphs:

'(5) In the case of a binding decision paragraph 1 does not stipulate as a precondition, for the international responsibility of an international organization to arise, that the required act be committed by member States or international organizations. Since compliance by members with a binding decision is to be expected, the likelihood of a third party being injured would then be high. It appears therefore preferable to hold the organization already responsible and thus allow the third party that would be injured to seek a remedy even before the act is committed. Moreover, if international responsibility arises at the time of the taking of the decision, the international organization would have to refrain from placing its members in the uncomfortable position of either infringing their obligations under the decision or causing the international responsibility of the international organization, as well as possibly incurring their own responsibility.

(6) A member State or international organization may be given discretion with regard to implementation of a binding decision adopted by an international organization. In its judgment on the merits in *Bosphorus Hava Yollari Turizm ve Ticaret AS v. Ireland*, the European Court of Human Rights considered conduct that member States of the European Community take when implementing binding EC acts and observed: "[...] [A] State would be fully responsible under the Convention for all acts falling outside its strict international legal obligations [...] [N]umerous Convention cases [...] confirm this. Each case (in particular, *Cantoni* at para. 26) concerned a review by this Court of the exercise of State discretion for which Community law provided."

Attention should be drawn to the fact that the ILC does not reflect the Commission's proposal to add a special rule by virtue of which, where Member States lack discretion in implementing an obligation under EU law, responsibility for their conduct should be attributed only to the EU.[85]

In addition, practice does not support the position of the Commission. It is true that in the *Protection of trademarks and geographical indications for agricultural products* case the WTO Panel accepted the explanation given by the European Commission according to which the enforcement of EU law through recourse to the authorities of its Member States means that these authorities act de facto as bodies of the Union, for which the Union would be responsible under WTO law and international law in general.[86] Even so, no definitive conclusion should be drawn either from this Report or from any other within the scope of the WTO's dispute settlement system. In fact, nothing prevents the WTO Members from presenting claims only against EU Member States, even when measures that have been taken by the EU in exercising exclusive competences are at stake. Nevertheless, in practice, the European Commission intervenes as co-defendant supporting a pragmatic solution that sets aside the internal competence discussion, which has the support of third countries that act as claimants.[87]

The situation is completely different as regards the European Court of Human Rights (ECtHR). It will suffice to mention the ruling on the *Bosphorus* case, in which, referring to measures implemented by the Irish authorities pursuant to an EU Regulation which left no margin of discretion whatsoever, the ECtHR stated that a Contracting Party is responsible 'for all acts and omissions of its organs regardless of whether the act or omission in question was a consequence of domestic law or the necessity to comply with international legal obligations'.[88] A different

(7) Paragraph 1 assumes that compliance with the binding decision of the international organization necessarily entails circumvention of one of its international obligations. As was noted in a statement in the Sixth Committee by the delegation of Denmark on behalf of the five Nordic countries: "[...] it appeared essential to find the point where the member State could be said to have so little 'room for manoeuvre' that it would seem unreasonable to make it solely responsible for certain conduct." Should on the contrary the decision allow the member State or international organization some discretion to take an alternative course which does not imply circumvention, responsibility could arise for the international organization that has taken the decision only if circumvention actually occurs, as stated in paragraph 2'.

Art 19 of the Draft Articles should also be borne in mind, since it establishes that 'This chapter is without prejudice to the international responsibility of the State or international organization which commits the act in question, or of any other State or international organization'.

[85] See G Gaja, *Seventh Report on Responsibility of International Organizations* (ILC, 2009), A/CN.4/610, paras 31 ff. See *Yearbook of the International Law Commission 2009*, vol II Part 1, p 73.

[86] WTO, *Protection of trademarks and geographical indications for agricultural products and foodstuffs*, Report of the Panel of 15 March 2005 (WT/DS174/R, para 7.98). See in the same sense WTO, European Communities—Measures Affecting the Approval and Marketing of Biotech Products, Report of the Panel of 29 September 2006 (WT/DS291/R, WT/DS292/R and WT/DS293/R, para 7.101).

[87] See I Blázquez, *Integración europea y diferencias comerciales en la OMC* (Madrid, Marcial Pons, 2006) 332 ff.

[88] In its unanimous judgment on the merits of 30 June 2005 in the case *Bosphorus Hava Yollari Turizm ve Ticaret AS v Ireland* (Application No 45036/98), the Grand Chamber of the European Court

question is whether the European court has adopted a deferential attitude towards the EU, in particular towards its Court of Justice. As is well known, while the ECHR acknowledges that the standard of protection of human rights granted by the EU is equivalent to the one provided by the European Convention on Human Rights, it presumes that a State has not deviated from the requirements of the Convention when it does no more than implementing legal obligations flowing from its EU membership.[89] This is a case law doctrine that will hardly be maintained, in my view, when the accession of the EU to the ECHR takes place.

One could consider invoking Article 64 of the ILC Draft, which preserves the possibility of having special rules of international law applicable to an international organisation, and notes that 'such special rules of international law may be contained in the rules of the organization applicable to the relations between an international organization and its members'.[90] However, it is unreasonable to think that the rules that govern the allocation of competences between the EU and its Member States constitute a *lex specialis* regarding international responsibility that can be invoked against third countries. It would be different if the Member States along with the third countries ended up accepting (despite the fact that it would make no sense) that investment agreements had to be concluded as purely EU agreements[91] or if they agree on special rules with respect to allocation of responsibility.

iii. EU Law Does not Support the Position of the Commission Either

Not even from an EU law perspective is it possible to defend that the international responsibility for a breach of future investment agreements should rest upon the EU at all events. Therefore, it is also unreasonable to think that those agreements should be concluded as purely EU agreements.

of Human Rights held (para 137): 'In the present case it is not disputed that the act about which the applicant complained, the detention of the aircraft leased by it for a period of time, was implemented by the authorities of the respondent State on its territory following a decision to impound of the Irish Minister for Transport. In such circumstances the applicant company, as the addressee of the impugned act fell within the "jurisdiction" of the Irish State, with the consequence that its complaint about that act is compatible *ratione loci, personae and materiae with the provisions of the Convention*'. See also the Decision of the European Commission of Human Rights of 9 February 1990 in *M & Co v Germany* (Application No 13258/87) (1990) 64 DR 138 and Decision of the European Court of Human Rights in *Kokkelvisserij UA v Netherlands* of 20 January 2009 (Application No 13645/05).

[89] See its Judgment in *Bosphorus v Ireland*, n 88 above, paras 149 ff.

[90] See PJ Kuijper and E Paasivirta, 'Further Exploring International Responsibility: The European Community and the ILC's Project on Responsibility of International Organizations' (2004) 1 *International Organizations Law Review* 111, 127; and Hoffmeister, 'Litigating against the European Union…', n 84 above, at 739.

[91] As noted by G Gaja in the *Seventh Report on Responsibility of International Organizations*, n 85 above (fn 203): 'Supposing that an international organization accepts an obligation towards a third State to ensure a certain result and that this result is not achieved because of the conduct of one of its member States, the organization would incur responsibility under the general rules, even if the relevant conduct was attributed to the member State', whereas 'the member State would not incur responsibility if it has not acquired a parallel obligation under international law towards the third State'.

Independently of the realm of the Union's exclusive competence regarding foreign investment, it should be recalled that paragraph (6) of article 207 TFEU states that the exercise of the competences conferred by this Article 'shall not affect the delimitation of competences between the Union and the Member States, and shall not lead to harmonisation of legislative or regulatory provisions of the Member States in so far as the Treaties exclude such harmonisation'.[92]

However, if only the EU were to be held internationally liable for the breach of an investment agreement, being the only one able to act as respondent in the relevant arbitration, it could be sued by an investor for acts carried out by Member States within the sphere of their own competences. As a consequence, the Union should make them modify their acts in order to comply with the arbitration award. It should be pointed out that this award would be the result of an arbitration in which the Member State would not have conducted its own defence.

As several reputed authors have noted,

> the international responsibility of the EU with regard to a very broad investment agreement touches upon internal competence of the MS which may result in the consequence that MS law has to be changed (harmonized) because of the international responsibility of the EU', adding to this that 'changes would be contrary to Article 207(6).[93]

The Commission itself falls into a blatant contradiction in its Proposal Regulation on financial responsibility: while stating that international responsibility would lie with the Union at all events, it does not pretend that the Union shall act as respondent in every claim brought by third country investors. On the contrary, as we will explain in section III.B, the proposal—as well as the Regulation finally approved – provides for the possibility of having a Member State acting as respondent in disputes concerning, fully or partially, treatment afforded by it. This solution obviously assumes that future investment agreements should be concluded as 'mixed agreements'.[94]

Needless to say, there is no way to understand that there is an 'arbitration agreement' in place between a foreign investor and a Member State within the framework of an investment agreement concluded only by the Union.

iv. Regulation No 912/2014

As indicated above, problems relating to liability for violation of future investment agreements are addressed in Regulation No 912/2014 based on the dissociation between international and internal responsibility (leaving unresolved who bears

[92] As regards Art 207(6) TFEU, see W Weiß, 'Common Commercial Policy in the European Constitutional Area: EU External Trade Competence and the Lisbon Decision of the German Constitutional Court' in *Common Commercial Policy after Lisbon, European Yearbook of International Economic Law* (Special Issue n 14 above) 29, 34.

[93] In this sense, Tietje, Sipiorski and Töpfer, *Responsibility in Investor-State-Arbitration in the EU*, n 79 above, at p 17.

[94] See Kleinheisterkamp, *Financial Responsibility...*, n 25 above, at p 7.

international responsibility in each case).[95] And so, after proclaiming in Article 1 that 'the adoption and application of this Regulation shall be without prejudice to the division of powers established by the Treaties', the Regulation provides in Article 3 the following allocation criteria proposed by the European Commission:

> 1. Financial responsibility arising from a dispute under an agreement shall be apportioned in accordance with the following criteria:
>
> (a) the Union shall bear the financial responsibility arising from treatment afforded by the institutions, bodies, offices or agencies of the Union;
> (b) the Member State concerned shall bear the financial responsibility arising from treatment afforded by that Member State;
> (c) by way of exception to point (b), the Union shall bear the financial responsibility arising from treatment afforded by a Member State where such treatment was required by Union law
>
> Notwithstanding point (c) of the first subparagraph, where the Member State concerned is required to act pursuant to Union law in order to remedy the inconsistency with Union law of a prior act, that Member State shall be financially responsible unless such prior act was required by Union law.

Furthermore, Regulation No 912/2014 gives decision-making powers to the European Commission in determining financial responsibility in accordance with such allocation criteria where the EU acts as respondent (Articles 3(2) and 19). It also provides that the Member State shall bear financial responsibility where the EU is the respondent and the State accepts potential responsibility during the proceedings (Article 3(3)).

Certainly, it will not always be easy to decide who bears the financial responsibility in the first case, especially if the measures that were declared incompatible with the investment agreement had been adopted by a Member State in the implementation of an act of the Union institutions—Let's say, for instance, in transposing measures of an EU directive.[96]

However we should not forget that any decision adopted by the Commission would be the subject of an action before the ECJ.[97]

B. What is the Role of the EU and its Member States in Investor-State Arbitration?

i. The Commission's Proposal

The Regulation Proposal on financial responsibility did not specify precise rules on the participation of the EU and its Member States in investor-State arbitration.

[95] See A Dimopoulos, 'The Involvement of the EU…', n 33 above, pp 1677 ff.

[96] See Tietje, Sipiorski and Töpfer, *Responsibility in Investor-State-Arbitration in the EU*, n 79 above, at p 22.

[97] See in this respect A Dimopoulos, 'The Involvement of the EU…' n 33 above, pp 1706 ff.

Article 4 provided that it should be the Union who acts as respondent where the dispute concerns treatment afforded by the institutions, bodies or agencies of the Union. Nonetheless, it also provided for the possibility of the EU acting as respondent in any other cases. Indeed, in conformity with Article 8 of the Proposal, the EU should act as respondent in disputes concerning treatment afforded by a Member State as long as the latter does not intend to act as respondent or in the event that the Commission decides so, taking into consideration certain circumstances that would allegedly justify it.

With regards to the second scenario, according to the Proposal the Commission could decide that the Union shall act as respondent where one or more of the circumstances listed in paragraph (2) occur:

(a) it is likely that the Union would bear at least part of the potential financial responsibility arising from the dispute …;[98]
(b) the dispute also concerns treatment afforded by the institutions, bodies or agencies of the Union;
(c) it is likely that similar claims will be brought under the same agreement against treatment afforded by other Member States and the Commission is best placed to ensure an effective and consistent defence; or,
(d) the dispute raises unsettled issues of law which may recur in other disputes under the same or other Union agreements concerning treatment afforded by the Union or other Member States.

Article 8(2) of the Proposal gave the Commission an enormous margin of discretion. Thus, pursuant to circumstances (a) and (b), the Commission would have the capacity to decide whether the EU acts as defendant as long as an EU measure is at stake, even if the final award could only assess a breach of the agreement resulting from measures undertaken by a Member State. However, in both circumstances the intervention of the Union could be justified: first, because its interests would be at stake, and secondly, as a means to ensure unity of external representation.[99]

It is harder, by contrast, to find a proper justification for scenarios listed in subparagraphs (c) and (d)[100] since they would give the chance to the Commission to act even when the dispute does not relate prima facie to EU law. In addition, by providing for EU action just because there could be other similar claims or issues of law which may recur in other disputes, the proposal started from a wrong premise: that arbitration tribunals are subject to precedent.

In any case, the Commission proposal posed, in my judgement, more problems than it intended to resolve.

First, it would lead to situations in which a Member State could not be able to conduct its own defence in relation to measures that fall outside of the scope of EU competences and despite having to assume financial responsibility resulting from

[98] See Art 3 of the Regulation quoted above in Section III.A.(iv).

[99] See to this effect COM(2012) 335 final, n 10 above, at p 7.

[100] The Commission also tries to justify subparagraphs (c) and (d) upon the need to ensure unity of external representation (ibid).

an award rendered against it.[101] It would be a different matter if the Member State did not confirm to the Commission in writing that it intends to act as respondent. In this scenario, it should be understood that the Member State waives the right to its defence bearing the consequences of this decision.

It could be considered that the first problem laid out would have been solved by the requirements of loyal cooperation—also addressed to the Commission[102]—resulting from article 4(3) TEU and complemented by the Regulation Proposal through mechanisms of consultation and joint implementation. It should be taken into consideration that, pursuant to Article 10 of the Proposal, where the Union is acting as a respondent, the Commission must prepare the defence in close cooperation with the Member State concerned. The latter may also form part of the Union delegation in the arbitration proceedings. Nevertheless, Article 10 did not ensure an adequate defence of the Member State—particularly so as regards Member State measures falling within the scope of EU law and considered by the Commission contrary to it.

Also, with respect to arbitration proceedings in which a Member State is a party, the Proposal went too far by providing in its Article 9(2) that 'the Commission may, at any time, require the Member State concerned to take a particular position as regards any point of law raised by the dispute or any other element having a Union interest'. The same applies to Article 9(3), which entitled the Commission to request the Member State to lodge an application for the annulment, appeal or review of the award, if such application is possible, 'where it considers that the consistency or correctness of the interpretation of the agreement so warrant'. It also stated that, in such circumstances, Commission representatives should form part of the delegation. On a general basis, even the obligation to provide the Commission with all documents relating to any proceeding in which a Member State is a party (Article 9(1)(a)) could be considered unjustified,[103] as would be the obligation to permit representatives of the Commission to form part of the delegation representing the Member State (Article 9(1)(c)), at least in the situations in which the dispute refers exclusively to the treatment afforded by the concerned Member State.

Be that as it may, the rules contained in the Regulation Proposal would not be enforceable against investors from third countries that are parties in future investment protection agreements, nor to the relevant arbitration tribunals if they were not covered by the agreement.[104] And it is probable that some of the

[101] Tietje, Sipiorski and Töpfer, *Responsibility in Investor-State-Arbitration in the EU*, n 79 above, at p 24.

[102] See Opinion 1/94 of the ECJ, of 15 November 1994, *on the Competence of the Community to conclude international agreements concerning services and the protection of intellectual property* (WTO), para 108, and Tietje, Sipiorski and Töpfer, n 79 above, p 23.

[103] Tietje, Sipiorski and Töpfer also note that the exchange of information may interfere with the respect for confidentiality in arbitral proceedings (n 79 above, p 22).

[104] In its Report on the proposal for a regulation establishing a framework for managing financial responsibility linked to investor-state dispute settlement tribunals of 26 March 2013, the Committee on International Trade of the European Parliament advocated the inclusion of a new paragraph 2a

solutions from the Proposal would not be accepted by the third countries that the Commission enters into negotiations with, particularly the provision of a possibly long waiting period if a Member State were to challenge the decision of the Commission on the status of respondent.

The third major problem that arises from the proposal is that the ICSID Convention is not open for the EU to participate in, and it is not easy to amend it to that effect. As a result, to the extent that future investment protection agreements provide for the participation of the EU in investor-State arbitration mechanisms, they could not provide only for recourse to ICSID arbitration.[105] As is generally known, ICSID arbitration has distinct advantages that make it a very attractive choice for European investors in claiming their rights against third countries, especially when it comes to enforcing awards.

The problem is really not in relation to other arbitration institutions, such as the ICC, nor with ad hoc arbitration pursuant to UNCITRAL rules, which are two other options offered to investors by BITs concluded by Member States (as well as the ICSID Additional Facility rules). The same applies to arbitration under ICSID Additional Facility Rules.[106]

Just as ICC arbitration and UNCITRAL rules are open to investor-State arbitration, we see no reason for these rules not to be applicable to settlement of disputes between the EU and foreign country investors.[107] The fact that the ICC Regulation or the UNCITRAL rules may require some kind of adaptation presents no particular problems.

ii. Regulation No 912/2014

The Legislative Resolution of the European Parliament concerning the Proposal Regulation on financial responsibility[108] and, as a consequence, Regulation No 912/2014 largely refocuses the European Commission's approach.

in Art 8 of the proposal, in the following terms: '2a. where the Union assumes to act as respondent pursuant to a decision of the Commission in accordance with paragraph 2 or the default rule set out in paragraph 1, such determination of the respondent status shall be binding on the claimant and the arbitration tribunal' (INTA Report A7-6124/2013, n 22 above; amendment No 24). This proposal is not contained in the European Parliament Legislative Resolution of 16 April 2014, n 15 above. The Commission's proposal went in the opposite direction, as appears from the first words of Art 8(1). See to this effect Kleinheisterkamp, *Financial Responsibility*..., n 25 above, at pp 8–9.

[105] See A Dimopoulos, 'The Involvement of the EU...', n 33 above, pp 1692 ff.

[106] See D Moura Vicente, 'El arbitraje de inversiones y las nuevas competencias de la Unión Europea conforme al art. 207 TFUE' (2012) V *Arbitraje. Revista de Arbitraje Comercial y de Inversiones* 759, 763.

[107] See ICC Commission Report: *States, States entities and ICC Arbitration*, (2012). In fact the 2012 ICC Rules of Arbitration contain provisions that are intended to facilitate the participation of states in ICC arbitration. As regards UNCITRAL Rules, nothing prevents their use by any type of entity, including private institutions or international organisations (see UNCITRAL Arbitration Rules as revised in 2010), as pointed out by Reinisch ('The EU on the Investment Path...', n 4 above, at p 19, fn 111), contrary to the European Parliament's view, which excludes it by mistakenly arguing that the EU is not part of the UN or UNCITRAL (European Parliament Resolution of 6 April 2011, n 21 above, para 33).

[108] Legislative Resolution of 16 April 2014, n 15 above.

The Regulation considerably reduces the Commission's margin of discretion in order to determine when the EU shall act as respondent in the event of disputes concerning treatment afforded by a Member State. In particular, it restricts that possibility to the following three cases:

— 'The Union would bear all or at least part of the potential financial responsibility arising from the dispute in accordance with the criteria laid down in Article 3' (Article 9(2)(a));
— 'The dispute also concerns treatment afforded by the institutions, bodies or agencies of the Union' (Article 9(2)(b)); and
— '[T]he Union is to act as the respondent where similar treatment is being challenged in a related claim against the Union in the WTO, where a panel has been established and the claim concerns the same specific legal issue, and where it is necessary to ensure a consistent argumentation in the WTO case' (Article 9(3)).

In addition, it requires the Commission to adopt its decision (within 45 days) following consultations with the affected Member State—'based on a full, balanced, factual analysis and legal reasoning provided to the Member States' according to the advisory procedure set forth in the 'comitology' Regulation in the first two cases and to the examination procedure in the third one (Article 9(2) and (3)).

Moreover, the Regulation also provides that the EU shall act as respondent when the Member State has notified the Commission in writing (within 45 days), and following consultations with the latter, that it does not intend to act as such (Article 9(1)(a)). By contrast, the Commission's proposal stipulated that the EU shall act as respondent if the Member State has not confirmed to the Commission that it intends to act as respondent (within 30 days) (Article 8(1)(a)).

As regards arbitration proceedings, the Regulation insists on the need to ensure close cooperation among the Commission and the Member States, taking due account not only of the interests of the EU but also of the Member States.[109] In this respect, we should highlight the inclusion of Article 6 that provides the following:

> (1) In accordance with the principle of sincere cooperation referred to in Article 4(3) TEU, the Commission and the Member State concerned shall take all necessary steps to defend and protect the interests of the Union and of the Member State concerned.
> (2) The Commission and the Member State concerned shall enter into consultations on the management of disputes pursuant to this Regulation, bearing in mind any deadlines set down in this Regulation and in the agreement concerned, and shall share with each other information where relevant to the conduct of disputes.

[109] See Art 9(4) and (6) and Arts10 and 11.

Concerning the settlement of disputes with foreign investors—which for reasons of space is not addressed in this study—the Regulation also reverses the excesses in the Commission's Proposal. Suffice it to mention that the Regulation suppressed the provision included in the Proposal providing that where the Member State wishes to settle the dispute in a dispute concerning exclusively treatment afforded by it, the Commission could oppose the agreement by claiming 'an overriding interest of the Union'.[110]

Notwithstanding the improvements made by the European Parliament and the Council on the Commission's Proposal, there are reasons to wonder if it was not possible to find more appropriate solutions. We have in mind especially the failed draft agreement on the accession of the EU to the European Convention for the Protection of Human Rights and, in particular, the co-respondent mechanism provided therein. It is true that this mechanism has been questioned by the ECJ in its Opinion 2/13 of 18 December 2014. However the objections raised by the Court could be easily saved in the field of investment arbitration.[111]

IV. EPILOGUE

Following the completion of this work, the European Union launched an investment chapter proposal for the TTIP (made public in November 2015) which presents some significant developments. In particular, it provides for the establishment of a First Instance Tribunal (in fact a list of arbitrators) composed of fifteen members appointed by the parties (five from the EU, five from the US and five from other countries). Under the proposal, for each dispute submitted to the Tribunal, its President should appoint three judges (a national of a Member State of the EU, a US national and a national of a third country, which would act as president) or, if the parties so agree, to a single judge (national of a third country). The proposal contains, as expected, the requirement that the members of the Tribunal qualified to be judges in their countries of origin (or deserve the consideration of 'jurists of recognised competence') and have demonstrated expertise in public international law.

In addition, the text presented by the EU also envisages the creation of an Appeal Tribunal composed of six members appointed by the parties (two nationals of EU Member States, two US nationals and two nationals from third countries) that would hear appeals from the awards issued by the Tribunal in chambers of three judges. The proposal provides that an appeal could be based not only on any of the grounds provided for in Article 52 of the ICSID Convention for the annulment of

[110] Art 14 of the Proposal. See Art 15 of the Regulation.
[111] Opinion 2/13, n 31 above (paras 215 ff).

an award, but also on an error in the interpretation or application of the law or on a manifest error in the appreciation of the facts. The appeals system provided for in the EU proposal rules out any other possibility of appeal, revision or annulment of the award.

Furthermore, the EU proposal for TTIP has resulted in a legal revision of the text of the CETA (the new version was published in February this year, 2016), which now also provides for the establishment of a (sort of) Permanent Tribunal and of an Appellate Tribunal.

15

From External Policy to Free Trade: The EU-Singapore Free Trade Agreement

ANTONIO SEGURA SERRANO*

Content:

I. INTRODUCTION

IN LESS THAN a decade, the EU has introduced a dramatic change in the approach initially taken in the field of international trade agreements with third parties. Originally, the EU (European Communities at the time) started with a practice consisting of negotiating agreements with ancient colonies of the European powers and other developing countries. These agreements necessarily took into account the extant economic situation of underdevelopment in these countries and were accordingly considered as part of the EU development policy. Similarly, the EU has also concluded international trade agreements with neighbouring countries, be they Eastern European nations or the group of countries on the Southern border of the Mediterranean. In both cases, there was a clear external policy-driven aim that justified the efforts made and often the economic facilities that those agreements entailed for third parties.

* Associate Professor of International Law and European Law, University of Granada.

However, the EU has radically changed its policy regarding these trade agreements with third countries. The intent and the rationale behind those agreements is not anymore animated by external policy interests, but by a solely economic interest consisting of gaining access to third-country markets and therefore benefiting the trade terms of the EU as a bloc. The legal instrument used by the EU is the so-called free trade agreement (FTA). FTAs are utilised by the EU either in relation to other regional economic blocs (often promoted by the EU itself)—and that is why they are called regional trade agreements (RTA)—or in relation to single countries in a more bilateral relationship. In fact, these bilateral FTAs are lately on the rise as the practice exemplified by the EU-Korea FTA (EUKFTA), the EU-Singapore FTA (EUSFTA) and the Comprehensive Economic and Trade Agreement (CETA) demonstrates. The EUSFTA was concluded only in December 2013, and other similar FTAs will follow suit. These recent FTAs are the central piece of the EU's 'deepening' approach regarding trade relations with third partners, whereby the EU seeks to foster economic integration through the incorporation of issues like services, competition and investment.

This chapter aims to briefly show the aforementioned change effected within the EU trade policy and to identify the logic behind it. It will then focus on the EUSFTA as one of the latest examples of this new and extremely economic-driven policy of the EU. A brief conclusion will evaluate this policy change undertaken by the EU and its possible consequences for the multilateral trading system at large.

II. THE EU'S FREE TRADE AGREEMENTS: POLICY IN MOTION

A. Outline of Agreements in Place

The EU's current trade agreements with third countries may be classified according to several criteria. Following a qualified description that takes into account their purpose, policy context, and the regulation of trade,[1] extant EU trade agreements could be ranged, together with those concluded with candidates and potential candidates, from those that group the different agreements concluded with neighbouring countries, to those where there is an underlying development objective, and finally the so-called 'global market access' agreements[2] that correspond to the new EU deep trade agenda.

[1] M Cremona, 'The European Union and Regional Trade Agreements' (2010) 1 *European Yearbook of International Economic Law* 245, 249; B Rigod, '"Global Europe": The EU's New Trade Policy in its Legal Context' (2012) 18 *Columbia Journal of European Law* 277, 282.

[2] See Cremona (n 1 above) 265.

First, leaving aside the Europe Association Agreements[3] and the Ankara Agreement with Turkey (establishing a customs union), the agreements with candidates and potential candidates to EU accession, such as the Stabilisation and Association Agreements (SAA) with the countries of the Western Balkans, are largely considered as FTAs. They include the liberalisation of trade in goods, but also an obligation to open up services and capital markets, together with provisions on competition policy and intellectual property.[4] Secondly, regarding the agreements concluded with neighbouring countries, the European Economic Area (EEA) agreement with Norway, Iceland and Liechtenstein is essentially an FTA that also extends the EU four freedoms to the EEA members, together with similar EU provisions on competition and State aid.[5] Similarly, the 1972 EU trade agreement with Switzerland provides for the liberalisation of trade in industrial goods, which has been improved by subsequent sectorial agreements covering, among other things, agricultural products, public procurement, and even free movement of persons. The Euro-Mediterranean Association (EMA) Agreements in force (with the Palestinian Authority, Tunisia, Morocco, Israel, Jordan, Egypt, Algeria and Lebanon) have been promoted by the Barcelona Conference since 1995 and provide for the establishment of a free trade area and the prospect of future liberalisation of trade in services and capital movement, launching a process of economic integration that could eventually lead to an EU-Mediterranean free trade area.[6] However, these EMA Agreements also establish a framework for political dialogue, and human, social and cultural dialogue, now integrated within the European Neighbourhood Policy (ENP) since 2004[7] and the Union for the Mediterranean process since 2008.[8] Finally, the Partnership and Cooperation Agreements (PCA) concluded with the states of the former Soviet Union are being terminated (they were concluded for 10-year periods) and replaced, at least for the states belonging to the ENP,[9] by new association agreements that are regarded by the EU Commission as 'deep and comprehensive free trade agreements' (DCFTA).[10] These DCFTAs

[3] These Europe Association Agreements served as a lever for the accession of the 10 countries of Central and Eastern Europe to the EU, and are now terminated.

[4] Roman Petrov, *Exporting the Acquis Communautaire through European Union External Agreements* (Baden-Baden, Nomos, 2011) 125.

[5] F Blankart, 'The European Economic Area, the bilateral agreements and Switzerland' in A Liebich and B Germond (eds), *Construire l'Europe: mélanges en hommage à Pierre du Bois* (Paris, Presses Universitaires de France, 2008) 189.

[6] European Commission and High Representative of the European Union for Foreign Affairs and Security Policy, 'A partnership for democracy and shared prosperity with the Southern Mediterranean', COM(2011) 200 final, 9, envisaging in the medium to long term the establishment of Deep and Comprehensive Free Trade Areas.

[7] European Commission and High Representative of the European Union for Foreign Affairs and Security Policy, 'A new response to a changing Neighbourhood', COM(2011) 303 final, setting out the main priorities and directions of a revitalised ENP strategy.

[8] S Blockmans and A Lazowski, *The European Union and Its Neighbours: A Legal Appraisal of the EU's Policies of Stabilisation, Partnership and Integration* (The Hague, TMC Asser Press, 2006).

[9] European Commission, 'Eastern Partnership', COM(2008) 823 final, 3.

[10] Ibid.

would entail not only the liberalisation of trade in goods (including regulatory approximation and mutual recognition), but also some liberalisation of services, establishment and capital. The EU has already concluded negotiations with Moldova, Georgia (both treaties provisionally apply since 1 September 2014), Armenia and Ukraine to set up an Association Agreement that encompasses a DCFTA,[11] although Armenia has decided to join the customs union of Russia, Belarus and Kazakhstan, and Ukraine suspended the preparations for signing, but later signed an Association Agreement with the EU in March 2014.[12]

Thirdly, the EU has concluded FTAs that also have a development objective. The European Partnership Agreements (EPA) with the seven regional groupings of African, Caribbean and Pacific (ACP) states are meant to replace the trade provisions of the Cotonou Convention concluded between the EU and 79 ACP states,[13] as the WTO waiver on the non-reciprocal preferences provided therein expired at the end of 2007. Starting in 2008, negotiations with ACP countries are under way with the aim of achieving WTO-compatible EPAs that will encompass reciprocal but asymmetric trade liberalisation. The only EPAs being applied are, first, the one with the CARIFORUM group of countries (a sub-group of the ACP Group comprising 16 Caribbean states, now completing the ratification process. The Pacific EPA as well as the Eastern and Southern African (ESA) EPA are also being implemented on an interim basis, and further progress is expected.[14] Negotiations have also been concluded with the Southern African Development Community's EPA group, the Eastern African Community, and West Africa (whose text was initialled on 10 July 2014). However, talks with the Central Africa region are delayed because of the current political conditions.[15]

There is a debate regarding the ability of FTAs,[16] and particularly EPAs,[17] to truly help achieve the aims of development cooperation. However, the EU considers[18]

[11] European Commission, 'The EU's bilateral trade and investment agreements—where are we?', 3 December 2013, at p 4, at: europa.eu/rapid/press-release_MEMO-13-1080_en.htm.

[12] Reuters, 'European Union signs landmark association agreement with Ukraine', 21 March 2014: www.reuters.com/article/2014/03/21/us-ukraine-crisis-eu-agreement-idUSBREA2K0JY20140321.

[13] As is well known, EU relations with the ACP group date back to the 1975 Lomé Convention, revised on four occasions until 1989. The Lomé Convention was replaced by the Cotonou Agreement in 2000, revised in 2005 in Luxembourg and in 2010 in Ouagadougou, and covers EU-ACP relations until 2020.

[14] K De Gucht, 'Economic Partnership Agreements (EPAs)—State of Play, Future Perspectives and Implementation', 11 October 2013, at: europa.eu/rapid/press-release_SPEECH-13-812_en.htm.

[15] European Commission, 'Overview of EPA Negotiations', 7 February 2014, at: trade.ec.europa.eu/doclib/docs/2009/september/tradoc_144912.2.14.pdf.

[16] E Valerdi Rodríguez, 'The European Union Free Trade Agreements: Implications for Developing Countries', *Real Instituto Elcano, Working Paper 8/2009*: www.realinstitutoelcano.org/wps/portal/rielcano_eng/Content?WCM_GLOBAL_CONTEXT=/elcano/elcano_in/zonas_in/europe/dt8-2009.

[17] M Geboye Desta, 'EC-ACP Economic Partnership Agreements and WTO Compatibility: An Experiment in North-South Interregional Agreements?' (2006) 43 *Common Market Law Review* 1343; R Perez, 'Are the Economic Partnership Agreements a First-best Optimum for the African Caribbean Pacific Countries?' (2006) 40 *Journal of World Trade* 999; J-J Hallaert, 'Economic Partnership Agreements: Tariff Cuts, Revenue Losses and Trade Diversion in Sub-Saharan Africa' (2010) 44 *Journal of World Trade* 223.

[18] European Commission, 'Trade, growth and development—Tailoring trade and investment policy for those countries most in need', COM(2012) 22 final, 2–3.

that trade is a powerful engine for development, which in turn accords to the EU principle of Policy Coherence for Development.[19] But also, effective development policy is critical in helping create better conditions for trade and investment in developing countries, as envisaged in the Agenda for Change.[20] EPAs are therefore regarded as instruments for development as much as they are trade agreements. In other words, EPAs are bilateral or regional trade agreements that aim to be comprehensive FTAs, but also modulated and tailor-made according to the level of development of each partner, introducing variable geometry or multiple-speed into the agreements.[21]

Finally, the EU has recently started to negotiate deep FTAs. Even if some EPAs have gone further than expected for a trade agreement that pursues development objectives,[22] the bulk of the EU deep trade agenda has been underway since 2006, following the Global Europe initiative.[23]

B. Rationale Behind the Policy Change

The Global Europe initiative has focused on enhanced market access, which works as the main rationale behind the change in the EU approach towards FTAs. Consequently, these agreements which are currently being negotiated and concluded are called either 'global', 'deep', or 'competitive' FTAs, reflecting the EU's policy shift in the trade arena.[24]

To start with, the aim of EU economic growth lies behind the Europe 2020s strategy,[25] which in turn ascribes a central role to EU trade policy.[26] In other words, boosting trade is nowadays considered one of the few means to bolster economic growth and create jobs within the EU.[27] In this respect, the Commission submits that the EU must remain open in the era of globalisation both because

[19] Article 208 of the Treaty of the Functioning of the European Union (TFEU) requires that the EU take into account the objectives of development cooperation, particularly poverty eradication, when it adopts policies that may affect developing countries.

[20] European Commission, 'Increasing the impact of EU Development Policy: an Agenda for Change', COM(2011) 637.

[21] European Commission (n 18 above) 13.

[22] Cremona (n 1 above) 265; Cf Rigod (n 1 above) 285, submitting that EPAs, PCAs and EMAs should clearly be assessed as a means of implementing foreign policy by using trade as leverage.

[23] European Commission, 'Global Europe: Competing in the World—A Contribution to the EU's Growth and Jobs Strategy', COM(2006) 567 final.

[24] Cf SJ Evenett, '"Global Europe": An Initial Assessment of the European Commission's New Trade Policy' (2006) 61 *Aussenwirtschaft* 384, submitting that the Global Europe initiative should be understood as an evolution rather than a revolution in the European Commission's thinking about the EU's external trade policy.

[25] European Commission, 'Europe 2020—A strategy for smart, sustainable and inclusive growth', COM(2010) 2020 final.

[26] European Commission, 'Trade, Growth and World Affairs—Trade Policy as a core component of the EU's 2020 strategy', COM(2010) 612 final.

[27] European Commission, Commission Staff Working Document 'External Sources of Growth—Progress report on EU trade and investment relationship with key economic partners', 18 July 2012, p 4: trade.ec.europa.eu/doclib/press/index.cfm?id=821.

it operates 'within a rules-based international framework',[28] where open and fair markets worldwide is the ultimate generally shared goal, and also in order to remain competitive.[29] However, at the same time the EU should not be naïve[30] and should assert itself more effectively on the world stage. The EU should seek to secure better market access for EU business, and a level playing-field regarding its external competitors.[31]

Secondly, the EU had systematically favoured the multilateral path towards the liberalisation of trade,[32] maintaining a de facto moratorium on preferential trade agreements.[33] The Doha Round was considered by the EU as a priority, mainly due to the expectation of reaping the benefits flowing from a global liberalisation similar to the one reached at the Uruguay Round negotiations. Therefore, FTAs were seen as a 'distraction from the far bigger prize of multilateral liberalisation'.[34] However, from the late 1990s the EU was unable to influence the multilateral trade agenda due both to opposition from leading developing countries and lack of support from the United States.[35] The Doha Round deadlock led the EU Commission to consider that the Doha negotiations would not deliver answers to the newer questions that international trade rules ought to take care of.[36] These issues are services, foreign direct investment (FDI), public procurement, competition, enforcement of intellectual property rights (IPR), together with regulatory barriers applicable thereto. Some of these issues are widely known as the 'Singapore issues',[37] which would not be agreed to within the WTO in the short to medium term,[38] and which reflect the trade policy challenges that the EU believes it needs to tackle as part of its smart growth.[39] Thus, the EU Commission submitted

[28] European Commission (n 25 above) 22–23.

[29] European Commission (n 23 above) 3–4, submitting that competitive markets within the EU Single Market, together with openness, are vital for the EU economic growth strategy to succeed.

[30] European Commission (n 26 above) 3.

[31] European Commission (n 25 above) 23.

[32] P Lamy, 'Stepping Stones or Stumbling Blocks? The EU's Approach towards the Problem of Multilateralism vs Regionalism in Trade Policy' (2002) 25 *The World Economy* 1412.

[33] S Woolcock, 'The EU and the Rise of Regionalism', *Working Paper No 2009/2, European Foreign Policy Unit*, London School of Economics (2009) 1.

[34] BA Melo Araujo, 'The EU's Deep Trade Agenda: Stumbling Block or Stepping Stone Towards Multilateral Liberalisation?' (2014) 5 *European Yearbook of International Economic Law* 272.

[35] Woolcock (n 33 above) 8.

[36] European Commission staff working document, Annex to the Communication from the Commission to the Council, the European Parliament, the European Economic and Social Committee and the Committee of the Regions, 'Global Europe: Competing in the World, A Contribution to the EU's Growth and Jobs Strategy', SEC(2006) 1230, p 9.

[37] At the WTO Ministerial Conference in Singapore four working groups were established on investment, competition, transparency in government procurement and trade facilitation: WTO, 'Singapore Ministerial Declaration', WT/MIN(96)/DEC, Singapore, 18 December 1996. However, developing countries were able to take off the agenda three out of those mentioned four issues in the so called 'July Package' (2004), leaving trade facilitation as the only one on the negotiating table: WTO, 'Doha Work Programme—Decision adopted by the General Council on 1 August 2004', WT/L/579, 2 August 2004, p 3.

[38] SJ Evenett, 'Five hypotheses concerning the fate of the Singapore issues in the Doha Round' (2007) 23 *Oxford Review of Economic Policy* 392.

[39] European Commission (n 26 above) 4–6; European Commission (n 23 above) 8.

in 2006 that 'FTAs, if approached with care, can build on WTO and other international rules by going further and faster ... by tackling issues which are not ready for multilateral discussion'.[40] Although still committed to the Doha Development Round, the Commission also declared in 2010 that the bilateral approach is not the enemy of the multilateral and that liberalisation fuels liberalisation, noting that a large part of the EU's energy would be spent on delivering FTAs.[41]

Thirdly, FTAs concluded by the EU before the Commission arrived at this new strategy, including those without a development oriented objective, did not serve the aim of furthering the EU's commercial interests and its economic growth.[42] To the contrary, and partially due to the EU exclusive competence in the field of external trade, EU foreign policy concerns fuelled the negotiation of FTAs, as seen above.[43] Politics rather than trade used to be behind most of EU FTAs, excepting the FTAs with Chile and Mexico, which were signed to offset the economic influence of the US and the North American Free Trade Agreement (NAFTA).[44] The European Commission therefore undertook that the new EU trade policy should incorporate a fresh wave of balanced FTAs. The EU's main trade interests were not well served by old FTAs so in order for trade policy to create growth, economic factors must play a pivotal role in the design of the next generation of FTAs. In particular, the Commission identified market potential and the level of protection against EU export interests as the key economic criteria that should drive eligibility regarding new FTA partners.[45]

Finally, as mentioned before, the new EU strategy regarding FTAs has to be evaluated against the EU's main competitors' practice. As noted,[46] already in 2006 the United States (and also Japan) had in place a trade policy focused on the negotiation of different FTAs, which was labelled as 'competitive liberalisation'.[47] Using its negotiating power, this policy aimed at putting in place a US-type of trade liberalisation.[48] This policy involved two kinds of competition: first, the US would be competing against other major economic powers through the negotiation of FTAs in order to regain its leadership in the trading system; secondly, trading partners would be competing against each other in order to have access to the US market

[40] European Commission (n 23 above) 8.

[41] European Commission (n 26 above) 3–4.

[42] European Commission (n 36 above) 9, stating that '[t]he current geography of EU FTAs mainly covers our neighbourhood and development objectives well, but our main trade interests less well'.

[43] O Cattaneo, 'The Political Economy of PTAs' in S Lester and B Mercurio (eds), *Bilateral and Regional Trade Agreements: Commentary and Analysis* (Oxford, OUP, 2009) 44–45.

[44] Woolcock (n 33 above) 5–6.

[45] European Commission (n 23 above) 8–9.

[46] Melo Araujo (n 34 above) 273.

[47] CF Bergsten, 'Competitive Liberalisation and Global Free Trade: A Vision for the Early 21st Century', *Working Paper no 96-15*, Institute for International Economics: www.iie.com/publications/wp/wp.cfm?ResearchID=171; SJ Evenett and M Meier, 'An Interim Assessment of the U.S. Trade Policy of "Competitive Liberalization"', *Discussion Paper no 2007-18*, University of St Gallen.

[48] A Sbragia, 'The EU, the US and Trade Policy: Competitive Interdependence in the Management of Globalisation' (2010) 17 *Journal of European Public Policy* 376–77.

on the basis of the depth of its commitments on market access.[49] With the US policy in mind, the EU could not but follow suit, if it did not want to experience new losses in market share for EU exporters.[50] Hence, FTAs are the latest protective tool used by the EU in order to avoid trade diversion affecting EU exporters and to restore the level playing-field in emerging markets with respect to the other big players.[51]

C. A New Generation of FTAs

Therefore, a new generation of global or 'deep' FTAs was felt to be necessary by the EU. However, the EU Global Europe initiative has developed two main indicators for prospective FTAs, ie market potential and protection against EU exporters,[52] which means that as opposed to the US approach, the EU will be selective in identifying its trade partners. First, market potential has to do with the size of the market and its prospective growth, which make emerging economies the natural objective of these new FTAs. Secondly, protection against EU export interests covers the new issues identified as the 'Singapore issues' or 'WTO-plus issues', ie, mainly non-tariff barriers (NTBs), services, intellectual property, public procurement, competition and investment.

Based on these criteria, the EU made a choice whereby ASEAN (Association of Southeast Asian Nations), Korea, MERCOSUR (Mercado Comun del Sur, comprising Argentina, Brazil, Paraguay, Uruguay and Venezuela), India, Russia and the Gulf Cooperation Council (even China, although recognising the difficulties) were initially selected as priorities for the launching of new negotiations.[53] However, the EU is only willing to invest its time and resources with those partners that have the same level of ambition 'to avoid the risk of negotiations later stalling because of a mismatch of expectations'.[54] Also, where those partners have already concluded FTAs with other countries that are competitors to the EU, the EU will expect no less than full parity in the trade concessions. Moreover, the EU assumes that different legal techniques, like regulatory convergence, mutual recognition, or regulatory transparency will be required for FTAs to address NTBs, depending on the partner.[55]

The EU has already concluded two global FTAs with Mexico and Chile. The agreement with Mexico is an Economic Partnership, Political Coordination and

[49] Evenett and Meier (n 47 above) 5, 20.
[50] European Commission (n 36 above) 9.
[51] Rigod (n 1 above) 289.
[52] European Commission (n 23 above) 9.
[53] Ibid.
[54] European Commission (n 36 above) 13.
[55] Ibid 12.

Cooperation Agreement and came into force in 2000 as an EU reaction to NAFTA. However, there are ongoing talks in order to modernise the free trade provisions of this agreement, the aim being to deepen the existing rules but also to cover areas not initially included, mainly services, investment, and public procurement.[56] The agreement with Chile is an Association Agreement, which came into force in 2003, and is a broad and comprehensive FTA, covering all the areas of EU interest (services, investment, procurement, competition, and IPRs, among others).

More recently, the EU has concluded three deep FTAs in the application of the Global Europe initiative. The first one is the EUKFTA which came into force in 2011. Its trade provisions cover all the WTO-plus issues, including a dispute settlement mechanism, and it has been praised as the second most significant bilateral trade agreement in trade terms after NAFTA.[57] The second is the EU-Colombia/Peru FTA, provisionally applied with Peru since 1 March 2013 and with Colombia since 1 August 2013. Together with a 'human rights clause' (Article 1), this FTA contains commitments on the implementation of essential labour standards and major environmental conventions (Articles 269–270). The third is the EU-Central America Association Agreement, whose trade provisions apply with Honduras, Nicaragua and Panama since 1 August 2013, with Costa Rica and El Salvador since 1 October 2013, and with Guatemala since 1 December 2013.[58] This is the first EU 'region-to-region' agreement after the EPA with CARIFORUM, but in terms of regional integration goes beyond the latter,[59] and it also includes the WTO-plus provisions as sought by the EU.

Nevertheless, even if emerging economies have been the immediate targets in order to apply its new trade policy regarding FTAs, the EU's trade agenda includes negotiating bilateral trade agreements also with other, developed partners. This new agenda is of an unprecedented scale and envisages the conclusion of FTAs with the US and Japan.[60] The EU has already concluded the CETA with Canada, at the end of 2014, which comprises all WTO-plus issues, including an investment chapter. If the EU eventually completes its current trade agenda, including the conclusion of FTAs with emerging and developed countries alike, two-thirds of EU trade will be covered by FTAs.[61]

[56] European Commission, 'The EU's bilateral trade and investment agreements—where are we?', MEMO 13/1080, 3 December 2013, 5–6: europa.eu/rapid/press-release_MEMO-13-1080_en.htm.

[57] CM Brown, 'The European Union and Regional Trade Agreements: A Case Study of the EU-Korea FTA' (2011) 2 *European Yearbook of International Economic Law* 297, 298.

[58] European Commission (n 56 above) 5.

[59] L Tuis and CM Brown, 'The European Union and Regional Trade Agreements' (2013) 4 *European Yearbook of International Economic Law* 254.

[60] The EU has recently started talks with the US with a view to concluding the Transatlantic Trade and Investment Partnership (TTIP) in July 2013, and has also launched negotiations for an FTA with Japan in April 2013, see European Commission (n 56 above) 2.

[61] European Commission (n 27 above) 13.

III. THE EU-SINGAPORE FREE TRADE AGREEMENT

A. Introduction

The negotiations towards an EU-Singapore FTA (EUSFTA)[62] were concluded in December 2012 and the agreement was initialled in Singapore on 20 September 2013.[63] It was expected that the procedures allowing this FTA to become effective would be completed by late 2014, but in October 2014 the Commission decided to request an Opinion from the Court of Justice.[64]

B. The Content of the EUSFTA

i. Structure of the Agreement

The EUSFTA presents many characteristics that resemble those of the EU-Korea FTA (EUKFTA). The EUSFTA is composed of 17 chapters that incorporate several Annexes, Appendices and Understandings, while the EUKFTA has 15 chapters. Equally, the EUSFTA numbering, like that of the EUKFTA, is not sequential, but by chapter, whereby annexes are attached to chapters, instead of to the agreement as a whole.[65] The chapters of the EUSFTA can be generally grouped into four. First, Chapters 2 to 7 are devoted to trade in goods, and so they regulate market access for goods, trade remedies, technical barriers to trade (TBTs), sanitary and phytosanitary measures (SPSs), custom and trade facilitation, and non-tariff barriers (NTBs) to trade and investment in renewable energy generation. Secondly, Chapters 8 and 9 are dedicated to services, establishment, electronic commerce and investment protection. Thirdly, Chapters 10 to 14 deal with rules associated with trade (regulatory measures affecting trade) like government procurement, intellectual property (including geographical indications), competition, trade and sustainable development, and transparency. Finally, Chapters 15 to 17 are devoted to the dispute settlement (to a large extent modelled on the WTO dispute settlement system) and mediation mechanisms, and the institutional, general and final provisions.

[62] Singapore is considered a pioneer in bilateral free trade agreements in East Asia, see L Low, 'A Case Study of Singapore's Bilateral and Cross-Regional Free Trade Agreements' in SN Katada and M Solís (eds), *Cross Regional Trade Agreements* (Berlin, Springer-Verlag, 2008) 47.

[63] The text of the EUSFTA assessed in this paper corresponds to the version published in September 2013 at: trade.ec.europa.eu/doclib/press/index.cfm?id=961.

[64] European Commission, 'Singapore: The Commission to Request a Court of Justice Opinion on the trade deal', 30 October 2014, at: trade.ec.europa.eu/doclib/press/index.cfm?id=1185. European Commission (n 56 above) 4.

[65] Brown (n 57 above) 299, in fn 10, submits that this structure is rather similar to a US FTA.

As in the case of the EUKFTA,[66] the EUSFTA is meant to eliminate trade barriers well beyond those addressed by Article XXIV of GATT and Article V of GATS. Implementing the Global Europe strategy, the EUSFTA regulates WTO-plus issues and, therefore, it does not seek merely to address measures affecting trade at the border, but also to modify the parties' regulatory internal measures or flanking policies that may hinder trade. In this respect, the EU is definitively setting the path towards the conclusion of a new generation of FTAs where the so-called Singapore issues become the ultimate goal of any trade negotiations with key partners.

ii. *Trade in Goods*

(a) Customs Duties

The text of the EUSFTA differs from that of the EUKFTA in that the National Treatment provision is stated right after setting out its Objective (to liberalise trade) and Scope (trade in goods) and so it apparently covers tariff and non-tariff measures. In any case, Article 2.3 of the EUSFTA is largely based on Article III of GATT as well.

As required by WTO rules, a free trade area may be exempted from the most favoured nation (MFN) principle only if it agrees to eliminate 'substantially all trade between the constituent territories in products originating in such territories' (Article XXIV(8)(a)(i) GATT). This aim is foreseen in Chapter 2. Specifically, Article 2.1, together with Article 2.6 and Appendices 2-A-1 and 2-A-2 of the EUSFTA, provides that Singapore commits to remove all tariffs from the entry into force of the FTA, and the EU assumes an obligation to eliminate all custom duties at the latest five years after that same date. In this respect, the EUSFTA is very similar to the EUKFTA.

As mentioned, Singapore has agreed to fully liberalise merchandise trade from the entry into force of the agreement. This is due to the fact that Singapore is a very open economy and has decided to unilaterally apply zero MFN duties on the bulk of its imports of any kind (industrial or agricultural). Nevertheless, the EU believes that there is still an advantage in the EUSFTA, especially for some EU manufacturing sectors that are export-oriented. About a third of the tariff lines in Singapore have not been bound at the WTO, and for those duties that have been bound at the WTO, these tariffs are generally bound at a considerably higher level than their present level of application. Thanks to the EUSFTA, Singapore wholly commits to its present level of open access to the benefit of EU exporters, and it also removes the residual duties on some alcoholic beverages, including beer. As for the EU, 50 per cent of Singapore exports to the EU are currently free of import tariffs. This high figure is due to the fact that an important proportion of EU imports from Singapore is focused in areas where there are WTO tariff elimination agreements applicable to

[66] Ibid 300.

special sectors (like products covered by the 1996 WTO Ministerial Declaration of Trade in Information Technology Products and the WTO Pharmaceutical Agreement). The EU has assumed through the EUSFTA the obligation to immediately remove 75 per cent of the import duties applicable to Singapore goods and on virtually all other merchandise trade over a three- or five-year transition period.[67]

The EUSFTA contains a Protocol, situated at the end of the text of the Agreement, devoted to the rules of origin, thus mirroring the EUKFTA that also includes a similar Protocol. The rules of origin set up by the EUSFTA have been simplified with regard to other agreements in order to promote the facilitation of trade between the two partners and, to a large extent, reflect the current renovation of the EU's preferential rules of origin. In this respect, the EUSFTA rules of origin allow for some degree of accumulation of origin inside the ASEAN region (as with the EU's General System of Preferences regulation), taking into account that Singapore's economy is very much integrated into supply chains across this region.[68]

(b) Non-Tariff Barriers (NTBs) and Technical Barriers to Trade (TBTs)

Chapter 2 of the EUSFTA comprises rules on NTBs and explicitly incorporates provisions like Article XI and Article XX of GATT. However, a major innovative feature already included by the EUKFTA is also reproduced in the EUSFTA and consists of the setting-up of sectoral provisions that apply to several non-tariff issues. Indeed, Article 2.13 of the EUSFTA refers to the 'Sectoral Annexes' that are attached to that chapter as Annex 2-B and Annex 2-C. The former contains provisions on Motor Vehicles and parts thereof and the latter is devoted to Pharmaceutical Products and Medical Devices. Chapter 4 on TBTs follows suit. Indeed, Chapter 4 seeks to achieve the objective of identifying and eliminating unnecessary barriers to trade, reaffirming the provisions of the WTO TBT Agreement, and sometimes going beyond it regarding marking and labelling. Thus, Chapter 4 also incorporates an Annex 4-A on Electronics, together with three Appendices.

There is a rationale to this innovation addressing specific sectoral NTBs and TBTs. In spite of the commitment to remove tariff barriers, it is often the case that real access to markets is hindered by national regulatory measures when imported products are unable to meet the requirements of the destination country. The EU believes this is particularly the case in some Asian countries, especially Japan.[69] Therefore, the EUSFTA embraces several sectoral annexes covering merchandise deemed critical for the EU, just as the EUKFTA did, with the aim of ensuring that EU standards will be accepted by Singapore, standards that in turn are mainly based on international standards.

[67] European Commission, 'The economic impact of the EU-Singapore Free Trade Agreement', September 2013, 34–35.

[68] Ibid 36.

[69] European Commission (n 56 above) 2.

The rules on motor vehicles set out in the agreement promote regulatory convergence and compatibility in this domain based on international standards. The text recognises that the car standards used in Europe, that is, those developed by the World Forum for Harmonisation of Vehicle Regulation within the United Nations Economic Commission for Europe (UNECE) are the relevant international standards. Therefore, Singapore accepts UNECE type-approval certificates as compliant with its domestic technical regulations and conformity assessment procedures with respect to both cars and car parts, without further testing or certification, and agrees to align its regulatory system with those international standards.[70]

With respect to pharmaceuticals and medical devices, as was the case with the EUKFTA, the EUSFTA sets out several commitments in order to improve the transparency in the way authorities set the prices and conditions for reimbursement, allowing for access to the remedies available under domestic law (the EUKFTA is more specific, as it allows for judicial review of those pricing decisions).

Regarding electronics, international standards and standard-setting bodies like the International Organization for Standardization (ISO), the International Electrotechnical Commission (IEC) and the International Telecommunication Union (ITU) are recognised in Annex 4-A of the EUSFTA as the relevant standards that national regulatory systems must use, just as the EUKFTA does. The aim of these rules on electronics is eliminating duplicative testing. Therefore, without prejudice to consumer safety, health and environmental concerns, the parties have agreed to the progressive replacement of mandatory third-party testing in favour of less burdensome forms of conformity assessment, which in fact are those applied by the EU, ie the supplier's declaration of conformity. Singapore has agreed to remove a first group of consumer electronics products from the list of products where third-party certification has been mandatory until now. Once the EUSFTA is in force, Singapore will review Appendix 4-A-2 (that includes the list of products still requiring third-party testing) with the aim of gradually reducing the number of products listed therein.

Chapter 7 of the EUSFTA contains another innovation, not included in the EUKFTA, regarding NTBs to trade and investment in renewable energy generation. In order to facilitate trade in this area, this chapter provides for the equal treatment of any supplier from both parties and, therefore, the granting of preferences to suppliers through local content rules (a very familiar occurrence in Asia) is forbidden. As in the other sectors described above, these rules promote the recognition of international technical standards and provide for Singapore's acceptance of EU declarations of conformity or test reports without further requirement, for the purpose of placing such equipment on its market. The EU will also accept Singapore suppliers' declarations of conformity under the same terms as from Union suppliers.

[70] During the EUSFTA negotiations, Singapore declared a change in its 'green rebate' programme supporting the buying of environmentally friendly cars. This change will allow cleaner combustion engines produced in the EU to be eligible for the green rebate as well, which will bring a cost advantage to the purchase of EU cars of up to €12,000 per car, thereby proving the importance of regulatory barriers to trade, see European Commission (n 67 above) 37.

(c) Trade Remedies

Following the approach taken in the EUKFTA, Chapter 3 of the EUSFTA regulates the implementation of trade remedies by parties. Sections A and B of this chapter expressly reaffirm their rights and obligations, first, under Article VI of GATT 1994, the Anti-Dumping Agreement and the Subsidies and Countervailing Measures (SCM) Agreement and, secondly, under Article XIX of GATT, the Safeguards Agreement and Article 5 of the Agreement on Agriculture. However, Section C sets out the bilateral safeguard mechanism, whose working is fundamentally based on the mentioned WTO Safeguards Agreement. If a party is to impose a bilateral safeguard measure then the latter could consist of either the suspension of further reduction of the rate of customs duty on the goods concerned, or an increase in the rate of customs duty on the goods concerned to a level which does not exceed the lesser of: (i) the MFN applied rate at the time the measure is taken, or (ii) the base rate specified in the schedules from which reductions are calculated (Article 3.10). It is important to note that the bilateral safeguard clause is operative only during the transition period.

(d) Sanitary and Phytosanitary Measures (SPS)

The EUSFTA also contemplates the regulation of non-tariff barriers such as SPSs in a more specific way than the EUKFTA. As is well known, trade in raw and processed products of animal or plant origin like meat or meat products or fruit and vegetables is ordinarily affected by regulatory measures that protect public goods like human, animal and plant life and health. However, the EU believes that, for most Member States, Singapore applies a costly and cumbersome system of authorising imports on an establishment-by-establishment basis, which eventually affects the ability of EU small and medium enterprises (SMEs) to trade with Singapore. Therefore, Chapter 5 of the EUSFTA is aimed at reducing the impact of SPSs and provides for the progressive introduction of a system by Singapore where this country will assess the performance of the inspection and certification systems put in place by the respective competent authorities of EU Member States.[71] Specifically, the mechanism designed by Chapter 5 and its two Annexes is based on a process of progressive acceptance by Singapore of the equivalence (Article 5.14) of the inspection and certification systems existing in EU Member States so that all meat exporters from a given Member State are in principle eligible to export meat products to Singapore. However, Singapore retains the right to carry out on-the-spot verifications at any time (Article 5.8) in order to maintain confidence in the effective implementation of Singapore's strict SPSs, and also the right to carry out import checks at the border (Article 5.7).

[71] European Commission (n 67 above) 40.

(e) Customs and Trade Facilitation

The EU is aware of the importance of Singapore's port, the second largest in the world in terms of container turnover, as a major transit point for imports and exports travelling between Europe and Asia. Many EU exporters are using Singapore's harbour area as a delivery centre from where they operate in the Asian region.[72] Chapter 6 of the EUSFTA seeks to set out efficient standards for customs processing and provides for cooperation between customs authorities in order to simplify, harmonise and modernise trade procedures at the interface between business and customs administrations. The EUSFTA goes beyond the EUKFTA in that the parties have strengthened the effort to achieve international standardisation, specifically assuming the Revised Kyoto Convention on the Simplification and Harmonisation of Customs Procedures, the International Convention on the Harmonized Commodity Description and Coding System, and the Framework of Standards to Secure and Facilitate Global Trade (SAFE Framework) of the World Customs Organization (WCO) (Article 6.2). Finally, the EUSFTA contains two understandings (numbers 3 and 4) devoted, respectively, to additional customs-related provisions and the mutual recognition of customs Authorised Economic Operators (AEO) Programmes.

iii. Trade in Services and Investment Protection

Reaffirming their respective commitments under the GATS, the EU and Singapore have agreed in Chapter 8 to the progressive reciprocal liberalisation of trade in services, establishment and electronic commerce, in many cases going well beyond their WTO schedules of services commitments. Following the structure and content of the EUKFTA, the EUSFTA sets out the provisions regarding the three modes of supply, ie, cross-border supply of services, establishment, and the temporary presence of natural persons for business purposes. However, with respect to the former two, it is to be noted that the Market Access (MA) and National Treatment (NT) commitments are not accompanied by a Most-Favoured Nation (MFN) clause similar to the EUKFTA, so that parties are not mandated to accord to services, services suppliers, establishments and investors of the other party, treatment no less favourable than that they accord to like services, services suppliers, establishments and investors of any third country in the context of an economic integration agreement signed after the entry into force of the EUSFTA. Perhaps, this can be explained by the introduction of a Review Clause contained in Article 8.63 (absent from the EUKFTA), where both parties agree to evaluate this chapter and their schedules of specific commitments no later than three years after the entry into force of the agreement. Section E of this chapter contains the regulatory framework, including an intended mutual recognition agreement

[72] Ibid 20, 39.

and provisions on domestic regulation, ie, internal measures relating to licensing requirements and procedures or qualification requirements. This Section also sets out the regulation applicable to specific services sectors such as computer services, postal services, telecommunication services, financial services, and international maritime transport services. Section F is devoted to electronic commerce. Section G encompasses the General Exceptions clause, modelled on Article XIV of GATS.

According to an assessment carried out in 2009,[73] the maximum benefits from an EU-ASEAN FTA, for both the EU and Singapore, would stem from the liberalisation of trade in services. Because it serves as the main hub in South East Asia for trade in services, Singapore alone attracts half of the EU-ASEAN trade in commercial services, which causes many EU companies to use it as the operating centre for carrying out business in the region. This context, together with the comprehensive liberalisation of services sectors achieved through the EUKFTA, explains why the parties have considered the aim of a wide-ranging liberalisation of services as a key issue regarding the EUSFTA. Therefore, taking into account their GATS level of commitments, the EUSFTA has significantly expanded EU commitments for Singaporean service operators in a broad range of business sectors, sometimes going beyond the EUKFTA (ie, on postal services). By the same token, Singapore has entered unqualified commitments (that is, without sectoral limitations) in a remarkably generous number of services sectors for the three modes of supply mentioned above.[74]

Specifically, Singapore has agreed to enter comprehensive commitments in the financial services sector, which it has traditionally regulated tightly, particularly retail banking, where EU banks will be able to double, under certain conditions, their number of customer locations. Another feature worth mentioning is that limitations, such as equity caps, to establishment in most non-services sectors, especially manufacturing, are not allowed in the EUSFTA. Moreover, the EUSFTA incorporates disciplines on non-discrimination and transparency in its sector-specific rules, as they are found in the *acquis communautaire*, which is of the outmost importance in sectors like telecommunication services and postal services.[75]

Finally, Chapter 9 of the EUSFTA is devoted to investment protection. As is well known, the EU has had competence to negotiate provisions on investment protection since the entry into force of the Treaty of Lisbon, as provided for in Article 207 TFEU. Unlike the EUKFTA, which was negotiated before, the EUSFTA includes an investment chapter in what is an absolute novelty in the EU's trade practice, as it will cover all significant topics of international

[73] Ecorys, 'Trade Sustainability Impact Assessment of the FTA between the EU and ASEAN—Final Report Volume I—Main Findings and Recommendations', 19 June 2009: trade.ec.europa.eu/doclib/docs/2010/april/tradoc_145989.pdf.

[74] European Commission (n 67 above) 30.

[75] Ibid 33.

economic law. This chapter is divided into two sections addressing, respectively, investment protection and investor-state dispute settlement.[76]

The first section sets out the gold standards in investment protection, namely, the principle of national treatment (Article 9.3) and other standards like fair and equitable treatment and full protection and security (Article 9.4). It also forbids expropriation (Article 9.6) except for public purposes, under due process of law, on a non-discriminatory basis, and against payment of prompt, adequate and effective compensation. Annex 9-A provides clarification on direct expropriation and indirect expropriation, both equally prohibited. Moreover, free movement of capital is guaranteed by Article 9.7.

The second section comprises alternative methods for investor-state settlement of disputes, including amicable resolution (Article 9.15), consultations (Article 9.16), mediation (Article 9.17, together with Annex 9-A), and of course, arbitration. Regarding arbitration, and taking into account that the EU is not a party to the ICSID Convention, the claimant has the choice of submitting the claim to the ICSID Convention (including the Additional Facility), UNCITRAL or any other forum (Article 9.19). In order to avoid frivolous suits, Articles 9.23 and 9.24 include provisions on claims 'manifestly without legal merit' or 'unfounded as a matter of law'. Articles 9.20 and ff provide detailed rules for the conditions applicable to the submission of a claim, the constitution of the Tribunal, the applicable law and the rules of interpretation. Moreover, Annexes 9-B and 9-C contain exhaustive provisions on the code of conduct for arbitrators and on transparency, including public access to documents and hearings as well as the possibility of third-party submissions.

The investment provisions set out in the EUSFTA are no different from those established in the CETA[77] or those currently under negotiation in the Transatlantic Trade and Investment Partnership between the US and the EU (TTIP).[78] These provisions are being very much criticised from several quarters,[79] even if the EU Commission is making huge efforts to highlight that the new investment rules will produce a significant improvement regarding old-fashioned investment treaties.[80]

[76] DRAFT EU-Singapore FTA, Version October 2014 (before legal revision) Chapter 9—Investment: trade.ec.europa.eu/doclib/docs/2014/october/tradoc_152844.pdf.

[77] Consolidated CETA Text, 26 September 2014: trade.ec.europa.eu/doclib/docs/2014/september/tradoc_152806.pdf.

[78] EU Negotiating Texts: trade.ec.europa.eu/doclib/press/index.cfm?id=1230.

[79] Mattias Kumm, 'An Empire of Capital? Transatlantic Investment Protection as the Institutionalization of Unjustified Privilege' (2015) 4 *ESIL Reflections*.

[80] EU Commission, 'Investment Provisions in the EU-Canada Free Trade Agreement (CETA)', 26 September 2014, p 1: trade.ec.europa.eu/doclib/docs/2013/november/tradoc_151918.pdf, stating that the CETA investment provisions introduce 'important innovations to investment protection, ensuring a high level of protection while preserving the EU and Canada's right to regulate and pursue legitimate public policy objectives such as the protection of health, safety, or the environment'. See also Catharine Titi, 'Investment Law and the European Union: Towards a New Generation of International Investment Agreements' (2015) 26 *European Journal of International Law* 639.

iv. Regulatory Provisions

Like the EUKFTA, the EUSFTA includes regulatory chapters dealing with a range of issues shaping the business environment, and whose goal is to ensure a level playing-field for EU firms, Singaporean ones, or those from third countries. These regulatory chapters incorporate cross-cutting rules on most of the so-called 'Singapore issues' or WTO-plus issues; specifically government procurement, intellectual property protection, competition and regulatory transparency.

(a) Government Procurement

As is well known, the WTO Agreement on Government Procurement (GPA) of 1994 entered into force on 1 January 1996. In December 2011, a decision on the outcomes of the re-negotiation of the Agreement, which had been ongoing for more than a decade, was taken at Ministerial level in Geneva.[81] This political decision was confirmed, on 30 March 2012, by the formal adoption of the Decision on the Outcomes of the Negotiations under Article XXIV:7 of the GPA.[82] Some two years after this Protocol amending the Agreement was first adopted, the Revised WTO GPA entered into force on 6 April 2014.

The EUKFTA incorporated by reference in Chapter 9 (which contains only three articles) the Revised WTO GPA even before its entry into force, somehow relying on its future implementation. By contrast, the EUSFTA explicitly includes the Revised GPA rules, almost article by article, in Chapter 10 and it does so after the entry into force in 2014 of the Revised GPA. The EUSFTA has even included a final adjustment clause (Article 10.20), whereby the EU and Singapore commit to amend this chapter following the potential modification of the Revised GPA.

The EUSFTA has also served to significantly expand the parties' commitments regarding their previous WTO commitments in public procurement. Thus, the EU and Singapore have agreed to include in their schedules additional central government entities as well as entities operating within the utilities sector. Moreover, 'public-private-partnerships' or concessions, which generate some of the major public tenders in the utilities sectors, will also be covered by the EUSFTA.

[81] WTO, Committee on Government Procurement, 'Ministerial-level meeting of the Committee on Government Procurement (15 December 2011)—Decision on the outcomes of the negotiations under Article XXIV:7 of the Agreement on Government Procurement', WTO/GPA/112, 16 December 2011.

[82] WTO, Committee on Government Procurement, 'Adoption of the results of the negotiations under article XXIV:7 of the Agreement on Government Procurement, following their verification and review, as required by the Ministerial Decision of 15 December 2011 (GPA/112), paragraph 5—Action taken by the parties to the WTO Agreement on Government Procurement at a formal

(b) Intellectual Property Rights

Chapter 11 of the EUSFTA regulates the protection of intellectual property rights (IPRs) in a way very similar to the EUKFTA, which already went beyond the protection offered by the WTO Trade Related Intellectual Property Rights (TRIPS) Agreement.[83] First, the EUSFTA offers a wide-ranging legal protection of copyright, including a rule (Article 11.6) providing protection equivalent to Article 15 of the 1996 World Intellectual Property Organization (WIPO) Performances and Phonograms Treaty (WPPT), ie the right of performers and phonogram producers to remuneration for broadcasting and communication to the public, which is not presently afforded by Singapore's Copyright Act.[84] But the EUSFTA also protects trademarks, geographical indications (GIs), designs, patents, and plant varieties. The Agreement also devotes Section F to test data submitted to obtain an administrative marketing approval to put both the pharmaceutical and agrochemical products on the market. GIs deserve a special mention, as Singapore has agreed to set up a national register (Article 11.17) to protect to a higher degree, not only wines and spirits, but also agricultural products and foodstuffs, therefore going to some extent beyond the rules included in the WTO TRIPS Agreement (as the EUKFTA does).

The EUSFTA also encompasses an extensive regulation on IPRs enforcement which goes beyond that provided for in the WTO TRIPS Agreement, but that falls short of the protection offered by the EUKFTA, which incorporates criminal enforcement measures. Indeed, the EUSFTA comprises measures for the civil enforcement of IPRs and border measures with an extended scope, but does not include rules on criminal enforcement. This is in line with the recent backlash suffered by the Anti-Counterfeiting Trade Agreement (ACTA), which has met with worldwide public opposition.[85] Both the EU and Singapore were among the signatories of the ACTA, which has however not been ratified by the EU due to the final veto of the European Parliament in July 2012. In any case, the enforcement rules contained in the EUSFTA reflect to a large extent the corresponding EU rules regulating the enforcement of IPRs within the internal market.[86]

(c) Competition and Related Matters

Like the EUKFTA, the EUSFTA has set out very specific rules on competition in Chapter 12. First, Section A is devoted to antitrust and mergers. Specifically,

meeting of the Committee, at the level of Geneva heads of delegations, on 30 March 2012', WTO/GPA/113, 2 April 2012.

[83] Brown (n 57 above) 303.

[84] European Commission (n 67 above) 45.

[85] Antonio Segura Serrano, 'El Acuerdo comercial de lucha contra la falsificación (ACTA): Una evaluación desde el Derecho de la UE' (2012) 28 *Revista General de Derecho Europeo* 1–40.

[86] Directive 2001/29/EC of the European Parliament and of the Council, of 22 May 2001, on the harmonisation of certain aspects of copyright and related rights in the information society, [2001] OJ L/167, 22 June 2001, p 10; Directive 2004/48/EC of the European Parliament and of the Council, of 29 April 2004, on the enforcement of intellectual property rights, [2004] OJ L157/45, 30 April 2004.

the parties recognise the importance of free and undistorted competition in their trade relations and commit to maintain in their respective territories comprehensive legislation to address horizontal and vertical agreements, decisions by associations of undertakings and concerted practices, abuses of a dominant position, and concentrations (Article 12.1). With respect to implementation, both the EU and Singapore agree to maintain authorities responsible for the effective enforcement of the aforementioned legislation, respecting the principles of procedural fairness and rights of defence. Secondly, Section B is devoted to ensuring that public undertakings and undertakings entrusted with special or exclusive rights do not use their special rights to engage in anti-competitive practices, and that no discrimination is exercised by state monopolies. Strikingly, as in the case of the EUKFTA, the dispute settlement and mediation systems of the EUSFTA do not apply to either of those Sections (Article 12.14).

Subsidies are regulated in Section C, which refers to the WTO Subsidies and Countervailing Measures (SCM) Agreement for the definition of measures to be considered as subsidies. The EUSFTA applies to subsidies irrespective of whether they are granted in relation to the production of goods or of services (the EUKFTA does not explicitly cover subsidies in services), but it does not apply to subsidies in the agriculture and fisheries areas. Without prejudice to the rights and obligations of both parties under the WTO SCM Agreement (regarding trade remedies and dispute settlement), the EUSFTA explicitly adopts the definition of prohibited subsidies in Article 3 SCM Agreement, but also goes beyond it through the prohibition of other categories of subsidies. Subsidies also prohibited are those which cover debts or liabilities of an undertaking without any limitation, in law or in fact, as to the amount or the duration, and those subsidies made to insolvent or ailing undertakings without a credible restructuring plan based on realistic assumptions. All prohibited subsidies contained in Article 12.7 are subject to the dispute settlement and mediation mechanisms, as opposed to the exclusion applicable to the rules on competition mentioned above.

(d) Trade and Sustainable Development

The EUSFTA, as did the EUKFTA, lays down very detailed obligations, together with a framework for cooperation on trade and sustainable development in Chapter 13. First, the agreement prescribes binding commitments to domestic levels of labour and environmental protection consistent with international standards and agreements. According to the EU, the thrust of this chapter essentially resides in refraining from 'race-to-the-bottom' practices as regards labour and environmental laws to attract trade or investment.[87] This is perhaps

[87] European Commission (n 67 above) 46.

reflected in Article 13.12 where the parties undertake a duty not to waive or fail to effectively enforce their environmental and labour laws in a manner affecting trade or investment between them.

In respect of labour, the parties commit to ratifying and effectively implementing the fundamental International Labour Organization (ILO) conventions and will also consider other ILO conventions, whereas in respect of the environment the parties reaffirm their commitment to the UN Framework Convention on Climate Change (UNFCCC) and its Kyoto Protocol. Compared to the EUKFTA, the EUSFTA goes beyond it in prescribing detailed rules on trade in timber and timber products, and trade in fish products, in order to avoid illegal trade. Moreover, Articles 13.4 and 13.10 set out a framework for cooperation on labour and environmental protection, respectively, which includes cooperating in international fora, sharing good practices, and exchanging views on the impacts of the agreement or on the promotion of ratification of multilateral agreements, among other things.

Among the general provisions (Section D) of this chapter, the agreement lays down disciplines that seek to enhance the contribution of trade and investment to sustainable development, such as those regarding development assurance schemes, like eco-labelling or fair and ethical trade, and corporate social responsibility (Article 13.11). Regarding the institutional provisions, the monitoring mechanism for the implementation of this chapter is based on the task of the Board on Trade and Sustainable Development (BTSD) (comprising senior officials), that will include a public session with the participation of stakeholders.[88] Secondly, the chapter provides for a specific mechanism for the settling of disputes, composed of a double track. First, there is the possibility of 'government consultations', which may be taken to the BTSD. Secondly, if the BTSD does not arrive at a solution, then it is possible unilaterally to trigger a third-party independent arbitration system, regulated in detail, and consisting of a 'panel of experts', which will deliver an interim and a final report with recommendations. The parties will discuss appropriate measures to be implemented, taking the report into account, while its follow-up will be monitored by the BTSD.

(e) Transparency

Chapter 14 of the EUSFTA follows very closely the regulation laid down in the EUKFTA. Article 14.2 of the former agreement recognises the impact that national regulatory environments may have on trade and investment and so the parties commit to complying with a number of transparency rules that go beyond the

[88] Although the parties have agreed to set up channels for inclusive consultations with stakeholders or the civil society (including employers, workers, environmental interests and business groups) in this chapter, the role of 'domestic advisory groups' is downplayed with regard to the EUKFTA, as they are not directly involved in the specific mechanism for the settlement of disputes provided by this chapter.

WTO requirements. Together with an obligation to publish measures of general application, the parties assume the duty to publish in advance any legislative proposal so that interested persons have reasonable opportunities to comment on such proposals, which in turn should be taken into account. Moreover, in order to facilitate the effective implementation of the agreement, the parties agree to establish contact points for responding to enquiries or seeking to resolve problems for those interested persons concerning any measures of general application. This chapter sets out as well due process obligations regarding administrative proceedings and the duty to establish impartial and independent tribunals or procedures for the prompt review of administrative actions.

v. *Institutional Provisions*

(a) Dispute Settlement and Mediation Mechanisms

Like the EUKFTA, the EUSFTA has incorporated a dispute settlement system in Chapter 15, which is modelled on the basis of the WTO system, together with a mediation mechanism in Chapter 16. Both FTAs deploy several improvements with regard to the WTO system, taking the bilateral setting of those agreements into account.[89] However, the EUSFTA includes some changes with respect to the EUKFTA that reflect the accumulated experience, that is, both mechanisms are more detailed in the former.

The dispute settlement system works on the basis of a permanent list of 10 arbitrators (Article 15.20), rather than ad hoc panellists, as happens within the WTO. Arbitration panels are composed of three arbitrators, selected by lot if there is no agreement by the parties. Arbitration procedures are quite speedy, as arbitration panels have to issue their ruling no later than 180 days after the date of their establishment, although not so quick when compared to the 150 days' deadline established in the EUKFTA. Unlike the WTO scheme, there is no appellate procedure. However, the transparency rules contained in the EUSFTA are remarkable compared to the WTO system, as they provide that hearings are open to the public and that the arbitration panel will accept *amicus curiae* submissions. These features correspond to a model of dispute settlement that the EU has sought to share with its trading partners since the beginning of the twenty-first century.[90] Finally, as in the case of the EUKFTA, the EUSFTA organises the relation between its dispute settlement system and the system established at the WTO. Without prejudice to the rights and obligations of both parties within the latter, Article 15.21 of the EUSFTA seeks to avoid the concurrent initiation of dispute proceedings under both systems with regard to a particular measure, unless substantially different obligations under each agreement are in dispute, or unless the forum initially selected fails for procedural or jurisdictional reasons.

[89] Brown (n 57 above) 306.

[90] Ibid.

The mediation mechanism provided for in Chapter 16 of the EUSFTA is meant to resolve any disagreement arising out of a regulatory measure adopted by one of the parties. In contrast to the EUKFTA, where the mediation procedure only addresses market access measures in goods (and explicitly excludes areas like trade in agricultural products, services and establishment, government procurement, competition, intellectual property rights, among others), the EUSFTA mediation mechanism is applicable to any measure covered by the agreement. This mediation system seeks to find a solution to any measure allegedly affecting trade or investment but is not intended to serve as a basis for dispute settlement procedures, although recourse to the dispute system is expressly preserved (Article 16.7). Within the quick mediation mechanism, a mediator is appointed by agreement or by lot from the list of arbitrators to offer advice or propose a solution (by contrast, the EUKFTA expressly provides that the mediator will issue an 'advisory opinion') that the parties will consider in order to reach a mutually agreed solution (60 days after the appointment, Article 16.5). Finally, as in the EUKFTA, the EUSFTA sets up a review clause providing for the modification of the mediation procedure according to the development of a corresponding mechanism in the WTO (Article 16.10), not yet adopted.

(b) Cross-cutting Provisions

Chapter 17 is devoted to the institutional, general and final provisions, which distill a more nuanced consideration of parties' sovereignty in comparison to the EUKFTA, ie, decisions are taken by the parties within the Trade Committee, but not by this Committee in its own right (Article 17.4). Article 17.1 sets up the Trade Committee, which is co-chaired by the Minister for Trade and Industry of Singapore and the European Commissioner for Trade. This Committee is ultimately responsible for the proper operation of the agreement and is the supreme body among the other specialised committees. It is to be noted that, in contrast to the EUKFTA, in the EUSFTA there is no Committee for Trade and Sustainable Development, nor are there Working Groups. Other novelties with respect to the EUKFTA are: the provisions on current account and capital movements, devoted to setting up a framework for long-term investment; the clause on confidential information; and the clause excluding the agreement's direct effect. The entry into force of the agreement will take place once all ratification procedures by parties have been completed (Article 17.12). In other words, as some of the issues addressed by the EUSFTA are of Member State competence, apart from EU conclusion and ratification, it will be necessary for Member States to accomplish their domestic procedures to ratify the agreement as well. This is the reason why provisional application of the agreement is foreseen upon the exchange of notifications, except for those provisions that cannot be provisionally applied. Provisional application of the EUSFTA might be authorised under EU law by the Council at the moment of its signature. However, as the Treaty of Lisbon has attributed a new prominent role for the European Parliament, it is unlikely that the provisional application will take place before the European Parliament has expressed its opinion on the agreement.

Finally, the EUSFTA is an integral part of the overall bilateral relations as governed by the Partnership and Cooperation Agreement (PCA). It constitutes a specific agreement giving effect to the trade provisions of the PCA (Article 17.17). Even though the text of the PCA with Singapore is not yet available, it is likely that, as in the case of the PCA with Korea, the former provides for the suspension of the EUSFTA if essential elements of the bilateral relationship between the parties are affected, including respect for democratic principles, human rights and fundamental freedoms and the rule of law.

IV. CONCLUSIONS

As this chapter has tried to show, the EU has now embarked on a clear-cut trade policy based on the conclusion of FTAs which in turn seek to obtain market openings abroad and the defence of EU exporters' interests. The EUSFTA is just the latest example of this trade policy officially launched through the Global Europe initiative which has sought to lay aside the old EU external policy. A final evaluation will now be carried out using two very different legal and political parameters.

First, the EU approach has some consequences for the multilateral trading system. Indeed, there is the question of whether the EUSFTA respects the EU legal commitments with regard to the WTO obligations, ie Article XXIV of GATT and Article V of GATS.[91] But this kind of assessment has never been made within the WTO for several reasons.[92] However, more importantly, through FTAs the EU (just as the US[93] or Japan) might be significantly affecting the multilateral trading system by way of introducing stumbling blocks (as opposed to building blocks) to multilateral free trade, as Bhagwati has consistently warned.[94] This outcome has recently been questioned by empirical economic literature though, which submits that RTAs/FTAs do not provoke a trade diversion effect and so do not act as substitutes for but as complements to multilateral free trade.[95] Further, the preferential treatment accorded in FTAs is often applied on a non-discriminatory basis and, therefore, can be multi-lateralised.[96] Still, even if regional/bilateral FTAs and

[91] JH Mathis, *Regional Trade Agreements in the GATT/WTO: Article XXIV and the Internal Trade Requirement* (Amsterdam, TMC Asser Press, 2001).

[92] PC Mavroidis, 'Always Look at the Bright Side of Non-delivery: WTO and Preferential Trade Agreements, Yesterday and Today' (2011) 10 *World Trade Review* 376.

[93] A Hilaire and Y Yang, 'The United States and the New Regionalism/Bilateralism' (2004) 38 *Journal of World Trade* 603.

[94] J Bhagwati, *The World Trading System at Risk* (Hemel Hempstead, Harvester Wheatsheaf, 1991).

[95] R Baldwin, '21st Century Regionalism: Filling the gap between 21st century trade and 20th century trade rules' (2011) *WTO Staff Working Paper ERSD*-2011-8, 18.

[96] R Baldwin, S Evenett and P Law, 'Beyond Tariffs: Multilateralizing Non-Tariff RTA Commitments' in R Baldwin and P Law (eds), *Multilateralizing Regionalism: Challenges for the Global Trading System* (Cambridge, Cambridge University Press, 2009) 79.

multilateral free trade may reinforce each other, the former trend is producing yet another worrying outcome; that is, the introduction of new deep disciplines in settings of great power asymmetries and, at the same time, the erosion of the WTO as a central forum.[97] The EU itself is aware of the risks that FTAs entail for the functioning of the multilateral trading system, in particular, regarding developing countries and economic operators.[98] However, the EU trade agenda is precisely seeking to shift the multilateral system by introducing regulatory convergence through the back door,[99] thus somehow undermining global efforts to negotiate solutions to regulatory incompatibilities.[100]

Secondly, the EUSFTA also needs to be assessed with respect to the EU trade agenda stated in the Global Europe initiative which is to promote market openness and deep disciplines on WTO-plus regulatory issues. After the EUKFTA, the EUSFTA is the second EU FTA in Asia that seeks to realise this trade agenda, therefore focusing on a sole economic rationale. But EUSFTA economic figures are less significant than those derived from the EUKFTA, as Korea is a highly advanced emerging economy. Moreover, the estimated economic effects make Singapore the most benefited partner, as predictions say its real GDP will grow five times the amount of that of the EU thanks to the FTA.[101] This means that there must also be a political goal. Indeed, the EUSFTA has been considered as the first building block towards an eventual agreement that would include the whole ASEAN region.[102] In this vein, the EUSFTA is another step in the long-standing goal of locking the highest number of countries into a specific set of EU-type regulatory rules. These EU rules are based on international standards negotiated in pluri-lateral fora and then exported abroad through its deep FTAs.[103] The aim is to influence the next round of multilateral trade negotiations or, in case the multilateral path fails, to gain an ample dissemination of EU rules. So the EUSFTA is somewhat justified on the basis of the 'race for leadership between the US and the EU to impose a set of rules and standards on the rest of the world'.[104]

[97] Baldwin (n 95 above) 31.

[98] See European Commission (n 36 above) 13.

[99] European Commission, 'Contribution from the Commission to the February 2013 European Council Debate on Trade, Growth and Jobs', p 10: trade.ec.europa.eu/doclib/docs/2013/april/tradoc_151052.pdf.

[100] G Martin Prada and A Rossi, 'The Regulatory Framework of Regional Trade Agreements' in W Lim and R Torrent (eds), *Multilateral and Regional Frameworks for Globalization: WTO and Free Trade Agreements* (Seoul, Korea Development Institute, 2002) 183.

[101] European Commission (n 67) 4. Singapore seems also to be interested in facilitating ASEAN's FTAs, see L Lai To and R Yi Hooi, 'The Politics of Singapore's Bilateral Free Trade Agreements: Enlightened Self-interest to Promote East Asian Regionalism in the New Millennium' in VK Aggarwal and S Lee (eds), *Trade Policy in the Asia-Pacific: The Role of Ideas, Interests, and Domestic Institutions* (Berlin, Springer 2011) 121.

[102] European Commission (n 67 above) 12.

[103] Melo Araujo (n 34 above) 283.

[104] Cattaneo (n 43 above) 36, 43.

16

The External Dimension of the Area of Freedom, Security and Justice: An Essential Part of the European Union's External Action

JOSÉ MARTÍN Y PÉREZ DE NANCLARES*

Contents:

* Professor of Public International Law at the University of Salamanca. Currently Director of the International Law Department at the Spanish Ministry of Foreign Affairs and Cooperation. This chapter forms part of a research project financed by the Spanish Ministry of Economic Affairs and Competitiveness of which the author is the main researcher (DER2012-36703). The opinions contained in this text are personal and do not bind the Ministry for whom the author works.

I. GENERAL ASPECTS: THE PROGRESSIVE CONFIGURATION OF AN EXTERNAL DIMENSION IN THE AREA OF FREEDOM, SECURITY AND JUSTICE

IN A COLLECTIVE work such as this, which concerns the external action of the European Union (EU), a place has to be found for the external dimension of the Area of Freedom, Security and Justice (AFSJ). Until recently, however, this might not have been the case. In fact, until the last decade it was very much seen as a secondary issue, by both EU institutions and academics. This was due to the specific nature of the matter, as well as the absolute pre-eminence of the internal dimension of the EU's competence in the AFSJ.

Thus, any study concerning the AFSJ must start by bearing in mind the very unusual nature of the subject-matter. Home affairs and justice have always been extremely delicate matters in the European integration process. This is not surprising, since it is one of the competences of the EU which most clearly goes to the heart of the concept of national sovereignty. There has always been an evident dialectical tension between the need for Member States to attribute competences to the EU in this area as a result of the existence of the internal market without borders and, at the same time, the resistance of the same Member States to losing control over questions that directly affect competences connected to national sovereignty. It is precisely for this reason that the path that the areas of home affairs and justice have had to take in the EU until they have achieved full 'communitisation' under the Lisbon Treaty has been so long and complex.

This path commenced with the case law of the Court of Justice of the European Union (CJEU) filling the void left by the initial silence of the founding treaties in this area and then went through three successive stages. First, the 'convention model' was used, whereby international treaties were entered into outside of the founding treaties (the Schengen Agreements, the Dublin Convention etc). Subsequently, the unique 'intergovernmental model' was preferred, based on the differentiation between Community and extra-Community pillars (the Maastricht Treaty). And, finally, the progressive attraction of the Community model (the Treaties of Amsterdam and Nice) held sway, leading, under the 'Community model', to an (almost) full 'Community regularisation' of the home affairs and justice areas (the Lisbon Treaty). At the same time as these stages have marked out on the EU constitutional route map the competences contained in the founding treaties in relation to the AFSJ, their specific application has been exhaustively laid down in practice in the Tampere Programme (1999–2004), the Hague Programme

(2005–09) and now the Stockholm Programme (2010–14), as well as in their respective Action Plans. These Programmes and Action Plans have successively planned for the adoption of a wide range of specific measures required to patiently weave together the different strands that form the dense network of secondary law which comprises the current content of the AFSJ.[1]

However, until not that long ago, the pre-eminence of the internal dimension was almost complete in this EU area of action, the external dimension being very much of secondary importance. During the 1990s, however, the idea of including within the AFSJ a degree of external action by the EU matured politically. However, the steps taken were very limited and focused almost exclusively on irregular immigration and the creation of effective return and readmission mechanisms. One had to wait until the Tampere European Council for this external dimension to become (formally) a political priority; and, even more importantly, the goal of taking what started to be termed a 'comprehensive approach' in relation to this area became a reality.[2] This idea of a 'comprehensive approach' became part of Community terminology and from then on was included as a goal of EU action on immigration.[3]

In fact, however, until the previous decade the external dimension of the AFSJ was of no importance whatsoever and was of secondary importance for academics. Thus, despite the political declaration made in this regard by the important Feira European Council in 2000, it was not until 2005 that the EU institutions considered for the first time the importance of this external dimension to achieve a coherent AFSJ.[4] On this basis, both the Hague Programme (2005–09) and the

[1] In fact, it is now practically impossible to keep abreast of the EU's intense action in areas as different and wide-ranging as visas, asylum, immigration, civil cooperation, police cooperation, criminal judicial cooperation, etc. One only has to skim through the thousand odd pages of the best textbooks on this subject to get a clear idea of the range and depth of the rules that currently make up the AFSJ. See, for example, the latest volume of the excellent book by S Peers, *EU Justice and Home Affairs Law*, 3rd edn (Oxford, Oxford University Press, 2011). Even some of the specific instruments adopted in this area are genuinely worthy of major treatises. The first of these instruments that comes to mind is probably the European arrest warrant, which has been the subject of numerous studies. See, for example, the comprehensive work of R Blekstook, *Handbook on the European Arrest Warrant* (The Hague, Asser Press, 2005).

[2] Conclusions of the Tampere European Council of 15–16 October 1999, point 11.

[3] Put succinctly, the 'comprehensive approach' may be defined as the goal of ensuring that this EU action combines in an equal manner the three parts of which it must be composed, namely the control of irregular immigration, the facilitation of legal immigration and its mobility, and the interlinking of immigration with development cooperation.

[4] In that year, the Commission approved an important Communication which contained a strategy relating to the dimension of the area of freedom, security and justice; COM(2005) 491 final of 12.10.2005. The Action Plan also examined this issue; COM (2005) 184 final of 10.5.2005. Nevertheless, the most prestigious academics in this area had started to consider the convenience of including the external dimension in the AFSJ. See, for example, G De Kerchove and A Weyembergh (eds), *Sécurité et justice: enjeu de la politique extérieure de l'Union européenne* (Brussels, Université Libre de Bruxelles, 2003); H Labayle, 'La politique extérieure de l'Union européenne en matière de justice et d'affaires intérieures: chimère ou réalité?' in AAVV, *Études en l'honneur de Jean-Claude Gautron—Les dynamiques du droit européen en début de siècle* (Paris, Pedone, 2004) 681–99; C Boswell, 'The "external dimension" of EU immigration and asylum policy' (2003) 79 *International Affairs* 619–38.

current Stockholm Programme (2010–14) have gone much further with respect to the goal of equipping the AFSJ with an external dimension to the point that this has become a genuine priority.[5]

Nevertheless, the decisive step in this regard was taken by the Lisbon Treaty.[6] In addition to the merger of the pre-existing European Union and the European Communities into the single European Union (Article 1 TEU) which was expressly recognised as having legal personality (Article 47 TEU),[7] external action was given greater visibility, clarity, coherence and effectiveness; at least from the substantive point of view, since the disappearance of the pillar structure in relation to the AFSJ[8] meant that the external competences pertaining to the AFSJ were assimilated to those existing in the rest of the areas which are within the competence of EU.[9] As a result, the unique situation of external action existing in relation to police and judicial cooperation in criminal matters prior to the Lisbon Treaty (former Article 38 TEU) disappeared. There still exists a possible overlapping of EU action as regards AFSJ which comes within the CFSP—for example, in relation to terrorism[10]—but this is very slight. In short, in general terms the Lisbon Treaty

[5] The European Council has already set the EU priorities in this area for the next 5 years; Conclusions of the European Council of 27 June 2014, point 4.

[6] S Peers, 'Mission accomplished? EU Justice and Home Affairs law after the Treaty of Lisbon' (2011) 48 *Common Market Law Review* 661–93; LC Rossi, 'From EU Pillar to Area: The impact of the Lisbon Treaty on the External Dimension of Freedom, Security and Justice' in C Flaesch-Mouguin and LS Rossi (eds), *La dimension extérieure de l'espace de liberté, de securité et de justice de l'Union européenne après le Ttraité de Lisbonne* (Brussels, Bruylant, 2013) 5–22; RA Wessel, L Marin and C Matera, 'The External Dimension of the EU's Area of Freedom, Security and Justice' in C Eckes and T Konstantinides (eds), *Crimen within the Area of Freedom, Security and Justice: A European Public Order* (Cambridge, Cambridge University Press, 2011) 272–300.

[7] Prior to the Lisbon Treaty, the European Community had express legal personality under the founding treaties (former Art 210 TEC), but academics debated at length whether the European Union had legal personality. In any event, from the moment that the founding treaties attributed to the EU the competence to enter into international treaties with third countries as regards matters coming within the third pillar in relation to police and judicial cooperation in criminal matters (Art 38 TEU)—and also in the second pillar with respect to common foreign and security policy (Art 24 TEU)—the debate became of much less practical interest.

[8] We have left on one side the competences relating to the CFSP because although formally this area has lost its status as an extra-Community pillar, the way that it is regulated under the Lisbon Treaty means that its clearly intergovernmental nature persists. It is formally included within the EU but it is not a normal EU competence (exclusive, shared or supporting), nor is it subject to ordinary decision-making processes or regulated through the ordinary legal acts of the EU or under the legal control of the CJEU, except with regard to those acts that directly affect individuals (Art 24(1) TEU and Art 275 TFEU).

[9] The institutional issue regarding how, in practice, the tasks of an external nature in the hands of the High Representative, the President of the European Council and the members of the Commission with external competences will be engaged in, together with the structuring of the work of the new European External Action Service, was discussed at length by academics when the Lisbon Treaty came into force. However, this question goes beyond the remit of this chapter. See M Gatti, 'The role of the European External Action Service in the external dimension of the Area of Freedom Security and Justice' in C Flaesch-Mouguin and LS Rossi (eds), *La dimension extérieure*, n 6 above, at 195–203.

[10] Current Art 43 TEU, which relates to the CFSP, expressly mentions terrorism in its first paragraph when it states that missions outside of the EU, which may have recourse to civil and military resources, 'may contribute to the fight against terrorism, including by supporting third countries in combating terrorism in their territories'.

has led to a degree of 'Community regularisation' of external action in the AFSJ or, as another author has put it, a 'normalisation' of the AFSJ.[11]

This does not mean, however, that action by the EU in this area is immune from both legal and political problems.[12] Quite the reverse is true. But now there is no doubt whatsoever about the indivisibility of the internal and external dimensions of the AFSJ if the goal is to achieve genuinely effective and coherent action in relation thereto, the latter being an instrumental part of the former.[13] First, this is so because, as is also the case with the other attributions of EU competences, all Community policies have an external dimension. But, secondly, this indivisibility manifests itself even more clearly with respect to the AFSJ because, due to the very nature of the area to be regulated (immigration, asylum, control of external borders, etc), the measures adopted inside the EU already have per se an external dimension that affects third countries. Thirdly, moreover, there are also certain actions that are in themselves a clear manifestation of this external dimension itself (eg readmission agreements, judicial cooperation agreements with third countries, agreements for the transfer of personal and financial data, etc). For this reason, as in other areas of EU action, to be able to measure accurately the scope of external action in the AFSJ, one must start by analysing the nature of the competence attributed to the EU in this area (2), examining how this competence has actually been exercised in the EU (3) and detecting the main problems that have arisen (4), before finally reaching some brief conclusions of a critical nature (5).

II. THE EXTERNAL COMPETENCE OF THE EU IN RELATION TO THE AFSJ: CONSEQUENCES OF THE COMMUNITISATION OF THE EXPRESS AND IMPLIED COMPETENCES IN THIS AREA

With the Lisbon Treaty, the goal of establishing

> an area of freedom, security and justice without internal frontiers in which the free movement of persons is ensured in conjunction with appropriate measures with respect to internal border controls, asylum, immigration and the prevention and combating of crime (Article 3(2) TEU)

[11] C Kaddous, 'Un nouveau cadre pour la dimension externe de l'espace de liberté, de securité et de justice' in C Kaddous and M Dony (eds), *D'Amsterdam à Lisbonne—Dix ans d'espace de liberté, de securité et de justice* (Berna, Heilbing & Lichtenhahn, 2010) 61–79 at 76.

[12] In our opinion, two interesting collective works which include an analysis of the external governance of AFSJ from a political science perspective are T Balzacq (ed), *The External Dimension of EU Justice and Home Affairs—Governance, Neighbours, Security* (Basingstoke, Palgrave McMillan, 2010) (with numerous references to academic texts at pp 249–76); and S Wolff, N Wichmann and G Mounier (eds), *The External Dimension of Justice and Home Affairs—A Different Security Agenda for the European Union?* (London, Routledge, 2010).

[13] J Santos Vara, 'The External Dimension of the Area of Freedom, Security and Justice in the Lisbon Treaty' (2008) 10 *European Law Journal* 577–97; C Flaesch-Mougin (ed), *Union européenne et sécurité: aspects internes et externs* (Brussels, Bruylant, 2009).

was defined as a shared competence with the EU (Article 4(2)(j) TFEU). This competence aims to guarantee the absence of internal border controls for persons and to develop a common policy on asylum, immigration and external border controls (Article 67(2) TFEU), and to ensure a high level of security through the prevention of crime and judicial and police cooperation regarding criminal matters (Article 67(3) TFEU) and mutual recognition of judicial and extrajudicial decisions in civil matters (Article 67(4) TFEU). It is a shared competence which encompasses sufficient express attributions of powers so as to achieve both a common policy as regards immigration (Article 77 TFEU), asylum (Article 78 TFEU) and judicial cooperation in civil matters (Article 81 TFEU), as well as the adoption of important actions regarding criminal judicial cooperation (Articles 82 to 86 TFEU) and police cooperation (Articles 87 to 89 TFEU). In short, after the Lisbon Treaty, in general terms, full 'communitisation' may be considered to have been achieved in this area. As a result, the nature of the competence as regards AFSJ does not differ substantially for the internal market, the environment or any other matter of a typically shared nature, and the position of the institutions is also the same. It is therefore for the Commission (as the 'legislative engine' of the EU) to propose the grant of a negotiating mandate by the Council; the European Parliament is included in the legislative procedure (prior approval); the Council normally decides by qualified majority (when, with respect to the internal dimension, the ordinary legislative procedure would be foreseen); and the CJEU exercises full judicial control over the AFSJ (above all, references for a preliminary ruling, action for annulment and prior control of the constitutional nature of international treaties).[14]

Nevertheless, it should be noted that certain minor vestiges of its intergovernmental past remain. Thus, the current regulation maintains the spatial exceptions for the United Kingdom, Ireland and Denmark. Nor is it easy to define, in each specific case, precisely what the competences of the EU and the Member States are, since the criteria of comparative efficiency and sufficiency arising from the application of the principle of subsidiarity to this area (Article 5(3) TEU) leave a lot of room for discretion, while at the same time, at a 'subconscious' level, Member States' memories of the association of this area with the concept of sovereignty have not entirely disappeared. Moreover, certain special rules with regard to police and judicial cooperation in criminal matters still exist (Member States' legislative initiative, loopholes where unanimity is required, etc) and there is even

[14] Under Art 218 TFEU, the procedure for the conclusion of international agreements is effectively negotiated with the Commission's proposal to be given a mandate to negotiate. Thereafter, the Council approves (or not) said mandate, the Commission carries out the negotiations and, where applicable, proposes to the Council the signature and ratification of the agreement. During this process, the Council will follow the same voting mechanism as required by the founding treaties for the internal dimension (which, in most cases, means a qualified majority and not unanimity). Probably the most important new feature of this process is the requirement for prior approval by the European Parliament (Article 218(6) TFEU).

a transitional period of five years in relation to the jurisdiction of the CJEU.[15] This has led authors such as Esther Zapater and Isabel Lirola to consider that there has been a 'limited removal of the pillar system'[16] with 'possible brakes and fragmentations'.[17] In any event, significant progress has been made.

What is of most interest to this paper is that the definition of the AFSJ as a shared competence of the EU and Member States has also had important consequences as regards its external dimension. The first and most obvious of these is the full applicability to the AFSJ of the general rules on international agreements of a general nature contained in the founding treaties (Articles 216 to 219 TFEU). Thus, to measure precisely the scope of the EU's external competence as regards the AFSJ, the possibility of entering into agreements 'where the Treaties so provide' (Article 216(1) TFEU) must be examined ie whether any express ad hoc attribution of external competence is contained in the regulation of the AFSJ. This is the case above all of the express competence with respect to immigration, which made it possible for the EU to

> conclude agreements with third countries for the readmission to their countries of origin or provenance of third-country nationals who do not or who no longer fulfil the conditions for entry, presence or residence in the territory of one of the Member States (Article 79(3) TFEU).[18]

And to a lesser extent, this is also the case as regards the curious attribution of competence introduced with respect to asylum (Article 78(2)(g) TFEU).[19]

[15] In general, this question in relation to the AFSJ following the Lisbon Treaty was treated in more detail in our previous work, entitled 'El espacio de libertad, seguridad y justicia en el Tratado de Lisboa' (2007) 70–72 *Revista de las Cortes Generales* 85–126. See also A Valle Gálvez, 'Espacio de Libertad, Seguridad y Justicia y Tratado de Lisboa' in J Martín y Pérez de Nanclares (ed), *El Tratado de Lisboa—La salida a la crisis constitucional* (Madrid, Iustel, 2008) 417–35.

[16] This author claims that under the formal communitisation carried out under the Lisbon Treaty, elements remain that 'make it possible to identify a *limited removal of the pillar system*'; E Zapater Duque and I Lirola Delgado, 'La dimensión exterior del Espacio de Libertad, Seguridad y Justicia en el Programa de Estocolmo: el reto de la integración y de la coherencia' in M Pi Llorens and E Zapater Duque (eds), *¿Hacia una Europa de las personas en el Espacio de Libertad, Seguridad y Justicia?* (Madrid, Marcial Pons, 2008) 19–44, particularly p 37.

[17] I Lirola Delgado, 'La cooperación judicial en materia penal en el Tratado de Lisboa: ¿Un doble proceso de comunitarización y consolidación a costa de posibles frenos y fragmentaciones?' (2008) 16 *Revista General de Derecho Europeo*: www.iustel.com.

[18] In this regard, former Art 63(3)(b) TEC, in the wording given to it by the Treaty of Amsterdam, limited itself to establishing that the Community would be competent to adopt measures regarding immigration policy with respect to 'illegal immigration and illegal residence, including the repatriation of illegal residents'. This, however, was not an *express* attribution of external action, at least not one with the clear wording required of such attributions of competence.

[19] This attribution of competence is not, however, so obvious, since if we read it carefully what it actually attributes to the EU is a type of *internal* competence to attain a goal that is per se external in nature and whose implementation requires the entering into of cooperation agreements with third countries. Specifically, it attributes a competence to adopt 'measures for a common European asylum system' which include 'partnership and cooperation with third countries for the purpose of managing inflows of people applying for asylum or subsidiary or temporary protection'.

A second consequence of the communitisation of the AFSJ is the full applicability to the ALSJ of the doctrine on implied competences as regards entering into international agreements, except in the above-mentioned case of readmission agreements, for which an express attribution exists. Thus, as regards AFSJ matters, the EU is competent to enter into an agreement with one or more third countries or international organisations when so required to achieve any of the goals laid down in the policy to attain an AFSJ, when this is provided for in a legally binding act of the EU or when this may affect common rules or alter the scope thereof (Article 216(1) TFEU). Prima facie this, in general, amounts to an express assumption by the Treaties of the case law doctrine of parallelism developed by the CJEU in the well-known case *AETR*[20] and subsequently completed by the Opinions 1/76[21] and 1/94,[22] as well as by later settled case law.[23] Nevertheless, although this paper is not the place to examine this issue, the way this rule is formulated is unfortunate and, in practice, the application of this case law continues to give rise to a good number of legal problems. That said, in general terms we can say that since the Lisbon Treaty there has been, through Article 216(1) TFEU and the case law of the CJEU, sufficient (implied) competence to enable the EU to enter into an international agreement pursuant to Article 216(1) when this is necessary to attain, in the context of the policies of the EU, any of the objectives laid down by the Treaties (Opinion 1/76), when this is foreseen in a legally binding act of the Union (Opinion 1/94) or when this 'may affect common rules or alter their scope' (*AETR*). And the procedure will be exactly the same as that under Article 218 TFEU. Nevertheless, with respect to the specific scope of the crossing of external borders, there is also a Protocol according to which the attribution of a competence to the EU as regards the measures relating to the crossing of external borders (Article 77(2)(b) TFEU) must be understood 'without prejudice to the competence of Member States to negotiate or conclude agreements with third countries as long as they respect Union law and other relevant international agreements'.[24] This Protocol may be understood by some to be a provision of

[20] In this case, the CJEU recognised the existence of implied external competences. As a result, the possibility of the EU entering into an international agreement may arise from both an express ad hoc attribution of the founding treaties and other treaty provisions or the internal acts adopted by the EU in these areas (theory of parallelism or *in foro interno in foro externo*); judgment of 31 March 1971, Case 22/70 *Commission v Council*, [1971] ECR 263 (*Accord européen sur les transports routiers* (*AETR*)), particularly para 16; see also judgment of 14 July 1976, Joined Cases 3/76, 4/76 and 6/76 *Kramer and Others*, [1976] ECR 1279, paras 20 and 33.

[21] Opinion 1/76 includes the requirement of the *necessity* of the international agreement in question to attain the goal pursued by the attribution of competence existing in the internal sphere; Opinion 1/76 of 26 April 1977, para 3.

[22] Opinion 1/94 clarifies that the EU may enter into an international agreement when *a binding act of the Union is foreseen*, this being an exclusive external competence; Opinion 1/94 of 15 December 1994, [1994] ECR I-5267, in particular para 95.

[23] For examples of this case law in external matters, see the following opinions of the CJEU: Opinion 2/91, of 19 March 1993, [1993] ECR I-1061; Opinion 1/94 of 15 November 1994, [1994] ECR I-5267; Opinion 1/03 of 7 February 2006, [2006] ECR I-1145.

[24] Protocol no 23 on external relations of the Member States with regard to the crossing of external borders.

primary law which would prevent the Union from attaining an implicit external competence of an exclusive nature in this area. However, it could also be interpreted as meaning that the possible exclusive nature of the EU competence would not be ab initio but only when exercised. This interpretation could be supported by the fact that this Protocol is in fact inherited from the Treaty of Amsterdam, when the founding treaties did not contain the provisions on competences which were introduced by the Lisbon Treaty.

Thirdly, with respect to police and judicial cooperation in criminal matters, as a result of its (almost) total communitisation, there has been a transformation from the former express competence in external matters (former Articles 24 and 38 TEU) into an implicit competence governed by identical rules to those seen in relation to the rest of the matters specific to the AFSJ. There is, nevertheless, a controversial Declaration on this subject which states that the Member States can enter into international agreements with third countries or with international organisations in these same matters 'in so far as such agreements comply with Union law'.[25] Therefore, despite the fact that Declarations are obviously merely interpretative, a doubt immediately arises. Does this statement mean that the consequence of the EU entering into such agreements is not the normal one of pre-emption (displacement of the possibility of Member States intervening) or does it simply transfer to the external dimension the fact that the intensity of the competence of police and judicial cooperation in criminal matters is less than that existing in relation to immigration and asylum? In our opinion, although the wording of the Declaration may be unfortunate or open-ended, it would not seem possible—in view of the fact that the AFSJ is considered to be a shared competence—to sustain the first reading There is no doubt, however, that the potential exists for conflicting interpretations.

Fourthly and finally, it is worth clarifying that the fact that the EU's competence as regards AFSJ matters is shared with Member States does not, in practice, prevent certain attributions of competences, existing in their external dimension, from having a degree of intensity which makes them exclusive or quasi-exclusive. Obviously, none of them has an exclusive nature ab initio since they are not on the 'closed list' which now exists in the founding treaties (Article 3(1) TFEU). But they may have an exclusive nature in the external dimension

> when its conclusion is provided for in a legislative act of the Union or is necessary to enable the Union to exercise its internal competence, or in so far as its conclusion may affect common rules or alter their scope (Article 3(2) TFEU).

This provision becomes particularly important with respect to the AFSJ because in the internal sphere the EU has been attributed with the competence of adopting a *common* policy on visas and other short-stay residence permits

[25] Declaration on Article 218 of the Treaty on the Functioning of the European Union concerning the negotiation and conclusion of international agreements by Member States relating to the area of freedom, security and justice [2010] OJ C83/489.

(Article 77(2)(a) TFEU), asylum policy, temporary protection, subsidiary protection and procedures to grant or withdraw the uniform status of asylum or subsidiary protection (Article 78(1) and 78(2)(a), (b), (c) and (d) TFEU), and even an immigration policy (Article 79(1) TFEU).[26] It may also be important if the EU were to carry out an exhaustive intervention in this area to the point that, in practice, it displaced (pre-emption effect) any possible intervention by Member States. In this regard, the attributions of (internal) competence that only permit the adoption of 'minimum rules' are obviously not affected by the debate about the exclusive nature of the external dimension. This is the case of the national criminal procedural rules required for the mutual recognition of judgments (Article 82(2) TFEU) or substantive criminal harmonisation (Articles 83(1) and (2) TFEU). In these areas, the EU's competence in the external dimension will always be shared in nature and, therefore, 'mixed agreements' will clearly be the order of the day.

Having examined the scope of the express and implied competences to act with regard to the external dimension of the AFSJ, the next section analyses exactly how the EU has exercised these competences in practice.

III. THE EXERCISE OF EXTERNAL COMPETENCES AS REGARDS THE AFSJ: MORE THAN JUST READMISSION AGREEMENTS

A. Readmission Agreements: The Most Visible Field of External Action in the AFSJ

The way in which the EU has exercised the express and/or implied competences attributed to it has largely focused on the control of immigration, particularly as regards readmission agreements.[27] Prior to the Treaty of Amsterdam, this was based on an implied external competence, and after it, the express attribution contained in the treaties, whether in the former version of Article 63(3)(b) TEC or now in the clear attribution of express competence contained in Article 79(3) TFEU. In line with the evolution referred to above, this type of agreement has also gone through different phases. Initially, they were not ad hoc international agreements; instead, the external action was set out in readmission clauses included in mixed cooperation and collaboration agreements entered into with certain countries from Eastern Europe and the Caucasus, first as a mere principle to be taken

[26] Take, for example, the association agreement with Kosovo, being negotiated t the time of writing, which will be an EU-only agreement and which contains various provisions relating to the AFSJ.

[27] Among the now abundant literature existing in this regard, see N Arenas Hidalgo, 'Los acuerdos europeos de readmisión de inmigrantes en situación irregular. Diez años de política europea de readmisión a debate' (2010) 43 *Cuadernos Europeos de Deusto* 53–90; R Cholewinsky, 'EC Readmission Agreements' in S Peers and N Rogers (eds), *EU Immigration and Asylum Law* (Leiden, Nijhoff, 2006) 881–983.

into account in the framework of these agreements (Russia,[28] The Ukraine,[29] or Moldavia)[30] and subsequently as specimen clauses specifically approved by the Council and included in such agreements (Armenia,[31] Azerbaijan,[32] Georgia[33] or Uzbekistan).[34] Thereafter, once the Treaty of Amsterdam came into force, an intermediate phase began in which the practice of including this type of clause continued, albeit on a transitional basis, while waiting for the EU to enter into a readmission agreement that expressly stated the EU's new competence in this matter (eg association agreements with Croatia[35] or Chile).[36] Similarly, during this same intermediate phase, with respect to other agreements with a wider content, provisions were included that expressly provided for the signing with these States of a readmission agreement the negotiation of which would start once the agreements in question came into force. This occurred with respect to the agreements with Egypt,[37] Algeria,[38] and the Lebanon[39] and the Cotonou Agreements with ACP countries.[40]

Finally, to date the EU has entered into more than a dozen 'pure' readmission agreements with countries as diverse as Hong Kong,[41] Macao,[42] Sri Lanka,[43] Albania,[44] Russia,[45] Moldova,[46] The Ukraine,[47] Macedonia,[48] Montenegro,[49] Serbia,[50] Bosnia and Herzegovina,[51] Pakistan,[52] Georgia,[53] Armenia[54] or Turkey.[55] In the same way, the Council has granted a mandate to the Commission to negotiate in a further half dozen cases, although in these the readmission agreement has

[28] [1997] OJ L327 of 28.11.1997 (Art 84).
[29] [1998] OJ L49 of 19.2.1998 (Art 27).
[30] [1998] OJ L181 of 24.6.1998 (Art 20).
[31] [1999] OJ L239 of 9.9.1999 (Art 72).
[32] [1999] OJ L246 of 17.9.1999 (Art 75).
[33] [1999] OJ L205 of 4.8.1999 (Art 75).
[34] [1999] OJ L229 of 31.8.1999 (Art 72).
[35] [2005] OJ L26 of 28.1.2005 (Art 77).
[36] [2002] OJ L352 of 30.12.2002 (Art 46).
[37] [2004] OJ L304 of 30.9.2004 (Art 69).
[38] [2005] OJ L265 of 10.10.2005 (Art 84).
[39] [2006] OJ L143 of 30.5.2006 (Art 69).
[40] [2000] OJ L317 of 15.12.2000 (Art 13).
[41] [2004] OJ L17 of 24.1.2004.
[42] [2004] OJ L143 of 30.4.2004.
[43] [2005] OJ L124 of 17.5.2005.
[44] [2005] OJ L124 of 17.5.2005.
[45] [2007] OJ L129 of 17.5.2007.
[46] [2007] OJ L334 of 19.12.2007.
[47] [2007] OJ L332 of 18.12.2007.
[48] [2007] OJ L334 of 19.12.2007.
[49] [2007] OJ L334 of 19.12.2007.
[50] [2007] OJ L334 of 19.12.2007.
[51] [2007] OJ L334 of 19.12.2007.
[52] [2010] OJ L287 of 4.11.2010.
[53] [2011] OJ L52 of 25.2.2011.
[54] [2013] OJ L289 of 31.10.2013.
[55] [2014] OJ L134 of 7.5.2014.

yet to be signed (Morocco, Cape Verde or Belarus) and in two cases the Commission has had great difficulties even starting negotiations (China and Algeria).[56]

In relation to this type of agreement it is worth mentioning, among others, the following issues. From the political perspective, there is the question of whether these EU actions are based on some type of strategy or, on the contrary, they are due to reasons of mere expediency. In our opinion, a strategy can be clearly seen in relation to countries from the former Yugoslavia that may meet the twin objectives of completing the pre-accession association agreements entered into so as to stabilise a particularly problematic area, while also intervening within the framework of the AFSJ in order to ensure the return of illegal immigrants to certain countries that are particularly close to the EU's external land borders. However, in other cases it is difficult to detect any strategy at all. In fact, it is hard to understand why the Commission was given a mandate to negotiate with a State without first being sure that it will at least be possible to start negotiations.

But also from the legal perspective such actions give rise to certain doubts regarding various issues. For example, the first thing that is striking is that the decisions adopted by the Council to conclude these international agreements do not show that they comply with the principle of subsidiarity (Article 5(3) and Protocol no 2). Moreover, it is perfectly legitimate to ask questions about the greater efficiency of the EU's intervention and, above all, the alleged insufficiency of the intervention of Member States. This question is even more relevant if we bear in mind that in practice the Commission is having enormous difficulties in some cases concluding—or even initiating—negotiations regarding certain treaties for which it has a mandate. Claiming that the mere selection of the States with which it has been decided to negotiate a treaty of this nature amounts to the added value required by the principle of subsidiarity would appear to us to be insufficient.

Secondly, fully in line with the new ad hoc attribution of competences and the case law of the CJEU as regards shared competences already exercised by the EU, Member States can no longer enter into agreements of this nature with third countries once this has been done by the EU (*pre-emption* or *occupation* of the territory) except where they are expressly authorised by the latter (which has never happened so far) or in relation to the implementation of the agreement (Protocols applicable to the agreement). As far as we know, this requirement is clearly being complied with once the agreements are concluded, although the same cannot be said of the situation in the preceding phases. In this regard, it is also worth noting that some Member States also undertake negotiations with respect to treaties in this area with third countries when the Commission has already been given a

[56] See A Roig and T Huddleston, 'EC Readmision Agreements: A Re-evaluation of the Political Impasse' (2007) 9 *European Journal of Migration and Law* 363–87; C Billet, 'EC Readmission Agreements: A Prime Instrument of the External Dimension of the EU's Fight against Irregular Immigration. An Assessment after Ten Years of Practice' (2010) 12 *European Journal of Migration and Law* 45–79.

mandate by the Council to negotiate with these same States. It is submitted that this practice may give rise to doubts about its compatibility with the principle of sincere cooperation (Article 4(3) TEU). Strictly speaking, it appears clear that pre-emption—which means the displacement of any possibility of entering into an agreement with the third country in question by a Member State—will not be effective until such time as an agreement is concluded. But a doubt may exist as to whether this parallel carrying out of negotiations by a Member State at the same time as the Commission could amount to a violation of the obligation to abstain from adopting 'any measure which could jeopardise the attainment of the Union's objectives' through the signing of said agreement.

Thirdly, doubts also exist about the compatibility of this type of agreement with the international commitments assumed by both the EU and its Member States in relation to asylum, human rights, extradition and other areas.[57] Particularly problematic are the provisions of these agreements that provide for the readmission of those who are nationals of States that are not parties to the agreement (or are even stateless persons) who have entered, or find themselves illegally in, EU territory. In the opinion of certain authors, the application of EU policy as regards border controls could be endangering non-negotiable aspects of asylum policy.[58] Nevertheless, in our opinion, the agreements in question comply with the standards laid down by the international commitments assumed by the EU. Thus, these agreements include the 'compatibility clause' in which it is established in general that '[t]his agreement shall not affect the rights, obligations and responsibilities of the Community [now Union], the Member States and [the State in question with which the readmission agreement is signed] arising from International Law'.[59]

And fourthly, in relation to the agreements already in force, from a substantive point of view it is worth noting that, in practice, the oft-mentioned 'comprehensive approach' has totally failed to take shape, being, in fact, more a goal than a reality.

[57] More specifically, some of the provisions of this type of agreement may give rise to doubts about the compatibility with the Convention relating to the Status of Refugees of 28 July 1951 and its Protocol of 31 January 1967. Equally, in some cases doubts may also arise with respect to the compatibility with the European Convention for the Protection of Human Rights and Fundamental Freedoms of 4 November 1950, for example in relation to the express prohibition on inhuman and degrading treatment; in such case, the Convention of 10 December 1984 against torture and other cruel, inhuman or degrading treatment or punishment would also be relevant. In certain very specific cases, one could also consider their very compatibility with the conventions and the multilateral international agreements on the readmission of foreigners. See, for example, N Coleman, *European Readmission Policy: Third Country Interests and Refugee Rights* (The Hague, Nijhoff, 2009) N Albuquerquer Abell, 'The Compatibility of Readmission Agreements with the 1951 Convention relating to the Status of Refugees' (1999) 11 *International Journal of Refugee Law* 60–83.

[58] S Klepp, 'A Contested Asylum System: The European Union between Refugee Protection and Border Control in the Mediterranean Sea' (2010) 12 *European Journal of Migration and Law* 1–21.

[59] See, for example, Art 17 of the Agreement between the European Community and Bosnia Herzegovina on the readmission of persons residing without authorisation, n 51 above.

B. Other Agreements on the Question of Immigration, Asylum and civil Cooperation: Doubts about the International Action of FRONTEX

It should be stressed that the EU has not just entered into admission agreements. With respect to external competences, then, life exists beyond this express attribution analysed above; the EU has also intervened as regards questions of the control of borders and the fight against illegal immigration. In 1998, the Council adopted the objective of attaining external action in this area. A High Level Working Group on Asylum and Immigration was set up in order to lay the foundations for the development of an external immigration policy and it became much more active after the Seville European Council of June 2002. However, at present it is probably the action of FRONTEX which gives rise to most legal problems.[60] This agency has entered into international agreements ('working arrangements') with countries from locations as diverse as Eastern Europe (Russia, Ukraine, Croatia, Georgia, Belarus, Serbia, Albania, Montenegro, Macedonia, Bosnia and Herzegovina, Moldova and Turkey), Africa (Cape Verde and Nigeria), Republics of the former Soviet Union (Armenia and Azerbaijan) or North America (the United States and Canada), and even with international organisations (International Organization for Migration) or other European Agencies (Agency for Fundamental Rights, European Maritime Safety Agency, Europol, etc).[61]

From the outset, then, these agreements have given rise to major legal issues. First, there is clearly a doubt about their legal status.[62] And, secondly, it is not clear whether entering into such agreements goes beyond the competences entrusted to FRONTEX in Articles 13 and 14 of the Regulation which created it.[63] It is even open to doubt whether the official publication of the agreements or of the mandates to negotiate is compatible with the principle of publicity which forms part of the EU legal system.[64]

Similarly, an interesting question in relation to the external dimension of the common immigration policy is that relating to the extraterritorial interception of irregular immigrants, particularly when this takes place at sea, beyond the 12 miles

[60] See, for example, M Urrea Corres, 'El control de fronteras como instrumento para la seguridad: una aproximación al nuevo marco jurídico de FRONTEX' (2012) 10 *Revista del Instituto Español de Estudios Estratégicos* 153–72.

[61] FRONTEX is also in negotiations with further seven countries, namely, Libya, Morocco, Senegal, Mauritania, Egypt, Brazil and Tunisia.

[62] See, in general, S Carrera, L Herzog and J Parkin, 'The peculiar nature of EU Home Affairs Agencies in Migration Control: Beyond Accountability verus Autonomy' (2013) 15 *European Journal of Migration Law* 337–58; J Santos Vara, 'The external activities of AFSJ Agencies: The Weakness of Democratic and Judicial Controls' (2015) 20 *European Foreign Affairs Review* 115–36.

[63] Council Regulation (EC) No 2007/2004, of 26 October 2004, establishing a European Agency for the Management of Operational Cooperation at the External Borders of the Member States of the European Union, [2004] OJ L349 of 25.11.2004; amended in 2007 ([2007] OJ L199 of 31.7.2007) and in 2011 ([2011] OJ L304 of 22.11.2011).

[64] See M Fink, 'Frontex Working Arrangements: Legitimacy and Human Rights Concerns Regarding Technical Relationships' (2012) 28 *Utrecht Journal of International and European Law* 20–35.

of territorial waters which, pursuant to the United Nations Convention on the Law of the Sea of 1982, belong to the coastal State (Article 3); or beyond the 24 miles of the contiguous zone over which the authorities of the coastal State may also adopt measures required to prevent illegal immigration (Article 33(1)).[65] Apart from the public international law dimension itself, specifically with respect to the external dimension of the AFSJ, the action that the EU carries out through FRONTEX in this regard in maritime areas adjoining the African continent co-exists with bilateral agreements that certain Member States have entered into in this matter with third countries. This is the case, for example, of Spain which, through agreements with six countries, has been able to organise effective common patrols on a joint basis by the Spanish *Guardia Civil* and the corresponding security forces of the African countries affected, to combat illegal immigration.[66] Nevertheless, pursuant to the above-mentioned doctrine of pre-emption laid down by the CJEU in relation to the shared competences of the EU, the actions of Member States would be compatible with EU law to the extent that the latter has not exercised its competence; where it has, Member States must fit in with what the EU does, except where the latter duly authorises them. It should also be recalled that one of the functions entrusted to FRONTEX is that of coordinating operational cooperation for the external control of borders and facilitating the cooperation between Member States and third countries, and concluding working arrangements with these third countries in this area.[67] Therefore, the risk of overlapping competences exists.

Finally, this type of agreement to carry out joint patrols with the authorities of African countries such as Guinea or Senegal gives rise, in the opinion of certain authors, to certain legal doubts as regards *non-refoulement* requirements arising, from an international perspective, under the Geneva Convention of 28 July 1958 and, from the EU perspective, the founding treaties themselves (Article 78(1) TFEU).[68] It does not appear, however, that this can be deduced from the agreements themselves. In any event, this would arise as a result of their being put into practice and, moreover, the fact that these are *joint* controls with the State in question should not be overlooked.

Before concluding this section, apart from the actions of FRONTEX, it would be worth stating at least the following four additional issues. First, in relation to the fight against illegal immigration, the EU also ratified (jointly with Member States) the Palermo Protocols against the smuggling of migrants and the trafficking of persons through the 'mixed agreement' mechanism; which is perfectly in

[65] See P García Andrade, 'Extraterritorial Strategies to Tackle Irregular Immigration by Sea: A Spanish Perspective' in B Ryan and V Mitsilegas (eds), *Extraterritorial Immigration Control* (Leiden, Brill, 2010) 311–46.

[66] This is the case of the agreements entered into with Morocco, Senegal, Mauritania, Cape Verde, Gambia and Guinea. For example, the agreement with Cape Verde has been published. See *Boletín Oficial del Estado* (Spanish Official Gazette) of 5 June 2009.

[67] As per Arts 2(1), 3 and 14 of Regulation 2007/2004, n 63 above.

[68] S Klepp, 'A Contested Asylum System: The European Union between Refugee Protection and Border Control in the Mediterranean Sea' (2010) 12 *European Journal of Migration and Law* 1–21.

accordance with the content of this agreement. Secondly, the EU has also engaged in some external action as regards visas, whether through treaties with certain micro-States of limited political importance (Barbados, Seychelles, Mauricio, Bahamas, Antigua and Saint Kitts & Nevis)[69] or through visa facilitation agreements with States with whom readmission agreements are being negotiated at the same time.[70] Thirdly, in relation to asylum, in some forums the question of whether the EU could ultimately adhere to the Geneva Convention is starting to be raised. Finally, as regards civil cooperation, the CJEU has ruled that, pursuant to the implied competences referred to earlier in this chapter, the EU effectively had the exclusive external competence in relation to the Lugano Convention, which extends to non-EU Member States the effects of the well-known Brussels Regulation I.[71] Thereafter, the European Community, followed by the EU, have been very active in this area.[72]

C. External Action in Criminal Matters: Continuity after Communitisation

Based on the former attribution of competence contained in the extra-Community pillar of Police and Judicial Cooperation in Criminal Matters (Article 38 TEU), the EU has carried out interesting international activity, the details of which have been analysed, as far as the Spanish literature in this area is concerned, by Carmen Martínez Capdevilla.[73] Now, following the disappearance of the ad hoc basis for external competence with the entry into force of the Lisbon Treaty and the extension of the general criteria of the EU's external action to this matter, international agreements have continued to be entered into with third countries based on the implied external competence arising under Article 216(1) TFEU mentioned earlier and the case law of the CJEU (*AETR* and Opinion 1/76). Logically, the basic problem has been the transition to the new post-Lisbon regime, particularly in relation to international agreements where negotiations have already commenced but which have not yet come into force.

Initially, four agreements of this nature were entered into. Two of them were to extend the Schengen *acquis* to Iceland and Norway,[74] in addition to Switzerland and Liechtenstein.[75] As regards the other two, one was with Japan with respect

[69] [2009] OJ L169 of 30.6.2009.

[70] See B Martenczuk, 'Visa Policy and EU External Relations' in B Martenczuk and S Thiel (eds), *Justice, Liberty and Security: New Challenges for EU External Relations* (Brussels, VUB Press, 2008) 21–53.

[71] Opinion 1/03, of 7 February 2006, [2006] ECR I-1145.

[72] See, for example, S Peers, *(EU Justice…)*, n 1 above, at 648–53.

[73] In relation to this subject, her interesting monograph in Spanish, C Martínez Capdevilla, *Los acuerdos internacionales de la Unión Europea en el tercer pilar* (Cizur Menor, Civitas-Thomson, 2009) is compulsory reading.

[74] [2009] OJ L353 of 31.12.2009.

[75] [2011] OJ L160 of 18.6.2011.

to judicial cooperation in criminal matters[76] and the other was with the United States, with respect to the transfer of financial payment messaging data.[77] The first three do not give rise to significant judicial problems and it is clear that they concern an external action in the context of a shared competence that cannot become exclusive, in relation to which the use of 'mixed agreements' is not in dispute. In fact, to avoid any doubt about the interpretation of the scope of the abovementioned Declaration no 36, all of them include express clauses that make it clear that Member States can continue to enter into agreements with third countries, provided that they do not infringe either the terms of those agreements or EU law. In our opinion, however, in the future it would be a good idea for the relevant Decisions of the Council and/or the agreement in question to refer expressly to the specific competence under Article 216(1) TFEU, which contains the legal basis for entering into the same. Otherwise, the argument that the Lisbon Treaty (Article 216(1) TFEU) has created more confusion than certainty in relation to the doctrine laid down in *AETR* and Opinion 1/76 would gain ground. However, it is the agreement with the US that has proved to be much more controversial, having given rise to quite a number of institutional and substantive problems.[78] From an institutional point of view, the switch to the post-Lisbon regime strengthens the position of the European Parliament—from merely bit part to centre stage, with the requirement of prior approval (Article 218(6)(a) TFEU)[79]—and its critical position with respect to this agreement created major difficulties.[80] And from a substantive point of view, various academics have pointed to the possible incompatibility of the mass transfer of personal data without any court intervention with basic human rights requirements, particularly Article 8 of the Charter of Fundamental Rights. Equally, the doubts about the legal form which the ad hoc provision should have had as regards data protection (Article 16 TFEU) are not unreasonable either.

Furthermore, the European Union also signed agreements with third countries which define the conditions and modalities for the transfer from the European Union-led Naval Force (EUNAVFOR) to the affected country of persons suspected of intending to commit, committing or having committed acts of piracy and detained by EUNAVNOR. Such is the case of the recent agreement between the EU and Tanzania.[81]

[76] [2010] OJ L39 of 12.2.2010.

[77] [2010] OJ L195 of 27.7.2010.

[78] In this regard, see J Escribano Úbeda-Portugués, 'El refuerzo de los mecanismos de cooperación entre la Unión Europea y los Estados miembros en el ámbito del tratamiento y la transferencia de datos de mensajería financiera en la UE a Estados Unidos en materia de lucha contra la financiación del terrorismo' (2011) 23 *Revista General de Derecho Europeo*; www.iustel.com. W Hummer, 'Die SWIFT-Affaire: US-Terrorismusbekämpfung versus Datenschutz' (2011) 49 *Archiv des Völkerrechts* 203–45, is extremely critical of this agreement.

[79] See I Bosse-Platière, 'Le Parlement européen et le volet externee de l'ELSJ' in C Flaesch-Mougin and LS Rossi (eds), *(La dimension…)*, n 6 above, 95–129.

[80] J Monar, 'The Rejection of the EU-US SWIFT Interim Agreement by the European Parliament: A Historic Vote and Its Implications' (2010) 15 *European Foreign Affairs Review* 143–51.

[81] [2014] OJ L108 of 11.4.2014.

Moreover, within the field of police and judicial cooperation in criminal matters, the international agreements entered into with other EU agencies with competences in relation to AFSJ are equally problematic. Thus, Europol has entered into operational agreements with neighbouring European countries, such as Iceland (2001), Norway (2001), Switzerland (2004), Croatia (2006), Bosnia Herzegovina (2007), Albania (2007), Serbia (2008) and Liechtenstein (2013) but also with countries outside Europe such as the US (2001), Canada (2005) or Australia (2007) and even with Interpol (2001). Similarly, Eurojust has signed agreements with third European countries such as Norway (2005), Iceland (2005), Croatia (2007), Switzerland (2008), Liechtenstein (2013) and Moldova (2014) and with non-European countries like the US (2006). It has also signed Memoranda of Understanding with several entities, like the United Nations Office on Drugs and Crime (2010) or Interpol (2013). The controversy does not relate so much to the existence, or not, of legal personality or whether or not it is possible to enter into relationships with third countries because the treaties themselves provide for this (eg Article 88(2)(a) TFEU). Rather, it relates to the doubts about the possibility that this attribution of legal personality within the internal sphere of the Union[82] may at the same time give rise, without the need for any further formality, to legal personality in external matters, quite apart from the doubts about the possible overlapping with the legal personality of the EU and the insufficient institutional control over this type of agreement.

Finally, the external action of the EU as regards specific issues relating to the AFSJ has not only involved third countries as counterparties but also international organisations. For example, the then European Community entered into an international cooperation and assistance agreement with the International Criminal Court.[83]

IV. CERTAIN RISKS OF EXTERNAL ACTION IN THE AREA OF FREEDOM, SECURITY, AND JUSTICE: THE PREDOMINANCE OF SECURITY AND CONTROL IN A FRAGMENTED SPACE

A. The Freedom *versus* Security Conundrum: A Combination that is Difficult to Reconcile

Probably one of the areas of the EU where the greatest divergence exists between the goals laid down by the European institutions and the reality of their specific acts is that of external action in the AFSJ. The AFSJ was designed in the founding

[82] In fact, there are (internal) agreements between Europol and the Commission, Eurojust, OLAF and FRONTEX, together with the agreements between Eurojust and OLAF that do not give rise to this problem.

[83] [2006] OJ L115 of 28.4.2006. The legal basis for entering into this agreement was the former Article 24 TEU specific to the CFSP. In any event, it is clear that its substantive content is directly related to the specific issues of the AFSJ.

treaties as a new concept that came into being following the disappearance of the internal borders between States that had created a single market in which its three basic features should be combined in a balanced manner: *freedom* of movement for all persons who find themselves inside that space, regardless of their nationality; *security* arising from the adoption of the necessary measures to compensate for the risks that may be caused by the disappearance of these borders between States; and *justice* to guarantee judicially compliance with the legal requirements and fundamental rights in a particularly delicate area. In line with this approach, the treaties define the AFSJ as 'an area without internal borders in which the free movement of persons is ensured', in which there will be 'a common policy on asylum, immigration and external border control based on solidarity between Member States which is fair towards third-country nationals' and in which, in any event, any action taken will be 'with respect for fundamental rights'.

In fact, however, the EU's actions in this matter are a long way from having achieved a balance between these three elements. That said, important steps have been taken. Thus, with the entry into force of the Lisbon Treaty, action in relation to the *justice* element has been extended since, in addition to giving the EU's Charter of Fundamental Rights the same status as the founding treaties (inclusion by reference) and making this legally binding (Article 5 TEU), the CJEU's judicial control over all parts of the AFSJ, including those that previously formed part of the extra-Community pillar and, therefore, with respect to the EU's external action in this area, has been completely regularised. In addition, when the EU accedes to the ECHR in the future, on the terms laid down in Article 6(2) TEU, the protection of human rights will be strengthened through the control that the European Court of Human Rights will be able to exercise.[84]

B. The Mirage of the 'Comprehensive Approach': A Goal that is Difficult to Achieve in Practice

As mentioned earlier, since Tampere the EU has in theory been inspired by what has been termed a 'comprehensive approach' to immigration policy; in other words, the desire to combine, in a balanced manner, control of irregular immigration, mobility of legal regulation and development cooperation. In fact, however, throughout the term of the Tampere Programme, immigration control comprised the bulk of the EU's action. Equally, during the period in which the Hague Programme was applied (2005–09) the European Council made—particularly during 2005 and 2006—various declarations in favour of the so-called 'comprehensive approach', but the rhetoric was not matched by action.[85] Last but not least, while

[84] At present, the proposed Accession Agreement of the EU to the ECHR is pending after the CJEU's declaration in Opinion 2/2013.

[85] Commission Communication of 2006 entitled 'The global approach to immigration one year on: towards a comprehensive European migration policy', COM(2006) 735 final, of 30.11.2006. Through

the Stockholm Programme for the 2010–14 period reiterated the theory, in practice the picture was, once more, quite different.[86]

As a result, the 'mobility partnership' instrument[87] has not lived up to the hopes placed on it and has ended up becoming another way to facilitate the control of migration policy.[88]

In short, the desired balance between the three elements that make up the 'comprehensive approach' has not (yet) been achieved. Nor has the sought-after consistency between the actions that make this up been achieved. Nor, probably, has the necessary coordination between the EU and the Member States which is sought.

C. Fragmentation into an '*À la Carte* Space': The Unsustainable Position of the UK, Ireland and Denmark

Continuing with the risks to consistent external EU action within the AFSJ, the exceptions contained in the primary law for the UK, Ireland and Denmark with respect to (internal) actions in the AFSJ[89] have serious negative consequences for the external dimension thereof. These negative consequences are striking for the fragmentation that they cause. But in practice, putting on one side the parallel issue of reinforced cooperation, this unusual set of rules has given rise to issues that are much thornier than those that may initially have been imagined. The opt-in and opt-out clauses have led to a wide range of legal problems that require an in-depth study to calculate the extent to which the resulting puzzle is compatible with the most basic requirements of legal certainty. Moreover, these exceptions have also resulted in certain practices which do not completely satisfy the requirements of the principle of sincere cooperation. In fact, anyone who examines in

this concept, the terms 'circular migration' and of 'mobility partnerships with third countries' have also been coined; COM(2007) 248 final de 16.5.2007.

[86] We would recommend reading the Commission's assessment in this regard in its Report entitled 'Global Approach to Migration and Mobility', COM(2011) 743 final 18.11.2011.

[87] See the Commission's assessment of this issue in its EU 2009 Report on Policy Coherence for Development, COM(2009) 461 final of 17.9. 2009. Comments such as 'efforts need to continue in order to embark upon the policy challenge of offering real migration and mobility options for nationals of developing countries legally seeking employment in the EU' or '[a]lso facilitating labour migration … remains important' (p 8) are examples of wishful thinking that are worthy of note.

[88] See F Esteve García, 'Las asociaciones de movilidad y la inmigración circular: ¿nuevos instrumentos de cooperación y nuevos derechos de movilidad en el enfoque global de la UE en materia de inmigraciones?' in M Pi Llorens and E Zapater Duque (eds), (*¿Hacia una Europa …*), n 16 above, at 69–104.

[89] The situation of these countries is governed by Protocols no 21 and 22 attached to the TEU and the TFEU. See, for example, S Carrera and F Geyer, 'El Tratado de Lisboa y un espacio de libertad, seguridad y justicia: excepcionalismo y fragmentación en la Unión Europea' (2008) 29 *Revista de Derecho Comunitario Europeo* 133–64; B Martenczuk, 'Variable Geometry and the External Relations of the EU: The Experience of Justice and Home Affairs' in B Martenczuk and S Thiel (eds), (*Justice, Liberty and Security…*), n 70 above, 493–524.

detail the operation of these exceptions in the post-Lisbon legal regime may detect the spirit of Kafka in, for example, the possibility of the UK and Ireland opting out of actions that develop a Schengen *acquis* that already binds them.

In addition, in practice, something as basic as determining the position of each of these three Member States is not a simple task. For example, with respect to readmission agreements, Ireland does not participate in them, apart from the one concerning Hong Kong. Denmark does not participate in any, but all of them include a Declaration that provides for the entering into of an agreement between Denmark and the third country in question on identical terms. And as for the UK, while it has signed these agreements, during the negotiations it used all sorts of tricks to exploit the political position afforded by its opt-in or opt-out position, as suited it best.

In short, in our opinion, the price paid for attributing the competence in these matters to the EU has been that of giving concessions to these three Member States that have given rise to a genuine '*à la carte* external action'.

V. FINAL CONSIDERATIONS: THE INDISSOLUBLE LINK BETWEEN THE INTERNAL AND EXTERNAL DIMENSIONS OF THE AFSJ

To conclude, the external action of the EU with respect to the AFSJ area continues to suffer from certain deficiencies that cannot be ignored. That said, in our opinion the Lisbon Treaty has meant substantial progress in the form of improved instruments, procedures and judicial control of this external dimension of the AFSJ. The consideration of police and judicial cooperation in criminal affairs as a shared competence of the EU subject to the Community method, the greater participation of the European Parliament in the process for entering into international agreements, or judicial control by the CJEU of all international agreements that the EU might sign in this field, are undoubtedly steps in the right direction. The same can be said of the full applicability to the whole of the AFSJ area of the general rules.

Nevertheless, the main conclusion in relation to the specific goal of this chapter is that, despite all of the unusual features and defects that can be found, the internal and external dimensions of the AFSJ are now inseparable. If the latter is not adequately developed, the former cannot be made consistent and effective. And, in view of the long and winding road taken to reach the Lisbon Treaty, this is no mean feat…

17

The EU Antiterrorist Sanctions

ENZO CANNIZZARO[1]

Content:

I. INTRODUCTORY REMARKS

THE FIELD OF antiterrorism indisputably constitutes one of those in which political needs constantly tend to condition and overshadow the legal dimension. This generic observation, far from rendering legal analysis superfluous, has the opposite effect: stressing the necessity of an impartial and objective legal analysis, unleashed from the constraint of political necessity.

One of the main problems which arise in this context is to determine the most appropriate way to control antiterrorist action: through the political process or rather through judicial review. In many modern legal orders, these two aspects are closely interrelated. Judges generally tend to attenuate the standard of review of highly politically motivated acts in the belief that the legality of these acts ought to be controlled mainly through the political process by organs endowed with political legitimacy.

[1] Professor of International and European Law, University of Rome 'La Sapienza'.

In the EU legal order, this relationship seems to be inverted. The ECJ has substantially upheld the view that antiterrorist action falls largely, if not exclusively, within the intergovernmental realm, where Member States' predominant role is still undisputed. However, it has refused to draw from this premise the consequences sought by the Member States and by the EU political institutions, namely the immunity of politically motivated acts from judicial control. Quite the contrary, in one of the boldest courses embarked upon in its over 40 years of activity, the ECJ has subjected antiterrorist sanctions to a strict judicial scrutiny. This course is carved out in this famous conclusion: '[t]he Courts of the European Union must ensure the review, in principle the full review, of the lawfulness of all European Union acts in the light of fundamental rights'.[2]

The relationship between political control and judicial control thus represents the invisible thread around which this chapter will unfold. In the first part, attention will be brought to the Treaty provisions which establish the EU competence in the field of antiterrorist sanctions. In spite of its technical character, this issue is of extraordinary interest even from a systemic viewpoint. The field of antiterrorist sanctions constitutes the only EU policy which explicitly straddles the foreign policy competence and the material competences of the EU. The exercise of this competence entails a sequence of acts based on different and perhaps irreconcilable decision-making procedures: a common foreign and security policy (CFSP) decision, to be taken through intergovernmental mechanisms, determines the conditions for the adoption of restrictive measures to be taken through the procedure laid down by Article 215, para (1). The complexity of this normative paradigm is at the origin of a number of legal problems, some of which still remain unsolved.

The second issue is perhaps even more interesting, as it goes to the heart of the troubled question of judicial control over the foreign relations power, an area traditionally apportioned to the executive and dominated by the harsh needs of foreign policy. In particular, the ECJ has ruled that restrictive measures adopted in order to give effect to Security Council (SC) resolutions are nonetheless subject, 'in principle', to the same standard of control applicable to measures of purely domestic origin. The course embarked upon by the ECJ, tenaciously defended in isolation against virtually all the powerful political actors of the EU, deserves great respect and appreciation. Beyond its uncontroversial virtues, however, this tendency is not without cost. It is based on a cultural paradigm, which tends to consider the domestic EU legal order as a safe area, based on respect for human rights and on the rule of law, as an ideal antagonist to the international legal order, which by contrast is considered as an arena dominated by the harsh needs of *raison d'état*. From a technical view point, it tends to insulate the internal legal order

[2] Judgment of 3 September 2008, Joined Cases C-402/05P and C-415/05P, *Yassin Abdullah Kadi and Al Barakaat International Foundation v Council of the European Union and Commission of the European Communities*, [2007] ECR I-6351, para 326.

and to assume that international rules are incapable, by themselves, of producing direct effects internally and need to be implemented by domestic rules, which are therefore subject, 'in principle', to the same standard of control applicable to other purely internal rules.

The development of each of these parts entails the need to enter into lengthy and complex technical arguments. This is almost unavoidable. If foreign relations law epitomises the complexities of the law of European integration, antiterrorist sanctions epitomise the complexities of foreign relations law. They represent an impenetrable conundrum, which seems to defy the technical skill and the political wisdom of every interpreter. In the present chapter, one will not attempt to attain the impossible: to lend coherence to an inherently incoherent system. More modestly, an endeavour will be made to sketch the contours of a frame of reference, which can be of avail for further analysis.

II. THE COMPETENCE OF THE EU TO ADOPT ANTITERRORIST SANCTIONS

A. Article 215 TFEU: A Rule or an Exception?

Antiterrorist sanctions are adopted under Article 215 TFEU which establishes, as is well known, a two-step procedure: a CFSP act directs the EU institutions to adopt the sanctioning act, which will be adopted by the Council, acting by a qualified majority on a joint proposal from the High Representative of the Union for Foreign Common and Security Policy and the Commission. The historical origin of that provision heavily affects its systematic coherence.

The predecessor of Article 215, namely Article 301 TEC, was drafted with a view to codifying a pre-existent practice whereby the Community's powers were used for sanctioning purposes after a decision of the Member States taken within the frame of political cooperation. As the ECJ said in *Bosphorus*

> by Regulation No 990/93 the Council gave effect to the decision of the Community and its Member States, meeting within the framework of political cooperation, to have recourse to a Community instrument to implement in the Community certain aspects of the sanctions taken against the Federal Republic of Yugoslavia by the Security Council of the United Nations.[3]

The procedure established by Article 215 still follows this scheme, based on a combination between CFSP and a specific substantive competence of the EU on restrictive measures. The uniqueness of this competence thus lies in the fact that the Treaties do not assign specific objectives to this act. Rather, the objectives are to be drawn from the CFSP act which constitutes a pre-condition for its enactment.

[3] Judgment of 30 July 1996, Case C-84/95, *Bosphorus Hava Yollari Turizm ve Ticaret AS v Minister for Transport, Energy and Communications and others* [1996] ECR I-3953, para 13.

The reasons for setting up a procedure combining these two acts lay in the circumstance that each of these acts is unable, by itself, to produce the desired result. There is, notoriously, a fundamental difference in nature between the CFSP and the other substantive EU policies. The first has a purely functional scope, in the sense that CFSP measures are qualified only by the political objectives pursued. Conversely, substantive policies have a material scope and can pursue only the specific objectives assigned by the Treaties. To avoid the danger of overlap, and primarily the use of the intergovernmental procedures of the CFSP to adopt measures substantively falling within one of the other policies of the EU, a normative barrier has been erected contextually with the inclusion of the CFSP within the system of the founding Treaties. This normative barrier was explicitly enshrined in Article 40 TEU, in the pre-Lisbon version, which envisaged that the exercise of the CFSP, 'shall not affect the application of the procedures and the extent of the powers of the institutions laid down by the Treaties for the exercise of the Union competences referred to in Articles 3 to 6 of the Treaty'.

Thus, restrictive measures could not be adopted by CFSP acts since they fell, by their substance, within the scope of other EU policies, most commonly within the scope of the commercial policy. As the ECJ said in *Centro-Com*,[4] 'the Member States cannot treat national measures whose effect is to prevent or restrict the export of certain products as falling outside the scope of the common commercial policy on the ground that they have foreign and security objectives'.[5]

This decision can hardly be read as entailing that restrictive measures fall plainly within the scope of the commercial policy. This construction was ruled out by the ECJ's plain words in *Kadi I*: '[h]aving regard to [their] purpose and object' (namely to combat international terrorism), restrictive measures do not relate 'to international trade in that [they are] essentially intended to promote, facilitate or govern trade'.[6] The Court concluded, in paragraph 187, that restrictive measures 'could not, therefore, be based on the powers of the Community in the sphere of the common commercial policy'.

On the other hand, substantive EU policies were prevented from entering the field reserved to the CFSP. This prohibition was an indispensable corollary of the principle of conferral, which assigned specific objectives to each competence of the Union, and reserved the pursuit of political objectives in the international arena to the CFSP.

Political motivation was, indeed, the hallmark of the CFSP. This EU policy was characterised by considerable indeterminacy, since it was virtually the only EU competence unleashed from a substantive field and purely functional in nature. Correspondingly, politically motivated actions could not be adopted under one of the other EU substantive policies.

[4] Judgment of 14 January 1997, Case C-124/95 *The Queen, ex parte Centro-Com Srl v HM Treasury and Bank of England*, [1997] ECR I-81.

[5] Para 26.

[6] Para 185.

In the light of this regime of segregation, the role of Article 301 TEC was precisely to establish a link—the only one expressly provided for in the normative plan—between the political and the substantive dimensions of the EU.[7]

This state of affairs, notably corresponding to the will of the Member States to maintain control over the politically motivated action of the Union, has not substantially changed with the Lisbon reform and with the setting up of a new, integrated system of external action. This new system undoubtedly attempts to attenuate the regime of mutual exclusion between CFSP and other EU substantive policies. However, the means employed are not fully appropriate to attain this aim. The impression is that the necessity to change the preceding system and to confer unity and coherence on the EU external system has not prompted a substantial change but stopped at the inescapable crossroads, from which many different routes depart: one leading to the full absorption of the CFSP in EU substantive policies on the external plane; one leading to the opposite extreme, to a creeping intergovernmentalisation of these substantive policies, with an indeterminate number of options in the middle.

Article 21, paragraph (2), TEU assigns a set of objectives, mainly of a political character, to the full range of policies which are part of the EU's external action, including the external aspects of all the EU's substantive policies. A textual interpretation of Article 21, paragraph (2) thus seems to indicate that the EU acts falling within the realm of external action can freely pursue the objectives assigned in that provision, including those which appear as purely political and which were, in the pre-Lisbon system, assigned only to the CFSP.[8]

Other provisions, among which is, pre-eminently, the revised Article 40 TEU, seem rather to indicate the maintenance of the pre-Lisbon system,[9] with the exclusive competence of the CFSP to pursue political objectives and the exclusive competence of the other EU policies to pursue the substantive objectives respectively assigned to them.[10]

[7] In legislative practice, this barrier proved not to be an absolute one. See E Cannizzaro, 'Unity and Pluralism in the EU's Foreign Relations Power' in *The Fundamentals of EU Law Revisited. Assessing the Impact of the Constitutional Debate* C Barnard (ed), *Collected Courses of the Academy of European Law* (Oxford, Oxford University Press, 2007) at 193.

[8] For a discussion on the interpretation of this provision, see L Bartels, 'The EU's Human Rights Obligations in Relation to Policies with Extraterritorial Effects' (2015) 25 *European Journal of International Law* 1071, and my reply, 'The EU's Human Rights Obligations in Relation to Policies with Extraterritorial Effects: A Reply to Lorand Bartels' (2015) 25 *European Journal of International Law* 1093, at 1093.

[9] See the opinion of AG Bot (Case C-658/11, *European Parliament v Council of the European Union*, delivered on 30 January 2014): this provision sets out the obligation 'to define the boundaries between the CFSP and the Union's other policies' (para 86). In the opinion of the Advocate General, the test to assign the objectives of Art 21, para (2), to the various competences of the Union is one of proximity: 'in so far as Article 21(2) TEU sets out the common objectives of the Union's external action, that provision should be read in conjunction with the more specific provisions applicable to each policy in order to determine the Union policy to which a certain objective is more specifically related' (para 88).

[10] Art 23 TEU assigns the pursuit of the objectives laid down by Art 21, para (2), to the primary competence of the CFSP, which 'shall be guided by the principles, shall pursue the objectives of, and be

Rather than defining the relationship between political objectives and substantive means of action, the new EU's external action seems to have created a crucible in which different, and possible antithetical, theoretical options have been put together with no single one clearly predominating over the others. This makes particularly difficult the search for the best interpretative option. Not surprisingly, the scholarship is sharply divided between conservation and innovation; the case law of the ECJ exhibits considerable uncertainty and practice continues to develop intermediate solutions through arrangements designed to establish informal means of communication between the political and the substantive dimension of the European integration.[11]

Yet, in all evidence, the construction of the provisions setting up the EU external action deeply affects the construction of Article 215 TFEU. Should one assume that the EU Institutions are empowered to pursue autonomously the objectives of Article 21, paragraph (2), the maintenance of a two-step procedure for the adoption of restrictive measures would represent an exception to that system since in that particular area the pursuit of political objectives would continue to be conditional on a previous CFSP deliberation. If the setting up of an integrated external action did not change the means-ends relationship at the basis of the exercise of EU competences prior to the entry into force of the Lisbon Treaty, Article 215 would still constitute an exception, but in the opposite sense: in a system still founded on the reciprocal isolation of the CFSP and, respectively, of the other EU's substantive policies, the Member States are nonetheless empowered to use the means of action transferred to the EU for sanctioning purposes.

conducted in accordance with' these. For the policies included in Part V of the TFEU, the wording is much more nuanced (see Art 207, which speaks of the 'the context of the principles and objectives of the Union's external action'; Art 208, para (1), Art 212, para (1), and Art 214, para (1), which speak of the 'framework of the principles and objectives of the Union's external action'). A difficult issue arises with regard to the objectives of the development cooperation policy. Under Art 208 TFEU, 'Union development cooperation policy shall have as its primary objective the reduction and, in the long term, the eradication of poverty'. Other objectives specifically assigned to the development cooperation policy under Art 177 TEC, such as the protection and the promotion of human rights, have been expunged from the terms of the provisions governing this specific substantive policy and included in Art 21, para (2), among the objectives assigned to the external action of the Union. This can hardly entail that development cooperation policy is barred from autonomously pursuing this objective, which has featured in that policy from its very beginning and which is one of its *raisons d'être*. Therefore, precisely this exclusion could constitute a formidable argument in favour of the autonomy of the EU in the pursuit of objectives included in Art 21, para (2), through its substantive policies. A more moderate position has been taken by the ECJ in Case C-377/12 *European Commission v Council of the European Union* (Judgment of 11 June 2014, EU:C:2014:1903), where the Court seems to say that the objectives of Art 21, para (2), TEU can be pursued by development cooperation acts only insofar as these acts are mainly designed to attain the primary objective assigned to that policy, namely the eradication of poverty. All in all, this conclusion seems to attenuate the famous decision of the ECJ in Case C-268/94, *Portuguese Republic v Council of the European Union* (Judgment of 3 December 1996, [1996] ECR I-6177), para 24.

[11] For a closer analysis, I refer to my work *Unity and Pluralism in the EU's Foreign Relations Power*, n 7 above.

In a different, evolutive, perspective, the decision of the drafters of the Treaty to leave unaltered the complex two-step procedure of Article 215 TFEU for the adoption of restrictive measures, in spite of the changing institutional and normative landscape of the EU external action, constitutes an element for the overall interpretation of other Treaties' provisions concerning the relationship between the CFSP and other substantive policies of the EU: namely to maintain the guardianship of the CFSP over the political use of substantive policies.[12]

B. The 'Bridge' Between the CFSP and Other EU Substantive Policies

In *Kadi I* the Court considered that Article 215 TFEU constitutes 'a bridge … constructed between the actions of the Community involving economic measures under Articles 60 EC and 301 EC and the objectives of the EU Treaty in the sphere of external relations, including the CFSP'.[13]

It would be erroneous, however, to assume that Article 215 is based on a combination of competences. One can hardly believe that a combination of two competences can produce a greater effect than that which may be produced by the sum of either competence. This would be tantamount to presuming that a combination of two shortcomings can exceed their sum.[14]

Even leaving aside mathematical analogies, a simple consideration of the structure of the decision-making procedure established by Article 215 clearly shows that it is not the result of a combination of legal bases. Under ECJ case law, a combination of competences entails a combination of their corresponding procedures. According to consistent case law, a measure 'that simultaneously pursues a number of objectives, or that has several components, which are inseparably

[12] On the relationship between CFSP and other substantive EU act, see, among the most recent contributions, ME Bartoloni, *Politica estera e azione esterna dell'Unione europea* (Napoli, Editoriale Scientifica, 2012); P Van Elsuwege, *EU External Action after the Collapse of the Pillar Structure: in Search of New Balance between Delimitation and Consistency* (2010) 47 *Common Market Law Review* 1007.

[13] See n 1 above, para 197.

[14] The idea that Art 215 simply constitutes a mere sum of pre-existing competences re-emerges periodically in literature and case law. This is probably what the ECJ had in mind when it said, in *Kadi I*, that 'a bridge has been constructed between the actions of the Community involving economic measures under Articles 60 EC and 301 EC and the objectives of the EU Treaty in the sphere of external relations, including the CFSP' (para 197). Were this metaphor meant to convey the idea that Art 215 is simply the intersection between two pre-existing competences, it would not be particularly felicitous. It would be quite a miraculous bridge, one which connects two shores, neither one capable of sustaining its pillars. In a different perspective, in Case C-548/09P, *Bank Melli* (Judgment of 16 November 2011, [2011] ECR I-11381, the Court, upholding the previous decision of the General Court, said that 'Art. 60 EC and 301 EC are provisions expressly envisaging that action by the Community may prove necessary in order to attain one of the objectives specifically assigned to the Union by Article 2 EU, namely the implementation of a common foreign and security policy' (para 58). From this passage, one can reasonably infer that these two provisions do not combine pre-existing competences but, rather, establish a new competence, which puts together the objectives assigned to the CFSP with specific means of actions.

linked without one's being incidental to the other … will have to be founded, exceptionally, on the various corresponding legal bases'.[15]

Article 215, like its predecessor, Article 301, does not combine the two legal bases and does not merge their respective procedures.[16] It rather establishes a sequence of acts, each based on its own legal basis and each adopted through its own procedure. The problem thus arises as to the legal nature of this strange procedure: if it is not a combination of legal bases, what else may it be?

The problem of the legal nature of the competence set up by Article 215 has been dealt with in short by the ECJ in *Bank Melli*.[17] The Court ruled out that the adoption of restrictive measures requires a combination of legal bases. It rather stressed the autonomy of each of the two acts, which have to be adopted each according to its own procedure. The CFSP act appears thus as a mere condition for the adoption of the restrictive measures by the Council, by a qualified majority, on a joint proposal of the High representative for CFSP and the Commission, whilst Parliament is merely informed.

The conclusion ought, therefore, to be drawn, that Article 215 TFEU is a competence of a new kind, whose decision-making procedure is based on a sequence of acts, one representing the condition for the adoption of the other.

C. Nature and Implication of the Bridge Constructed by Article 215, paragraph (2)

The holding of the ECJ in *Bank Melli* seems to entail the full autonomy of the two component parts of Article 215. The former, the CFSP decision, should determine the political objectives only; the second should provide the means of action. Neither of these two dimensions of the European integration would be thus subordinate to the other.

As pointed out in the preceding paragraph, this model has inspired, in other areas, practical arrangements implemented where the need was felt, to establish an informal coordination between the CFSP and other EU substantive policies. In areas of shared consent, the EU supranational institutions have largely agreed to act within a framework of political objectives laid down by CFSP acts.[18]

[15] See, inter alia, Judgment of 11 June 2014, Case C-377/12, *Commission v Council*, para 34, EU:C:2014:1903.

[16] According to the well-settled case law of the ECJ, a combination of competences cannot disrupt the logic of the system. Moreover, as the Court said in *ECOWAS* (Judgment of 20 May 2008, Case C-91/05, *Commission v Council*, [2008] ECR I-3651), para 76, a combination of legal bases 'is impossible with regard to a measure which pursues a number of objectives or which has several components falling, respectively, within (a substantive EU policy), and within the CFSP'.

[17] See n 14 above.

[18] See, inter alia, Council Decision 2012/123/CFSP of 27 February 2012 amending Decision 2011/523/EU partially suspending the application of the Cooperation Agreement between the European Economic Community and the Syrian Arab Republic ([2012] OJ L54, 28 February 2012, p 18). In spite of this heading, the Council decision is founded on the basis of article 217 TFEU.

However, this is not precisely the model upheld by the Court in *Bank Melli*. Having asserted the formal autonomy of the two acts which formed the sequential procedure established by Article 215, the Court abstained from dealing with the insidious issue of their substantial autonomy and did not seize the opportunity to clarify the respective roles of the two components of the 'bridge' constructed by that provision.

This appears highly regrettable. If the CFSP act were empowered to determine the content of the restrictive measures, the formal autonomy of the substantive EU act adopting restrictive measures, designed to pursue the objectives set by the CFSP act, would be not much more than an optical illusion. As the claimant in *Bank Melli* rightly observed, the list of the individuals addressed by the measures, annexed to the Regulation adopted under Article 301 TEC, merely reproduced the list annexed to the CFSP act. Consequently, to amend that Regulation, the procedure laid down by Article 215, paragraph (1), second sentence, would not be sufficient. A new act would need to be adopted on the basis of the CFSP procedure.

Thus, far from having a different object and content, the two acts, the CFSP act adopted on the basis of an intergovernmental procedure, and the Regulation, adopted by the Council by qualified majority, tend substantially to coincide. The coincidence between the measures adopted by the CFSP act and those adopted by the regulation envisaged by Article 215, paragraph (1), second sentence, is confirmed by the analysis of the legislative practice, which shows that the CFSP generally predetermines the contents of the restrictive measures, which only nominally are adopted by the Council, on majority voting.

D. Antiterrorist Sanctions between Intergovernmental and Supranational Method

The idiosyncratic features of Article 215 TFEU as a legal basis for EU action should warn against assigning to it a broader scope than necessary. It should instead be considered an exceptional legal basis, to be used only in the absence of other viable alternatives.

The scope of Article 215 has been the subject of the litigation between the Parliament and the Council decided by the ECJ in Case C-130/10.[19] The Court was asked to see whether Article 215 was the proper legal basis for a regulation aimed at amending the famous Regulation (EC) No 881/2002 on restrictive measures directed against individuals connected with terrorist networks, and to bring that regulation into line with the EU standard of protection of human rights. In the Parliament's view, this amended regulation ought to be adopted, instead, under Article 75 TFEU.

[19] Judgment of 19 July 2012, Case C-130/10 *Parliament v Council*, EU:C:2012:472.

As is well known, the two twin-competences originally envisaged under Article 301 and Article 60 TEC have been transposed by the Lisbon Treaty in Article 215 and Article 75 TFEU. However, their respective decision-making procedures diverged dramatically. Whereas Article 215 TFEU still remained based on a combination of CFSP and substantive policies acts, Article 75 TFEU underwent a different evolution and has been fully drawn up within the realm of substantive EU competences. Its text now reads:

> [w]here necessary to achieve the objectives set out in Article 67, as regards preventing and combating terrorism and related activities, the European Parliament and the Council, acting by means of regulations in accordance with the ordinary legislative procedure, shall define a framework for administrative measures with regard to capital movements and payments, such as the freezing of funds, financial assets or economic gains belonging to, or owned or held by, natural or legal persons, groups or non-State entities.

Thus, albeit radically different as to their legal nature and their decision-making procedures, both provisions, Article 75 and Article 215, paragraph (2), TFEU, provide for a legal basis for the adoption of antiterrorist sanctions. It is therefore necessary to identify the distinctive character of the two respective competences.

At first sight, the distinction is self-explanatory. Article 75 is included in Title V of Part III of the TFEU, concerning EU policies and internal actions, and is specifically designed to prevent and combat terrorism and related activities. Article 215 is included in Part V of the TFEU, concerning the EU external action and concerns, more generically, restrictive measures.[20] At first sight, Article 75 applies to measures designed to address internal threat, whereas international threats require the more engaging procedure laid down by Article 215.

Although intuitively appropriate, this conclusion is not free from ambiguity. Indeed, the identification of the internal or international nature of a terrorist threat is not an easy task. A number of tests may be employed, considering, for example, the origin of the threat, their targets, the objectives pursued by terrorism and so on. No one, however, appears to be capable of distinguishing unequivocally between internal threat and international threat. This is probably due to the fact that the internal/international divide is particularly inappropriate to determine the nature of the EU competence with regard to antiterrorist sanctions, which, almost inevitably, straddles this line. Sanctioning measures against terrorists, indeed, possess a dual component: they are taken and performed internally but often are designed to produce their effect internationally.

In Case C-130/10, the Court adopted a formal test. In response to the objection of the Parliament, concerning precisely the difficulty of distinguishing internal from external terrorism, the Court—after recalling that the contested regulation

[20] Less distinctive appears the qualification of the measures enacted under Art 75 as 'administrative', a word not employed elsewhere in the founding treaties, and whose precise meaning appears to be controversial; the more so as the administrative measures under Art 75 have to be adopted through the ordinary legislative procedure and, therefore, constitute legislative acts.

was aimed at modifying a previous regulation adopted under Article 301 TEC, the predecessor of Article 215—concluded that the international dimension of that particular threat emerged from the existence of a CFSP act, precisely to give effect to a Security Council decision.[21]

Attractive as it may be, this argument begs the question. Due to the indeterminacy of the material scope of CFSP, it is illogical to deduce the international nature of a terrorist threat from the existence of a CFSP act, and to identify, on that ground, the legal basis of the EU action. This is tantamount to saying that the Member States, acting on a unanimous vote, in the context of a CFSP, are empowered to determine the legal basis of an EU act.

But was there a different option available? I submit that there was. The ECJ could have acknowledged that the objective of the contested regulation was not so much to adopt sanctioning measures, but rather to enhance the protection of fundamental rights for individuals already targeted by antiterrorist sanctions, and, by so doing, to contribute to creating an area of freedom, security and justice with respect for human rights, in the sense of Article 67 TFEU. This conclusion would have minimised the scope of Article 215 and, therefore, of the only EU competence based on the combination of the CFSP and one of the other EU substantive policies, according to the *ECOWAS* doctrine.[22]

By following the opposite path, the ECJ seems to indicate that the existence of a CFSP act is sufficient to draw the EU action entirely into the intergovernmental realm,[23] namely that when foreign policy objectives are at stake, even indirectly, the decision-making procedure must be intergovernmental in nature.

III. JUDICIAL REVIEW AND ANTITERRORIST SANCTIONS

A. Limits to the EU Power to Adopt Antiterrorist Sanctions

The second part of this chapter will deal with the limits to antiterrorist sanctions with regard to the protection of fundamental rights. For the purposes of the current study, as part of a collection of writings on the external dimension of European integration, this analysis will be limited to sanctions originating from

[21] Case C-130/10, n 19 above, see para 76. After recalling that the difference between these two legal bases depends on the existence of 'a bridge … between the actions of the Community involving economic measures … and the political objectives of the EU Treaty', the Court went on to say that 'Article 215 TFEU expressly provides such a bridge, but this is not the case with Article 75 TFEU, which creates no link with decisions taken under the CFSP' (para 59). The judgment of the ECJ, 14 June 2016, Case C-263/14 *European Parliament v Council of the European Union*, nyr, is based on an analogous rationale.

[22] See n 16 above. Judgment of the ECJ, 20 May 2008, Case C-91/05 *Commission v Council* [2008] ECR I-3651 (*ECOWAS*).

[23] This impression emerges from a passage incidental to the line of reasoning of the judgment. The Court explained, in para 82, that 'the difference between Article 75 TFEU and Article 215 TFEU, so far as the Parliament's involvement is concerned, is the result of the choice made by the framers of the Treaty of Lisbon conferring a more limited role on the Parliament with regard to the Union's action under the CFSP'.

international law and, more precisely, from SC resolutions. Does the EU encounter in this field the same limits put on its other policies or actions? Is the international origin of the most part of antiterrorist sanctions relevant in attenuating these limits?

These and other related issues have been dealt with in the complex and thoughtful case law of the ECJ, among which are the worldwide celebrated *Kadi* decisions.[24]

All of them are very well known in full detail and there is no point in dwelling upon them at any length. Reference to these cases will be restricted to what is strictly necessary to complete the analysis undertaken in the preceding section.

The ECJ case law seems to be based on a chain of assumptions, most of which are of a theoretical character. The basic assumption is that the UN Charter does not impose a particular model of implementation of SC resolutions and, therefore, the EU is permitted to transpose SC resolutions through implementing legislation instead of according direct effect to the resolutions. In the view of the ECJ, this process has the effect of severing the link between the obligations flowing from SC resolutions and the legislation enacted to give effect to it.

EU legislation designed to give effect to SC resolutions, consequently, is to be treated as ordinary legislation, subject to domestic, not international standards of review, including domestic principles which protect individual fundamental rights. Finally, insofar as the application of these domestic standards does not affect the effectiveness of EU law, the standard is, in principle, a full standard with regard to the scope as well as to the intensity of review.[25]

In spite of the ECJ's considerable effort, this impressive theoretical framework does not decisively contribute to the solution of the questions asked above. Regardless of whether the EU is among the direct addressees of the SC resolutions, as some could be inclined to believe, or whether it is only indirectly bound by the resolutions, by virtue of the reference made to them by the CFSP acts, the fact remains that the effects of SC resolutions within the EU legal order, direct or indirect as they may be, are conditional upon their compliance with primary EU law. If the SC resolutions are entitled to produce a direct effect within the EU legal order, they have to be directly in compliance with EU primary law; if the resolutions do not have a direct effect, nonetheless, they have to be 'indirectly' in compliance therewith, through the means of their implementing legislation.

Nor does the direct or indirect character of the reference to international law constitute an element for determining whether SC resolutions enjoy immunity

[24] Judgment of 3 September 2008, Joined cases C-402/05P and C-415/05P, *Yassin Abdullah Kadi and Al Barakaat International Foundation v Council of the European Union and Commission of the European Communities (Kadi I)*, see n 2 above; Judgment of 18 July 2013, Joined cases C-584/10 P, C-593/10 P & C-595/10 P, *Commission v Yassin Abdullah Kadi (Kadi II)*, EU:C:2013:518.

[25] See A Cuyvers, '"Give me one good reason": The Unified Standard of Review for Sanctions after Kadi II' (2014) 51 *Common Market Law Review* 1759; P Leino, '"In Principle the Full Review": what Justice for Mr Kadi?' in R Liivoja and J Petman (eds), *International Law-making: Essays in Honour of Jan Klabbers* (London, Routledge, 2014) 225.

from domestic judicial scrutiny. Neither international law nor the UN Charter establishes the obligation to grant immunity to SC resolutions within domestic orders. International law and the UN Charter only require the parties to abide by SC resolutions. Article 103 of the UN Charter establishes the additional obligation to grant priority to obligations flowing from the Charter over other conflicting obligations. By no means does this obligation entail that SC resolutions must be granted primacy vis-à-vis constitutional principles in domestic legal order. From a domestic perspective indeed, the application of Article 103 ultimately relies on domestic constitutional rules and principles.

Thus, the only remaining question is one of standards: namely whether the standards of legality applicable to purely domestic norms are equally applicable to norms having an international origin, designed to regulate international situations and to produce their effects primarily in their own legal environment.

Trends in comparative law show that domestic judges tend to adjust internal standards of review when international rules are at stake. Many techniques have been developed to take into account the international origin of certain rules when subject to domestic scrutiny. Let me briefly recall the well-known principle of *völkerrechtsfreundlichkait*, which has inspired a number of contemporary legal orders. An analogous principle, which can be well indicated as a principle of 'openness' of the EU legal order, emerges from Article 3, para (5), TEU.[26]

Issues regarding the normative contents of this provision have been extensively discussed in legal scholarship. However, for the limited purpose of the present contribution, there is no need to enter into this learned discussion and to determine precisely the various possible effects produced by such a provision. It is sufficient to refer to the main view shared among scholars, according to which such a provision has the effect of enlarging the set of fundamental values and interests of the EU legal order by including respect for international law and for the UN Charter. We can safely conclude, therefore, that compliance with international law and with the UN Charter corresponds to a constitutional interest of the EU legal order and concurs with others in determining the standard of review for underlying legislation.

The principle of 'openness' of the EU legal order may have significant implications for domestic judicial review of international rules. First, it may mean that domestic judges should abstain from reviewing the internal validity of international rules in the light of the domestic standard of protection of human rights if a mechanism of judicial review exists at the international level, substantially equivalent to the standard applied domestically.

[26] 'In its relations with the wider world, the Union shall uphold and promote its values and interests and contribute to the protection of its citizens. It shall contribute to peace, security, the sustainable development of the Earth, solidarity and mutual respect among peoples, free and fair trade, eradication of poverty and the protection of human rights, in particular the rights of the child, as well as to the strict observance and the development of international law, including respect for the principles of the United Nations Charter'.

This is the well-known doctrine of equivalent protection, increasingly applied by domestic and international judges as a cross-border conflict-settling technique. In *Kadi I*, the ECJ seems to have implicitly contemplated the possibility of employing such a technique.[27] In *Kadi II*, the ECJ expressly referred to the insufficiency of the administrative procedure of review instituted at the UN level and known as 'delisting', and indicated that by no means did such a procedure satisfy the engaging requirement of the domestic principles of effective judicial protection.[28] One could speculate, *a contrario*, that, if the UN delisting procedure were substantially equivalent to EU domestic principles, the ECJ could have decided to decline its jurisdiction.

The principle of equivalent protection may be considered as the procedural articulation of the 'openness' of a legal order. There is, however, another substantive articulation. Before reviewing international law in the light of domestic standards, domestic courts must primarily assess its validity within the same international legal order.[29] It would be preposterous to assume that the process of implementation of international law entails severing its ties with its original legal context. For example, before applying a treaty, a domestic judge ought to assess that it is still in force under the grounds of invalidity or termination enshrined in the Vienna Convention on the Law of Treaties and in general international law. Thus, domestic judges are empowered also to consider the existence of substantive higher standards of the international legal order and employ them to review the lawfulness of international 'ordinary' law.

The theoretical interest of this technique lies in the fact that it tends to decouple the substantive from the procedural competence to determine the legality of international law. When reviewing the validity of inferior international law, domestic judges act, within their own legal order, as decentralised organs of the international community. In a certain sense, such a doctrine still recognises the primary competence of the international legal order to determine the legality of its rules from a substantive viewpoint, whilst the domestic legal order only supplies the procedural machinery.

The idea that the European judicature has the power to review SC resolutions in the light of international peremptory law was put forward by the CFI in *Kadi I*[30] but subsequently reversed by the ECJ.[31] The CFI's decision paved the way

[27] This has been noted by a number of scholars. See J Kokott and C Sobotta, 'The Kadi Case—Constitutional Core Values and International Law—Finding the Balance?' (2012) 23 *European Journal of International Law* 1015.

[28] See Joined cases C-584/10 P, C-593/10 P & C-595/10 P, *Commission v Yassin Abdullah Kadi (Kadi II)*, n 24 above, para 133.

[29] See E Cannizzaro, 'Security Council Resolutions and EC Fundamental Rights: Some Remarks on the ECJ Decision in the Kadi Case' (2009) 28 *Yearbook of European Law* 593.

[30] Judgment of 21 September 2005, Case T-315/01, *Yassin Abdullah Kadi v Council and Commission*, [2005] ECR II-3649, para 226.

[31] In para 287 of the *Kadi I* decision (n 24 above), the ECJ said: 'With more particular regard to a Community act which, like the contested regulation, is intended to give effect to a resolution adopted

to dismiss the applicant's claim, since, in the view of the General Court, international peremptory law did not include an individual right to effective judicial protection. Arguably, the ECJ must have felt that the reference to the uncertain category of peremptory law was improper to secure full protection of individual fundamental rights. In consequence of this perception, the ECJ sought shelter in the most comfortable categories of domestic review. In *Kadi II*, the ECJ said, albeit in passing, that

> [s]uch a judicial review is indispensable to ensure a fair balance between the maintenance of international peace and security and the protection of the fundamental rights and freedoms of the person concerned, those being shared values of the UN and the European Union.[32]

In consequence thereof, the ECJ proceeded to assess the legality of SC resolutions against a purely domestic standard of review. Whereas the ECJ was fully legitimated to do so, in terms of judicial policy this choice does not seem the most appropriate one. It is not based on the superior legitimacy coming from international law and, quite the contrary, contributes to spreading mistrust on the capacity of international law to impose itself on reluctant States and ultimately disrupts its capacity to control their conduct. In a systemic perspective, the unilateral determination of the legality of SC resolutions on the basis of a purely domestic standard may further have a legitimising effect of analogous claims by other States, including those based on different conceptions about individual fundamental rights.[33]

B. *Jus Cogens* as a Limit to the Domestic Application of Antiterrorist Sanctions

A different course could have been grounded on the consideration that the effects, direct or indirect as they may be, of SC resolutions within the EU legal order primarily depend on the effects of the resolutions within their own legal order. This means that the balance between collective security interests and individual interests ought to be struck primarily within the international order.

By no means does this conclusion depend on the particular mechanisms of implementation of international law within domestic legal orders. As said before, once implemented in domestic legal orders, international law must be administered and adjudged by domestic courts, regardless of whether it can be applied directly

by the Security Council under Chapter VII of the Charter of the United Nations, it is not, therefore, for the Community judicature, under the exclusive jurisdiction provided for by Article 220 EC, to review the lawfulness of such a resolution adopted by an international body, even if that review were to be limited to examination of the compatibility of that resolution with jus cogens'.

[32] Ibid para 131.

[33] On the ECJ's perception of its role in the international legal order, see, recently, V Fikfak, 'Kadi and the Role of the Court of Justice of the European Union in the International Legal Order' (2013) 15 *The Cambridge Yearbook of European Legal Studies* 587.

or through implementing legislation. In the case at hand, SC resolutions had to be considered by the ECJ as part of EU law through the reference made by EU acts implementing them. It follows that the ECJ was empowered to determine the international legality of these resolutions as part of its overall assessment aimed at determining the conditions under which the EU implementing legislation ought to be applied within the EU legal order.

There is a case to be made that those SC resolutions conflicting with peremptory rules of international law are invalid. This argument is grounded on two premises: first that the activity of the SC to maintain and restore international peace and security is not free from legal restraints and that, on the contrary, it is bound to respect peremptory rules; secondly that peremptory law includes also rules protecting individual fundamental rights which the same SC has contributed to promoting and to bringing into existence.

The assessment of the international validity of SC resolutions by the ECJ would have produced a number of beneficial consequences both in terms of legal technique and of judicial policy. First, it would have contributed to the further development of standards of protection of human rights within the international legal order as a limit to the discretionary powers of the SC. Secondly, this course of action would have had a beneficial effect also on the role of the SC as a global institution entitled to govern individual conduct relevant for the maintenance and restoration of international peace and security. The progressive transformation of the SC from an entity addressing only the States, and imposing obligations on them, to an entity which aspires to govern individual conduct, would have been accompanied by a corresponding evolution of the set of values and interests which constitute a limit to its powers.[34] Finally, the adoption of an international standard of review of SC resolutions would have contributed to dispelling the fear that the EU aims to impose its own standards and its own values on the rest of the world.

By seeking refuge in the comfortable categories of its own legal order, the ECJ has not only made an impeccable exercise of dualism; it has also crystallised the present state of international law, and has missed an opportunity to sow the seeds for its further development. A *völkerrechtsfreundlicher* position may have constituted a more resolute step in the direction of the desired change; it would have presented the EU as a leading authority championing the development of a sphere of international human rights law as an antidote against the exercise of power at the international level. It would have contributed to the development of an international rule of law against the somewhat disquieting idea of a rising international global authority unleashed from legal restraint.

[34] I have developed this idea in more details in my article 'A Machiavellian Moment? The UN Security Council and the Rule of Law' (2006) 13 *International Organisations Law Review* 195.

18

The European Union's Arms Trade Control and European Civil Society

INMACULADA MARRERO ROCHA[1]

Content:

I. INTRODUCTION

THE EUROPEAN UNION (EU) has developed the most advanced regime for the control of the conventional arms trade existing in international society. This control regime has inspired procedures such as the First United Nations (UN) Conference on the Arms Trade Treaty (ATT), held in July 2012 in New York, which led to such an advanced treaty, in terms of control criteria and mechanisms, that it failed to be open for signature because some of the most powerful States in the global arms trade rejected the adoption of the text.[2]

[1] Lecturer in International Relations, Granada University.

[2] Unofficial text of the President of the International Conference on the Arms Trade Treaty, 14 July 2012, A/CONF.217/, Annex II: www.un.org/ga/search/view_doc.asp?symbol=A/CONF.217/CRP.1&Lang=E, accessed 18 May 2015. Draft submitted at the Final United Nations Conference on the Arms Trade Treaty, 18–28 March 2013, A/CONF.217/2013/L.3*: www.un.org/disarmament/ATT/docs/ATT_text_(As_adopted_by_the_GA)-E.pdf. The ATT is in force from 24 December 2014, accessed 8 May 2015.

Likewise, the EU has become a constant advisor in technical and administrative matters as well as a generous sponsor of initiatives aimed at improving control mechanisms or, rather, establishing control mechanisms in States and regions where the arms trade is unrestrained and the danger it poses to human security is increasing.

However, what is most striking is not the EU arms trade regime itself but rather its origin, nature and development, especially taking into account that EU Member States have an interest in the international arms trade equal to, or perhaps even greater than, other major arms exporters, and yet they have gradually decided to renounce these interests in order to alleviate the negative consequences of an unregulated, or poorly regulated, arms trade. Such a decision is no doubt motivated by many different factors, but this chapter seeks to demonstrate that one of the most decisive factors in determining the characteristics of such a regime has been the activism of European civil society, developed by significant non-governmental organisations (NGOs) in the territory of the Union. These have implemented information and awareness campaigns of such importance that they have gradually influenced the internal and external action of EU and its Member States on the trade in conventional weapons.

In order to prove this initial assumption mentioned above, this chapter will first analyse Member States' political, economic, commercial and strategic interests in the arms trade as well as the position they occupy in the global market. Secondly, an overview of the EU arms trade control regime and its evolution over time will be provided in order to illustrate its development and increasing sophistication, to the point of becoming the most advanced regime of its kind in international society. Thirdly, it will address the main reactions of European civil society to the consequences of the arms trade, the reasons that strengthen Europe's participation in arms trade matters, and the instruments used to influence EU institutions and the governments of Member States. Finally, it presents some conclusions about the relations between the EU arms trading system and European civil society activism on arms trade controls.

II. EUROPEAN UNION MEMBER STATES' INTERESTS IN THE CONVENTIONAL ARMS TRADE

Since the 1990s the international arms trade has turned into an increasingly open, smooth and wide market, as the once strict controls on each superpower bloc were lifted after the Cold War.[3] The arms trade now operates on a global level with a significant increase in the number of participating States and intermediaries. Even

[3] SG Sample, 'Arms Race and Dispute Escalation: Resolving the Debate' (1997) 34 *Journal of Peace Research* 7.

more worrying are the illegal actors which, whether or not supported by governments, are unlawfully taking over a growing share of the international arms trade.[4]

In this context, multinational arms-producing companies are undergoing more and more changes, in the form of mergers and acquisitions, with the sole purpose of maintaining their turnover and profit in relation to new producers, with either public or private capital, that have entered the market.[5] These constant changes in the arms-producing companies cause a series of difficulties when one tries to conduct research into the significance of certain EU Member States in the arms trade for a number of reasons.[6] First, not all arms companies registered in Europe have exclusively European capital and in some cases, even have a major public capital shareholding. Secondly, companies in this sector have recently undergone frequent changes in order to adapt to global arms market developments.[7] And

[4] This supply is obviously due to military expenditure made by the states, even though military expenditure fell in 2014 to $1776 billion, i.e. by 0.4 per cent of GDP in real terms. This fall in 2014 is essentially attributable to a 6.5 per cent decrease in USA military expenditure, but is till 69 per cent higher than in 2001. In addition, Western and Central European countries reduced military spending by 8.3 per cent between 2005 and 2014. However, this period ended in positive figures because Russian military expenditure rose by 8.1 per cent and further rises are planned, and China's military expenditure increased by 9.7 per cent. Likewise, there were significant increases in military spending in the Middle East and North Africa, while in sub Saharan Africa it fell for the first time since 2003. In 2015, military expenditure rose by 1.0 per cent in real terms and was estimated in $1.676 billion. Military spending decreased in North America, Western Europe, Latin America and the Caribbean, and Africa. Military expenditure in the USA fell by 2.4 per cent to $596 billion—a slower rate of decline than in recent years, mainly due to steps taken by the US Congress to mitigate the impact of the spending reductions imposed by the 2011 Budget Control Act. The decline in military spending in Western Europe slowed to 1.3 per cent, while countries in Central Europe increased spending by 13 per cent, largely prompted by fears of Russian aggression following the Ukraine crisis (Sam Perlo-Freeman, Aude Fleurant, Pieter D Wezeman and Siemon T Wezeman, 'Trends in World Military Expenditure, 2014', (April 2015), *SIPRI Fact Sheet*, books.sipri.org/files/FS/SIPRIFS1504.pdf; and 'Trends in World Military Expenditure, 2015', (April 2016), *SIPRI Fact Sheet*, books.sipri.org/files/FS/SIPRIFS1604.pdf, accessed 19 April 2016).

[5] In fact, the increase in competitiveness of the industry together with economic constraints as a result of the economic crisis and the gradual drawdowns in Iraq and Afghanistan—in addition to embargoes imposed on Libya and Syria since 2011—have led many of these companies to make a number of adjustments in order to stay in the market. The general fall in US and Western European companies' revenues is partially offset by a 25.1 per cent growth in revenues for 36 companies in the Top 100 based in other parts of the world, including Russia. In 'SIPRI Top 100 Arms Sales Decreased in 2014: Companies Pursue Diverse Strategies in Response to Austerity Measures', *SIPRI in the Media*, 18 February 2013. Many of these companies, especially American and Western Europeans, accounted the 84.2 per cent of the total arms sales. In 'The SIPRI Top 100 Arms-Producing and Military Services Companies, 2014 (excluding China)', December 2015, *SIPRI Fact Sheet*, www.sipri.org/research/armaments/production/Top100, accessed 17 April 2016.

[6] 'In the Union, defence industries are marred by economics and structural problems such as fragmentation and divergence of capabilities, excess production capability in certain areas and shortages in others, duplication, short productions runs, and failure to engage in increasingly costly research': P Koutranos, *The EU 2013 Common Security and Defense Policy* (Oxford, OUP, 2013) 250.

[7] After all these changes, 43 American companies are still in the Top 100 list of arms-producing companies in the world, which accounts for 60 per cent of total worldwide sales. 37 companies based in Western Europe, which remained mostly stable at the regional level with a very slight decrease of 0.9 per cent, are also in the Top 100, accounting for 29 per cent of global exports, most of them British, French, German or Italian. 'The SIPRI Top 100 Arms-Producing and Military Services Companies, 2014', (2014) *SIPRI Fact Sheet*: www.sipri.org/research/armaments/production/Top100), accessed 15 May 2015.

thirdly, it is always a difficult task to interpret data on total sales and the different product categories within the arms market.[8]

In any case, the EU's regime for the control of the arms trade requires Member States to provide information on their exports, in the same way as they must with their political institutions under the democratic control processes they are subject to. Finally, the UN Register of Conventional Arms (UNROCA) requires Member States to provide a report of their purchases and sales. These elements are sufficient to aver, as is done by the researchers at the Stockholm International Peace Research Institute (SIPRI) in its Exporters Database 2015, that three Member States of the EU rank among the six largest arms exporters in the world. Germany ranks third as a global arms exporter with a turnover of US$12.332 million over the period 2008–14. France is the fourth-largest exporter, with a turnover of around US$11.326 million over the same period, and United Kingdom ranks sixth, just after China, with US$8239 million turnover. Spain and Italy rank seventh and eighth respectively, and among the world's 25 largest arms exporters are EU States, such as the Netherlands, Belgium, Austria, Finland, Sweden or Poland. These figures indicate that, after the US and Russia, a significant number of EU countries accounts for a considerable part of the global arms market.[9]

Of course, the figures referred to above are linked to a number of Member States' commercial interests, and they have social and employment implications as well, because the activity of these companies has a significant economic and social impact in many EU regions, especially in the current context of the socio-economic crisis.[10] It should also be kept in mind that the arms trade remains a major external policy instrument that Member States have been using, even today, as shown by arms embargoes on countries in the Middle East, like Iran or Syria, while stimulating sales to other countries in the region like Saudi Arabia or Qatar.[11]

[8] That is why the operative provision 5 of the European Union Code of Conduct stated as a priority the adoption of a common list of military equipment, approved on 13 June 2000. Council Declaration of 13 June 2000, issued on the occasion of the adoption of the common list of military equipment covered by the European Union Code of Conduct on Arms Exports ([2000] OJ C191/1) and Common Military List of the European Union (equipment covered by the European Union Code of Conduct on Arms Exports, [2003] OJ C314/1). The last updating and replacing of the common military list was adopted by the Council on 9 February 2015 [2015] OJ C129/1).

[9] The five biggest exporters in 2011–15 were the USA, Russia, China, France and Germany. Together, they accounted for 74 per cent of the total volume of arms exports. Combined, the USA and Russia supplied 58 per cent of all exports. French arms exports decreased by 9.8 per cent between 2006–10 and 2011–15, and German exports fell by 51 per cent. The five biggest importers in 2011–15 were India, Saudi Arabia, China, the UAE and Australia. Together, they received 34 per cent of all arms imports (SIPRI Arms Transfers Database), http://armstrade.sipri.org/armstrade/html/export_toplist.php, accessed 18 May 2015; and Trends in International Arms Transfer 2015, February 2016, /books.sipri.org/files/FS/SIPRIFS1602.pdf, accessed 19 April 2016.

[10] See the interview with B Rammell, British Minister of State for Foreign and Commonwealth Affairs 'Toward a Legally Binding Arms Trade Treaty' (2009) 39 *Arms Control Today* 12.

[11] Saudi Arabia accounted for 30 per cent of the UK's exports. The UK's arms sales policy has been strongly criticised by public opinion, especially after the presentation of the Government's review of arms exports to the Middle East and North Africa, and wider arms control issues. Joint Report of Session 2012–13, vol I (London, Stationery Office July 2012). The UK government's plans aim at

This will undoubtedly have an impact on the fight for dominance in the region between Sunnis and Shias. EU Member States, using the instruments provided by the Common Foreign and Security Policy of the EU, have applied arms embargoes imposed by the UN Security Council. They have even adopted individual decisions where they undertake the commitment not to transfer arms to States not subject to such actions, just as they have decided to transfer arms to non-governmental groups, as has been the case with Syria.[12] However, despite the economic, commercial, political and strategic interests of Member States in this area, the EU was one of the largest promoters of the ATT. Since the General Assembly launched that initiative, the EU has taken part in the working groups and submitted proposals on the draft text.[13] In addition, the EU made efforts to export its arms control regime to other regions, funding training seminars and providing consulting and

seeking new export markets in the Gulf States; in November 2012 David Cameron visited Saudi Arabia, Oman and the United Arab Emirates. German companies are also exploring business opportunities with Saudi Arabia—a sale of 600–800 Leopard-2A7 battle tanks, plus 200 to Qatar. They also sold Algeria 1200 Tpz-1 armoured vehicles and two MEKO frigates. Saudi Arabia also received 11 per cent of French arms exports, but this did not cause as much of a debate as it did in Germany. Military spending in the Middle East amounted to US$196 billion in 2014, an increase of 5.2 per cent over 2013, and 57 per cent since 2005. Saudi Arabia's expenditure has increased since 2005 by 112 per cent (P Holtom, M Bromley, PD Wezeman and ST Wezeman, 'Development in Arms Transfers, 2012' (2013) *SIPRI Yearbook* 251 and S Perlo-Freeman, A Fleurant, PD Wezeman and ST Wezeman, 'Trends in World Military Expenditure, 2014' (April 2015), *SIPRI Fact Sheet*: books.sipri.org/files/FS/SIPRIFS1504.pdf, accessed 15 May 2015.

[12] In September 2011, the European Union suspended the Cooperation Agreement signed with Syria in 1977 (Council Decision 2011/523/EU of 2 September, partially suspending the application of the Cooperation Agreement between the European Economic Community and the Syrian Arab Republic, [2011] OJ L228/9). Some months later, the then-27 Member States agreed a set of sanctions, including a ban on trade in gold and precious metals with Syrian public bodies, a freeze on the assets of the Central Bank of Syria within the EU, an import ban on crude oil and petroleum products from Syria into the territories of the European Union—which represent 90 per cent of Syria's exports—as well as limiting the entry into the EU of a number of individuals linked to the Syrian government, freezing assets and, of course, banning the trade of arms and equipment which might be used for internal repression in Syria. See Council Decision 2011/782/CFSP of 1 December 2011 concerning restrictive measures against Syria [2011] OJ L319/ 56), Council Regulation (EU) No 442/2011 concerning restrictive measures in view of the situation in Syria [2011] OJ L121/1) and Council Regulation (EU) No 36/2012 of 18 January concerning restrictive measures in view of the situation in Syria and repealing Regulation (EU) No 442/2012 [2012] OJ L16/1). This former regulation has been modified many times with the intention of strengthening and extending the restrictive measures. For example, Council Regulation (EU) No 36/2012 was changed by Regulation (EU) No 867/2012 of 24 September [2012] OJ L225/1, as a result of Council Decision 2012/420/CFSP of 23 July amending Decision 2011/782/CFSP. The latest amendment effected was Council Regulation (EU) No 1323/2014 of 13 December [2014] OJ L358/1, as a result of Council Decision 2014/901/CFSP of 13 December [2014] OJ L358/28.

[13] Conclusions on the Arms Trade Treaty, 3026th Agriculture and Fisheries Council Meeting, Brussels, 12 July 2010. See also the report prepared by the Open-Ended Working Group on 20 July 2009, *Report of the Open-ended Working Group towards an Arms Trade Treaty: establishing common international standards for the import, export and transfer of conventional arms*, second substantive session, New York, 13–17 July 2009 (A/AC.277/2009/1). It is expressly provided in Council Joint Action 2008/230/CFSP of 18 March [2008] OJ L75/81, which reiterates support for the General Assembly Resolution 61/89 on the adoption of an arms trade treaty, and €500,500 was allocated from the general budget of the European Union to assist and train third countries in order to prevent and combat illicit trafficking in conventional arms.

technical services to help put control systems in place in countries that have none or have one but wish to improve it.[14] And, finally, it encouraged all UN Member States to sign and ratify the ATT adopted in April 2013.[15]

In those circumstances, it is interesting to analyse the views on arms trade control defended by Member States, especially compared to the remaining States with interests in this field. If we consider the views expressed by the Participating States at the two Conferences on the ATT in July 2012 and March 2013, in addition to the results of the voting which took place at the General Assembly for the adoption of the text of the ATT, it may be concluded that there are two major groups of States with different positions with regard to the international regulation of the arms trade.[16]

The first group consists of those countries in favour of a strict international regulation of the arms trade—the countries with no strong commercial interests in this field and that are not top-ranked exporters or importers but which suffer the negative consequences of an unregulated arms trade within their territories, notably in terms of criminal violence and human rights violations. This is the case of many Latin American and African States, which supported regulation with more restrictive criteria when approving licence applications and even proposed that when accepting or refusing a licence the impact of an export on the protection of human rights and the development of the importing States should be included as an evaluation criterion. Within this same group, but with more moderate positions, are States that do not occupy a prominent position in the global arms trade but also do not suffer the consequences of the lack of international controls in the arms trade within their territories to an alarming extent.[17]

[14] Thus, technical and legal assistance is crucial, as has been recognised by the UN and the EU; the two bodies have been organising and funding information and training seminars for several years to staff from Participating States in the 2012 Conference. But it is very likely that the control of brokering is not one of the easiest aspects to deal with and a priority for the Arms Trade Treaty—as underlined in the conclusions drawn up by the Group of Governmental Experts. W Bauwens, EU Statement in International Cooperation and Assistance, *First Session of the Preparatory Committee for the United Nations Conference on the Arms Trade Treaty*, New York, 21 July 2010, paras 3–5. The EU Council subsequently adopted a series of decisions necessary for the implementation of the EU Action Plan where corresponding budget items were approved for the organisation of training seminars on arms trade control to third countries (Decision 2009/1012/CFSP), and also for activities in support of the Arms Trade Treaty (Decision 2010/336/ CFSP).

[14] In the Council Joint Action on the EU's contribution to combating the destabilising accumulation and spread of small arms and light weapons and repealing Joint Action 1999/34/CFSP (2002/589/ CFSP, [2002] OJ L191/1).

[15] The EU adopted in December 2013 under Council Decision 2013/768/CFSP, 'a programme to support the Treaty's implementation by third countries' (Statement on the forthcoming entry into force of the Arms Trade Treaty, Brussels, 25 September 2014, 140925/01).

[16] Compilation of Views on the Elements of an Arms Trade Treaty, Background Document Prepared by the Secretariat, May 10 2012, A/CONF.217/2: www.un.org/ga/search/view_doc.asp?symbol=A/ CONF.217/2&Lang=E, accessed, 18 May 2015.

[17] The number of deaths caused by small arms as a result of criminal violence is alarming; this figure amounts to 490,000 a year, especially in Latin America, the Caribbean, and the West and South-East African region. In Mexico alone it is estimated that 50,000 people have died as a result of firearms over the past six years 'Urban Armed Violence' (2012) 23 *Small Arms Survey* 1. See also the data on violence against women and girls—with a focus on post-conflict Liberia and Nepal—K Krause, *Small Arms Survey* (Cambridge, Cambridge University Press, 2014).

The second group is composed of those countries which are more reluctant to accept the global regulation of the arms trade. The countries which have been firmly against arms trade control are those involved in an international conflict situation; they are even subject to sanctions imposed by other States and international organisations too. This is the case with Syria, North Korea and Iran, which regard arms trade control merely as a mechanism for foreign powers to interfere in their internal affairs. Therefore, these three countries were the only ones to vote against the ATT.[18] Also included in this group are large-scale arms exporters like the United States, Russia and China; their opposition to the proposed text at the First Conference in 2012 led to its failure, the change of the Chairperson and the convening of a new international conference. Those three States are the world's first-, second- and fourth-largest arms exporters respectively. Their interest in being free to decide with whom to trade is not only for economic and commercial purposes but also for the geo-strategic reasons behind their foreign and security policies. States, especially international powers, have traditionally used arms transfers as an instrument of foreign policy to influence events outside their territories. Finally, there is another group of countries reluctant to bring the arms trade under control—those occupying a significant position as new buyers or sellers; they regard the Treaty as a present or future obstacle for their political and economic interests. This is the case with India, Pakistan and other countries which voted against the 2012 draft text and abstained from the vote on the ATT approved and open for signature on April 2013.[19]

States with strong interests in the international arms trade that do not suffer the consequences of an unregulated trade in arms within their territories are usually against imposing tighter restrictions on arms transfer; this should in theory be the position of the EU and its Member States. Indeed, in the EU Treaty itself, the arms trade is subject to exception in the field of the common commercial policy because it is considered a sensitive issue for Member States' security. For this reason, from the very beginning, the Member States decided to have the greatest possible freedom when using conventional arms transfers as an instrument to protect their trade and foreign security policy interests. However, as the effects of the end of the Cold War had a significant impact on diversification, lack of control and expansion of the global arms market, the Member States—fully consistently with the principles and values that inspire the EU Common Foreign and Security

[18] C Craft, *Weapons for Peace, Weapons for War. The Effects of Arms Transfer on War Outbreak, Involvement and Outcomes* (Routledge, New York, 1999) and J Sislin and F Pearson, *Arms and Ethnic Conflict and Ethic Conflict* (Lanham MD, Rowman and Littlefield, 2001). See also K Booth and P Vale, 'Critical Security Studies and Regional Insecurity: The Case of Southern Africa' in K Krause and M Williams (eds), *Critical Security Studies* (Minneapolis MN, University of Minnesota Press, 1997) 329.

[19] In addition to the States voting against—Syria, North Korea and Iran—23 countries abstained, including Russia, China, Cuba, Bolivia, Belarus, Egypt, India, Indonesia and Ecuador, while 154 voted in favour. The treaty opened for signature on 3 June 2013, and entered into force from 24 December 2014. In May 2015, 130 States had signed it and 67 had ratified (States voting against or abstaining and the United States have not ratified the treaty yet).

Policy—decided to develop a non-legally binding Code of Conduct. The aim was to establish a number of criteria to limit export licensing and provide an internal procedure of information and cooperation in order to ensure the uniform application of those criteria by all Member States. Since the adoption of this Code of Conduct in 1988, the EU has been improving its control mechanisms to the point of giving binding effect to this Code.[20]

The behaviour of Member States regarding arms trade control can be explained by a number of ethical constraints governing their foreign policies. These have been firmly demanded by European civil society, which is fully aware of the need for EU Member States—which include some of the world's major arms exporters—to help ward off the evil effects of unregulated arms transfers. The next section explains how Member States and the EU itself have had to implement the governing principles when adopting decisions to approve or refuse certain arms export licences and supporting international initiatives favouring international arms trade control.

III. THE EUROPEAN UNION'S IMPROVEMENTS IN ARMS TRADE CONTROL

Since the 1990s the UN, through the General Assembly, has continuously made proposals to design a control system for conventional weapons, the most important milestones being the Plan of Action for the Prevention of Light Weapons and Small Arms of the UN Conference held in 2001[21] and the subsequent establishment of an Expert Group through its Resolution 61/89 of 6 December 2006, responsible for assessing the possibility of measures that would regulate the arms trade on the basis of consensus and balance that benefits all States.[22] The group conducted the preliminary work for the two conferences for the conclusion of an ATT that took place in 2012 and 2013 and ended with the adoption of a draft treaty open for signature and ratification from 3 June 2013, in force from 24 December 2014.[23]

The EU has distinguished itself by assisting and promoting within and outside its borders the UN's proposals to control trade in conventional arms with a much

[20] COREPER, on 30 June 2005, agreed at the technical level the text of a Common Position with the aim of transforming the Code into an efficient instrument to control arms exports from EU territory and by EU companies (Council Joint Decision 2008/944/CFSP of 8 December [2008] OJ L335/99).

[21] 'UN Conference on Illicit Trade in Small Arms' (2001) 95 *American Journal of International Law* 901.

[22] Action Programme to combat and eradicate the illicit trade in small arms and light weapons in all its aspects in Doc A/CONF. 192/15 (9–10 July 2001). See the following resolutions of the General Assembly on the conventional arms trade: 46/36 L of 9 December 1991, 51/45 N of 10 December 1996, 51/47B of 10 December 1996, 56/24 V of 24 December 2001 60/69 and 60/82 of 8 December 2005.

[23] Before 2001, the United Nations had already promoted several actions in the field of small arms and light weapons, as can be seen in the following General Assembly Resolutions /RES/50/70B (1995), A/58/298 (1997) and A/54/258 (1999). See 'Illicit Trade in Small Arms and Light Weapons in all its Aspects Program of Action (POA)' (2012) Inventory of International Nonproliferation Organizations and Regimes, Center for Nonproliferation Studies: cns.miis.edu/inventory/pdfs/sarms.pdf, accessed 4 May 2015.

higher intensity and rhythm than other regional and international organisations participating in these processes.[24] Backed by its progress in the design of control measures of the arms trade, the EU has contributed largely to promoting similar processes in other regions of international society. However, Member States never intended to develop a system for controlling conventional weapons subject to Union law. In addition, they wanted to make it clear that the trade in conventional weapons should not be part of the common market, considering that arms transfers were a matter of political significance and had serious implications for security and State defence, as stated in Article 346 of TFEU (former Article 296) and in fact, on 15 April 1958, the Council developed a list of products subject to that exception.[25] However, the changing international political circumstances, from the 1990s onward, destroyed the legitimacy of secrecy and freedom which the Member States had enjoyed throughout the Cold War. National parliaments began demanding information on arms sales, which sometimes were justified as part of cooperation to development, and thereafter, it was the NGOs that linked such sales with the suffering of the recipients as a consequence of the use of such weapons. The result was none other than serious violations of human rights and the perpetuation of violence and conflict.[26] Many of the arms sales operations

[24] *Statement of Behalf of the European Union at the Preparatory Committee for the Arms Trade Treaty*, Nueva York, 12 de Julio de 2011, paras 5–11: www.nonproliferation.eu/activities/adhoc/att.php, and accessed 18 May 2015, the EU and its Member States made the greatest number of interventions and proposals in the sessions of the Preparatory Committee for the Conference. Note especially the speeches of the EU Representative that highlight the need to consider that the future international arms trade regime will have an evolutionary basis and must improve in the various review conferences that may be held every five years. Werner Bauwens, EU Statement in International Cooperation and Assistance, *First Session of the Preparatory Committee for the United Nations Conference on the Arms Trade Treaty*, New York, 21 July 2010, paras 3–5; Annalisa Giannella, *Statement*, EU Statement in International Cooperation and Assistance, *First Session of the Preparatory Committee for the United Nations Conference on the Arms Trade Treaty*, New York, 21 July 2010, paras 3–5; Annalisa Giannella, *Statement on Behalf of the European Union on Final Provisions of the Arms Trade Treaty*, Preparatory Committee for the Arms Trade Treaty, New York, 13 July 2011, Attila Zimonyi, *Statement on Behalf of the European Union on Parameters on the Arms Trade Treaty*, Preparatory Committee for the Arms Trade Treaty, New York, 1 March 2011; Eszter Sandorfi, *Statement on Behalf of the European Union on General Comments on the Revised Chair's Draft Paper*, Preparatory Committee for the Arms Trade Treaty, New York, 3 March 2011 and EU Opening Statement by Mr Thomas Mayr-Harting. Head of the Delegation of the European Union to the United Nations at the UN Conference on the Arms Trade Treaty, New York, 5 July 2012.

[25] 'The provisions of the Treaties shall not preclude the application of the following rules: (a) no Member State shall be obliged to supply information the disclosure of which it considers contrary to the essential interests of its security; (b) any Member State may take such measures as it considers necessary for the protection of the essential interests of its security which are connected with the production of or trade in arms, munitions and war material; such measures shall not adversely affect the conditions of competition in the internal market regarding products which are not intended for specifically military purposes'. (Art 346, TFEU, former Art 296 TEC). Between 1991 and 1992, in the European Councils of Luxemburg and Lisbon, the Member States had agreed certain 'Common Criteria' for the export of arms, which served as the basis for the Code of Conduct on the Arms Trade adopted on 5 June 1998.

[26] John Stanley, 'Scrutiny of arms export controls', (2012) Scrutiny of the Government's UK Strategic Export Controls Annual Report 2011, published in July 2012, Stationery Office.

being undertaken by Member States were inconsistent with the principles and values underlying the external action of the EU, so the first step taken in this regard was the development of a Code of Conduct, in 1998, which only consisted of a political agreement by which the parties agreed to respect a number of criteria when authorising the export of arms.[27]

In 2002 the need to develop a policy of controlling the trade in weapons consistent with all EU principles and activities in the field of conflict prevention resulted in a Joint Action by which the Member States were committed to combating destabilising action and the proliferation of light weapons and small arms in response to the UN Programme of Action to Prevent, Combat and Eradicate the Illicit Trade in Small Arms and Light Weapons (SALW) in all aspects, adopted in 2001. Given the disturbing facts that campaigns for the control of trade in light weapons and small arms offered to the public, the EU decided to adopt a strategy to combat illicit accumulation and trafficking of SALW and their ammunition, adopted by the European Council on 15 and 16 December 2005.[28] This had as its main aim the implementation of an action plan, subject to review every six months, calculated to ensure consistency between the common foreign and security policy of the EU and its cooperation to development policy, through a series of actions at national, international and domestic level. Thus, Member States had made a legally binding commitment in the framework for the control of light weapons; however, for the rest of the categories of conventional weapons it only had the political agreement offered by the Code of Conduct. This situation ended when in 2008 the Council decided to translate the Code of Conduct it had been using since 1998 into a Common Position 2008/944/CFSP, giving it a legal and therefore binding character on all Member States.[29]

Among the benefits of the system of arms trade control that the EU has developed over the last 16 years is the scope of those criteria that Member States have to consider when authorising exports and the control measures established to unify the interpretation of the criteria, thus being able to develop an effective control

[27] The main acts adopted by the European Union for control of the arms trade are European Union Programme for Preventing and Combating Illicit Trafficking in Conventional Weapons, 9057/97 E—CFSP DG IV, 26 June 1997; Joint Action of 17 December adopted by the Council on the basis of Article J.3 of the TEU on the European Union's contribution to combating the destabilising accumulation and spread of small arms and light weapons (1999/34/CFSP), [1999] OJ L9/1, 15.01.99; Council of the European Union, Joint Action 2002/589/CFSP of 12 July on the European Union's contribution to combating the destabilising accumulation and spread of small arms and light weapons and repealing Joint Action 1999/34/CFSP, [2002] OJ L191/1 and Council of the European Union, Strategy to Combat Illicit Accumulation and Trafficking of SALW and their ammunition, 5319/06, 16 December 2005: register.consilium.europa.eu/pdf/en/06/st05/st05319.en06.pdf, accessed 25 April 2015. Z Yihdego, 'The EU's Role in Restraining the Unrestrained Trade in Conventional Weapons' (2009) 10 *German Law Journal* 281.

[28] EU Strategy to combat illicit accumulation and trafficking of SALW and their ammunition, adopted by European Council on 16 December 2005 (3066/05 CFSP 833 CODUN 19 COARM 38). See also Council Conclusions on the inclusion of a SALW article in agreements between the EU and third countries, 17 December 2008.

[29] Council Joint Decision 2008/944/CFSP, 8 December [2008] OJ L335/99.

over the arms trade.[30] Indeed, the criteria that Member States have to consider when authorising an export licence are much more stringent than those contained in any of the similar existing international instruments on the control of the arms trade, including that of the ATT itself. The Common Position 2008/944/CFSP reminds Member States that they must comply with the resolutions of the UN Security Council containing sanctions against third countries in the field of arms transfers, as well as the sanctions that have been agreed in the framework of the Organization for Security and Co-operation in Europe or the EU itself. Similarly, the criteria set out in the Common Position remind Member States of their obligations undertaken in cooperation forums in which they participate that are intended to ensure international security through arms control, in addition to international agreements which have been concluded on the same subject. Moreover, the criteria also take into account the situation of the States to which it is intended to send the weaponry, especially in terms of violations of human rights that can be caused by such weapons, the possibilities that they may serve to continue an armed conflict that endangers the stability of the area, that the recipient may be an intermediary of or sponsor international terrorist groups or organised international crime, which will use the weapons for offensive and not defensive purposes and to act as an intermediary for a State to obtain weapons indirectly that would never be able to receive them under the terms of the criteria. Finally, the criteria address the need to prevent Member States' transactions from impairing their foreign relations and those of the Union itself. Moreover, the EU also has mechanisms for consultation, information and transparency that allow States to progress to an increasingly homogeneous interpretation of the criteria contained in the Common Position and always to know the reasons why other States have denied an export licence, thus having more information about the circumstances of the recipients and ensuring widening compliance with the Code of Conduct.[31]

As mentioned previously, despite the importance of the Member States' positions in the international arms trade and its most advanced arms trade control system, many of its shortcomings have been revealed thanks to the political control that European citizens exercise over their States and Union institutions. The involvement of European citizens in matters relating to the arms trade in the form

[30] The ideas that follow were set out at length in I Marrero Rocha, 'El régimen de comercio de Armas de la Unión Europea' (2012) 40 *Revista de Derecho Comunitario Europeo* 669.

[31] Operative Provision 8 of the Code mentioned the need for Member States periodically to submit their reports on the implementation of the eight criteria contemplated in the Code and, in turn, an annual global report would be drawn up for all the Union (Annual Report according to Article 8(2) of Council Common Position 2008/944/CFSP defining common rules governing control of exports of military technology and equipment. The last report was the Sixteenth Annual Report [2015] OJ C103/1 (eeas.europa.eu/non-proliferation-and-disarmament/arms-export-control/index_en.htm). Such reports form an overall assessment of the implementation of the Code, now the Common Position, where the major weaknesses are identified and, more importantly, propose a series of targets for improvement including specific mechanisms to achieve them in the following year.

of movements, associations and campaigns, among others, is a determining factor in the development of the Union's control system over the arms trade and its implementation and improvement by those applying it, for the reasons set forth in the following section.

IV. EUROPEAN CIVIL SOCIETY'S REACTION TOWARD AN UNCONTROLLED CONVENTIONAL ARMS TRADE

Changes in the international arms trade since the end of the Cold War have contributed to the increase in the number of actors involved in the business, and moreover, have worsened the security of individuals, since many parts of the world are engaged in protracted conflicts, where the weaponry is not subject to any control, especially in the case of so-called failed States.[32] This increase in conflict areas, accompanied by greater involvement of civilians and combatants who are not part of regular armed forces, has expanded the demand for conventional weapons, especially small arms and light weapons. The spread of conventional weapons creates a culture of violence that greatly hinders peace processes. Afghanistan is a case in point, since there are over 10 million small arms and light weapons in circulation within its territory.[33] These arms in practice have greater lethal power, are easy to carry and hide, so that their transfer has increased as compared to operations of heavy conventional weapons. And, in response to that growth in demand there has also been an increase in supply by the arms industry and even the emergence of small arms industries in undeveloped countries.[34]

In this context, the aim of the EU is that the weapons coming from its territory should reach the right hands and be legally acquired; although determining who are the legitimate and legal recipients is always a complex issue. However, European civil society has refused to remain aloof from the progress made by the Union in developing an efficient and effective control system in the

[32] If to this we add the fact that the States still do not provide complete and reliable information about their transactions, it is not surprising that it results in situations that are as complex as set out in the *Small Arms Survey* which indicates the relationship that occurs between the prices of black market weapons in Lebanon and deaths in Syria's internal conflict ('Price Watch: Arms and Ammunition at Illicit Markets', *Small Arms Survey 2013*, chapter 11; H Ramadansyah, 'Controlling the Circulation of Small Arms in International Law' (The University of Kaiwato, 2013): researchcommons.waikato.ac.nz/, accessed 28 April 2015; NR Jenzem-Jones, 'The Headstamp Trail: An Assessment of Small-calibre Ammunition Documented in Syria', *Small Arms Survey, Working Paper 18* (2014): www.smallarmssurvey.org/fileadmin/docs/F-Working-papers/SAS-WP16-Headstamp-Trail-Ammunition-Libya.pdf; and N Huktin, 'Leaky Humanitarianism: The Anthropology of Small Arms Control in the Gambia' (2015) 42 *American Ethnologist* 68.

[33] M Schroeder and B King, 'Surveying the Battlefield: Illicit Arms in Afghanistan, Iraq, and Somalia', *Small Arms Survey 2012: Moving Targets*: www.smallarmssurvey.org/fileadmin/docs/A-Yearbook/2012/eng/Small-Arms-Survey-2012-hapter-10-EN.pdf, accessed 10 May 2015.

[34] C García Segura, 'Transformaciones de la conflictividad armada y la seguridad internacional: las implicaciones políticas de la privatización de la seguridad' in DJ Liñán Nogueras (ed), *Las crisis políticas y económicas. Nuevos escenarios internacionales* (Madrid, Tecnos, 2014) 19.

weapons trade.[35] Europe has a long tradition of involvement and desire for citizen participation in public affairs. Since 1968 there have been various movements of Europeans citizens that have spread to other parts of the globe and have been the subject of major studies by the academy. As Flesher and Cox have said: 'European social movements have been central to European history, politics, society, and culture and have had a global reach and impact'.[36] More recently, European social movements have been the forerunners of contemporary movements such as the anti-globalisation movement or global justice movements. And in recent years, especially in Greece, Iceland, the UK, Spain or Portugal, European citizens have staged major protests against the measures of financial austerity that have spread to other societies like the US, through the 'take Wall Street' movement.[37] However, these new movements coexist with others with decades of experience that have been involved in major campaigns on issues of peace and disarmament. Both new and old European social movements have made Europe a 'contagious' space which has given birth to transnational protests that have served as sources of inspiration, information and learning, and undoubtedly have led to a network of international promotion and condemnation.[38] Moreover, in the case of the control or the disappearance of certain types of weapons, the efforts of European citizens have not proved to be an abstraction but a framework of action with important implications.[39]

The social initiatives for the control of the arms trade are rooted in the 1990s, in a context of European pacifism, which demanded the end of military conscription and a fundamental reduction in defence expenditure that had cornered much of the budgets of EU Member States belonging to the North Atlantic Treaty Organization.[40] It is true that the effects of weapons of mass destruction remained a major concern, especially with regard to the spread of uncontrolled nuclear material in the territory of the former Soviet Union, as well as the need to enforce

[35] Mary Kaldor defines civil society as 'a concept linked to the notion of reducing the violence of social relations, the public use of reason to manage human affairs' in M Kaldor, *The global civil society. An answer to war* (Barcelona, Tusquets Publishers, 2005) 16 and 17–19. (Author's translation).

[36] C Flesher Fominaya and C Laurence, *Understanding European Movements* (London, Routledge, 2013) 7.

[37] D della Porta and S Tarrow, *Transnational Protest and Global Activism* (Lanham MD, Rowman and Littlefield Publishers Inc, 2004); R Cohen and S Rai, *Global Social Movements* (London, The Athlone Press Co, 2000); I Sommier, *Le renouveau des Movements Contestatataires à l'Heure de la Mondialization* (Paris, Flammarion, 2003); A Starr, *Global Revolt: A Guide to the Movements against Globalization* (New York, Zed Books, 2005) and *Transnational Social Movements* (Cambridge, Cambridge University Press, 2005) and E Romanos, 'Collective Learning Processes within Social Movements' in C Flesher Fominay and C Laurence, n 36 above, 203.

[38] C Scholl, 'Europe as a Contagious Space' in C Flesher Fominay and C Laurence, n 36 above, 27.

[39] L Davies, 'Global Citizenship: Abstraction or Framework of Action?' (2006) 58 *Educational Review* 5.

[40] On the Post Cold-War pacifist movements and their influence on the International Relations structure of their times see D Levy, M Pensky and J Torpey, *Old Europe, New Europe, Core Europe: Transatlantic Relations After Iraq War* (London, Verso, 2005) and J Smith, C Chatfield and R Pagnucco, *Transnational Social Movements and Global Politics: Solidarity Beyond The State* (Syracuse NY, Syracuse University Press, 1997).

existing treaties that prohibit the transfer, development and storage of chemical, biological and nuclear weapons. However, the new factor consisted in exposing the damage that conventional weapons caused, especially their uncontrolled sale.[41] Conventional weapons are not questioned as an essential tool for national defence, but their irresponsible transfer to territories in conflict, States suffering criminal structural violence or in any other circumstances in which these weapons, directly or directly, cause serious violations of human rights, is a matter of grave concern. The first campaigns against conventional weapons were designed within the framework of various NGOs, in the early 1990s, and were aimed at eliminating from International Relations some types of weapons that were particularly harmful to humans, such as anti-personal mines, cluster bombs and blinding lasers.[42] Once these campaigns ended with the signing of international agreements prohibiting such weapons, the next target focused on the control of trade in other conventional weapons, in particular, light and small arms, which are the easiest to transfer and divert for uses other than to ensure strictly the security of States.[43]

The group of NGOs that became interested in the consequences of conventional weapons and the need to put some limits on their transfer is called the 'Arms NGOs Community' and its main activities are in the field of research, design of public policy, assessment, advising, protest, awareness and education.[44] NGOs implementing activities in the field, besides information, awareness or protest campaigns, belong to this community as do a series of think tanks that are dedicated to research, analysis and preparation of independent reports on security, arms control and disarmament. The Arms NGOs Community identifies more with the characteristics of all social movements that began in the 1960s, such as environmentalism, feminism or anti-militarism,[45] and makes use of the established

[41] See the report on the dissemination of Fissile Material in the territory of the former Soviet Union 'Confirmed proliferation: Significant Incidents of Fissile Material Trafficking in the Newly Independent States (NIS)' 1991–2001, (2002) *CNS Reports*, Center for Nonproliferation Studies.

[42] L Monin and A Gallimore, *The Devil's Garden: The Story of the Landmines* (London, Random House Books, 2002).

[43] These instruments are the Convention on Cluster Munitions, opened for signature and ratification in December 2008; the Ottawa Convention on anti-personnel mines, opened for signature and ratification in 1997; and the Protocol on Blinding Lasers within the Treaty on the Prohibitions or Restrictions on the Use of Certain Conventional Weapons whose damage is excessive and have indiscriminate effects, 10 April 1981. About these types of weapons and their international regime see B Rappert and R Moyes, 'The Prohibition Of Cluster Munitions: Setting International Precedents for Defining Inhumanity' (2009) 16 *The Nonproliferation Review* 249. On the involvement of the campaigns against these types of weapons and their prohibition in the sphere of International Public Law in J Brunnée and S Toope, 'Constructivism and International Law' in JL Dunoff and MA Pollack, (eds), *Interdisciplinary Perspectives on International Law and International Relations* (Cambridge, Cambridge University Press, 2013) 119–45.

[44] In P Batchelor, 'NGO Perspectives: NGOs and the Small Arms Issue' (2002) 1 *Disarmament Forum* 37.

[45] See the description and comparison between the old and new social movements, in S Hutter, 'Globalization and the Transformation of National Protest Politics' in H Kouki and E Romanos (eds), *Protest Beyond Borders. Contentious Politics in Europe since 1945* (New York/Oxford, Berghahn Books, 2013) 181; R Falk, 'The Global Promise of Social Movements: Explorations at the Edge of Time' (1987)

media and direct contact with institutions to enforce its demands and put pressure on States with the aim of addressing the appropriate legislative changes at national and international level.[46] This is in contrast with more contemporary social movements that are a form of collective action, based on the pre-existence of a conflict, due to structural tensions, organised informally with participation based on equality, and which reject established channels to voice their demands. These often use unconventional means, such as civil disobedience, questioning the ability of institutions to exercise their power against individual autonomy, rejecting the very division between public and private, and disputing the system of norms and established values. Moreover, since 1989, European civil society has participated in that more global concept of civil society in the context of groups and networks using worldwide social media, enabling formal and informal organisations to negotiate, cooperate and join together to achieve a common goal and connect people who belong to different worlds, with various training and professional developments but which ultimately conduct an activity of advocacy centred on what and on whom the States have forgotten.[47]

The UN, especially its General Assembly, has enhanced the activities of the Arms NGOs Community from the time in which it uses the information it provides on the relationship between the increase in the volume of transactions of different types of weapons, many them beyond government control, and the increase in violence, human rights violations and the loss of human lives, especially civilians. Previously, other initiatives developed within the UN framework on certain types of weapons like anti-personnel mines, cluster bombs or blinding lasers have used the reports and proposals submitted by the NGO Arms Community. The NGO Committee on Disarmament, Peace and Security has been responsible for over 30 years for facilitating the contact and the relationship between UN activities in this field and that carried out by hundreds of citizens, associations and groups.[48] Among conventional weapons, small arms and light weapons are those that began to seize the attention of many participants in the NGOs Arms Community. In fact a large group of NGOs, some with previous experience in the campaign for the prohibition of anti-personnel mines, decided to create the International Action Network on Small Arms (IANSA). This network began its work in May 1999 and, according to its founding document, its activity is to facilitate civil society's capacity to act in order to improve the security of individuals and prevent the growth

12 *Alternatives* 173; W Lance Bennett, 'Social Movements Beyond Borders: Organization, Communication, and Political Capacity in Two Eras of Transnational Activism' in D della Porta and S Tarrow (eds), *Transnational Protest and Global Activism* (n 36 above) 203 and E Grau and P Ibarra, *Anuario de movimientos sociales* (Madrid, Icaria Editorial, 2012) 26.

[46] S Hutter, 'Globalization and the Transformation of National Protest Politics' in H Kouki and E Romanos (eds), n 45 above, 181.

[47] M Kaldor, *La sociedad civil global* (n 35 above) 105–18 and E Echart Muñoz, *Movimientos Sociales y Relaciones Internacionales. La irrupción de un nuevo actor* (Madrid, Catarata, 2008) 26.

[48] See NGOs Community activities during the ATT Pre- Committee in 2010: disarm.igc.org/index.php?option=com_content&view=category&layout=blog&id=148&Itemid=80, accessed 10 May 2015.

and spread of small arms, creating a network of important civil organisations capable of achieving the objectives set. But within this broad spectrum, as Rogers points out, not all organisations and not all citizens of IANSA have participated and collaborated in the campaign with the same intensity. IANSA has carried out advocacy and lobbying activities and has offered to inform and advise government officials, although not all governments have given the same response to this invitation. Throughout its work one of the most significant results have been two reports entitled *Biting the Bullet Project*, through which IANSA assessed States' compliance with the existing international legislation on small arms and implementation of the UNPoA in the light of the UN Small Arms Review Conference of 2006.[49] Since 2003, IANSA has formed part of a larger network called the Arms Control Coalition (ACC), which has brought together a very large number of NGOs and NGO networks to promote the adoption of ATT. The main features of ACC are its geographic scope that crosses State borders and reaches more than 100 countries,[50] its global objectives, and its composition, in which organisations with ties to other institutions (trade unions, political parties, churches or education centres) are included, as well as NGOs and more informal citizen movements that communicate through the network.[51]

ACC is not a movement only of European civil society, but also, since the 1990s, the term civil society is used in a different way from the past, and is not restricted geographically. But while ACC has a wide geographical distribution of participants, it can be said that an important part of the weight of the network is formed by partnerships, organisations and networks of EU citizens, also called the European Arms NGOs Community, who have managed to develop an influence quantitatively and qualitatively superior to the institutions of the EU and its Member States more than other ACC participants in their respective States and regional organisations.[52] In this context, it is necessary to explain why this has happened and how this influence has manifested itself throughout the development of the EU arms trade control system and the conclusion of the ATT.

[49] disarm.igc.org/, accessed 10 May 2015. Programme of Action to Prevent, Combat and Eradicate the Illicit Trade in Small Arms and Light Weapons in All Its Aspects (UNPoA).

[50] ACC has been working for more than a decade and has collected millions of signatures of citizens from all over the world in favour of controlling the arms trade. See D Rogers, *Postinternationalism and Small Arms Control, Theory, Politics, Security* (London, Ashgate Publishing Group, 2009) 173.

[51] On the characteristics of these types of social movements, see M Shawn, 'Civil Society and Global Politics: Beyond a Social Movements Approach' (1994) 23 *Millennium. Journal of International Studies* 647.

[52] Within the European Arms NGO Community there are certain differences, above all, featuring the European Network against Arms Trade, which carries out Campaigns Against Arms Trade (CAAT) that are particularly strong in the UK. Their aim is not to develop an effective monitoring of the arms trade but rather to end it. In A Stavrianakis, *Taking Aim At The Arms Trade. NGOs, Global Civil Society and the World Military Order* (New York, Zed Books, 2010) 33.

A. Reasons for European Civil Society's Influence on European Union Arms Trade Controls

The ability of European civil society to mobilise their governments politically and to exercise the necessary influence on the processes of national decision-making and in the framework of the Union is the main reason why it can be considered an actor in international relations. And its participation in the development of foreign policy decisions of the Member States can be analysed from a Kantian logic, which interprets the action of citizenship as a fulfilment of moral duties contracted with future generations and other citizens who are outside the EU space.[53] Obviously, this conception of European citizenship is far from the idea that strictly links it with the State in terms of political, social and economic rights, and which European citizens have gone beyond as a result of their experience of participating in the process of European integration and their desire to influence the development of its external action, including the arms trade, although this continues to be considered one of the sensitive areas of security and defence policy of the States where no limitations on sovereignty are allowed.[54] The campaign of the European Arms NGOs Community in favour of an ATT was developed not only in the holding of the conference but was also the product of a long process of prior awareness directed to the Member States, especially those with greater weight in the international arms trade, and recently building on a commitment among ATT parties to ensure an effective implementation.[55] The regional context of the Union has a number of features and offers a set of opportunities that European citizenship has taken advantage of to make their voices heard on issues of such importance as the control of the arms trade. Three elements can be identified that differentiate

[53] As Linklater says: 'the political theory of cosmopolitan democracy and recent accounts of possible futures for Europe argue that the nation-state is neither the sole nor the most important moral community. Post-sovereign arrangements which increase the role of sub-state and transnational political authorities in Europe have been defended as a normative ideal by exponents of a range of different ethical and political arrangements ... The ethical principles which require the development of a transnational citizenry in Europe invite deep concerns about the harms and injustices which the region can do to outsiders. To take the project of world citizenship seriously, any European societies which embark on the experiment of breaking the nexus between citizenship, sovereignty, territoriality and nationality have to display compassion in their dealing with the non-European world, but they have to do more than that for the reasons already mentioned' (A Linklater, 'Cosmopolitan Citizenship' (1998) 2 *Citizenship Studies* 25 and 30).

[54] E Echart Muñoz, *Movimientos Sociales y Relaciones Internacionales* (n 47 above) 55.

[55] On the influence of European movements and society in the development of the Union's participation in the first Conference on an Arms Trade Treaty, see S Deapauw, 'The European Union's Involvement in Negotiating an Arms Trade Treaty' *Non-proliferation Paper 23* (2012): www.sipri.org/research/disarmament/eu-consortium/publications/Nonproliferation_paper_23, accessed 12 May 2015. Arms NGOs Community is also involved on First Conference of ATT States Parties and its preparation (www.un.org/disarmament/ATT/csp1/, accessed 16 May 2015) and many have elaborated documents to assist States to apply sustainable development standards when making decisions regarding international arms transfers through the application of a clear and consistent procedure ('Practical Guide: Applying Sustainable Development to Arms-Transfer Decisions, Oxfam International Technical Brief' (2015): www.oxfam.org/sites/www.oxfam.org/files/tb-practical-guide-arms-trade-decisions-apr09.pdf, accessed 17 May 2015).

the EU context from other national or regional contexts, and that make it more permeable and receptive to the participation of civil society.

First, unlike other States, EU Member States have a long tradition of citizen participation in public affairs. European civil society has always played a very important role in the political, economic and social life, a consequence of the liberal political philosophy that inspired European political systems and bourgeois societies. This participation has been slowly spreading to more areas of the internal and external policies of States, and hence from the beginning of the process of European integration, civil society has claimed an increasing intervention in the competences the States have attributed to the supranational organisation. Therefore, the growing desire of citizens to participate in political affairs is no surprise to EU institutions, which have had to articulate mechanisms to meet these aspirations. If, at first, civil society was more sensitised to the promotion of human rights from the EU and its cooperation to development, it later also focused on a line of pacifist action centred on the elimination of certain types of weapons and now on the control of trade in conventional arms.[56] While campaigning for an ATT does not have a clear territorial demarcation, the truth is that organisational impulses have a major Western base, especially from the meeting of civil movements in Western Europe and Eastern Europe from the late 1980s, in a pacifist context endorsing what happened in the Helsinki process.[57] This explains why most of the organisations that make up the ACC have a very strong European dimension, such as the relevance of the offices that have been established in EU member countries and the number of EU citizens who participate, support or simply sympathise with their activities.[58] On the contrary, some part of civil society participating in an

[56] We must bear in mind that Europe was the birthplace of the concept of civil society, understood as a polite, well-mannered and peaceful society. Bourgeois society was the centre of public life between the State and the family, a model that was gradually exported to Eastern Europe during the 1970s and1980s. Thus, it was a phenomenon associated with liberalism, where associational life was an important sector of activity (A Ferguson, *Ensayo sobre la historia de la sociedad civil* (Barcelona, Akal, 2010)). However, postmodern civil society, by associationism, attempts to correct the problems facing victims of globalisation. In this new civil society associations of individuals and their actions are based on tolerance, pluralism and contestation, but some postmodernists criticise the concept of civil society, considering it Eurocentric.

[57] On the union of social movements in Western and Eastern Europe at the end of the Cold War, the study by H Kouri and E Romans, *Protest beyond Borders Contentious Politics in Europe since 1945* (n 45 above) is recommended.

[58] In the case of IANSA, the European base is very important, and fundamentally consists of the NGOs registered in the Union territory: Belgium (Africa Europe Faith & Justice Network (AEFJN), Groupe de Recherche et d'Information sur la Paix et la Sécurité (GRIP), Pax Christi Vlaanderen, Pax Christi International); Finland (Civil Society Conflict Prevention Network (KATU), Committee of 100); France (Action Sécurité Éthique Republicaines, Caritas—France); Germany (Aktions buend nis Amoklauf Winnenden); Netherlands (IKV Pax Christi, Transition International); Portugal (Observatory on Women and Armed Violence); Spain (Fundacio per la Pau, Plataforma per la Pau Lloret); Sweden (Amnesty International—Sweden, Swedish Fellowship of Reconciliation (SweFOR)); and United Kingdom (Institute for Disarmament Diplomacy, Action on Armed Violence (AOAV), Africa Center For Prevention and Resolution of Conflict (ACPRC), Amnesty International—International Secretariat, Amnesty International—UK, Gun Control Network, Omega Research Foundation, Oxfam International, Saferworld).

ACC and that suffers the consequences of irresponsible and uncontrolled trade in conventional arms is found in regions where there is no tradition of citizen engagement in matters of foreign and security policy and where political elites are against this happening, so participation mechanisms are virtually non-existent and citizens have no opportunity to assert their claims against the political institutions closest to them.

Secondly, civil society in the European Union, unlike other societies, has the ability to enforce their ideas, proposals and claims against State institutions exercising external political control. For example, we can mention some of the actions that have taken place in the United Kingdom, the Member State where ACC and IANSA exerted the greatest influence and where the pressures on State institutions regarding the control of the arms trade are strongest. Amnesty International called on leaders of the major political parties in the UK to commit to supporting a strong and effective Arms Trade Treaty. In Belgium, activists including IANSA members, Pax Christi Vlaanderen, will mark Belgian National Peace Week and they focused 'on the harm caused by the uncontrolled trade and diversion of arms, and the call for a strong and robust ATT' and organised a roundtable that was held at the Belgian parliament where civil society met politicians and urged the Belgian government to speak out for a robust ATT. In Sweden, the Swedish Fellowship on Reconciliation (SweFor), in June 2012, developed a campaign to collect signatures of Swedish parliamentarians in favour of an ATT, which were later handed over to the Swedish government delegation at the ATT conference. But the pressure of European civil society is not only developed in State offices;[59] the European Arms NGOs Community also makes use of the mechanisms of access to Member States' institutions, especially through the participation of citizens' associations in national parliamentary scrutiny processes to enable them to assert their opinions and spread information. It also has some access to the EU institutions, especially the Commission and the European Parliament.[60]

Within the institutional framework of the Union, it is the Commission that has paid most attention to the issues of citizen participation as a remedy for the crisis of legitimacy, assigning a key role to civil society in the good governance of

[59] The actions of IANSA, ACC and its participating organizations have been the most relevant in involving the governments of some States and even the main political parties. This was the case of the marketing campaigns such as Gun Destruction Day in 2004, which resulted in some governments conducting the destruction of weapons, such as South Africa and Cambodia, as well as in Latin American States. In addition, regular meetings and collaborations with western Governments are maintained, capable of curbing the trade in small arms, mainly from European countries, such as Holland, Norway, Finland, Switzerland and the UK, which have included advisors from civil society as represented in IANSA (D Rogers, *Postinternationalism and Small Arms Control, Theory, Politics, Security* (n 50 above) 175–78).

[60] A Stavrianakis has carried out important research on the means European NGOs working in the field of arms control have used to influence State Institutions (A Stavrianakis, 'Missing the Target: NGOs, Civil Society and the Global Arms Trade' (2011) 15 *Journal of International Relations and Development* 224: www.palgrave-journals.com/jird/, accessed 26 April 2015).

the Union, as stated in the White Paper on European Governance, 2001,[61] and encouraging its participation in the development of legislative initiatives, given that the challenges that the Union faces are increasingly complex and the participation of civil society organisations in governance is becoming ever more relevant.[62] Furthermore, the European Parliament, especially in the context of the Subcommittee on Security and Defence, regularly listens to the views, information, and claims of the European Arms NGOs Community, particularly useful for the exercise of its function of political control over the Common Foreign and Security Policy.[63]

The third reason that justifies the role of European civil society in monitoring the arms trade is the absence of weighty civil organisations in favour of the free trade in weapons, contrary to what happens in the US and Canada whose pacifist social movements are very active. However, ACC and IANSA encounter resistance there from what is known as the 'Fireman Community', represented mainly by the World Forum on the Future of Sport Shooting Activities (WFSA), which includes associations of hunters, target shooters and manufacturers of firearms and ammunition from 13 countries, although the predominant network organisation is the American National Rifle Association.[64] And indeed, both ACC and WFSA have played an active role in two international conferences for the conclusion and entry into force of an ATT. In the first conference alone, 177 NGOs applied for accreditation and over 40 participants went to the special meeting of 13 January 2012 with the intention of making critical comments, offering opinions and information, but the only action that changed the position of a government during the conference was the opinion of the US National Rifle Association.[65] The sudden disagreement

[61] ec.europa.eu/dgs/communication/pdf/comm-initiatives/2001-european-governance-white-paper-com2001_0428_en.pdf, accessed 14 May 2015.

[62] There is a wide doctrinal debate on the crisis of legitimacy and civil society's participation in European governance. In B Finke, 'Civil Society Participation in EU Governance' (2007) 2 *Living Review in European Governance* 1.

[63] This was the case of Cédric Poitevin who participated on 28 November 2012 at a public hearing before the Subcommittee on Security and Defence of the European Parliament in order to defend the ATT project, submitted by the Chairperson of the International Conference held in July 2012 (C Poitevin, 'Traité sur le commerce des armes. Priorités EU pour l'avant les négociations mars 2013' (2012) *Note d'Analyse du Groupe d'Information sur la paix et Reserche et Sécurité*, Bruxelles: www.grip.org/sites/grip.org/files/NOTES_ANALYSE/2012/na_2012-11-28_fr_c_poitevin.pdf, accessed 6 May 2015.

[64] M Kaldor, *La sociedad civil global* (n 35 above) 38–39.

[65] In this sense, see List of Non-Governmental Organizations, Preparatory Committee for the United Nations Conference on the Arms Trade Treaty, New York, 13–17 February 2012, A/CONF.21/PC.IV/INF/2, and the interventions of the NGO group who made a speech in favour of the conclusion of an ATT in Control Arms Coalition NGO Speeches for the Final Diplomatic Conference on ATT, March 2013 (controlarms.org/en/wp-content/uploads/sites/2/2013/03/March-DipCon2-NGO-Speeches_Mar21.pdf, accessed 13 May 2015). See, too, the speeches of some of the organizations favourable to free trade in the arms trade: Statement by Ted R Bromund, The Heritage Foundation Leadership for America, United Nations Conference on The Arms Trade Treaty, New York, 2–27 July 2012; Statement of the Defense, Small Arms Advisory Committee. Arms Trade Treaty Final Negotiations Conference, 21 March 2013; Statement by Johanna Reeves, Executive Director of Fire Arms Importer/Exporter Roundtable (FAIR) Trade Group, New York, 9 July 2012; Statement by The International Committee of

with the Obama administration's first draft treaty presented at the conference in July 2012, and which without doubt contained a much stricter control regime over the arms trade, was a result of the support the National Rifle Association had managed to gather internally, which made it impossible for the US government to get approval from the Senate to ratify the future treaty.[66]

B. European Arms NGOs Community's Contribution to the European Union Regime on Arms Control

As the concern of European arms companies is to increase their sales of materiel, and especially since there is overproduction and some duplication of goods produced in the territory of the Union, requiring States to develop more adequate control mechanisms for their arms trade has not been easy. This is especially so considering that in the conventional arms trade not all States play the same game; not everyone has arms industries and among those who have them, there are great differences, leading to different levels of compliance with the criteria and procedures of the control system of the EU arms trade.[67]

However, since the late 1990s, the European Arms NGOs Community has exercised an important external control over the activities carried out by Member States, identifying situations in which the interpretation of the criteria of the system of control and transparency of the actions of States has been very inadequate. This contributes to the progress and improvement of the system of arms trade control by Member States, especially those who are tempted to apply internal political and economic criteria in their transactions rather than humanitarian principles.[68] The European Arms NGOs Community has developed its activity

Museums and Collections of Arms and Military History, Arms Trade Treaty Final Negotiations Conference, 20 March 2013; Statement by Wayne La Pierre, Executive Vice President, Arms Trade Treaty Conference, July 2012: www.un.org/disarmament/ATT/statements/docs/20130321/ngo/20130321_wfsa.pdf, accessed 11 May 2015.

[66] Global Solutions has concluded upon analysis that US failure to ratify ATT generates high costs in terms of global leadership, including loss of international credibility and weaker political authority (A Chelseth, F Nasir, J Steies and P Lobejko, *United States on the Road to Isolation: The Coast of Non-Ratification* (Minneapolis MN, University of Minnesota, 2004).

[67] The interests of the Member States relating to the arms trade are so important that they affect military capabilities of the Common Security and Defence Policy of the Union. Panos Koutranos explains the difficulties in developing EU peacekeeping missions if Member States' arms companies are determined to continue producing and selling, following a business logic and are not planning on security (P Koutranos, *The EU Common security and Defence Policy* (Oxford, OUP, 2013) 253. After ATT entry into force, European think tanks, such as Chatam House, have been trying to involve European defence industries in the implementation of the ATT: 'As a global supply chain continues to spread and evolve, the ATT is an opportunity for the new emerging power and future exporter and importers of defence material to develop their control systems so that they are ATT-compatible, reliable and effective'. In E Kytömäki, 'The Defence Industry, Investors and the Arms Trade Treaty' (December 2014), *Research Paper*, Chatham House, p 3.

[68] Z Yihdego (n 27 above) 281.

in several areas among which are, first, research and advice[69] and, secondly, the lobbying and denunciations that have been crucial in detecting faults in the EU control system of the arms trade, improving their mechanisms and procedures and ensuring consistency, as shown by some examples.

Regarding *research and advice* a number of recent cases can be highlighted that show that without the work of the European Arms NGOs Community on the regime of controlling arms the Union would have remained the most advanced but on paper only, since, in some cases, Member States have been particularly benevolent with the incorrect application of the system made by some of its

[69] EU Non-Proliferation Consortium is a European Network of Independent Non-Proliferation Think Tanks, which houses a number of think tanks very superior to those of other international regions. The network includes: Aberystwyth University—David Davies Memorial Institute of International Studies, United Kingdom; Institute for Disarmament Diplomacy, United Kingdom; British American Security Information Council (BASIC), United Kingdom; British Pugwash Group, United Kingdom; Carnegie Europe, Belgium; Center for International Security and Arms Control Studies (CESIM), France; Center for Transnational Studies, Foreign and Security Policy (ATASP), Germany; Centro interuniversitario Machiavelli (CIMA), Italy; Danish Institute for International Studies (DIIS), Denmark; Egmont—The Royal Institute for International Relations, Belgium; European Centre for Space Law (ECSL), France; European Leadership Network for Multilateral Nuclear Disarmament and Non-Proliferation (ELN), United Kingdom; European Space Policy Institute (ESPI), Austria; European Union Institute for Security Studies—EUISS, France; Flemish Peace Institute, Belgium; Foundation for Strategic Research (FRS), France; French Institute of International Relations (IFRI), France; Geneva Centre for Security Policy (GCSP), Switzerland; German Institute for International and Security Affairs (SWP), Germany; Group for research and information on peace and security (GRIP), Belgium; Hungarian Institute of International Affairs (HIIA), Hungary; Institute for International Legal Studies (ISGI), Italy; Institute of International Relations Prague (IIR), Czech Republic; International Affairs and Foreign Policy Institute (INCIPE), Spain; International Centre for Defence Studies (ICDS), Estonia; International Institute for Strategic Studies (IISS), United Kingdom; International Security Information Service Europe (ISIS Europe), Belgium; Istituto Affari Internazionali (IAI), Italy; King's College London—Centre for Science and Security Studies (CSSS), United Kingdom; King's College London—International Centre for Security Analysis (ICSA), United Kingdom; Landau Network Centro Volta (LNCV), Italy; Latvian Institute of International Affairs—LIIA, Latvia; Luxembourg Institute for European and International Studies (LIEIS), Luxembourg; Netherlands Institute of International Relations 'Clingendael', Netherlands; Observatoire des armements, France; Peace Research Institute Frankfurt (PRIF / HSFK), Germany; Research Center of the Slovak Foreign Policy Association—RC SFPA, Slovakia, Royal Higher Institute for Defence—RHID, Belgium, Royal United Services Institute for Defence and Security Studies—RUSI, United Kingdom, School of International Studies—University of Trento, Italy (SIS), Italy; Stockholm International Peace Research Institute (SIPRI), Sweden; The Austrian Institute for International Affairs—oiip, Austria; The German Council on Foreign Relations—DGAP, Germany; The Hague Centre for Strategic Studies (HCSS), Netherlands; The Hellenic Foundation for European & Foreign Policy (ELIAMEP), Greece; The Institute for Peace Research and Security Policy (IFSH), Germany; The Polish Institute of International Affairs (PISM), Poland; University of Aarhus—Department of Political Science and Government, Denmark; University of Antwerp—Research Group in International Politics, Belgium; University of Hamburg—Carl Friedrich von Weizsäcker Centre for Science and Peace Research (ZNF), Germany; University of Innsbruck—Department of Political Science, Austria; University of Kiel—Institute for Security Policy (ISPK), Germany; University of Liège European Studies Unit, Belgium; University of Ljubljana—Defence Research Centre, Slovenia; University of Southampton—Department of Politics and International Relations, United Kingdom; University of Warsaw—Institute of International Relations, Poland; University of Westminster—School of Law, United Kingdom; University Pantheon-Assas Paris II—Centre Thucydide, France; Verification Research, Training and Information Centre (VERTIC), United Kingdom; Vienna Center for Disarmament and Non-Proliferation—VCDNP, Austria; Wilton Park, United Kingdom.

partners. For example, the European Network of Independent Non Proliferation Think Tanks warned that third States that were recipients of economic and humanitarian assistance from the Union were also the final destination of exports of small arms from Member States, bearing in mind that such weapons could only worsen the humanitarian circumstances of the recipients and that such operations are contrary to the European Union Programme for Preventing and Combating Illicit Trafficking in Conventional Weapons and the Strategy to Combat Illicit Accumulation and Trafficking of SALW and their Ammunition.[70] Nicolas Rousseau's work, in the same line of research on the EU and small arms and light weapons in Africa, revealed inconsistencies between the foreign policy of the EU and the business of its armaments companies, which contravenes the objectives and principles of European law on arms trade control.[71]

As regards the *lobbying and denunciations* developed by European Arms NGOs Community, its contribution to the EU is outstanding and the Union remains the region that provides most information to the United Nations Register of Conventional Arms (UNROCA). The information UNROCA obtains is crucial to analyse the individual and regional capacities of States, while eliminating suspicions and developing confidence-building measures. However, in recent years there has been a dramatic decline in the States offering reports to UNROCA. Only 37 of the UN Member States have deposited their reports in the Registry each year, 174 have done so once or more between 1992 and 2013, and 22 have never made that report. Of the 50 European countries that have made their UNROCA reports, 25 have done so every year, including the main EU exporters. It is true that there is no obligation to include light weapons and small arms in these reports, but it is useful to contrast them with the information provided by other States and to locate inconsistencies. European think tanks, such as SIPRI, often develop analyses of the registration data provided by Member States and data from countries in other regions that have been involved in such transactions and indicate the manifest inconsistencies between the resulting figures.[72] Similarly, the Groupe

[70] C Poitevin, 'European Union Initiatives to Control Small Arms and Light Weapons: Towards a More Coordinated Approach', *Non-Proliferation Papers* 33 (2013), and *European Union Program for Preventing and Combating Illicit Trafficking in conventional Weapons*, 9057/97 DG E-CFSP IV, 26 June 1997; Joint Action of 17 December 1998 adopted by the Council on the basis of Article J.3 of the Treaty on European Union on the European Union's contribution to combating the destabilising accumulation and spread of small arms and light weapons (1999/34/CFSP), [1999] OJ, L9/1 and Council of the European Union, Joint Action 2002/589/CFSP of 12 July on the European Union's contribution to combating the destabilising accumulation and spread of small arms and light weapons and repealing Joint Action 1999/34/CFSP, [2002] OJ L19/1; and Council of the European Union Strategy to combat illicit accumulation and trafficking of SALW and their ammunition, 5319/06, 16 December 2005 (n 27 above).

[71] Nicolas Rousseau, 'L'UE et les armes légères et de petit calibre en Afrique subsaharienne' (2011) *Note d'Analyse du Groupe de Recherche et d'Information sur la Paix et la Sécurité*, www.nonproliferation.eu/documents/other/nicolasrousseau4f7187a377e4e.pdf, accessed 2 May 2015.

[72] P Holtom, L Béraud-Sufreau and H Weber, 'Reporting to the United Nations Register of Conventional Arms', *SIPRI Fact Sheet* (2011): www.sipri.org/research/armaments/transfers/transparency/un_register, accessed 25 April 2015. Since ATT entry into force European NGOs Community has been

d'Information et Reserche sur la Paix et la Sécurité (GRIP) denounced subterfuges used by States like Italy to circumvent the system of export licences to Libya, selling €6,000,000 in light weapons and small arms in 2009, but doing so via Malta, making it seem that the latter State was the beneficiary of the transaction without informing the EU, because according to the Italian authorities, 7,500 revolvers and automatic pistols and 3706 rifles and carbines sold to Tripoli cannot be considered military materiel. Although this transaction was not discovered until 2011, thanks to UNROCA detection of the sale, the only State that appears as the principal arms dealer to Libya, worth €79,689,691 is Malta, which has no military industry and in fact only granted transit licences for Italian exports. Some of the Italian NGOs such as *Rete per il Disarmo* or *Tavola per la Pace* denounced the situation, bearing in mind that the Italian government did not even report these sales to its own parliament. GRIP has also exposed some arms transactions from Belgium to Tripoli, where the arms ended up in Sudan and were used in the conflict in Darfur, as a result of a number of gaps in the end-user certificates that Libya should have required.[73] Moreover, after the publication of the Thirteenth Annual Report on Exports Control of Military Technology and Equipment, published on 30 December 2011, European Arms NGOs Community discovered that the Member States had increased the value of their weapons sales by 21 per cent compared to 2009, designed especially for emerging powers, but also for totalitarian regimes in the Middle East and North Africa, so that the transfers were contrary to the criteria of the EU's arms trade.[74]

V. FINAL CONCLUSIONS

1. Some EU Member States occupy a key position within the group of major arms exporters in the world and want to continue producing and selling conventional arms to increase their margin of economic gain and maintain the ability to influence the course of crises and conflicts elsewhere in the international society in which they have interests. The principles and criteria underlying the external

concentrated in transparent to monitoring the adherence of signatory States to the criteria of the ATT. See MM Mutschler and Jan Grebe, 'Transparent Reporting for a Successful Arms Trade Treaty', Policy Brief 1/2015, (Bonn International Center for Conversion, 2015) 1; M Bolton, H Guerra, R Acheson and O Sprague, 'The Road Forward for the Arms Trade Treaty: A Civil Society Practitioner Commentary' (2014) 10 *Global Policy* 1; and Y Fukui, 'The Arms Trade Treaty: Pursuit for the Effective Control of Arms Transfer' (2015) 20 *Journal of Conflict and Security Law* 301.

[73] F Santopinto, 'Le contrôle du commerce des armes par l'UE. UN cas emblématique venu de Libye', (2011) *Note d'Analyse du Groupe de Reserche et d'Information sur la Paix et la Sécurité*, www.nonproliferation.eu/documents/other/federicosantopinto4f717297b4dd9.pdf, accessed 2 May 2015 and L Géhin, 'Union européenne: plus d`exportations d'armes, mois de transparence?', Éclairage, 14avril 2016, www.grip.org/fr/node/1991, accessed, 19 April 2016.

[74] See: www.centredelas.org/index.php?option=com_content&view=article&id=840:el-nuevo-informe-oficial-de-la-ue-sobre-exportaciones-de-armas-demasiado-tardio-e- incompleto&catid=43:industria-i-comerc-darmes&Itemid=64&lang=en, accessed, 16 May 2015.

action of the EU and its control system for arms trade do curb many of the import licences that third parties request of the Union's States and that could directly or indirectly lead to serious violations of human rights or end up by diverting the weapons to an unauthorised destination. In other cases, Member States either do not properly interpret or apply these criteria, and yet the EU still has the most advanced control system of trading weapons that exist in international society.

2. At the European level there is a strong tradition of civil society's participation in domestic and international affairs. Many of Europe's civil movements in the field of human rights, environmentalism, disarmament and social justice have even influenced citizens elsewhere. Within the international networks of NGOs and think tanks that promote arms control, European leadership is indisputable. Furthermore, European NGOs have channels and mechanisms to access national and European institutions that can seldom be found in other States and regions. Moreover, within the Union, associations in favour of unfettered arms trade are virtually non-existent or do not have sufficient force to counteract the efforts of the European Arms NGOs Community. This is in marked contrast to what happens in the US and Canada, whose NGOs and networks in the area of disarmament and non-proliferation are also very active but are counterbalanced by the Fireman Community.

3. The European Arms NGOs Community has offered alternative and independent information on the consequences of some of the arms sales operations undertaken by Member States, and reported the violations of the control regime which have been committed, and offers advice to improve procedures and mechanisms. Thus, Member States are subject to an external control which is able to highlight inconsistencies and incoherencies of their actions much more strictly and independently than the EU institutions and the Member States themselves can develop.

4. The work of the European Arms NGOs Community has been fundamental in improving the system of arms control in the EU, and the representatives of the Member States and the Union have proved to be the most progressive group among the participants at the two conferences on ATT when designing the Treaty, despite the interests of the international arms trade. However, other organisations and networks of citizens active in the control of the arms trade have neither the experience nor the channels of participation in their own States and regions to be able to transform or influence the policies of their States and boost the control of the international arms trade to the same extent and results that have been obtained in Europe.

Index